THE

GRENVILLE PAPERS.

VOL. III.

THE

GRENVILLE PAPERS:

BEING

THE CORRESPONDENCE

OF

RICHARD GRENVILLE EARL TEMPLE, K.G.,

AND

THE RIGHT HON: GEORGE GRENVILLE,

THEIR FRIENDS AND CONTEMPORARIES.

EDITED, WITH NOTES,

By WILLIAM JAMES SMITH

IN FOUR VOLUMES.—VOL. III.

AMS PRESS
NEW YORK

Reprinted from the edition of 1953, London
First AMS EDITION published 1970
Manufactured in the United States of America

International Standard Book Number:
   complete set: 0-404-06150-8
   volume 3: 0-404-06153-2

Library of Congress Catalog Card Number: 72-119154

AMS PRESS, INC.
New York, N. Y. 10003

CONTENTS

OF

THE THIRD VOLUME.

ADDENDA ET CORRIGENDA.

Vol. i. p. 383, Note, *for* Thomas Robinson Earl of Grantham, *read* Henry de Nassau, Earl of Grantham, who was more probably the person alluded to in Lord Egremont's letter.

Vol. ii. p. 65. Almon's letter to Lord Temple of Sunday [June 23, 1765], should have been placed according to its date in Vol. iii.

Vol. ii. p. 192, *for* Tuesday the 18th of August, *read* Thursday the 18th of August.

Vol. iii. p. lxvi., line 18, *for* wo, *read* wod

Vol. iii. p. 105, *for* Sir Cliff. Withrington, *read* Sir Clifton Wintringham.

Vol. iii. p. 187, subnote [a], *for* Memoirs, *read* Life.

Vol. iii. p. 189, in the fifth line of the Note, place a *comma* after the word " hold."

Vol. iii. p. 192. At the end of the Note, *add*, where the Frankland interest was predominant.

Vol. iii. p. 282, Note, *for* Buckingham Street, *read* York Buildings, near Buckingham Street.

Vol. iii. p. 319. In the penultimate paragraph of Lord Clive's letter, line 3, *for* adding more to my own fortune, *read* adding nothing more to my own fortune.

Vol. iii. p. 321, Note 2, *add*, and this volume, p. 296.

Vol. iii. p. 344. In the last paragraph of Lord Temple's letter, George, means George Grenville, jun., afterwards Earl Temple and Marquess of Buckingham.

Vol. iv. p. 4, line 6 of Lord Suffolk's letter, *add Note on the words* " unavailing grief : "—Lady Suffolk, a daughter of Lord Trevor, had very recently giving birth to her first child.

Vol. iv. p. 321, line 3, in note, *for* Junius, *read* the Author of Junius.

Vol. iv. p. 481, in line 9 of Mr. Whately's letter, *for* imposible *read* impossible.

Vol. iv. p. 517, in note 3, *for* Stationary office *read* Stationery office.

1. *The Author of Junius: see Vol. IV. p. 254.*

this observations contained in the inclosed papers are thrown
together and sent to you upon a supposition that the Tax therein referred

2. *The Author of Junius: see Vol. IV. p. 256.*

It is a melancholy consideration that, when every commodity, which can admit of a Tax,
is loaded to the last point, it sh.d still be necessary for Government to contrive new Taxes.

3. *The Author of Junius: see Vol. IV. p. 261.*

At least if frauds are committed in this way, they
ought to be corrected by regulations, not the thing itself restrained
or suppressed by a tax, which, in many instances, must amount to a
prohibition, & when that happens, will at once defeat itself & injure
the publick.

John Murray, Albemarle Street.

Pl. II.

1. The Author of Junius : see Vol: IV: p. 381.

The Grand Council was mine, [I] may say, with truth, almost every thing that, for two years past, has attracted the attention of the publick.

2. The Author of Junius : see Vol: IV: p. 256.

The only Condition, which I presume to make with you, is that you will not only not shew these papers to any body, but that you will never mention your having received them.

6

John Murray, Albemarle Street.

Some late papers, in which the Cause of this Country, and the defence of your Character and. Measures have been thought not ill maintained; — others, signed Lucius, and one or two upon the new Commission of trade, with a Multitude of others, came from this hand. They have been taken Notice of by the Publick.

2. Mrs Grenville, afterwards Lady Temple.

Nugent will have all your Patriots that come to the Bath drawn by my man & there is to be verses put under your Pictures Mr — Pope says they ought to be drawn out of hand for fear some of them shou'd — change sides, my Lord Gifford is here. Mrs Pulteney is gone

John Murray Albemarle Street

Pl. IV.

1. *Miss Chamber, afterwards Lady Temple.*

I don't understand what you mean by indifference, I think I have performd all
promisd you, in permitting you freely to discourse to me

your humble servant

Anne Chamber

2. *Mrs Grenville, afterwards Lady Temple.*

me thing above all others must allways make me
happy be— where I will, & that is the knowing you
are my husband tho' I can't be perfectly easy while
you are absent

3. *Mrs Grenville, afterwards Lady Temple.*

the black boys dined
with Lady Betty last Sunday & we carryed them
to the Duke of Dorsets in the afternoon & a
they were much pleased.

 # His Grace had lately married a Miss Wrottesley,
Niece of the good Gertrude, Dutchess of Bedford.

2# Miss Liddell, after her divorce from the Duke, married
Lord Upper Ossory.

2. *Junius from Mr Woodfall's collection.*

pray let this be announced,

Memoirs of Lord Barrington in

our next.

keep the Author a secret.

3. *Lady Temple. 1768.*

Oberon Imp!

To

Miss Hotham

Ob: Rex.

Sent by a Sylph, unheard, unseen,
A new Years-Gift from Mab our Queen;
But tell it not, for if you do,
You will be pinch'd all black & blue.
Consider well what a Disgrace,
To show abroad your motled Face,
Then seal your Lips, put on the Ring,
And sometimes think of Ob: the King.

fairy Pallace

4. *Mrs Grenville afterwards Lady Temple.*

To

Richd Grenville. Esq

at his house.

in Pallmall

London

5. *Junius: from Mr Woodfall's collection.*

Mr Woodfall, Printer, in

Paternoster Row.

INTRODUCTORY NOTES

LORD TEMPLE AND THE AUTHORSHIP OF JUNIUS.

In these concluding volumes of the GRENVILLE CORRESPOND-ENCE will be found Three Letters addressed to Mr. Grenville in the year 1768, by that anonymous writer who afterwards became, and who still continues, so celebrated as the Author of the LETTERS OF JUNIUS.

It has been long expected that upon the publication of these Papers the real name of that writer would become *certainly* known. In that expectation I regret to say the public will be disappointed. The letters to Mr. Grenville not only do not dis-close the author's name, but it can scarcely be said that they afford even a clue to its discovery; on the contrary, it may per-haps be considered that they create additional difficulties, and that they were intended by the author to render his concealment the more effectual.

I have before stated that there was no mystery in the preserva-tion of these letters, by Mr. Grenville or his descendants, and it was necessary to say thus much in contradiction to the various rumours which have been circulated respecting alleged discoveries at Stowe, of "*a box with three seals*," containing "the original letter from Junius to the King, signed with the real name of the author;"—"the original letter to Lord Mansfield;"—and at another time, "a letter confirming the claims of Charles Lloyd to the authorship, *beyond all possibility of doubt;*"—besides other letters said to have been found *" in concealed places, behind the shelves of the library,"* &c.

All these reports are entirely fabulous. The only letters which have been found addressed to Mr. Grenville by the Author, are those now for the first time printed in these volumes; they are unquestionably in the handwriting of Junius: two of them are signed with the initial C., the other has no signature. They do not appear to have been in any respect distinguished by Mr. Grenville; each of them is endorsed in his usual careful manner, and they were tied up with other letters in packets arranged in alphabetical order: these letters, being anonymous, were placed under letter A.

In January, 1827, I assisted the Rev. Dr. Charles O'Conor, my predecessor as librarian at Stowe, in the arrangement of a portion of Mr. Grenville's correspondence which had been brought from Wotton to Stowe many years before. These papers were parcelled up and docqueted by Mr. Grenville himself, and from their appearance I believed them to have remained unopened since his death in 1770. The letters from the Author of Junius were found at this time, and in this collection. Dr. O'Conor was well acquainted with the facsimile specimens of the handwriting of Junius in Woodfall's edition of the Letters, and upon compari-son he suspected that these were in the same hand. He com-municated his discovery to the late Duke of Buckingham, by whom the papers were immediately shown to me for my opinion, and also with reference to a comparison of them with some letters from the Honourable Augustus Hervey, who, from similarity of handwriting, Dr. O'Conor too hastily imagined to have been the author. If there were, however, no other circumstances which rendered that theory quite untenable, it would be sufficient that Mr. Hervey was at Lisbon for the recovery of his health in De-cember, 1769, at a time when Junius was in active correspondence with Woodfall, and occupied in some of his most famous pro-ductions.

It has been asserted on the authority of Pinkerton in the *Wal-poliana*, that Mr. Grenville once told Sir John Irwin that he had that morning received a letter from Junius, saying that he esteemed Mr. Grenville, and might soon make himself known to him. The author of *Junius Identified*[1] has mentioned also, but without giving any authority, that—

—" there is preserved at Stowe a private unpublished letter written by Junius to Mr. George Grenville, wherein he desires him to refrain from making any attempt to discover the author, as it might do him harm, but could produce no satisfactory result; adding, that in proper time he would declare himself."

This latter report is probably derived from the same source as that mentioned in the *Walpoliana*. No such letter was preserved at Stowe.

Having had the honour of living in the very intimate confidence of the late Duke of Buckingham for many years, and up to the period of his death, I am enabled most positively to affirm that his Grace was not aware of the existence of any other letter or letters addressed by the Author of Junius to Mr. Grenville, except those which were discovered by Dr. O'Conor, and which for the first time became known to the Duke in the manner above mentioned.

It is true that Mr. Grenville was very intimate with Sir John Irwin, but it does not seem probable that he would have communicated to him any part of those letters from his anonymous correspondent, who had expressed his earnest wish to serve him, and who had most emphatically desired that he would not only not show them to anybody, but that he would never mention his having received them. Besides, it is by no means certain that Mr. Grenville ever knew that these letters signed C. were by the same writer who subsequently adopted the signature of Junius[2].

[1] 8vo. 1818. Supplement, page 398.

[2] It has been supposed that the late Mr. Thomas Grenville had some peculiar knowledge respecting the authorship of Junius. I have no reason to join in that belief, for I never heard him speak upon the subject, nor did I ever hear it mentioned in his presence. He had not seen these letters addressed to his father, until they were shown to him by myself at Stowe, about ten or twelve years ago, I believe in October 1840. After having appeared to read them with great attention, he returned them to me without any observation whatever,—it is possible because he felt no interest in the subject, or that I did not presume to ask him any questions upon it. I remember considering that his manner upon this occasion was significant, because it was unusual. I revert with very great pleasure to the many hours which I had the honour and advantage of spending with him at various times in the library at Stowe, and he always

It was not until the end of the year 1829, after the late Duke of Buckingham's return from a tour on the Continent, that I first suggested to his Grace the possibility that Lord Temple might have been the author of Junius. Although it had not occurred to him, nor had he heard it as a family tradition, the Duke did not discourage the supposition; and in all our subsequent conversations upon the subject, we found no reasons for considering it in any respect improbable. In the year 1831, a book was published in America by Mr. Newhall, in which the claims of Lord Temple to be Junius are advocated in a series of letters to a friend at Salem.

I have read with more or less attention nearly all the numerous publications on the authorship of Junius; and nothing which has been written upon the subject has in any respect shaken my conviction, that of all the persons hitherto named, the probabilities are greatly in favour of Lord Temple.

Since the publication of the first or author's edition of the Letters in 1772,[1] about forty persons have at various times been proposed as candidates for the authorship. Very few, however, of these claims have survived the lapse of time; indeed, scarcely any have been recently mentioned except those of Sir Philip Francis, which have certainly found some influential supporters, chiefly, I believe, from the very ingenious and positive manner in which the

---

appeared to be much pleased in giving me the benefit of his extensive and most accurate information upon the books and manuscripts which I produced, either for his amusement, or upon which I desired to ask his opinion or advice.

[1] The references in these volumes, to the Letters of Junius, are to Woodfall's *second edition*[a], 3 vols. 8vo., 1814 [edited by Dr. Mason Good]. I am not however disposed to agree in opinion with the Editor in his presumption that *all* the letters which he has ascribed to the Author of Junius are *indisputably genuine*, but it may be admitted that, under all the circumstances, at the period of his publication (without any exclusive information, and without the lights which modern discoveries might have rendered to him), he exercised a very fair discretion in the selection he has made. He would, I think, have done better to have omitted some, and he might have extended his selections from the newspapers to an earlier date than that which he has assigned to the first communication supposed to have been made by the author to the printer of the *Public Advertiser*.

[a] It may be useful to mention that the *Table of Contents* in this edition is the same as that used for the first edition in 1812, and that the paging is consequently incorrect. Beginning with the Dedication, at page 341 of the *second* edition, the numerical order of the pages should subsequently be taken from the *first* edition.

arguments in his favour were first placed before the public more than thirty years ago[1]. They appear to have almost convinced Sir Philip himself that he was Junius, even after he had declared that the fact of imputing the authorship of the letters to him, was "giving currency to a silly and malignant falsehood."

Lord Campbell, in his most amusing work, the *Lives of the Lord Chancellors of England*, after discussing the claims of Mr. Wedderburn, considers that "there is a claim against Francis as the real Junius which would convict him before any fair and intelligent jury;" and his Lordship has added, but without producing any authority for the assertion, that "there is *overwhelming evidence* to prove that Sir Philip delivered the manuscript to Woodfall." Whenever any portion of this very re-

---

[1] In a work entitled *The Identity of Junius with a distinguished living Character established.* [By John Taylor.] 8vo. 1818. The subject was so comprehensively treated, and so entirely exhausted, in this book, that although the claims of Sir Philip Francis have since been advocated and supported by many writers, nothing whatever has been added either to the arguments or the evidence originally adduced by Mr. Taylor. Great stress is laid upon the parallel passages and phrases which are mentioned as having been used by Junius and Sir Philip Francis ; but these so-called *parallels* are *all* taken from the writings or speeches of Francis *long subsequent to the period when Junius wrote.* Not a single instance has been given of any passage either written or spoken by Francis previous to, or even contemporary with, Junius ; and therefore I pronounce them to be entirely worthless as regards the question of the authorship. They prove nothing more than that Francis, like many others, had been a diligent reader of Junius ; an admirer, and an extensive imitator of his writings.

Here are one or two specimens of the parallel passages which are to identify Francis with Junius :—

In 1769 Junius wrote—"And laws you know are intended to guard against what men *may* do, not to trust to what they *will* do."—I. 539.

More than *sixteen years* afterwards, in a speech, Francis said,—"But laws are made to guard against what men *may* do, not to trust to what they *will* do."

In 1769 Junius, quoting the words of Sir Richard Steele, wrote,—"We are governed by a set of drivellers, whose folly takes away all dignity from distress, and makes even calamity ridiculous."—I. 570.

And Sir Philip Francis wrote, *more than forty years afterwards,*—"Such authors of such ruin take away all dignity from distress, and make calamity ridiculous."

Again, Junius writes,—"It was on a consideration of this kind of character that a great poet says with a singular emphasis, ' Beware the fury of a patient man.' "

And Francis, *nearly fifty years* afterwards, in a pamphlet on Reform, says—"Agreed. Then look to the proverb for instruction before it be too late. *'Beware the fury of a patient man.' "*

And then with regard to the speeches in Parliament of Lord Chatham and others so confidently stated to have been reported by Sir Philip Francis, and *not printed, though preserved in notes, till twenty years afterwards;* as the same speeches, in the same words, have been subsequently discovered in contemporary newspapers, it is unnecessary to dwell upon that part of the *Identity.*

markable *evidence* shall have been suffered to transpire, the public will be enabled to form an opinion with respect to its value; and if it should be generally considered so overwhelming as his Lordship describes it, it will perhaps be sufficient to settle the question at once and for ever. In its absence, however, we must be content to know that there is at least abundant evidence to prove that Sir Philip was very desirous that his young wife Lady Francis should believe him to be Junius, though (no doubt for very prudent reasons) he never made any distinct and candid avowal of the fact, yet " by *telling circumstances,*" which, in the opinion of Lady Francis, "*none but Junius could know,*" he succeeded in inducing her to consider it beyond the shadow of a doubt. "He never avowed himself," says Lady Francis, "more than saying he knew what my opinion was, and never contradicting it." Like the dissembling Richard Duke of Gloucester to the mayor and citizens of London, when they besought him to accept the crown which he so ardently desired, Sir Philip might have said : —

> " Since you will buckle Junius on my back,
> To bear *his* burden whether I will or no,
> I must have patience to endure the load :
> But if black scandal or foul-faced reproach
> Attend the sequel of your imposition,
> Your mere enforcement shall acquittance me
> From all the impure blots and stains thereof:
> For Heaven knows, and you may partly see,
> How far I am from the desire of this."

To have coveted the fame of Junius was, however, a weakness which Sir Philip Francis shared in common with several other candidates, even with no less distinguished a man than his friend Edmund Burke : for Junius (C.), in one of his letters to Mr. Grenville, in allusion to his incognito, says : "The town is curious to know the author. Everybody guesses, some are quite certain, and all are mistaken. . . . . Mr. Bourke denies it, as he would a fact, which he wished to have believed."

I have mentioned Sir Philip Francis now, because it appeared to me that of all the candidates hitherto named, he stood highest in the public favour. It is not my intention to attempt any minute refutation of his claims, but it will be necessary occasionally to refer to them in connection with those of Lord Temple. I have never, at any time, believed in the validity of the claims of Francis. To some of those distinguished men who have declared themselves in his favour, " I listen," to use the language of Junius, " with diffidence and respect, but without the smallest degree of conviction or assent." Every argument which has been advanced in support of Francis, has been most minutely sifted and examined, and, as I think, most completely and satisfactorily disposed of and destroyed, in some admirable Essays on the Authorship of Junius, which have occasionally appeared in the *Athenæum* from the pen of an acute and accomplished critic, who has evidently devoted the greatest attention to the subject. It seems to be impossible, after having read these papers attentively, to retain any lingering belief that Junius and Sir Philip Francis were one and the same person.

The writer of a recent article in the *Quarterly Review*[1], who maintains that Thomas Lord Lyttelton was Junius, and whose ingenuity and talent are indeed worthy of a better subject, has also contributed some very excellent remarks in opposition to the Franciscan theory.

" A simple test," says a writer in the *Edinburgh Review*[2], " ascertains the political connection of Junius. He supported the cause of authority against America, with Mr. Grenville, the Minister who passed the Stamp Act. He maintained the highest popular principles on the Middlesex Election, with the same statesman, who was the leader of Opposition on that question. No other party in the kingdom but the Grenvilles combined these two opinions : and it is very unlikely that a private writer, unpledged and unconnected, should have spontaneously embraced political doctrines, which, though ingenuity might reconcile them in reasoning, were, in the disputes of that period, the opposite extremes."

It is certain, then, that Philip Francis was not of the Grenville connection, for his politics did *not* combine these two opinions : it is equally surprising that his claims to the authorship of Junius have not hitherto been more closely examined with reference to this very *simple test*.

---

[1] Vol. xc. December, 1851. [2] Vol. xliv. June, 1826.

In a speech made by Francis on the 11th of April, 1796, in the House of Commons, on his motion respecting the Regulation of Slaves in the West Indies (*Parl. Hist.* vol. xxxii. pp. 944–992), he very distinctly stated his views and opinions on the subject of the taxation of America, and he declared them to be in strict accordance with those of Lord Chatham. These are his words:—

"I know where that fatal question [the taxation of America] originated. No part of the argument which divided this country on the merits of the Stamp Act, or of the events which followed it, has escaped me. With all those transactions in my view, I declare now, *on the principles and in the language of Lord Chatham, that I rejoice that America resisted.* * * * I rejoice that America resisted with success, because it was a triumph of unquestionable right over outrageous wrong, of courage and virtue over tyranny and force. * * * *

"The claim which they [the Americans] resisted, was that of direct taxation by a House of Commons in which they were not represented. They asserted truly, that taxation and representation were inseparable; that the right grew from the fact, and could not exist without it."

Is this *supporting the cause of authority against America?*

Is it possible that this could be the language and these the sentiments of JUNIUS, the invariable friend and partizan of Mr. Grenville, *the Minister who passed the Stamp Act?* or these the sentiments of that same Junius who denounced Mr. Pitt as a *lunatic,* as *the high priest himself who with more than frantic fury offered up his bleeding country a victim to America?* Could this be the Junius who, "when Lord Chatham affirms that the authority of the British Legislature is not supreme over the colonies, *in the same sense in which it is supreme over Great Britain,* listens without the smallest degree of conviction or assent?"

Junius was ever clear and decided in his opinions with regard to the right of taxing the colonies by an Act of the British Legislature, though with the knowledge of recent events he subsequently considered it, for the future,—

"As a speculative right merely, never to be exerted, nor ever to be renounced. To his judgment it appears plain, that the general reasonings which were employed against that power [the right of taxation] went directly to our whole legislative right, and that one part of it could not be yielded without a virtual surrender of all the rest."

Junius in Parliament would have voted *in favour* of Lord Rockingham's Declaratory Bill, which declared the abstract right to tax, and *against* the repeal of the Stamp Act. If Philip Francis had been in the House of Commons, he would have done exactly the reverse: he would have followed *the principles and language of Lord Chatham,* and with Mr. Pitt, he would have *opposed* the Declaratory Act, and he would have voted *in favour* of the repeal of the Stamp Act.

It will be remembered that Junius has recorded a very decided opinion on the subject of the Game Laws; in his letter of the 2nd of November, 1771, he writes:—

"As to the Game Laws, he never scrupled to declare his opinion that they are a species of the *Forest Laws ;* that they are oppressive to the subject, and that the spirit of them is incompatible with legal liberty ; that the penalties imposed by these laws bear no proportion to the nature of the offence ; that the mode of trial and the degree and kind of evidence necessary to convict, not only deprive the subject of all the benefits of a trial by jury, but are in themselves too summary, and to the last degree arbitrary and oppressive ; that in particular the late Acts to prevent dog-stealing, or killing game between sun and sun, are distinguished by their absurdity, extravagance, and pernicious tendency. If these terms are weak and ambiguous, in what language can Junius express himself?"—Vol. ii. p. 396.

Twenty-five years afterwards, in the months of March and April, 1796, Mr. Philip Francis delivered his opinion upon the same subject in the House of Commons, when he made two short speeches on Mr. Curwen's Bill for the repeal of the Game Laws. The Bill was rejected on the second reading by a majority of 65 to 17; and as far as can be ascertained from Mr. Francis's very brief observations, it is probable that he voted in the majority. At all events, what he said upon this occasion is not very characteristic of the language or opinions of Junius as quoted above.

Mr. Francis began by confessing—

"that *he was not much acquainted with the subject,* but as he considered it of great importance, he begged leave to make a few observations.

There was one principle which the Legislature ought always to keep in view in their deliberations, and which he rose principally for the purpose of stating. Though no sportsman himself, he wished that the game should be preserved for the sake of sportsmen. To discourage poachers, therefore, was certainly important. The reason why he was particularly desirous for the preservation of game was, that while the capital presented so many attractions as it did at present to country gentlemen, and while it was at the same time of so much consequence to the country that they should reside for some time upon their estates, he was anxious that the country should present as many attractions as possible, to render a return to their rural residence desirable."

This bears no resemblance to the energetic style of Junius, nor is it like that of a man of mature age, who in his younger days had studied the subject in a constitutional point of view; Junius would not, twenty-five years afterwards, have asserted that *he was not much acquainted with the subject.*

Another circumstance, very much relied upon by those who advocate the claims of Sir Philip Francis, is a supposition that Junius was favourable to or had " *spared*" Lord Holland, because, through his patronage, Philip Francis, when a youth of less than eighteen years of age, had been appointed to a small clerkship in the Secretary of State's office.

Dr. Francis, the father of Philip, had been one of Lord Holland's chaplains, but they had quarrelled several years before Junius began to write under that signature; and this worthy Doctor had even furnished Churchill the Satirist with information for the purpose of ridiculing his patron, because he had refused to recommend him for an Irish bishopric.

It is possible, however, that the gratitude of the younger Francis may have been more conspicuous towards Lord Holland, than towards others to whom both he and his father owed much greater obligations. Mr. Welbore Ellis, the Secretary at War, for instance, was designated by Junius as "little mannikin Ellis:"— "the most contemptible little piece of machinery in the whole kingdom;" and yet to this gentleman, upon whom Junius delighted to heap the most contemptuous abuse, was Mr. Francis indebted for his appointment to a place in the War Office, which he held from 1763 to 1772, at a salary of 300*l.* or 400*l.* a year.

If Mr. Francis were Junius, he certainly did not *spare* King George III., although his father, Dr. Francis, had not only been kindly noticed by the King, but he received more substantial marks of His Majesty's goodness in being placed upon the English pension list for an annuity of 300*l*., in addition to a pension of double that amount on the Irish establishment, both of which he enjoyed from about 1762 until his death in 1773.

To Lord Chatham, also, Sir Philip Francis professed to be under great obligations. In one of his speeches he says :—

" In the early part of my life I had the good fortune to hold a place very inconsiderable in itself, but immediately under the late Earl of Chatham. He descended from his station to take notice of mine, and he honoured me with repeated marks of his favour and protection."

In some of the earlier letters of the Author of Junius, under various signatures, few of his victims have been more scurrilously abused than Lord Chatham. He was *"an abandoned profligate;" "a patron of sedition;" "a traitor;" "a man purely and perfectly bad;" "so black a villain that a gibbet would be too honourable a situation for his carcase."* Even his infirmities are heralded forth—he is *"a lunatic brandishing a crutch;"* or *"a miserable, decrepit, worn-out old man;"* and this is but a moderate selection from the epithets which were so liberally bestowed upon him by his grateful young friend, and all this without any motive either assigned or to be conjectured.

But to return to Lord Holland. The first occasion on which he is mentioned is in one of the private notes from Junius to Woodfall, on the 21st of July, 1769 :—

" I wish Lord Holland may acquit himself with honour. If his cause be good, he should at once have published that account to which he refers in his letter to the Mayor."

If Lord Temple were Junius, there was no reason why he should combine in running down Lord Holland, or that he should step out of his way to do injustice against a man with whom he had at that time no personal or political anger. What he said to Woodfall, therefore, was merely from an impulse of justice and good feeling towards a statesman, who, when he was designated by the

Livery of London in their petition to the King, as a public de-
faulter of unaccounted millions, he knew to be the object of an
exaggerated accusation, founded upon a gross perversion of the
truth. No man had more experience of, or knew better than
Lord Temple, the nature of the official accounts which were still
in arrear, and that Lord Holland was not singular in that respect.
He knew perfectly well that Lord Chatham's accounts, ending with
the year 1755, were even then unsettled, and the accounts of his
brother, George Grenville, as Treasurer of the Navy, an office
which he had quitted for seven years, were not yet closed, and in
fact remained unsettled at the time of his death in 1770.

In the letter addressed to the Printer of the *Public Advertiser*,
on the 16th of October, 1771, and signed "Anti-Fox," which has
by general agreement been attributed to Junius, he says:—

" I know nothing of Junius, but I see plainly that he has *designedly
spared* Lord Holland and his family. Whether Lord Holland be
invulnerable, or whether Junius should be wantonly provoked, are
questions worthy the Black Boy's consideration."

This letter was evidently intended as a friendly warning (or
even a threat, for it implies that Lord Holland was *not* invulnerable) to the Black Boy (meaning Charles James Fox, Lord Holland's second son), who was suspected by Junius of having been
the author of some recent communications to the newspapers, as
well as that Junius knew that the Black Boy had made himself
busy in the affair of Luttrell and Wilkes, in favour of the former.
Charles Fox was at this time M.P. for Midhurst, and a subaltern
in the Tory ranks : it was not until he quarrelled with Lord North,
two or three years later, that the Whigs were able to detach him
from their adversaries, and it will not be forgotten what a valuable
acquisition he became to that party.

If Junius had any particular object to accomplish in wounding
Lord Holland, he would have found no difficulty in ascertaining
the *vulnerable* point in his character ; but the truth is that at this
period Lord Holland had almost ceased to be a public character.
He said not long before, in a letter to George Selwyn, "The
newspapers, I am told, have forgot me." He had in a great measure retired from public life, he was an old man in miserable

health, he took no part in the intrigues of the day, he held no
office, and it was not even suspected that he desired any. After
his dismissal from the Paymastership of the Forces in 1765, an
office which he had held during the Administration of Mr. Pitt
and Lord Temple, as well as while Mr. Grenville was in power,
he had not incurred the resentment of Lord Temple by accepting
any employment under Lord Rockingham or the Duke of Grafton;
but, residing chiefly on the Continent, he did not return to England until the autumn of 1768, and not then to take any part in
politics or public life. He again visited Italy in 1769, and remained at Genoa, Nice, or Naples during the whole of the following year. It has been supposed that he was occasionally consulted by the King as a person capable of giving advice, as well
from his talents as from his great political experience and sagacity; but this does not seem to rest on any good authority, for,
according to his own account, he was not in favour with the King.
In a letter to George Selwyn, dated from Nice, in January, 1768,
he writes :—

" I cannot help sometimes asking myself, dear Selwyn, why I am in
such disgrace with the King? Have I deserved it? I am now the
only mark left of irrevocable displeasure, and I vow to God I cannot
guess why."

He had, besides, some resentments in common with Junius and
Lord Temple : he had quarrelled with the Duke of Bedford and
with Rigby; of the former he wrote to Selwyn early in the year
1768 in no very complimentary terms :—

" It cost the Duke of Bedford very little to declare off with Grenville. He would do that, or anything else, ten times as dishonourable,
if he was bid, with a grace that is surprising, and an air as if he was
doing something indisputably right."

The ingratitude of Rigby was a constant source of grief to
Lord Holland ; he complains in his letters to Selwyn, often and
bitterly, of Rigby's unkind behaviour :—

" I never hid anything from him when he was my friend. I had
nothing to hide from him on my part when he ceased to be so. *   *
I am sometimes weak enough to think that if Rigby chiefly, and some
others had pleased, I should have walked down the vale of years more

easily; but it is weak of me to think so often as I do of Rigby, and you will be ashamed of me."

Nor does it appear that Lord Holland had any influence at this time either with Lord Bute, or the Duke of Grafton, or Lord Mansfield,—all persons against whom Junius was most inveterate.

To amass riches was the principal object of Lord Holland's life, and in that he succeeded. He was not ambitious of power; in his latter years he was very desirous of obtaining an Earldom, but the King had constantly refused it. He supplicated Horace Walpole to intercede for him with the Duke of Grafton, who applied to the King in his favour; but George the Third could never be persuaded to give Lord Holland this step in the Peerage.

Besides, Junius did not always *spare* Lord Holland: he indirectly censured him by his support of Dr. Musgrave, who accused Lord Holland, in concert with Lord Bute and the Princess Dowager[1], of having received a large bribe from France, for giving undue advantages to French influence in the peace of 1763. Though Dr. Musgrave's information was voted by the House of Commons to be frivolous, yet Junius describes him as

" A firm and honest man, whose examination was most curious and interesting, and who, with no other support but truth and his own firmness, resisted and overcame the whole House of Commons."

That Lord Holland was not more frequently attacked by Junius, I believe to have been solely caused by the circumstances I have stated, without the slightest reference to Mr. Philip Francis or his supposed gratitude. With all his faults, Lord Holland had more friends than enemies. His apparent frankness of disposition gained him many adherents, who were attached to him by strong personal friendship; his agreeable manners and constant good humour rendered him ever a welcome companion in social life.

He spent his latter years in retirement between Holland House and his villa at Kingsgate, in the Isle of Thanet; his health continued gradually to decline until his death on the 1st of July, 1774, aged 69.

---

[1] Junius very unfairly implicated the Duke of Bedford in this imputation, although he was not even named or alluded to in Dr. Musgrave's charge.

The Edinburgh Reviewer before quoted[1] continues :—

" It is not to be understood that other persons may not have held opinions adverse to the cause of the Americans, and favourable to that of Wilkes. The value of the criterion depends on the improbability that on the two most important questions which occurred for ten years, a writer of great ability should zealously, frequently, and for a long period, write in support of the popular side of one, and of the unpopular on the other, unless he, or those whom he supported, had been pledged to these opposite opinions by measures of so public and decisive a nature, as to cut off all retreat. It may be observed also, that Junius, who is unfriendly to Lord Chatham, in the beginning, loads that noble man with panegyric after he was reconciled to Lord Temple and Mr. Grenville. Whoever revives the inquiry, therefore, unless he discovers positive and irresistible evidence in support of his claimant, should show him to be politically attached to the Grenville party, which Junius certainly was, and must also produce some specimens of his writings of tolerable length, such as might afford reasonable grounds for believing that he could have written these letters."

I shall endeavour to prove that the political opinions, the friendships, the animosities, and the resentments of Lord Temple, coincided very exactly with those of the Author of Junius, judging of the latter by the tendency of his writings, and of the former from the opinions of his friends and contemporaries, as well as from the compositions which are known to have proceeded from his pen.

Lord Temple's character was a compound of contradictions : he was certainly capable of the warmest and most generous attachments, while he was most bitter and rancorous in his personal resentments ; of a very haughty and apparently impracticable temper, yet easily conciliated by kindness and small attentions :—

" Lofty and sour to them that loved him not,
But to those men that sought him, sweet as summer."

" The natural disposition of this noble Lord," says Almon, the bookseller, who was often confidentially employed by Lord Temple, " was the most amiable that can be conceived, to his friends; but when offended, his disapprobation was warm and conspicuous, his language

[1] See *ante*, page xix.

flowed spontaneously from his feelings, his heart and his voice always corresponded."—*Anecdotes of the Life of Lord Chatham*, vol. ii. p. 29[1].

With a disinterested patriotism, and genuine love of liberty, Lord Temple is supposed to have delighted in faction, and the libellous abuse of men in power. He was no doubt extremely ambitious of political influence, and yet, whenever it seemed within his grasp, he invariably found some difficulty which prevented his acceptance of office, probably because the estimate which his pride had induced him to form of his own importance to an Administration was not confirmed by the opinions of his political associates. But even Smollett, a writer notoriously in the pay of his political adversaries, describes him as "a nobleman of distinguished abilities, and the most amiable disposition ; frank, liberal, humane, and zealously attached to the interest and honour of his country."

Horace Walpole, who was for many years intimately acquainted with Lord Temple, has, in his Memoirs and Letters, made frequent allusions to his character and habits. The following passage very aptly illustrates the concealment of which he was even at that time suspected :—

" This malignant man (Lord Temple) worked in the *mines* of successive factions for near thirty years together. To relate them is writing his life."[2]

Mr. Macaulay, in one of his Historical Essays[3], has more recently drawn the character of Lord Temple with no favourable hand:—

---

[1] Almon relates in his *Memoirs*[a], that when Lord Chatham came into office in 1766, and upon that occasion had differed violently from Lord Temple, Mr. Charles Townshend had offered him some office, and desired him to ask Lord Temple's leave to accept it. Almon has printed his reply.

" After the maturest consideration, pardon me, Sir, if I say, that I cannot think of going to Stowe upon this subject. If Lord Temple consents, he must look coldly upon me ever afterwards ; and if he refuses, it is putting him under an obligation to do something better whenever he comes into office. You know his Lordship's temper ; he is warm and decided, particularly at the present moment. I must therefore continue to lament in silence this unfortunate division, anxiously looking forward to better days."

[2] *Memoirs of George III.*, vol. ii. p. 359.

[3] *Edinburgh Review*, No. 162, January, 1834.

[a] *Memoirs of an Eminent Bookseller.*

" The head of the Grenvilles was Richard Earl Temple. His talents for administration and debate were of no high order; but his great possessions, his turbulent and unscrupulous character, his restless activity, and his skill in the most ignoble tactics of faction, made him one of the most formidable enemies that a Ministry could have. * * * It was supposed that Lord Temple secretly encouraged the most scurrilous assailants of the Government. In truth, those who knew his habits, tracked him as men track a mole. It was his nature to grub underground. Whenever a heap of dirt was flung up, it might well be suspected that he was at work in some foul crooked labyrinth below. * * Pamphlets made up of calumny and scurrility, filled the shops of all the booksellers; and of these pamphlets the most galling were written under the direction of the malignant Temple."

Horace Walpole says again :—

" But while the wit and revelry of Wilkes and Churchill ran riot, and were diverted by their dissipation to other subjects of pleasantry or satire, they had a familiar at their ear, whose venom was never distilled at random, but each drop administered to some precious work of mischief. This was *Earl Temple, who whispered them where they might find torches, but took care never to be seen light one himself.* Characters so rash and imprudent were proper vehicles of his spite, and he enjoyed the two points he preferred even to power—vengeance and a whole skin."[1]

Upon another occasion he describes him as—

" accustomed to run and meet faction in the highways," and " who never wanted fear, where there was room for it, and who had no taste for anything that did not lead directly home to faction;" as one in whom " the love of confusion predominated even over his ambition." * *

" In truth nothing could be more offensive than Lord Temple's conduct, whether considered in a public or private light. Opposition to his factious views seemed to let him loose from all ties, all restraint of principles."

Upon Lord Temple's refusal to join Mr. Pitt, in June, 1765, Walpole again exclaims :—

" But what could excuse the conduct of Lord Temple, who, having an opportunity of redressing all the breaches of the constitution, against which he had been so clamorous, now not only waived that duty, but leagued with the very men whom their own guilt, and his voice and pen, had pointed out as the criminals."[2]

---

[1] *Memoirs of George III.*, vol. i. p. 182.   [2] *Ibid.*, vol. ii. p. 188.

In a letter to George Montague, dated July 21, 1766, Walpole writes :—

" You may strike up your sackbut, psaltery, and dulcimer, for Mr. Pitt comes in and Lord Temple does not.   Can I send you a more welcome affirmative or negative.   My sackbut is not very sweet, but here is the Ode I have made for it :—

> " When Britain heard the woeful news
> That Temple was to be Minister,
> To look upon it could she choose
> But as an omen most sinister ?
> But when she heard he did refuse
> In spite of Lady Chat., his sister,
> What could she do but laugh, O ! Muse ?
> And so she did, until ———.

If that snake had wriggled in, he would have drawn after him the whole herd of vipers : his brother Demogorgon and all.   'T is a blessed deliverance."

In his *Memoirs of the Reign of George the Second,* Walpole described Lord Temple to be—

"indecently forward to come into place, and having always hated by the scale of his ambition, he had only passions to sacrifice, not principles, when the terms of his advancement were to be adjusted."

The attachment of Lord Temple to Wilkes has been seen by the correspondence between them in these volumes, and upon several occasions Junius displays the same personal feelings of kindness towards Wilkes.

" I have served Mr. Wilkes, and am still capable of serving him."—*Junius,* vol. i. p. 295.

" I love the cause independent of persons, and I wish well to Mr. Wilkes independent of the cause."—*Ibid.,* vol. i. p. 326.

" Continue careful of your health.   Your head is too useful to be spared, and your hand may be wanted."—*Ibid.,* vol. i. 314.

" Depend upon it, the perpetual union of *Wilkes* and *mob* does you no service.   Not but that I love and esteem the mob.   It is your interest to keep up dignity and gravity besides.   I would not make myself cheap by walking the streets so much as you do. *Verbum sat.*"—*Ibid.,* vol. i. p. 317.

When Wilkes's complaint of a breach of privilege was taken

into consideration by the House of Commons, Mr. Pitt said, in allusion to the *North Britons*, that—

"he condemned the whole series of them. The author did not deserve to be ranked among the human species; he was the blasphemer of his God, and the libeller of his King. He had no connection with him. He had no connection with any such writer. He neither associated nor communicated with any such. It was true that he had friendships, and warm ones: he had obligations, and great ones; but no friendships, no obligations, should induce him to approve what he firmly condemned. It might be supposed that he alluded to his noble relation (Lord Temple). He was proud to call him his relation: he was his friend, his bosom friend, whose fidelity was as unshaken as his virtue. They went into office together, and they came out together: they had lived together, and would die together. He knew nothing of any connection with the writer of the libel. If there subsisted any, he was totally unacquainted with it."[1]

Lord Temple had also, in the House of Lords,

"disculpated himself from encouraging the general satire in the *North Britons*, and said he had always condemned the attack on the Scotch, and on the Tories, in that paper."[2]

Notwithstanding these denials, Lord Temple was generally believed to be a contributor to the *North Briton,* and in some of the papers the style of Junius is certainly perceptible. In one of his letters to Wilkes he pretends to condemn the wholesale abuse of the Scotch nation, but upon another occasion his antipathy shows itself, when Wilkes, as Lieutenant-Colonel of the Bucks Militia, had written to him respecting the appointment of a surgeon to the regiment, Lord Temple ironically replied, "I hope he is a Scotchman."

Upon occasion of one of the debates in the House of Commons respecting Wilkes,

"Rigby, looking at Lord Temple, who was sitting at the end of the House to hear the debate, as he constantly practised, drew a picture of that incendiary Peer, described him in his blue riband encouraging mobs from windows of coffee-houses, and more particularly as the instigator of Wilkes. James Grenville rose in amazing heat to defend

---

[1] *Almon's Anecdotes of Lord Chatham,* vol. ii. p. 94.
[2] *Walpole's Memoirs of George III.,* vol. i. p. 329.

his brother, and vomited out a torrent of invectives on Rigby, telling him of his interested ignorance," &c. [1]

In a debate in the House of Lords on the ESSAY ON WOMAN,

" Warm words passed between Lord Temple and Lord Marchmont, the latter of whom said, that though Wilkes was gone, he had left his gang behind him." [2]

Lord Barrington writes to Mr. Mitchell, in May, 1763 :—

" I am sorry and ashamed to say that Lord Temple has on this, and all similar occasions, united himself to Mr. Wilkes and the mob." [3]

These passages have been selected with the view of displaying, in their own words, the estimation in which the character of Lord Temple was held by some of his contemporary politicians, as well with regard to his opinions as his talents, and in order to show how much he was disliked by the principals of his party, and the motives which might actuate him in the literary vengeance which he afterwards, in his character of Junius, inflicted upon them. Although he seems upon all occasions to have been very desirous of conciliating the Rockinghams and Bedfords, neither of those connections ever evinced any disposition to serve with him or under him; and his long exclusion from office may be ascribed to the disinclination which existed among the statesmen of all parties, in the various negotiations which took place from the year 1763 to 1768, to admit him to any share of power, while they would willingly have connected themselves with Mr. Grenville, if there had been any means of detaching him again from Lord Temple.

In the transactions of 1763 and 1765, it was much more the haughtiness and impracticability of Lord Temple, than any other difficulties encountered by Mr. Pitt, which prevented him from forming a strong and lasting Administration, and this was no doubt seen and felt by Mr. Pitt. It was observed by Horace Walpole in 1764, during a visit which he made to Stowe, how little cordiality subsisted between them, and from about that time

---

[1] *Walpole's Memoirs of George III.*, vol. i. p. 327.

[2] *Ibid.*, vol. i. p. 355.

[3] *Ellis's Original Letters*, 2nd Series, vol. iv. p. 465.

Lord Temple had leaned towards his brother George Grenville, and—

"as if the love of confusion predominated over his ambition, he selected the important moment in May, 1765, to clog Mr. Pitt's measures by openly rushing into connection with his brother George."[1]

The coolness between Lord Temple and Mr. Pitt most probably took its rise from the intimate association of the former with Wilkes and his companions, an alliance of which Mr. Pitt very much disapproved, as it was no doubt the cause of great anger and dislike on the part of the King towards Lord Temple, which had been shown in a variety of ways, officially by dismissal from the Lord Lieutenantcy of Bucks, and afterwards more personally by his being forbidden the Court[2].

Subsequently, when the King had been induced to send for Lord Temple to form an Administration with Mr. Pitt, the pleasure which the King evinced upon his declining to do so, is thus mentioned by Lord Temple himself, in a letter to his brother George, dated July 18, 1766 :—

"I had my last audience of the King yesterday at three o'clock. I stayed with him an hour: very gracious, and I believe not a little delighted with my declining."[3]

---

[1] *Walpole's Memoirs of George III.*, vol. ii. p. 173.

[2] Letter from Lord Egremont to Mr. Grenville, *ante*, vol. ii. p. 52.

[3] George the Third has not only been said to have disliked the Grenvilles, but to have even extended his dislike to Lord Chatham, after his reconciliation with Lord Temple; though that may perhaps in some measure be attributed to the part taken by Lord Chatham in opposition to the Court, on the question of the Middlesex election, and subsequently to his politics on the subject of America. In August, 1775, Lord North having proposed that Lord Chatham's pension should be settled in reversion on his younger son, the King replied :—"The making Lord Chatham's family suffer for the conduct of their father is not in the least agreeable to my sentiments. But I should choose to know him to be totally unable to appear again on the public stage, before I agree to any offer of that kind, lest it should be wrongly construed into a fear of him; and indeed his political conduct the last winter was so abandoned, that he must in the eyes of the dispassionate have totally undone all the merit of his former conduct. As to any gratitude to be expected *from him or his family*[a], the whole tenor of their lives has shown them void of that most honourable sentiment. But when decrepitude or death puts an end to him as a trumpet of sedition, I shall make no difficulty in placing the second son's name instead of the father's, and making up the pension £3000."—*Lord Brougham's Sketches, George III.*, p. 15.

[a] *His family* could only refer to the Grenvilles, for the Pitts were too young at that time to have incurred the charge of ingratitude.

In the evening of the same day Lord Temple told Lord Northington that " the farce was at an end, and the masque was off :
his Lordship need not have sent for him from the country, for
there was no real wish or intention to have him in the Administration."[1] Lord Temple very keenly felt the treatment he experienced on this occasion, as well as the provoking silence with
which his resignation in October, 1761, had been accepted : when
a Peerage to Lady Hester, and a pension to himself[2], were the
rewards of Pitt, not the slightest notice was taken either at that
time or afterwards of the loss of Lord Temple's services ; he
retired without regret, his opinion slighted, and his opposition
disregarded. Walpole writes to Conway in October, 1761,—
" Lord Temple is all hostility, and goes to the Drawing-room to
tell everybody how angry he is with the Court :" and at the same
time Rigby writes to the Duke of Bedford :—

" I saw Lord Egremont at Court, and wished him joy. I saw it
indeed in his countenance. The reverse was as visible in Lord Temple's, who, Mr. Elliot informs me, does not take all this business in
the same manner Mr. Pitt does, and gave Mr. Elliot notice that he
meant to appeal to the public for his justification."

This business, as Rigby calls it, was no doubt the cause of deep

---

[1] *Almon's Anecdotes*, vol. ii. p. 179.

[2] At this time was published a Satirical Poem called RODONDO, *or the State Jugglers.*
It had on the title-page the motto, subsequently adopted by Junius :—" Stat magni
nominis umbra."—*Lucan.* The author was a Mr. Hugh Dalrymple, who also wrote
Woodstock, an Elegy ; he was Attorney-General of the Grenadas, and died in 1774[a].
This satire is chiefly devoted to abuse of Lord Temple and Pitt ; it is frequently in
very coarse language, and much resembling in style the writings of Peter Pindar.
The following is a specimen :—

> " When even Temple grew a wise man,
> And gauged the State like an exciseman :
> Imbibing sympathetic wit
> And eloquence from brother Pitt,
> Then great Rodondo left the steerage,
> And took a pension and a peerage ;
> Yet warned by patriot Pulteney's fate,
> He kecked and boggled at the bait :
> Nor would he touch a single tester,
> But left all that to Lady Hester."

[a] See MS. note by Isaac Reed, prefixed to a copy of *Rodondo* in the British
Museum.

resentment in a mind constituted like that of Lord Temple, and his subsequent dismissal from the Lord Lieutenantcy of Bucks conveyed in a letter from Lord Halifax in terms so strictly official, and so evidently contemptuous, must have filled up the cup of his bitterness.

Supposing that Lord Temple were Junius, these were sufficient causes, even if there were no others, for his rancorous hatred to the King: scarcely any other object of his scurrilous abuse was more severely dealt with than the King himself, for although he declared that the Duke of Grafton should be "the pillow on which he was determined to rest all his resentments,"[1] yet he certainly divided his favours with the King.

"While I remember," says Junius, "how much is due to *his* sacred character, I cannot with any decent appearance of propriety call you the meanest and the basest fellow in the kingdom. I protest, my Lord, I do not think you so."

It is due to the honourable forbearance of Mr. Woodfall and his descendants, to mention that some of the most violent language of Junius against the King has not hitherto been published; particularly the latter part of a letter signed *Vindex*, written in February, 1771, which still remains in manuscript[2].

There were many channels through which, particularly with the assistance of Lady Temple and her close intimacy with the Princess Amelia, Lord Temple could become well acquainted with all the interior details of Court gossip, and he would learn by this means how much he shared with his protégé Wilkes the active

---

[1] When Junius wrote this sentence, he had perhaps in his mind a saying of Lord Coke's, that the Chief Justiceship of the Common Pleas was the "*pillow whereon the Attorney doth rest his head.*" Some extracts from the works of Lord Coke still remaining in Lord Temple's autograph, show that he was a reader and admirer of his writings.

[2] Mr. Sergeant Rough, by whom the original letters from Junius to Wilkes were communicated to the late Mr. Woodfall for publication in 1812, mentions in a letter to Mr. Barker, dated in 1827, that he suppressed "*a line or two in which the King was spoken of upon alleged personal knowledge, with much bitterness.*" He adds, "They belonged to Mr. P. Elmsley, the late Principal of St. Albans [Oxford], who, as I believe, possessed them as executor to his father. His knowledge of me as a brother Westminster with me, and the circumstance of my having married an acknowledged daughter of Mr. Wilkes, induced him to decline letting Mr. Woodfall have them without my assent. They came to me from my friend Mr. Hallam, to whom they were afterwards returned for Mr. Elmsley." It is not known who is now in possession of these letters.

c 2

indignation of George III., which was so well known to have been raised to its utmost height by the cry of *Wilkes and Liberty.*

The Duke of Grafton had formerly been the very intimate friend and associate of Temple and Wilkes; he completed the desertion of both by joining the Rockingham Administration, although he had offended Lord Temple long before, when he seceded from the cause of Wilkes by refusing to become his bail in May, 1763[1]. The tenor of the Duke's letter on this subject to Lord Temple would clearly account for the "first and the unconquerable disgust" which Junius subsequently displayed towards the Duke of Grafton.

It was a remarkable feature in Lord Temple's character that he warmly and generously adopted injuries or affronts to his friends as if they were personally inflicted upon himself. With these feelings he earnestly resented the treatment Wilkes had experienced from the Duke of Grafton: it seems to have inflamed his anger even more than the Duke's ingratitude towards Lord Chatham. Many times does Junius return with invigorated rancour to the subject of the abandonment of Wilkes by the Duke of Grafton, and the persecution he had suffered from his former friend and associate.

" As for Mr. Wilkes, it is perhaps the greatest misfortune of his life that you should have so many compensations to make in the Closet for your former friendship with him. Your gracious Master understands your character, and makes you a persecutor because you have been a friend."—*Junius*, vol. i. p. 484.

"Was not Lord Chatham the first who raised him [the Duke of Grafton] to the rank and post of a Minister, and the first whom he abandoned? Did he not join with Lord Rockingham and betray him? Was he not the bosom friend of Mr. Wilkes, whom he now pursues to destruction?"—*Ibid.*, vol. i. p. 494.

" The Duke of Grafton has always some excellent reasons for deserting his friends: the age and incapacity of Lord Chatham, the debility of Lord Rockingham, or the infamy of Mr. Wilkes. There was a time, indeed, when he did not appear to be quite so well acquainted, or so violently offended with the infirmities of his friends."—*Junius*, vol. i. p. 500.

[1] See letter from the Duke of Grafton to Lord Temple, *ante*, vol. ii. p. 53.

It will be seen also from many letters in this collection, that in the negotiation with Lord Rockingham and the Duke of Bedford through the medium of the Duke of Grafton, it was his Grace who always objected to the nomination of Lord Temple; even the commission to Lord Rockingham in 1767 was supposed to be unlimited, except as to the exclusion of Lord Temple and Mr. Grenville; and in a letter from Mr. Grenville to his brother at that period, he mentions the Duke of Grafton's *jockey tricks*.

As early as August, 1766, he was assisting Lord Chatham by endeavouring to detach the Duke of Bedford from the Grenville connection, and upon this Gerard Hamilton observes to Lord Temple,—

"their" [the Bedfords'] "difficulty is not occasioned by the nature of their engagements, but by some dispute about the disadvantageousness of the terms."

The final abandonment of the Grenvilles by the Duke of Bedford and his party, at the end of the year 1767, was certainly contrived by the Duke of Grafton, and would be sufficient to account for the extreme animosity of Junius against those two Dukes. It was at a time, too, when Lord Temple was desirous of coalescing with the Bedfords, and his expectations were disappointed by the intrigues of the Duke of Grafton[1].

The following passage, founded upon the letters of Miss Wrottesley[2] to the Duke of Bedford, is quoted from Wiffen's *Memoirs of the House of Russell* : —

" In the midst of the agitation arising from the General Election in March, 1768, Mr. Wilkes returned from his exile to add new strength to the tempest. Lord Temple was early disposed to avow himself his champion and patron. He said publicly that he loved faction, and had a great deal of spare money, and he held meetings at his house, whence many of those civic patriots drew their inspiration, and afterwards when the frenzy for Wilkes was at the highest, distinguished themselves in what may not unsuitably be called the Saturnalia of Freedom. Mr. Grenville, justly alarmed at his brother's conversation, sent Whately and Lord Suffolk to him : they attacked him at the Opera[3], and got

---

[1] See a letter from Lord Temple to Mr. Grenville, *post*, vol. iv. p. 178.

[2] Miss Wrottesley, the writer, was a niece of the Duchess of Bedford.

[3] Lord and Lady Temple went very frequently to the Opera, as I find from this and other contemporary letters. At the time the above was written, Junius, in a letter to

him to say that he would do nothing at present, but would make no promises for the future. It was not long before he entered into all the mazes of City politics, and gambolled in the mischief which he so studiously sought."

The animosity of Lord Temple, however, towards the Duke of Bedford commenced at an earlier period. He had accepted the office of Lord Privy Seal upon the resignation of the former in 1761, and he was subsequently employed to negotiate the Peace of Paris, of which it is well known Lord Temple and Mr. Pitt so much disapproved. In a letter from the Duke of Bedford to Mr. Neville, dated Woburn Abbey, September 5, 1763, in allusion to the recent changes in the Ministry, and the negotiation with Mr. Pitt and Lord Temple, he says :—

"You may easily imagine that I and my friends were to be made examples of; and Mr. Pitt did not scruple to tell the King, that events might possibly arise in consequence of the Peace which might make it *criminal* in me to have signed it, and that I never more should be trusted in an efficient place in the King's service, but that it might be hereafter possible to give me a place of honour, but no trust."[1]

Horace Walpole compares the Duke of Bedford to Don Carlos, "who could be made to take half of what he meant for the whole;" he adds that the Duke was—

"clamorous against a Spanish war, and as he always compensated for the arguments he leaped over, by excess on the other side, he told

the Duke of Grafton, mentions his appearance at the Opera with Miss Nancy Parsons, in a passage which I have subsequently quoted [vol. iv. p. 276], and the minute details of his accusation against the Duke seem to imply that the writer was himself present, and witnessed the delinquencies which he describes.

Lord Temple's fondness for the Opera is alluded to in some verses on Wilkes and Churchill having gone to France, printed in the *Public Advertiser* of Tuesday, January 17, 1764 :—

> " But say, ye matchless couple, was it kind
> To fly and leave dear *Tiddy-Doll*[a] behind ?
> Now you are gone, life's hardly worth his care ;
> Where shall he find him such another pair.
> Not his lov'd Opera *now* can give him ease,
> Nor popularity itself can please.
> The peerless Peer arraigns the partial Fates
> And droops and mourns the absence of his mates."

[1] *Bedford Correspondence*, vol. iii. p. 240.

[a] Tiddy-Doll is a *sobriquet* applied to Lord Temple in the satirical poem of *Rodondo*, see *ante*, page xxxiv.

Bussy, he was sorry for his departure, as we were no longer in a situation to make war." [1]

On the 6th of November, 1761, after the King's Speech, in the debate on the Address in the House of Lords,—

"Lord Temple rose, and opened on his own and Mr. Pitt's resignations, the motives to which he explained; found fault that no mention was made of the Militia, and that the Parliament had not been thanked for establishing it. He talked on Court favour, and on those who disposed of all things, endeavouring to provoke Lord Bute to rise. He said the crisis for a war with Spain had been most advantageously held out to this country, *and complained of those who had betrayed the secrets of our situation to Bussy.*" [2]

In a note to this passage Walpole adds :—

"It is certain that M. de Bussy told different persons what the Duke of Bedford had said to him, particularly to Lady Hervey, from whom I had it."

Junius thus expresses himself with regard to the Duke of Bedford, in a private note to Woodfall, dated *Thursday night* [October 5, 1769] :—

"I reserve some things expressly to awe him in case he should think of bringing you before the House of Lords. I am sure I can threaten him privately with such a storm, as would [make] him tremble even [in] his grave." [3]

---

[1] *Memoirs of George III.*, vol. i. p. 78.

[2] *Memoirs of George III.*, vol. i. p. 89. See also the *Letters of Mary Lepel Lady Hervey*, 8vo, 1821, p. 279, where the same story is alluded to, but the editor of that publication was not then able to explain its meaning. Lady Hervey entirely corroborates Walpole's information, although the Duke of Bedford is only mentioned as "a great rich person." She adds,—"Perhaps you may guess at him, when I tell you 't is one who has some parts, at least verbal ones, in a particular assembly, but has no judgment anywhere, but great heat, violence of temper, and an obstinate wrongheadedness, which is, however, twisted and turned about to serve the views and interests of one [meaning Rigby probably] who entirely governs him, and, as it has been for some time reported, sold him to one whom you may remember I have always despised and hated."

[3] When Junius wrote that passage to Woodfall, he probably had in his mind the following lines from Churchill's dedication of his poem, the *Rosciad*, to Bishop Warburton—

> "Methinks I hear the deep-toned thunders roll,
> And chill with horror every sinner's soul——
> In vain they strive to fly—flight cannot save :
> *And Potter trembles even in his grave.*"

These words were likely to occur to Lord Temple, as both Potter and Churchill had been his very intimate friends.

Lord Temple had probably derived some secret information relative to the negotiations for the Peace in his subsequent conversations with Mr. Grenville, with whom it should be remembered he was not upon speaking terms at that period [1763], and the remarks made by Junius respecting the "callous pride," the "Tory principles," and the "English stuff" of Lord Egremont, favour that supposition. They evince also a knowledge of his correspondence with Mr. Grenville, and that Lord Egremont very frequently disapproved of the proceedings of the Duke of Bedford while he was at Paris[1]. In allusion to Lord Egremont's sudden and untimely death, Junius says, in his letter to the Duke of Bedford,—

" He saw and felt his own dishonour in corresponding with you ; and there certainly was a moment at which he meant to have resisted, had not a fatal lethargy prevailed over his faculties, and carried all sense and memory away with it."—Vol. i. p. 581.

At the date of the above-mentioned note to Woodfall, Junius was aware also that the rumours circulated by Dr. Musgrave on the subject of the Peace would become matter of consideration at the ensuing meeting of Parliament. The accusations of Dr. Musgrave were accordingly brought forward at the opening of the Session in January following, when they were voted *frivolous* by the House of Commons. Junius was no doubt disappointed at the result of the inquiry, which he had most unreasonably expected would have damaged the political as well as private character of the Duke of Bedford, whose name he artfully wished to include in the charges of Dr. Musgrave, whereas in truth the Duke was not even alluded to. The persons accused of having been bribed by the French Court were the Princess Dowager, Lord Bute, and Lord Holland.

The anger and resentment of Lord Temple against the Duke became furious after the Bedford party had completely separated from the Grenvilles, and we need seek no further to find reasons for the virulent abuse, and gratification of personal revenge, with which the Duke was subsequently assailed in the writings of Junius.

---

[1] See *ante*, vol. i. p. 475, *et seq.*

The Duke of Bedford had never been in private life upon more than civil terms with Mr. Grenville or Lord Temple, and the civility was tempered with much coldness and suspicion. There was ever a want of cordiality in their communications: their mutual visits at Stowe, Wotton, and Woburn, were merely formal and complimentary. Mr. Grenville was more inclined to think well of the Duke of Bedford and his friends, than Lord Temple, who often expressed to his brother a suspicion of their insincerity. The Bedfords certainly disliked Lord Temple. Mr. Grenville mentions in his Diary, under the date of November, 1766, that Rigby told him Lord Temple had said :—

"*that the Bedfords were hungry*, but it did not much signify, for they all, as a Party, desired to have it understood that their wishes went to Mr. Grenville, not to Lord Temple."

The Duke of Bedford's disinclination towards the Grenvilles had rapidly increased after the failure of the negotiations with Lord Rockingham and the Duke of Grafton in July, 1767, and it is evident that all these leaders of parties had equal dislike of Lord Temple.

The opinions of Junius would be very consistent with those of Lord Temple at the period of the accession of George III., for Lord Temple would naturally speak with satisfaction of the political aspect of the country, and the situation of public affairs, under an Administration in which he had himself been a prominent member, and by which the flourishing state of the country had been produced.

Junius says,—

"When our gracious Sovereign ascended the throne, we were a flourishing and contented people."—[Vol. i. p. 390.]

And again,—

"He [the King] found this country in that state of perfect union and happiness which good government naturally produces, and which a bad one has destroyed."—[Vol. iii. p. 371.]

At any period previous to their mutual resignation in October, 1761, it may be safely inferred that Mr. Pitt and Lord Temple were upon the most amicable and affectionate terms, upon all public as well as private questions. Mr. Pitt, during the whole of his Administration, relied entirely upon the advice and opinions of Lord Temple in the management of the War, and, indeed, entirely confided in him on the adoption of all measures of importance.

Murray and Pitt had always been rivals in the House of Commons, and they continued so in the Cabinet after Murray became Lord Mansfield and Lord Chief Justice. Lord Temple, as was his custom, adopted the rivalry of his friend Pitt, and he had from an early period disliked Lord Mansfield.

In the year 1758, Temple took an active part in the proceedings in the House of Lords to explain and amend the Habeas Corpus Act, in opposition to Mansfield, who, in a speech which he made upon the occasion, ridiculed Lord Temple's misplaced zeal, and his total ignorance of the subject, in terms which Lord Temple could not easily forget, and if he wrote the Letters of Junius, certainly did not forgive. The following are the speeches of Lord Temple and Lord Mansfield, taken from Lord Hardwicke's Papers :—

" Earl Temple spoke much and warmly of the importance of Liberty, and of this Bill to the security of it, and regretted that his own ill state of health, as well as slender abilities, would not allow him to dó justice to the subject. He hoped that the House would not suffer itself to be too much influenced on such questions by the authority of two Lords [Hardwicke and Mansfield] whose eminence in the knowledge of the law he acknowledged; and he desired still more importunately, that it would not depart from its own dignity by referring questions to the Judges, which their Lordships' ancestors had already determined, and in which those Judges themselves were interested, and by the determination of which they might acquire a power formidable to the Peers themselves, who might suffer by it even for their conduct in that House. That he would not take the law from the Judges, as to the main principles of it [1], any more than he would ask the bench of Bishops

---

[1] " It is a point of fact, on which every English gentleman will determine for himself. As to lawyers, their profession is supported by the indiscriminate defence of right and wrong, and I confess I have not that opinion of their knowledge or integrity, to think it necessary that they should decide for me upon a plain constitutional question."— *Junius*, vol. i. p. 498.

" Without pretending to reconcile the distinctions of Westminster Hall, with the

about the great outlines of his religion. He then desired that the journals of the Lords concerning the liberty of the subject in the years 1628, 1641, 1677, and 1704 [1], should be read; the resolutions of their Lordships in 1704, in the case of *the Aylesbury men* [2], being drawn up by Lord Somers."

Lord Mansfield spoke half an hour, and began with—

" excusing the great zeal shown by many persons for the Bill, from their total ignorance of what it was, and their groundless imagination that Liberty was concerned in it, which had no more connection with the Bill than with the Act of Navigation, or that for encouraging the cultivation of madder. *That ignorance on subjects of this kind was extremely pardonable, since the knowledge of positive laws required a particular study of them,* and the greatest genius, without such study, could no more become master of them, than of what was contained in the Japanese history without understanding the language of the country." [3]

Temple suspected Lord Mansfield of doing him ill offices in the Closet with George II. Lord Waldegrave relates [4], that when the King gave Mansfield full powers to negotiate with Pitt and the Duke of Newcastle, he insisted that Temple should have no employment that required frequent personal attendance on the Sovereign, and it was even with great difficulty that George II. was persuaded to give Lord Temple the Garter [5].

After the accession of the new King, Lord Mansfield's political importance had considerably increased, and scarcely any individual member of the Cabinet possessed and exercised greater in-

---

simple information of common sense, or the integrity of fair argument," &c., &c.—*Ibid.*, vol. ii. p. 176.

" When law and reason speak plainly, we do not want authority to direct our understandings."—*Ibid.*, vol. i. p. 369.

" When the laws, plain of themselves, are illustrated by facts, and their uniform mean-ing illustrated by history, we do not want the authority of opinions, however respect-able, to inform our judgment, or to confirm our belief."—*Ibid.*, vol. ii. p. 427.

[1] The Resolutions of the House of Lords, here alluded to by Lord Temple, of the years 1628 and 1704, are both quoted in full by Junius in his 48th Letter, Vol. ii. 238–39.

[2] The case of *the Aylesbury men* is also mentioned by Junius, see vol. i. p. 529, and vol. iii. p. 362.

[3] As Junius, Lord Temple replied to this some years afterwards, when, in a Letter to Lord Mansfield, he says :—" To investigate a question of law demands some labour and attention, though very little genius or sagacity. As a *practical profession, the study of the law* requires but a moderate portion of abilities."—*Junius*, ii. 412.

[4] *Memoirs*, p. 128.

[5] See *ante*, vol. i. p. 337–38.

fluence over the councils of George III. during the early years of
his reign.

Lord Brougham, in his *Sketches of Statesmen*, says,—

" He [Mansfield] not only acted as Speaker of the House of Lords for
above a year, but for a much longer time he had a seat in the Cabinet,
and took a part in the business of Government, *all the more objectionable in his position, that it was much more active than it was open,and
avowed.*" [1]

He was now closely connected with Lord Bute's Administration, against which Lord Temple was an active and energetic
leader of Opposition, and a bitter personal animosity sprung up
between them, which was much inflamed by the supposed partiality of Lord Mansfield as a judge in all cases where the liberty
of the press was concerned ; and his subsequent conduct in the
several cases of Wilkes, Woodfall, Almon, &c., in which Lord
Temple took so much active and personal interest, added to the
intensity of his hatred.

Walpole relates, that on the Regency Bill debate in the House
of Lords, after Lord Mansfield's speech,—

" Lord Temple shrewdly and bitterly, with allusion to Lord Mansfield's
friends, family, and supposed principles, asked him, supposing the
Parliament had left to Queen Anne the secret nomination of her
successor, whom his Lordship thought she would have appointed?"

The Bill was carried by 120 to 9, and, continues Walpole,—

" Thus Lord Temple, with his small faction, and one or two of Mr. Pitt's
friends, was deserted, after the most sanguine expectations of a vigorous
opposition. He resented this desertion with his *usual intemperance;*
yet what claim had he on the concurrence of those with whom he
had sedulously declined all connection? His resentment on this
occasion was, I doubt not, a leading step to a new alliance, into which
he soon after hurried." [2]

Almon asserts, that after Lord Temple's resignation in 1761,
Lord Bute had made more than one unsuccessful attempt at re-

---

[1] Junius says to Lord Mansfield, —" Instead of acting that open, generous part,
which becomes your rank and station, *you meanly skulk into the Closet,* and give your
Sovereign such advice as you have not spirit to defend. *You secretly engross the power
while you decline the title of Minister.*"—Vol. ii. p. 179.

[2] *Memoirs of George III.*, vol. ii. p. 114–15.

conciliation with him. Upon the motion in the House of Lords
for papers relative to the rupture with Spain,—

" Lord Temple observed, concerning the Family Compact, that it had
been signed in August, had been ratified in September, and the written
advice of Mr. Pitt and himself was given and dated on the 18th of that
month. Upon which Lord Bute rose in much heat, and gave to Lord
Temple the most flat and unqualified contradiction. He declared
upon his *honour* that there was no intelligence of such a fact so constituted at that time. These words brought up Lord Temple again,
who likewise declared upon his *honour* that there was intelligence of
the highest moment relative to these matters at that time ; that he
was not at liberty to declare it publicly, but he would refresh his Lordship's memory in private. In a private conference between them,
Lord Bute admitted that he recollected the facts as they had been
stated, but when he returned into the House of Lords, he did not,
which as a gentleman he ought to have done, stand up in his place and
acknowledge his mistake. It will not be thought improbable that
Lord Temple's enmity to Lord Bute was embittered by this circumstance ; and it was not the only occasion on which the lie direct was
given by Lord Bute. On the 28th of March, 1763, Lord Temple's
speech in the House of Lords on presenting the City Petition against
the Excise Laws, mentioned the circumstance of Lord Bute's tampering
with the City Committee. Upon which Lord Bute got up and assured
the House that the whole was a FACTIOUS LIE. An inquiry having
been instituted by the Corporation of London, it was made indisputably
clear," continues Almon, " *who was the liar.*"

" Nor will it be improper to take notice of another circumstance
which was indeed of less moment, but not less personally insulting to
the feelings of Lord Temple and Mr. Pitt. On the first Court-day
after the accession of George III., and while the late King lay dead in
his palace, Lord George Sackville made his appearance at St. James's,
and was admitted to kiss the King's hand. This was such an outrage
on the memory of the late King, and on the honour of those who had
the conduct of the war, that they were perfectly astonished at it, and
made inquiry into the cause of it, when, to their no less surprise, they
found that Lord George had been invited to Court by .the Earl of
Bute." [1]

To these causes of animosity against Lord Bute may be added

[1] *Almon's Biographical and Political Anecdotes, passim.*

that the characters and persons of Mr. Pitt and Lord Temple were reviled and ridiculed in the publications of the *Briton*, the *Auditor*, &c., supposed to be by writers in the pay of Lord Bute, such as Smollett, Shebbeare, Guthrie, &c.

To counteract the venom of these papers, the *North Briton* was projected by Wilkes and Churchill. Almon admits that Lord Temple was not ignorant of the design, and certainly approved of it, although he pretended that the severity of some of the reflections upon the Scotch did not meet with his entire approbation.

" He frequently assisted his friends in the production of these papers, not indeed with his pen, but with his information and line of reasoning."

There can be very little doubt but that Lord Temple wrote several of the papers in the *North Briton;* there are evident traces of his style, particularly in the celebrated Number Forty-five, and the account which Almon gives in his *Memoirs of Wilkes,* of the origin of that Number, corroborates the supposition that Lord Temple assisted Wilkes upon that occasion, more, perhaps, than the latter would consider it honourable or right to have admitted.

Mr. Grenville being obliged to ask his brother's permission to be re-elected for the borough of Buckingham, upon his being appointed First Lord of the Treasury, and the two brothers being then upon ill terms, the letter was carried by Charles Lloyd, Mr. Grenville's secretary, and it enclosed, by way of compliment, a copy of the King's Speech, as it was intended to be delivered from the throne on the following day.

Mr Pitt was with Lord Temple in Pall Mall when the message arrived, and Almon says that they were—

" much displeased on reading the King's Speech, which they had thus received. Mr. Pitt spoke with warmth and indignation on the passage respecting the King of Prussia; and Lord Temple adopted his sentiments. At this instant Mr. Wilkes happened to call upon his Lordship, having just returned from Paris. Mr. Wilkes agreed in sentiment concerning the speech ; and when he returned home, he wrote a sketch of the conversation which passed on the subject while he was present.

From this sketch, and some additions of his own, he wrote this celebrated paper, the forty-fifth number, which was published on Saturday,
the 23rd of April, 1763."[1]

Lord Temple wrote what Almon calls " a fair and constitutional
Defence of this paper of the *North Briton*." A few copies only
of this Defence were printed, and not published. I have never
been able to meet with one, but some extracts are given by
Álmon[2], which sufficiently indicate that, by cultivation and improvement, the writer would subsequently become capable of being
the Author of Junius.

It appears to me extremely probable that Lord Temple was also
the writer of—

" A FRAGMENT, which it is said was found in the pocket of one of the
printers who were apprehended by the King's messengers, supposed to
have been intended for Number xlvi. of the *North Briton*, to be
published on the following Saturday, April 30, 1763."

The general style is very similar to that of Junius. It commences thus:—" It is a very melancholy consideration," &c., &c.
The paper enclosed by the Author of Junius to Mr. Grenville, in
February, 1768, commences precisely in the same manner[3]. It
may be stated also, upon the authority of Almon, who, it should
be remembered, derived his information principally from Lord
Temple himself, that in March, 1763, Lord Bute caused an offer
to be made to Lord Temple and Mr. Pitt, by Mr. Hans Stanley,
that if they would withdraw from the Whigs, he would make an
opening to them to return to Administration. He was, however,
unsuccessful, and he then returned to Mr. Grenville, and that this
was the cause of the sudden succession of Mr. Grenville to the
Ministry[4].

Again, in January, 1766, Lord Bute is said to have made
another unsuccessful attempt at a reconciliation with Lord Temple,
through the medium of Lord Eglintoun; and Almon asserts that,
notwithstanding the failure of this project, Lord Bute found
means through one of the Princess's confidants to amuse Lord

---

[1] *Almon's Memoirs and Correspondence of Wilkes,* vol. i. p. 95.
[2] *Anecdotes,* vol. ii. p. 16.   [3] See vol. iv. p. 256.
[4] See *ante,* vol. ii. p. 32, *note.*

Temple with assurances, that a *carte blanche* would shortly be offered to him, and this manœuvre succeeded so well that Lord Temple was completely duped by it, and for some time believed the assurances. That Lord Bute should have been more successful in gaining Lord Chatham is thus alluded to by the Author of Junius, in one of the earliest letters attributed to him, dated June, 1767:—

" It was then his good fortune to corrupt one man, from whom we least of all expected so base an apostacy. Who, indeed, could have suspected that it should ever consist with the spirit or understanding of that person, to accept of a share of power under a pernicious Court minion, whom he himself had affected to detest or despise, as much as he knew he was detested and despised by the whole nation? I will not censure him for the avarice of a pension, nor the melancholy ambition of a title. These were objects which he perhaps looked up to, though the rest of the world thought them far beneath his acceptance."—*Junius,* vol. ii. p. 467.

It seems to be an indispensable qualification in a candidate for the Authorship of Junius, that he should be proved to have had the means of knowing the technical forms of the Secretary of State's office, and that he should have been intimately acquainted with the business of the War Office. In these respects, Mr. Philip Francis fulfils in some degree the required conditions.

Between the ages of seventeen and twenty-three, he spent a certain number of months at intervals, when he was not otherwise employed, in the Secretary of State's office, and therefore he had the opportunity of learning something, however little, of its forms; and having been more than eight years in the War Office, at a more mature age, he may be presumed to have been well informed in every department of its business, although it does not appear that he rose above the situation of a subordinate clerk. He aspired to be Deputy Secretary at War, and having failed to obtain that appointment, he resigned, or, as Junius describes it, Lord Barrington contrived to *expel* him—an expression very unlikely to be employed by Francis, in speaking of himself on such an occasion.

Upon this subject, however, I need not dwell; but I beg to

refer the reader to the *Athenæum* and the *Quarterly Review*, where, as I have before mentioned, the claims of Sir Philip Francis are very conclusively settled.

My present object is to show that Lord Temple was much more intimately acquainted with the Secretary of State's Office than Mr. Francis could be, and that he had also the opportunity of knowing very particularly everything that passed in the War Office.

During the Seven Years' War, which had been carried on with so much vigour and success, Mr. Pitt held the seals of Secretary of State, and at the same time his brother-in-law Lord Temple was in office, either as First Lord of the Admiralty, or Lord Privy Seal, and in Mr. Pitt's frequent attacks of gout, which prevented his attention to public business, he entirely confided to Lord Temple the duties of the Secretary's office, he invariably consulted his opinion, and much of the success of the war has been attributed to Lord Temple's management of it. At the same period Lord Barrington was Secretary at War, and would consequently have much business to transact with Lord Temple, who would thus have ample opportunity of becoming acquainted with every detail of the War Office.

Lord Barrington had been a very early friend of the Grenvilles: he sat at the same Board of Admiralty with George Grenville, they entered public life about the same time, and they formed part of that band of youthful *patriots* who assisted to destroy the Administration of Sir Robert Walpole. Lord Temple had therefore been acquainted with Lord Barrington from the earliest period of his official life.

These circumstances are of some importance in connection with the authorship of Junius, because they account for the accurate information which Junius evidently possessed respecting the details of the army, and they explain the origin of the numerous military phrases which pervade his writings.

In the beginning of the year 1772, Junius, under the various signatures of *Veteran, Nemesis, Scotus*, &c., made some bitter reflections on the character of Lord Barrington :—

" He and I have been old acquaintance, and considering the size of

his understanding, I believe I shall be able to prove that no man in
this kingdom ever sold himself and his services to better advantage
than Lord Barrington. * * * A man whose whole life has been
employed in acting the part of a false, cringing, fawning, time-serving
courtier: a man who never had a different opinion from the Minister
for the time being, and who has always contrived to keep some lucrative
place or other under twenty different Administrations."

He gives a review of Lord Barrington's political career from its
commencement, with a minuteness of detail which could only proceed from one who had been intimately acquainted with the circumstances he describes. After the resignation of Mr. Pitt and
Lord Temple, he not only continued in office under the successive
Administrations of Lord Bute and Mr. Grenville, as Chancellor of
the Exchequer and Treasurer of the Navy, but he also adhered
to the Rockingham Administration. In 1765, says Junius
(Nemesis),—

" he gave himself back body and soul to the Duke of Cumberland and
Lord Rockingham. The last manœuvre restored him to the War
Office, where he has continued ever since with equal fidelity to Mr.
Pitt, the Duke of Grafton, and Lord North, and now he modestly tells
the whole world that *he gets nothing* by his services."

These were sufficient causes of offence to Lord Temple from
one with whom he had been for so many years on terms of intimate and confidential association, as well in private as in official
capacities.

But Lord Barrington had committed a still greater crime in the
eyes of Lord Temple, even than that of having deserted the Grenville connection. He presumed to hold an adverse opinion on
the subject of the Middlesex Election, and he it was who moved
the expulsion of Wilkes from the House of Commons, in February, 1769: the speech he made on that occasion is reported
in the *Cavendish Debates.* Lord Temple was present in the
House of Commons, and gives an account of this debate in a
letter to his sister, Lady Chatham[1].

Mr. Calcraft, who had amassed a large fortune as an army contractor, and whose business would necessarily oblige him to go

---

[1] See *Chatham Correspondence*, vol. iii. p. 349.

often to the War Office, was at this time in very intimate and confidential communication with Lord Temple, and in the course of conversation could furnish him with all the gossip which he derived from his protégé Philip Francis, one of the clerks under Lord Barrington, and therefore Lord Temple would have the means of being acquainted with all the intrigues of the office, which enabled him to gratify, under a variety of signatures, his personal pique against Lord Barrington, very likely increased by other private motives, which it may not now be possible to trace to their source.

With respect to Chamier, Bradshaw, and "such small deer," they were "insignificant creatures, not worth the generous rage of Junius," and it is quite evident that they had only the misfortune to be mentioned as a means of further annoyance to Lord Barrington and the Duke of Grafton, who were to receive more effectual stabs from their anonymous assailant, through the sides of these their subordinates.

It could be of no importance to Junius that D'Oyly and Francis were superseded or removed, or expelled from the War Office, to make room for Chamier the broker, and brother-in-law of Bradshaw, except that their grievances created some additional reasons for attacking—

"that * * * * * *   * * * * * * Barrington, whom he [Junius] proposed to entertain himself and the public with torturing, having nothing better to do."

Mr. Bradshaw, who had been lately promoted to a seat at the Board of Admiralty, was therefore in a somewhat higher capacity than the other clerks I have mentioned, and he may have been the object of some personal resentment on the part of Lord Temple, as more particular pains have been taken in the delineation of his character, for which, indeed, Junius has used some of his darkest colours.

But these men were merely the tools used by Junius in manufacturing his attacks upon their principals, in the same fashion in which he adopted the case of that petty-larceny rogue Eyre, as a means of "pulling to the ground" Lord Mansfield, or with still more reprehensible malignity, the unfortunate Miss Parsons, as a means of annoying, and exposing the private life of the Duke of Grafton.

The EARL of HILLSBOROUGH was not the object of so much virulent invective and personal abuse from Junius, as most of the other persons he attacked: he was very leniently dealt with considering that he, like Barrington, had been an early friend of the Grenvilles, and that he also had abandoned their party. His letters to Mr. Grenville are very numerous, and show that they were on very intimate terms of acquaintance[1], but they do not possess any public interest; they relate chiefly to money transactions between them.

"The Earl of Hillsborough," says Junius, under the signature of Atticus, "set out with a determined attachment to the Court party, let who would be Minister. He had one vice less than other courtiers, for he never even pretended to be a patriot. The Oxford election[2] gave him an opportunity of showing some skill in Parliamentary management, while an uniform obsequious submission to his superiors introduced him into lucrative places, and crowned his ambition with a Peerage. He is now what they call a King's man, ready, as the Closet directs, to be anything or nothing, but always glad to be employed. A new department, created on purpose for him, attracted a greater expectation than he has yet been able to support. In his first act of power, he has betrayed a most miserable want of judgment. A provision for Lord Botetourt was not an object of importance sufficient to justify a risk of the first impression which a new Minister must give of himself to the public. For my own part, I hold him in some measure excused, because I am persuaded the defence he has delivered privately to his friends is true, 'that the measure came from another and a higher quarter.' But still he is the tool, and, ceasing to be criminal, sinks into contempt. In his new department, I am sorry to say, he has shown neither abilities nor good sense. His letters to the colonies contain nothing but expressions equally loose and violent. The minds of the Americans are not to be conciliated by a language, which only contradicts without attempting to persuade. His correspondence, upon the whole, is so defective in design and composition, that it would deserve our pity, if the consequences to be dreaded from it did not excite our indignation. This treatment of the colonies, added to his

[1] Bubb Dodington, in his Diary, p. 269, speaks of them as "bosom friends."
[2] See *ante*, vol. i. p. 132, *note*.

refusal to present a petition from one of them to the King (a direct breach of the Declaration of Rights) will naturally throw them all into a flame. I protest, Sir, I am astonished at the infatuation which seems to have directed his whole conduct. The other Ministers were proceeding in their usual course, without foreseeing or regarding consequences; but this nobleman seems to have marked out by a determined choice the means to precipitate our destruction." [1]—*Junius*, vol. iii. p. 172.

When Lord Hillsborough accepted office as Secretary for the Colonies under the Duke of Grafton's Administration, he thought proper to write a sort of apologetic letter to Mr. Grenville, explaining his reasons for doing so, and this he probably considered necessary because he had previously concurred in all the measures and political opinions of Mr. Grenville.

By this desertion of his former friends, he (Lord Hillsborough) incurred the anger of Lord Temple, which was subsequently much increased by the circumstances attending the dismissal of Sir Jeffry Amherst from the Government of Virginia, for the purpose of making provision for Lord Botetourt. Sir Jeffry Amherst had been a very old friend of Lord Temple. He was appointed to a command in America during the War, by Mr. Pitt, and for his great successes there he was rewarded with the Government of Virginia, if not at the recommendation, at least with the concurrence of Lord Temple. Contemporary letters prove that he was a frequent visitor at Stowe.

Under these circumstances it is not surprising that when he was suddenly deprived of his Government, to make room for this courtier Lord, his cause should be warmly adopted and advocated by Lord Temple, under a variety of signatures, with all the zeal and vehemence of personal friendship. The letters of Mr. Whately, Mr. Knox, and Mr. Augustus Hervey, to Mr. Grenville, all advert to the subject while it was pending [2].

Colonel Norbonne Berkeley, afterwards Lord Botetourt, had been formerly an intimate friend of Lord Temple and Wilkes. In the duel between Lord Talbot and Wilkes he was second to the former, and was entrusted by Wilkes with a letter he had just

---

[1] See *post*, vol. iv. p. 380, a note relating to this passage.
[2] See *post*, vol. iv. p. 326.

written to be delivered to Lord Temple in the event of his falling[1].

Lord Botetourt, having ruined himself by gambling, was now become, says Junius,—

" the best of courtiers," and " if bowing low, and carrying the Sword of State, constitute merit and services, there are few men to whom Government are more indebted than to his Lordship."

Lord Hillsborough made a long speech against the Resolutions proposed by the Duke of Richmond in the House of Lords, in May, 1770, and Lord Temple spoke in support of them. Upon that occasion he recorded his opinion of Lord Hillsborough and his colleagues in the following terms:—

" My Lords, I have been engaged for many years in public business, I have been in office myself, and have seen Administrations that were highly obnoxious to the people, but such a set of Ministers, so lost to all sense of shame, so eminently above the mere pretence of regard for justice, I never saw. They are not satisfied with trampling on our rights, they must add insult to oppression, they must make us feel our chains, as well as labour to enslave us, and despise our resentment, while they provoke our execration."[2]

I have now mentioned the principal persons who were distinguished by the rancorous abuse of Junius, and I have endeavoured to show that there were particular reasons also why these persons had each of them incurred the political or personal resentment of Lord Temple. Besides the King, the Dukes of Grafton and Bedford, Lords Mansfield, Bute, Hillsborough, and Barrington, there were other persons included in the number of those designated as the *King's friends,* and the Bedfords, or *Bloomsbury gang*[3], to all of whom, as is well known, Lord Temple was

---

[1] See *ante*, vol. i. p. 477.

[2] " I cannot express my opinion of the present Ministry more exactly than in the words of Sir Richard Steele : 'that we are governed by a set of drivellers, whose folly takes away all dignity from distress, and makes even calamity ridiculous.'"—*Junius,* vol. i. p. 570.

[3] " The Bedfords, or, as they were called by their enemies, the Bloomsbury Gang, professed to be led by John Duke of Bedford, but in truth led him wherever they chose, and very often led him where he never would have gone of his own accord. He had many good qualities of head and heart, and would have been certainly a respectable, and possibly a distinguished man, if he had been less under the influence of his friends,

equally opposed; and North, Weymouth, Gower, Rigby, Jerry Dyson, and Sandwich, were invariably and constantly the objects of the contemptuous sarcasm and ridicule of Junius[1].

Soon after the death of George Grenville in November, 1770, the Grenville party, so called, was entirely dispersed. Lord Temple cannot be said to have had any adherents; he was rather himself an adherent of Lord Chatham, in whom all that remained of the Grenville connection was thenceforth concentrated.

Of the more intimate personal and political friends of Mr. Grenville, Lord Suffolk had joined the Administration as Lord Privy Seal, and became in a few months afterwards Secretary of State, with Whately for his Under Secretary; Wedderburn[2] was made Solicitor-General; Augustus Hervey a Lord of the Admiralty; Lord Hyde and Lord Buckinghamshire also supported the existing Government. Lord Temple alone continued acting with Lord Chatham in bitter opposition to—

" those wretches called Ministers, who have brought themselves and their master where ordinary ability never arrives, and nothing but firstrate geniuses in incapacity can reach : I mean a situation in which there is nothing they can do, which is not a fault." [3]

or more fortunate in choosing them. Some of them were indeed, to do them justice, men of parts. But here we are afraid eulogy must end. Sandwich and Rigby were able debaters, pleasant boon companions, dexterous intriguers, masters of all the arts of jobbing and electioneering, and both in public and in private shamelessly immoral. Weymouth had a natural eloquence which sometimes astonished those who knew how little he owed to study. But he was indolent and dissolute, and had early impaired a fine estate with the dice-box, and a fine constitution with the bottle."—*Macaulay's Essay on Lord Chatham, Edinburgh Review,* January, 1834.

[1] " Is it *bonâ fide* for your interest or your honour to sacrifice your domestic tranquillity, and to live in a perpetual disagreement with your people, merely to preserve such a chain of beings as North, Barrington, Weymouth, Gower, Ellis, Onslow, Rigby, Jerry Dyson, and Sandwich? Their very names are a satire upon all government, and I defy the gravest of your chaplains to read the catalogue without laughing."—*Junius,* vol. ii. p. 131.

[2] " The part of Wedderburn" (writes Lord Chatham to Calcraft on the 22nd of January, 1771) " is deplorable ; of Lord Suffolk, pitiable."—*Chatham Correspondence,* vol. iv.

" To sacrifice a respected character, and to renounce the esteem of society, requires more than Mr. Wedderburn's resolution; and though in him it was rather a profession than a desertion of his principles (I speak tenderly of this gentleman, for, when treachery is in question, I think we should make allowances for a Scotchman), yet we have seen him in the House of Commons overwhelmed with confusion, and almost bereft of his faculties."—*Junius,* vol. ii. p. 205.

[3] Lord Chatham to Colonel Barré, March 21, 1771, *Chatham Correspondence.*

Lord Suffolk wrote to Lord Temple on the 22nd of January[1], announcing the fact of his having kissed hands for the Privy Seal, and received a reply in which there is nothing remarkable but its coldness, and the similarity of its commencement to an expression used by Junius in one of his private letters to Lord Chatham :— "Retired and unknown I live in the shade,"[2] &c. ; and Lord Temple says,—"Retired as I am, and wish to be," &c.

Junius, under the signature of Henricus, attacked Lord Suffolk, in two letters dated the 15th of April and the 21st of May, in which he says :—

" The singularity of your late conduct seemed to claim some attention from the public, which you do not, I presume, think you have escaped ; but since, by their silence, they either think you superior to shame, or below the dignity of revenge, I cannot help giving to them what I owe on this occasion, which, had I only considered the gratification of a passion, I should have sooner done. * * * * * Before I arraign your subsequent conduct, which I mean to do pretty freely, I must admire the simple *candour* with which you have declared yourself without principle. In the most destructive Administrations, composed of men perhaps more profligate than your Lordship, care has generally been taken to save, in some measure, appearances with the public ; and although the destruction of this Constitution has been pretty clearly their object, they have never ventured openly to avow it : even the Duke of Grafton did not condemn his own principles, though he avowed and gloried in such measures as no man with principle could undertake. Your Lordship is the first man who ever saved others the trouble of accusation. Your Protests must remain to all posterity a monument of your infamy ; and one would almost imagine you designed they should." * * * * * ." Thus we see a hopeful young Peer possessed of an independent fortune, with an only child, a daughter, connected with the most honourable characters in this kingdom, prostituting his honour, and every valuable consideration of the public, for that of an office, independent even of those sweet allurements which could, one would imagine, make the bitter pill go down. For shame, my Lord, to throw yourself away under such circumstances, at the discretion of *such* an Administration. Had you, like poor Whately, been reduced from a state of independence to the humiliating necessity of soliciting your support from Administration, our reproach would be only turned against those who creditably took advantage of such a

---

[1] See *post*, vol. iv. at that date.   [2] *Chatham Correspondence*, vol. iv. p. 194.

situation, and gratified themselves with the purchase of an honest man's reputation ; and though we congratulated them on the acquisition which they had prudently secured, we should sincerely pity the object of their triumph. I am neither surprised nor shocked at any inconsistency in Mr. Wedderburn : his profession sets his principles at auction, and it is reasonable that the highest bidder should command them ; but that the Earl of Suffolk should act such a part, I own astonished me : a man who had everything to lose and nothing to gain by prostitution ; that an independent Peer of England should voluntarily pledge himself to his country for the exertion of every right and every power, with which the Constitution had vested him for their service, and should after this betray every interest of the public and desert that service ; that he should in one Session repeatedly declare to this purport, if not to this tenor, that he would *never hereafter* be induced, for *any* consideration, to herd with men whom he considered as enemies to their King and country, and in the next deliver over his conscience, his right, and his powers, into their hands at their discretion, and thereby include himself in every odious term of reproach which he had so liberally bestowed upon them." * * * * " You have had time to reflect on your situation, and I would not wish to add more to embitter the sweets of office. Had this address appeared sooner, while you was *fortunâ dulci ebrius*, you would perhaps have laughed with Lord Sandwich at the undertaking of one who endeavoured to prove that honesty and virtue had any real existence. You would, like the Duke of Grafton, have perused it at your tea-table, and perhaps taken a pride, like Lord Hillsborough, that you was dignified with an enemy, though you had not, like him, preserved a friend. But I think, my Lord, a sufficient time is elapsed, during which some intervals of private reflection and remorse must have interfered, and the flattery of those who purchased must have subsided, and left your conscience and Mr. Grenville to reproach you. For I still believe you to consist of that composition, which, without virtue enough to avoid prostitution, has still feeling enough to be ashamed of it." * * * * " There are few men, except Mr. Wedderburn and your Lordship, who would have gone through the difficulty of exposing themselves to those who had such evidence against them, with that happy indifference which we have experienced from you both. To preserve the hypocrisy of patriotism, after you had openly made your compact with corruption ; to profess consistency in adhering to the words of a Protest, on the tenor of which your whole conduct is the grossest ridicule, and to possess the characteristical firmness of administration in reviving so ignominious a consideration, requires more courage and intrepidity than most men have the good fortune to possess ; but I allow your friend Wedderburn has outstripped you. He has modestly ventured not only virtually, but directly, to attack Opposition for measures which he himself concurred in promoting ; and hears himself despised, execrated, detested, without fear and without anger. Let him excuse me when I assure him, with some very allowable pride, that I do not think he has a claim to any notice beyond my advice to consider, that the power from whence he derives very superior abilities, will expect and must receive an account to what purposes they have been employed."

In conclusion, Junius seems to point out what he might consider to be his own (Lord Temple's) situation with regard to the Court :—

" But I must congratulate you, my Lord, on that ambition which has led you to inquire into those desirable *arcana* of a Court, by which you have learned a sort of loyalty distinct from duty to His Majesty or affection to his family, by which you have found that it will be for your interest, and consequently for your honour, to attach yourself hereafter to men, who, while they act directly contrary to the interest of their countrymen, and are indifferent with regard to their confidence or esteem, can hug themselves among the highest of mankind, and ridicule the contemptible folly of those whose virtue has excluded them from their share in the plunder of the public."—*Junius*, vol. iii. p. 381, *et seq.*

I have ventured to make these long extracts, because they appear to contain language and opinions so entirely characteristic of the feelings which might be supposed to actuate Lord Temple under the peculiar circumstances of Mr. Grenville's recent death, and the desertion of Lord Suffolk from the Grenville connection, as well as Wedderburn, Whately, and others, all of whom had been in such close and intimate alliance with Mr. Grenville, and that section of the Opposition which acknowledged him for its leader.

Horace Walpole describes Lord Suffolk as—

" a young man of thirty-two, totally unpractised in business, pompous, ignorant, and of no parts, but affecting to be the head of Grenville's late party." [1]

Wedderburn, who became Solicitor-General, was indebted for his seat in Parliament to Lord Clive's friendship for Mr. Gren-

[1] *Memoirs of George III.*, vol. iv. p. 261.

ville[1], and it was natural, therefore, that his defection should be resented by Junius with peculiar severity.

Whately had been Secretary of the Treasury during Mr. Grenville's Administration, and was always most affectionately attached to him. His letters to Mr. Grenville are very numerous, and relate to the passing occurrences of the day, and the most secret and confidential arrangements of party politics. He was also a very industrious purveyor of news and political gossip to Lord Temple, with whom he was in frequent communication and correspondence[2].

Junius confessed that he was not conversant in the language of panegyric, and indeed he was singularly sparing of his commendation; it was extended to very few of his political contemporaries. Mr. Grenville, however, was his especial favourite; his conduct was always defended by Junius; no vulnerable part was to be found in Mr. Grenville's character; his policy was invariably approved of in every minute particular; his was the patriot voice which was raised in defence of the laws and constitution, which always declared the way to safety and to honour.

If Lord Temple were not himself the Author of Junius, it would be still more remarkable that a writer whose partiality to Mr. Grenville was so conspicuous upon every occasion, should have never mentioned his brother Lord Temple, with whom he lived upon the most affectionate terms, and with whom he at this time entirely coincided in political opinions. Under the signature of Junius, Lord Temple is not even named; twice only in the Miscellaneous Letters is he slightly alluded to, as if the Author were influenced by the rule which he has laid down in his Preface, with respect to Philo-Junius, that the subordinate should never be guilty of the indecorum of praising his principal, or, in other words, of praising himself.

Lord Temple was unquestionably a political leader of considerable note and influence, a very active and zealous partizan, more or less connected with every public question of his time, who had

---

[1] On the 23rd of January, Calcraft writes to Lord Chatham,—" Lord Clive is full of indignation at the desertion of Wedderburn," &c.—*Chatham Correspondence.*

[2] See *post*, vol. iv. p. 278, *note.*

long held a high office in the State, who had been at least twice
solicited to undertake the Administration of the Government himself, and yet Lord Temple is the only person of any political
distinction who is never mentioned in the pages of a writer by
whom his brother was held in so great estimation, and who professed to discuss and criticise the conduct and characters of the
chief political men of his time.

Upon the formation of the new Ministry in the summer of 1766,
a violent quarrel ensued between Lord Temple and Mr. Pitt,
which continued with great bitterness, at least on the part of Lord
Temple, until a reconciliation was effected between them through
the mediation of their mutual friend Calcraft, in the autumn of
1768, and during this interval Mr. Pitt (now become Lord Chatham) was attacked by the Author of Junius, under a variety of
signatures, and he was the object of the most scurrilous abuse.

In a letter from Charles Lloyd to Mr. Grenville, written during
this interval, he says,—"Mr. Pitt (Lord Chatham) complains that
Lord Temple is the encourager of all the abuse against him."[1]

It is remarkable, however, that soon after the reconciliation
Junius finds occasion to say of Lord Chatham, that "he began to
like him," and at last, in a letter dated August 13, 1771, he
says,—

"I did not intend to make a public declaration of the respect I bear
Lord Chatham. I well knew what unworthy conclusions would be
drawn from it. But I am called upon to deliver my opinion, and
surely it is not in the little censure of Mr. Horne to deter me from
doing signal justice to a man who, I confess, has grown upon my
esteem."

George Grenville had been reconciled to Lord Chatham for
some months previous to his death in 1770, but there was no very
cordial feeling between them. Grenville was not a man ever to
forget, or entirely to forgive, the public ridicule which had been
cast upon him by Pitt, and he well knew that the latter had
always despised him as a politician, and depreciated his talents as
a statesman.

---

[1] See *post*, p. 312. Horace Walpole says, "The Duke of Grafton, too, reproached
Temple with blackening a most respectable character (Lord Chatham's) from revenge."
—*Memoirs of George III.*, vol. ii. p. 449.

The reconciliation of Chatham and Temple was much more
sincere, because there was a foundation of real affection and gratitude in the mind of the former: he had always lamented the
temporary estrangement of his "noble brother," who, he said,
"had indeed abused him, in the warmth of his temper, but almost
everybody else had *betrayed* him."

It is not likely that an unknown friend and partizan of George
Grenville, particularly so constant and partial a friend such as
Junius certainly was, should have displayed so much warmth of
feeling towards Lord Chatham: such expressions as are used by
Junius, the great friend of Grenville, towards Chatham, would
only be consistent if Lord Temple were the author of them, for
Lord Temple was most affectionately attached to both; and the
same argument would equally apply to the case of Wilkes. Temple was devoted to his brother George, but he had also a very
strong friendship, amounting almost to affection, for Wilkes. It
could scarcely happen that a stranger to both, as Junius *pretended*[1] to be, should have evinced so strong a partiality, personally and politically, towards two men, differing in every respect, and in so remarkable a manner, as George Grenville and
John Wilkes.

Lord Temple had all those powerful motives of party zeal and
patriotism, as well as private feelings of deep personal resentment
and warm friendship for individuals, under the influence and impressions of which, the Letters of Junius were unquestionably
composed. He was a man whose ambition had been disappointed, whose pride had been wounded and provoked by neglect,
who had been long excluded from office by the supposed dislike
of the King, and the chief statesmen of all parties; who had
laboured long and in vain for the attainment of objects in
which he felt the most intense interest—the destruction of the
Grafton Administration, and the restoration of Lord Chatham and
the Grenvilles to power and popular applause. He had "a motive
and a cue for action," and in sacrificing his time and thoughts to

[1] Of Mr. Grenville he said, "I have neither the honour of being *personally known*
to him," &c.—*Junius*, vol. i. p. 533.

And to Wilkes,—"I willingly accept of as much of your friendship as you can impart to a man *whom you will assuredly never know.*"—*Ibid.*, vol. i. p. 314.

these favourite designs, he was supported by his hopes of success, by the wincing of his antagonists, by the satisfaction of his
revenge, and by his gratified vanity.

Lord Temple was most probably often in familar intercourse
with the very persons who were the objects of the most severe
invective of Junius, and from this intimate and personal knowledge of the private character of his victims, he was the better
enabled to direct his satire towards the most acute feelings of the
individual.   He knew, for instance, that George III. was " as callous as Stockfish to everything but the Reproach of *Cowardice*,"[1]
and he pointed his darts accordingly.

The Author of Junius was not only an anonymous writer, but
it is evident that he always intended to remain so; he wrote with
every design and desire of concealment[2], and therefore he might

[1] See *Junius*, vol. i. p. 221, and Mr. Grenville's Diary, *post*, p. 176.

[2] Horace Walpole mentions the " unparalleled remonstrance of Junius to the King,
the most daring insult ever offered to a Prince but in times of open rebellion, and aggravated by the many truths it contained.   Nothing could exceed the singularity of this
satire but the impossibility of discovering the author.   Three men were especially suspected, Wilkes, Edmund Burke, and William Gerard Hamilton.   The desperate hardi-
ness of the author, in attacking men so great, so powerful, and some so brave, was re-
concileable only to the situation of Wilkes; but the masterly talents that appeared in
those writings were deemed superior to his abilities : yet in many of Junius's letters an
inequality was observed ; and even in this remonstrance different hands seem to have
been employed.   The laborious flow of style, and fertility of matter, made Burke believed the real Junius; yet he had not only constantly and solemnly denied any hand
in those performances [a], but was not a man addicted to bitterness, nor could any one
account for such indiscriminate attacks on men of such various descriptions and professions.   Hamilton was most generally suspected.   He, too, denied it, but his truth was
not renowned.   The quick intelligence of facts, and the researches into the arcana of
every office, were far more uncommon than the invectives ; and men wondered how
any one possessed of such talents could have the forbearance to write in a manner so
desperate, as to prevent his ever receiving personal applause for his writings : the venom
was too black not to disgrace even his ashes."[b]

Sir Nathaniel Wraxall, in his *Historical Memoirs*, speaking of Junius, says,—" Lord
North either did not know, or professed not to know, his name.   The late Lord Temple
protested the same ignorance.   Every evidence, internal and external, proves him to have
been a person of pre-eminent parts, admirable information, high connections, living almost
constantly in the metropolis, and in good company ; ignorant of nothing that was done
at St. James's, in the two Houses of Parliament, in the War Office, or in the Courts of
Law, and personally acquainted with many anecdotes or facts, only to be attained by
men moving in the first ranks of society."

[a] " I now give you my word and honour that I am not the author of *Junius*, and
that I know not the author of that paper, and I do authorize you to say so."—*Burke to
C. Townshend, November 24th, 1771.*

[b] *Memoirs of George III.*, vol. iii. p. 401.

perhaps have considered that any particular regard to consistency of opinion or candour in argument was unnecessary; he might violate either to suit the purpose of the moment; the principle he denounced to-day he might under another signature advocate to-morrow; and yet it must be admitted, that after he assumed the name by which he is most known, he desired to be consistent, and in his character of Junius, he replies to Mr. Horne,—

"I cannot recall to my memory the numberless trifles I have written, but I rely upon the consciousness of my own integrity, and defy him to fix any colourable charge of inconsistency against me."— *Junius*, vol. ii. p. 306.

Lord Temple was so generally known, or so continually suspected, to be the author or encourager of libellous publications, that it appears strange he should not have been more directly charged with the Authorship of Junius[1]. He did not, indeed, altogether escape suspicion, but the very bold and daring nature of the Letters, and the ruinous consequences which a discovery of the Author of them would have entailed upon a man of Lord Temple's rank and station, must have deterred many people even from the imagination that he should have undertaken such incessant literary labour, or have incurred so great a risk, added to the extreme difficulties he must necessarily encounter in successfully preserving his concealment.

It will be considered still more surprising that Almon the bookseller, who was so much in Lord Temple's confidence, as to be familiarly called "Lord Temple's man," and who was besides a great speculator about Junius, should never have suspected or at least have never made known his suspicions of Lord Temple, instead of supporting (as he did in an edition of the Letters published by him) the very absurd theory that Boyd was the Author of Junius, merely, as it would seem, because he (Boyd), like Sir Philip

[1] In the autumn of 1766 was published "A Letter to the Right Honourable Earl Temple upon his Conduct in a late Negotiation, and its Consequences; to which is prefixed a curious Dialogue between a certain Right Honourable Author and his Bookseller." 8vo. The dialogue is between Lord Temple and Almon (the latter designated as "*Mr. Vamp*"), with respect to certain publications in which Lord Temple is supposed to be interested. It shows that, even at this time, suspicion was attached to Lord Temple wherever libellous papers were in question.

Francis and some others, was very desirous that the Authorship should be attributed to him.

I confess that Almon's silence with regard to any suspicion of Lord Temple would have had some adverse effect upon my own opinion in his favour, if I did not believe that Lord Temple had taken considerable pains to mystify Almon, and had succeeded in doing so, by continually asserting and insisting that he never *wrote* anything, and therefore it will be seen, that whenever Almon presumes to attribute the authorship of any paper or pamphlet to Lord Temple, he always does so with a sort of respectful reservation,—with doubtful phrases, such as:—"*principally written by Lord Temple;*"—or, "*at least he dictated the greatest part of it;*"—or, "*though not literally by Lord Temple, was entirely written under his eye, and nearly every line dictated by him.*"

He allows that he even assisted in the *North Briton* and other publications,—"*not indeed with his pen, but with his information and line of reasoning;*"—again, "*Lord Temple dictated, or nearly so, but did not write any part of it himself;*"—or, "*Lord Temple wrote, or perhaps it will be correctly stating, that his Lordship dictated to an amanuensis.*"

These phrases are selected from Almon's *Biographical and Political Anecdotes*, and it should be remembered that the author professed to have received the most interesting of these anecdotes from Lord Temple himself.

It seems to me almost an impossibility that any man, even the Author of Junius, should have the fortitude and industry to persevere for a long series of years in a course of anonymous political letter-writing, without some private and friendly encouragement and assistance, some kindred spirit upon whom he could rely, with whom he could share his triumphs, and who would glory in the successful popularity of his slander, who would revel in the mischief, and cheer him on to his revenge. Such a friend Lord Temple found in his wife[1], the partner of his joys,

---

[1] "It appears to our view that the writings of Junius emanated *from one mind, and yet not without assistance.* Some person must have been privy to them, but this aid must have been confined to the *writer's own household, to his nearest family connections,* subordinate to one great over-ruling mind. Otherwise the transcription and the immediate transmission of those letters to one and the same printer could not have been ac-

his sorrows, and his labours, who was not only his amanuensis, but who had talent enough to assist him in the composition of his writings, whose praise was sufficient to support his vanity,—for a vain man Junius must have been, although it might be true, as he asserted, that his vanity was confined within a narrow compass: so indeed it was, but it was not the less *vanity*, that absorbing passion which goads us on to the fulfilment of all that is good and all that is evil in our nature. The imperious necessity of concealment, however, superseded all the claims of vanity. Concealment became the grand object of his unceasing care and vigilance, not only because his personal safety so entirely depended upon it, but because it so essentially contributed to the success of his writings :—

" Besides every personal consideration, if I were known, I could no longer be an useful servant to the public. At present there is something oracular in the delivery of my opinions. I speak from a recess which no human curiosity can penetrate, and darkness we are told is one source of the sublime. The mystery of Junius increases his importance." [1]

" When Junius had once provided for his safety," says Dr. Johnson, " by impenetrable secrecy, he had nothing to combat but truth and justice, enemies whom he knows to be feeble in the dark. Being then at liberty to indulge himself in all the immunities of invisibility, out of the reach of danger he has been bold, out of the reach of shame he has been confident."

Nor does the theory of Lady Temple being the amanuensis in any way invalidate the solemn declaration of Junius, that he was the *sole* depositary of his own secret. I believe that declaration to have been true,—with this reservation only, that Junius considered his wife to be part of himself, in accordance with the highest authority, bone of his bones, and flesh of his flesh. He could not, without danger, have confided the secret to any human

complished : a service that could not be purchased with money or enforced by authority. *It must have been done by kindred aid alone*, it being that kind of concern in which the stranger doth not intermeddle. Without such *domestic aid*, and *affectionate conspiration*, we cannot conceive that such an extraordinary and dangerous correspondence could possibly have been carried on three years undetected, and have remained undivulged to this time."—*Essay on Junius by Dr. Waterhouse*, p. 97. I concur entirely in these opinions, so well expressed by Dr. Waterhouse.

[1] *Junius*, vol. i. p. 314.

being but his wife; with her it was safe: their very existence depended upon concealment—a discovery would have entailed upon them shame and disgrace: no doubt Junius spoke from the anguish of his heart when he exclaimed to Woodfall,—

"I sh^d. not survive a Discovery three days;—Act honorably by me, & at a proper time you shall know me. I am persuaded you are too honest a man to contribute in any way to my destruction."

To Wilkes, Junius said,—

"I have faithfully served the public without the possibility of a personal advantage. As Junius, I can never expect to be rewarded. The secret is too important to be committed to any great man's discretion. If views of interest or ambition could tempt me to betray my own secret, how could I flatter myself that the man I trusted would not act upon the same principles, and sacrifice me at once to the King's curiosity and resentment?"—*Junius*, vol. i. p. 295.

The participation of Lady Temple would account for the expression in one of his private notes to Woodfall:—

"The Truth is, there are people about me, whom I wo. wish not to contradict, & who had rather see Junius in the papers ever so improperly, than not at all."—*Junius*, vol. i. p. 199.

It may be imagined that he was often urged on in his laborious task with more zeal than discretion. In some of the letters to the Dukes of Grafton and Bedford may certainly be found expressions very characteristic of the playful and spiteful mischief of Lady Temple's pen, particularly with reference to the Duke of Grafton and the "lovely Thais" at the Opera House; to the Duke of Bedford and the alleged sale of Lord Tavistock's wardrobe; or the "venerable Gertrude," her rout at Bedford House a fortnight after Lord Tavistock's death, and her disposal of the gowns and trinkets of the Marchioness of Tavistock; the peculiar and dreadful nature of the malady with which the Princess Dowager was afflicted, and the supposed extraordinary treatment of it, as further described in an additional note, still suppressed by Mr. Woodfall; these are matters to a knowledge of which, his information could scarcely have extended without the gossiping assistance of Lady Temple.

To the honourable integrity of Mr. Henry Sampson Woodfall, Junius was unquestionably indebted for the success of his incognito. He must have had many opportunities of watching the persons who applied for the parcels and letters which were left at the various coffee-houses, according to the directions of Junius, or he might have instructed the waiters to obtain information which would have enabled him to detect the Author, if he had been inclined to act treacherously towards his anonymous friend. But Junius seems to have had considerable confidence in his printer, and to the credit of the latter it was never betrayed; he never attempted to penetrate the secrecy of the Author, nor did he instigate or permit others to do so; but although Mr. Woodfall did not know who *was* the Author of Junius, he had many opportunities of knowing who *was not.*

Junius was no doubt frequently in great fear of being discovered. In one of his letters to Mr. Grenville, dated September, 1768, he says, I have " present important reasons for wishing to be concealed." Those reasons became still more important in 1769. In his earliest private note to Woodfall, dated April 20th[1], he says, " If any enquiry is made about these papers, I shall rely upon y^r giving me a hint." And on the 15th of July[2], " tell me candidly whether you know or suspect who I am." It seems to me that there is a consciousness—a tone of rank and notoriety in this expression " *who I am,*" which an obscure person would not have adopted.

On the 21st of July[3], Junius, in a private note to Woodfall, says :—

---

[1] Woodfall must have received previous communications from the author, but they have not been preserved. The date of this note is supplied by Dr. Mason Good, the editor of *Woodfall's Junius* in 1812. The original has no date. It may be worthy of remark that of the *sixty-three* private notes from Junius to Woodfall, *thirty-one* are without any date; *twenty-eight* have the day of the week only; *two* have the month and the day of the month; *one*, the month, the day of the month, and the day of the week; *one* with the date of the year only, but in this single instance it is wrong—1770 being substituted for 1771. Mr. Woodfall has unfortunately lost the Note No. 6. In the above calculation I have assumed it to be dated the day of the week only. Out of *one hundred* letters from Lord and Lady Temple, I find *sixteen* without any date; *fifty-three* have the day of the week only; *twenty-three* have the month and day of the month; *three*, the month, the day of the month, and the day of the week; *five*, the year, the month, and the day of the month.

[2] The original is only dated " Saturday."

[3] The original is dated " Friday night " only.

"That Swinney[1] is a wretched but a dangerous fool. he had the impudence to go to Lord G. Sackville, whom he had never spoken to, & to ask him, whether or no he was the Authour of Junius—take care of him."

The contemptuous manner in which Junius mentions *that Swinney*, seems to imply some former knowledge of, or previous communication either from him or respecting him. Perhaps he may also have made some inquiries of Woodfall, or offered some assistance to Junius on the subject of his writings, with a view to the discovery of the Author. It is, at all events, not difficult to account for his visit to Lord George Sackville becoming known to Lord Temple, for besides that they were now intimate acquaintances, and lived in Pall Mall within fifty yards of each other, they were at this time in the habit of meeting daily at the house of their mutual friend Lady Betty Germain, in St. James's Square. This venerable lady, who was in her 86th year, was then extremely ill, and Lady Temple, who was her niece, was in constant attendance upon her. Lady Betty had been her guardian from earliest childhood, and she had always, previous to her marriage, resided with her in St. James's Square, frequently corresponded with her when absent, and spent much of her time with her when in London.

Lady Betty and her late husband Sir John Germain, had been the very intimate friends of Lionel Duke of Dorset, and his son Lord George Sackville was destined to inherit, at Lady Betty's death, a very considerable property, including the estate of Dray-

---

[1] The Reverend Dr. Sidney Swinney was of Clare Hall, Cambridge, a Fellow of the Royal Society and of the Society of Antiquaries. He is described as a gentleman of uncommon generosity and benevolence, with an extensive knowledge of ancient and modern languages. He visited several of the Courts of Europe, and resided some years as Chaplain to the British Embassy at Constantinople. He is said also to have been some time Chaplain to the British Forces in Germany, under the command of Lord George Sackville. He was the author of a Poem called the *Battle of Minden* (in which, by the way, the Battle of Minden is never named), and one or two sermons. He died at Scarborough, November 12, 1783. Daniel Wray, in writing to Lord Hardwicke on the 18th of November, 1771, an account of a meeting of the Royal Society, mentions that " Dr. Swinney, your Lordship's friend, presented his father-in-law Holwell's works." Swinney had married the daughter of John Zephaniah Holwell, who was some time Governor of Bengal, and the author of some Tracts relative to the affairs of India. See *Mr. Justice Hardinge's Memoirs of Daniel Wray*, in *Nichols's Illustrations of Literature*, vol. i. p. 144.

ton, in Northamptonshire, and therefore he was frequently in St. James's Square, in attendance upon an aged friend from whom he had such great expectations.

Nothing could be more probable than that Junius, who was then in the full career of his popularity, should be the subject of occasional conversation at these meetings, and in this manner Lord or Lady Temple would hear from Lord George, as a matter of gossip, that a person of the name of Swinney, who had never spoken to him upon the subject before, had asked him whether or no he was the Author of Junius. Even if Lord Temple himself had not been present, he would of course have been immediately informed by Lady Temple, who would be very glad to find the suspicion resting upon Lord George, and the more so as, in repeating the gossip, it would afford her a favourable opportunity of encouraging such a report.

Junius, considering Swinney to be an inquisitive, troublesome person, or, as he described him, "*a wretched but a dangerous fool,*" thought it necessary to desire Woodfall to be on his guard. Swinney probably said much more on the subject than Junius thought advisable to communicate to Woodfall. Lord George might have added that Swinney was endeavouring to find out the Author, an additional reason that Woodfall should "*take care of him.*"

But if, as it has been stated, Swinney was once Chaplain to the Forces under Lord George Sackville, it would certainly be strange that he should never have *spoken* to Lord George. Phrases in conversation, however, are so seldom correctly reported, that what was really said might have been, and most likely was, as I have ventured to interpret it as above, viz. that he had *never before spoken to him upon that subject.*

Hitherto Junius had been known to Woodfall as "Mr. William Middleton," but *that Swinney* seems to have been the cause of his changing his name to "Mr. John Fretley." In the same note to Woodfall he adds,—

"Whenever you have anything to communicate to me let the hint be thus—C., *at the usual place*, and so direct to Mr. John Fretley, at the same Coffee House, where it is absolutely impossible I sh^{d} be known."

This expression implies that he sometimes went himself to receive his parcels, that he was himself "*the gentleman who transacts the conveyancing part of our correspondence.*"[1]—*Junius,* vol. i. p. 245. He could not mean that Mr. John Fretley, a mere imaginary person, should not be known.

In his note of October 5th[2] he seems to be more confident:

" As to me, be assured that it is not in the nature of things that they or you, or anybody else, should ever know me unless I make myself known. All arts, or Inquiries, or rewards, would be equally ineffectual."

On the 26th of December[3],—

" I doubt much whether I shall ever have the pleasure of knowing you; but if things take the turn I expect, you shall know me *by my Works.*"

He did not personally know Woodfall;—nor was it probable that Lord Temple knew him, otherwise than by name, as the printer of the *Public Advertiser.*

In February[4], 1770, he writes,—

" When you consider to what excessive enmities I may be exposed, you will not wonder at my caution. I really have not known how to procure your last."

This, again, does not seem consistent with a person of obscure condition, who would be little affected, or rather whose vanity would be flattered, by the *excessive enmities* of men in the rank of Sir William Draper, of the Duke of Grafton, of the Duke of Bedford, or even of the King himself.

To Sir William Draper, Junius said,—

" As to me, it is by no means necessary that I should be exposed to the resentment of the worst and most powerful men in this country, though I may be indifferent about yours. Though *you* would fight, there are others who would assassinate."—*Junius,* vol. ii. p. 7.

At the beginning of 1771 Junius seems to have anticipated

---

[1] See vol. iv. p. 281, *note.*
[2] The original is dated " Thursday night " only.
[3] The original has no date.
[4] The original has no date.

more danger of discovery. In his note to Woodfall of the 11th of February[1], he says:—

" Our correspondence is attended with difficulties."

And again, on the 21st of February[2],—

" it will be very difficult, if not impracticable, for me to get your Note."

On the 25th of September[3],—

" I have not been able to get y^{rs} from that place, but you shall hear from me soon."

On the 8th of November[4],—

" Shew the Dedication & Preface to Mr. Wilkes, and if he has any *material* Objection, let me know. I say *material* because of the difficulty of getting your letters."

In a *secret* postscript to the same letter, he says,—

" beware of David Garrick. he was sent to pump you, & went directly to Richmond to tell the king I sh^{d} write no more."

Two days afterwards Junius enclosed to Woodfall the well-known letter to Garrick, accompanied by a private note.—*Junius*, vol. i. p. 231.

At no period during the whole of his correspondence with Woodfall does Junius evince more alarm and fear of discovery than upon this occasion of Garrick's " impertinent inquiries."

The curiosity and eagerness of the King upon every subject connected with Junius was no doubt well known to Lord Temple, and he would readily believe that the report sent by Garrick, coming with such an air of authenticity direct from Woodfall, was received at Richmond with " triumph & exultation."

Such an important piece of Court gossip would be very rapidly circulated, even by the King himself, and is likely to have spread in political circles. Besides, as Gunnersbury was so near to Richmond, it may almost immediately have reached the ears of the Princess Amelia, with whom Lady Temple, always extremely intimate, was at this time in constant communication, either visiting or by letter, and therefore it is not surprising that Lord Temple

---

[1] The original is dated " Monday," only.
[2] The original has no date.
[3] The original is dated " Wednesday noon " only.
[4] The original is dated " Friday " only.

should have very soon become acquainted with a report so particularly interesting to himself.

There were no doubt other reasons why Junius should endeavour to deter Garrick from "meddling," and therefore it is natural he should somewhat exaggerate his own rapidity and exactness in procuring the earliest information, in order to impress Woodfall with a notion that he knew more about Garrick's "cunning and activity" than it was necessary to enlarge upon, except generally and impressively, to put Woodfall upon his guard:—"Beware of David Garrick!"

Not only did Garrick send the information to Ramus, the King's page, that "Junius would write no more," but, according to his own apologetical letter to Woodfall, he did the same to other parties.

"Now let us examine," says Garrick, "into the cause of this dreadful denunciation. Mr. Woodfall, the first informer, informs me in a letter in no ways relative to the subject, without any previous *impertinent inquiries* on my part, or the least desire of secrecy on his, that *Junius would write no more.* Two or three days after the receipt of yours, being obliged to write a letter upon the business of the theatre to one at Richmond, and after making my excuses for not being able to obey His Majesty's commands, I mentioned to him that Junius would write no more. And so far was I from thinking that there was a crime in communicating what was sent to me without reserve, that I will freely confess that I wrote no letter to any of my friends without the mention of so remarkable an event. I will venture to go farther, and affirm that it would have been insensible and unnatural, not to have done it."

Garrick's well-known intimacy with Lord Chatham[1], Lord Lyttelton, and Lord Camden[2], renders it probable that he wrote to

---

[1] Very soon after this time, Lord Chatham sent Garrick a poetical invitation to Burton Pynsent. See letters on the subject from Lord Lyttelton and Garrick in the *Chatham Correspondence*, vol. iv. p. 197.

[2] Boswell relates the following,—" I told Dr. Johnson that one morning when I went to breakfast with Garrick, who was very vain of his intimacy with Lord Camden, he accosted me thus,—' Pray now, did you—did you meet a little lawyer turning the corner, eh?'—' No, Sir,' said I, ' pray what do you mean by the question?'—' Why,' replied Garrick, with an affected indifference, yet as if standing on tiptoe, ' Lord Camden has this moment left me ; we have had a long walk together.' JOHNSON : ' Well, Sir, Garrick talked very properly. Lord Camden *was* a *little lawyer* to be associating so familiarly with a player.' "—*Boswell's Life of Johnson.*

them also upon this occasion, and from them, as well as from others of his acquaintance, Lord Temple would be certain to hear, upon the authority of Garrick, that Junius would write no more. With this view, therefore, it was important that Garrick should not be in possession of the handwriting of Junius: "I would avoid having *this* hand too commonly seen." He might show it in quarters where it would be examined and scrutinised, and possibly guessed at, or even detected. The original autograph was therefore retained, and a *copy* of the letter sent to Garrick[1].

It is evident, nevertheless, that Garrick had seen the original, because, in his letter to Woodfall, he quotes the words " *impertinent inquiries,*" which Junius subsequently desired, in the copy sent to Garrick, should be altered into "*practises.*"

Junius knew the gossiping nature of Garrick[2], and he suspected him of questioning Woodfall with respect to the mode of their communications : "he was sent to pump you." He was acquainted with Wilkes also[3] ; in short, David Garrick was altogether a very dangerous person.

Junius had hitherto received his letters from Woodfall, addressed to " *Mr. John Fretley,*" or to " *Mr. William Middleton,*" at the New Exchange Coffee House ; but upon this occasion,

---

[1] Both letters are still extant; the original is in Mr. Woodfall's possession : the copy was purchased with the *Garrick Correspondence,* by the late Mr. Upcott, of the London Institution, in whose collection it came to sale a few years ago. Barker, in his *Letters on the Authorship of Junius,* p. 191, has printed a second note which Junius is supposed to have written to Garrick, upon the authority of Park the antiquary, who states that he found it in a contemporary newspaper, and the same note is alluded to by Butler in his *Reminiscences,* as having been mentioned in a conversation with Wilkes upon the subject of Junius, between the years 1776 and 1784. No such note, however, was found among Garrick's papers, although that which he received through the medium of Woodfall had been carefully preserved, and he would have been much more likely to have kept a note which was stated to be in the *identical handwriting* of the author, than one which he knew to be only a copy from the original retained by Woodfall. I believe it to be a forgery, but by whom, I cannot guess, nor do I know when or where it was first printed.

[2] It is possible he may have also known the fact that Garrick had a share in the property of the *Public Advertiser,* by the expression he had used to Woodfall, " *I understand you are ingaged with other Proprietors.*"

[3] Almon relates that Garrick accompanied Mr. Fitzherbert when he went to call on Wilkes by desire of the Duke of Grafton, on the 13th of November, 1768, to endeavour to persuade Wilkes not to present the Petition on the state of his case, which he had threatened, and which Mr. Fitzherbert was not able to prevail upon him to forego. The Petition was presented the next day.

after cautioning Woodfall against Garrick, he adds, "Change to the *Somerset Coffee house*, & let no mortal know the alteration."

The New Exchange Coffee House stood on the south side of the Strand, between Durham Yard and Adam Street. Garrick, at that time, lived in Southampton Street, on the west side, in a house now occupied as Eastey's Hotel, but he had just taken one of the houses recently erected by his friends the Adams (the "Adelphi"), No. 5, on the Terrace; and being on the point of removing there, he would frequently have occasion, on his way from Southampton Street to the Adelphi, to pass the door of the New Exchange Coffee House, where he was probably well known, and this may, for some reason which it may now be in vain to conjecture, have influenced Junius in removing his "conveyancing" department a little further off, to the Somerset Coffee House, which stood about a quarter of a mile to the east, near the present entrance to King's College, in the Strand. There he continued to receive his letters until the 10th of February, when he gave new directions to Woodfall :—

"If you have any thing to communicate, you may send it to the original place for once, N. E. C. [*i.e.* New Exchange Coffee House], & mention any new place you think proper, west of Temple bar."

After Garrick had got fairly settled in his new house, Junius ventured nearer to the old locality, and in March he said to Woodfall,—

"Pray let the *two* sets be well parcelled up, & left at the bar of Munday's Coffee house, Maiden lane, with the same Direction," &c.

Under the influence of the panic caused by the *impertinent inquiries* of Garrick, Junius wrote privately to Woodfall,—

"I must be more cautious than ever. I am sure I sh^d. not survive a Discovery three days, or, if I did, they wo^d. attaint me by bill."[1]

---

[1] The passage I have quoted had not, as far as my observation extends, been explained by the commentators on Junius, until the author of a recent article in the *Quarterly Review* (No. clxxix. p. 100) has thus alluded to it :—

"In general terms it may be said that a Bill of Attainder is a mode of convicting a person of high treason by Act of Parliament. But to justify such a stretch of power, it is understood that the offender, by either flight or concealment, cannot be reached by any ordinary Court of Justice. When Junius says, ' I am sure I should not survive a discovery three days,' he obviously refers to the private vengeance which would pursue

This alarm has all the appearance of being genuine and without affectation, but it is such as would only be felt by a man conscious of his rank and station, being of sufficient importance to induce the Government to have adopted such a measure against him.

Junius was a reader of Montesquieu[1], and has quoted him— once directly, and indirectly more than once. So also has Lord Temple quoted Montesquieu, in his pamphlet entitled *Conduct of the late Administration Examined*[2], &c., &c.

In the " Esprit des Loix" (Liv. xii. chap. 19) will be found

him, and when he adds, ' Or if I did, they would attaint me by bill,' he as obviously means that if he sought safety by flight, the Government would take the means of visiting him with those penalties of treason, as the forfeiture of estate, which are independent of injury to the person.   *   *   *   *   *   From the very nature of the proceeding, it must be aimed at the position and fortune, rather than at the person of the obnoxious party.   Junius had probably the cases of Ormonde and Bolingbroke in his mind ; and if his rank was in any degree equal to theirs, we can well understand his alarm at the thought of incurring that forfeiture which was decreed against them."

[1] " It is easy to perceive that Junius had added to the study of the ancient Classics, that also of the best French writers.   Montesquieu, whose style and manner of composition had been, for about five and twenty years before Junius wrote, highly popular in England, had undoubtedly been in a very particular manner the subject of his study. And it is evident that he was no stranger to the wit of Voltaire, nor always averse from imitating it."—*Preface to Heron's (i. e. Pinkerton's) Edition of Junius*, p. 45.

[2] " But they are to be told, that to describe their master as *surprised*, and as *highly provoked*, is not a proof of their knowledge of the duties of Administration.   The President Montesquieu, when he condemns this mixing of passion with the royal authority [a], which, he says (Liv. xii. chap. 25), *est un grand ressort, qui doit se mouvoir aisément et sans bruit*, could not more exactly have described their dispatches, if he had read them.   *Un ministre malhabile ne sçait vous dire ou vous écrire, si ce n'est que le Prince est faché, qu'il est surpris, qu'il mettra ordre.*   The reason of the impropriety of this kind of style he had given before—*Dans nos monarchies toute la felicité consiste dans l'opinion que le peuple a de la douceur du gouvernement.*   The King is the father of his people, and he views their errors and their crimes with that compassion with which parents regard the misconduct of their children : it is with reluctance that he lifts his hand to punish, and it is not the being *provoked*, it is the necessity of preventing greater evils, it is justice, it is his paternal care for his obedient subjects, which draws from him any mark of correction and chastisement.   It is by this character that he preserves the reverence of his people, and therefore to attribute to him those little passions, which may perhaps at some times agitate the minds of his Ministers, is to diminish his dignity, the confidence which his subjects place in him, and the happiness of his people.   This is so self-evident that I doubt not the Secretary himself will be the first to acknowledge it ; and to confess that he could not, without betraying equally the truth and his duty, represent his master as *highly provoked*."—*Conduct, &c.*, p. 131.

[a] " Les rois ne se sont reservé que les graces.   Ils renvoient les condamnations vers leurs officiers."—*Montesquieu.*   Quoted by *Junius*, vol. i. p. 448 ; see also *Junius*, vol. ii. p. 126, and vol. iii. p. 59, where the same subject is referred to.

the following passage, which Junius had probably in his mind when he expressed to Woodfall his fears that they would *attaint him by bill*:—

"Il y a dans les êtats où l'on fait le plus de cas de la liberté, des loix qui la violent contre un seul pour la garder à tous. Tels sont en Angleterre les *bills* appelés *d'attainder*."

And then is added, in a note, as follows :—

"Il ne suffit pas, dans les tribunaux du royaume, qu'il y ait une preuve telle que les juges soient convaincus ; il faut encore que cette preuve soit formelle, c'est à dire, légale : et la loi demande qu'il y ait deux temoins contre l'accusé ; une autre preuve ne suffiroit pas. Or, si un homme, presumé coupable de ce qu'on appelle haut crime, avoit trouvé le moyen d'écarter les temoins, de sorte qu'il fût impossible de le faire condamner par la loi, on pourroit porter contre lui un *bill* particulier *d'attainder*, c'est à dire, faire une loi singulière sur sa personne. On y procède comme pour tous les autres *bills :* il faut qu'il passe dans deux chambres, et que le roi y donne son consentement, sans quoi il n'y a point de *bill*, c'est à dire, de jugement. L'accusé peut faire parler ses avocats contre le *bill ;* et on peut parler dans la chambre pour le *bill*."

After a lapse of more than eighty years it has not hitherto been discovered that the Author of Junius corresponded *directly* with more than four persons ; viz. Mr. Grenville, Lord Chatham, Wilkes, and Woodfall.

Assuming Lord Temple to have been Junius, George Grenville was his own brother, and Lord Chatham the husband of his only sister ; to both of whom, with the exception of a short period in their lives, he had been most affectionately attached.

Wilkes was under great pecuniary and personal obligations to Lord Temple, and had been for many years one of his most intimate and confidential friends.

Woodfall, as the printer of his works, was necessarily trusted with his private correspondence.

There is certainly no person to whom the Letters of Junius have at any time been attributed, except Lord Temple, who can claim the same degree of intimate connection or relationship with .the three first-mentioned persons.

No other letters or papers in the handwriting adopted by the

Author, are now known to be extant, but those in the possession of Mr. Woodfall, the two letters which are printed in the *Chatham Correspondence*, those which are to be found in the present volumes, and those which were addressed to Mr. Wilkes, and first printed in Woodfall's edition of Junius in 1812. It is uncertain in whose custody the latter now remain, many unsuccessful attempts having been recently made to ascertain the place of their deposit.

It will very naturally be asked, why should Lord Temple, if he were the Author of Junius, and so desirous of concealment, incur the risk of discovery by so bold and hazardous, and apparently so useless an experiment, as that of addressing anonymous letters in the handwriting, however carefully disguised, of Lady Temple, to his brother, his brother-in-law, and to a man who had been his most intimate friend?

This question would, *primâ facie*, seem to present an insuperable obstacle to the theory of Lord Temple being the Author of Junius; but however extraordinary, and however improbable, such a proceeding on the part of Lord Temple may appear, yet I will venture to assert that it is much more in favour of the theory than against it.

It is absolutely certain that the letters were addressed by Junius to these persons, and it would surely be still more improbable, and still more extraordinary, that Junius, if he were an unknown and obscure individual, should have selected these three persons, and no others, each in his degree standing in such intimate relationship or connection towards Lord Temple, for such private and such confidential communications.

The obvious reason, too, for writing these letters might be assigned to the probability that he considered these three persons were the most likely to suspect him to be the author of certain papers, because they would more easily perceive their resemblance to his known political opinions and conversations, and his intention was therefore to divert their suspicions into another channel, from the extreme improbability that if he were the Author he would adopt so daring a course as that of sending communications to them in a handwriting which, although carefully feigned, might still contain some traces of the original character of Lady Temple's autograph.

The writing is, however, entirely in an acquired hand, and sufficiently distinct from her usual hand to escape detection, without the most close and careful examination.

There are, indeed, few things more difficult, even to the most experienced eyes, than to form a correct judgment upon a question of disguised handwriting; it is one upon which there will always be a variety of opinions, and I confess that after having, during a long course of years, examined and copied with accuracy the handwritings of some hundreds of remarkable persons of all classes, and all times, I am still very slow in forming a decided opinion where there is any question of comparison. Some fac-similes are appended to these volumes, in order to afford an opportunity for arriving, in that respect, at a due appreciation of the theory which I have endeavoured to support; viz. that Lord Temple was the Author of Junius, and Lady Temple his amanuensis. I shall have another opportunity of alluding to the handwriting of Junius.

Another reason, too, might have influenced Lord Temple in sending these letters to his brothers; that knowing or believing himself to be suspected, he would therefore endeavour by this means to prevent any embarrassing questions, or any allusion to the subject in conversation, by making it a point of honour, as he did most emphatically to Mr. Grenville, " *that you will not only not shew these papers to any body, but that you will never mention your having received them ;*" and that " *at a proper time he will solicit the honour of being known to you: he has present important reasons for wishing to be concealed.*" He adds that "*if an earnest wish to serve you gives me any claim, let me entreat you not to suffer a hint of this Communication to escape you to* ANY BODY." To *any body;*—as if he would say, not even to your brother, or your most intimate friend.

Two letters were addressed by the Author of Junius to Lord Chatham, one in January, 1768, and the other in January, 1772. Until Lord Chatham received the last, which was signed JUNIUS, he could not know that the letter of January, 1768, was also from the same writer, because it was without any signature and before the Author had adopted the signature of Junius. There is no evidence whatever that Lord Chatham ever mentioned the receipt of either of these letters, but the writer of them had not bound him to secrecy as he did Mr. Grenville, unless, indeed, the opening paragraph of the second letter can be so considered :—

"Confiding implicitly in your Lordship's honour, I take the liberty of submitting to you the enclosed paper, before it be given to the publick."

The existence even of these letters was not known until the publication of the *Chatham Correspondence*, and then they were found to be without any accompanying remark either by Lord or Lady Chatham, although it would have been supposed that a letter from a writer who had become so celebrated even in his own time, and whose successful concealment had baffled all attempts to penetrate the mystery of the Authorship, would have received some remark from Lord Chatham, who lived for six years after it was written, or from Lady Chatham, who was herself so ardent a politician, and who lived for many years afterwards.

The motive which might have influenced Lord Temple in writing to Lord Chatham on the second occasion, was evidently the strong desire he had of *pulling Lord Mansfield to the ground*, and his wish to enlist the talents and energy of Lord Chatham and Lord Camden to assist him in that work.

As Junius was known to be so extremely hostile to Lord Mansfield, it would have awakened suspicion in Lord Chatham's mind, if Lord Temple had shown the same anxiety in his own person and character, as he was enabled to do under the signature of Junius, and therefore he took this mode of enforcing his opinions and of trying to gain over Lord Chatham to his designs, and submits the plan he wished should be adopted, well knowing too that Lord Chatham would have no objection to *pull Lord Mansfield to the ground*, if a fair opportunity were afforded him.

The "*cunning Scotchman,*" however, contrived to defeat the designs of his enemies; he "*whittled away*" the charge, and Junius, disappointed, and perhaps disgusted at his want of success, in this his last and favourite project, wrote no more,—at least not under that signature.

Junius had great confidence also in the honour of Wilkes, but it would seem not altogether unalloyed with suspicion. When the latter requested that the Author would prescribe the mode of communicating an answer to his first and second letters, Junius replies:—

"You may intrust Woodfall with a letter for me. Leave the rest to his management. I expect that you will not enter into any explanation with him whatever."

He would not trust Wilkes as he did Woodfall, with an address to any coffee-house, lest his curiosity should be tempted to make inconvenient inquiries.

In a following letter, Wilkes says,—

"I have not had a moment's conversation with Woodfall on the subject of our correspondence, nor did I mean to mention it to him."

And again:—

"After the first letter of Junius to me, I did not go to Woodfall to pry into a secret I had no right to know." . . . .

"I do not mean to indulge the impertinent curiosity of finding out the most important secret of our times, the Author of Junius. I will not attempt with profane hands to tear the sacred veil of the sanctuary. I am disposed, with the inhabitants of Attica, to erect an altar to the unknown God of our political idolatry, and will be content to worship him in clouds and darkness."

It is in relation to Wilkes that he displays a little distrust even of Woodfall. Perhaps he thought it possible that Wilkes might suspect his correspondent, and might hazard a hint, or a guess, or in some way allude to the Authorship; therefore he wrote to Woodfall,—

"I wo.ᵈ have you open any thing that may be brought to you for me, (except from Mr. W.) [Wilkes]."

The letters from Junius to Wilkes show an intimate personal knowledge of his character, and the allusions to his daughter mark something more than a stranger's interest in him:—

"I appeal to Miss Wilkes, whose judgment I hear highly commended." . . . . . "Ask that amiable daughter whom you so implicitly confide in: is it possible that Junius should betray me?"

Miss Wilkes had been noticed by Lady Temple, and had been received by her at Stowe[1]. It has been seen, too, that Wilkes, only a few minutes before he went out to fight with Lord Talbot, wrote a letter to Lord Temple[2], recommending, in very affectionate terms, his daughter to the care of Lady Temple in the event of his death. Lord Temple had besides been the guest of Wilkes at Aylesbury, and thus had the opportunity of becoming acquainted with his daughter, his family, and his domestic arrangements.

In a letter to Mr. Horne, also, Junius alludes to Miss Wilkes:—

" You say you are a *man*. Was it generous, was it manly, repeatedly to introduce into a newspaper the name of a young lady with whom you must heretofore have lived on terms of politeness and good humour ? "

It is evident that Junius appreciated the literary acquirements of Wilkes, by his desiring Woodfall to submit to him the proof-sheets of the Dedication and Preface, and by afterwards sending his thanks to Wilkes for what he had done, and wishing he had done more.

Junius evinces also a personal attention and even kindness to Wilkes (vol. i. pp. 314–17), and it is certain that Lord Temple assisted him at various times with large sums of money[3]; he was the first to visit him after his arrest under the General Warrant, and on his imprisonment in the Tower, and in the King's Bench Prison; he applied in person, immediately upon his committal, for the writ of Habeas Corpus; he accompanied him into the Court of Common Pleas; he offered to become bail for him to any amount that might be necessary, and in every way stood forth openly as his champion and defender, as one in whose honour and integrity he placed the highest confidence.

---

[1] Wilkes to Humphrey Cotes, November, 1764, in *Almon's Memoirs of Wilkes.*
[2] See *ante,* vol. i. p. 477.
[3] " Lord Temple not only gave him money from his own pocket, but he also instigated his friends to send him presents. At his instance the Duchess of Queenberry and Lady Betty Germain, each transmitted to him 100*l.* This was done with the knowledge of Almon, who says that Wilkes did not know from whom those sums came, until Lord Temple died, and then he thought himself at liberty to inform him."—*Almon's Memoirs of Wilkes.*

Wilkes returned this attachment with implicit devotion to Lord Temple. In addition to the repeated expressions of gratitude which are to be found in his letters in this collection, he says in a letter to Humphrey Cotes, dated February 17, 1764 :—

" I love only Lord Temple ; him I almost adore, and I grieve that I have been the cause of so much disquiet to the most excellent and most amiable man alive."

Again, in December, 1765 :—

" I beg you will tell Lord Temple from me, how much I am devoted to him, and that my mean faculties shall ever be exerted in any manner he wishes and will vouchsafe to prescribe."[1]

In his letter to the Duke of Grafton in December, 1766, he mentions Lord Temple as—

" one of the greatest characters our country could ever boast."

The interest which Junius continued to take in City politics induced him to correspond with Wilkes as a person who could be rendered instrumental to his designs ; and although no letters dated at this time between Wilkes and Lord Temple are now extant, and it is even doubtful whether they corresponded, or whether there was any personal communication between them, yet the letter from Mr. Dayrell[2] in September, 1771, relative to the ensuing election for Lord Mayor, proves at least that there was no quarrel, and it completely identifies the feelings and interest of Lord Temple in City politics at that juncture, with the letters between Junius and Wilkes upon the same subject.

Mr. Dayrell begins by informing Lord Temple that he had " communicated his answer to the Friends of Liberty;" but I have not been able to find any clue to the nature of the answer, or the communication which occasioned it.

He then enters at once into the question of the pending Election for Lord Mayor, from which it appears that both he and Lord Temple wished for the success of Sawbridge ; and here should be remembered the observation of Junius in his first letter to Wilkes :—

---

[1] *Almon's Memoirs of Wilkes.*

[2] See vol. iv. *post.* The letter has no date, but from internal evidence it may be safely ascribed to the time above-mentioned.

" I will not scruple to declare at once *that Mr. Sawbridge ought to be Lord Mayor.*"

Mr. Dayrell continues thus :—

" Mr. Alderman Bridgen's refusal brought great confusion, as your Lordship will observe, and I firmly believe will lose the present Lord Mayor his re-election. *The Shelburne party will be totally ruined in less than forty-five hours.*"

Junius writing to Wilkes, September 18th, says,—

" You seem to have no apprehension but *lest the friends of Lord Shelburne should get possession of the Mansion House. In my opinion they have no chance of success whatsoever.* The real danger is from the interest of Government, from Harley, and the Tories.—If, while you are employed in counteracting Mr. Townshend, a Ministerial Alderman should be returned, you will have ruined the cause." . . . . . .

" If, then, upon a fair canvass of the Livery, you should see a probability that Bridgen may not be returned, let that point be given up at once, and let *Sawbridge* be returned with *Crosby :*—a more likely way in *my* judgment to make *Crosby* Lord Mayor."—*Junius,* vol. i. p. 307.

To return to Mr. Dayrell's letter : he adds,—

" Nash is most likely to be Mayor, which we do not secretly dislike, as he is more likely to be with us, than any of the Shelburnes can be. If that should be the case, a certain person [1] whom your Lordship knows has a trap for him, which he longs to communicate to your Lordship, with many other important things, now in plan, *particularly an attack upon the privilege of commitment the House of Lords has lately exercised upon the printers,* and Mr. Bull [2] has agreed to act with him in everything."

In allusion to the attack upon the House of Lords in the matter of the printers, Junius, in his letter to Wilkes, dated September 18th, has the following paragraph :—

" Nothing can do you greater honour, nor be of greater benefit to the community, than *your intended attack upon the unconstitutional powers assumed by the House of Lords.* You have my warmest applause, and, if I can assist, command my assistance. The arbitrary power of fine and imprisonment assumed by these men, would be a disgrace to any form of legal government not purely *aristocratical.*

[1] Wilkes is the person alluded to.
[2] Wilkes and Bull were at this time the Sheriffs of London and Middlesex.

f 2

Directly it invades the laws, indirectly it saps the Constitution. Naturally phlegmatic, these questions warm me. I envy you the laurels you will acquire. Banish the thought that Junius can make a dishonourable or an imprudent use of the confidence you repose in him. When you have leisure, communicate your plan to me, that I may have time to examine it, and to consider what part I can act with the greatest advantage to the cause. The constitutional argument is obvious. I wish you to point out to me where you think the force of the *formal legal* argument lies."—*Junius,* vol. i. p. 308.

If it were Lord Temple's object to destroy any suspicion that might be lurking in the mind of Wilkes, or to bind him to silence if he suspected, he entirely succeeded in his desire, for upon no occasion is it mentioned that Wilkes ever pretended to be acquainted with the secret.

Mr. Charles Butler, in his *Reminiscences*[1], speaking of the Authorship of Junius, relates, that having been intimately acquainted with Wilkes, upon some occasion of their meeting the conversation accidentally turned upon the subject of Junius, and that Wilkes totally disclaimed the Authorship for himself, and treated the supposition with ridicule. Upon Mr. Butler expressing a wish to see the originals of the letters which Junius had addressed to Wilkes, they were produced, *together with a card of invitation to dinner, from old Lady Temple, written in her own hand, and upon comparing it with Junius's letters, they thought there was some resemblance between them.* Mr. Butler does not assert that any conversation passed with respect to the possibility of Lord Temple being the Author, but it may be considered rather a significant fact, that *the handwriting of Lady Temple* and *the original letters of Junius* should happen to be found together, and that they should have been so readily produced by Wilkes for comparison[2].

---

[1] Two vols. 8vo, 3rd edition, 1822, p. 81.

[2] There is another *Reminiscence* mentioned by Mr. Butler, in which I think it probable his memory was not correct,—indeed he relates it with some degree of doubt. He states that he and Wilkes examined the originals of Junius's letters more than once with great attention. "All of them," he adds, "*except the Letter to the King,* are, if I remember rightly, in the same handwriting." How should the original of Junius's letter to the King, written in December, 1769, come into the possession of Mr. Wilkes? It is not likely that Woodfall would have given it to Wilkes without the permission of the Author. It is, however, not impossible, nor even improbable, that Junius might

It must be mentioned that there is one other person with whom Junius *indirectly* corresponded, and that person was the Reverend Mr. Horne, with whom I have no reason to believe that Lord Temple had any private acquaintance. I have said *indirectly*, because the letter was sent through the medium of Woodfall, as appears from a note prefixed by Junius himself to the first collected edition of his Letters in 1772 :—

"This letter was transmitted privately by the printer to Mr. Horne, by Junius's request. Mr. Horne returned it to the printer, with directions to publish it."[1]

The private note from Junius to Woodfall, which accompanied the letter, says :—

" to prevent any unfair use being made of the inclosed, I intreat you to keep a Copy of it. then seal & deliver it to Mr. Horne.—I presume you know where he is to be found."—C[2].

Mr. Horne does not appear to have had any curiosity about the autograph, for he immediately returned the letter to the printer for publication, and the copy still remains in the possession of Mr. Woodfall: the original, when returned by Horne, was probably delivered over to the compositor, and so shared the fate of nearly all the other letters of Junius.

There is so much apparent sincerity and consistency in the frequent assertions of Junius with respect to his *rank and fortune*, and his being *far above all pecuniary views*, that we are in a manner constrained to give him credit in this instance, and to believe that he did not press this circumstance upon Woodfall for the mere purposes of deception.

In his private notes, he says to Woodfall :—

himself have submitted a copy of it to Wilkes, for his revision and opinion previous to publication, as we know he did with respect to his Dedication and Preface. If such a remarkable document had been found among the correspondence of Junius and Wilkes, when it was entrusted to Mr. George Woodfall and his editor, Dr. Mason Good, for publication in 1812, he, the latter, would scarcely have omitted to mention so interesting a circumstance in his Preliminary Essay, particularly if he found it to be in a writing different from the usual hand of Junius.

[1] *Junius*, vol. ii. p. 276.　　　　[2] *Ibid.*, vol. i. p. 225.

"In point of money, be assured you never shall suffer." [1]   . . .

"If your Affair sh^d come to a trial, and you sh^d be found guilty, you will then let me know what expence falls particularly on yourself; for I understand you are ingaged with other Proprietors. Some way or other *you* shall be reimbursed." . . . .

"What you say about the profits is very handsome; I like to deal with such men. As for myself, be assured that I am far above all pecuniary views, & no other person I think has any claim to share with you. Make the most of it therefore, & let all your views in life be directed to a solid, however moderate independence. Without it, no man can be happy, nor even honest.—"

And in a letter signed JUNIUS, in April, 1769, but which, for some unexplained reason, he did not think proper to include in his collected edition of 1772, he says,—

"It is true I have refused offers which a more prudent, or a more interested man would have accepted. Whether it be a simplicity or a virtue in me, I can only affirm that *I am in earnest:* and you I think, Sir, may be satisfied that my *rank and fortune* [2] place me above a common bribe."—*Junius,* vol. iii. p. 202.

And to Wilkes he wrote:—

"Though I do not disclaim the idea of some personal views to future honour and advantage (you would not believe me if I did), yet

---

[1] However profuse in promises, there is no evidence that Junius ever furnished Woodfall with money. It would not have been easy to do so, for, besides the difficulty of conveying a sum in cash, without detection, bank notes might have been traced to the hands of a former possessor; and perhaps Junius knew that Woodfall was satisfied with the profits which he had derived from the increased circulation of the *Public Advertiser.* Junius would not have recommended Woodfall to give money to the waiters at the coffee-houses where his letters were deposited, but that he should have incurred danger by attempting to do it himself, and if he had not been certain that Woodfall was quite able and willing to do so.

[2] "It is not possible for the Crown to prevent the appointing of some men of low *rank and fortune,* and when any one such is appointed, gentlemen of superior *rank and fortune* disdain to serve with such officers," &c.—*Lord Temple's Speech on the Militia Bill,* 1756.

"A matter of such difficulty that some have pretended it is too high to be entrusted to a special jury of the first *rank and condition.*"—*Lord Temple's Protest,* November 29, 1763.

" —— a further reason for never committing such an office to any but men of the *first rank and fortune.*"—*Junius,* vol. iii. p. 5.

"To a man of your Lordship's *high rank and fortune.*"—*Ibid.,* vol. iii. p. 203.

"The equity of the verdict must be measured by the distinctions of *rank and fortune.*"—*Ibid.,* vol. iii. p. 312.

I can truly affirm, that neither are they little in themselves, nor can they by any possible conjecture be collected from my writings."— *Junius*, vol. i. p. 264.

Junius was evidently a man of leisure, who had no particular pursuit or employment, either of profit or advantage, for his time must have been fully occupied by the labour to which he had devoted himself in the composition of his Letters[1], and consequently his circumstances were such as to render him independent of any exertion necessary for the support of his position in life.

He said in one of his letters to Wilkes,—

" I offer you the sincere opinion of a man who, perhaps, has more leisure to make reflections than you have, and who, though he stands clear of all business and intrigue, mixes sufficiently for the purposes of intelligence in the conversation of the world."—Vol. i. p. 265.

Junius has very exactly described the origin and progress of his mysterious employment in one of his letters to Mr. Grenville :—

" It began with amusement, grew into habit, was confirmed by a closer attention to your Principles and Conduct, & is now heated into Passion."

This passage was written in 1768 : if he was then only "heated into Passion," what must have been the degree of his fury two years later ! In the same letter he affirms that almost everything that had for two years past attracted the notice of the public came from the same hand, and there is now little doubt but that he was a practised writer even before the accession of George III.

In the letter to Mr. Grenville, above quoted, he says also,— "the *Grand Council*[2] was mine;" and this is a very important acknowledgment, because many persons have doubted the authen-

---

[1] Junius frequently adverts to the laborious nature of his employment:—

" I am heartily weary of writing."—*Junius*, vol. i. p. 274.

" I am overcome with the slavery of writing."—*Ibid.*, vol. i. p. 335.

" The pains I took with that paper upon Privilege were greater than I can express to you. Yet after I had blinded myself with poring over journals, debates, and parliamentary history," &c., &c.—*Ibid.*, vol. i. p. 309.

" Is there no merit in dedicating my life to the information of my fellow subjects ? Is there no labour in the composition of these letters ? "—*Ibid.*, vol. ii. p. 308.

[2] *Junius*, vol. ii. p. 482.   See, also, *post*, vol. iv. p. 171, *note*.

ticity of that Paper. It is dated 22nd October, 1767, and was first attributed to Junius by Dr. Mason Good, in Woodfall's edition of 1812.

This question being settled, it becomes almost a matter of certainty that he was also the Author of a Letter to an Honourable Brigadier-General[1], published in 1760. The subject of this letter was first mentioned by a correspondent of the *Gentleman's Magazine* in 1817 ; and again, without any previous knowledge of its having been there attributed to Junius, the Letter was reprinted in 1841 by Mr. Simons, one of the librarians in the British Museum, with some judicious editorial remarks and illustrations, which very satisfactorily established the fact that these two productions emanated from the same writer, and that writer the Author of the Letters of Junius.

The Honourable Brigadier-General George Townshend, to whom this Letter was addressed, had succeeded to the chief command at the siege of Quebec, after the death of Wolfe, and it devolved upon him to receive the capitulation of that important acquisition. It was the letter written from thence by General Townshend to Mr. Pitt, when Secretary of State, which excited the strong indignation of Lord Temple, because the whole merit of the affair seemed to be appropriated by General Townshend to himself, without one kind expression of esteem or affection with regard to the person, or one civil compliment to the memory of General Wolfe, whose appointment to the expedition against Quebec had been made by Mr. Pitt and Lord Temple, and principally, it is believed, at the recommendation of the latter. The great interest taken in the fate of General Wolfe by Lord Temple is traditionally known by the following anecdote, so well related by Lord Mahon in his *History of England*, vol. iv. p. 228 :—

"A slight incident connected with these times is recorded by tra-

---

[1] " A Letter to an Honorable Brigadier-General, Commander-in-Chief of His Majesty's Forces in Canada." 8vo, London, 1760. " A pamphlet," says Walpole, " reflecting bitterly on the vanity with which he had assumed a principal share in the conquest of Quebec, though the honour of signing the capitulation had only fallen to him by the death of Wolfe, and the wounds of Monckton ; an honour so little merited, that he had done his utmost to traverse Wolfe's plans."

dition, and affords a striking proof, how much a fault of manner may obscure and disparage high excellence of mind. After Wolfe's appointment, and on the day preceding his embarkation for America, Pitt, desirous of giving his last verbal instructions, invited him to dinner, Lord Temple being the only other guest. As the evening advanced, Wolfe, heated perhaps by his own aspiring thoughts, and the unwonted society of statesmen, broke forth into a strain of gasconade and bravado. He drew his sword, he rapped the table with it, he flourished it round the room, he talked of the mighty things which that sword was to achieve. The two Ministers sat aghast at an exhibition so unusual from any man of real sense and real spirit. And when at last Wolfe had taken his leave, and his carriage was heard to roll from the door, Pitt seemed for the moment shaken in the high opinion which his deliberate judgment had formed of Wolfe : he lifted up his eyes and arms, and exclaimed to Lord Temple, ' Good God ! that I should have entrusted the fate of the country and of the Administration to such hands ! '

" This story was told by Lord Temple himself to a near and still surviving relation : one of my best and most valued friends."[1]

The want of appreciation on the part of General Townshend of the merits of Wolfe, and that peculiar feature of Lord Temple's character which always induced him to adopt and resent the quarrels of those whom he had loved or protected, would account for the attack upon Townshend in the Letter to a Brigadier-General[2], added, perhaps, to some other real or fancied provoca-

---

[1] The venerable person alluded to by Lord Mahon was the late Right Honourable Thomas Grenville, from whom I had also the honour of receiving the same anecdote, and I have frequently heard the circumstances repeated by him to others, as having occurred at the house of his uncle Lord Temple, in Pall Mall. Lord Temple erected an obelisk of stone about sixty feet high in a conspicuous part of the Park at Stowe, where it still remains, to the Memory of General Wolfe, with the following inscription :—

" Ostendunt terris hunc tantùm fata."

[2] General Townshend, having failed in his attempt to trace the author of the pamphlet, and believing the attack upon his character to have been encouraged by the Duke of Cumberland, immediately challenged Lord Albemarle, as the nearest friend and representative of the Duke. Horace Walpole, in a letter to Montagu (*Collected Edition*, vol. iv. p. 109), has related the circumstances of the intended duel, which was prevented by the timely interference of Mr. Caswall, the Captain of the Guard at St. James's, to whom it became known through the information of Lord Buckingham, who was Townshend's second, and " who," adds Walpole, " loves a secret too well not to tell it."

tion, of which it would now be a hopeless task to endeavour to ascertain the cause. It is not a very improbable conjecture that Townshend's well-known talent for Caricature might have been exercised at the expense of Lord Temple, whose tall and awkward figure would have afforded him ample opportunity for ridicule.

Almon, in his Biography of Lord Camden[1], alluding to the Corn Bill and the suspension of the law in 1766, for preventing the exportation of corn[2], has the following passage:—

"Lord Temple[3] contrasted Lord Camden's doctrines when Lord Chief Justice in the affair of General Warrants, with the doctrines he had delivered upon the present occasion: in the first he had declared, that an hour's loss of liberty to an Englishman was inestimable: in the last, he had said that the suspension of the law was only *a forty days' tyranny* at the outside."[4]

This, continues Almon, provoked Lord Camden exceedingly, and in the moment of his irritation, he drew a character of Lord Temple, hypothetically, and concluded, that *if* the character he had described applied to any person, "it must be one of the narrowest, most vindictive, and most perfidious of human beings."

Many months afterwards these words were repeated by a writer in the *Public Advertiser*, under the signature of Scævola, who undertook the defence of Lord Camden in opposition to Junius,

---

[1] *Biographical Anecdotes*, vol. i. p. 378.

[2] See Lord Temple's Speech on the Suspending and Dispensing Prerogative, in *Parliamentary History*, vol. xvi.

[3] Mr. Pitt had written to Lady Chatham on the 10th of February preceding,—"I just learn that the world is at the House of Lords to-day, where mighty things are doing. I am sorry to say Lord Temple rises in passion, and sinks in consideration. Lord Camden grows in fame and public confidence."—*Chatham Correspondence*, vol. ii.

And about the same time Gerard Hamilton, writing to Calcraft, says,—"Lord Temple pointed most part of what he said personally to Lord Camden, who, I observe, avoids upon all occasions studiously the least altercation with his Lordship."—*Ibid.*, vol. ii. p. 385, *note*.

[4] Junius, under the signature of *Bifrons*, writing in April, 1768, says,—"By this rule, a man may say as a judge, that the loss of an Englishman's liberty for twenty-four hours only is grievous beyond estimation; and then as a minister may declare, that *forty days' tyranny* is a trifling burthen, which any Englishman may bear."—*Junius*, vol. iii. p. 43.

and, as the latter considered, in a very injudicious and unnecessary manner[1].

He did not usually "think it any way incumbent upon him to take notice of the silly invectives of every simpleton who writes in a newspaper,"[2] but, among all the very numerous and most bitter opponents of Junius, few of them seem to have incurred his anger, or to have moved him to an intemperate expression, more than this Scævola, and for reasons which I shall presently endeavour to explain.

In a private note to Woodfall on the 10th of December, 1771, Junius says,—

" I sho^d not trouble you or myself, about that Blockhead Scævola, but that his absurd fiction of *my* being Lord C's [Camden] Enemy has done harm.—Every fool can do mischief.—therefore signify to him what I said."

Again on the 17th,—

" Make your mind easy about me. I believe you are an honest man, and I never am angry.—say to morrow, ' We are desired to inform Scævola that his private note was received with the most profound indifference & contempt.'[3] I see his design. The duke of Grafton has been long labouring to detach Camden. This Scævola is the wretchedest of all fools ; & dirty knave."—

It was true that Lord Camden had been frequently wavering in his adherence to Lord Chatham. He had absented himself from the House of Lords upon occasions when Lord Chatham was much interested, particularly upon a motion relative to the Falkland Islands question. The subject is often mentioned in

---

[1] " Scævola, I see, is determined to make me an Enemy to Lord Camden. If it be not wilful malice, I beg you will signify to him that when I originally mentioned Lord C's Declaration about the Corn bill it was without any view of discussing that Doctrine, & only as an instance of a singular Opinion maintained by a man of great learning & integrity.—Such an instance was necessary to the plan of my letter :—I think he has in effect injured the man whom he meant to defend."—*Junius, private note to Woodfall*, No. 45, and see also *Junius*, vol. ii. p. 361.

[2] *Junius*, vol. ii. p. 6.

[3] This was perhaps a mode of expression usual with Lord Temple. I have mentioned in the Preface to vol. i. p. vi. a sketch of his portrait drawn by Lady Mary Grenville, as he was supposed to be saying in the House of Lords, " I am come to express my *highest indignation and contempt*," &c., &c.

Calcraft's correspondence with Chatham, in which I consider Temple to be a party equally concerned. On the 24th of March Calcraft writes suspiciously of Lord Camden :—

" 'T is most certain Lord Camden dined in company with Rigby on Wednesday : probably at the Duke of Grafton's. He (Rigby) returned to the House afterwards, and loudly proclaimed his company."

Chatham replies :—

" Lord Camden's dinner grieves me for his sake : consequence I believe it will have none ; but I am prepared not to be astonished at anything."

On the 7th of April Chatham writes :—

" The reports of Lord Camden grieve me : his indiscretion in appearances is unpardonable ; but I yet trust that he will not dishonour himself, by deserting the Constitution, however he has blemished his patriotism by such silly coquetry with the Court."

The newspapers, about this time, having insinuated that Lord Camden was deserting Lord Chatham, and making his court to the Duke of Grafton, Chatham writes to Calcraft, on the 8th of April :—

" I have seen Lord Camden to-day, by my bedside, but not a word from him with regard to any intercourse of the nature imputed to him. I would hope there has been nothing, but I own I have my fears."

At the end of the Session of Parliament, Camden did not concur with Chatham and Temple in approving the measure of pressing by a Motion for an immediate dissolution of Parliament.

There is sufficient in this correspondence to justify the expression of Junius, that " *the Duke of Grafton had been long labouring to detach Camden.*" There is certainly not anything very *foolish* or very *knavish* in the letters of Scævola, and nothing which apparently could warrant the very harsh terms applied to him by Junius in his private note to Woodfall ; unless, indeed, it were, as I believe, that the assertions of Scævola approached too near the real truth of the case, and that Junius was not, at any time, so near being unmasked as by this *wretched fool*, and *dirty knave* SCÆVOLA, who had the unpardonable temerity to accuse

Lord Temple[1] of being the *patron* of Junius, and William Gerard Hamilton[2] the writer.

[1] Upon another occasion Lord Temple was pointed at as the Author of Junius by a writer in the *Public Advertiser* (October 11, 1769), under the signature of *Poetikastos,* a name said to have been assumed by Sir John Macpherson, but I know not whether he was the writer of the following letter addressed "to the BROTHERHOOD of STOWE."

" If you have secretly endeavoured to misrepresent the virtue of the Sovereign to the subject, you justly forfeit the confidence of the one and the regard of the other ; and if you have made grievances to be felt, where they could only affect in idea, and apprehensions to arise from imagination only, you cannot, with reason, complain, if you are lashed for crimes of which you are guiltless, and if iniquity is demonstrated in your present intentions or principles of political speculation." . . . . . . " But it were unworthy of the cause of order and Government to reverberate upon you the strokes of your satire, or to play back upon you your own engines of imposition. *Let Junius avail himself of delusive antithesis, and may you continue to feed, under the veil of secrecy, the flames of sedition. To alarm with ideal apprehensions, to torture with imaginary grievances, and deceive with fictitious patriotism, are acts worthy of you.* Beware how their effect will revert." . . . . " The credulity of the public will not receive repeated imposition. You have not the charm of novelty ; and though a few circumstances have tended to extinguish the memory of your former behaviour, Britain can never forget the sacrifices of her dignity for a Ribbon, and the loss of her Colonies for a stupid experiment in financing. . . . . . . " Remember, C——[a], the transactions of the year 1752[b]. The soul that was then resolved in the torture of crushed ambition to ——, has not yet forgot its passion. The place is known—the hour is remembered, when on the bended knee God was implored to assist the scheme. But let the transaction be forgot, and let not the infirmities of age suffer for the deception of youth."

[2] It will be seen in these volumes that William Gerard Hamilton was in very frequent and most confidential correspondence with Lord Temple, and there is no reason to doubt but that their intimacy continued up to this time at least, but only one letter (in 1768) from Hamilton to Temple has been found of a later date than 1767. So, also, with respect to Calcraft, it is equally certain that his intimacy with Temple continued during the life of the former, but no letter from Calcraft to Temple is extant, dated in

[a] It is worthy of observation, that the initial letter C, by which Lord Temple is here addressed, was the signature used by Junius in his private communications to Woodfall and Mr. Grenville.

[b] It was in the year 1752 that Lord Temple, then Lord Cobham, succeeded to the former title upon the death of his mother, the Countess Temple, but I cannot form any conjecture with regard to the *transactions* here alluded to, unless indeed they have reference to " a *Memorial of several noblemen and gentlemen of the first rank and fortune,*" upon the subject of the education of the Prince of Wales ; a copy of it was sent *anonymously* to General Hawley, in December, 1752, and by him shown to the King and the Duke of Cumberland. This paper has been attributed to Lord Temple, and I think it not improbable that he had some hand in it, for it is in every respect consistent with his opinions. A copy of it is inserted in Horace Walpole's *Memoirs of George II.,* and in a note subsequently added, and supposed to be by Walpole himself, the Memorial is stated to be his own production ; but Walpole's observations upon it in the text would scarcely warrant the supposition that it was written by him. If the note were added by the editor, the late Lord Holland, as a mere assertion unsupported by any authority, it would be of little value, because Lord Holland could have no exclusive information upon the subject.—See *Walpole's Memoirs of George II.,* vol. i. p. 298 ; *Bubb Dodington's Diary,* and *Newhall's Letters on Junius.*

In a letter addressed to Junius in the *Public Advertiser* of Saturday, November 9th, 1771, Scævola says,—

" You call yourself a man of rank and wealth. To say the truth, there are some perhaps over-acute, who will have it that you belong to a *certain malcontent Peer of this realm* [Lord Temple], *who is said to have put the same false colours upon this very doctrine of Lord Camden's, in a pamphlet full of wretched invective soon after the opinion was delivered ;* that your politics are to make every public man either odious or despicable : that you have uncommon malignity, except as to Mr. Grenville : that all these particulars (the exception included) are, when taken collectively, speaking proofs, not of the writer (whose abilities are his own), but of the *Patron of Junius.* Let the public ruminate upon this idea ; but let charity check the judgment, and resist every confirmation short of proof. I, for one, declare that I shall wait for mathematical demonstration before I can agree to associate Junius with *one of the narrowest, most vindictive, and perfidious of human beings.*" [1]—Scævola.

And again, on the 18th of November, Scævola writes,—

" I have dropped a hint with regard to the patron of Junius. The fair way to examine this hint is to read the whole series of Letters attributed to Junius, applying them to the supposed patron or party, and so correcting and establishing the idea. However, to give the reader some excuse for my arrogance in suggesting a notion, which differs from the most prevalent one [2] ; let me observe, that Junius never speaks of Mr. Grenville with disrespect : that when he speaks of times, and measures, in which Mr. Grenville bore a principal share, and which he attacks with great freedom, he avoids even the name of Mr. Grenville ; for he describes his Grace as called in ' to support an Administration which Lord Bute had pretended to leave in full possession of authority ; but which (as he would have us believe) became servile to my Lord Bute from the moment of his Grace's accession to the system, and by means of stipulations between the Duke and the

the years when Junius was writing. Nor are there any letters *at this time* from Almon, a certain and constant purveyor of news to Lord Temple ; not one from Wilkes, from Humphrey Cotes, from Beardmore, from Mackintosh, one only from Dayrell, all intimate friends of Temple, and all, as I believe, unconscious instruments in his hands to serve the purposes of the Letters of Junius. For special reasons Lord Temple must certainly have destroyed the greater part of his correspondence at this period. In a letter from Calcraft to Almon, dated *Ingress, December* 29, 1771, he says,—" Many thanks to you for your correct and constant intelligence. If Mr. Hamilton is in town, I should like to hear what he thinks will be the consequence. What childish stories do they propagate ! You *cannot conceive either the questions I am asked, or the innumerable reports about Lord Temple.*"

[1] See *ante*, p. xc.   [2] Edmund Burke was generally suspected.

favourite.' Here he transfers all the odium of that servility from his friend Mr. Grenville, to the Duke of Bedford ; though in truth it belongs equally to both. What is the ground of his inveteracy to the Duke of Bedford? He shall tell you in his own words :—' Apparently united with Mr. Grenville, you waited until Lord Rockingham's feeble Administration should dissolve in its own weakness. The moment their dismission was suspected, &c., you thought it no disgrace to solicit once more the friendship of Lord Bute, &c.' [1] *Hinc illæ lacrymæ.* The Duke of Bedford forsook Mr. Grenville, and therefore Junius persecutes him with such rancour. But his panegyric upon the Stamp Act in his very first Letter, and his anxious vindication of Mr. Grenville [2], from the most vulnerable and most indefensible part of his political life, announce to us that gentleman's attached and partial friend. Out of many other passages that point out the suspected person [3], I must remind the reader of two or three instances which evince that Junius, at two critical periods, disclaims Lord Rockingham and Lord Chatham :—' When the Duke of Cumberland's first negotiation failed, and when the Favourite was pushed to the last extremity, you saved him by joining in an Administration in which Lord Chatham had refused to engage. Lord Chatham formed his last Administration *upon principles which you certainly concurred in,* or you could never have been placed at the head of the Treasury. By deserting *those principles* (in which he found you were secretly supported in the closet), you soon forced him to withdraw his name from an Administration which had been formed upon the credit of it.' [4] What caution is here used to avoid a compliment to Lord Chatham, or to those unstated *principles,* in the midst of invectives upon the Duke of Grafton for deserting them. I presume the conclusion is not a rash one from these premises (to omit for the present several others), that the patron of Junius is the person [5] characterized in my last." [6]

In one of his replies to Sir William Draper, Junius says :—

" You are a scholar, Sir William, and if I am truly informed, you write Latin with almost as much purity as English."

And subsequently he added :—

" Will you forgive me if I insinuate to you, that you foresaw some

---

[1] *Junius,* vol. i. p. 538.

[2] Letter xviii. addressed to Mr. Justice Blackstone.—*Junius,* vol. i. p. 531.

[3] William Gerard Hamilton.

[4] Letter xii. addressed to the Duke of Grafton.—*Junius,* vol. i. p. 484.

[5] Lord Temple.   [6] *Public Advertiser,* November 18, 1771, signed SCÆVOLA.

honour in the apparent spirit of coming forward in person, and that you were not quite indifferent to the display of your literary qualifications ? "

Lord Temple had probably been informed, either by Lord Chatham or his sister, that only a few months before Sir William Draper had written a long and very formal Latin inscription in honour of Lord Chatham as a statesman, of which he had sent him a copy, and which he proposed to place upon a triumphal column in his garden at Manilla Hall, near Bristol.

Lord Chatham, in his reply[1], "hopes Sir William will give him leave most earnestly to entreat that, of an inscription so infinitely partial, the four last lines alone may remain ;" and accordingly the inscription on the column was a simple dedication only to Lord Chatham, by Sir William Draper.

A continual interchange of very intimate correspondence and communication was kept up during the years 1769, 1770, and 1771, between Mr. Calcraft, Lord and Lady Chatham, and Lord Temple[2], and it will appear that in many instances the information conveyed in this correspondence coincided with that used by Junius in his public Letters, as well as in his private notes to Woodfall.

It is well known that Lord Granby always regretted the vote he gave in favour of the expulsion of Wilkes, in May, 1769, contrary to the advice of Lord Chatham. He made a visit to Hayes about a week before the debate on that question. Lord Temple was aware of this interview and the object of it; he alludes to it in a letter to Lady Chatham, dated May 6th : —

"Lord Granby has made his report to the Duke of Grafton of what passed with Lord Chatham."

On the day previous, May 5th, Junius, in one of his private notes to Woodfall, writes,—

---

[1] *Chatham Correspondence*, vol. iii. p. 327.

[2] The letters from Calcraft in the *Chatham Correspondence* are very numerous. Considering their intimacy, it can scarcely be doubted that he also wrote very frequently to Lord Temple, but, as I have before stated, not a single letter written at this time has been preserved.

" it is essentially necessary that the inclosed should be published to-morrow, as the great Question comes on on Monday, & *Lord Granby is already staggered.*"[1] as if Junius knew exactly the tenor of the conversation which had passed at Hayes between Lord Chatham aud Lord Granby, and that the latter was, at least, undetermined and wavering ("staggered") as to the nature of the vote he intended to give on the important question to be decided on the Monday following.

The enclosure above alluded to by Junius was a letter addressed to Lord Granby, under the signature of "YOUR REAL FRIEND,"[2] which thus concludes :—

" One short question will determine your character for ever. Does it become the name and dignity of Manners to place yourself upon a level with a venal tribe who vote as they are directed, and to declare upon your honour, in the face of your country, that Mr. Luttrell is, or ought to be, the sitting Member for the County of Middlesex? I appeal *bonâ fide* to your integrity as an honest man :—I even appeal to your understanding."

On the 7th Calcraft writes from Ingress, to Lord Chatham at Hayes, sending the best account he could obtain of the King's intended Speech, with some other paragraphs of intelligence, which are placed within inverted commas, as if they were the words of his correspondent, who, it may be assumed, was Lord Temple, as Lord Chatham is subsequently referred to him for *additional* information.

" 'T is said the Duke of Ancaster and Lord Jersey are to move in the Lords (the Earls of Carlisle and March having refused), Mr. Payne and Lord Robert Spencer in the Commons. The view[3] in getting Payne is to convey an impression of Lord Mansfield's support, &c."

---

[1] The original is dated "friday" only.

[2] *Junius,* vol. iii. p. 203.

[3] *The view is,* &c. I do not find this to have been an ordinary mode of expression, but the word *view* is often used by Junius in the sense of *the object is,* or *the motive is ;* thus, for instance, he writes to Woodfall (private note No. 46), "*I have no view but to serve you,*" &c. Lord Temple has used the same word in the same sense in some Collections in his handwriting, which were evidently made for the compilation of the speech on *the Suspending and Dispensing Prerogative,* subsequently published in the form of a pamphlet. The passage runs thus,—" Salus populi suprema lex. His Lordship (Lord Camden) goes to common sense. He wants no statute. The Law of England, he hitherto thought perfect, but if so destitute of sense and reason, &c., &c. he would move for a Bill to enact it; *the view is to hold forth to the public* that there has been a violation of the constitution, &c." I shall have occasion to revert to these Collections hereafter.

In his own words, Calcraft continues :—

" A letter is just arrived from Lord Granby to desire he may see me to-morrow afternoon, and it will give me pleasure to convey any commands of your Lordship ; in particular such as may aid his conduct at this crisis: . . . . *Lord Temple will give your Lordship the best information*."

Lord Chatham replies on the same day; he mentions Lord Temple's arrival at Hayes, and, with respect to Lord Granby, suggests,—

"for Mr. Calcraft's judgment, whether the proposing a refreshing interview between the Marquis and my Lord Chancellor, might not be a good measure."

Lord Chatham and Lord Temple had been long endeavouring to detach the Marquess of Granby from the Government, and they were at this juncture using the most urgent entreaty to persuade him to resign his employments and join the Opposition.

On the following morning, January 8th, 1770, Chatham writes to Calcraft, and, after mentioning Lord Temple's intention

" to use endeavours that some proper words of addition to the Address should be moved in the House of Commons to engage debate," at the meeting of Parliament next day,

he adds,—

" Notwithstanding all report, the opinion at Hayes is, that Lord Chancellor will not be removed; and he certainly will not have the unpardonable weakness to resign in such a crisis. His Lordship is firm, and in the rightest resolutions. Lord Chatham entertains not the least doubt that Mr. Calcraft will find Lord Granby in the same dispositions. The expectation of the public was never more fixed upon two great men than upon the Marquis and Lord Camden."

Calcraft in reply, on the same day, informs Lord Chatham that—

" he has seen Lord Granby, who goes to the Chancellor's (by an appointment of Lord Granby's asking) this morning. His Lordship seems very properly disposed, and I hope Lord Chancellor will fix him to take his part to-day, if an opportunity arises in the course of the Debate."

On the 15th of January Lord Temple writes to Lord Chatham :—

" I am this instant returned from Calcraft's. Lord Granby is there. The King, it seems, and the Duke of Grafton, are upon their knees to Lord Granby, not to resign. He remained to the Duke of Grafton inflexible as to that, but has yielded for twenty-four hours. Calcraft does most earnestly wish, and so do I, that you may take the trouble of writing, either to Lord Granby himself, or to Calcraft, your opinion and warm desire that his Lordship may to-morrow morning go to the Queen's house, desire to see the King, and carry into execution what had been so much better done yesterday. . . . . . . The Ministry live upon moments. . . . Heaven and earth are in motion." [1]

The letters on the following days between Chatham, Calcraft, and Temple, show how pressingly they continued to urge Lord Granby, until at last, on the morning of the 17th instant, he resigned all his employments except the command of the regiment of Horse Guards.

Having accomplished the resignation of Lord Granby, the next grand object of these Correspondents was the City Remonstrance and Petition, upon which also Junius was particularly interested.

On Tuesday, the 13th of March, Calcraft writes to Chatham,—

" Lord Temple will have communicated my intelligence of last night. It is since confirmed, and I believe Thursday will be the day on which the Remonstrance is to be attacked in Parliament. . . . *The alarm at Court is beyond imagination. If our friends stand firm, they own all is over with them.* Every temptation is, or will be, held out to Lord Rockingham. There, is their only hope. I wish your Lordship could contrive to see Lord Granby to-morrow, and talk over with him the state of the times, and the Remonstrance."

Chatham replies on the same evening, and on Saturday, the 17th of March, Calcraft again writes :—

" The fright at Court continues, and they are not only puzzled, but undetermined, what to do with the Remonstrance, now 't is got to Parliament. . . . . . The Ministers dread a Resolution of the Common Hall against the advisers of the strong words in His Majesty's answer."

---

[1] Junius was very busy at this time ; his communications with Woodfall were interrupted : on the 12th he says,—"You must not write to me again, but be assured I will never desert You. I received your letters regularly, but it was *impossible* to answer them sooner. You shall hear from me again shortly."—C.

On this same day, Saturday, March 17th, Junius writes to Woodfall:—

"to-morrow before 12 you shall have a Junius, it will be absolutely necessary that it should be published on Monday. Would it be possible to give Notice of [it] to night, or to morrow, by a dispersing a few Hand-bills. Pray do whatever You think will answer this purpose best, for now is the Crisis."—C. [1]

The promised Junius [2] was sent to Woodfall on the following day: it is upon the subject of the City Address and Remonstrance, and the King's answer. It was accompanied by the following private note:—

"this letter is written wide, & I suppose will not fill two Columns. for God's sake, let it appear to-morrow.—I hope you received my note of yesterday. *Lord Chatham is determined to go to the Hall to support the Westminster Remonstrance. I have no doubt that we shall conquer them at last.*"—C. [3]

Probably before the above note was dispatched to Woodfall by Junius, Lord Temple had received from Calcraft the following, *dated Sunday,* 20 *minutes past nine, March* 18, 1770,—

"Just as your Lordship left me, a friend [4] came in, who says he hears a strong report that they disagree amongst themselves, see the difficulties they may be involved in, and have resolved not to proceed upon the Remonstrance to-morrow. *Lord Chatham's proposal about Westminster adds to their alarm. The greatest person requires cordials.* We should not be the less upon our guard for this rumour."

On the following day there was a debate in the House of Commons, on the Address to the King, in reprobation of the Remonstrance, which was carried by a large majority. Lord Temple wrote to Lady Chatham on the "20th, past 11, at night," that he—

"had the grace to stay in the House of Commons 'till three o'clock this morning. . . . . I have kept open my letter for news from the House, to which I have sent, but in vain. *Impeachment* seemed to be the measure resolved on at dinner time."

Junius subsequently added as a note to his xxxviiith Letter—

"About this time, the Courtiers talked of nothing but a Bill of pains and penalties against the Lord Mayor & Sheriffs, or Impeachment at the least."

---

[1] The original is dated "Saturday" only.   [2] Letter xxxviii., vol. ii. p. 123.
[3] The original is dated "Sunday" only.   [4] Perhaps William Gerard Hamilton.

In the same note, and as if in allusion to Calcraft's letter mentioned above, Junius has added—

" The Minister took fright & at the very instant that little Ellis was going to open, sent him an order to sit down. All their magnanimous Threats ended in a ridiculous vote of Censure, & a still more ridiculous Address to the King. This shameful Desertion so afflicted the generous mind of George the third, that he was obliged to live upon potatoes for three weeks, to keep off a malignant fever.—Poor man! *quis talia fando temperet a lacrymis!*"

The " *shameful desertion* " is another echo from one of Calcraft's letters to Chatham. On the 24th of March he writes:—

" The Court think the Ministers have stopped too short in the persecution of the City Magistrates, and the language of Thursday was, ' *my Ministers have no spirit: they don't pursue measures with any spirit.*' There is great confusion among them, and if we stand by the people as we ought, and take another early opportunity to show it, it will have the best effect, for notwithstanding high words, there is real alarm."

Again, on the 27th, Calcraft says,—

" The anger of the Court and Bute party, at being given up, as they term it, after the strong answer to the City Remonstrance, has been so violent, that thoughts of going further have been resumed, but I do not believe they will be carried into execution."

Lord Chatham replies :—

" As for the anger you mention in a certain quarter, at being given up, as they call it, after the silly answer to the City, I can only say, they have nothing to be angry with but their own *folly* and the *wisdom* of the Constitution, expressed with so much precision in the Bill of Rights. As for all talk of going further, I can only look on it with the contempt it deserves."

These passages correspond with the general tone and sentiment of the Letter which Junius was then writing, and which appeared on the 3rd of April; it contains a further consideration of the King's Answer to the City Address[1].

---

[1] The following is an extract :—" Let it be taken for granted that an occasion may arise in which a King of England shall be compelled to take upon himself the ungrateful office of rejecting the petitions, and censuring the conduct of his subjects ; and let the City Remonstrance be supposed to have created so extraordinary an occasion. On this principle, which I presume no friend of administration will dispute, let the wisdom and spirit of the Ministry be examined. They advise the King to hazard his dignity by a positive declaration of his own sentiments :—they suggest to him a language full of

The above correspondence sufficiently indicates the very great interest taken by Lord Chatham and Lord Temple in City politics, and at this conjuncture particularly, with respect to the Address and Remonstrance presented to the King by the Lord Mayor and Aldermen, on the 14th of March. Upon this subject Junius has written two letters, dated March 19th and April 3rd. I have found among Lord Temple's papers a document which I think is certainly connected with the composition of these two letters. It is a printed copy of the Address and Remonstrance, cut from one of the newspapers of the day, carefully pasted down on a quarter of a sheet of foolscap paper, and folded, with an endorsement in Lord Temple's hand, "REMONSTRANCE and ANSWER." Within this paper, and folded precisely in the same size and form, was a half sheet of small quarto paper, containing also, in Lord Temple's hand, some extracts from Chapter xix. of Locke's *Essay on Civil Government.*

The Remonstrance and Answer are reprinted in the note below [1]

severity and reproach. What follows? When His Majesty had taken so decisive a part in support of his Ministry and Parliament, he had a right to expect from *them* a reciprocal demonstration of firmness in their own cause, and of zeal for *his* honour. He had reason to expect, (and such I doubt not were the blustering promises of Lord North) that the persons whom he had been advised to charge with having failed in their respect to him, with having injured parliament, and violated the principles of the constitution, should not have been permitted to escape, without some severe marks of the displeasure and vengeance of parliament. As the matter stands, the Minister, after placing his Sovereign in the most unfavourable light to his subjects, and after attempting to fix the ridicule of his own precipitate measures upon the Royal character, leaves him a solitary figure upon the scene, to recall, if he can, or to compensate, by future compliances, for one unhappy demonstration of ill-supported firmness, and ineffectual resentment. As a man of spirit, his Majesty cannot but be sensible, that the lofty terms in which he was persuaded to reprimand the city, when united with the silly conclusion of the business, resemble the pomp of a mock tragedy, where the most pathetic sentiments, and even the sufferings of the hero, are calculated for derision."—*Junius,* vol. ii. p. 127.

[1] " The humble Address, Remonstrance, and Petition of the Lord Mayor, Aldermen, and Livery of the City of London, in Common Hall assembled.

" To the King's most excellent Majesty.

" May it please your Majesty,

" We have already in our Petition dutifully represented to your Majesty the chief injuries we have sustained. We are unwilling to believe that your Majesty can slight the desires of your people, or be regardless of their affection, and deaf to their complaints : yet their complaints remain unanswered : their injuries are confirmed : *and the only judge whom the Revolution has left removable at the pleasure of the Crown has been dismissed from his high office for defending in Parliament the law and the Constitution.* We therefore venture once more to address ourselves to your Majesty, as to the father of your people, as to him who must be *both able and willing to redress our griev-*

in order to shew the passages in *Italics*, and Capitals, which in this copy have been *underlined or noted by Lord Temple's* hand,

ances : and we repeat our application with the greater propriety, because we see the instruments of our wrongs, who have carried into execution the measures of which we complain, more particularly distinguished by your Majesty's royal bounty and favour [a].

"UNDER THE SAME SECRET [AND] MALIGN INFLUENCE, WHICH THROUGH EACH SUCCESSIVE ADMINISTRATION HAS DEFEATED EVERY GOOD, AND SUGGESTED EVERY BAD INTENTION, THE MAJORITY OF THE HOUSE OF COMMONS HAVE DEPRIVED YOUR PEOPLE OF THEIR DEAREST RIGHTS [b].

"They have done a deed, more ruinous in its consequences than the levying of Ship money by Charles the first, or the dispensing power assumed by James the second [c]. *A deed which must* VITIATE *all the future proceedings of this Parliament : for the acts of the Legislature itself can no more be valid without a legal House of Commons, than without a legal prince upon the throne* [d].

"*The representatives of the people are essential to the making of laws ; and there is a time when it is morally demonstrable, that men cease to be represented.* THAT TIME IS NOW ARRIVED [e]. The present House of Commons do not represent the people. We owe to your Majesty an obedience, under the restrictions of the laws, for the calling and duration of Parliaments : and your Majesty owes to us, that our representation, free from *the force of arms or corruption*, should be preserved to us in Parliament.

"It was for this we successfully struggled under James the second ; for this we seated and have faithfully supported your Majesty's family on the throne.

"The people have been invariably uniform in their object; though the different mode of attack has called for a different defence.

"Under James the second they complained that the sitting of Parliament was interrupted, because it was not corruptly subservient to his designs. *We complain now, that the sitting of this Parliament is not interrupted, because it is corruptly subservient to the designs of your Majesty's Ministers. Had the Parliament under James the second, been as submissive to his commands, as the Parliament is at this day to the dictates of a Minister, instead of clamorous for its meeting, the nation would have rung, as now, with outcries for its dissolution.* The forms of the Constitution, like those of religion, were not established for the form's sake, but for the substance. And we call God and men to witness, that as we do not owe our liberty to those nice and subtle distinctions

[a] "The *grievances* of the people are aggravated by insults : *their complaints not merely disregarded, but checked by authority,* and every one of those acts against which they remonstrated, confirmed by the King's decisive approbation."—*Junius,* vol. ii. p. 110.
[b] "The King's answer to the Remonstrance of the City of London, and the measures since adopted by the Ministry, amount to a declaration that the principle on which Mr. Luttrell was seated in the House of Commons, is to be supported in all its consequences, and carried to its utmost extent. *The same spirit which violated the freedom of election, now invades the declaration and bill of rights, and threatens to punish the subject for exercising a privilege, hitherto undisputed, of petitioning the Crown.*"—*Junius,* vol. ii. p. 105.
[c] "That the principle on which the Middlesex Election was determined, is *more pernicious in its effects,* than either *the levying of ship money, by Charles the First, or the suspending power assumed by his son,* will hardly be disputed by any man who understands or wishes well to the English Constitution."—*Junius,* vol. ii. p. 116.
[d] "If any part of the representative body be not chosen by the people, *that part* VITIATES *and corrupts the whole.*"—*Junius,* vol. ii. p. 115.
[e] "The time is come," &c.—*Junius,* vol. ii. p. 115.

and it will be seen that these particular passages contain the *points*, and some of the same expressions, to be found in the two Letters of Junius which I have mentioned.

The extracts from Locke are as follows; and it appears to me that they also contain the germs of some passages in the Letter of Junius, dated March 19th, and that they were used by Lord

which places and pensions, and lucrative employments have invented : so neither will we be deprived of it by them : *but as it was gained by the stern virtue of our ancestors, by the virtue of their descendants it shall be preserved.*" [a]

" Since, therefore, the misdeeds of your Majesty's *Ministers*, in violating the freedom of election, and *depraving* the noble constitution of Parliament are notorious, as well as subversive of the fundamental laws and liberties of this realm ; *and, since your Majesty, both in honour and justice, is obliged inviolably to preserve them, according to the oath made to God and your subjects at your Coronation;* We, your Remonstrants, assure ourselves that your Majesty will restore the constitutional government and quiet of your people, *by dissolving this Parliament, and removing those evil Ministers for ever from your Councils.*"

[" HIS MAJESTY'S ANSWER.]

" *I shall always be ready to receive the requests and to listen to the complaints of my subjects* [b]; but it gives me great concern to find that any of them should have been so far misled, as to offer me an Address and Remonstrance, *the contents of which I cannot but consider as disrespectful to me,* injurious to Parliament, and *irreconcileable to the principles of the Constitution* [c].

" *I have ever made the law of the land the rule of my conduct* [d], esteeming it my chief glory to reign over a free people : with this view *I* have always been careful, as well to execute faithfully the trust reposed in me, as to avoid *even the appearance of invading* any of those powers which the Constitution has placed in other hands [e]. It is only by persevering in such a conduct, that I can either discharge my own duty, or secure to my subjects the free enjoyment of those rights *which my family were called to defend ;* and while I act upon these principles, I shall have a right to expect, and I am confident I shall continue to receive, the steady and affectionate support of my people." [f]

[a] " The time is come when the body of the English people must assert their own cause : conscious of their strength, and animated by a sense of their duty, *they will not surrender their birthright to ministers, parliaments, or kings.*"—*Junius*, vol. ii. p. 115.

[b] " His Majesty is pleased to say that he is always ready to receive the requests of his subjects."—*Junius*, vol. ii. p. 117.

[c] " Whether the Remonstrance be or be not *injurious to Parliament,* is the very question between the Parliament and the people, and such a question as cannot be decided by the assertion of a third party, however respectable. That the petitioning for a dissolution of Parliament is *irreconcileable with the principles of the constitution* is a new doctrine."—*Junius*, vol. ii. p. 117.

[d] " His Majesty proceeds to assure us that *he has made the laws the rule of his conduct.*"—*Junius*, vol. ii. p. 118.

[e] " His Majesty, we are told, is not only punctual in the performance of his own duty, but *careful not to assume any of those powers which the constitution has placed in other hands.*"—*Junius*, vol. ii. p. 120.

[f] " To talk of *preserving the affections,* or *relying on the support of his subjects, while he continues to act upon those principles,* is indeed paying a compliment to their loyalty, which I hope they have too much spirit and understanding to deserve."—*Junius*, vol. ii. p. 119.

Temple, in other words, but to the same effect, in the composition of that and some others of the Letters—

" Extracts from Mr. Locke's (nineteenth) chapter on the Dissolution of Government.

" Besides this overturning from without, *Governments are dissolved from within.*

" *When the Legislative is altered. The Constitution of the Legislative* is the first & fundamental Act of Society, whereby provision is made for the continuation of their union, under the Direction of persons & the *Bonds of Laws* made by Persons *authorised* thereunto, by the consent & appointment of the People, without which no one Man, *or number of Men* amongst them, can have Authority of making Laws that shall be binding to the rest. When any one *or more* shall take upon them to make Laws, whom the People have not appointed so to do, they make Laws without authority which the People are not therefore bound to obey. This being usually brought about *by such* in the commonwealth who *misuse* the Power they have, it is hard to consider it aright, & know at whose door to lay it, without knowing the form of government in which it happens.

" Let us suppose, then, the Legislative placed in the concurrence of three distinct persons. *Whoever introduces new laws, not being thereunto authorised by the fundamental appointment of the Society, or subverts the old, disowns & overturns the power by which they were made* [1].

---

[1] " Even that assertion, which we are told is most offensive to Parliament, in the theory of the English Constitution is strictly true. *If any part of the representative body be not chosen by the people, that part vitiates and corrupts the whole. If there be a defect in the representation of the people, that power which alone is equal to the making of laws in this country is not complete, and the acts of Parliament under that circumstance are not the acts of a pure and entire legislature.* I speak of the theory of our constitution, and whatever difficulties or inconvenience may attend the practice, I am ready to maintain, that as far as the fact deviates from the principle, so far the practice is vicious and corrupt."—*Junius,* vol. ii. p. 115.

And in this same letter, in which the above passages, extracted from Locke by Lord Temple, are paraphrased by Junius, I find other ideas and expressions also applied by Junius, from the Essay on Civil Government : thus, for instance, in his 12th Chapter, Locke says :—

" For though in a commonwealth the members of it are distinct persons still, in reference to one another, and as such are governed by the laws of the society, yet in reference to the rest of mankind they make one body, which is, as every member of it before was, still in the state of nature with the rest of mankind."

Junius changes this into the following :—" However *distinguished by rank or property,* in the rights of freedom *we are all equal.* As we are Englishmen, *the least considerable man among us has an interest equal to the proudest nobleman, in the laws and constitution of his country,"* &c.—vol. ii. p. 113.

Locke continues :—

" Hence it is, that the controversies that happen between any man of the society with

Thirdly, *when* by the arbitrary Power of the Prince [or of either of the other branches of the Legislature], *the electors, or ways of election, are altered without the consent, &* contrary to the common interest *of the People, there also the Legislative is altered. for if others than those whom the Society hath authorised thereunto, do chuse or in any other way than what the society hath prescribed, those chosen* are not the Legislative appointed by the People [1]. The Legislative [& a fortiori every part thereof], act against the Trust reposed in them when they endeavour to invade *the property* of the subject, & make themselves or any part of the Community masters or arbitrary disposers of the Lives, Liberties, or fortunes of the People." [2]

those that are out of it, are managed by the public, and *an injury done to a member of their body, engages the whole in the reparation of it.*"

And Junius said :—

" It is a common cause, in which we are all interested, in which we should all be engaged."—*Junius*, vol. ii. p. 114.

" We hold it, Sir, that an injury offered to an individual is interesting to society." —*Junius*, vol. i. p. 532.

And the expression, *power without right* (to be found in Lord Temple's Speech on the *Suspending and Dispensing Prerogative*, published early in 1767), subsequently more than once used by Junius, and emphatically claimed by Sir Philip Francis, because he said he heard it from Lord Chatham, was originally derived from Locke, as will be seen by the following extracts :—

" And where the body of the people, or any single man is deprived of their right, or is under the exercise of a *power without right*, and have no appeal on earth, then they have a liberty to appeal to heaven, whenever they judge the cause of sufficient moment."—Chap. xiv. And again —" As usurpation is the exercise of power, which another hath a right to, so tyranny is the exercise of *power beyond right*, which nobody can have a right to."—Chap. xviii.

It is evident that Locke is one of the authors upon which the style of Junius was partly formed. When he wrote the following passage in one of his letters about this same time, he had been probably reminded of the well-known saying of Caligula, which is quoted by Locke in the same chapter of his Essay, from which Lord Temple's extracts were derived.

" The Ministry have realized the compendious ideas of Caligula. They know that the liberty, the laws, and property of an Englishman have, in truth, but *one neck*, and that to violate the freedom of election, strikes deeply at them all."— *Junius*, vol. ii. 153.

[1] " The right of election is the very essence of the Constitution. To violate that right, and much more to *transfer it to any other set of men*, is a step leading immediately to the dissolution of all government. So far forth as it operates, it constitutes a House of Commons *which does not represent the people*."—*Junius*, vol. i. p. 475.

" The arbitrary appointment of Mr. Luttrell invades the foundation of the laws themselves, as it manifestly transfers the right of legislation from those *whom the people have chosen*, to those whom they have rejected."—*Junius*, vol. i. p. 509.

[2] " We can never be really in danger until the forms of Parliament are made use of to destroy the substance of our civil and political liberties; until Parliament itself *betrays its trust*, by contributing to establish new principles of Government, and

The following draft of the *second* Remonstrance and Petition from the City of London, is from the original in the handwriting of Lady Chatham. It was probably the joint composition of Lord Chatham and Lord Temple; the passages within brackets of this form [ ] are interlined in the handwriting of the latter. It differs in some respects from that which was subsequently adopted, and which was printed in the newspapers of the day.

The King's reply to this Remonstrance produced the well-remembered rejoinder from the Lord Mayor Beckford, which is engraved under his statue in the Guildhall of the City of London.

One paragraph of the Remonstrance, including the words added by Lord Temple, was adopted *verbatim* by Lord Chatham for the Resolution moved by him in the House of Lords on the 4th of May [1], the Remonstrance itself not having been presented to the King until the 23rd of May.

MAY IT PLEASE YOUR MAJESTY.

Labouring under the weight of that Displeasure which your Majesty has been advised to lay upon us, in the Answer given from the Throne to our late Humble Address, Remonstrance, and Petition, we cannot but feel ourselves constrained, with all Humility, to request Permission once more to approach the Royal Father of his People.

Conscious, *Sire*, of the purest sentiments of Veneration for your Majesty's Person, we grieve, that unskilfulness in the expression of Courts, from men used only to speak with plainness that which (to their understandings) the *Law* allows, and the *Constitution* teaches [& the necessity of the Times requires], hath been misconstrued by Ministers, instruments of that Influence which shakes the Realm, into Disrespect to your Majesty.

We stand, *Sire*, perplexed [agitated] and well nigh confounded in

employing the very weapons committed to it by the collective body to stab the Constitution."—*Junius*, vol. ii. p. 116.

" Yet surely it is not a less crime, nor less fatal in its consequences, to encourage a flagrant breach of the law by a military force, than to make use of the forms of Parliament to destroy the Constitution."—*Junius*, vol. ii. p. 35.

"When the Constitution is *openly invaded*, when the *first original right of the people*, from which all laws derive their authority, is *directly attacked*," &c.—*Junius*, vol. ii. p. 35.

" We are far from thinking you capable of a direct deliberate purpose to *invade those original rights of your subjects, on which all their civil and political liberties depend.*"—*Junius*, vol. ii. p. 65.

[1] See *Parliamentary History*, vol. xvi. ; and *Chatham Correspondence*, vol. iii. p. 452.

our thoughts, by the awful *Sentence* of *Censure* lately past upon us, in your Majesty's answer from the Throne : nevertheless we cannot, without surrendering all that is dear to Englishmen, forbear most humbly to supplicate that your Majesty will deign to grant a more favorable interpretation to the dutiful though *persevering Claim* of our *invaded Birthrights;* nothing doubting [but] that the Benignity of your Majesty's nature will, to our unspeakable comfort, at length break through all the secret and visible *Machinations* to which we owe our *severe Repulse;* and that your Kingly Justice, and Fatherly Tenderness, will disclaim the Malignant and pernicious *advice* which suggested that Answer which we deplore ; 'an *advice of most dangerous tendency:* in as much as thereby the exercise of the clearest Rights of the Subject, namely, to petition the King for Redress of Grievances, to complain of violation of the freedom of Election, to pray Dissolution of Parliament, to point out male (*sic*) Practices in Administration, and to urge the Removal of Evil Ministers, hath under [pretence of reproving certain parts of the said Remonstrance and Petition by] the generality of *one compendious word* [Contents] been, indiscriminately, checked with Reprimand ; and we your Majesty's afflicted Citizens of London have heard from the throne itself [instead of a gracious answer to the Prayer], that the *Contents* of our humble Address, Remonstrance, and Petition, laying our *complaints* and *injuries* at the feet of our Sovereign, as *Father of his People, able* and *willing* to *redress our Grievances,* cannot but be considered by your Majesty as Disrespectful to Yourself, Injurious to your Parliament, and Irreconcileable to the Principles of the Constitution.'

May your Majesty then deign to approve, that *we here reclaim* the *clearest Principles* of this *Constitution,* against the insidious attempt of evil Counsellors, to *perplex, confound,* and *shake* them ; and in virtue of those Rights and Liberties which our *Forefathers* bravely vindicated at the ever-memorable Revolution, and which their *Sons* will ever defend, vouchsafe, *Sire,* that we now again renew, at the Foot of the Throne, the claim of our *indispensable Right* to a *full, free,* and *unmutilated Parliament, legally chosen in all its Members.* A right which this House of Commons have manifestly violated, by depriving, at *their Will* and *Pleasure,* the County of Middlesex of one of its *Legal Representatives,* and, in his place, *arbitrarily nominating,* as a Knight of the Shire, a Person not elected by a majority of the *Freeholders* of the said County ; and as the only constitutional means of Reparation now left for these oppressed *Freeholders,* and for the injured Electors of Great Britain, that we again pray, with the most urgent supplications, *the Dissolution* of this present Parliament, together with the *Removal of evil ministers :* and *the total extinction of that fatal Influence which has caused such National Discontent.*

In the mean time, SIRE, we offer our constant Prayers to Heaven that your Majesty may never cease to reign *in* and *by* the Hearts of a Loyal, Dutifull, and Free people.

On the 10th of November, 1770, Lord Chatham wrote to Calcraft:—

"Lord Mayor has just left me; the object of his visit was the Press warrant. His Lordship's discourse was candid and manly. I frankly declared *the fullest opinion against striking at this necessary means of public safety, be the popularity of it what it may.*"[1]

This was no doubt also the opinion of Lord Temple, as will presently be seen from Calcraft's reply: and Junius, some months later, in allusion to the right of pressing seamen, says:—

"I *too* have a claim to the candid interpretation of my country, when I acknowledge an involuntary compulsive assent to one very unpopular opinion. I lament the unhappy necessity, whenever it arises, of providing for the safety of the State, by a temporary invasion of the personal liberty of the subject. Would to God it were practicable to reconcile these important objects in every possible situation of public affairs! I regard the legal liberty of the meanest man in Britain as much as my own, and would defend it with the same zeal. I know we must stand or fall together. But I never can doubt, that the community has a right to command, as well as to purchase, the service of its members. I see that right founded originally upon a necessity, which supersedes all argument. I see it established by usage immemorial, and admitted by more than a tacit assent of the Legislature. I conclude there is no remedy in the nature of things for the grievance complained of: for if there were, it must long since have been redressed."—*Junius*, vol. ii. p. 350.

On the 11th of November Calcraft writes:—

"As your Lordship is to see Sergeant Glynn to-day, it may be proper to inform you of a paragraph in a letter of this morning: 'Within a day or two Mr. Beardmore is to put a question to Mr. Sergeant Glynn,

---

[1] Lord Chatham's opinion on this subject is still stronger expressed in a letter to Lord Shelburne of this date:—"There is also, I perceive, reason to fear a race of frivolous and ill-placed popularity about press warrants. I am determined to resist this ill-judged attempt to shake the public safety. In this state of things, I shall persevere to do my duty to my country, determined by principle, though unanimated by hope. As to what the city now intends to do, I wish to hear nothing of it; resolved to applaud and defend what I think right, and to disapprove what shall appear to me wrong and untenable."—*Chatham Correspondence*, vol. iii. p. 485.

Mr. Dunning, and the Common Sergeant, whether the Lord Mayor ought by a requisition from the Privy Council, or Admiralty, to back the Press warrants; and if he refuses, what they apprehend will be the consequence?' "[1] . . . "On my return last night, I found intelligence of Lord Mansfield's refusal to be Speaker of the House of Lords; *which has occasioned great consternation among the Ministers*, both on account of the mode, and the time of doing this. His words were, '*he would not*.' Just at the meeting, and *after frequent audiences in the Closet*, the measure does seem strong; in his Lordship it may be *timidity*."[2]

In the *Chatham Correspondence* a letter from Gerard Hamilton is quoted, addressed to Calcraft on the 10th instant,—

"Wheel within wheel: Lord Mansfield never surely would have kept his intention secret to the very day before the meeting of Parliament, if it had not been so understood by the Closet."

On the 12th of November Junius wrote a private note to Woodfall, which was accompanied by a Letter to Lord Mansfield, and it would seem that he considered it of some importance that it should be published immediately upon the meeting of Parliament, which was fixed for Tuesday the 13th instant. Junius says:—

"the inclosed, tho' begun within these few days, has been greatly laboured. It is very correctly copied, & I beg you will take care that it be literally printed as it stands. I don't think you run the least Risque. . . . this paper sh.d properly have appeared tomorrow, but I co.d not compass it. so let it be announced tomorrow & printed Wednesday. "if you sh.d have any Fears, I intreat you to send it early enough to Miller, to appear tomorrow night in the London Ev.g Post.—In that Case, you will oblige me by informing the public tomorrow, in *Your own Paper*, that a real Junius will appear at Night in the London. Miller, I am sure, will have no scruples. Lord Mansfield has thrown Ministry into Confusion, by suddenly resigning the Office of Speaker of the H. of L.ds"[3]

The directions of Junius were implicitly obeyed, the letter was announced on *Tuesday*, and published in the *Public Advertiser* on *Wednesday* the 14th.

I presume that the note to Woodfall was written by Lady

---

[1] As Beardmore was Lord Temple's confidential " man of business," it may be safely assumed that the letter quoted by Calcraft came from Lord Temple.

[2] Junius says—" Your *fears* have interposed at last," &c.

[3] The original is marked "private," and dated "Monday evening" only.

Temple, who had herself so "*correctly copied*" the Letter, the composition of which may have occupied Lord Temple's leisure during the previous week up to Saturday night, as it includes a paragraph[1], evidently added at the last moment, in allusion to Lord Mansfield's resignation, which it will have been seen by Mr. Calcraft's correspondence quoted above, had only become known within the previous day or two.

It must be here particularly observed that the above-mentioned note to Woodfall is dated *Monday evening* [November 12th, 1770], and that the death of Mr. George Grenville took place on the following day, *Tuesday*, November 13th.

I am aware that on these dates may be founded an objection to the theory of Lord Temple's Authorship. It is, however, a mere question of the feelings, it involves no impossibility; and I think that after a fair consideration of all the circumstances, it will be admitted that where many other reasons combine in favour of it, this objection alone will be found to have very little weight in the opposite scale.

Mr. Grenville had been in a declining state of health ever since the loss of his wife in the previous December, but his death was nevertheless, at the time it happened, somewhat unexpected.

The only account of his illness is to be gleaned from Lord Chatham's letters to Mr. Calcraft. On *Saturday*, November 10th, he writes:—

" The account of last night is such, as for the first time, seems to Lady Chatham and myself a ground of some solid hope. Dr. Addington's judgment that a fever suppressed is Mr. Grenville's case, was yesterday happily verified by the appearance of a considerable eruption on the face: the pulse kept up sufficient for nature, aided by Dr. Addington's plan, to throw off the evil. Lady Chatham is gone to town to-day full of hope: pray God! the evening account may confirm and increase this happy gleam."

[1] " Though you dare not be Chancellor, you know how to secure the emoluments of the office. Are the seals to be for ever in commission, that you may enjoy 5000*l.* a year? I beg pardon, my Lord; your fears have interposed at last, and forced you to resign. The odium of continuing Speaker of the House of Lords, upon such terms, was too formidable to be resisted. What a multitude of bad passions are forced to submit to a constitutional infirmity! But though you have relinquished the salary, you still assume the rights of a Minister."—*Junius*, vol ii. p. 179.

On *Sunday* Lord Chatham says :—

" By a note just received, poor Mr. Grenville is only rather better. His state is very precarious. Lady Chatham went to him again this morning."

On *Tuesday* night, after the event, Lord Chatham again writes :—

" The favour of your kind note reached me at Lord Temple's, whither I was just returned from Bolton Street, after assisting in some family duties there; and a most sad assembly it was. Lady Chatham is, thank God, as well as her strength permits her to be, after being up the greatest part of the night in such a scene. Lord Temple is deeply affected, but I have the pleasure to tell you he seems otherwise well."

There can be no doubt but that Lord Temple had the greatest attachment to his brother, both personally and politically, and that he very sincerely lamented his loss; but grief for the loss of a brother is not usually of that absorbing and overwhelming nature which would be caused by the death of a wife or child; nor is it such as should necessarily preclude a man from following the ordinary avocations of his life. Besides, it should be remembered that Lord Temple and Mr. Grenville had not *always* been upon even friendly terms; for several years previous to their reconciliation in 1765, there had existed between them a bitterness of feeling, amounting almost to rancorous hostility.

Although so much family and domestic correspondence has been preserved, there is not a single letter extant, between Lady Temple and Mr. or Mrs. Grenville, nor is there any evidence that there was much cordiality between them.

Lady Temple was affectionately attached only to her husband, and it was her duty, as it was no doubt her pleasure, to do all in her power to assuage his grief; and she could adopt no better mode of distracting his thoughts, and diverting his mind, than by encouraging him in the pursuit of that employment in which they were mutually engaged, and which had become the business of their lives: an employment described by Junius himself, to have begun with amusement, to have grown into habit, and to have become, at last, more than heated into passion. The political occupation of Junius was a passion much more violent, and much more engrossing, than an affection arising from any of the ties of relationship.

The forms of society would necessarily cause his seclusion for a short time, and accordingly it will be seen that before the end of the year he had sent communications, under several signatures, to the *Public Advertiser*, but nothing appeared under the name of Junius until the 30th of January, 1771, when his celebrated letter on the Falkland Islands was published.

The following are extracts from Calcraft's letter to Lord Chatham, on the 21st of November:—

"Lord Barrington is *heartbroken at his nonsensical speech in Parliament; the Army affronted*, and *Harvey full of resentment*, at being hung out in the envious colours his Lordship chose for him . . . . . I have received a most affectionate letter from Lord Temple, which gives very great satisfaction to me ; not only from the love and respect I bear his Lordship, but because it portends, as I sincerely hope, future good. I hear *Lord Mansfield maintained his old doctrine in the Court of King's Bench yesterday, that Juries were not judges of the criminality or innocence of the fact.*"

The first part of this letter Mr. Calcraft received from a "well-informed correspondent;"[1] the second part was no doubt contained in the letter he mentions from Lord Temple.

It is certainly a curious fact, that these two subjects, differing in every respect from each other, but both communicated in the same letter to Lord Chatham, should, *on the same day*, be also both of them communicated by Junius to Woodfall. In a private note dated *Wednesday night*, [*November* 21, 1770,] Junius says,—

" I will never rest 'till I have destroyed or expelled that Wretch[2].— I wish you Joy of yesterday[3].—The fellow truckles already."—C.

On the outside of the note, Junius wrote,—

"the inclosed strikes deeper than you may imagine. C."

It contained the letter signed TESTICULUS, which appeared in the *Public Advertiser* of the 24th. It is evident that this letter

---

[1] Probably William Gerard Hamilton.   [2] Lord Mansfield.

[3] On the day before, the Court of King's Bench had granted Woodfall a new trial on the indictment for printing Junius's Letter to the King.

was not to be supposed to come from the writer of *Junius*, for it commences thus :—

" I have never joined in the severe censures which have lately been thrown upon Lord Barrington [1]. The formal declaration he was pleased to make (for the information of the House of Commons and of this country) with respect to the *shameful ignorance and incapacity of all the general officers without exception*, may for aught I know be extremely well founded; and if it were not so, I do not consider the Viscount as a free agent. He undoubtedly meant no more than as a dutiful servant to obey the orders, and express the sentiments of his Royal Master.". . . . " If it be the King's intention (as we have sufficient reason to think it is) to govern the army himself (by which means the disposal of commissions, like everything else, will ultimately centre in Carlton House), the first step is to possess the public with an opinion that this measure is. not of choice but necessity. When the Secretary at War has informed the House of Commons, in the name of his gracious Master (for it is not to be suspected that he spoke for himself), that all his general officers were no better than drivellers, it follows of course, that the Secretary at War, with the Adjutant-General's advice, must be the ostensible manager of the army, and then you see, Sir, everything goes on as Her Royal Highness the Princess Dowager of Wales would have it."—*Junius*, vol. iii. p. 280.

The latter part of this extract had also been alluded to by Calcraft on the 11th instant, in a letter to Lord Chatham :—

" At 11 o'clock on Friday, the Duke of Argyll died; by 12 Lord Barrington had a letter from the King, ordering the Grey Dragoons to Lord Panmure, the Scotch Fusileers to Mackay; Mackay's to Urmston of the Guards, the Government of Limerick to Colonel Hale, and his Light Dragoons to Colonel Preston. All this without any communication with Ministers or Lord Lieutenant of Ireland ! "

---

[1] On the 19th instant Junius had written upon the same subject under the signature of TESTIS, thus :—" A few days ago I was in a large public company, where there happened some curious conversation. The Secretary at War [Lord Barrington] was pleased to express himself with unusual simplicity and candour. He assured us that after having carefully considered the subject, he did not know a single general officer (out of near an hundred now in the service) who was in any shape qualified to command the army; and for fear we should not believe him, repeated and inforced his assertion five several times. You will allow, Sir, that at the eve of a foreign war, this is pretty comfortable intelligence for the nation, especially as it comes from authority. He gave us some consolation, however, by assuring us that he and General Harvey would take excellent care of the army, &c."—*Junius*, vol. iii. p. 278.

Lord Chatham observes upon this:—

"*The military line of business is new.*"

The next communication which I have to notice, from Calcraft to Lord Chatham, is the following anonymous letter received by the former on Sunday, December 9th, 1770, and by him inclosed to Lord Chatham on the same day:—

"Should anything more be said in Parliament concerning the Administration of Justice [1], the following fact may be worth attending to. It is more extraordinary and of more consequence than you, or any man not acquainted with the course of proceedings in the Court of King's Bench, can imagine.

"In the cause of the King against Woodfall, the verdict was, '*guilty of printing and publishing only.*' A motion was made in arrest of judgment by the defendant's counsel, upon this ground, that the verdict was so ambiguous, that judgment could not be entered upon it. On the other hand it was moved, that the verdict might be entered up according to the legal import of the words of the verdict, which, as the Solicitor-General contended, amounted to 'guilty.' In the consideration of this matter, the Court, *strictly and regularly*, could do no more than determine upon the legality of the verdict, as it appeared upon the face of the record of the proceedings at *Nisi Prius*. They could not (as is universally known in Westminster Hall) *travel out of the record*. But Lord Mansfield, in delivering the opinion of the Court, did that which is never done except when a new trial is moved for. He went regularly through the evidence which was given at the trial, and very particularly rehearsed the charge which he had given to the jury. Now all this is flatly irregular, extra judicial, and unprecedented. His reason for this proceeding was, that he might have an opportunity of saying, what he had no right to say on that occasion, that the three other judges concurred with him in the doctrine laid down in his charge to the jury."—*Chatham Correspondence*, vol. iv. p. 48.

To this letter the Editors of the *Chatham Correspondence* have appended a note that "the writer is *understood* to be Mr. Calcraft's friend and correspondent Philip Francis."

Having, through the obliging intervention of Lord Mahon,

---

[1] He refers to a debate which had taken place in the House of Commons on the Thursday previous (December 6) on Mr. Sergeant Glynn's motion for a Committee to inquire into the Administration of Criminal Justice.

h 2

been allowed by the Editors to examine the original paper, I am compelled to differ from the conclusions to which they have arrived upon the subject of it.

Although I think it extremely probable to have been the composition of the Author of Junius, yet I can discover no reason for supposing that it was either written or sent by Francis. It differs entirely in point of style from other communications attributed to Francis[1], and which contain precisely the common-place sort of information which might be expected from a clerk in the War Office who was desirous of sending the gossip of the office to his friend and patron the army contractor; but in the anonymous letter above quoted, there is a lofty tone of authority, a decided expression of opinion, that the facts it contains are "*worth attending to, and more extraordinary and of more consequence than you, or any man not acquainted with the course of proceedings in the Court of King's Bench, can imagine.*"

This is not the style in which Francis would (even anonymously) address a man of Calcraft's experience, so much older, and so much more likely to be better "*acquainted with the course of proceedings in the Court of King's Bench*" than himself.

Moreover, the handwriting of this paper is certainly not that of Francis; it is without disguise, a common business-like sort of hand, no resemblance to that of Junius, and it has the appearance of having been freely and rapidly written, as if transcribed from the author's copy. It is neither dated nor addressed, but it is endorsed, apparently in Mr. Calcraft's hand—"*Anonymous, received December 9, well worth attention.*"

It appears also, that Lord Chatham considered it to be *well worth attention*, for he adopted the subject and substance of it in a speech which he made in the House of Lords on the following day, Monday, December 10th, when Lord Mansfield, who had desired that the Lords should be specially summoned, informed them that he had left a Paper with the Clerk of the House, containing the opinion of the Court of King's Bench in the case of the King *v.* Woodfall.

---

[1] *Chatham Correspondence*, vol. iii. p. 444, and vol. iv. p. 128.

The chief part of the debate on this occasion which has been preserved is comprised in the few sentences reported as the speech of Lord Chatham. Up to within a recent period it was supposed that the earliest report of this speech was given by Junius, in a letter to the Printer of the *Public Advertiser*, under the signature of "Phalaris,"[1] and dated December 17th, and which contains a version almost verbatim of the anonymous letter to Calcraft; and the same version with some, but trifling, alterations, was again used by Junius as a Note in the Preface to the first collected edition of his Letters, where it is described as "*a quotation from a speech delivered by Lord Chatham, taken with exactness; curious in itself, and very fit to be inserted here.*"

The writer of some Essays upon the Authorship of Junius, in the *Athenæum*, to whom I have been so frequently indebted for information, has however lately discovered, that a brief report of Lord Chatham's speech was given as follows, in the *London Evening Post* of December 11th, the day after that upon which it was delivered :—

"Lord Chatham rose, and observed that the verdict of the jury in that case, was guilty of printing and publishing only ; that (if the newspapers told him true, for he had only newspaper information of that transaction) two motions had been made in the Court upon the verdict : one was on behalf of the defendant for an arrest of judgment, the other was on behalf of the prosecutor, to enter up the words of the verdict according to their legal import. How comes it then that the judges, *who had nothing but the record before them*, and could not, or ought not to consider anything else ; I say, how comes it, that the judges who ought not to give judgment upon anything but what is strictly, regularly, and legally before them ; I say again, how comes it that the judges *travelled out of the record*, to give their judgment upon matters not contained in that record? The proceeding is *irregular, unprecedented, and extrajudicial.*"

This report is much more likely to be a correct version of what was really said by Lord Chatham than that given by Junius, because Lord Chatham could not in his place in Parliament speak with so much *exactness* the very words set down by an anony-

---

[1] *Junius*, vol. iii. p. 302.

mous correspondent, unless he had either committed them to memory, or had read them from a written paper. He might use the *substance* of a communication which he thought *worthy of attention*, but he would scarcely commit himself so far as to adopt the opinion of the anonymous writer, by alluding in Lord Mansfield's presence, to his conduct in such terms as these :—

" His *real* [*apparent* in the Preface] motive for doing *what he knew to be wrong*, was, that he might have an opportunity of telling the public extrajudicially that the other three judges concurred in the doctrine laid down in his Charge."

Although an anonymous writer might accuse Lord Mansfield of doing deliberately on the judgment-seat what *he knew to be wrong*, yet it does not seem probable that Lord Chatham would hold such language in the House of Lords.

But if Junius were the Author of the anonymous letter, and if Lord Temple were Junius, he would certainly know that Lord Chatham had partly availed himself in the House of the substance of his remarks, and therefore he might safely give the whole of them two years afterwards as a quotation from Lord Chatham's speech *taken with exactness.*

Lord Temple was probably not in the House of Lords on the 10th of December, as a month had not elapsed since the death of Mr. Grenville, but he would be very exactly informed of all that transpired on that occasion, both from Lord Chatham and Calcraft, and the anonymous communication would, as certainly, be shown to him.

The reasons are obvious, why Lord Temple, if he were Junius, should not have made this communication *direct* to Lord Chatham : he would not wish it to be known either to him or to Calcraft, that he took so great an interest in all that concerned the trial of Woodfall.

Assuming that Lord Temple was not in the House of Lords on Tuesday, the 11th of December, he would doubtless be informed by Lord Chatham of everything which took place there, and consequently we find Junius using the very words of Lord Chatham in the following instance.

In a paper attributed to Junius, entitled *A Second Chapter of Facts, or Materials for History*[1], the debate is thus alluded to :—

"The Earl of Chatham having asserted on Tuesday last in the House of Lords, that Gibraltar was open to an attack from the sea, and that if the enemy were masters of the Bay, the place could not make any long resistance, he was answered in the following words by that *great Statesman*, the Earl of Sandwich :—' Supposing the noble Lord's argument to be well-founded, and *supposing Gibraltar to be unluckily taken*, still, according to the noble Lord's own doctrine, it would be no great matter; for *although we are not masters of the sea at present, we probably shall be so sometime or other; and then my Lords, there will be no difficulty in taking Gibraltar.*'"

On the 16th of December, Lord Chatham writes to the Countess Stanhope :—

"Your Lordship and Lord Stanhope may have heard that an idea has prevailed strongly here, of designs against Gibraltar. Some intelligence even, on that head, having reached me, I made use of it in the House of Lords. The intelligence was not quite slighted; but a *great Statesman* comforted us by saying, that *if that place were at present to be taken by sea, we should retake it by sea, when we have a fleet there.*"[2]

Under the signature of "Domitian," Junius again alludes to the debate in the House of Lords on the 11th of December :—

"Lord Sandwich declared a month ago, in full Parliament, that Gibraltar was a place of no consequence, and immediately afterwards the Princess Dowager makes him Secretary of State. Whoever compares the sale of Dunkirk with this nobleman's character, must be very much of a sceptic, if he entertains any doubt about the fate of Gibraltar."[3]

Calcraft's information to Lord Chatham on the 16th of Decem-

---

[1] *Junius*, vol. iii. p. 292.

[2] It should be remembered that upon this occasion, no strangers, not even the Members of the House of Commons, were permitted to be present; strict orders having been given to all the officers and door-keepers of the House of Lords, not to admit for the future any person or persons whatsoever, except such members of the House of Commons as should come to present Bills, and they to depart as soon as they had made their usual obediences.

[3] *Junius*, vol. iii. p. 323.

ber, again runs parallel with that which Junius communicates to Woodfall. Calcraft says :—

" Lord North told us our situation was precarious, but *war was too probable*: that so many more ships were ordered to be fitted as would take nine thousand additional seamen, and though Spain should come into terms of accommodation, it would be unwise to disarm whilst the warlike preparations of France and Spain continued."

He then mentions, that—

" Sir Edward Hawke attended to comfort us about the state of our Navy :" and that, " Barré described the riot in the Lords, as a mob broke in, headed by Lords Marchment and Denbigh."

Two days previously, Junius wrote, that—

" Sir Edward Hawke, on Wednesday last, gave the House of Commons a very pompous account of the Fleet," and that " the riot in the House of Lords has shocked the delicacy of Sir Fletcher Norton."

Again, Junius says,—

" Lord North informed the House of Commons, on Wednesday last, that although he wished for an honourable accommodation, he thought it his duty to tell the House that he feared *war was too probable;* that he intended to move for a further augmentation of ten thousand seamen, and that at any rate he should advise the keeping up the naval and military force upon the augmented establishment, for that notwithstanding the language held by the French and Spanish Ministers, there was all over France and Spain the greatest appearance of hostile preparations." [1]

On the 14th of January, 1771, Calcraft writes :—

" War, according to my intelligence, is more and more certain :"

And Junius, in a private note to Woodfall, dated the 16th :—

" Without regarding the language of ignorant or interested people, depend upon the assurance I give you, that every man in Administration, looks upon *war as inevitable.*"

On the Monday following Calcraft's correspondence is less warlike: he sends Lord Chatham an extract from a letter, but he does not name the writer [2] :—

---

[1] *Junius,* vol. iii. 294.

[2] There are phrases in it which lead me to infer that Lord Temple (Junius) was the writer. Upon more than one occasion he professed to Mr. Grenville to have *secret channels of information, &c.* See *post,* page 366, *note.*

" My *intelligence* of the French Court's having raised it's tone, is *strictly true*[1]; and it seems they have done so very effectually. Our honest Ministers have lowered theirs in proportion. At *this very moment*, I believe, the *compromise is concluded*[2]. My own judgment assures me, it is the most ignominious one that ever was made for this country, and I have the *surest information* to confirm me in my opinion. I am now convinced that *there are no conditions to which Lord North was not determined to submit*[3]. If there had been *one spark of shame*[4], a single atom of honour in the composition of our Ministry, *war was inevitable*[5]. Look to yourselves, *you gentlemen who have something to lose*[6]! *The Ministry have views of conquest, though not over the enemies of England*[7]. The French and Spanish Ministers tendered preliminaries to Lord North, and told him stiffly, that unless they were accepted, they would not proceed to explain themselves in regard to *terms of accommodation*[8]. *Our Ministry have received the law in every sense*[9]. I know this by the *strangest and surest channel*[10]. Perhaps,

---

[1] " He applies that description with the *strictest truth* and justice to the Spanish Court."—*Junius*, vol. ii. p. 201.

" Even that assertion, which we are told is most offensive to Parliament, is *strictly true*."—*Ibid.*, vol. ii. p. 115.

" Admitting this last assertion to be *strictly true*."—*Ibid.*, vol. ii. p. 121.

[2] " As far as the probability of argument extends, we may safely pronounce that *a conjuncture which threatens the very being of this country*, has been wilfully prepared and forwarded by our own Ministry."—*Ibid.*, vol ii. p. 191.

[3] " In these circumstances we might have dictated the law to Spain. *There are no terms to which she might not have been compelled to submit.*"—*Ibid.*, vol. ii. p. 190.

" If the actual situation of Europe be considered, the treachery of the King's servants, particularly of Lord North, who takes the whole upon himself, will appear in the strongest colours of aggravation."—*Ibid.*, vol. ii. p. 190.

[4] " He might perceive the snare laid for him by his Ministers, and feel *a spark of shame* kindling in his breast."—*Ibid.*, vol. ii. p. 192.

[5] " ——— every man in administration looks upon *war as inevitable.*"—*Private note to Woodfall, Junius*, vol. i. p. 216.

[6] " Woe to the property of England !"—*Ibid.*, vol. iii. p. 54.

[7] " If any ideas of strife or hostility have entered his Royal mind, they have a very different direction.—*The enemies of England have nothing to fear from them.*"—*Ibid.*, vol. ii. p. 189.

[8] " I told you *war was too probable* when I was determined to submit to any *terms of accommodation.*"—*Ibid.*, vol. ii. p. 193.

[9] " *Rather than suffer the execution of that scheme to be delayed or interrupted,* the King has been advised to make a public surrender, a solemn sacrifice, in the face of all Europe, not only of the interests of his subjects, but of his own personal reputation, and of the dignity of that crown which his predecessors have worn with honour."—*Ibid.*, vol. ii. p. 183.

[10] See *post*, page 366, *note*.

" I suspect the *channel* through which you have your *intelligence.*"—*Private note to Woodfall, Ibid.*, vol. i. p. 208.

after all, this very measure they have plunged into to save themselves from ruin, may hasten their destruction."

In reply, Lord Chatham thanks Calcraft for—

"intelligence so material, and seemingly authentic."

On Tuesday, the 22nd of January, Calcraft writes to Lord Chatham:—

" Poor Lord Lyttelton does not seem to be in very high spirits. He desires me to tell your Lordship, this is the best Peace ever made for England; other people say the most disgraceful: my Lord's information is that the Ministers have got everything they ever asked. No paper from Lord Mansfield delivered to-day."

Lord Chatham replies on the same evening:—

" I grieve that so good a man as Lord Lyttelton has fallen into the snare of a Court who cover so clumsily the gross and palpable imposition, but a fatality seems over us when integrity pins its faith on the sleeve of duplicity, and the virtuous become the indirect instruments of the wicked."

A few months later Junius says,—

" Lord Littleton's [1] integrity and judgment are unquestionable, yet he is known to admire that cunning Scotchman [Lord Mansfield] and verily believes him an honest man."—Vol. ii. p. 305.

The correspondence between Lord Chatham and Calcraft in March and April, 1771, refers to the subject of the dispute between the House of Commons and the Lord Mayor and Aldermen of London, in consequence of Mr. Onslow's Resolutions in the matter of the Printers; and at this time Junius was occupied in the preparation of his Letter on the Privilege of Parliament, which appeared on the 22nd of April, and alluding to it some months afterwards in a letter to Wilkes, he says,—"the pains I took with that letter on Privilege were greater than I can express to you, &c."

Wilkes refused to obey the summons of the House of Commons to answer for his conduct as an Alderman. Calcraft writes, on the 24th of March:—

---

[1] This is the only occasion on which the name of Lord Lyttelton is mentioned by Junius, and it is written as above. On the same page, in one of Lady Temple's letters, the name is twice mentioned, and it is written *Littleton*, and Lyttelton.

" The Ministers avow Wilkes too dangerous to meddle with. He is to do what he pleases, we are to submit. So His Majesty orders. *He will have 'nothing more to do with that devil Wilkes.'* The Treasury Bench are sick of the other parts of this business : reprimand only is now the language. *When I saw Lord Temple two days since he was the eagerest politician in London, and resolved to come out on this business.*"

On the same subject Junius writes,—

" It is remarkable enough that the very men who advised the Proclamation, and who have arraigned it every day, both within doors and without, are not daring enough to utter one word in its defence, *nor have they ventured to take the least notice of Mr. Wilkes* for discharging the persons apprehended under it."—*Junius*, vol. iii. p. 375.

On the 26th of March, *Tuesday morning three o'clock*, Calcraft writes to Chatham :—

" I cannot go to bed without giving your Lordship some account of last night's business. The Lord Mayor attended *without counsel*, adhered to his former defence, read the oaths of office, and City Charter. . . . *Late as it was*, they proceeded against Alderman Oliver, who made his defence very short indeed, was firm in the opinion of having acted right according to his oath."

Lord Chatham, in reply, declared his opinion thus :—

" That the discharge of Miller, taken under the Speaker's warrant, I think contrary to the established jurisdiction of the House with regard to printers of their proceedings and debates; but I hold also as fully, that in a conflict of jurisdiction, the Lord Mayor and City Magistrates, acting under an oath of office and their Charter, cannot be proceeded against criminally by the House, without the highest injustice and oppression. The House might well assert its claim of jurisdiction, as a counter right, without punishing their Member for what he has done *as Magistrate*."

On the 9th of April, Junius coincides very minutely in the opinion of Lord Chatham.

" These gentlemen, [the Lord Mayor and Mr. Oliver] *as Magistrates*, had nothing to regard but the obligation of their oaths and the execution of the laws. . . . . *They were tried and condemned at midnight*, without being heard by themselves or their counsel, on the only point on which their justification could possibly depend. In short, a question strictly of jurisdiction, was referred to numbers, and carried like a common Ministerial measure."—*Junius*, vol. iii. p. 376.

On the 7th of April, Lord Chatham writes to Calcraft,—

"The misfortune is, that the City is wrong in the matter of the Speaker's warrants to bring the printers before the House. The House seems to be aware that they have been wrong in all the rest: the House will desist from their wrong, and the City persist in theirs." . . . . .

"I need not say, my dear friend, how little is left to keep up my animation towards public affairs : the desultoriness and no-plan of our friend in Pall Mall[1] : the poor weakness of Lord Camden : the no-weight of such advice as I can give either in the City, or in Grosvenor Square[2], are circumstances not very encouraging."

Calcraft, in reply, says :—

"The want of a steady system in Pall Mall touches me nearly. His Lordship is roused. Cannot we flatter ourselves good may follow? Could he tread steadily in your Lordship's steps, I must own the childishness of Grosvenor Square would not disturb my mind."

The apparent *desultoriness and no-plan of our friend in Pall Mall,* and *the want of a steady system,* arose most probably from the manner in which Lord Temple's attention was devoted, and his time occupied, in the preparation of the elaborate letter by Junius on Privilege, as Junius himself describes it in a subsequent letter to Wilkes :—

"In pursuing such inquiries, I lie under a singular disadvantage. Not venturing to consult those who are qualified to inform me, I am forced to collect everything from books or common conversation. . . . . . . Yet after I had blinded myself with poring over journals, debates, and parliamentary history, I was at last obliged to hazard a bold assertion, &c."—*Junius to Wilkes,* vol. i. p. 308.

Several letters also between Lord Shelburne, Lord Chatham, and Lord Temple, prove that the opinion of the latter with respect to the dissolution of Parliament, was in accordance with that expressed by Junius in his letter on Privilege ; thus :—

"If he [the King] loves his people, he will *dissolve a Parliament,* which they can never confide in or respect."

And also, under the signature of "A Whig," Junius says, on the 9th of April :—

"I most truly lament the condition to which we are reduced, and

---

[1] Lord Temple.   [2] Lord Rockingham's.

the more so, because there is but one remedy for it, and that remedy has been repeatedly refused. A *dissolution of the Parliament* would restore tranquillity to the people, and to the King the affections of his subjects: the present House of Commons have nothing to expect, but contempt, detestation, and resistance."—Vol. iii. p. 379.

On the 9th of April also Lord Shelburne writes to Lord Chatham,—

" Since I saw your Lordship, I hear that *Lord Temple has declared, some time since, his intention of moving for a dissolution :*"

And Lord Chatham replies :—

" I rejoice to hear what you understand of *Lord Temple's resolution to move a dissolution. . . . .* As to the idea of shortening the duration of Parliaments, I still wish that it may rest with your Lordship, until I have an opportunity of communicating with Lord Temple upon it, and also with Lord Lyttelton, the Duke of Northumberland and some others."

Lord Temple, in a letter to Lord Chatham, dated April 18th, says :—

" I totally agree with you in respect to the City transactions. I lamented with those of the City whom I first saw, that they did not content themselves with standing upon the impregnable ground of the illegal Proclamation; however, that since they were in the scrape, it must be covered and got out of as well as they could. The incredible imbecility and rashness of the idiot Ministry have been very helpful to them ; and upon the whole, the embarrassment and disgrace to the Court put them in a lower and more distressful light than if my Lord Mayor had not interfered at all.

" I am clear, likewise, that at the very end of the Session, a motion for a dissolution would come with the greatest propriety, and with a proper and forcible protest, should point out the proper line for the City. If anything, my dear Lord, could call me down to the House of Lords, it would be that measure, and I had almost determined upon it in my own mind ; but I confess the general state of the Opposition, the *implacable division in the City,* which the demon of discord hath so plentifully scattered, have, without blaming either side particularly, *reduced me to a state of despondency for the public, which makes me think it almost unmanly to step again into any public transaction."* [1]

---

[1] "In the present state of things, If I were to write again, I must be as silly as any of the horned Cattle, that run mad through the City, or as any of your wise Aldermen. I meant the Cause & the public. both are given up. I feel for the honour of this

Lord Chatham thus expresses himself to Lord Shelburne respecting a dissolution of Parliament:—

" Lord Temple entirely approves of it, but at the same time has not engaged to come to the House of Lords. Time and further reflection may still bring him."

By a passage in a letter from Lord Chatham to Calcraft, on the 22nd of September, 1771, considerable sensation seems to have been created on account of a visit made by Lord and Lady Temple to the Duke of Grafton:—

" All Stowe, I learn, honoured the race at Wakefield Lodge. These appearances puzzle West Saxon understandings, and put an end to any hope for the public ; but without hope, there is a thing called *duty*, and room enough left for the philosophy of opposition, though very little for activity."

Calcraft, still more *puzzled* and astonished, and, as if doubtful of the *possibility* of such an occurrence, writes on the 28th to Almon (" Lord Temple's man "),—

" Is it true that Lord Temple and his family were at Wakefield Lodge Races ? "

Wakefield Lodge, in Whittlebury Forest, four or five miles from Stowe, is the official residence of the Duke of Grafton, as Hereditary Ranger.

Whether, upon the occasion of this visit of Lord and Lady Temple, they had happened to hear any gossiping story relative to the King's timber in the Forest, and of the Duke of Grafton's proceedings in that matter, can only now be conjectured; but it is worthy of observation, that the letter which Junius addressed to the Duke of Grafton [1] on that subject, is dated *on the* 28*th of*

Country, when I see there are not ten Men in it, who will unite & stand together upon any one question."—*Junius*, vol. i. p. 255.

[1] In this letter Junius distinctly says,—

" I *have examined the original grant*, and now in the face of the public, contradict you directly upon the fact. The very reverse of what you have asserted upon your honour, is the truth. The grant, *expressly, and by a particular clause*, reserves the property of the timber for the use of the crown."

It is not very probable that this assertion is *literally* true, because if the Author of Junius himself had examined the *original* grant in the Record Office where it is deposited, his name, and the object of his search, must have been known to the keepers or

September, a few days only after this visit from "all Stowe" to Wakefield Lodge Races.

As a specimen of powerful and eloquent invective, this letter is, perhaps, one of the finest of the productions of the Author.

Lord Temple very frequently attended the debates in the House of Commons; and it would appear, from expressions in the letters of his contemporaries, that it was notoriously his habit to do so : this is another necessary qualification for the Authorship of Junius. He is always found to have been present at any proceedings relative to Wilkes, and the question of the Middlesex Election.

Horace Walpole, in a letter to Lord Hertford, in giving a description of the debate on General Warrants, in February, 1764, mentions that—

" not only my Lord Temple, *whom you may swear never budged as a spectator*, but old Will Chetwynd, now past eighty, and who had walked to the House, did not stir a single moment out of his place from three in the afternoon, till the division at seven in the morning."

Upon another occasion of a debate respecting Wilkes, Walpole says that :—

" Rigby looking at Lord Temple, who was sitting at the end of the House to hear the debate, *as he constantly practised*, drew a picture of that incendiary peer, &c." [1]

clerks, and when the transaction was mentioned in the newspapers soon afterwards, it would have afforded too obvious a clue to his discovery. But as Lord Temple was the owner of property closely adjoining the boundaries of the Forest, and perhaps originally a part of it, it would be much more likely that he was in possession of *a copy of the Grant*, which may have been formerly procured for some purpose connected with the peculiar rights or privileges of the land in question, which had belonged, before the Reformation, to the monks of Luffield Abbey ; and among the multitudinous contents of the evidence room at Stowe, the accumulation of nearly three centuries and several generations, it is not impossible but that such a document may still exist, although in my former researches I cannot now recollect having seen it there.

[1] Lady Suffolk speaks of this occurrence in a letter to her nephew Lord Buckinghamshire (then in Russia), dated November 29th, 1763,—" Jemmy Grenville and Mr. Rigby were so violent against each other, one in his manner of treating Lord Temple who was in the House, and the brother in justification of his brother, that the House was obliged to interpose to prevent mischief [a]. *Lord Temple comes to me ; but politics is the bane of*

[a] *Parliamentary History*, vol. xv. p. 1362.

In a letter dated *Saturday night, 9 o'clock,* February 4, 1769, Lord Temple writes to Lady Chatham :—

" The House of Commons was up about two this morning: the expulsion carried by no more than eighty-two, though Conway retired without voting, and the gallant Marquis [of Granby] voted for it.   The numbers were 137 to 219.   My brother made what was universally deemed the best speech he ever made, against expulsion." [1]

And again, dated " *Friday, past eight,*" [April 14, 1769] :—

" *I am this instant come from the House of Commons,* who have voted the election of Wilkes void.   The Sheriffs, after waiting for them long, at last appeared, and the poll is brought up : but by consent the House is to adjourn till Saturday or Monday, upon which they are now debating.   The resolution is to bring in Luttrell." .   .   .   .   .

" Middlesex will address the King to dissolve the Parliament, which will be instantly followed by the Lord Mayor and Livery of London.   *I suppose I shall be in the House of Commons till Sunday Morning* [2].   Calcraft hears that the Ministry are altogether by the ears, and that a change is resolved."

In another letter to Lady Chatham, dated *Tuesday night, May 9, 1769,* Lord Temple wrote as follows :—

" Yesterday turned out again a most glorious day : not the shadow of an argument against the disqualification, by precedent or otherwise. Wedderburn made a most excellent speech with us.   It has cost him his seat in Parliament, which he has this day vacated in consequence of Sir Laurence Dundas's reproaches and desire, from what I think too generous a delicacy.   .   .   .   .   .   Things tend apace to coalition amongst us.   Sir Fletcher [Norton] was brutal and impertinent to George Grenville last night.   *I am half dead with my attendance of yesterday.*"

There was no report of the proceedings upon this occasion until the recent publication of Sir Henry Cavendish's Debates, where the speeches of Burke, Wedderburn, George Grenville, and others,

---

friendship, and when personal resentments join, the man becomes another creature; when you return, experience will convince you of the truth of what I say."[a]

[1] Mr. Grenville's speech was afterwards printed and published in the form of a pamphlet by Almon.

[2] The debate lasted till three o'clock on Sunday morning, when Mr. Luttrell was declared duly elected by 197 against 143.

[a] *Suffolk Correspondence,* vol. ii. p. 287.

are given at considerable length. It is, nevertheless, extremely probable that Lord Temple took notes of this debate, particularly of Mr. Wedderburn's speech, and that the materials were used by Junius in his Letters xvi. xvii. xviii. and xix., written in the July following, upon the subject of Wilkes's expulsion. In Letter xix. the description of what passed between Dr. Blackstone and Mr. Grenville is undoubtedly that of an eye-witness:—

"The truth of the matter is evidently this. Dr. Blackstone while he was speaking in the House of Commons, never once thought of his Commentaries, until the contradiction was unexpectedly urged, and stared him in the face. Instead of defending himself upon the spot, he sunk under the charge in an agony of confusion and despair. It is well known that there was a pause of some minutes in the House, from a general expectation that the Doctor would say something in his own defence ; but it seems his faculties were too much overpowered to think of those subtleties and refinements which have since occurred to him. It was then Mr. Grenville received that severe chastisement which the Doctor mentions with so much triumph. *I wish the honourable gentleman, instead of shaking his head, would shake a good argument out of it.* If to the elegance, novelty, and bitterness of this ingenious sarcasm, we add the natural melody of the amiable Sir Fletcher Norton's pipe, we shall not be surprised that Mr. Grenville was unable to make him any reply."

The reference to Sir Fletcher Norton's conduct to George Grenville, alluded to in Lord Temple's note to Lady Chatham, quoted above, strengthens the supposition that Junius himself was present in the person of Lord Temple.

In discussing, however, these questions of Wilkes's expulsion, and the Middlesex Election, upon which it was well known that Lord Temple had taken so great personal interest, and upon which Junius had bestowed so much pains in the several Letters on that subject, he considered it necessary, in order to divert public attention from himself, to make the following declaration in his letter to Dr. Blackstone:—

"It is not my design to enter into a formal vindication of Mr. Grenville, upon his own principles. I have neither the honour of being personally known to him, nor do I pretend to be completely master of all the facts. I need not run the risk of doing an injustice to his opinions, or to his conduct, when your pamphlet alone carries, upon the face of it, a full vindication of both."

It is very possible that this assertion may be true: *in his assumed character of Junius* he was not personally known to Mr. Grenville.

On the 26th of January, 1770, Lord Temple writes to Lady Chatham :—

" A glorious day indeed! The House [of Commons] was not up 'till near three. *I was there the whole time.*"

And again, on the 20th of March, he says :—

" *I had the grace to stay in the House of Commons 'till three o'clock this morning* [1].   *   *   * I take it for granted it [the Address] will come up to us [the House of Lords] tomorrow, and that we shall be to debate it on Thursday : purposely meant to interfere with the Lord Mayor's dinner."

Mr. Daniel Wray, who was a Deputy Teller of the Exchequer, and a person likely to obtain authentic political information, writes thus to Lord Hardwicke, in a letter dated November 22nd, 1772 :—

" The divisions are great in the besieger's camp ; particularly between Lords Temple and Camden, about the author of Junius's Letters."

On this passage, which is quoted in a Memoir of Mr. Wray [2], written by his friend Mr. Justice Hardinge, there occurs the following remark :—

" These words are of no trivial import : and they wonderfully confirm a passage in a conversation between Lord Camden and me. He told me that many things in *Junius* convinced *him*, that the *materials* were prompted by Earl Temple, and he mentioned in particular a confidential statement which had been made in private between Lord Chatham, Lord Temple, and Lord Camden, which, from the nature of it, could *only* have been disclosed by *Lord Temple*, through *Junius*, to the public."

---

[1] This was upon the debate on the City Remonstrance. The letter of Junius on the subject was dated on the 19th of March, the same day.

[2] See Nichols's *Illustrations of Literary History*, vol. i. p. 146.

In the third volume of Mr. Justice Hardinge's Miscellaneous Works[1], he further says:—

"I know enough of Junius to know that he was of Lord Temple's school, and that he wrote that paper from hints or materials prompted by him. So far he was betrayed in one of the letters to the first Lord Camden, for in that letter he touched upon a fact, known only to three persons, Lords Chatham, Camden, and Temple. The latter, during almost the whole period of the *Junius*, was bitter against the two former: and so was Junius, though with an air of guard and candour.

"Lord Temple had not eloquence or parts enough to have written. Junius; but I have no doubt that he knew the author."

Junius addressed only one of his Letters to Lord Camden, No. lxix., the last in the series of his acknowledged writings, and in this Letter there is only one sentence in which, by any possibility, such *a fact* can be involved.

"After the noble stand you made against Lord Mansfield, upon the question of libel, we did expect that you would not have suffered that matter to have remained undetermined. But it was said that Lord Chief Justice Wilmot had been *prevailed upon* to vouch for an opinion of the late Judge Yates, which was supposed to make against you; and we admit of the excuse. When such detestable arts are employed to prejudge a question of right, it might have been imprudent at that time to have brought it to a decision. In the present instance you will have no such opposition to contend with."

The above passage, therefore, probably contains *the fact* to which Mr. Justice Hardinge alludes, as being known only to Lords Chatham, Camden, and Temple. In what manner Lord Chief Justice Wilmot was *prevailed upon*, or what was the opinion of Mr. Justice Yates, or upon what occasion it was given, I regret that, after most diligent search, I have hitherto been unable to discover.

Upon a former occasion, in a letter to Lord Chief Justice Mansfield, Junius seems to refer to some similar circumstance:—

"The name of Mr. Justice Yates will naturally revive in your mind some of those emotions of fear and detestation with which you

---

[1] Miscellaneous works in Prose and Verse of George Hardinge, Esq., &c., Senior Justice of the counties of Brecon, Glamorgan and Radnor. 3 vols. 8vo, Nichols, 1818.

always beheld him. That great lawyer—that honest man, saw your whole conduct in the light that I do. After years of ineffectual resistance to the pernicious principles introduced by your Lordship, and uniformly supported by your *humble friends* upon the bench, he determined to quit a Court [1] whose proceedings and decisions he could neither assent to with honour, nor oppose with success."—*Junius*, vol. ii. p. 165.

At the commencement of the Session of Parliament in January 1770, great indignation was expressed by the Opposition against the Duke of Grafton, because no notice was taken in the King's Speech of the numerous petitions which had been presented, praying for a dissolution of Parliament, in consequence of the proceedings of the House of Commons on the subject of the Middlesex Election.

"We were taught to expect," says Junius (in his letter to the Duke of Grafton, upon his resignation of office), "that you would not leave the ruin of this country to be completed by other hands, but were determined either to gain a decisive victory over the constitution, or to perish bravely at least behind the last dyke of the prerogative. You knew the danger, and might have been provided for it. You took sufficient time to prepare for a meeting with your Parliament, to confirm the mercenary fidelity of your dependents, and to suggest to your Sovereign a language suited to his dignity at least, if not to his benevolence and wisdom. Yet, while the whole kingdom was agitated with anxious expectation upon one great point, you meanly evaded the question, and instead of the explicit firmness and decision of a King, gave us nothing but the misery of a ruined grazier [2], and the whining piety of a Methodist. We had reason to expect that notice would have been taken of the petitions which the King has received from the English nation; and although I can conceive some personal motives for not yielding to them, I can find none, in common prudence or decency, for treating them with contempt. Be assured, my Lord, the English people will not tamely submit to this

[1] He left the Court of King's Bench, and accepted a junior judgeship in the Court of Common Pleas, in May 1770, and died about a month afterwards.
"At the same time, no man reverences the present set of judges more than myself, ... insomuch that it would be difficult to make a change for the better, unless you could pick out another YATES from the bar."—*Another Letter to Almon*, p. 173.
[2] "There was something wonderfully pathetic in the mention of the *horned cattle*."— *Junius*.

unworthy treatment ; they had a right to be heard, and their petitions, if not granted, deserved to be considered."—*Junius*, vol. ii. p. 92.

Lord Temple had previously obtained a copy of the intended Speech, probably through the medium of Lord Camden. I found it, in manuscript, among his papers, with some passages under-lined by himself, particularly the words with which the Speech concludes:—

" Such a conduct on your part will, above all things, contribute to maintain in their proper lustre, the strength, the reputation, and the prosperity of this country ; *to strengthen the attachment of my subjects to that excellent constitution of Government, from which they derive such distinguished advantages, and to cause the firm reliance and confidence which I have in the wisdom of my Parliament, as well as in their zeal for the true interest of my people, to be justified and approved both at home and abroad.*"

The following paragraph is added, in the handwriting of Lord Temple:—

" As I have made, and ever shall make, our excellent constitution the rule of my own conduct, so shall I always consider it as equally my duty, to exert every power with which the Constitution hath entrusted me, for preserving it safe from violation of every kind, being fully con-vinced that in so doing, I shall most effectually provide for the true interest and happiness of my people."

I have considered it not improbable that this passage was the result of a communication between Lords Temple, Chatham, and Camden, and prepared in order that it should be suggested by the latter to his colleagues, as an amendment for the conclusion of the King's Speech, but the adoption of which had been overruled by a majority in the Cabinet. It is at least such as would have been in accordance with the opinions subsequently expressed by Lord Camden, as well as in concurrence with those of Lords Chatham and Temple, and, I may add, of Junius also.

The Great Seal was soon after taken from Lord Camden, and Junius writes:—

" We now see the Chancellor of Great Britain tyrannically forced out of his office, not for want of abilities, not for want of integrity, or of attention to his duty, but for delivering his honest opinion in Par-liament, upon the greatest constitutional question that has arisen since the Revolution."—*Junius*, vol. ii. p. 96.

Lord Camden was at this time also accused of having made known to Lord Chatham the secret discussions of the Cabinet, and, indeed, on the subject of the Middlesex Election, Lord Chatham admitted that Lord Camden had in conversation frequently declared his opinion upon that question to be hostile to the Government of which he formed a part.

In June 1771 Junius, in a letter to the Duke of Grafton, says :—

"You did not neglect the magistrate, while you flattered the *man*. The expulsion of Mr. Wilkes, *predetermined* in the Cabinet, &c."

There must be some meaning in this passage beyond the common acceptation of the words, because it is obvious that all the measures of an Administration must, in one sense, be necessarily *predetermined* in the Cabinet. It was made known to Wilkes by a message from the Duke of Grafton, a few days before the meeting of Parliament in November, that if he persisted in opening his case by presenting a Petition to the House of Commons, his expulsion would be the result. But it was said that Lord Camden had long before informed Lord Chatham, and consequently Lord Temple also [1], of the intentions of the majority of the Cabinet with regard to Wilkes, and which could not be prevented by his single voice; that the Parliament was not to be dissolved; that the expulsion was a measure *predetermined*, a mandate to be implicitly obeyed, not a measure merely proposed for discussion, but to be forced through the House of Commons, in opposition to popular opinion, by the absolute power of a Government majority, and, according to the insinuations of Junius, not without considerable bribery :—

"In former times the most venal parliaments made it a condition, in their bargain with the Minister, that he should furnish them with some plausible pretences for selling their country and themselves. You

---

[1] Probably the information conveyed in a letter from Lord Temple to his brother George Grenville, dated *Sunday morning* [May 15, 1768], was derived from Lord Camden. "I called upon you last night to ask whether you had heard any thing authentic *with regard to intended expulsion;* I have, and with such an appearance of authority, that I have for that and other reasons writ to Harry to come up."

Subsequently, in a debate on the Middlesex Election, Lord Camden said,—"A secret influence had said the word, *Mr. Wilkes shall not sit*, and the *fiat* was to be obeyed though it tore out the heart-strings of this excellent Constitution."

have had the merit of introducing a more compendious system of government and logic. You neither address yourself to the passions nor to the understanding, but simply to the *touch*. You apply yourself immediately to the *feelings*[1] of your friends, who, contrary to the forms of Parliament, never enter heartily into a debate, until they have *divided*."—*Junius*, vol. i. p. 479.

And again :—

" I am not versed in the politics of the north; but this I believe is certain, that half the money you have distributed to carry the expulsion of Mr. Wilkes, or even your Secretary's share in the last subscription, would have kept the Turks at your devotion."—*Junius*, vol. i. p. 490.

Junius sent to Woodfall on the 31st of January, 1771, a private note, accompanied by four short paragraphs, to be inserted on successive days in the *Public Advertiser*, all to the same effect, and intended to instigate the Ministry to open the doors of the Houses of Parliament to strangers, on the following Tuesday, February 5th, when the debate on Lord Chatham's motion relative to the Falkland Islands question was expected to take place.

It has been taken for granted, from this communication to Woodfall, that Junius was not a member of either House of Parliament. It *proves* nothing, but I consider it much more in favour of, than against, my theory that Lord Temple was Junius.

In each of the four paragraphs sent for insertion in the newspapers, he speaks of the *Houses* of Parliament, but in his private note to Woodfall, he says :—

" it is of the utmost importance to the Public Cause that the Doors of the *H? of Lords* sh? be opened on Tuesday next."

Lord Temple knew that a very important debate would arise in the House of Lords, on the Motion which Lord Chatham intended to make on that day. He would, of course, be present himself to support Lord Chatham, and he would, as certainly, desire that the debate should be reported in the newspapers. However capable

---

[1] " Prospects, promises, and provision draw away the hungry, the greedy, and the gaping; virtue alone can carry the virtuous and upright. When those who carry the *bag* show the way, the *feeling* interest will always be on that side."—*Lord Temple's Letter from Albemarle Street to the Cocoa Tree.*

he might be of doing this himself, it is obvious that he could not have done it in this instance without detection, because if all strangers were excluded, any report which appeared in public must necessarily be known to emanate from a peer, and more particularly from any peer who was in the habit of taking notes, or who had been seen to take notes upon this occasion.

It is more than probable that Lord Temple did sometimes furnish Almon, Woodfall, and Miller with reports of speeches in Parliament, particularly those of Lord Chatham. I have already mentioned his frequent attendance in the House of Commons on all occasions of interest, and some of his notes of speeches in the House of Lords are still extant, written first in pencil, and afterwards corrected with a pen.

The paragraphs in the *Public Advertiser* failed in the desired effect: the public were not admitted to the House of Lords, and it is believed that no report is preserved of the debate which took place on the 5th of February, relative to the Falkland Islands. The Opposition Peers in the House of Lords were desirous that the public should not be excluded, as appears by their Protest[1] of the 10th of December previous, when Lord Gower having suddenly moved, while the Duke of Manchester was speaking, that the House should be cleared, so great a clamour and uproar ensued, that Lord Chatham, unable to gain a hearing, left the House, followed by many peers.

Lord Temple was no doubt absent, as his name is not appended to the Protest, but it is certain that his sentiments on the subject of it would have coincided with those of Lord Chatham.

Several of Lord Chatham's letters about this period allude to the " *Tapestry*," with reference to the exclusiveness of the House of Peers.

Writing to Lady Stanhope on the 16th of December, 1770, he says,—

---

[1] This paragraph forms part of the protest. " We must consider this proceeding (too manifestly premeditated and prepared) to have been for no other purpose than to preclude inquiry, on the part of the Lords; and under colour of concealing secrets of State, to hide from the public eye the unjustifiable and criminal neglects of the Ministry, in not making sufficient and timely provision for the national honour and security."

[2] His absence would be accounted for by the death of his brother, George Grenville, having happened less than a month before.

"Attendance in the House of Lords, and hourly businesses out of it, but relative to it, have possessed my time wholly. The labours within the House, are now the labours of Hercules ; for the House being of late kept clear of *hearers*, we are reduced to a snug party of unhearing and unfeeling Lords, and the *tapestry hangings;* which last, mute as Ministers, still tell us more than all the Cabinet on the subject of Spain, and the manner of treating with an insidious and haughty power."[1]

And on the 22nd of January following :—

" I take it for granted that the same declaration will be laid before the Tapestry on Friday, which will be offered to the live figures in St. Stephens."

On the 25th to Lady Chatham, he says,—

" I am just returned from the Tapestry."

In one of the private letters to Wilkes, dated September 7th, 1771, Junius writes,—

" I should be glad to mortify those contemptible creatures who call themselves noblemen, whose worthless importance depends entirely upon their influence over boroughs."

This passage has been frequently quoted, and, as I think, a very erroneous inference drawn from it, that Junius could not have been a member of the Upper House of Parliament, because if he were himself a nobleman, he would not have spoken in so disparaging a manner of noblemen or great men.

I do not, however, understand that the language of Junius in this instance is intended to apply to the Peers generally as an Order. There may be, and we know there are, peers and noblemen, who are quite as worthless as any Commoner may be ; it is not their Order alone that makes them less *contemptible,* if their conduct and character do not otherwise render them good members of society.

The remarks of Junius appear to me to be very distinctly expressed, and particularly directed against those noblemen *only* " whose worthless importance depends entirely upon their in-

---

[1] It will be remembered that the Defeat of the Spanish Armada formed the subject of the Tapestry in the old House of Lords, which was destroyed by the fire in 1834.

fluence over boroughs:" that is boroughmongers in the literal
sense, men or noblemen, who buy and sell boroughs. Lord Hertford would seem, by a subsequent part of the letter, to have been
pointed at, but the remarks were also probably aimed at such men
as Lord Clive for instance, who, although he was a *Heaven-born
General* in India, was nevertheless a great boroughmonger in
England. It is notorious that a considerable portion of the
enormous wealth which he acquired in India was applied to the
purchase of boroughs, and several members were sent to the
House of Commons entirely through the influence so obtained.
Lord Verney, too, might be one of those " contemptible creatures."
His *worthless importance* was notoriously increased by his parliamentary influence in the boroughs of Wendover and Carmar-
then. A few years later, Lord Temple, in allusion to Lord Verney,
and under a supposition that he wished to persuade the Corporation of Buckingham[1] to sell themselves to Lord North, said,—

" Such a hint partakes less of the generous and disinterested sentiments which should animate the representative of an independent
county, than of *that meaner sort which sometimes recommends Court
Members to poor boroughs for a valuable consideration, when the poor
are sold, and a profit made on their perjury.*"—See *post*, vol. iv.

Sir Laurence Dundas was another person whose *worthless importance* was derived solely from his very extensive parliamentary
influence; and others might be named, better entitled to be called
noblemen, who were in the same predicament with respect to their
importance.

I do not believe, therefore, that Junius meant to speak in disrespectful terms of the Peers generally, and Lord Temple was
certainly not likely to depreciate his Order; he was proud of his
peerage; he had sought and obtained for his family the promotion
to an earldom, and it is supposed that he was ambitious of still
further advancement.

Although it is probable that two or three members were returned to Parliament by Lord Temple's influence, yet he was no

---

[1] Lord Verney was at this time one of the Members for the County of Buckingham,
and he was engaged in building a large house at Claydon, near Buckingham, which was
intended to rival Stowe in magnificence, but only a small part of it was completed.

boroughmonger. The honourable influence which he possessed in the borough or the county of Buckingham, had descended to him by inheritance from his ancestors, through several generations; it was an influence neither bought nor sold, but obtained by, and enjoyed solely as the result of, the personal affection and kindness of his friends and neighbours.

A very elaborate Essay was written by Dr. Busby, the learned translator of Lucretius, to prove that De Lolme, the author of the well-known Essay on the English Constitution, was also the Author of the Letters of Junius, and the Doctor has completely succeeded in establishing the fact to his own entire satisfaction.

Although I consider it extremely improbable—I might even say impossible—that De Lolme could be Junius, yet there is a mysterious connection between Junius and that author which has not hitherto been satisfactorily explained.

The Preface to the original edition of the Letters concludes with a paragraph translated from the French edition of De Lolme's Essay, which is at the same time recommended by Junius to the public "*as a performance, deep, solid and ingenious.*"

The Preface containing this quotation was sent, in manuscript, by Junius to Woodfall, in November, 1771; the Essay itself having been printed *in French*, at Amsterdam, in the same year[1], and it was not published *in English* until the year 1775.

Dr. Busby says:—

" Did the *words* of the paragraph given in the Preface of Junius, however faithful to the sense of the original, differ from those in De Lolme's English edition, and the style of the paragraph vary from the general style of the work, little difficulty would accrue, because the Essay was published in French at the time Junius wrote, and he might have translated the passage with which he concludes his preface. But the paragraph as sent by Junius to Woodfall in 1771, and as first published by De Lolme in 1775, is verbally the same, syllable for syllable, and in style perfectly correspondent with the rest of the Essay.

" It need scarcely be observed that were twenty French scholars to translate a passage equal in length to that paragraph, however closely

---

[1] The French edition is dated à Amsterdam, chez E. van Harrevelt, 1771.

they might all adhere to the *meaning* of the original, no two versions of the twenty would coincide *literally*,—expression for expression. If Junius himself translated the paragraph and De Lolme adopted it, De Lolme did so, either from respect to the writer who had in so marked, so conspicuous a manner, extolled and recommended his work, or because the passage was given in a style superior to his own. . . . . If, again, De Lolme transcribed the passage from Junius, not from a motive of grateful politeness, but purely on account of his own inability to execute it equally well, all the other parts of his translation would have been palpably inferior, and the paragraph of Junius, a reproach to the general style. But not only are the other portions as successfully performed, as faithfully, as forcibly, and as elegantly expressed as the paragraph presented to us by Junius, but many of the passages are even superior."[1]

Besides the paragraph which has been mentioned, Junius has quoted De Lolme in another part of the Preface :—

" While this censorial power is maintained, to speak in the words of a most ingenious foreigner, both Minister & Magistrate is compelled, in almost every instance, *to choose between his duty & his reputation*."[2]

Nearly the same words are repeated by Junius in his letter to Lord Camden,—

" When the contest turns upon the interpretation of the laws, you cannot, *without a formal surrender of all your reputation*, yield the post of honour, even to Lord Chatham."

Many instances might be adduced to show that Junius was a diligent reader of De Lolme's Essay on the English Constitution, and that he used it in the composition of his Letters. Two or three instances will suffice to show that he probably translated a considerable part of the English version which was published in 1775.

In his *Dedication*, Junius says:—

" When Kings and Ministers are forgotten, when the force and direction of personal Satyr is no longer understood, &c."

---

[1] Arguments and facts demonstrating that the Letters of Junius were written by John Louis De Lolme, LL.D., &c., by Thomas Busby, Mus. Doc. 8vo, London, 1816, p. 223.

[2] The words in the French edition of De Lolme, are—" *d'opter entre son devoir, et le sacrifice de toute sa reputation d'intégrité*," p. 230. And in the English edition, 8vo, 1821, the words are,—" *to choose between his duty and the surrender of all his former reputation*," p. 217. The substance of this passage was appropriated by Sir Philip Francis either from Junius or De Lolme, in a speech which he made in the House of Commons in 1786.

In De Lolme :—

" This torrent is compelled by the general arrangement of things, finally to throw itself into a vast reservoir, where it mingles, and loses its *force and direction.*"—P. 150.

In the *Preface* of Junius :—

" The Laws of England provide, as effectually as any human Laws can do, for the protection of the subject, in his reputation, as well as in his person & property."

De Lolme says :—

" *The laws* which so effectually *provide* for the safety of the people."
—P. 67. . . . " The same laws that protect the *person and property* of the individual, do also *protect his reputation.*"—P. 213.

Again in the *Preface* of Junius :—

" If it be really a part of our Constitution, and not a mere *dictum* of the Law, *that the King can do no wrong,* it is not the only instance, in the wisest of human institutions, where theory is at variance with practice.—That the Sovereign of this Country is not amenable to any form of Trial known to the Laws, is unquestionable. But exemption from punishment is a singular privilege annexed to the royal character, & no way excludes the possibility of deserving it. How long, & to what extent a King of *England* may be protected by the forms, when he violates the Spirit of the Constitution, deserves to be considered."— Vol. i. p. 382.

And De Lolme, at p. 51 of the *Essay :* —

" It is a fundamental maxim *that the King can do no wrong;* which does not signify, however, that the King has not the power of doing ill, but only that he is above the reach of all courts of law whatever, and *that his person is sacred and inviolable.*"

Dr. Busby has enumerated many examples of parallel passages in the writings of Junius and De Lolme.; and although I think he was certainly mistaken in his views respecting the Authorship of Junius, yet his " *Facts and Arguments* " are worthy of attentive consideration with reference to the subject which he discusses with so much ingenuity.

It appears extremely probable that several chapters of De Lolme's Essay on the Constitution, particularly those on the Liberty of the Press, were entirely translated by the Author of Junius.

In the *Advertisement* prefixed to the first English edition of the Essay printed in 1775, there is the following note by De Lolme :—

" Though all the booksellers in London had at first refused to have anything to do with my English edition (notwithstanding the French work was extremely well known), yet, soon after I had thought of the expedient of a subscription, I found that two of them, who are both living [1], had begun a translation, on the recommendation, as they told me, of a noble Lord, whom they named, who had, 'till a few years before, filled one of the highest offices under the Crown. I paid them ten pounds in order to engage them to drop their undertaking, about which, I understood, they already had been at some expense. Had the noble Lord favoured me with his subscription, I would have celebrated the generosity and munificence of my patron ; but as he did not think proper so to do, I shall only observe that his recommending my work to a bookseller cost me ten pounds."

The description of the noble Lord, abovementioned, applies very exactly to Lord Temple, who had only a few years before been Lord Privy Seal, an office which, in point of precedence, ranks as one of the highest under the Crown ; and from his well-known political opinions, he would be very likely to recommend such a work to the notice of the booksellers, Almon and Kearsley, who were both known to him, and Lord Temple had perhaps sent them, or caused to be sent to them, that portion of the work translated, which cost De Lolme ten pounds to purchase.

Lord Temple was an accomplished French scholar : he had spent several years in the acquisition of the language, under a French tutor, during his travels on the Continent from 1728 to 1733, and in his letters at that time he mentions his anxious wish to acquire both the French and Italian languages. In one of his letters to his uncle Lord Cobham, dated from Florence, he says :—

" Je serois bien aise de pouvoir passer quelque tems à Paris, afin de me perfectionner, car je ne puis penser sans beaucoup de regret, aux deux années et demie employées à apprendre avec des mauvais maîtres à Lausanne, ce qui deviendra mon premier soin d'oublier aussitôt que j'en aurai de bons." [2]

[1] Probably Almon and Kearsley.

[2] Lord Temple's correct knowledge of the French language would enable him to detect

I have found no mention of De Lolme among Lord Temple's papers, nor anything to show that there was a personal acquaintance between them; and although Lord Temple, when a young man, had spent between two and three years in Switzerland, chiefly at Lausanne and Geneva, which last named was De Lolme's native place, yet it was before De Lolme was born.

It was the opinion of Dr. Parr, and other learned critics, that the compositions of Junius contained many Gallicisms, and Dr. Busby founded one of his principal arguments in favour of De Lolme as the Author of Junius, on the fact of there being so many idiomatic phrases and expressions in the Letters, which were evidently derived from the French.

This opinion is again very consistent with the claims of Lord Temple, who, from the age of eighteen to twenty-three, was travelling in various parts of France, Switzerland, and Italy, chiefly, as I have shown, with the view of making himself intimately acquainted with the French and Italian languages.

At this early period of life, the studies which occupied his mind, and the impressions he then received, would be likely to have considerable influence upon his subsequent style of composition.

Dr. Busby has entered very minutely into this subject, for the purpose of showing that Junius very frequently made use of language which was not purely English, but had its origin in foreign sources [1].

From the frequent and not very reverent allusions made by Junius to the Priests, and ceremonious absurdities of the Roman

the "*barbarous French*" of Lord Rochford, which Junius mentions in a note to his letter on the Falkland Islands question (vol. ii. p. 191), and the intimate acquaintance with the business of the Secretary of State's Office, which he had acquired during Mr. Pitt's Administration, entitled him also to say under the signature of "Lucius" (vol. iii. p. 89), " We are a little better acquainted than he imagines with the style of the Secretary of State's Office."

[1] Lord Brougham says of Junius,—" Writing at a time when even good or even correct composition was little studied, and in the newspapers hardly ever met with, his polished style, though very far from being a correct one, and further still from being good pure English, being made the vehicle of abuse, sarcasm, and pointed invective, naturally excited a degree of attention, which was further maintained by the boldness of his proceedings."

Catholic Church, the " logic of St. Omers," and the *" morâle relachée "* professed and inculcated by Loyola, Malagrida, and other distinguished members of the Society of Jesus, it may be inferred that he was very minutely acquainted with the character of the Jesuits, and the *sound casuistry* of their religious and political doctrines.

In one of the Miscellaneous Letters under the signature , of " Bifrons," he writes, with evident satisfaction,—

" I am not deeply read in authors of that professed title [the soundest casuists], but I remember seeing Busembaum, Suarez, Molina, and a score of other Jesuitical books burnt at Paris for their *sound casuistry*, by the common hangman."—*Junius*, vol. iii. p. 46.

The ceremony here alluded to probably took place in or about the year 1732, when the disputes between the King of France and his Parliaments relative to the Jesuits had arrived at the highest point of acrimony. Several burnings of obnoxious and prohibited books and writings are described by contemporary authorities[1] at this time ; and as Lord Temple (then Mr. Richard Grenville) was in France, and chiefly at Paris from the autumn of 1731 to the spring of 1733, he had consequently many oppor-

---

[1] Among other instances I have selected the following :—In the *Daily Courant*, April 28th, 1732. " An Arrêt of the Council of State was affixed up some days ago, ordering that two libels, entitled the second and third letters of the Abbot de Lisle, concerning the Miracles of M. de Paris, should be torn and burnt by the hands of the common hangman in the churchyard, before the great portico of the Church of Notre Dame [at Paris], as being defamatory and seditious, which was executed the 26th past."

In the *Country Journal* or *Craftsman*, May 20th, 1732. " A paper entitled *Nouvelles Ecclesiastiques, &c.*, was burnt by the common hangman, by order of an Arrêt of the Parliament of Paris, *au bas du grand escalier du Palais.*"

Craftsman, No. 316, quoted in the *Gentleman's Magazine* for July, 1732, mentions that the Parliament of Paris had ordered some ecclesiastical mandates to be suppressed, and one of them was proposed to be burnt by the common hangman.

Daily Courant, Monday, August 14, 1732. " On the 13th N. S. the Parliament issued an Arrêt against a printed book, entitled the *" Origin of the Parliament and its Prerogatives,"* which was condemned to be burnt by the hands of the common hangman, as prejudicial to the royal authority, which was executed the same day in the court yard of the Palais. That book had the same fate some days before at Rouen, pursuant to an Arrêt of the Parliament of Normandie."

Daily Courant, Monday, March 19th, 1732-3. " On the 20th N. S. the Parliament [of Paris] made an Arrêt, ordering a pamphlet, entitled a ' Letter from Louis XIV. to Louis XV.,' to be burnt by the hands of the common hangman, which was done accordingly the same day."

tunities of witnessing the ceremonies of the burning of *scores of Jesuitical books* by the common hangman, as described by Junius[1].

In a letter to his brother George Grenville, dated from Paris, [August?] 1732, he says:—

"The King of France has at last exerted himself, and banished no less than 160 Members of his Parliament in different parts of his kingdom, for pretending to advise him not to let the Pope domineer him; at least that has been the beginning of the quarrel : an example which I believe our King will think of twice before he follows. This has been a stroke of the Jesuits, who are all in all at this Court."

And to his aunt Lady Cobham, dated from "Bourdeaux ce 24me Juin, 1732," he writes, with contemptuous sarcasm, a description of some Romish ceremonies resembling a scene of the witches in *Macbeth* :—

"On m'a appelé dans ce moment pour voir une cérémonie à la Romaine, qui ne ressemble pas mal à la scéne des sorcières en Macbeth, des prêtres qui font une procession avec des crucifixes autour d'un feu de joie fait en honneur de St. Jean, de la fête duquel ce soir est la veille. Ils y ont mis le feu avec des chandelles de cire, portées pour cet effet en procession, après quoi ils ont fait le tour trois fois en chantant, et tout le peuple y a jeté des branches."[2]

It can, I think, scarcely be doubted that the Author of Junius, whoever he might have been, did frequently send, or cause to be

---

[1] Voltaire describes the ceremony of burning obnoxious books at Rome, in August, 1731 : "L'exécution se fit avec la grande cérémonie extraordinaire. On dressa dans la place, vis à vis le couvent de la Minerve, un vaste échafaud, et à trente pas un grand bûcher. Les Cardinaux montèrent sur l'échafaud; le livre fut présenté, lié et garrotté de petites chaînes de fer, au cardinal doyen. Celui-ci le donna au grand inquisiteur, qui le rendit au greffier : le greffier le donna au prévôt, le prévôt à un huissier, l'huissier à un archer, l'archer au bourreau. Le bourreau l'éleva en l'air et en se tournant gravement vers les quatre points cardinaux : ensuite il délia le prisonnier; il le déchira feuille à feuille; il trempa chaque feuille dans la poix bouillante ; ensuite on versa le tout dans le bûcher, et le peuple cria anathème aux Jansenistes," &c.—*Œuvres de Voltaire*, tome v. p. 1020.

[2] In another part of the same letter, he says,—"Après avoir vu la plûpart des villes dans le sud de France, je suis arrivé enfin à Bourdeaux depuis avant-hier : il n'y a pas ici beaucoup de bonne compagnie, de sorte que je partirai dans deux ou trois jours pour Paris. Les villes que j'ai trouvé le plus à mon goût sont Aix et Avignon. Je ne me suis arrêté dans la première que trois jours ; mais ce tems m'a suffit pour découvrir que les étrangers y etoient bien vus ; mais j'ai demeuré dans la dernière une dixaine de jours, & je suis tout à fait charmé de leurs politesses et bonnes manières, & en meme tems surpris de voir, qu'étant Sujets du Pape, ils n'aient pas pris la même fierté

sent, to Almon, Woodfall, Miller, Bingley, and other publishers, reports of debates in the House of Lords, more particularly of some of the speeches of Lord Chatham.

There are many very remarkable instances of similarity in phrases and expressions in the Letters of Junius and the Speeches of Chatham, and for this reason, chiefly, many persons have been deluded into a belief that Philip Francis was Junius, because it was insisted that he, Francis, first "wrote" these speeches for publication by Almon in 1792, in the *Anecdotes of Lord Chatham*, and that he compiled them from his own notes taken at the time, but preserved in manuscript for more than twenty years. This evidence would be startling,—*if it were true.*

Lord Chatham's Speeches, which were professed to be written from the original notes, and to be published *for the first time in* 1792, are to be found in the contemporary newspapers a few days after they were spoken, not only the same in substance, but word for word, as they were pretended to have been first compiled by the "gentleman with a strong memory," in 1792, and said to have been again "*revised*" by him in 1813 for the *Parliamentary History*, edited by the late Mr. Wright[1].

The conclusion of a very short debate which took place in the House of Lords, on the 2nd of February, 1770, upon a Reso-

que le reste des peuples de ses Etats.   Le Languedoc est un très beau pays, mais je ne puis pas dire que je l'aie trouvé tout à fait un paradis terrestre, comme on me l'avoit vanté.

" Depuis Montauban, ville assez agréable par sa situation, et à ce que j'ai ouï dire par sa politesse envers les étrangers, nous avons pris un bateau pour descendre la Garonne, l'Ippocrène des Gascons, belle rivière, bordée d'un beau pays. Je ne sais autre nouvelle qu'une aussi désagréable, qu'elle est mal fondée à ce que j'espère : on dit que la flotte Espagnole a fait voile vers l'Angleterre, avec dessein d'y mener le prétendant : je m'imagine pourtant que ce n'est autre chose qu'un bruit populaire.

" Je suis bien aise, Madame, que vous avez été si charmée de la musique de Handel avec les paroles Angloises, mais je ne puis pas trop bien comprendre comment les Italiennes ont fait pour réussir si bien dans la prononciation : apparemment ceci mettra quelqu'un en tête de composer un Opera Anglois."

And on the 8th of August, 1732, writing from Paris, he says,—" Je suis allé Lundi passé à Versailles, & Mardi j'y vis l'entrée du Nonce, dans laquelle assurément il n'a pas brillé. Il harangua le Roi & la Reine en Italien, & Monsieur le Dauphin en François. Le Roi a l'air de ce qu'il est, la Reine paroit très bonne princesse, et le Dauphin, à mon avis, ressemble assez au Roi. Le château de Versailles est magnifique par son immense grandeur, mais je ne trouve pas que l'architecture y répond. Les jardins sont beaux, mais d'une beauté forcée ; on y reconnoit facilement la part que l'Art y a eue. Je trouve Marli un endroit bien plus charmant."

[1] See Essay upon Junius, in *Athenæum*, September 21, 1850.

lution proposed by Lord Marchmont, is distinguished by Almon[1] as being copied from the *London Museum* (a contemporary publication which was once supposed to have in part belonged to Almon), and he adds, "It is not known that any other account of this debate was taken;" consequently it was not appropriated by the "gentleman with the strong memory," who, it was said, *wrote* the other speeches of Lord Chatham twenty years after they were delivered.

I agree with the Author of *Junius Identified*, that this debate bears internal evidence of having been reported by Junius, and as Lord Temple was in the House of Lords upon that occasion, it may not unfairly be assumed that it was communicated either by him, or through his means, to Almon.

It commences thus:—

"It should seem that the Scotch kept this Motion in their pockets, and that they reserved themselves for it, as neither the Earl of Marchmont, who made it, nor Lord Mansfield, who supported it, opened their mouths 'till now, when they both spoke with great vigour." . . . .

. . . . . "He (Lord Chatham) quoted Lord Somers and Chief Justice Holt in support of his law, and drew their characters very finely. He called them *honest men*, who knew and loved the English Constitution."—

Then, turning to Lord Mansfield, he said,—

"I vow to God! I think the noble Lord equals them both,—*in abilities*."[2]

Towards the conclusion, he complained strongly of the Motion's being sudden, and made at midnight, and pressed the necessity of an adjournment of only two days. He said, among other things,—

---

[1] *Anecdotes of Lord Chatham*, 8vo, 1792, vol. ii. p. 304.

[2] "When I acknowledge your *abilities*, you may believe I am sincere."—*Junius to Lord Mansfield*, vol. ii. p. 181.

"Junius never pretends to be a better lawyer than Lord Mansfield; on the contrary, he takes every opportunity to acknowledge his superior learning and *abilities*."— *Junius*, vol. iii. p. 430.

"But with a sound heart, be assured you are better gifted, even for worldly happiness, than if you had been cursed with the *abilities* of a Mansfield."—*Ibid.*, vol. i. p. 237.

" if the *Constitution must be wounded*, let it not receive its *mortal stab*, at this dark and midnight hour." [1]

A writer in the *Edinburgh Review* [2], before quoted, has observed that,—

" whoever revives the inquiry relating to the Authorship of Junius, unless he discovers positive and irresistible evidence in support of his claimant, should show him to be politically attached to the Grenville party, which Junius certainly was, *and must also produce some specimens of his writings of tolerable length*, such as might afford reasonable grounds for believing that he could have written these letters ; which must be allowed to be finished models, though not of the purest and highest style of composition."

In the known and acknowledged productions of Lord Temple will be found many passages of comparative excellence, quite sufficient to show that he was capable of writing the Letters of Junius ; and some of the peculiarities of the style, as well as similarity of thoughts and expressions, will be found in the specimens hereafter given of the fragments which are still extant in his handwriting.

It can scarcely be expected that *"the highest style of Junius"* should ever be discovered under a real name : the withering sarcasm, the bitter personal satire, the rancorous invective, and other remarkable peculiarities by which it was distinguished, were

---

[1] —"and employing the very weapons committed to it by the collective body, *to stab the Constitution.*"—*Junius,* vol. ii. p. 117.

" Nothing less than a repeal as formal as the resolution itself can heal the *wound that has been given to the Constitution.*"—*Ibid.,* vol. ii. p. 73.

" They loved the *Constitution* they had saved so much, that they would not suffer the very act of saving it to have the appearance of giving it a *wound.*"—*Lord Temple's Pamphlet on the Suspending and Dispensing Prerogative,* 1766.

—"not to be compared with one thrust at the *Constitution,* let the instrument be never so harmless, or the intention never so innocent, for she may be *wounded* even in the house of her friends."—*Lord Temple, ibid.*

" I will consent to giving any reward, but that of *wounding the Constitution* further."—*Ibid.*

" The *stab* he had so unadvisedly made at the vitals of *the constitution* itself."—*Candor to the Public Advertiser,* p. 23.

—"*wounding the Constitution* under pretence of regard to royalty."—*Lord Temple's Defence of the North Briton ; Almon's Anecdotes,* vol. ii. p. 118.

[2] June, 1826, vol. xliv. p. 1.

as much the result of cultivation and acquirement, and as carefully to be concealed, as the disguised handwriting: to have employed either the one or the other for any purposes but those of the Letters of Junius, would be at once to have defeated the grand object of his life—his desire of absolute concealment.

It is only by diligent perseverance that a style of composition, or a mode of writing, can be acquired or altered; they are both extremely difficult, but not impossible; the original features of either can never be so entirely effaced but that some occasional traces can be discovered by those who study the peculiarities of each.

Lord Temple's compositions consist of his Speeches in Parliament, and his Protests; Petitions, Pamphlets, &c.

The only speech now known, which, as Mr. Richard Grenville, he made in the House of Commons, was on the 12th *of February,* 1748, upon the Bill for holding the Summer Assizes at Buckingham.

Of Lord Temple's speeches in the House of Lords only the following have been reported :—

November 15, 1753.—On the Repeal of the Jews' Naturalization Bill.

December 10, 1755.—On a Motion for a Vote of Censure on the Treaties with Russia and Hesse Cassel.

May 24, 1756.—On the Militia Bill.

June, 1758.—On the Bill to explain and amend the Habeas Corpus Act.

December 10, 1766.—On the Suspending and Dispensing Prerogative.

February 7, 1770.—On the Complaint against a Printer for publishing Protests.

May 18, 1770.—On the Duke of Richmond's Resolutions relating to America.

The Protests composed and signed by Lord Temple are as follow :—

November 13, 1755.—Protest against that part of the Address which relates to the King's German Dominions.

March 5, 1756.—Protest against the Bill for granting Commissions to Foreign Protestants.

June, 1758.—Protests on the rejection of the Bill to explain and amend the Habeas Corpus Act.

November 29, 1763.—Protest against the Resolution that the Privilege of Parliament does not extend to the case of Libels.

March 17, 1766.—Protest against passing the Bill to repeal the American Stamp Act.

February 2, 1770.—Protest on the rejection of a Resolution moved by the Marquess of Rockingham, that the House of Commons, in the exercise of its judicature in matters of Elections, is bound to judge according to the law of the land, and the known and established law and custom of Parliament, which is part thereof.

Lord Temple was also either known or supposed to be the Author of several Tracts or Pamphlets, viz. :—

1. A Letter to an Honourable Brigadier-General, Commander-in-Chief of His Majesty's Forces in Canada.[1] 1760.

2. A Letter to the Earls of Egremont and Halifax, His Majesty's principal Secretaries of State, on the Seizure of Papers. 1763.

3. A fair and constitutional Defence of the *North Briton*, No. 45. 1763.

4. A Letter from Albemarle Street to the Cocoa Tree. 1764.

5. A Letter from Candor to the *Public Advertiser*, published on the 22nd of September, 1764.

6. An Enquiry into the Doctrine lately propagated concerning Libels, Warrants, and the Seizure of Papers, in a letter to Mr. Almon, from the Father of Candor, published 29th November, 1764.

7. The Principles of the late Changes impartially examined by a Son of Candor. 1765.

8. A Speech on the Suspending and Dispensing Prerogative. 1766.

9. Conduct of the late Administration relative to the Repeal of the American Stamp Act. 1767.[2]

---

[1] I have ascribed this performance to Lord Temple, for the reasons assigned, *ante*, p. lxxxviii.

[2] On the authority of Almon, in his *Biographical Anecdotes*, Charles Lloyd, Mr. Grenville's private secretary, is said to have been the author of this Tract, and yet after describing it as "an able composition," he adds, that the greatest part of it, if not all of it, was dictated by Mr. Grenville. As Almon was himself the publisher of it, it was probably true that Charles Lloyd was the medium of communication, and the person from whom he actually received the manuscript, and that Mr. Grenville himself had some participation in the authorship; but I venture to attribute the greater part of it to Lord Temple, as the Author of Junius, whose early style it certainly resembles, particularly when compared with some of the Miscellaneous Letters which were written during the years 1767 and 1768, upon the subject of the Stamp Act and the dispute with America. I was induced to form this opinion, by finding among Lord Temple's papers, and in his own handwriting, very extensive collections relating to the same subjects, and extracts from the correspondence between the Secretary of State, the Governors, and various persons in the provinces of North America, evidently com-

10. A Letter to the Duke of Grafton on the present Situation of Public Affairs. Published about June, 1768.

11. The Buckinghamshire Petition, in September, 1769.

12. A Word at Parting. Published in December, 1767.

13. Another Letter to Mr. Almon in matter of Libel, in August, 1770.

14. A Summary of the Law of Libel, in four Letters, signed Phileleutherus Anglicanus, published in February, 1771.

Lord Temple is also supposed to have assisted Wilkes in the *North Briton* in 1762-3, and to have contributed to the *History of the late Minority* in 1765, and to an *Enquiry into the Conduct of a late Right Honourable Commoner* in 1766.

It may perhaps be said that I have attributed more labour to Junius than is consistent with the rank and station which I have claimed for the Author. I must, therefore, again remind the reader, that Junius in describing his own pursuit so early as 1768, says that it began with amusement, grew into habit, and at length became heated into passion : it became, in fact, the business of his life—his sole employment for many years. All that he did, therefore, was nothing more than could easily be accomplished by a man who was gifted with, or who had acquired, a certain facility of composition ; who possessed a sufficient knowledge of the subjects on which he wrote, and, above all, of a man who, like Lord Temple, had ample leisure to devote himself to the task, and ample fortune to work out his designs by all the means which might be necessary to preserve his concealment, with the assistance of well-paid, but unconscious and unsuspicious agents.

From the foregoing list of Lord Temple's writings, beginning with the year 1760, it will be perceived, that, without taking into consideration the Letters of Junius, and those under various other signatures, there is only moderate employment for each succeed-

---

piled for the purpose of writing this pamphlet, as nearly all the numerous quotations which it contains are to be found in these autograph collections of Lord Temple, and generally in the order in which they are quoted. The Tract itself is now exceedingly rare, and therefore some extracts will hereafter be given ; and I have appended also in the notes some passages from the writings of Junius, which seem to me to contain the same thoughts, and frequently the same expressions, besides that the style altogether bears, as I have said, a very strong resemblance to the Letters of the Author of Junius at the same period.

ing year. In the years 1770 and 1771, besides the Letters of
Junius, &c., he wrote only the pamphlet entitled *Another Letter
to Mr. Almon in the matter of Libel, with a Postscript;* a
Second Postscript to that Letter; and the short tract entitled, *A
Summary of the Law of Libel, &c.*

The following is an extract from the *Letter to an Honourable
Brigadier-General:*—

"Although I have justly given you the sole honour of your capitulation of Quebec, independent of fortune, or her influence, yet let us not
totally disclaim her favour and protection. Among heroes of ancient
days, the favour of the Gods was always esteemed a pious proof of
merit, and shall we not acknowledge it most fortunate, and consequently
meritorious, that you were necessarily appointed to be the historian of
your own exploits; Alexander passionately lamented that he had not,
like Achilles, another Homer to give immortality to his conquests.

"I know that our ingenious moderns have been reproached with
plundering the shrines of antiquity, and ransacking the virtues of the
dead, to erect a lying monument to the fame of the living. I shall not
be apprehensive of this reproach when I assert, that the noblest praise
ever given to Cæsar, *that of writing with the same spirit with which he
fought,* is equally due to you for the letter you wrote from Quebec to
the Secretary of State. Some malignant spirits indeed were offended
at your not having paid one civil compliment to the memory of General
Wolfe, or used one kind expression of esteem or affection with regard
to his person. Surely some people are never to be satisfied. Permit
me, Sir, in your name to ask them, whether your warmest encomiums
could have added to that universal good opinion which the public had
conceived of Mr. Wolfe's abilities and courage?" . . . . .

"But they must have known very little of the expedition to Quebec,
who expected that you would bear testimony to the conduct of a
General whose plan of operations you had the honour, both in public
and private, to oppose; and against whose last desperate attempt you
protested in form. True, this attempt succeeded; but not the most
fortunate success should alter an opinion founded, like yours, in calm
deliberate judgment. You were not prejudiced in favour of this attack,
by having any share in the execution. You were at a *safe and honourable* distance from the scene of action, when you were *told that you
commanded.*"[1]

---

[1] "Bout-de-ville [Lord Townshend], *sulky.* I was quiet enough at Rainham, when
I was told that I was Lord Lieutenant of Ireland. For a man *to be told that he com-*

In the Preface to the first volume of this Correspondence, I have already quoted a passage from Lord Temple's pamphlet on the *Seizure of Papers.* Here are some other extracts equally worthy of the Author of Junius:—

"But what was the pretence of this late violation of rights so sacred in their nature, this invasion of property, in a critical point, which *comprehends*[1] every valuable interest a man can have? A person is suspected of being the author of a printed paper, which, in the judgment of the Secretaries of State, was a seditious libel, and the proof of the fact is to be sifted out of his own papers; for your Lordships have said in your letter which is published, that such of the papers seized, as tend to make out the guilt of the owner, are to be kept and used for that purpose." . . . .

"The reason is most inadequate, and must appear so to every man who is not beat out of his senses by the jargon of lawyers, or confounded in his own ideas with the quibbles of legal nonsense."[2] . . . .

"There is indeed hardly anything so wicked and unconstitutional, but a *precedent* may be found for it, if the records of the Star Chamber[3], or the memorials of tyranny, are resorted to as authorities." . . . . . .

"Legal *precedents* are those whose authority stands upon trial, and judicial decisions of courts of law, in times of liberty and justice." . . . .

mands a kingdom, or an army, when he dreams of no such matter, forms a situation too difficult for such a head as mine. *Upon another occasion, indeed, I found the business done to my hand, by a person who shall be nameless.*"—*Junius ; Grand Council,* vol. ii. p. 482.

"How easy, how *safe and honourable,* is the path before you !"—*Junius,* vol. ii. p. 82.

[1] "The free election of our representatives in Parliament *comprehends,*" &c.—*Ibid.,* vol. ii. p. 153.

"A clear unblemished character *comprehends* not only the integrity," &c.—*Ibid.,* vol. ii. p. 194.

[2] "As to lawyers, their profession is supported by the indiscriminate defence of right and wrong, and I confess I have not that opinion of their knowledge or integrity to think it necessary that they should decide for me upon *a plain constitutional question.*"—*Ibid.,* vol. i. p. 498.

"But other men are willing to take the law upon trust. They rely upon authority, because they are too indolent to search for information ; or, conceiving that there is some mystery in the laws of their country which lawyers are only qualified to explain, they distrust their judgment, and voluntarily renounce the right of thinking for themselves."—*Ibid.,* vol. ii. p. 408.

[3] "Had there been no Star Chamber, there would have been no rebellion against Charles the First. . . . I am no friend to the doctrine of *precedents,* though lawyers often tell us, that whatever has been once done may lawfully be done again."—*Ibid., Preface,* vol. i. p. 384.

"One *precedent* creates another. . . . Examples are supposed to justify the most dangerous measures, and where they do not suit exactly, the defect is supplied by analogy."—*Ibid.,* vol. i. p. 342.

" *Precedents* which have the show of authority, from the sanction of courts, though of arbitrary and unjust judges, in times too of tyranny and oppression, can only be mentioned to be scorned and inveighed against, in days of liberty and justice ; or to be set up as beacons to warn against the shipwrecks which the rocks and quicksands of arbitrary power have occasioned in former ages.

" But in the halcyon days of liberty, when justice is administered with purity, care will be had to avoid precedents of seeming authority, to give to proceedings that are arbitrary and oppressive, the appearance of being legal." . . . .

" That no such badge of slavery does yet exist in this country, is still believed. That it never may exist, will naturally be the wish of every Englishman [1]. The expectations of liberty are, that if the late most extraordinary, and, as it is thought, unprecedented and illegal seizure of papers, produces a legal trial, it will be found to have been manifestly against law ; and that all the subjects of this kingdom will have the satisfaction to be assured by a judicial determination, that as their houses are their sanctuaries, their closets are the sanctum sanctorum of that sanctuary."

And the following passages are from the LETTER FROM ALBEMARLE STREET TO THE COCOA TREE :—

" Our national parties sprang up in days when the encroachment of the Crown threatened the subversion of the Constitution. James I. taught a system of prerogative consistent with nothing but slavery ; and his descendants, corrupted with false principles, obstinately pursued his perverse plan. The unbridled attempts of arbitrary power necessarily produced opposition, then resistance, and at last ended in the expulsion of a race of tyrants [2], a succession of which had disgraced the throne, and all but destroyed this country : if there are yet amongst us any wretched remains of those parties, they are the tattered rags of a direful warfare between the faithful friends of a limited mixed monarchy, and the traitorous advocates for absolute and arbitrary sovereignty ; but the fortunate change in the circumstances of the nation should now soften into general harmony all former animosities, and eradicate unnatural and destructive prejudices.

" The Protestant succession is now so firmly established in the hearts of a free people, as to be beyond the reach of any attempt. The

---

[1] " That he is the king of a free people, is indeed his greatest glory. That he may long continue the king of a free people, is the second wish that animates my heart. The first is, THAT THE PEOPLE MAY BE FREE."—*Junius*, vol. ii. p. 122.

[2] " In one glorious act of substantial justice."—*Ibid.*, vol. ii. p. 216.

liberties of the subject too, that other Herculanean pillar of the Constitution, are now so well understood, and the foundations of them so immoveably fixed, as to be, I hope, in no immediate danger: the Ministers of this free Government may therefore stand on sure ground, while they pursue an unshaken attachment to these great objects; but *it will always be dangerous to despise the clamours of the people, when there is the least appearance of ground for them in matters of liberty.* The spirit of liberty is a jealous spirit: authority, which is a match for all other opposition, is scarcely equal to its strength; and power itself will not subdue its energy without a struggle too hard to be endured."[1]

I must resist the temptation of making longer extracts from this pamphlet, although it contains many other passages not unworthy of having been written by the Author of Junius, and therefore I beg to commend it to the attentive perusal and consideration of the reader.

In August, 1764, Almon received for publication a pamphlet in manuscript, entitled a LETTER TO THE PUBLIC ADVERTISER, signed CANDOR, and dated from *Gray's Inn, August 31st,* 1764. It was published on Saturday, the 22nd of September, with the following motto on the title-page—

" Honi soit qui mal y pense."—*St. George of England.*

On the reverse of the title-page there is a note from the Author to Almon, which commences thus:—

" CANDOR presents his compliments to Mr. Almon, and desires he

---

[1] " Whatever style of contempt may be adopted by Ministers or Parliaments, *no man sincerely despises the voice of the English nation.* The House of Commons are only interpreters, whose duty it is to convey the sense of the people faithfully to the Crown. If the interpretation be false or imperfect, the constituent powers are called upon to deliver their own sentiments. Their speech is rude but intelligible; their gestures fierce, but full of explanation. Perplexed by sophistries, their honest eloquence rises into action. The first appeal was to the integrity of their representatives; the second, to the King's justice; the last argument of the people, whenever they have recourse to it, will carry more perhaps than persuasion to Parliament, or supplication to the throne."—*Junius,* vol. ii. p. 133.

Here is a very similar passage from De Lolme's *Essay on the English Constitution :—*

" Hence, though the complaints of the people do not always meet with a speedy and immediate redress (a celerity which would be the symptom of a fatal unsteadiness in the Constitution, and would sooner or later bring on its ruin), yet when we attentively consider the nature and the resources of this Constitution, we shall not think it too bold an assertion to say, *that it is impossible but that complaints in which the people persevere* (that is, *well-grounded complaints*), will sooner or later be redressed."— Book ii. chap. xiii.

will convey [1] for him the following Letter, a small part of which has been printed already." [2]

A few pages of the first part of this pamphlet had been sent in a Letter addressed to the printer of the *Public Advertiser*, and it appeared in that paper on Saturday, the 2nd of August, under the signature of CANDOR.

It was probably the intention of the Author to proceed with his subject in a series of Letters to the *Public Advertiser*, but in that paper of the 7th of August, among the notices to correspondents, is the following, which was no doubt intended as a communication to CANDOR:—

"If our correspondent C. will make himself known to us, we shall perhaps be induced to comply with his request; but if he is unwilling to step forth and avow himself the author, or indemnify us for any charge whenever we are called upon by *authority*, the printer does not choose to run the risk of an expensive prosecution, and perhaps a personal trouble into the bargain. No one certainly can blame him for this caution, who avails himself of the same by being concealed. C. will understand our meaning when we hint to him that *enough* has been said already. We wish for a continuance of his correspondence on any future occasion."

In consequence, therefore, of the fears of the Printer, no more letters from CANDOR appeared in the *Public Advertiser*, but the pamphlet was sent to Almon, and published as I have stated above.

Before I speak of the subject of this pamphlet I will mention some other works by the same writer.

[1] When Junius, in one of his private notes to Woodfall, alluded to "the gentleman who transacts the *conveyancing* part of our correspondence," he did not mean the person who merely conveyed (or *carried*) the letters, but he probably used the word in the same almost obsolete sense in which the word *convey* is evidently here employed by Candor.

According to one of the definitions given by Johnson, *convey* means *to manage with privacy;* and *conveyance*, in the same sense, he defines to be *secret management.*

[2] It may be inferred that Almon did not know the author, from the following note, which was prefixed to the advertisement in the *Public Advertiser* of October 19th, 1764, announcing the second edition of this letter:—

"+‖ The Letter dated October 17th was received yesterday. Every request is complied with, and an answer is ready; *where shall it be sent.*"

Besides, as the author had declined making himself known to Woodfall, it is not likely that he should do so to Almon.

Almon, writing to Lord Temple, on the 12th of November, 1764, says:—

"I have received another pamphlet from CANDOR, which is very long, very severe, and very good; it is upon juries, libels, warrants, &c."

This refers to the celebrated tract which was soon after (on the 29th of November) published by Almon, entitled,—

"An Enquiry into the Doctrine lately propagated concerning Libels, Warrants, and the Seizure of Papers, with a view to some late Proceedings, &c., in *a Letter to Mr. Almon* from the FATHER OF CANDOR."

> "The child may rue that is unborn
> The hunting of that day."—*Chevy Chase.*

The letter is dated *Westminster, October 17th,* 1764, and signed the FATHER OF CANDOR—*Libertas et natale solum.*

In the second and all the subsequent editions, amounting to at least six or seven, within as many months, the title is altered to *A Letter concerning Libels, Warrants, &c.,* and, for some unexplained reason, *Almon's* name, and the FATHER OF CANDOR, are removed from the title-page, but the letter is still signed at the end as above. It is now best known by the latter title—the *Letter concerning Libels, &c.,* and so I shall in future call it.

The commencement runs thus:—

"Sir, some weeks after my son's sending you a *Letter to the Public Advertiser,* I was surprised with the sight of a pamphlet[1]. wherein a contrary doctrine is conveyed," &c.

Now, as Almon wrote to Lord Temple that he had received *another letter* from CANDOR, it is evident that he made no distinction between CANDOR and the FATHER OF CANDOR, but that probably, for reasons known to himself at the time, he considered them to be the same writer. The handwriting, or the mode in which he received them, or other circumstances, may have induced him to arrive at that conclusion.

But it suited the FATHER OF CANDOR to assume the guise of an old man, that the former letter might be supposed to come from his son, *the* SON OF CANDOR.

In the autumn of the following year there appeared a pamphlet,

---

[1] The pamphlet alluded to was the *Defence of the Majority,* of which Charles Lloyd is the reputed author.

published also by Almon, entitled *The Principles of the late Changes impartially examined, by a* SON OF CANDOR; and this pamphlet was subsequently attributed by Almon himself, in his *Political Anecdotes*, to Lord Temple: therefore Lord Temple may be considered, on the authority of the publisher, to be one of the *sons*, if not *the* SON OF CANDOR[1].

Lord Temple may have adopted this cognomen either from his admiration of the writings of CANDOR, and that he concurred in his doctrines and opinions, or, as I think most probable, because he was not only the SON OF CANDOR, but that he was also CANDOR, and the FATHER OF CANDOR, in his own individual person; and moreover, that all the generations of CANDOR were concentrated in the initial letter C. by which he was first addressed by Woodfall, the Printer of the *Public Advertiser*, on the 7th of October, 1764, and which continued to be used by Junius, in his communications to Mr. Grenville, as well as in all his future private correspondence with Woodfall, and consequently that C. was Junius and Junius was Lord Temple.

The LETTER CONCERNING LIBELS, WARRANTS, &C., was one of the most important of the political pamphlets which were written in that very pamphlet-writing age; it attracted the especial notice of the public, and it was attributed to Dunning, afterwards Lord Ashburton, and to Lord Chief Justice Pratt, afterwards Lord Camden. There is, however, quite as much mystery with respect to its Authorship, as to that of the Letters of Junius. It is very evident that Almon did not know by whom it was written. At one time he says:—

"This valuable Law Tract was very generally ascribed to Lord Camden and Mr. Dunning: sometimes distinctly, and sometimes

---

[1] In the list of Almon's publications, prefixed to his pamphlets in 1766, these three tracts follow each other in succession, thus :—

    III. The Principles of the late Changes impartially Examined. By a Son of Candor.

    IV. A Letter concerning Libels and Warrants, &c. By the Father of Candor.

    V. A Letter from Candor to the *Public Advertiser*.

This advertisement affords some corroboration to the belief that Almon considered the publications to be by the same author.

united. But a learned and respectable Master in Chancery[1] was not entirely ignorant of the composition."

Upon the rule for showing cause why the writ of Attachment should not issue for the publication of the *Letter on Libels*, Almon says,—

"Mr. Dunning burst out with astonishing splendour, which gave rise to the report that he was the Author of the Tract. By many people the Tract was supposed to be written by Lord Camden. It certainly contained the whole of his Lordship's doctrine concerning Libels. There was a third gentleman concerned."[2]

In a letter to the *Political Register*, written anonymously by Wilkes, upon the subject of his own public conduct, he alludes to this *Letter concerning Libels*, and quotes the following passage from it :—

"I do not think myself at liberty to scan the *private actions* of any man, but have a right to consider the conduct of every man in public, and to approve or condemn his doings, as they appear to me to be calculated either for the good or the hurt of his country."[3]

Wilkes remarks upon this,—

"I shall not now stay to show how far the equity of this rule was violated by the concealed author himself before he got half through his work, in a manner equally unjust to a sick and absent friend, whom he cruelly wounded."[4]

---

[1] If Almon knew anything of this Master in Chancery, it is strange he did not mention his name. He very likely alludes to Mr. Robert Pratt, the nephew of Lord Camden. This gentleman was elected member for the borough of Horsham, in 1763, through the influence of Lord Irwin, and at the recommendation of Mr. Pitt. He died in 1775, in the fiftieth year of his age. He had been married, but left no issue.

[2] *Biographical and Political Anecdotes*, vol. i. p. 80 and 244.

[3] "As the indulgence of *private malice* and personal slander should be checked and resisted by every legal means, so a constant examination into the characters and conduct of Ministers and magistrates should be equally promoted and encouraged."—*Junius, Preface*, vol. i. p. 352.

"In this paper you will find no reflections upon persons but what are unavoidably connected with things. If your Grace's private advantages can be reconciled to those of the nation, may you enjoy them long. If not, the sacrifice of the public to one man's interest or ambition would, in language at least, be too bad even for modern depravity."—*Letter* [from the Author of Junius] *to the Duke of Grafton*, in 1768, p. 4.

[4] Almon has a note on this passage :—"This celebrated tract has been ascribed to many gentlemen, but the real author has not been named. *He was a noble peer.*"—*Memoirs and Correspondence of Wilkes*, vol. i. p. 245.

Who was the noble peer here alluded to by Almon? It could not be either Lord

The LETTER TO THE PUBLIC ADVERTISER under the signature of
CANDOR is a very spirited and clever composition, written, as the
author professes, because he thinks it high time to show some im-
partiality by letting the world see what may be said in favour of
some of the great men in office; but it is in reality a very sarcastic and bitter attack upon the Ministry, and the author's spleen
is particularly directed against Lord Mansfield, under an ironical
defence of the legal part he acted upon the trials of the Printers of
the *North Briton*. He is said to have—

"clearly instructed the Jury, that the words in the information,
charging the paper to have been published with the most wicked intent,
in order to excite His Majesty's dutiful subjects to sedition, and charging
it to be a false, libellous, and seditious libel, were words of course, like
corrupt in an indictment for perjury, or like those in an indictment for
murder, charging the murder to have been committed *at the instigation
of the devil* [1], and that the Jury ought not to regard them at all, but to
consider merely whether the defendants had published the paper. His
Lordship's summing up was particularly long, pathetic, and explanatory,
and abounded with well-adapted observations and *ingenious distinctions*." [2] . . . . . "In short, the language of law touching libels,
was, in the Court of King's Bench, the same before the Revolution as
it is now. And Lord Jeffreys and Lord Mansfield not only concur
in sentiment, but in expression. But although both of these great
men are remarkable for the abilities they have shown when presiding
in the King's Bench, yet there is a wide difference between their manners and characters. The former was always reckoned a lawyer *bold*
and *courageous*, whereas I never heard any one of these terms applied
to the latter [3]; and in particular, his agreeable and conciliating de-
meanor to a jury is universally admired: . . . . . and he has
withal had the advantage of having ever practised in Courts of Equity;

Camden or Lord Ashburton, because Almon had himself at one time suspected and
named both, and he now, *in his latest publication*, distinctly asserts that *the real author
has not been named*. I believe he did not, with any certainty, know the author, but it
is possible he may here have pointed at Lord Temple, as a conjecture.

[1] "All this, I suppose, too, we shall be told is mere fiction, mere inference of law,
and *the suggestion of the devil*."—*Junius*, vol. iii. p. 300.

[2] "Without pretending to reconcile the *distinctions* of Westminster Hall with the
simple information of common sense, or the integrity of fair argument."—*Ibid.*,
vol. ii. p. 176.

[3] It should be remembered that Candor is writing ironically, and Lord Mansfield is
described by Junius in the *reverse* of these terms, as "*timid, vindictive*, and *irresolute*."
—Vol. ii. p. 168.

which circumstance alone surprisingly softens the rigour of the old common law, and accommodates it more to the humour and turn of the age. In short, he perceives how little regard the old adjudications deserve from a change in the times. He is besides so peculiarly *acute, refined, and logical,* in his *distinctions* between cases of law, which to ordinary men seem to be the same, and to be cases in point; and in trials by jury, he is so able in separating or assembling (as the cause may require) the different parts of the testimony, and in passing over or slurring one fact as immaterial, and enforcing another as material; that he never fails of carrying to every auditor at the time, the appearance of *right or wrong* [1] along with him. What a happiness, therefore, it is to have one's suit determined or tried by a person of so nice a discernment, and of so much judgment and capacity!" . . . . . . "But, as the end of all law is *substantial justice* [2], if *that* be obtained, *in spite of old rules or old cases,* is it not so much the better for the subject, especially if it be compassed in less time and in a more summary way?"

The Author then refers to the practice of requiring sureties for good behaviour in matters of Libel:—

" The two Houses of Parliament concurred in declaring that privilege of Parliament does not extend to the case' of writing and publishing seditious libels, nor ought to be allowed to obstruct the speedy and effectual prosecution of so heinous and dangerous an offence. It was the more necessary to come to such a Resolution, because there was no express case adjudged in the Courts below, wherein sureties for the good behaviour in matters of Libel had been enforced, when opposed by the party accused, although three or four cases of private men, not mem-

---

[1] " The pure and impartial administration of justice is perhaps the firmest bond to secure a cheerful submission of the people, and to engage their affections to Government. *It is not sufficient that questions of private right and wrong are justly decided,* nor that judges are superior to the vileness of pecuniary corruption. Jeffries himself, when the Court had no interest, was an upright judge."—*Junius,* vol. i. p. 399.

" As to lawyers, their profession is supported by the indiscriminate defence of *right and wrong.*"—*Ibid.,* vol. i. p. 498.

" The indiscriminate defence of *right and wrong* contracts the understanding while it corrupts the heart."—*Ibid.,* vol. ii. p. 412.

[2] " Instead of *those certain positive rules* by which the judgment of a court of law should invariably be determined, you have fondly introduced your own unsettled notions of equity and *substantial justice.*"—*Junius to Lord Mansfield,* vol. ii. p. 164.

" One glorious act of *substantial justice.*"—*Ibid.,* vol. ii. p. 216.

"If there were no other way to obtain *substantial justice* for the people."—*Ibid.,* vol. ii. p. 222.

"Easily deceived by the imposing names of equity and *substantial justice.*"—*Ibid.,* vol. ii. p. 392.

" To him at least they will do *substantial justice.*"—*Ibid.,* vol. i. p. 378.

bers of either House, had happened within the memory of all the great
lawyers now living, where surety for keeping the peace had been
strongly insisted upon by the Attorney General, and refused by the
supposed libellers, and wherein, in order to try the point with the
Crown, these last, whilst in custody, sued out writs of Habeas Corpus,
and upon the Attorney General's desiring and obtaining time, but not
coming in consequence of it to make good the point for the Crown,
demanded and obtained their liberty thereupon."

Alluding to Bishop Warburton and the bench of Bishops, on
the subject of the late Peace, he says, —

" And I believe everybody is ready to acknowledge, with a great
Prelate, the truth and excellency of *the Alliance between Church and
State;* and is therefore obliged to him for applying his episcopal
abilities, not long ago, in drawing up a curious piece, wherein he
asserted that the late Peace was *adequate* to our successes [1], and then
sending it for publication to his Great Patron, and surprising him with
this handsome instance of his good faith and gratitude." [2] . . . .
" It is, I trust, the principle of piety which makes them [the Bishops]
concur so cheerfully, and unanimously for the most part, with all
Ministers, observing no worldly distinctions of persons or parties.
They live in brotherly love with all mankind, and worship alone
the Father of Peace; or to speak more according to their own em-
phatical language, *the Great Peace-maker.* And, indeed, their conduct
is of much force, and must make a strong impression, as it is always
accompanied with a decent holy deportment; which induces the be-
holder to consider it as proceeding entirely from the true spirit of the
Gospel. The manner of doing things is certainly of great moment;
and such among the best men is the force of example, that you scarcely
ever see two bishops dissenting from their brethren in a debate. They
are ever resigned to the will of *the Great Disposer of all things.*
Twenty-six such men who would not only act unanimously, but be
earnest also in their respective dioceses in preaching up unanimity and

---

[1] The Address from Bath in favour of the Peace had been sent for presentation to
Mr. Pitt, who then represented that city in Parliament. The Address was drawn up
by Bishop Warburton, and communicated to Mr. Pitt by his friend Mr. Allen, of Prior
Park, to whom he writes upon that subject—" The epithet of *adequate* given to the
Peace, contains a description of the conditions of it so repugnant to my unalterable
opinion concerning many of them, and fully declared by me in Parliament, that it was
as impossible for me to obey the commands of the Corporation in presenting their Address, as it was unexpected to receive such a commission."—*Chatham Correspondence,*
vol. ii. p. 224. There is also an ironical allusion to Bishop Warburton in *Another
Letter to Almon,* p. 151.

[2] It was through the patronage of Mr. Pitt that Warburton had been made Bishop of
Gloucester.

true concord to all men, and in recommending the same doctrine to their inferior and subordinate clergy, might, in my poor apprehension, do a great deal of good in a few years, in these degenerate times; and therefore it is with infinite pleasure that I see *an appearance of piety* so encouraged and countenanced at Court, and the spirit of *the Great Lord* so strongly diffusing itself, by degrees, in this kingdom [1]. We have had nothing like it since the time of Charles the First, excepting a little gleam of short-lived duration, under Queen Anne."

The Author then proceeds with several pages of remarks upon General Warrants, the Seizure of Papers, and the evasion of the writ of Habeas Corpus in the case of Wilkes, in which there are many passages containing phrases and opinions similar to those of the Author of Junius, as well as to those of Lord Temple, particularly in his pamphlet on the *Seizure of Papers*.

He afterwards passes on to an ironical description of the disadvantages of trial by jury, and in allusion to the general purpose of Lord Mansfield to contract the power of juries:—

"For, as the law now stands, *let a juror be ever so inflexible to the direction of a judge, or adhere ever so obstinately to his own opinion; it is* not in the power of that judge to discard him, and have another sworn; nor even, when the next trial comes on, to order the officer, who calls the jury, *to pass him over, if his name should again be drawn*, and to take care that he be never more upon another jury."[2] . . . . .

---

[1] All these scriptural phrases are of course used ironically, and in a political sense. "The *piety* of St. James's," "the *unfeigned piety*, the sanctified religion of George the Third," "the *unforgiving piety* of the Court," "the implacable resentment of a priest," or the "supercilious hypocrisy of a bishop," were always favourite themes with Junius: it may indeed be said, that the irreverent treatment of subjects appertaining to religion was one of his general characteristics.

[2] This is a subject frequently alluded to by Junius: "You ask me, what juryman was challenged by Lord Mansfield? I tell you his name was Benson. *When his name was called, Lord Mansfield ordered the clerk to pass him by.* As for his reasons, you may ask himself, for he assigned none. But I can tell you what all men thought of it. This Benson had been refractory upon a former jury, and would not accept of the law as delivered by Lord Mansfield, but had the impudence to pretend to think for himself." —*Junius*, vol. ii. p. 375.

"When Mr. Benson's name was called, Lord Mansfield was observed to flush in the face (a signal of guilt not uncommon in him), and cried out, *Pass him by*."—*Ibid.*, vol. ii. p. 387. See also *ibid.*, vol. ii. p. 176.

"Or if any Chief Justice should arbitrarily order a juror *to be set aside without any cause of challenge, and forbid his ever being put upon another panel, only because such juror had withstood his directory opinion in a former trial, upon a matter of fact, whereof by his oath he was to form his own judgment.*"—*Letter concerning Libels, &c.*, p. 108.

1 2

" The civil government and the interpretation of the laws and charters of the land, should ever be attentively regarded by all moderate men, let the factious and ambitious of either party struggle as much as they will about who shall be foremost in favour at St. James's, or how to get the best place. A trick, a fraud, or a job, is nothing more than a transitory evil, but *a solemn decision on any constitutional point* is what will be either a lasting security, or an irreparable infringement, of *the liberties of us and our posterity to the remotest generation.*" [1]

In a criticism of Hume's *History of England*, which had been recently published, the Author describes it as—

" in reality *a performance new, entertaining, and singular* [2], and will reconcile any man to the reigns of the Stuarts, who reads it free

---

[1] " Let me exhort and conjure you never to suffer *an invasion of your political constitution, however minute the instance may appear,* to pass by, without a determined persevering resistance. . . . . Be assured that the laws which protect us in our civil rights grow out of the Constitution, and that they must fall or flourish with it. This is not the cause of faction or of party, or of any individual, but the common interest of every man in Britain."—*Junius*, vol. i. p. 342.

" If, when the opportunity presents itself, you neglect to do your duty *to yourselves and your posterity,* to God and to your country, I shall have one consolation left, in common with the meanest and basest of mankind—civil liberty may still last the life of JUNIUS."—*Ibid.,* vol. i. p. 348. . . . . See also the *Letter concerning Libels, &c.,* p. 78.

[2] Junius, in his Preface, recommends *De Lolme's Essay on the English Constitution,* in similar terms, as a " *performance deep, solid,* and *ingenious.*"

Several other instances of the use of three adjectives consecutively, may be found in this pamphlet, as—" His Lordship's summing up was particularly *long, pathetic,* and *explanatory.*" " He is besides so peculiarly *acute, refined,* and *logical.*" " The most *learned, diligent,* and *laborious* inquisitors."

Among many other similar phrases in Junius are the following :—

" A verdict *perplexed, absurd,* or *imperfect.*"—Vol. i. p. 360. " His discourse was *impertinent, ridiculous,* and *unseasonable.*"—Vol. i. p. 374. " Women, and men like women, are *timid, vindictive,* and *irresolute.*"—Vol. ii. p. 168. " Your conduct has been *uniform, manly,* and *consistent.*"—Vol. iii. p. 195. " It was allowed to be *irregular, unprecedented,* and *extrajudicial.*"—Vol. iii. p. 290. " A misrepresentation of Junius, equally *pert, false,* and *stupid.*"—Vol. iii. p. 410.

In the *Letter concerning Libels, &c.,* the same peculiarity may very frequently be found. I select the following :—

" The publication of what is *false, scandalous,* and *seditious.*"—P. 10. " A very *long, refined,* and *elaborate* speech."—P. 18. " The arguments were so *artificial, qualified,* and *verbal.*"—P. 35. " And where there is a charge against one particular paper, to seize *all,* of every kind, is *extravagant, unreasonable,* and *inquisitorial.*"—P. 59. " instead of pursuing the course of established precedents, *inviolably, intrepidly,* and *openly.*"—P. 85. " nor any more general blessing than an *able, uniform, firm,* and *incorruptible* Chief Justice."—P. 110. " It is an *inglorious,* a *disheartening,*

from the prejudice of other histories; that is, who knows no facts but what are related in Mr. Hume, or any other relation of them, and is void of any political or religious principles relative to this Constitution; in short, whose mind is free from the shackles of previous information. It is amazing what a new light he has thrown upon everything: nay, one need but read this author to be satisfied, that we are mistaken in our opinions of all the people of those times, both as to their hearts and their understandings."

CANDOR describes Lord Mansfield as—

" so happy likewise, in a memory, that he forgets nothing, and therefore wants no repetition of matters that have been once laid before him ; nay, I have heard of one familiar and domestic, but remarkable instance of the faithfulness of his recollection, and that is, that he can even remember *all the healths* [1] *he himself has drunk* since his being twelve, or at most fourteen, years of age."

The Author concludes his letter thus :—

" As to the praise of fine writing and ingenuity, let it go where it list,

and a *disadvantageous* thing, to have a successful war followed by an inadequate or insecure peace."—P. 111. " If they are wilfully false they are certainly *malicious, seditious,* and *damnable.*"—-P. 40.

In *Another Letter to Almon,* also :—
" The verdict being *clear, usual,* and *legal.*"—P. 104. " The questions cannot be too direct, *leading,* and *pointed.*"—P. 183. " All this is *fair, equal,* and *just.*"—P. 185. " It cannot be too *pointed, personal,* or *particular.*"—P. 188. " But I grow *old, lazy,* and *stupid.*"—P. 198.

In Lord Temple's pamphlet on the *Seizure of Papers :*—
" They are very ready to purchase exemption from a *hard, expensive,* and *dangerous* prosecution."

In Lord Temple's *Letter from Albemarle Street to the Cocoa Tree :*—
" Content to drag on, like a wounded snake, a *weak, disgraced, disreputable* existence."

In the *Principles of the late Changes,* by Lord Temple :—
" An unexampled encroachment upon the most *inherent,* most *fundamental,* and most *essential* rights of Parliament."

In Lord Temple's *Defence of the North Briton, No.* 45 :—
" Ever since the Favourite's influence became predominant, the *staunch, known,* and *tried* friends of the Royal Family have been depressed."

[1] Junius, in a letter to Lord Mansfield, says,—" The liberal spirit of youth prevailed over your native discretion. Your zeal in the cause of an unhappy Prince was expressed with the sincerity of wine, and some of the solemnities of religion." And in a note he adds,—" This Man was always a rank Jacobite. Lord Ravensworth produced the most satisfactory evidence of his having frequently *drunk the Pretender's health upon his knees.*" When the charge of Jacobitism was originally brought against Lord Mansfield (at that time Mr. Murray), Lord Temple was certainly inclined to enter warmly into the question against him, and his opinions on that question coincided exactly with those of Junius. See *ante,* vol. i. p. 101.

I never had a thought about it, and can be perfectly content with having my words *as plain and artless as my purpose.*" [1]

The LETTER CONCERNING LIBELS, &c., obtained so much notoriety at the time of its publication, and received so much praise, that the Author would certainly have been discovered, or, disregarding consequences, he would have subsequently avowed himself, if there had not been, as was the case with Junius, some strong motives for concealment, and some reasons why he could afford so large a sacrifice of personal vanity.

No individual has ever laid claim to the Authorship of this, or either of the other pamphlets which I have now ventured to attribute to Lord Temple, as the Author also of the Letters of Junius.

The publisher must have gained considerably by the popularity of this tract (for it went through many editions), but he suffered also in purse and person by the prosecution to which he was subjected for the libellous portions of it. Almon, however, was patronized and protected by Lord Temple, and there can be little doubt but that his generous patron contrived in some way to indemnify him for any temporary losses he may have sustained.

If this tract had been really written by Dunning or Chief Justice Pratt, the fact would have become known long ago, but there are no sufficient reasons why it should have ever been supposed to emanate from the pen of a lawyer. It is true, that it abounds in an appearance or affectation of legal research, and many legal opinions are quoted, but there is much more display of law authorities [2], "legal nonsense," and law *jargon*, in the letter of Junius to Lord Mansfield, which might with much greater probability be attributed to a lawyer; but Junius said with all outward appearance of sincerity, and as I believe with perfect truth,—

"*I am no lawyer by profession*, nor do I pretend to be more deeply read than every English gentleman should be in the laws of his country."—*Junius*, vol. i. p. 350.

---

[1] "I speak," says Junius in his Preface, "to *the plain understanding of the people*, and appeal to their honest liberal construction of me."

"For I am a *plain unlettered man.*"—*Ibid.*, vol. i. p. 440.

"I do not presume to instruct the learned, but simply to inform the body of the people."—*Ibid.*, vol. i. p. 553.

[2] Whether of good or bad law is not now the question.

And again he exclaims to Wilkes,—

"Though I use the terms of art, *do not injure me so much as to suspect I am a lawyer.*—I had as lief be a Scotchman.—It is the encouragement given to disputes about titles, which has supported that iniquitous profession at the expense of the community."—*Junius,* vol. i. p. 312.

There is much justice in Horace Walpole's opinion of this tract. He says,—"It is bitter, has much unaffected wit, and is the only tract that ever made me understand law;" and Walpole knew that it could not be the wish or the interest of a lawyer to make law intelligible[1]. Gray, too, in a letter to Walpole on the subject of this tract, asks,—"Is the old man and the lawyer put on, or is it real? Or has some real lawyer furnished a good part of the materials, and another person employed them? This I guess." And probably a good *guess.* Lord Temple no doubt gathered much from books, but he mixed also " sufficiently for the purposes of intelligence, in the conversation of the world." Besides other legal acquaintances, his brother James Grenville was a barrister of Lincoln's Inn, and his intimate friends were the

---

[1] Sir Denis Le Marchant, in mentioning this tract, says that, " As a literary composition, it can claim but moderate praise. The style is loose and careless, and wants the easy flow, the perspicuous diction and classical tastes which may be found in some other contemporary tracts—such, for instance, as Mr. Charles Yorke's *Considerations on the Law of Forfeiture.* In parts it is rather dull, and the materials, valuable as they are, might have been arranged with more effect. They appear to have come from different and unequal hands ; for if the acuteness, wit, and learning of Dunning may be traced through many pages, remarks occasionally occur which could hardly have proceeded from a practising lawyer. I can find no authority in support of the general belief of his being the author. I suspect he only revised it, and that Lord Chatham did the same. There are passages strongly partaking of the spirit and peculiar mode of expression of the latter."—*Note in Walpole's Memoirs of George III.,* vol. iii. p. 166. This opinion rather corroborates my theory of Lord Temple's authorship. Several instances have been mentioned in which Junius uses the peculiar expressions of Lord Chatham, and who so likely to use them as Lord Temple? The authorship of Junius has been by several writers attributed to Lord Chatham, and the best and most intelligent commentator upon, and editor of, the Letters, insisted in 1802, that the Author was no other than Dunning : " He alone," says Heron (*i.e.* Pinkerton), " possessed that knowledge of the constitutional law of England, which Junius has so eminently displayed." But no one in these times believes in the claims of Dunning, and surely none but a writer in the *Dublin Magazine* would *now* venture to assert that Lord Chatham was Junius.

barristers Dayrell[1] and Mackintosh, and these, with Beardmore
his attorney, might be the unconscious purveyors of his legal information; and the collections that remain in his own handwriting show his extensive researches into old law books and
authorities, as well as the public records and journals of Parliament.

The subjects, too, which are treated of in this pamphlet—
General Warrants, the Law of Libel, and the Seizure of Papers
—were all of them those in which Lord Temple had greatly interested himself, and upon which his opinions are as well known
as his friendship for Wilkes, and his devotion to what he conceived to be the cause of truth and constitutional liberty. The
apparently contemptuous notice of Wilkes, both in this Letter and
in that from CANDOR to the *Public Advertiser*, was part of his
plan of concealment, and it will be remembered that the same
plan was sometimes adopted in the Letters of Junius, but it was
only to serve a special purpose, which "wrought to his designs,"
as he afterwards privately confessed to Wilkes:—

"Think no more of what is passed. You did not then stand so well
in my opinion; and it was necessary to the plan of that letter to rate
you lower than you deserved. *The wound is curable, and the scar shall
be no disgrace to you.*"[2]—*Junius*, vol. i. p. 314.

The circumstances mentioned in the following paragraph from
the *Letter concerning Libels, &c.*, are related in a letter to Lord
Temple from Sir John Phillipps[3], and therefore also tend to

---

[1] Dayrell lived in an old Manor House, which formerly stood in the village of Lamport, within half a mile of Stowe : it was pulled down about a dozen years ago, and
its site is now included in Stowe gardens.

There has always been a tradition at Stowe, that Dayrell furnished Junius with
the legal argument for his letter to Lord Mansfield ; I have heard it frequently from the
late Duke of Buckingham, and it is very possible to have been true, for if it were enclosed to Woodfall and addressed to Junius, it would have reached the hands of Lord
Temple, and have been used by him, without any suspicion on the part of Dayrell, who
might indeed have been even urged by Lord Temple to send it to Junius. Dayrell died
at Lamport Manor House, in May, 1816, at the age of seventy-three, and was buried
in the church at Stowe.

[2] Lord Temple made use of the same figurative expression in his pamphlet on the
Principles of the late Changes, by a Son of Candor: " The wound would soon have
closed, without leaving a scar where the shaft passed."

[3] "Sir John Phillipps's compliments wait on Lord Temple, and has underneath

strengthen the probability of Lord Temple's authorship of the pamphlets in question:—

" If by virtue of any resolution of theirs [the House of Commons], whether the same may be pleaded in a regular plea or not, a man be committed to Newgate, the Court of King's Bench will never venture to question the legality of the proceeding. When the Honourable Alexander Murray was so committed, a late great patriot, Sir John Phillipps, put on his gown, and came into the Court on purpose ' to make a motion,' as he phrased it, ' in the cause of Liberty,' and prayed a Habeas Corpus for the said Mr. Murray; which was accordingly granted of course. The cause of his imprisonment returned by the gaoler, was only an order of the House of Commons, without any crime alleged. The Judges said they could not question the authority of that House, or demand the cause of their commitment, or judge the same; and therefore refused to discharge the prisoner, maugre all the patriot's arguments to the contrary, and so remanded him."—P. 75.

The well-known antipathy of Junius to Scotland and Scotchmen finds a parallel in this pamphlet. The author says,—

" And such a horror have I, particularly of the introduction of any new *criminal* law into this country, that, were it to happen, rather than

obeyed his Lordship's commands in regard to the case of Mr. Murray, as far as his memory will serve him, having left the notes he took of that case in the country, and therefore can't remember the particular term or year, but it was some time during the last Parliament."

" In Banco Regis. The King and Alex. Murray.

" Mr. Murray being committed to Newgate by order of the House of Commons, for a contempt, Sir J. P. moved the Court for a writ of Habeas Corpus, to be directed to the Keeper of Newgate to bring Mr. Murray into Court, in order to his being bailed, and upon Sir J. P.'s attempting to give reasons to induce the Court to grant the writ, he was stopped by Mr. Justice Wright (who then presided there in the absence of Lord Chief Justice Lee), and he said, *it was a writ which the subject was entitled to, ex debito justitiæ, therefore take your writ.* Accordingly the writ was granted, and Mr. Murray was brought up in a day or two, when Sir J. P. moved the Court that he should be bailed, and produced an affidavit on that occasion, from his physician, of his ill state of health, which was read, but *the Court refused to bail him, as he was committed by the House of Commons for a contempt, and remanded him to Newgate.* In this case it is to be noted, that the Court of King's Bench granted the writ of Habeas Corpus without any probable cause showed by affidavit, or any affidavit produced at all (the affidavit of the physician being not produced till after the body was brought up), and therefore it appears to have been then the opinion of the Court that the writ should issue of course upon motion."

This letter is not dated: the writer died in the year 1764, some months before this pamphlet was published.

The same case of the Honourable Alexander Murray is also alluded to by Junius in one of his Miscellaneous Letters on Privilege, *Junius*, vol. iii. pp. 362-4.

submit thereto, I should be even for accompanying a noble Law-lord to *Ultima Thule*, which, by the shiver he spoke it with, I guess must be Scotland, the very northern scrag, or bleakest bare bone of the island. A man would fly anywhere in such a case."—P. 30.

*   *   *   *   *   *

" A King of England may be considered in two respects, either in a public or a private capacity. In the latter, he may, as a man, indulge his own humour, in the *establishment of his household, and the choice of his immediate servants*." [1]—P. 5.

On the maxim that *the King can do no wrong*, the author says,—

" In order, however, to preserve a proper respect and chastity of idea with respect to the crowned head, *the royal name is never to be introduced into any question of public transactions*. And therefore it is established as a maxim, *the King can do no wrong*, as doing nothing by himself, but everything by the advice of his Counsel and Ministers. . . . . . As nothing can be done in a limited monarchy but what somebody is to be accountable for it, so every Minister in his department is to be responsible accordingly and to act on his peril." [2]—P. 6.

The author then, in allusion to the *Star Chamber*, observes that —

" The faces of the subject are so ground by this proceeding, that everybody at length is alarmed, *and the people, in struggling with the Crown, happening to get the better*, the patriots of the time seized an occasion, towards the latter end of the reign of *Charles the First*, to extort from that martyr to obstinacy, an Act for the abolition of this most oppressive jurisdiction." [3]—P. 7.

On the liberty of the press, the writer says,—

" There is one great reason why every patriot should wish *this sort*

---

[1] " I should be sorry to confine him [the King], *in the choice of his footmen or his friends*."—*Junius*, vol. ii. p. 257.

[2] " When the Character of the Chief Magistrate is in question, more must be understood, than may safely be expressed. If it be really a part of our Constitution, and not a mere *dictum* of the Law, *that the King can do no wrong*, it is not the only instance, in the wisest of human institutions, where theory is at variance with practice. That the Sovereign of this Country is not amenable to any form of Trial, known to the Laws, is unquestionable. But exemption from punishment is a singular privilege annexed to the royal character, & no way excludes the possibility of deserving it."—*Junius*, vol. i. p. 381.

[3] " Had there been no Star-chamber, there wo.^d have been no Rebellion against Charles the first. The constant Censure & admonition of the press wo.^d have corrected his Conduct, prevented a Civil War, & sav(d him from an ignominious death."—*Junius*, vol. i. p. 384.

of writings to be encouraged; which is, that animadversions upon the *conduct of Ministers, submitted to the eye of the public in print,* must, in the nature of the thing, be *a great check upon their bad actions,* and at the same time an incentive to their doing what is praiseworthy." [1]— P. 39.

" When men find themselves aggrieved by the violence or the misconduct of the persons appointed to the Ministry, it is natural for them to complain, to communicate their thoughts to others, to put their neighbours on their guard, and to remonstrate in print against the public proceedings. . . . . . The liberty of exposing and opposing a bad Administration by the pen is among the necessary privileges of a free people, and is perhaps the greatest benefit that can be derived from the *liberty of the press.* But Ministers, who by their misdeeds provoke the people to cry out and complain, are very apt to make that very complaint the foundation of a new oppression, by prosecuting the same as a libel on the State. Now, the merit of these publications must arise from their being true or false : if they are true, they are highly commendable ; if they are wilfully false, they are certainly malicious, seditious, and damnable." [2]

" —— Although it were obvious to every indifferent person that the unlucky writer had no such intention, nay, had been ready on a former occasion voluntarily to associate *for the defence of His Majesty's title, and to venture his life in the field to support it* [3]. And yet I am fully convinced that were it not for such writings as have been prosecuted by Attorney Generals for libels, we should never have had a revolution, nor his present Majesty a regal crown ; nor should we now enjoy a Protestant religion, or one jot of civil liberty."—P. 41.

The substance of the following passage is borrowed by the

---

[1] Junius on the same subject :—" As the indulgence of private malice & personal slander should be checked & resisted by every legal means, so a constant examination into the Characters and Conduct of Ministers and Magistrates should be equally promoted & encouraged. They, who conceive that our Newspapers are no restraint upon bad men, or impediment to the execution of bad Measures, know nothing of this Country."—Vol. i. p. 352.

[2] Among other passages to the same effect, Junius has the following :—" In that state of abandoned servility & prostitution, to which the undue influence of the Crown has reduced the other Branches of the Legislature, our Ministers and Magistrates have in reality little punishment to fear, & few difficulties to contend with, beyond the Censure of the press, & the spirit of resistance, which it excites among the people."—Vol. i. p. 352.

[3] " Sir, the Man who addresses You in these terms is your best friend. He wo⁴ willingly hazard his Life in defence of your title to the Crown."—*Junius,* vol. i. p. 384.

Author from himself, in his *Letter to the Public Advertiser, by*
CANDOR :—

" But, even if the usage had been both immemorial and uniform, and
ten thousand similar warrants could have been produced, it would not
have been sufficient; because the practice must likewise be agreeable
to the principles of law, in order to be good, whereas this is a practice
inconsistent with, and in direct opposition to, the first and clearest
principles of law. Immemorial uniform usage will not even support
the bye-law of a corporation, if it be flatly repugnant to the fundamentals of the common law; much less will it authorize the secret
practice of a political office." [1]—P. 49.

In speaking of the Lord Chancellor Hardwicke, who had recently died, the Author mentions particularly three great measures,
in all of which he was opposed to the opinions of Lord Temple,
viz. the *Militia Bill*, the new *Habeas Corpus Bill*, and the
Marriage Act. He adds that—

" the same illustrious personage was blessed with a good temper and
great worldly prudence, which are the two handmaids in ordinary to
prosperity; that his whole deportment was amiable, and that he possessed in general the soundest understanding in matters of law and
equity, and the best talents for judicature I had ever seen, that he
might be cited as an example, in this country, of the perfect picture of
a good judge, which my Lord Bacon hath so admirably drawn; and
that he was, in short, a truly wise magistrate. He was free from the
levities, vices, and expenses, which are so commonly the product of a
lively and prurient fancy. His station did not require, nor his genius
furnish him with imagination, wit, or eloquence. And, perhaps, had
he possessed a true taste for the fine arts and the politer parts of
literature, he would never have been so extensive a lawyer, to which,

---

[1] " For after the utmost researches, no one case could be found by the most learned,
diligent, and laborious inquisitors, wherein such a ,warrant had been adjudged legal;
and as to the various forms used from time to time by the clerks of statesmen, ten
thousand of such would not avail, when in direct opposition to the first and clearest
principles of law. Nay, uniform usage will not even support a by-law of a corporation
that is flatly repugnant to the principles of the common law, and much less the secret
and multiform practice of an unconstitutional political office."—*Letter of Candor to the
Public Advertiser*, p. 27.

A repetition of his own phrases and opinions is one of the peculiarities of Junius, and
Dr. Busby, in his work, advocating the claims of De Lolme to be Junius, observes also
that Junius was the constant copyist of himself, and the plagiarist of his own letters,
and that many of the arguments and much of the diction in those letters were borrowed
from other of his productions.

however, the plainness of his education might have somewhat contributed. In short, one might say that Lord Somers and he seem to have been the reverse of each other in every respect."—P. 37.

With respect to Wilkes, the Author says,—

" I must, however, declare, *had I been his constant comrade*, and my doors open to him at all hours, much more the partaker of his loosest pleasures and of his most shameful blasphemies, I should not have stood forth, either in the one House or the other, as the immediate mover of *the poor devil's* public disgrace, censure, prosecution, and ruin, or as the mercenary advocate of his pursuers, unless I had an inclination to convince mankind, that I was regardless of all principle whatever, excepting that of serving a party for my own private interest, and from that motive was willing to act upon any stage, the most inconsistent and most abandoned of all parts, even against the companions of my happiest moments ; and to imprint this lesson upon the world, that no motive whatever of public good or private friendship was at the bottom of my conduct, or even the smaller restraint of common decorum." [1]—P. 32.   . . . .

" When it was directly advanced that it would be *an insult on the understanding* [2] *of* mankind," &c.—P. 19.

[1] In a Letter to the Duke of Grafton, Junius says,—" I have frequently censured Mr. Wilkes's conduct, yet your advocates reproach me with having devoted myself to the service of sedition. . . . . . Remember, my Lord, that you continued your connection with Mr. Wilkes long after he had been convicted of those crimes, which you have since taken pains to represent in the blackest colours of blasphemy and treason. . . . . . For my own part, my Lord, I am proud to affirm, *that if I had been weak enough to form such a friendship, I would never have been base enough to betray it.*"—Vol. i. p. 460.

" Is this [the Duke of Grafton] the man who dares to talk of Mr. Wilkes's morals ? . . . . . Was he not the bosom friend of Mr. Wilkes, whom he now pursues to destruction ?"—*Junius*, vol. i. p. 494.

[2] " To exaggerate the enormity of such proceedings would be to *insult the lowest understanding* in this country."—*Lord Temple on the Seizure of Papers.*

" To expatiate on the terrible consequences of seizing papers would be to *insult*, not *the understanding*, but the feelings, of the meanest capacity."—*Letter from Albemarle Street to the Cocoa Tree, by Lord Temple.*

" If they invaded the rights of the people, they did not dare to offer a direct *insult to their understanding.*"—*Junius*, vol. i. p. 479.

" I fear you would consider it as a mockery of your established character, and *an insult to your understanding.*"—*Ibid.*, vol. i. p. 572.

" I reverence the character of Charles the First as little as Mr. Horne, but I will not *insult his misfortunes* by a comparison that would degrade him."—*Ibid.*, vol. ii. p. 309.

" You violate your own rules of decorum when you do not *insult the man whom you have betrayed.*"—*Ibid.*, vol. ii. p. 402.

" To say that they are, is an *insult to the common understanding of mankind.*" — *Ibid.*, vol. iii. p. 31.

" Nor do a public injury without *insulting the public understanding.*"—*Ibid.*, vol. iii. p. 91.

With respect to the Seizure of Papers—

"Many gentlemen have *secret correspondences*[1], which they keep from their wives, their relations, and their bosom friends. Everybody has some private papers that he would not on any account *have revealed*. A lawyer hath frequently the papers and securities of his clients; a merchant or agent of his correspondents."—P. 54. . . . . .

"But I would have such things as *emergent*[2] necessities applied to his pardon, and not to his justification."—P. 50. . . . .

"Some old gentleman of the same Tory *kidney*."[3]—P. 52. . . . .

"They can never be brought to act fairly by the people, let the ground be *ever so good*."—P. 99. . . . .

"Let liberty in general be *ever so much concerned*, or his own fortune be *ever so great*, or his expectancies *ever so vast*."—P. 99. . . .

"Wherever the law was clear, they would not suffer it to be violated by any person, *ever so high, or ever so great*."[4]—P. 78. . . . . .

[1] "Every man who has papers has his *secret* and confidential *correspondences*. . . . The merchant has his *secrets* of trade, the philosopher his discoveries in science. . . . Secrets that may cost a man his life; secrets, of which there are many, that though they can neither affect life nor liberty, yet some men would rather die than *have discovered;* the *revealing* of which may render life insupportable," &c.—*Lord Temple's Pamphlet on the Seizure of Papers.*

[2] "Because no point of time, nor *emergent* circumstance, can alter the Constitution, or create a right not antecedently adherent."—*Lord Temple's Speech on the Suspending and Dispensing Prerogative.*

[3] "The writer is of that *kidney*."—*Principles of the late Changes*, p. 19.

[4] "Any verdict, *ever so deficient*, may be good at that rate."—*Another Letter to Almon*, p. 79.

"Let the name of the judge be *ever so respectable*."—*Ibid.*, p. 145.

"At any price, *ever so exorbitant;* let the inconveniency to the public be *ever so grea*."—*Ibid.*, p. 150.

"Let a juror be *ever so inflexible*, or adhere *ever so obstinately*."—*Candor to the Public Advertiser*, p. 41.

"Let men, however, differ *ever so widely* in other respects."—*Ibid.*, p. 11.

"And the greatest man, be he *ever so cautious*."—*Ibid.*, p. 11.

"But, strictly speaking, injustice cannot be justified, let it be committed *ever so unwittingly*."—*Ibid.*, p. 23.

"Nor will they join in a cry against any man, were he *ever so culpable* in other respects," &c.—*Lord Temple's Defence of the North Briton.*

"Supposing them *ever so regardless* of what they owe to the public."—*Junius*, vol. ii. p. 48.

"And now let the judicial decisions of the House of Commons be *ever so extravagant*, let their declarations of the law be ever so flagrantly false," &c.—*Ibid.*, vol. ii. p. 142.

"If a member of the House of Commons were to conduct himself *ever so improperly*."—*Ibid.*, vol. ii. p. 229.

"There are people about me whom I would wish not to contradict, and who would rather see Junius in the papers *ever so improperly* than not at all."—*Ibid.*, vol. i. p. 199.

"That no officer, let his age and infirmities be *ever so great*, and his services *ever so distinguished*."—*Ibid.*, vol. iii. p. 441.

In a Postscript to the *Letter concerning Libels, &c.*, the author replies to a pamphlet entitled *Considerations on the Legality of General Warrants.* He quotes a resolution of the House of Commons :—

" *That the searching and sealing of the chambers, studies, and papers of Mr. Holles, Mr. Selden, and Sir John Elliot, being members of Parliament, and issuing out warrants for that purpose, are breaches of privilege.*" [1]—*Postscript,* p. 8.

The subject of sureties for the good behaviour in matters of Libel is particularly alluded to by CANDOR in his letter to the *Public Advertiser,* and also in the *Letter concerning Libels, &c.* The former says,—

" Because there was no express case adjudged in the Courts below, wherein sureties for the good behaviour in *matters of libel had been enforced, when opposed by the party accused,* although three or four cases of private men, not members of either House, had happened within the memory of all the great lawyers now living, *where surety for keeping the peace had been strongly insisted upon by the Attorney General, and refused by the supposed libellers,* and wherein in order to try the point with the Crown, these last, whilst in custody, sued out writs of Habeas Corpus, and *upon the Attorney General's desiring and obtaining time, but not coming in consequence of it, to make good the point for the Crown, demanded and obtained their liberty thereupon.*"— P. 15.

And in the *Letter concerning Libels, &c.,* as follows :—

" It is further observable, that there is no adjudged case where this demand of surety for the peace in libel, has been determined to be legal : the Crown hath in some cases, as in that of *Mr. Amherst and others, after insisting upon it, avoided having the point determined, and*

---

[1] Among other collections from the Journals of Parliament relating to privilege, I found the following in Lord Temple's handwriting, and the extract was probably made for this pamphlet :—

" July 6, 1641. " Resolved, upon the question that the issuing out of warrants from the Lords and others of the Privy Council, compelling Mr. Hollis and the rest of the members of that Parliament (3 Car.) during the Parliament to appear before them, is a breach of the privilege of Parliament by those Lords and others.

" *That the searching and sealing of the chamber, study, and papers of Mr. Hollis, Mr. Selden, and Sir J. Elliot, being members* of this House, and during the Parliament, *and issuing of warrants to that purpose, was a breach of the privilege of Parliament,* and by those that executed the same."

relinquished the claim to it, but not till the last minute; it is contrary to the general principles and notions of law; and it may be the means of great oppression." [1]

Again, in the *Letter concerning Libels, &c.*:—

" Already almost anything that a man writes may, by the help of that useful and ingenious key to construction, an *inuendo*, be explained to scandalize Government, and of course be a libel; and could ' the last-mentioned impediments (*i. e.* juries) be totally removed, instead of being only now and then got the better of by the dexterity of a judge, no writing whatever could possibly escape conviction." [2]—P. 10.

There is still another publication which I would attribute to the same author—the Author of Junius. It is entitled, ANOTHER LETTER TO MR. ALMON, IN MATTER OF LIBEL, and was not published until 1770 [3], when Junius was in the full bloom of his popu-

---

[1] I have found among Lord Temple's papers a memorandum of " *Bails taken in Trinity vacation,* 1754," and, according to a note in his own handwriting, he procured them from " Mr. Athorpe, one of the principal officers in the Crown Office, who was concerned for *Mr. Amherst* as his Clerk in Court."
In the case of " Nicholas Amherst, Mr. Athorpe says that this was spoke to at Sergeant's Inn Hall, when Chief Justice Willes declared it was *oppressive and against law* to demand security for good behaviour." " N.B. In Easter term, 10th George II., about the time of Mr. Amherst, but previous to his case, many recognizances were taken by the Secretaries of State where security was given for good behaviour; *but Mr. Amherst absolutely refusing, they gave it up as to him.* One general observation Mr. Athorpe makes, that security for good behaviour has *always been insisted upon, but as constantly given up, where the party has disputed the legality of the demand.*"
It will have been seen from the above, that the *fact* of Mr. Amherst's having refused to give the required security, and of its being consequently not insisted upon, as well as the *opinion* that to require it was *oppressive and against law,* corresponds exactly with the statement in the *Letter of Candor,* and in the *Enquiry, &c.,* and therefore, I think that this memorandum by Lord Temple corroborates my theory, that he was the Author of those pamphlets.

[2] In Lord Temple's *Defence of the North Briton, No.* 45, as quoted by Almon, there is the following parallel passage :—" A political paper wrote a great many years ago to expose the danger of making writings criminal by *inuendoes,* proved a treatise on the small-pox to be the blackest treason, by translating the word *variol* to mean *government,* and adapting every other term according to the same dictionary. Sure no other method can succeed in proving that there is an insult aimed at the King in this Paper."

[3] It is dated August 5th, in that year, and it must have occupied the author's attention for some weeks previously. There are no private communications from Junius to Woodfall between the months of March and October, nor any Letter under the signature of " Junius " between May and November, except a short one to Lord North, published on the 28th of August, and two or three under other signatures in June and July. The Letter to Lord North was probably sent to Woodfall about the 26th or 27th, at which time Lord Temple was on his way through London from Stowe to Dorsetshire. Lady Chatham writes to Mr. Grenville on the 27th,—" By my last letter from Stowe

larity [1]. The same subjects, the same political opinions, the same phrases, and the general similarity of style, sufficiently identify the writer of this letter with the publications already mentioned, although it is neither signed CANDOR nor the FATHER OF CANDOR. He speaks of himself as " formerly of Gray's Inn," from whence the Letter of CANDOR to the *Public Advertiser* in 1764 was dated. In this pamphlet he affects a tone of more than usual humility, and professes to—

" fling out his disinterested reflections, grounded as to names and doctrines upon the magazines and registers, without being at all sure that they are genuine or just ; but an old and feeble man, *no barrister, though formerly bred for one of the Inns of Court*, and still intimate with lawyers, may perhaps here and there suggest what is more worthy of observation than the rabble of Gazetteers, or the 'listed writers of a party. I do not pretend to be free from prejudice, although I wish to be so, but every man is insensibly warped by the company he keeps. An occasional residence in town, and dinner parties at law taverns, and meetings at law coffee-houses, furnish me with most of my information, for I have not, thank God! seen the inside of a Law Court for many a year, and being above want, and past ambition, I care not *three straws* [2] who is Minister."—P. 138.   .   .   .   .

" Twenty absurd or unjust verdicts will not weigh *as a straw*," &c. —P. 131.

As if to anticipate and destroy any suspicion which might arise from a comparison of his style, he says :—

my brother Temple is to be at Eastbury [Dorsetshire] to-morrow, but I don't understand from it that it is his purpose to extend his excursions any further this year, so that the visit to Hagley will not take place." And in a letter from Burke to Lord Rockingham, dated *Gregories*, September 8th, he says :—" Lord Temple was not at the races [Aylesbury]. Lady T. had been taken ill in Dorsetshire." In the same letter Burke mentions that Lord Chatham had been three days at George Grenville's at Wotton.

[1] " I have lately read a good part, not the whole, of a pamphlet on the late verdicts. It is called *A Letter to Almon.* They give it to Lord Camden [a]. If it be his I think his rancour far outran his judgment. Though there are good hits in it, and some part, as I imagine, very sound doctrine, he would certainly have answered his purpose much better if he had shown less malevolence and personal enmity in the cause."—*Burke to Lord Rockingham*, Sept. 23, 1770.

[2] " No indifferent man would care *three straws*," &c.—*Candor*, p. 25.

" Would be, if attempted, worth *one single straw*."—*Letter concerning Libels, &c.*, p. 78.

[a] It will be remembered that the *Letter concerning Libels, &c.*, had also been by some, and with as little probability, attributed to Lord Camden.

"*The deficiency of deep professional learning and practice, must excuse my want of neatness in legal expression*[1], and the seeming elaborate verboseness of my style may crave some pardon, as it is partly occasioned by the desire of being fully understood, and *partly by disguise of writing*, a natural scantiness of expression, and a very confined sphere of conversation. And I need not add, that if I did not regard some persons as superior beings, and capable therefore of doing much good or hurt, I should not have so much attended to their proceedings, so that my making them the topic of observation is panegyric, as far as *my poor words*[2] can scatter either praise or blame."—P. 198.   .   .

—— " The sole sensible construction of the verdict, in *my poor opinion*, is."—P. 119.   .   .   .   .

" Having really and truly *no connection with great political men*[3] I am very little concerned about their sentiments with respect to myself. The only matter that creates any uneasiness, in my desultory way of writing, is, lest I should draw a suspicion upon any other person of being the Author, which I should be heartily sorry for. It might injure such man with his friends. And yet where a story is told one, or a sentiment thrown out, or particular ways of reasoning, or modes of expression used, which happen to strike, it is difficult to avoid the repetition of them with one's pen, in such a manner as to create with others a surmise, that they, the original ventors of them, are the printing author, or to induce a belief in themselves, that some companion may have made an unfair use of what hath been dropped by

---

[1] " I shall not think myself answered though I should be convicted of a mistake in terms, or *of misapplying the language of the law*."—*Junius*, vol. i. p. 351.

" And though it may be bold for one of those not entitled, and not expected to be so learned in the Constitution, and *with still less pretensions to be learned in the law*."—*Lord Temple's Speech on the Suspending and Dispensing Prerogative.*

[2] " Might in *my poor apprehension*."—*Candor to the Public Advertiser*, p. 19.

" In my *poor opinion*, if the resolution had been agreed to."—*Letter concerning Libels, &c.*, p. 78. " It would in *my poor opinion* be of infinite use."—*Ibid.*, p. 65. " And in *my poor opinion* had they done so."—*Ibid.*, p. 14.

" If, however, *my poor attempt*."—*Junius*, vol. iii. p. 47. " Mine, I confess, are *humble* labours."—*Ibid.*, vol. i. p. 553.

[3] " Lord Temple said he was himself of *no party, nor connected with any party*."—*Walpole's Mem. Geo. III.*, vol. ii. p. 113.

" Be assured that he is a man quite unknown and *unconnected*."—*Junius, private Letter to Mr. Grenville*, see vol. iv. p. 354. " I have no *connection with any party*."—*Ibid.*, see vol. iv. p. 381.

" In short, *I am of no party*."—*Candor*, p. 24.

" If I were *a party writer*."—*Junius*, vol. iii. p. 166. "*If I were only a party man, I should naturally concur in any enterprise likely to create a bustle without risk or trouble to myself*."—*Junius to Wilkes*, No. 77.

them in private conversation [1], and from thence to be uneasy and to suspect, perhaps, several of their occasional intimates.   Let me, therefore, protest, that I wish to be guilty neither of betraying [2] what has fallen under the general sanction of free gentlemanly discourse, nor to hurt any particular man; but to plead for myself, that a thorough scrupulous attention to such delicacies would prevent my writing at all, and that I trust is more than any individual has a right, upon such ground, to exact from me.   Indeed, the more I relish a man's discourse, the worse I shall use him at this rate.   Now, I am not given to talk much, but I sit a great many hours in coffee-houses, where I cannot help listening to the discourse of young disputatious barristers, who are inclined to show their talents in argument, and their ingenuity in observations on what has passed, to whet their tongues for the bar, by discussing points, and to acquire a little modest assurance in speaking before company.   These staid counsellors of no business, retainers to great men, idle Members of Parliament, old benchers, and other loquacious, legal, political gentry, that newspapers and nothing to do bring in my way, are, I confess, my best sources of intelligence, and the oracles I consult for the better understanding of what I read in political pamphlets.   Being unaccustomed to gain my subsistence by my pen, and not having acquired the knack of writing, I am fain very often to use the words of the persons from whom I derive my knowledge, from a poverty of expression that I labour under, and an unreadiness in law-language, a propriety in which, nothing but practice at the bar will give.   My fearfulness, therefore, in misreporting what I have heard, must in some measure apologize for my not having varied so much as I could wish, the habit, dress, and peculiarity of the relations which I retail.   For I solemnly declare, I should be ashamed, wantonly, to make any illiberal use of what men of honour have very unadvisedly uttered in my presence.   But what is said in a coffee-

---

[1] Several writers upon the Authorship of Junius have noticed the very numerous and striking proofs of identity in peculiar phrases and opinions which are to be found in the writings of Junius and the Speeches of Lord Chatham.   They are so remarkable as to render it almost certain that some of the Speeches attributed to Lord Chatham must have been reported by Junius.   These circumstances, however, are easily accounted for, when it is considered that the materials of which they were composed were probably the result of *conversations* between Lord Chatham and Lord Temple, perhaps even partly suggested by the latter, and afterwards communicated by himself to the journals he desired to patronize.   With the exception of a short period in their lives, it is well known that a very close intimacy existed between them, cemented, too, by the affection which the latter always evinced towards his sister, Lady Chatham.

[2] " I mean neither to *betray private conversations*. . . . . I pretend to no anecdotes of Cabinets, nor will I indulge myself even in conjectures on past stipulations."— *Word at Parting.* See *post,* vol. iv. p. 202.

house, a public walk, or at a mixed dinner, cannot be deemed a perfect secret, and I have foreborne alluding in the least to any of them, and have delivered everything in my own anonymous person. What I here say, I apply to the middling gentleman, who, perhaps, is of a particular party, and though a retainer to it, a man of worth ; for as to the leading men of all parties, I have long ceased to think they mean anything but power, places, wealth, and titles, without caring at all for the public, and if they do the State any good, it is by accident, or because it suits some present purpose of their own, and not for the sake of the com· munity, or of pure patriotism itself."—P. 142.

" If any private reflections have escaped from me, I shall lament the lapse, for I bear no personal enmity to any man breathing, and wish only to advert to their public conduct, meaning to die in the same mediocrity and obscurity I have lived, and whilst I stay here to judge of men's actions by my own understanding, and not by the political glosses, either of their admirers or their satirists."—P. 198.

In allusion to Lord Mansfield's conduct, in the case of Wood-fall, the author says :—

" But I will not animadvert upon so miserable a ground for the punishment of any fellow-creature. To call such a determination law, or sense, would be doing an injury to both. *The poverty of human language*[1] *is such, that it does not produce any expression sufficiently demeaning*, to give the proper name or epithet to so pitiful a degradation of the talent of rationality."—P. 28.

And again :—

" Supposing, however, that a jury, finding no special verdict, should not find a general verdict in the usual phrase, guilty, or not guilty, as they ought to do, but in some other words, such words must certainly be entered on the record, if the Judge accepts them. Where their meaning is dubious, or incomplete, the Judge may refuse to accept them, and it must always be his fault, if any uncertain verdict be taken. It is *his duty* to point out to them the defect, whatever it be, and to make them explain themselves, or to *send them back* for further consideration."[2]—P. 59.

" Where the paper is not *like a law instrument, drawn in technical,*

---

[1] *Our language has no term of reproach,* the mind has no idea of detestation, which has not already been happily applied to you and exhausted."—*Junius to Lord Mansfield,* vol. ii. p. 160.

[2] " If he (Lord Mansfield) had known *his duty, he should have sent the jury back.* I speak advisedly, and am well assured that no lawyer of character in Westminster Hal will contradict me."—*Junius,* vol. i. p. 363.

legal expressions, nor the devise of property (the *creature*[1] of law), *it wants no comment of lawyers*[2], and it is the proper province of laymen to put a proper construction thereon," &c.—P. 128. . . . .

"Constructive guilt, the *creature* of the bench, will not be endured." —P. 144. . . . . .

"In the King *against Bingley*, the defendant was obstinate, and would not be examined; the consequence of which was, his being committed to prison for his contempt, in not submitting to be examined, and there lay for two years, till the Crown thought the matter might by and by occasion some serious complaint, and therefore he was let out, in the same *contumacious* state he had been put in, with all his sins about him, unanointed and unannealed. If my memory does not fail me, there was some coquetry between the Court and the Attorney-General upon this very article, about who should undergo the ridicule of letting him escape."[3]—P. 189.

The following passages are also selected from "*Another Letter to Almon*,"—

[1] In a letter to Mr. Grenville, in February, 1770, Lord Temple uses this expression: —"As far as justice will permit against two *creatures* of the Court." "They declared themselves to be mere *creatures* of execution."—*Junius*, vol. iii. p. 17.

[2] "When the laws, plain of themselves, are thus illustrated by facts, and their uniform meaning established by history, *we do not want the authority of opinions, however respectable, to inform our judgment, or to confirm our belief.*"—*Junius*, vol. ii. p. 427.

"Though I do not pretend to be as infallible a lawyer as Lord Chief Justice Willes, nor even as Lord Chief Justice ———, yet, *if I am to use the forbidden weapons in law, common reason, and common interpretation of words*," &c.—*Lord Temple to Wilkes.* See *ante*, vol. i. p. 328.

"*He would not take the law from the judges, as to the main principles of it*, any more than he would ask the Bench of Bishops about the great outlines of his religion." —*Lord Temple's Speech on the Habeas Corpus Bill in* 1758.

[3] The above is the passage quoted by Junius as a note in his Letter to Lord Mansfield; not, however, *verbatim*, but with such alterations as an author would make in his own composition. In the manuscript copy of the note, still extant in Mr. Woodfall's possession, the word *contumacious* was originally written *contumelious*, and subsequently altered, but in such a manner as to leave it doubtful which word was intended to remain, and consequently, in the Author's edition of 1772, the word stands *contumelious*. In Woodfall's editions of 1812 and 1814 it is *contumacious*. Junius was probably indifferent which word was used; he thought them synonymous. But this apparently trifling alteration furnishes presumptive evidence that *Another Letter to Almon* was written by Junius.

In another part of the pamphlet (p. 170) the author says:—"The vulgar sense of the word *contempt* has created the confusion. All *contumacy* of, or *contumely* upon, the person, expressions, and sentiments of a judicial officer and magistrate, by word of mouth or writing, is, in common parlance, a *contempt*." See also p. 164.

" *In God's name* [1], is there to be no certainty from henceforth in the law?"—P. 123. "*In God's name,* let the treatment of any judge," &c. —P. 171. " Can any man of *common sense* and honour say ?"—P. 84. " By what maxim of law or *common sense ?*"—P. 14. " For my own part, being *one of the people.*" [2]—P. 178. " It was in truth a mere *oratorial* [3] excrescence."—P. 183. "*Come forth* [4], therefore, and answer directly,"—P. 61. "There is a report, too, whether *well or ill founded.*" [5] —P. 111. " They will resist it as Hampden did the *pittance of ship money* demanded from him, or as the Americans do the payment of the paltry *tea duty.*" [6]—P. 137.

The Author concludes his letter at p. 158, " *And so, Mr. Almon, I wish you good night.*" And again in the postscript, " *And so, once more, good night.*" [7]

---

[1] " *In God's name,* what business have private men," &c.—CANDOR *to Public Advertiser,* p. 11. " *In the name of common sense.*"—*Ibid.,* p. 41. " *In the name of God* and the laws."—*Junius,* vol. iii. p. 31. " *In God's name,* let him retire."—*Ibid.,* vol. ii. p. 380. " *For God's sake,* Sir."—*Ibid.,* vol. iii. p. 399. " But *in the name of common sense.*"—*Ibid.,* vol. iii. p. 183. " In *the name of decency and common sense.*"—*Ibid.,* vol. iii. p. 331.

" Is this now, *in the name of common sense.*"—*Letters concerning Libels, &c.,* p. 48. " But, *in God's name,* what have damages to do with the great point," &c.—*Ibid.,* p. 66. " *I vow to God* I am astonished at it."—*Ibid.,* p. 111.

[2] " I speak to the people as *one of the people.*"—*Junius,* vol. ii. p. 346.

[3] " I promise you you will be as well able to judge of his *oratorial* powers."—*Ibid.,* vol. iii. p. 287.

[4] " *Stand forth,* my Lord, for thou art the man."—*Junius,* vol. i. p. 506. " *Come forward,* thou worthy representative of Lord Bute."—*Ibid.,* vol. ii. p. 155. " *Come forward* to your people."—*Ibid.,* vol. ii. p. 87. " *Come forward,* thou virtuous Minister."—*Ibid.,* vol. ii. p. 53.

[5] " What do we care *whether* this dormant and antiquated claim of the Crown *be well or ill founded.*"—*Junius,* vol. iii. p. 55. " *Whether* you have guessed *well or ill,*" &c.— *Ibid.,* vol. i. p. 196. " How *well or ill* we have argued."—*Ibid.,* vol. iii. p. 147.

[6] I have quoted this passage because, in one of the Letters of Junius, written almost at the same date, the two subjects of *Ship money* and *Tea duty* occur within a few lines of each other, thus—" Had *Mr. Hampden* reasoned and acted like the moderate men of these days, instead of hazarding his whole fortune in a law-suit with the Crown, he would have quietly paid *the twenty shillings demanded of him.* In the repeal of those acts which were most offensive to America, the Parliament have done everything but remove the offence. They have relinquished the revenue, but judiciously taken care to preserve the contention. It is not pretended that the continuance of *the tea duty* is to produce any direct benefit whatsoever to the mother country."—*Junius,* vol. ii. p. 146-7.

[7] This mode of ending a letter has been noticed as a peculiarity in Junius. In the private note (No. 5) to Woodfall, he ends,—" *And so I wish you a good night.*" And in No. 46,—" *So farewell.*" The same peculiarity, if such it can be called, occurs several times in the letters of Lord and Lady Temple.

Some months afterwards, in December of the same year, was published, by *Miller*, "A SECOND POSTSCRIPT to a late Pamphlet, entitled A LETTER TO MR. ALMON IN MATTER OF LIBEL, by the Author of that Letter;" with the following motto :—

"*And thus was fulfilled the* LAW, *and the* PROPHETS."[1]

The Postscript is written in the same style as the Letter itself, and was occasioned by the delivery of the unanimous judgment of the Court of King's Bench, in the King against Woodfall. Several phrases may be found in it similar to some used by Junius. At p. 30, the Author affects ignorance of Woodfall. Alluding to the *Letter to the King*, he says, " *One* Woodfall, it seems, originally printed the paper in question, in the *Public Advertiser*."

In the Memoirs of Almon, published under the title of the *Memoirs of an Eminent Bookseller*, at page 74, there is a quotation from a letter signed *Phileleutherus Anglicanus*, on the subject of Almon's trial for the publication of the well-known *Letter concerning Libels, Warrants, &c.*, and which, upon the authority of Almon, is there said to have been written by the author of that celebrated tract[2].

A series of four letters, signed *Phileleutherus Anglicanus*, had recently appeared in the *Public Advertiser*—the first on Saturday, the 15th of December, 1770, and the others on the three succeeding Saturdays; and on Saturday, the 2nd of February, 1771, they were collected and published in the form of a tract, under the following title:—"A SUMMARY OF THE LAW OF LIBEL: in Four Letters, signed PHILELEUTHERUS ANGLICANUS, addressed

---

[1] This phrase was used by Lord Temple in a reply to his sister Lady Chatham, who, in August, 1775, had asked him for the loan of £1000, in consequence of the illness of Lord Chatham and his inability to attend to any affairs of business. In complying with her request, Lord Temple says :—

"Though nothing can be more contrary to my own sacred *Law, and to my own Prophets*, than entering into an account of the nature you propose, yet the great distress you describe in the present moment is too grievous for me not, in this instance, to be my own Pope, and give myself absolution ; I have therefore sent an order to Mr. Coutts," &c.

[2] I mention Almon's authority for as much as it is worth. I have already stated my belief that he did not with any *certainty* know who was the author.

to, and printed in, the *Public Advertiser*, by H. S. Woodfall. London: Printed for S. Bladon, in Paternoster Row. 1771."

It is presumptive evidence that Woodfall considered these Letters to be written by the author of *Another Letter to Almon in Matter of Libel*, because he has prefixed to his advertisement of the above-mentioned tract, a notice that it was printed in type of the same size as *Another Letter, &c., to which it will be a very proper supplement.* For this and other reasons, I have no doubt that *Phileleutherus* was *Candor*[1], and I repeat my belief that *Candor* was *Junius.*

Phileleutherus describes himself to be "*a speculative and not a practising lawyer,*" and it will be remembered that Junius, among other similar expressions, said, "*I am no lawyer by profession;*" and the author of *Another Letter to Almon*, &c., calls himself "*no barrister, though formerly bred for* [not in] *one of the Inns of Court, and still intimate with lawyers.*"

Phileleutherus says too, in allusion to certain legal doctrines,—

"But I trust men will not, in a plain matter, suffer themselves to be *talked out of their senses.*"

And Lord Temple, in his pamphlet on the *Seizure of Papers*, has the following passage to the same effect:—

"The reason is most inadequate, and must appear so to every man who is not *beat out of his senses* by the jargon of lawyers, or confounded in his own ideas with the quibbles of *legal nonsense.*"[2]

Several other phrases and words used by *Phileleutherus* will occur to the reader as in some degree peculiar to Junius; as, for instance, "whether their opinions be *well or ill founded;*"— "*a multitude* of variable circumstances;"—"*In the name of common sense,*" &c.—"Now, if this be his sincere opinion, and that it is possible, *I am well assured*, from what I know of very sensible men in particular *points,*" &c.

There is also a passage in the third letter of *Phileleutherus*

---

[1] I have before mentioned (*ante*, page clix) that the productions of Candor have been attributed to Lord Camden, and so appears to have been the opinion of "*A Candid Enquirer*," in the *Public Advertiser* for January 10, 1771, who addresses Phileleutherus as *alias* Lord Camden.

[2] See other parallels from Junius, &c., *ante*, page clxxxii.

which appears to me very conclusively to connect him with the Author of Junius, and with an anonymous letter addressed to Calcraft on Sunday, the 9th of December, 1770, and by him immediately communicated to Lord Chatham, who made use of the substance of it in his speech in the House of Lords on the following day[1]. *Phileleutherus* says :—

" There were *two motions made to the Court*, in consequence of the verdict in the *King against Woodfall; the one* was, ' *to stay the entering up of judgment on the verdict;*' and *the other,* ' *that the verdict might be entered up according to the legal import of the finding of the jury.*'[2] On the latter motion, *the counsel were encouraged to go into what passed at the trial,* and the Chief Justice declared it was *necessary to report the whole* "[3].

" Now, these things pass my understanding[4]. Because nothing can be requisite for the Court to determine such motion but the charge, the plea, and the finding of the jury. It was known, and is allowed to be clear law, that the verdict must be entered in the words it was delivered. . . . The report of the evidence, the arguments of counsel, or directions of the Judge, cannot be of any use. No such collateral matter ought to be admitted. *The Court cannot travel out of the record*[5] in quest of something to ground their opinion upon : they must *confine themselves to the very words of the finding,* applying them to the information and plea, and then see what will be their effect."

" Such report, therefore, was unnecessary and impertinent, the legality of the Judge's directions was not in judgment before the Court, and they could not give any opinion thereon without doing what was

---

[1] For an account of this letter, and Lord Chatham's speech, see *ante,* page cxv.

[2] "The verdict given in Woodfall's trial was ' guilty of printing and publishing *only,*' upon which *two motions were made in Court:* one, *in arrest of judgment,* by the defendant's counsel, grounded upon the ambiguity of the verdict; the other, by the counsel for the Crown, for a rule upon the defendant to show cause *why the verdict should not be entered up according to the legal import of the words.*"—*Junius,* vol. i. p. 369, and vol. iii. p. 302.

[3] "On both motions a rule was granted, and soon after *the matter was argued before the Court of King's Bench.* The noble judge, when he delivered the opinion of the court upon the verdict, went *regularly through the whole of the proceedings,*" &c.—*Junius,* vol. i. p. 369, and vol. iii. p. 302.

[4] "I *vow to God* this sort of reasoning *passes my understanding.*"—*Second Postscript to a late Pamphlet,* &c., p. 24.

[5] "And the court, in considering whether the verdict shall be established or not, are so *confined to the record,* that they cannot take notice of anything that does not appear on the face of it; in the legal phrase, they cannot *travel out of the record.*"—*Junius,* vol. i. p. 369, and vol. iii. p. 303.

extrajudicial and irregular[1]; and consequently this determination was
a rash and voluntary act, and can carry no legal authority whatever
with it.   Did not we know that Lord Mansfield's practice needs no
support, one would be tempted to suppose that these directions were
first *slid in upon the Court for the sake of procuring their sanction*[2],
*and afterwards into a superior judicature for the like end.   .   .   .   .
Nothing but a motion for a new trial, upon the ground of misdirections
to the jury, could bring the matter before the Court*[3].   .   .   .   .

"But if what was ruled in the *King against Woodfall* be intended,
as I conceive it is, for a complete code of the Law in Libel, I am surprised to read in the newspapers, that the noble Penner[4] hath declined
answering some plain questions put for the more clear ascertainment of
his doctrine, and its binding force as a judgment.   When four months
had been taken finally to settle it, and it was officiously intruded upon
the great world as complete, the intimation of a doubt about its meaning, especially from a peer of the same profession[5], should have produced an immediate explanation[6].   But *that* is refused[7], and the opinion
is to remain a dark lanthorn for political application hereafter.   It was
asserted in another place that the noble Judge avowed to everybody his
adjudication, and wished for nothing more than an opportunity of fully
declaring it, for the sake of certainty in so agitated a question.   All
this only serves to show the man[8]!   For an explicit resolution of the
Queries must and will come, after six weeks more consultation, and one
or two farther intermediate, ambiguous answers."

---

[1] "The noble judge did travel out of the record, and I affirm that his discourse
was *irregular, extrajudicial,* and unprecedented."—*Junius,* vol. i. p. 369, and vol. iii.
p. 303.

[2] "His apparent motive for doing what he knew to be wrong was, that he might
have an opportunity of telling the public *extrajudicially* that *the other three judges concurred* in the doctrine laid down in his charge."—*Ibid.,* vol. i. p. 369, and vol. iii. p. 303.
This concluding part of the before-mentioned anonymous letter to Calcraft was used
by Junius, as well under the signature of "Phalaris," as in the speech of Lord Chatham
which is quoted as a note in the Preface to the Letters, and it is here also alluded to by
Phileleutherus, but it should be particularly observed that it did not form part of the
newspaper report of Lord Chatham's speech, probably for the simple reason that *it was
not spoken;* nevertheless it was known to Junius, and this circumstance is an additional
proof that Junius was the writer of the anonymous letter to Calcraft, and of the Letters
of Phileleutherus.

[3] "This proceeding would have been very proper *had a motion been made of either
side for a new trial,* because either a verdict given contrary to evidence, *or an improper
charge by the Judge at Nisi Prius, is held to be a sufficient ground for granting a new
trial.*"—*Junius,* vol. i. p. 369, and vol. iii. p. 303.

[4] Lord Mansfield.   [5] Lord Camden.
[6] See *Junius,* vol. iii. p. 300–301.   [7] See *Junius,* vol. iii. p. 301.
[8] "I can find but one way of reconciling the fact with the cunning understanding of
the man."—*Junius,* vol. iii. p. 300.

The following are some extracts from the pamphlet entitled THE CONDUCT OF THE LATE ADMINISTRATION EXAMINED, &c., and which, for reasons before stated, I have attributed to Lord Temple :—

" They may call too late for the efforts of that warmth of *affection*, which such a partial exemption tends to *alienate* from them. It tends too to *alienate* [1] from them this *affection*, from which they have received such advantages, that they have been represented to have some peculiar claims to a freedom which they purchased by peculiar fortitude ; a representation which is most untrue. We have been told, that having *fled to that country from our oppression*, their migration to America [2], as it argued in them a love, so it gave them a title to freedom superior to that of their fellow-subjects who remained in England." . . . .

" If their *flight* argued in them a love of *freedom* [3], their countrymen who remained in England showed by their actions an equal love of it, supported with more resolution and success ; they took arms to oppose the tyranny from which the others fled, averted it by the civil war, and abolished it by the revolution." . . . .

" But even this degree of exertion is not to be resorted to till the last extremity ; *lenient and persuasive methods, the utmost lenity* [4], these are the terms which he directs the Governors and the Commander-in-Chief to oppose to the revolt which he saw so universal." . . . .

" To be convinced of the evil effects which these his dissertations upon prudence and *lenity* must have had in the midst of so much tumult, let us suppose for a moment that the procrastinating Secretary had still

---

[1] " In one view behold a nation overwhelmed with debt; her revenues wasted ; her trade declining ; *the affections of her colonies alienated.*"—*Junius*, vol. i. p. 401. " It is not then from the *alienated affections* of Ireland or America."—Vol. ii. p. 77. " A series of inconsistent measures had *alienated* the colonies from their duty as subjects, and from their natural *affection* to their common country."—Vol. i. p. 394. "The Duke of Grafton idly irritates the colonies, wickedly *alienates* their affections from their mother country."—Vol. iii. p. 212.

[2] " If emigration be no crime to deserve punishment, it is certainly no virtue to claim exemption; and, however it may have proved eventually beneficial, the mother country was but little obliged to the intentions of the first emigrants."—*Junius to Wilkes*, No. 79.

[3] " They left their native land in search of *freedom*, and found it in a desert."— *Junius*, vol. ii. p. 77.

[4] " What effect can we hope for even from a vigorous measure, when the execution of it is committed most probably to one of the persons who have professed themselves the patrons of *lenient* moderate measures, until the very name of *lenity* and *moderation* became ridiculous?"—*Junius*, vol. iii. p. 78.

" While the gentle Conway breathed into his ear, he was all *lenity* and *moderation*." —*Ibid.*, vol. iii. p. 185.

procrastinated, even his delay or his neglect would have been less pernicious to his country than dispatches of so much *Caution*."[1] . . . . . .
" It were ever to be wished that inquiries of this sort could be made
without descending to personal accusations : for the subjects are much
lessened when the reputations of particular men, the praise or censure
of some *Minister*, becomes a considerable part of them. But on this
occasion, it is feared that this reserve is impossible; when we judge of
the merits of measures, we necessarily judge of those by whom they
were planned and executed. If however, in the course of the inquiry,
blame shall be thrown on particular persons [2], the writer can truly say,
that this was not in his first intention, and that it is only the necessary
result of the subject he treats ; a subject of so much importance, that
he has not suffered the dislike which he feels in common with almost
all mankind to *personal censure* [3], to stifle that information which the
public has a right to receive upon a point which goes up to the very
first principles of our Constitution, and involves in it questions upon
which the existence of all government depends. The reader easily sees
that the subject I mean is the *Stamp Act*." . . . . .
" The declaratory law asserting the power of Great Britain to tax the
Americans, will hold forth *only a delusive and nugatory affirmance of
the right of the Legislature of this kingdom* [4], if not followed by some
bill which shall exert it. The surrender of so unalienable a jurisdic-

---

[1] " The word *Caution*, in Italics, and with a capital letter, indicates the *sobriquet* of
General Conway, which it will be recollected is applied to him by Junius in his anonymous paper, written about the same time, and entitled *Grand Council*," &c.—*Junius*,
vol. ii. p. 482.

[2] " At a crisis like this, Sir, I shall not be very solicitous about those idle forms
of respect, which men in office think due to their characters and station : neither
will I descend to a language beneath the importance of the subject I write on. When
the fate of Great Britain is thrown upon the hazard of a die, by a weak, distracted,
worthless Ministry, an honest man will always express all the indignation he feels. This
is not a moment for preserving forms, and the Ministry must know that the language of
reproach and contempt is now the universal language of the nation."—*Junius*, vol. iii.
p. 74.
" In this paper you will find no reflections upon persons but what are unavoidably connected with things."—*Letter to the Duke of Grafton* [by the Author of Junius],
p. 4.

[3] " Reflections on characters, merely private, ought, I own, to be discouraged."—
Junius, vol. iii. p. 90. " As the indulgence of private malice and personal slander
should be checked and resisted by every legal means, so a constant examination into
the characters and conduct of Ministers and magistrates should be equally promoted
and encouraged."—*Ibid.*, vol. i. p. 352.

[4] This passage is quoted from the Protest against the Repeal of the Stamp Act,
signed by Lord Temple, followed by twenty-seven other Peers, on the 17th March,
1766. The Protest was drawn up by Lord Temple, assisted by Mr. Grenville and Lord
Lyttelton.

tion, when this surrender might, and certainly in America would be attributed to such motives, demands a subsequent vigour and firmness; if now, when time for recollection has been given, you neglect to pursue those measures, which justice and necessity demand from you; and to which duty, gratitude, and interest ought to secure obedience from them, the whole new world ceases for ever to be subject to your authority."[1]

" The first and *great principle* of all government, and of all society, is that *support* is due in return for protection; that every subject should *contribute* to the common defence, in which his own is included."

" It was necessary and it was just to recur to this principle at the close of the last war. It was found necessary to maintain upwards of 10,000 men for the defence of our colonies; an expense of between 300,000 and 400,000 pounds per annum, great part of which was entirely new, was on that account to be incurred; it was just that the colonies which had profited so much by the war, whose interests, commerce, and security had been the first objects of the peace, and of whose ability to bear at least some proportion of that new expense there neither was nor is any reason to doubt, should contribute (not to support or defend Great Britain, but) about a third part of the expense necessary for their own defence and protection."[2]

" Upon this general and acknowledged principle, and upon this application of it, which was just in itself, and which the situation of this country made necessary, and which it might have been expected would

---

[1] " The enterprises of the Americans are now carried to such a point, that every moment we lose serves only to accelerate our perdition. If the present weak, false, and pusillanimous Administration are suffered to go on in abetting and supporting the colonies against the mother country, if the King should take no notice of this last daring attack upon our commerce, the only consequence will be that the contest, instead of being undertaken while we have strength to support it, will be reserved, not for our posterity, but to a time when we ourselves shall have surrendered all our arms to the people with whom we are to contend, nor will that period be distant."—*Junius*, vol. ii. p. 516.

" If, when the opportunity presents itself, you neglect to do your duty to yourselves and your posterity," &c.—*Junius, Dedication.*

[2] " When Mr. Grenville was placed at the head of the Treasury, he felt the impossibility of Great Britain's supporting such an establishment as her former successes had made indispensable, and at the same time of giving any sensible relief to foreign trade, and to the weight of the public debt. He thought it equitable that those parts of the empire which had benefited most by the expenses of the war, should contribute something to the expenses of the peace, and he had no doubt of the constitutional right vested in Parliament to raise that contribution."—*Junius*, vol. i. p. 394.

" The other, to serve the purposes of party, repealed that Act, yet showed by their conduct that they approved of the equitable principle on which it was founded, that America should contribute a little to the *support* of the public expense."—*Ibid.*, vol. iii. p. 86.

appear neither unreasonable nor unpleasing to an English ear, *the Stamp Act was planned.*" . . . .

" It is time, therefore, to return to measures undertaken upon public grounds and permanent principles; what those are, the perusal of this tract may in some degree have suggested; and if any senator should condescend to turn it over, he may perhaps, by the evidence it contains, be prepared to hear himself addressed by his constituents in some such manner as this :

" When I entrusted to you the care of my interests, and the power of granting some part of my property for the services of the State, I entrusted it in confidence that this power would never be used but on the calls of necessity, and would ever be exercised with justice," [1] &c.

The great variety in the style of the handwriting used by the Author of Junius would alone justify the assertion that it was certainly not the undisguised and ordinary hand of the writer, and therefore it can scarcely be expected that the handwriting of any individual should now be discovered that will correspond *exactly* with that adopted by Junius. I believe it to have been a style of writing acquired for the express purpose of these and other anonymous papers. It became in the course of time, and after long practice, as it were, a second and totally distinct hand, which the writer could assume at pleasure, not perhaps without some occasional appearances of the character of the original style of writing becoming perceptible through the disguise, and these instances varied according to the circumstances of the moment, and the degree of care used.

---

[1] Dr. Busby has observed, that Junius is remarkably addicted to personification, or that dramatic form of appeal called in rhetoric the figure *Prosopopœia.* The above is an instance of it, and it occurs very frequently in the Letters ; as, for instance, in his Address to the King, when he supposes " an honest man to be permitted to approach a King," and who, " unacquainted with the vain impertinence of forms, would deliver his sentiments with dignity and firmness, but not without respect, &c."—*Junius*, vol. ii. p. 64.

It occurs again in the Letter on the King's answer to the City Address, *Junius*, vol. ii. p. 131, and it is also to be found in the several pamphlets attributed to Lord Temple : the *Letter concerning Libels, &c. ; Another Letter to Mr. Almon ;* in the *Letter from Albemarle Street to the Cocoa Tree;* and in the *Letter to the Duke of Grafton* in 1768.

It probably became more or less laboured as the writer was influenced by the fear of discovery, and a wish to render the disguise the more effectual. Although it had always essentially the same character, yet it was sometimes partially changed in a very remarkable manner, as may be seen in the specimens engraved in Woodfall's edition of the Letters [1]. Compare, for instance, those numbered 6 and 10. The general appearance is very different, but, upon closer examination, the identity will be at once acknowledged. So also numbers 2 and 3 are equally unlike to numbers 8 and 27, and yet it is impossible to doubt that they proceeded from the same pen.

It should always be mentioned as a requisite qualification in a candidate for the Authorship of Junius, that either he or his amanuensis should have had considerable proficiency in the art of penmanship. In the correspondence of Junius with his printer Woodfall, are some very elaborate specimens of minute and delicate writing, such, for instance, as the letter addressed to Garrick. The fac-simile of it which is engraved in Woodfall's edition is copied with great accuracy, but it fails to give an adequate idea of the *beauty* of the original: it must have been written with an extremely fine pen, and the letters are very elegantly and correctly formed. Indeed, all the manuscripts of Junius are remarkable for their clearness and perfect legibility. They are usually written with a fine and hard pen, which must have been frequently changed, for there is seldom any perceptible difference in the fineness of the strokes at the beginning and end of a letter, and I believe that metal pens had not then been invented. There is seldom any appearance of haste; every letter is so deliberately, distinctly, and accurately formed, that there could never be any chance of a word being mistaken through any fault of the writer. The punctuation is always most carefully attended to, and I have not been able to discover more than one or two instances in which the *dot* over the letter *i* has been omitted.

The upright style of the writing is such as would be the result of holding the pen inclined from the right shoulder at an angle

---

[1] Three vols. 8vo, 1812, and second edition, 1814.

of about 45 degrees, and this mode of writing will be found to encourage a tendency to join several words together, as was frequently, but not invariably, the case with Junius, for in some of his letters to Woodfall, the words not only stand distinct from each other, but in some instances each particular letter in a word is completely detached from those on each side of it.

There are many peculiarities in the writing of Junius, but scarcely any that can be said to be uniform and invariable: it would rather seem to have been a study to display as much variety as possible. The notes to Woodfall are sometimes commenced with a small letter instead of a capital, and close to the left-hand edge of the paper. Particular letters, as the *m* and *n*, are often extremely narrow in form, as it were compressed, and the spaces between them disproportionately wide, sometimes three or even four times as wide as the letters themselves. Occasionally the loops to the letters *l*, *g*, *k*, and *h*, are extravagantly large, and again they are exactly the reverse; sometimes the letters have very round turnings, and at others the turnings are very acute and angular; the letter *i* has sometimes a round dot over it, and sometimes a grave accent; there is much variation also in the mode of connecting the letters *t* and *h*, and infinite variety in the form of the capital letters.

If, without any preconceived notions upon the subject, the autographs of the Author of Junius had been placed before me for my opinion as to the age of the writer, I should have pronounced them, for several reasons, to have been the handwriting of a person who had arrived at the middle period of life. Although the general appearance of them is firm, clear, and regular, yet, upon a close examination, it will be seen that the words are seldom written upon a straight line, but that if a line were drawn across the paper, through the centres of the first and last word, it would be found that most of the intermediate words were either above or below that line. This I have observed to be most frequently the case when the sight is beginning to be impaired by approaching age. But even this peculiarity is not invariable with Junius; it is sometimes less apparent, as in the second and third letter to Mr. Grenville, in both of which it seems as if great pains had been taken, and the resemblance to some of the notes to Woodfall is so slight as to be only sufficient to render it certain that they are by the same hand.

Another reason which would have strongly influenced my judgment, is the very frequent omission of single letters in words, thus:—infomed *for* informed; anoymous *for* anonymous; receve *for* receive; alteratins *for* alterations; inclosd *for* inclosed; not *for* note; frinds *for* friends; histoy *for* history; salent *for* salient; exection *for* execution; wordly *for* worldly; and many other similar instances. This I know, from personal experience and observation, to be an invariable sign of the sight becoming uncertain, and the arrival of a period of life when the assistance of spectacles usually becomes indispensable.

After having very carefully examined the original manuscripts[1] which Mr. Woodfall, the present possessor of them, in the most obliging manner, permitted me to retain in my possession for several weeks, and having devoted my attention particularly to the corrections and alterations which occur in them, it is my opinion that they are not in the handwriting of the Author himself, but that some of them were transcribed from a copy, and others written from the Author's dictation. The omissions are frequently such as I think could scarcely have occurred to a person writing down his own thoughts, though they might happen to a transcriber, while some of the corrections were evidently made at the moment of writing, and were merely the result of mistake or misapprehension on the part of the dictator or his amanuensis, and are such as might very naturally be suggested, either as alterations or improvements.

Junius never acknowledged the writing to be his own, and from

[1] Besides the letters which were privately addressed to Woodfall by Junius, there remain also in manuscript, the original autograph of the Dedication and Preface, the letters signed *Scotus* and *Vindex*, the *Postscript* which concludes the second volume, and all the Notes contributed by the Author. The latter were chiefly written on the margins of a copy of Wheble's pirated edition of some of the Letters of Junius, which the Author corrected and sent to Woodfall for his edition of 1772. When the notes were too long to be written on the margins, they are on separate pieces of paper, and some are also written on the newspaper slips of the letters of Philo-Junius, which were sent by Junius to be inserted in the complete edition. The corrected proof of the last letter to Lord Mansfield is also in Mr. Woodfall's possession.

some of his expressions it might be inferred that it was not. He desired Woodfall to copy the letter to Garrick, because he "would avoid having *this hand* too commonly seen." In another private note he says,—" You shall have it some time to-morrow night; it cannot be corrected and *copied* sooner." And again:—"The inclosed tho' begun within these few days has been greatly laboured. It is very correctly *copied*."

Upon the supposition that Lord Temple was the Author of Junius, I believe that Lady Temple was the amanuensis, by whose hand all the writing part of the correspondence was executed. Lord Temple's autograph was evidently not capable of being adapted to the handwriting of Junius; he wrote with difficulty: the letters are large and badly formed, and the whole appearance of it such as his person is described to have been, awkward and ungainly.

Lady Temple, on the contrary, had very considerable facility in the use of the pen. In her handwriting, at several periods of her life, are to be found many of the characteristics of the writings of Junius—the minute and delicate fineness of the letters, the regularity and clearness, the perfect formation of every letter, the unevenness of the lines, the peculiarity of commencing with a small letter instead of a capital, and close to the left-hand edge of the paper, the habit of occasionally omitting small words and single letters in words, the invariable attention to the dotting of the letter *i*, the similarity in the form of individual letters, and the general appearance of her *early* handwriting as compared with the feigned hand which she subsequently adopted for the writing of Junius.

I am aware that one of the objections which would obviously be made to the theory of Lady Temple being the amanuensis of Junius is the extreme improbability that her handwriting should be sent in anonymous letters to her brothers-in-law, Mr. Grenville and Lord Chatham, to whom it might be intimately known, and immediately recognised, and that if I were able now, at this distance of time, to detect it through the attempted disguise, *à fortiori*, so would Lord or Lady Chatham, or Mr. and Mrs. Grenville. This objection, however, plausible as it seems, has in reality no foundation, and is easily removed. If either of the persons to whom Junius sent private letters had at the same time received a letter from Lady Temple, written in the ordinary hand which she then used in her own character, it would not alone have caused any suspicion of its identity with the letter of Junius, there would not even have been sufficient general resemblance to have provoked comparison.

It is probable, however, that Lady Temple wrote very little else after she had devoted her hand to political letter-writing. I have never met with any of her letters except those which are in the Grenville collection, and they are nearly all addressed to her husband. There is not one extant addressed either to Mr. or Mrs. Grenville, and not one is to be found printed in the *Chatham Correspondence.* The comparison which I have made of her handwriting with that of Junius, is from her letters dated from ten to twenty or even thirty years before the time of Junius; and towards this latter period her ordinary writing had gradually assumed a more stiff and formal character than that which she had previously used, as if it were written very slow, and with a careful intention of making it laboured and precise, and, in short, as different as possible from that which she had acquired for the Letters of Junius. The strong peculiarities of her usual hand became still more prominent, while the same peculiarities were carefully avoided in the feigned hand.

I have selected the following specimens from the omissions and corrections which appear upon the original manuscripts; they have not hitherto been noticed in any of the editions of Junius.

In the private note to Woodfall, No. 41, respecting David Garrick, there is an error into which it seems to me very improbable that the Author himself could have fallen, because it so entirely alters, and even destroys, the meaning of the sentence in which it occurs. Junius says,—"The aspersions thrown upon my Letter to the Bill of Rights should be refuted by publication,"—but the word refuted was originally written *refused,* and such an error as this is, I think, a proof that the writing was that of an amanuensis, who was in this instance transcribing from a copy, and had mistaken the word without considering the sense of the passage.

In the following sentences the words placed between brackets were omitted in the original manuscript; those words which are in italics were *subsequently* added :—

" Let me know if the [books] are ready."

" That . . . . . would never have taken a step so absurd if there were [not] some wicked design in it."

" I am sure I can threaten him privately with such a storm as would [make] him tremble even [in] his grave."

" One of the first acts of the present [reign] was to dismiss Mr. Legge, because [*he*] had some years before," &c.

" There was some[thing] wonderfully pathetic in the mention of the horned cattle."

The word *than* is frequently substituted for *that*, and *vice versâ*.

" With[out] regarding the language of ignorant or interested people, depend upon the assurance I give you," &c.

" To save the worthy [*Judge*] from this perplexity, and the no less worthy [*Duke*] from impeachment," &c.

" But that [*he would act*] under Lord Chatham in any office."

" He invariably [*asserted*] that the decision must be legal," &c.

" Dowagers may [*be*] chaste," &c.

" May God protect me from doing any[*thing*] that [*may*] require such defence," &c.

" The courtiers [*talked of nothing*] but a bill of pains and penalties."

" But the man does not even [*know*] the stile of [*his*] office," &c.

" If [*he*] were even acquainted," &c.

" This shameful desertion [*so*] afflicted the generous mind of George the Third," &c.

" If there be [*in reality*] any such law in England as the law of Parliament [*which*] under the exceptions," &c.

" Nor can it be collect*ing* [altered into *collected*] from the Resolutions of either House."

" The suffering this charge to pass without any inquiry, fixes [*shameless*] prostitution upon the face of the House of Commons."

" Viscount Townshend sent over on the plan of being resident Governor. The history of this [*ridiculous*] Administration shall not be lost to the public."

" It will appear by a subsequent letter that the Duke's precipitation proved fatal [*to the grant*]."

" That very system of [*political*] conduct which Junius had held forth to the disapprobation of the public."

"A little experience [*however*] soon showed [*him*] how shamefully he had been treated."

In the two following instances it is evident that the alterations were subsequently made by the Author himself:—

"The death of Lord Granby [*will secure*] Junius."

The words *will secure* were changed to *was lamented by*.

" His mistakes in public conduct did not arise either from want of sentiment, or want of judgment, but [merely] from the difficulty of saying *no*," &c.

The word *merely* was changed to *in general*.

Junius and Lady Temple had frequently the same peculiarity in the mode of spelling certain words ; thus, for instance, they both wrote :—

endeavor,	*instead of*	endeavour.	cloaths,	*instead of*	clothes.
compleat	,,	complete.	wast	,,	waste.
extream	,,	extreme.	farther	,,	further.
stile	,,	style.	french	,,	French.
		irish,	*instead of*	Irish.	

They both write Dutchess more correctly than Duchess, and both use the abbreviation Xmas for Christmas.

They both wrote the following words indifferently :—

public *and* publick.　　　　　　inquire *and* enquire.

honour and favour with the letter *u*, but honorable and favorable always without it.

In some peculiar instances of spelling in Junius, I cannot find the same words for comparison in Lady Temple's autographs, but Junius writes—

lye *instead of* lie.

And Lady Temple writes—

dyed *instead of* died.

Junius writes incorrectly,—

inlightened, inlarges [1], and independance.

---

[1] This word was corrected by Junius, but in such a manner as to leave it in doubt whether inlarges or enlarges was intended to remain.

Lady Temple writes, with equal incorrectness,—

injoys, ingaged, and condolance.

Junius invariably wrote council instead of counsel, but I have not been able to find the word used in the same sense by Lady Temple. It was always written correctly by Lord Temple, except in one instance, and then the alteration leaves it in doubt which was first written, council or counsel. Mr. Dayrell, who was himself a barrister and the intimate friend of Lord Temple, always commits the same error of substituting council for counsel.

Junius always writes—

practises, *instead of* practices.   satyr *instead of* satire.
satyrical *instead of* satirical.

He writes indifferently—

until *and* untill.   unadvisable *and* unadviseable.
packet *and* pacquet.

His assumed names are written—

Iunius *and* Junius.   Fretly *and* Fretley.

Wheble printed the word *style;* but Junius, in the copy of Wheble's edition which he corrected for Woodfall, altered it into *stile*, as it is also written by Lady Temple.

The name of Lord Lyttelton is mentioned only once in the Letters of Junius, and then it is printed Littleton, and in *one* of Lady Temple's letters I find it written both Littleton and Lyttelton; so in *one* of the notes from Junius to Woodfall, he spells the name of the printer Newberry and Newbery.

Junius altered Wheble's spelling of the name of General Hervey into Harvey, the latter being correct. Lady Temple writes it indifferently Harvey, Harvy, and Hervey, and even the names of some of Lord Temple's most intimate friends, with which she must have been well acquainted, are once written Pit, Wilks, and Dorrel, instead of Pitt, Wilkes, and Dayrell. The latter name, which Lady Temple has written Dorrel, as it is still pronounced, shows her attention to *sound* rather than correctness, and not because she was ignorant of the proper mode of spelling the name; and, *apropos* of this circumstance, I have now to mention a remarkable instance of incorrect spelling by Junius in the following note:—" Miss Liddell, after her divorce from the Duke, married Lord Upper Ossory," but in the original autograph, the word divorce is written *difforce* [1]. The *ff* was subsequently altered into a *v*, but not at the time it was written, because the *v* is evidently made with a different pen, and the ink is of a darker colour. Once only in Lady Temple's letters does this word occur, and then it is correctly written divorce; but Lady Temple has very frequently written *off* instead of *of*, and the latter word being pronounced *ov*, it will be observed that the error made by the amanuensis of Junius is exactly equivalent in point of *sound* to Lady Temple's habit of substituting *off* for *of* (ov).

The instance just mentioned affords an additional argument in favour of the supposed employment of an amanuensis, for it seems impossible that the Author of Junius could himself have made so remarkable an error in spelling the language in which he could write so well. I may here observe that incorrect spelling is extremely uncommon in Lord Temple's manuscripts, and the instances which occur in Lady Temple's writings appear to arise more from carelessness than ignorance, as she writes indifferently a pair tree *and* a pear tree, bear *and* beer, acknoledge *and* acknowledge; also, herse *for* hearse, coucil *for* council, yestayday *for* yesterday, directy *for* directly, fashioble *for* fashionable, and other such trifling mistakes.

Junius also writes:—bust *for* burst, deel *for* deal, route *for* rout, confidante *for* confidant, Phlo *for* Philo, soliloque *for* soliloquy, nords *for* words, &c., &c.

Junius and Lady Temple used several forms of the note of interrogation; some of those used by Junius are peculiar as well as capricious and affected.

The mark of admiration is made in the same manner by Junius and Lady Temple; it is a clumsy stroke of uniform thickness, not as it is usually formed, commencing thick and tapering off to a point. It occurs at the end of the poem by Junius called *Harry and Nan*, and also in the manuscript of Lady Temple's poems, as well as another peculiarity common to both, a short dash, thus —, after the punctuation at the ends of some of the lines.

<hr>

[1] See the facsimile in Plate v.

There is another remarkable peculiarity to be found twice or
thrice in the Junius manuscripts, which I have never discovered
in any other writings except in those of Lord Temple, who has
also used it two or three times. Where a single mark of omission
only is necessary, they both use it double, thus—$_\wedge^\wedge$, and both without any apparent reason.

Too much reliance, however, must not be placed upon handwriting in the consideration of this question. Taking it for
granted, as I think will now be generally admitted, that the hand
of Junius was the feigned and not the natural hand of the writer,
there are yet certain points in this respect, the possession of which
are indispensable in a candidate for the Authorship.

There must be an appearance of facility in the penmanship, and
a certain original similarity of character or style in the writing,
which show a capability of being converted into the disguised
hand.

Now I conceive that these qualifications are so absolutely
wanting in the writing of some of the candidates who have been
named, as to render it almost an impossibility that they could
have produced the handwriting used by Junius. Such, for instance, as the writing of Edmund Burke, of William Gerard
Hamilton, of Lord George Sackville, of Glover, of De Lolme,
and of many other persons, including Sir Philip Francis, whose
pretensions have at various times formed the subject of inquiry.

It is right, however, to mention that I have not had the opportunity of examining the original autographs of the last-named
gentleman; my judgment is formed upon the fac-similes which
have been engraved, and in which there may be found a similarity
in the shape of certain letters, common to almost every handwriting of the period, but nothing approaching to the original
character of that of Junius.

On the contrary, I have found the handwriting of several persons, some almost unknown to fame, and having really no other
qualification for the Authorship, to be so remarkable in resemblance to that of Junius, that if all other circumstances combined
in favour of it, there would be a strong presumption that either of

them might have been the Author or his amanuensis. Such, for instance, are the handwritings of the first Lord Carysfort, a Lord of the Admiralty; of Mr. Claudius Amyand, some time Under Secretary to Lord Holdernesse, and subsequently a Commissioner of Customs; of the Honourable Augustus Hervey, afterwards Earl of Bristol; and, although in a somewhat less degree, of Hester Grenville, Countess of Chatham.

It would be impossible now to ascertain the modes which Junius adopted for the "conveyancing part" of the correspondence with his printer, Woodfall; it was probably similar to that used by Lord Temple in a secret correspondence with his sister Lady Chatham [1]. Junius sent many of his letters to Woodfall by the penny post, and they were always *post-paid*. Several appear to have been sent from the same office, as the post-mark is "*peny post payd*," a peculiarity of spelling not likely to occur often.

The ample fortune of Lord Temple would have enabled him to resort to so many contrivances, by the employment of a variety of well-paid agents, who might be rendered entirely unconscious of the nature of the services in which they were engaged, and the assistance of Lady Temple, and that of her servants, was no doubt made available for the same purpose. Servants in those days were not so knowing as they are now and reading and writing were then very uncommon accomplishments. It is not unlikely that part of the "conveyancing" was performed by Lady Temple herself; although a leader of fashion, she appears to have been

---

[1] Vide vol. iv. p. 281. Even so early as his days of wooing, Lord Temple (then Mr. Richard Grenville) was engaged in a secret correspondence with Mistress Anna Chamber, the future Lady Temple; and I find he was, upon one occasion, in disgrace with the lady, in consequence of some of his letters having wandered from their destination. In allusion to it he says,—" I am under apprehensions of all kinds, and though I think it impossible I can be suspected one moment of anything more than not being quite particular enough in the direction, yet that is by no means sufficient. I have always been, dear madam, so extremely cautious (and you may believe I study to be so more now than ever), that *I have sent all the letters* I ever writ you out of the country *to the same person in town* that I trusted them with when I was there. This I did to prevent the remarks of my own and other people's servants, and I have *sometimes directed them myself*, and *sometimes ordered him to direct them*, to hinder as much as possible any observation in your own family from constantly seeing the same hand."

very independent in her habits, for in one of her letters she says :—

" I make good use of my time, I go to the Mint at ten in the morning, and afterwards to the Lions, and to the other Curiositys to be seen in the Tower, and dine at a Chop-house." [1]

The greatest difficulty experienced by Junius in the "*convey-ancing part of our correspondence*," must have been in procuring the letters and packets which were sent by Woodfall to the several Coffee-houses according to his directions. It is often alluded to in his private notes to Woodfall :—

" I really have not known how to procure your last. if it be not of any great moment, I would wish you to recall it."

" it will be very difficult, if not impracticable, for me to get your Note."

" I have not been able to get y^{rs} from that place."

" I think you sh^d give money to the Waiters at that place, to make them more attentive."

" Shew the Dedication & Preface to Mr. Wilkes [2], and if he has any *material* Objection, let me know. I say *material* because of the difficulty of getting your letters."

" Upon no account, nor for any reason whatsoever are you to write to me, untill I give you notice."

" The gentleman, who transacts the Conveyancing part of our Cor-respondence, tells me there was much difficulty last night."

[1] Horace Walpole, in a letter to Lord Hertford, iu March, 1764, mentions Lady Temple :—

" Of all public places, guess the most unlikely one for the most unlikely person to have been at. I had sent to know how Lady Macclesfield did : Louis brought me word that he could hardly get into St. James's Square, there was so great a crowd to see my Lord lie in state. At night I met my Lady Milton, at the Duchess of Argyle's, and said in joke, ' Soh ! to be sure, you have been to see my Lord Macclesfield lie in state ! ' thinking it impossible ; she burst out into a fit of laughter, and owned she had. She and my Lady Temple had dined at Lady Betty's, *put on hats and cloaks*, and *literally waited on the steps of the house in the thick of the mob*, while one posse was admitted, and let out again for a second to enter, before they got in."

[2] Junius afterwards wrote to Woodfall :—" When you see Mr. Wilkes, pray return him my thanks for the trouble he has taken, I wish he had taken more." The *trouble* taken by Mr. Wilkes in the matter does not appear. There was certainly no addition or alteration made by him in the autograph copies of the Dedication and Preface ; with two or three trifling exceptions (probably mere caprices of the printer), they were printed exactly as the Author sent them to Woodfall.

"Your letter was twice refused last night, & the waiter as often attempted to see the person who sent for it." . . . .
"Pray let the *two* sets be well parcelled up & left at the bar of Munday's Coffee-house, Maiden lane, with the same Direction, & with orders to be Delivered to a Chairman, who will ask for them in the Course of to-morrow Evening." [1]

And on the 5th of March, 1772, he says:—

" your letters with the books are come safe to hand. The difficulty of corresponding arises from Situation & Necessity, to which we must submit."

If Lord Temple were the Author of Junius, the "sole depositary of his own secret," and determined that it should "perish with him," it might be expected that he would intend to destroy every vestige of his papers which might lead to a discovery. I have carefully collected all the scattered fragments in his handwriting which have escaped destruction; and those among them of a poli-

---

[1] If Mr. Woodfall had been inclined to pry into the secrets of his correspondent, this was perhaps one of the most favourable opportunities; but he did not avail himself of it; and it is so much the more honourable, because at this time Junius had declared in the Dedication, that he was "the sole depositary of his own secret, and that it should perish with him."—It is clear that the books were sent, for the receipt of them was acknowledged by Junius on the following day. How easy it might have been for Woodfall to have set a watch upon the person who applied for the parcel, and to have tracked him home to his retreat. The books here alluded to were the "*two sets in blue paper covers*," mentioned in the Note from Junius (No. 47), in December, 1771 : but at the same time he also desired Woodfall to send him one set "*bound in vellum gilt*," and with respect to the latter, it is very doubtful whether the manner of the binding [a] was not altogether forgotten by Woodfall, or whether they were ever sent, or if sent, still more doubtful whether they were applied for, or received by the Author. If Woodfall *did* send them to "*the last address*," fifteen months afterwards, in March, 1773, there is presumptive evidence that they were subsequently reclaimed by him because no application had been made for them, in the fact, that the original letter (No. 64), in the handwriting of Henry Sampson Woodfall, which is supposed to have accompanied them, is now in the possession of his grandson, and its having been sealed shows that it is the original, and not a copy. This letter is dated March 7, 1773. The last communication which Woodfall received from Junius is dated "19 Jan." [1773], and that was after a silence of eight months. It is a curious fact, that so little did Woodfall think of his "*old friend and correspondent*," that his letter remained without notice until its receipt was acknowledged in the *Public Advertiser* of the 8th of March following.

[a] Woodfall mentions the books in his letter (No. 64), but says nothing of the *vellum* binding : " I did not get them out of the bookbinder's hands till yesterday ; nor, though I desired them to be finished in the most elegant manner possible, are they done so well as I wished."

tical nature consist chiefly of extracts from the Journals of Parliament, from the Institutes of Sir Edward Coke, from Locke's *Essay on Civil Government*, from Petyt's *Jus Parliamentarium*, from Rushworth's Collections, &c., relating to the Privileges of Parliament[1], the Habeas Corpus Act, the proceedings against Wilkes, the case of the Aylesbury men and Mr. Justice Holt, the Suspending and Dispensing Prerogative, the power and discretion of the Judges with respect to bail, all of them upon subjects more or less treated of, and some of the extracts copied, almost verbatim, in the Letters of Junius. The cases of Lord Shaftesbury and the Honourable Alexander Murray are also referred to, and there are numerous collections from the correspondence of the several Governors and others in the Colonies, on the Stamp Act, and the Taxation of America.

Among the collections from the Journals of the House of Commons are the resolutions of 1628 and 1704, which are quoted by Junius[2], respecting the writ of Habeas Corpus, and their own power and privileges.

I shall now proceed to make the following extracts from Lord Temple's MANUSCRIPT COLLECTIONS, and, in the notes, to point out some passages in the Letters of Junius to which they seem to refer:—

"Aylesbury. Lord Chief Justice Holt. 1704–1705. *Aylesbury Case.*"—"Commons vote that it was contrary to the declarations they had made. Address the Queen not to grant a writ of Error, though ten Judges held it to be a petition of right. The Lords resolve to proceed in the matter by sure and regular steps; they first came to some general resolutions.

"1st.—*That neither House of Parliament could assume or create any new privilege that they had not been formerly possessed of.*"[3]

---

[1] "Not venturing to consult those who are qualified to inform me, I am forced to collect everything from books or common conversation. The pains I took with that paper upon privilege were greater than I can express to you. Yet after I had blinded myself with poring over journals, debates, and Parliamentary history," &c., &c.—*Junius to Wilkes*, vol. i. p. 308.

[2] *Junius*, vol. ii. p. 238–39.

[3] In the course of the proceedings upon *the Aylesbury Election, the House of Lords resolved: " That neither House of Parliament had any power by any vote or declaration to create to themselves any new privilege that was not warranted by the known laws and customs of Parliament."* And to this rule the House of Commons,

" That the imprisoning the men of Aylesbury for acting contrary to a Declaration made by the House of Commons was against Law."

" Their resolutions were communicated to the House of Commons at a Conference."

" They made a long answer to them : in it they set forth that *the right of determining Elections was lodged only in them, and that therefore they only could judge, who had a right to elect. They only were the judges of their own privileges ; the Lords could not intermeddle in it.*"[1]

" They, the Commons, had discovered on many occasions, and very manifestly what lay at bottom, with most of them, *but they had not skill enough to know how to manage their advantages, and to make use of their numbers.*"[2]

Journals, p. 554.—The Lords desire a present conference with the House of Commons in the Painted Chamber, about some ancient fundamental liberties of the kingdom. [Here follows the Resolution of the House of Lords in the proceedings upon the Aylesbury Election, as quoted by *Junius*, vol. i. p. 529.]

That the House of Commons, in committing to Newgate, D. Horne, Hen. Barte, and John Paton, junr., *John Paty and John Oviat for commencing and prosecuting an action at common law against the late constables at Aylesbury,* for not allowing their votes in election of members to serve in Parliament, upon pretence that their so doing was contrary to a declaration, a contempt of the jurisdiction, and a breach of the Privilege of the House, *have assumed to themselves alone a legislative authority, by pretending to attribute the force of a law to their declaration,* have claimed a jurisdiction not warranted by the Constitution, and have assumed a new privilege, to which they can show no title by the law and custom of Parliament, and have thereby, as far as in them lies, subjected the rights of Englishmen, and the

---

though otherwise they had acted in a very arbitrary manner, gave their assent, *for they affirmed that they had guided themselves by it in asserting their privileges.*"—*Junius,* vol. i. p. 529.

" *As for the law of Parliament, it is only another name for the privilege in question, and since the power of creating new laws has been formally renounced by both Houses,*" &c.—*Ibid.,* vol. ii. p. 212.

[1] " In my opinion they would consult their real dignity much better by appealing to the laws when they are offended, than by *violating the first principle of natural justice, which forbids us to be judges when we are parties to the cause.*"—*Ibid.,* vol. ii. p. 218.

" One of the greatest privileges assumed by either House of Parliament, is that of having their privileges (as they call them) examined and inquired into *in their own Houses only.*"—*Ibid.,* vol. iii. p. 361.

[2] " The man who is conscious of the weakness of his cause, is interested in concealing it ; and on the other side, it is not uncommon to see a good cause mangled by advocates who do not know the real strength of it."—*Ibid.,* vol. i. p. 513.

freedom of their persons, to the arbitrary votes of the House of Commons [1].

Resolved, that *Privilege of Parliament does not extend to the case of writing and publishing seditious libels,* nor ought to be allowed to obstruct the ordinary course of the laws in the speedy and effectual prosecution of so heinous and dangerous an offence [2].

— *in all cases, my Lords, where any right or liberty belongs to the subject by any positive Law, written or unwritten, if there were not also a remedy by Law, for the enjoying or remaining, of this right or Liberty, when it is violated or taken from him, the positive Law were most vain, & to no purpose* [3] for any man to have right in any Land or other inheritance, if there were not a known remedy, that is an action of writt, by which in some court of ordinary justice he might recover it; and in this case of right of liberty of the person, *if there were not a remedy in the Law for regaining it when it is restrained, it were of no purpose to speak of Laws that ordain it should not be restrained,* therefore, in this case also, I shall first observe the remedy that every freeman is to use for the regaining of his Liberty, when he is against Law imprisoned, that so, upon the legal course & form to be held in using that remedy, the precedents, or judgments upon it, for all precedents of record arise out of this remedy, may be easily understood, there are in the Laws, &c.

Commons Journal, April 3, 1628.—" Resolved, upon question, *that the writ of Habeas Corpus may not be denied, but ought to be granted to every man that is committed or detained in prison, or otherwise restrained, though it be by the command of the King, the Privy Council, or any other,* he praying the same, without one negative."

Commons Journal, March 8, 1704.—" *Resolved that no Commoner of England committed by the House of Commons for breach of privilege,*

---

[1] " I think the liberties of England ought to stand upon a more solid basis than presumptions, or the arbitrary voice of one branch of the Legislature only."

" The cases to prove that the assumed privileges of either House of Parliament are not examinable elsewhere than in their own Houses, are Lord Shaftesbury's case, 29 Car. 2 in B. R. The Queen *v.* Paty & alias, 3 Ann, in B. R., and the Hon. Alexander Murray's case, 24 Geo. 2, in B. R."—*Junius,* vol. iii. p. 362.

[2] " When Mr. Wilkes was to be punished, they made no scruple about the privileges of Parliament, and although it was as well known as any matter of public record and uninterrupted custom could be, that the members of either House are privileged, except in cases of treason, felony, or breach of the peace, they declared without hesitation that *privilege of Parliament did not extend to the case of a seditious libel,* and undoubtedly they would have done the same if Mr. Wilkes had been prosecuted for any other misdemeanour whatsoever."—*Ibid.,* vol. ii. p. 222, and vol. iii. p. 372.

[3] " *It is a leading maxim of the laws of England (and without it all laws are nugatory), that there is no right without a remedy, nor any legal power without a legal course to carry it into effect.*"—*Ibid.,* vol. ii. p. 216.

or contempt of that House, ought to be, by any writ of Habeas Corpus, made to appear in any other place, or before any other judicature, during that session of Parliament, wherein such person was so committed." [1]

Lord Digby's Speech in the House of Commons, 1640.

" It hath been a maxim among the wisest legislators, that *whoever means to settle good laws must proceed in them with a sinister opinion of all mankind."—Petyt, Jus Parliamentarium.*

James 1st, part of his Speech to both Houses of Parliament.

" Where there is variety and uncertainty in cases of law, *although a just judge may do rightly, yet an ill judge may take advantage to do wrong,* and then are all honest men that succeed him tyed in a manner to his unjust and partial conclusions. *Therefore leave not the Law to the pleasure of the Judges."* [2]

Petyt, page 27. *Discretion.*—" The Lord Chief Justice Popham, in his argument touching the union of both kingdoms in King James 1st's

---

[1] " You will not wonder, Sir, that with these qualifications, the declaratory resolutions of the House of Commons should appear to be in perpetual contradiction, not only to common sense, and to the laws we are acquainted with (and which alone we can obey), but even to one another. I was led to trouble you with these observations by a passage which, to speak in lutestring, *I met with this morning in the course of my reading,* and upon which I mean to put a question to the advocates for privilege :—on the 8th of March, 1704 (*vide* Journals, vol. xiv. p. 565), the House thought proper to come to the following resolution :—'*That no commoner of England committed by the House of Commons for breach of privilege or contempt of that House, ought to be, by any writ of Habeas Corpus, made to appear in any other place, or before any other judicature, during that session of Parliament, wherein such person was so committed.'* . . . . .

" If there be in reality any such law in England *as the law of Parliament,* which (under the exceptions stated in my letter on privilege) I confess, after long deliberation, I very much doubt, it certainly is not constituted by, nor can it be collected from, the resolutions of either House, whether *enacting or declaratory.* I desire the reader will compare *the above resolution of the year* 1704, *with the following of the 3rd April,* 1628.—' RESOLVED, *that the writ of Habeas Corpus cannot be denied, but ought to be granted to every man that is committed or detained in prison, or otherwise restrained by the command of the King, the Privy Council, or any other, he praying the same.'"—Junius,* vol. ii. p. 233. . . . . This resolution of 1628 was also quoted by Lord Temple in his Protest, on the rejection by the House of Lords of the Bill to explain and amend the Habeas Corpus Act, June 2, 1758.

[2] " The Government of England is a Government of law. We betray ourselves, we contradict the spirit of our laws, and we shake the whole system of English Jurisprudence, whenever we entrust *a discretionary power over the life, liberty, or fortune of the subject, to any man, or set of men whatsoever, upon a presumption that it will not be abused."—Junius,* vol. ii. p. 236.

" He (Lord Mansfield) assumes *an arbitrary power of doing right, and if he does wrong, it lies only between God and his conscience."—Ibid.,* vol. ii. p. 433.

" The distinction between doing wrong and avoiding to do right, belongs to Lord Mansfield : Junius disclaims it."—*Ibid.,* vol. ii. p. 397.

" —— to a situation so unhappy, that you can neither do wrong without ruin, nor right without affliction."—*Ibid.,* vol. ii. p. 72.

time, cited a resolution in Parliament where himself served as Speaker, that whereas it was proposed to have a law made that *the Judges might use their discretion* in appointing trials in foreign countrys [counties?] in respect the meaner sort of people were outweighed with the power of great men in some shires, that were parties to the suits, *it was upon grave advice and consultation denied, with this answer, that it was better to live under a certain known law, though hard sometimes in a few cases, than to be subject to the alterable discretion of any Judges.*" [1]

Discretion.—" Mr. Hyde's, afterwards Lord Chancellor Clarendon's, argument before the Lords in the Upper House of Parliament, April, 1641, the Courts of the Presidents and Council of the North, says he, or as it is more usually called the Courts of York, which by the spirit and ambition of the Ministers trusted there, or by the natural inclination of Courts to enlarge their own power and jurisdiction, hath so prodigiously broken down the banks of the first counsel in which it ran, hath almost overwhelmed that country under the sea of arbitrary power, and involved the people in a labyrinth of distemper, oppression, and poverty."

In another part of the same Speech:—" Now these jurisdictions tell you you shall proceed according to your *discretion*, that is, you shall do what you please, only that we may not suspect this *discretion* will be gentler and kinder to us than the law, special provision is made, no fine, no punishment, shall be less than by the law is appointed, but as much greater, as your *discretion* shall think fit, and indeed in this improvement we find *arbitrary courts* are very pregnant. *If the law requires my good behaviour, this discretion makes me close prisoner:* if the law sets me upon the pillory, this *discretion* appoints me to leave my ears there. But this proceeding, according to *discretion*, is no new opinion: it was in the first Commission I told your Lordships of, in 31 Hen. 8., that they should proceed secundum legem et consuetudinem regni Angliæ, vel aliter secundum sanas discretiones vestras, which in the interpretation of the Law, and that is the best interpretation, signifies the same thing, *to proceed according to discretion, is to proceed according to law, which is summa discretio, but not accord-*

---

[1] " Even in matters of private property we see the same bias and inclination to depart from the decisions of your predecessors, which you certainly ought to receive as evidence of the common law. *Instead of those certain positive rules by which the judgment of a court of law should invariably be determined, you have fondly introduced your own unsettled notions of equity and substantial justice.* Decisions given upon such principles do not alarm the public so much as they ought, because the consequence and tendency of each particular instance is not observed or regarded. " In the mean time the practice gains ground, the Court of King's Bench becomes a Court of Equity, and *the judge, instead of consulting strictly the law of the land, refers only to the wisdom of the Court, and to the purity of his own conscience.*"—*Junius*, vol. ii. p. 164.

ing to their private conceit or affection; for talis discretio, says the law, discretionem confundit, and such a confusion hath this *discretion* in these instructions produced, as if *discretion* were only removed from rage and fury: no inconvenience, no mischief, no disgrace that the malice, or insolence, or curiosity of these Commissioners, had a mind to bring upon that people but through the latitude and power of this *discretion,* the poor people have felt: *this discretion* hath been the quicksand which hath swallowed up their property, their liberty. I beseech your Lordships rescue them from *this discretion.*"

" *Law of England abhors discretion.*" [1]

" Former opinions in many cases differ from recent ones. *Jurors are to try the fact, and the judges ought to judge according to the law that ariseth upon the fact.*" [2]—[Coke] 1 Ins. 226.

" *But if they will take upon them the knowledge of the law upon the matter, they may. Yet it is dangerous, for if they mistake the law, they run into danger of an attaint, therefore to find the special matter is the safest way where the case is doubtful.*" [3]—[Coke] 1 Ins. 228.

[1] " If there be judge or lawyer of any note in Westminster Hall, who shall be daring enough to affirm that, according to the true intendment of the laws of England, *the discretion of an English judge is merely arbitrary, and not governed by rules of law,* I shall be glad to be acquainted with him."—*Junius,* vol. ii. p. 442.

" *The discretion of an English judge is not of mere will and pleasure; it is not arbitrary;* it is not capricious ; but as that great lawyer (whose authority I wish you respected half as much as I do) truly says, ' *Discretion,* taken as it ought to be, is *discernere per legem quod sit justum.* [Coke] 4 Inst. 41. 66. If it be not directed by the right line of the law, it is a crooked cord, and appeareth to be unlawful.' *If discretion were arbitrary in the judge, he might introduce whatever novelties he thought proper;* ' but,' says Lord Coke, ' *Novelties without warrant of precedents* are not to be allowed : some *certain rules* are to be followed :—*Quicquid judicis authoritati subjicitur, novitati non subjicitur,*' and this sound doctrine is applied to the Star Chamber, a Court confessedly arbitrary."—*Ibid.,* vol. ii. p. 410.

[2] " We are told that the Judge & Jury have a distinct Office ; that the Jury is to find the fact, & the Judge to deliver the Law. *De jure respondent Judices, de facto jurati.* The *dictum* is true, tho' not in the sense given to it by *Lord Mansfield.* The Jury are undoubtedly to determine the fact, that is, whether the Defendant did or did not commit the crime charged against him. The Judge pronounces the sentence annexed by Law to that fact so found ; and if, in the course of the trial, any question of Law arises, both the Council & the Jury must, of necessity, appeal to the Judge, & leave it to his decision."—*Ibid.,* vol. i. p. 376.

" You may know perhaps, though I do not mean to insult you by an appeal to your experience, that the language of truth is uniform and consistent. To depart from it safely requires memory and discretion. In the two last trials your charge to the jury began as usual, with assuring them *that they had nothing to do with the law,—that they were to find the bare fact,* and not concern themselves about the legal inferences drawn from it, or the degree of the defendant's guilt."—*Ibid.,* vol. ii. p. 174.

[3] " Thus far you were consistent with your former practice. But how will you account for the conclusion ? You told the jury, that *if after all they would take upon themselves to determine the law,* they might do it, *but they must be very sure that they determined*

" Safe if you find according to the Judge's direction, though the judge is mistaken."—" N.B.—Attaint is disused.   New trials moved."

" whereas, *the late King, James II., by the assistance of divers evil counsellors, judges, & ministers employed by him, did endeavor to subvert & extirpate the Protestant religion, & the laws & liberties of this Kingdom,* 1.—*by assuming & exercising a Power of dispensing with & suspending of laws, & the execution of Laws without consent of Parl!.*" [1]

" Mr. Locke.   The freedom of men under Government is to have a *standing Rule to live by,* common to every one of the Society, & made by *the Legislative Power created in it.*" [2]

" In cases of necessity, *the K., with the advice of his P. C.* [Privy Council], *may suspend the execution of any Law during* the recess *of Parl!.,* that is when Parl! cannot be conveniently assembled, & this was to be proved by Bill of Rights, Acts of Parliament, & usage of P. C. [Privy Council]." [3]

" ' Salus populi suprema lex.' [4]   His L. [Lordship] goes to common sense ; He wants no statute.   the Law of England he hitherto thought

according to law, for it touched their consciences, and they acted at their peril."—Junius, vol. ii. p. 175.

[1] " Lord Somers, in his excellent tract upon the rights of the people, after reciting the vote of the convention of the 28th of January, 1689, viz. that *King James the Second having endeavoured to subvert the constitution of this kingdom, by breaking the original contract between King and people, and by the advice of Jesuits and other wicked persons, having violated the fundamental laws, and having withdrawn himself out of this kingdom, hath abdicated the Government."—Ibid.,* vol. ii. p. 226.

[2] " The submission of a free people to the *executive authority of Government,* is no more than a compliance with *laws which they themselves* have enacted. While the national honour is firmly maintained abroad, and while justice is impartially administered at home, the obedience of the subject will be voluntary, cheerful, and I might almost say, unlimited."—*Ibid.,* vol. i. p. 387.

[3] " Lord Camden, it is agreed, did certainly maintain that, *in the recess of Parliament* the King (by which we all mean *the King in Council, or the executive power*) *might suspend the operation of an act of the Legislature,* and he founded his doctrine upon a *supposed necessity,* of which the King, *in the first instance,* must be judge. The Lords and Commons cannot be judges of it in the first instance, for they do not exist." —*Ibid.,* vol. ii. p. 361.

[4] These notes are evidently part of Lord Temple's collections for the pamphlet which he afterwards compiled from the several speeches, including his own, on the *Suspending and Dispensing Prerogative,* in December, 1766.   It was upon this occasion that Lord· Temple attacked Lord Camden for his phrase of forty days' tyranny, which, says Junius, "*I myself heard.*"—"*Forty days' tyranny* over a nation by the crown ! who can endure the thought ?   My Lords, less than forty days' tyranny, such as this country has felt in some times, would, I believe, bring your Lordships together, without a summons, from your sick beds, faster than our great patriots themselves, to get a place, or a pension, or both, and for aught I know, make the subject of your consultation that appeal to heaven which has been spoken of.   Once establish a dispensing power, and you cannot be sure of either liberty or law for *forty minutes.*" See *Lord Campbell's Lives of the Chancellors,* vol. v. p. 266.

perfect but if so destitute of sense & reason &c., He would move for a Bill to enact it, the view is *to hold forth*[1] *to the Public* that there has been a violation of y.ᵉ Constitution ; *if so He ought to cry mercy, will not be so mean as to skulk*[2] *under a Pardon.* It is not only the Right, but duty of the Crown, to *suspend* the execution of a Law *for the safety of the People, as much as to keep them from starving.* Prerogative, *says another,* is nothing but a Power to protect them. Brutus would have entrusted Nero himself with such a Power. *It is but 40 days' Tyranny at the outside.*"[3]

Denies dispensing or suspending power in the article of raising money without consent of Parliament.

SIR E. LYTTELTON. "Quando salus regni periclitabatur salus populi suprema lex." I shall ground my reason upon the law. First, of Nature ; 2nd, of State ; 3rd, public safety & conveniency, neither shall it be against the statute Law, Common law, or any of the Hereditary Rights & Liberties of the subjects of England, but consonant to & warranted by all. Quicquid necessitas cogit defendit. *Necessity is the Law of Time & action. Many things are lawful by necessity which otherwise are not. necessitas est Lex Temporis. whatever is done for public safety is best. The Laws are tributary, & must give place to the Law of Necessity;* what talk we of Formalities when we

---

[1] " The Duke of Bedford and his friends have uniformly *held forth* Sir Jeffry Amherst."—*Junius,* vol. iii. p. 106. " A pompous list of names is *held forth to the public.*" —*Ibid.,* vol. iii. p. 70.

[2] " Instead of acting that open generous part, which becomes your rank and station, you meanly *skulk* into the Closet."—*Junius,* vol. ii. 179. " It has been possible for a notorious coward, *skulking* under a petticoat, to make a great nation the prey of his avarice and his ambition."—*Ibid.,* vol. ii. p. 466. " —— we see the First Lord of the Admiralty *skulking* into the House just before a division."—*Ibid.,* vol. iii. p. 250. " Now will I *skulk* away."—*Ibid.,* vol. ii. p. 492.

" —— yet upon any call of a pushed Minister, he will contrive to *skulk* down to the lobby."—*Letter on Libels, &c.,* p. 96.

" They should not be permitted in any case to *skulk* under ambiguous or indirect terms."—*Another Letter to Almon,* p. 59.

"I will not disgrace their heroism so much as to say they *skulked* under a pardon." —*Lord Temple's Pamphlet on the 'Suspending and Dispensing Prerogative.'* See also, *ante,* vol. i. p. 20.

[3] " With regard to Lord Camden, the truth is, that he inadvertently overshot himself, as appears plainly by that unguarded mention *of a tyranny of forty days, which I myself heard.* Instead of asserting that the proclamation was *legal,* he should have said, ' My Lords, I know the proclamation was *illegal,* but *I advised it because it was indispensably necessary to save the kingdom from famine, and I submit myself to the justice and mercy of my country.*'"—*Junius,* vol. ii. p. 364.

" By this rule a man may say, *as a judge,* that the loss of an Englishman's liber for twenty-fours only, is grievous beyond estimation, and then, *as a Minister,* may declare *that forty days' tyranny is a trifling burthen which any Englishman may bear.*"— *Ibid.,* vol. iii. p. 43.

are like to lose the Kingdom, when the Keeping the Laws would end the Commonwealth [1].

State tryals, p. 158. Proceedings at the Court of Queen's bench on the habeas Corpus.—In Mich.* vac.* they (viz. the 5 partys) pray'd a habeas Corpus upon the stat, 31 Car. 2^dl, upon the return of which all the Judges met & advised whether they were bailable by that statute who were unanimously of opinion that they were not, & accordingly they were not, & accordingly they were remanded, & in Hillary term following they *moved the Court of Queen's Bench for a habeas Corpus by the Common Law which was granted;* upon the return whereof, the Judges of the Queen's Bench desired the assistance of the rest of the Judges, *who were all of opinion, except the Lord Chief Justice Holt, that they ought to be remanded* [2].

Subjoined are a few passages which have been selected from the writings of Junius and Lord Temple, as being more or less remarkable for similarity in phrases and opinions, in addition to the many other coincidences of language which have been occasionally quoted in the Notes throughout these volumes :—

" My Lord, you should not encourage *these appeals to Heaven.* The pious prince from whom you are supposed to descend, made such frequent use of them in his public declarations, that at last the people also found it necessary *to appeal to Heaven* in their turn." —*Junius,* vol. i. p. 458.

" The collective body of the

" And when the obstinacy of unhappy princes, enslaved with the notions of arbitrary power, which they called Prerogative, left no other option but to submit to the usurpation of the crown, or to fight, *they drew their swords, and Heaven to which they appealed,* propitious to English liberty, justified their cause and crowned it

---

[1] " When Lord Camden supposes *a necessity* (which the King is to judge of), and *founded upon that necessity,* attributes to the Crown *a legal power* (not given by the Act itself), *to suspend the operation of an Act of the Legislature,* I listen with diffidence and respect, but without the smallest degree of conviction or assent, &c."—*Junius,* vol. ii. p. 350. " General arguments against the doctrine of *necessity,* and the dangerous use that may be made of it, are of no weight in this particular case. *Necessity includes the idea of inevitable. Whenever it is so, it creates a law, to which all positive laws, and all positive rights must give way.*"— *Junius,* vol. ii. p. 395.

[2] " In the case of *the Queen v. Paty & alias,* 3 *Ann:* the defendants ["the 5 partys"] having been committed to Newgate by a warrant of the Speaker of the House of Commons, *were brought by Habeas Corpus into the Queen's Bench,* and prayed to be discharged upon the illegality of the commitment. The three puisne judges refused to interfere upon the authority of Lord Shaftesbury's case, *and the prisoners were remanded contrary to the opinion of Lord Chief Justice Holt,* one of the ablest judges that ever presided in that Court."—*Junius,* vol. iii. p. 365.

people form that jury, and *from their decision there is but one appeal.*"—*Junius,* vol. i. p. 505.

" *The first appeal* was to the integrity of their representatives; the second to the King's justice; *the last argument of the people,* whenever they have recourse to it, will carry more perhaps than persuasion to parliament, or supplication to the throne."—*Ibid.,* vol. ii. p. 134.

" If this last resource should fail us, our next and *latest appeal must be made to Heaven.*"—*Ibid.,* vol. iii. p. 165.

" Either the laws and constitution must be preserved by *a dreadful appeal to the sword,*" &c.— *Ibid.,* vol. iii. p. 379.

" If, following the glorious example of their ancestors, they should no longer *appeal* to the creature of the constitution, but to that high Being who gave them the rights of humanity."—*Ibid.,* vol. ii. p. 75.

" Delusions of this sort have indeed been long since *exploded,* but there are other *diabolical arts* which certainly do exist."—*Junius,* vol. iii. p. 39.

" An ostensible engagement, with a mental reservation, is the first principle of the *morale relachée professed and inculcated by the Society of Jesus.*"—*Ibid.,* vol. iii. p. 70.

" I am not deeply read in authors of that *professed title,* but I remember seeing Busembaum, Suarez, Molina, and a score of other *jesuitical books* burnt at Paris, for their *sound casuistry,* by the hands of the common hangman."—*Ibid.,* vol. iii. p. 46.

with success."—*Lord Temple's Speech on the Suspending and Dispensing Power,* 1766, p. 25.

" I concur with Mr. Locke's sentiments that when that great question does arise (and it must be the greatest of misfortunes when it does) between an executive and legislative power, constituted as our's are, *there is no judge on earth to decide it; and therefore the only remedy is the appeal to Heaven, that is, to the sword.*"—*Ibid.,* p. 24.

" For, as Mr. Locke truly says, the people have by a law antecedent, and paramount to all positive laws of men, reserved that ultimate determination to themselves, which belongs to all mankind, when their lies *no appeal on earth,* viz., to make their *appeal to Heaven;* and this judgement they cannot part with."—*Lord Temple's Speech on the Suspending and Dispensing Power,* p. 25.

" I might have said that it is condemned and *exploded by all morality* and sound *divinity;* avowed and professed only by *Jesuits, and such diabolical casuists.*"—*Lord Temple's Speech on the Suspending and Dispensing Prerogative,* p. 32.

— " perhaps a fit *state casuist* might for once at least," &c.   *   *   *

" Suppose only the King to be advised by the *casuists of state necessity,*" &c.— *Ibid.,* p. 52.

" They saw the very first opportunity
laid hold on to revive the doctrines of
a *dispensing power, state necessity,* arcana
of government, and all that clumsy machinery of *exploded prerogative,* &c."—
Junius, vol. iii. p. 9.

" The influence which makes *a septennial parliament* dependent upon the
pleasure of the Crown," &c.—*Ibid.,* vol. ii.
p. 211.

" When *the Septennial Act passed,* the
Legislature did, what apparently and
palpably they had no power to do ; but
they did more than people in general
were aware of ; they, *in effect, disfran-
chised the whole kingdom for four years.*"
—*Ibid.,* vol. i. p. 289.

" The prospect of your resentment is
too remote, and although the last Session
of a *Septennial parliament* be usually
employed in courting the favour of the
people," &c.—*Ibid.,* vol. i. p. 347.

" The *shortening the duration of Parliaments* is a subject on which Mr. Horne
cannot enlarge too warmly. If I did not
profess the same sentiments, I should be
shamefully inconsistent with myself.
It is unnecessary to bind Lord Chatham
by the written formality of an engagement. *He has publicly declared himself
a convert to triennial parliaments.*"—
Ibid., vol. ii. p. 311.

" They ought to insist upon a *triennial,* and banish the idea of an *annual
parliament.*"—*Ibid.,* vol. i. p. 284.

" If that bill had not been
passed, I am ready to maintain,
in direct contradiction to Lord
Camden's doctrine (taken as Scævola states it) that a litigious ex-
porter of corn, who had suffered

— " and leads to a dis-
trust of the uprightness of
judicature by introducing
jesuitical casuistry, in lieu
of plain, obvious, common
sense."—*Another Letter to
Almon,* p. 144.

" They passed the *Sep-
tennial Act,* which was indeed an extraordinary step,
and such a one as I hope
no parliament will ever again
be obliged to make, for we
must allow it was some-
thing extraordinary in a
*House of Commons chosen
by the people for three years
only, to continue themselves
for seven.*"—*Lord Temple's
Speech on the Repeal of the
Jews' Naturalization Bill in
1753.*

" As to the other points
of *shortening the duration
of Parliament, and increas-
ing the knights of the shire,*
my general notion of the
former, your Lordship
knows, and for the latter,
in general, I should wish
it success when matured
and ripened."—*Lord Tem-
ple to Lord Chatham, April*
18, 1771.

— " what can justify an act
questioned in any court of law
inferior or superior, but a legal
defence ? For certainly if the
embargo itself is *not a legal act,
within the known powers of the*

in his property in consequence of the proclamation, *might have laid his action against the custom-house officers, and would infallibly have recovered damages.* No jury could refuse them ; and if I, who am by no means litigious, had been so injured, I would assuredly have instituted a *suit in Westminster Hall,* on purpose to try the question of right. *I would have done it upon a principle of defiance of the pretended power of either or both Houses to make declarations inconsistent with law, and I have no doubt that with an act of Parliament on my side, I should have been too strong for them all.*"— *Junius,* vol. ii. p. 363.

" You have no enemies, Sir, but those who persuade you to aim at *power without right,*" &c. —*Ibid.*, vol. i. p. 384.

" The mere insulting assertion of *power without right.*"—*Ibid.*, vol. ii. p. 407.

" When no circumstances whatsoever are alleged in favour of the prisoner, it is a *power without right,* and a daring violation of the whole English law of Bail."— *Ibid.*, vol. ii. p. 419.

prerogative, it can afford no legal defence against any action brought into the Courts of Westminster Hall. I am sure the noble Lord on the woolsack can neither have forgot, nor can he differ from a very well founded opinion, which he knows well has been given in one of these courts, and not a great while ago, ' that *judges can decide only according to law, and are upon their oaths to pronounce what is law, and that they can regard nothing but law, not even votes of Parliaments.*'"—*Lord Temple's Speech on the Suspending and Dispensing Prerogative,* p. 50.

" I objected to the words *Royal authority,* as I hold *authority* to be *legal power,* whereas the embargo is, in my opinion, *power without law,* and *against law,* consequently is not authority in a just sense." —*Ibid.*, p. 36.

" The laws trampled upon and transgressed by the people ; Acts of Parliament, from a *careless necessity,* broken and suspended by *power without right,* Royal authority, that is unfounded prerogative, Royal authority exerted *against law.*"— *Ibid.*, p. 64.

" But rashly and wilfully to claim or exercise as Prerogative, *a power clearly against law,* is too great boldness for this country."—*Ibid.*, p. 55.

" *I speak to facts,* with which all of us are conversant. I speak to men, and to their experience." —*Ibid.*, vol. ii. p. 305.

" *These are facts,* Mr. Woodfall, which I promise you no gentleman in the guards will deny."—*Ibid.*, vol. ii. p. 46.

" But I shall not descend to a dispute about words. *I speak to things.*"—*Ibid.*, vol. iii. p. 137.

" *I speak to facts ;* and it is well they are proved, for I should not be believed without evidence." —*Ibid.*, p. 64.

" I do not know that they (*the Jesuitical books*) have yet found their way to England, unless perchance it be to the library of His Grace the Duke of Grafton, where they probably stand with the chapter of promises *dog-eared* down for the perusal of scrupulous statesmen."—*Junius*, vol. iii. p. 46.

" My Lord Privy Seal [Lord Chatham] and the Secretary of State [the Duke of Grafton] went to statute books before unopened, not *dog-eared*, and there made the amazing astonishing discovery," &c.—*Lord Temple's Speech on the Suspending and Dispensing Prerogative*, p. 62.

" If Lord Camden admits that the subsequent sanction of parliament was necessary to make the proclamation legal, why did he so *obstinately oppose the Bill which was soon after brought in for indemnifying all those persons who had acted under it ?*"—*Ibid*, vol. ii. p. 363.

— "ministers are ashamed or afraid to own that an act they advised *was not legal, though they say it was necessary.* . . . . . . " They will defend the act done as *strictly legal, at the expense of maintaining a degree of the dispensing power*, I say a degree, for I will not make it worse than they do themselves. They are so much more delicate or infallible than King William's Ministers and privy councillors, *that they are affronted with the offer of an indemnity, and one noble Lord says timeo Danaos et dona ferentes.*"—*Ibid.*, p. 34.

" I confess *I should be contented to renounce the forms of the constitution once more*, if there were no other way to obtain substantial justice for the people."—*Ibid.*, vol. ii. p. 222.

" I believe *I should not scruple to break the law if I could, in a proper case*, and trust to the justice of my country."—*Ib.*, p. 48.

" The *noble spirit* of the metropolis."—*Ibid.*, vol. ii. p. 115.

— " the Mansion House, that *seat of liberty and spirit.*"—*Lord Temple to Lord Chatham*, April 2, 1770.

" The submission of *a free people* to the *executive authority of Government* is no more than a compliance with laws which *they themselves have enacted.*"— *Ibid.*, vol. i. p. 387.

" *The freedom of men under Government is to have a standing rule to live by*, common to every one of the Society, and *made by the Legislative power created in it.* So says Mr. Locke who is appealed to as a great authority."—*Lord Temple's Speech on the Suspending and Dispensing Prerogative*, p. 4.

" The plan of tutelage and future dominion over the heir apparent laid many years ago at Carlton House between the Princess Dowager and her favourite the Earl of Bute,

" When the arrangements were all made (in 1763), Lord Bute retired to his

was as gross and palpable as that which was concerted between *Anne of Austria and Cardinal Mazarine to govern Louis XIV.*, and in effect to prolong his minority until the end of their lives."—*Junius,* vol. ii. p. 65, *note.*

"Although the *favourite* was at the present moment abroad, *yet his influence by his confidential agents, was as potent as if he were present.* Who does not know the *Mazarinade of France ;* that *Mazarine absent was Mazarine still.* What is there to distinguish the two cases?"—*Lord Chatham's Speech, March 2, 1770, of which the report is attributed to* JUNIUS.

" *With respect to the appointment of Mr. Luttrell,* the Chancellor (Lord Camden) *has never yet given any authentic opinion.*" —*(June,* 1769.) *Junius,* vol. i. p. 498.

" The spirit of the Favorite had some *apparent influence upon every Administration,* and every set of Ministers preserved an appearance of duration, so long as they submitted to that influence." —*Ibid.,* vol. i. p. 506.

" They who object to detached parts of Junius's last letter either do not *mean him fairly,*" &c. — *Ibid.,* vol. ii. p. 223.

" The question to those who *mean fairly,*" &c.— *Ibid.,* vol. ii. p. 342.

" That he is *the King of a free people* is indeed his greatest glory. That he may long con-

estate in Bedfordshire, and the Ministers boasted that they had exiled him. Lord Temple called it a Ma- *zarinade, alluding to a similar conduct of Cardinal Mazarine, who governed France as absolutely when absent from Court as when in it.*"[1]—*Almon's Biographical Anecdotes,* vol. ii. p. 36.

" It is now certain Lord Mansfield and *Lord Camden have never given any opinion concerning the disqualification,* since they say so themselves." — *Lord Temple to Lady Chatham, May,* 1769.

" Under the same *secret* and *malign influence which through each successive Administration,*" &c.— *City Address, as marked by Lord Temple.*

" The Duke of Devonshire I believe has been pretty direct to the King, and I dare say *means us very fairly.*"—*Lord Temple to Mr. Pitt, November* 11, 1756.

" *Deal with me fairly,* and I will come to you sooner or later, or in *any shape* that may be most agreeable."—*Lord Temple to Mr. Grenville, July* 9, 1759.

" We are a FREE PEOPLE, and I am for a FREE KING."—*Conclusion of Lord Temple's Speech on the Suspending and Dispensing Prerogative.*

— "friends to that system of liberty, which was founded in the expulsion of the House of

---

[1] It should be remembered, that Almon professes that he has endeavoured in his Anecdotes, to " *state facts as nearly as possible in the original language,* and in the original colouring in which they were spontaneously given at the moment."

tinue *the King of a free people* is the second wish of my heart. The first is THAT THE PEOPLE MAY BE FREE." — *Conclusion of Letter* xxxvii. *Junius,* vol. ii. p. 122.

Stuart, and secured by the accession of that of Hanover, under which, *their title being founded in freedom, it is our own fault, if we are not free."* —*Conclusion of Lord Temple's Letter from Albemarle Street to the Cocoa Tree.*

" That no such BADGE of SLAVERY does yet exist in this country is still believed. That it never may exist will naturally be the wish of every ENGLISHMAN."—*Conclusion of Lord Temple's Letter on the Seizure of Papers.*

" *The silence of Junius portends no good to the Ministry.* When he honours them with his notice, it is not a momentary blast. *He gathers like a tempest, and all the fury of the elements bursts upon them at once.*"—*Ibid.,* vol. iii. p. 241.

" *The people of England* are by nature somewhat phlegmatic . . . Their anger is not easily kindled, nor easily extinguished ; it is dark and gloomy ; it is nourished to a gigantic size and vigour, under *a silent meditation* on their wrongs, *until at last it arrives at such a mature and steady vehemence, as becomes terrible indeed.*"—*Ibid.,* vol. iii. p. 18.

" *The silence of an injured people is the calm before an earthquake,* and the despots have this moment perhaps reason to tremble, little as they apprehend *a storm that will sweep them to destruction.*" — *Lord Temple's Speech on the Resolutions relating to America, May* 18, 1770.

" I own I am concerned to see, that the great condition which ought to be the *sine quâ non* of parliamentary qualification, which ought to be the basis as it will assuredly be the only support, of *every barrier raised in defence of the Constitution.*"— *Ibid.,* vol. i. p. 284.

" If they will hold out a power, unconstitutional and destructive of the vitals of the Constitution, they must excuse others for holding up the *barrier against such a power, and defending the Constitution.*"—*Lord Temple's Speech on Suspending and Dispensing Prerogative, &c.,* p. 44.

— "who thinks he cannot spend the last remains of his health in a better cause, than *struggling to maintain the great barriers of the Constitution.*"—*Lord Temple's Letter from Albemarle Street to the Cocoa Tree.*

" The precise evil against which *the Constitution had contrived the trial by jury as its barrier.*" —*Another Letter to Almon,* p. 14.

" The great question comes on on Monday, and Lord Granby is already *staggered.*"—*Ibid.,* vol. i. p. 170.

" Gascoyne thinks that if Mr. Pitt comes, many of the Tories will be *staggered.*"—

"I never had a doubt about the strict right of pressing, until I heard that Lord Mansfield had applauded Lord Chatham for delivering something like this doctrine in the House of Lords. That consideration *staggered* me not a little."—*Junius*, vol. ii. p. 354.

"So curious an assertion would *stagger* the faith of Mr. Sylla."—*Ibid.*, vol. ii. p. 393.

— "contradict their own advice, and endeavour to *stagger* his resolution, at the moment when he has most occasion for it." — *Ibid.*, vol. iii. p. 379.

"*Appearances justify suspicion*, and when the safety of a nation is at stake, *suspicion is a just ground of inquiry.*"— *Ibid.*, vol. i. p. 388.

"It would raise and *justify suspicions*," &c.—*Ibid.*, vol. i. p. 218.

"When the Duke of Grafton has exhausted the Treasury, he will find that *every other power departs with the power of giving.*"— *Ibid.*, vol. iii. p. 189.

Lord Temple to Lady Chatham, November, 1762.

"I am a little *staggered* from so many circumstances." —*Lord Temple to Mr. Grenville, December* 13, 1757.

— "to *stagger* the judge who tried the cause," &c.— *Letter concerning Libels, &c.,* p. 66.

"Those who set about a private examination, especially *of one side*, after a public trial had, in order to stagger a jury," &c. — *Another Letter to Almon,* p. 65.

"Such a proposition carries with it an *appearance* which *justifies any suspicion.*"—*Lord Temple's draft of a Letter to Trustees of Buckingham Church.*

— "nothing could be done in such a situation, except giving away some things that fell, by the disposition of which the Ministers could not but see *the power was departed from them.*"—*Principles of the late Changes, by Lord Temple,* p. 34.

It is well known that the Author of Junius wrote a Poem on the Loves of the Duke of Grafton and Miss Parsons. The original manuscript is still extant in the possession of Mr. Woodfall. I believe it to have been sent to the Printer of the *Public Advertiser* in March, 1768 [1], shortly before the first Letter addressed by the

---

[1] Among Mr. Woodfall's collections of Junius manuscripts, there is an envelope addressed, "*To the Printer of the Public Advertiser, March* 14*th.*" It is folded in an oblong form, and suits exactly the size of the paper on which the poem of *Harry and Nan* is written. This I take to have been the original cover of it, but it has been misplaced, and now encloses the private note, No. 39, which was written in November, 1771. It is, besides, the only communication addressed "*to the Printer ;*" all the other private notes are addressed personally "*to Mr. Woodfall.*"

Author of Junius (but without signature) to the Duke of Grafton, in which his appearance at the Opera House with Miss Parsons is particularly alluded to[1]. The Poem was, however, first printed in Almon's *Political Register* for June, 1768, but whether from a copy sent to Almon for that purpose by Mr. Woodfall, because he did not wish it to appear in the *Public Advertiser*, or whether it was communicated to him by the Author, can only now be matter of conjecture[2].

It is entitled HARRY[3] *and* NAN, *an Elegy in the Manner of Tibullus*, and consists of six verses, commencing thus:—

" Can Apollo[4] resist, or a poet *refuse*
When Harry and Nancy solicit the *Muse*[5].
A Statesman, who makes a[6] whole Nation his care,
And a Nymph, who is almost as chaste, as she 's fair."

The second verse begins:—

" Dear Spousy had led such a damnable *life*,
He determin'd to keep any —— but his *wife*."[7]

[1] *Junius*, vol. iii. p. 41.

[2] This is not the only instance in which a communication refused by Woodfall finds its way to Almon, who proves less fearful of consequences. It will be remembered that the *Letter from Candor to the Public Advertiser*, which Woodfall declined to print unless the author would avow himself and abide the consequences, was immediately accepted and published by Almon, as if Lord Temple kept Almon in reserve for anything that Woodfall was afraid of.

[3] The Duke of Grafton's Christian name was Henry, but Junius always calls him *Harry*. It may be remarked that Junius has *twice* mentioned King Henry VIII., and on both occasions[a] has styled him *Harry the Eighth*. So, also, in *Another Letter to Mr. Almon*[b], he is called *Harry VIII.*; and Lord Temple, in a letter of condolence to Thomas, Lord Lyttelton[c], upon the death of his father, mentions *Harry the Fifth*. It is, to be sure, less remarkable that he should call his own brother Henry Grenville[d], *Harry* also, but it proves the habit of altering the name.

[4] Apollo was a very favourite Deity with Lady Temple ; he is mentioned very often in her Poems—for instance,—
" Apollo, facetious and merry, no doubt."—" Apollo as fine and perfumed as a beau."
—" Apollo and his tuneful maids."—" Apollo tuned the sounding lyre."—" Apollo soothed the mournful king."—" What but Apollo's lyre express."—" Aid me, ye nine, Apollo's sacred band."

[5] " To such a dream can I assent *refuse* ?
Forbid it, God of Love, and every *muse*."
                    Lord Temple's Poem, entitled a " Midsummer Night's Dream."

[6] So in the original MS., but in the printed copies it is *the* whole nation, &c.

[7] In Lady Temple's Poems are the following similar rhymes,—
" What ! dare before me to make love to my *wife*,
I can't be good-humoured again for my *life*."

[a] *Junius*, vol. i. p. 346, and vol. ii. p. 202.   [b] P. 154.
[c] *Chatham Correspondence*, vol. iv. p. 222.   [d] See *ante*, p. cxxxiv. *note*.

The fifth verse runs thus:—

> " So lucky was Harry that nothing could mend
> His choice of a mistress, but that of a friend ;—
> A Friend so obliging, and yet so sincere,
> With pleasure in one eye, in t'other a tear." [1]

And the sixth begins:—

> " My Friend holds the Candle ;—the Lovers *debate*,
> And among them God knows how they settle the *State*." [2]

My present object is to show that "Harry and Nan" may have been written either by Lord or Lady Temple. A small quarto volume of Poems by the latter, was printed by Horace Walpole at the Strawberry Hill press [3], and some of them, as well as those which still remain in manuscript, are similar in style and metre to the Elegy on Harry and Nan : thus, *On the Birth of Pallas and Mars* begins,—

> " If all should be true that old Histories tell,
> Jove lived with his wife like the d—— in h——."

Lord Temple also wrote some Poems ; several are extant in his handwriting, corrected and interlined. The following lines, on the return of Wilkes to England, are not without merit :—

> '" His wished return the Sons of Freedom claim
> In shouts as loud as his increasing fame.

" Against my consent, Vulcan took me for *life*,
Now considering my youth, do I make a bad *wife ?*"
" But I who long to save the *life*
Of the best mother, friend, and *wife*."

[1] Mr. Bradshaw is the *friend* who is thus *honourably* distinguished. He was Secretary to the Treasury under the Duke of Grafton's Administration, and was hated by Junius with the greater intensity, because he had been formerly his friend. It will be remembered that Mr. Bradshaw's *tears* furnished Junius with a subject of sarcastic ridicule upon another occasion.—See *Junius*, vol. iii. p. 263.

[2] The following similar rhymes are from Lady Temple's Poems :—

" Hath introduced unkind *debate*,
And topsy-turvy turned our *State*."

" To save their fortunes and secure the *State*,
Which scheme the best occasioned wise *debate*."

" Can enter into high *debate*,
And settle all their little *State*."

[3] See, *ante*, vol. ii. p. 257.

Waft him, propitious gales! to Albion's shore,
Never to quit his much loved country more.
What though he knows tyrannic power prepares
All that or insolence or meanness dares.
Though fierce oppression at the Statesman's nod
Shakes over Liberty her iron rod;
Though foul corruption be prepared to try,
And christen in mock trial, Truth a lie;
Though rank Hypocrisy with cankered heart
Points at his head her most envenomed dart;
Though persecution's mercenaries stand
With Informations armed in either hand;
His steadfast purpose terrors cannot shake,
Nor his unconquerable spirit break.
So Regulus to Carthage once returned,
And fired with patriot zeal, their torments spurned.
WILKES trusts to Freedom's, values Freedom's cause,
And cannot suffer, but with England's Laws.
From Court to Court through various perils tost,
While Juries yet remain, ALL is not lost.
For proud Prerogative at last may see,
Britons, though loyal, WILL *continue free.*" [1]

In the Introduction to that admirable edition of the Letters of Junius [2], by Pinkerton, under the name of *Robert Heron, Esq.,* the author asks,—

" Whence had Junius that readiness of disrespectful allusion to the Bible and the ceremonies of religion, which is so often displayed in these Letters? Perhaps from familiar acquaintance with the Holy Scriptures, the Book of Common Prayer, and the ordinary services of the Church.   .   .   .   .

" Or shall I venture to conjecture that Chillingworth and Pascal were much studied by him, even while he was engaged in the composition of these Letters; and that like every other writer, he insensibly transferred into his own works some striking allusions from the books

---

[1] " That he may long continue the King of a free people, is the second wish that animates my heart. The first is THAT THE PEOPLE MAY BE FREE."—*Junius,* vol. ii. p. 122.

[2] 2 vols. 8vo.   London, 1802.

which he read? His allusions to religion, so far as they are contemptuous, relate chiefly to the absurdities of the Roman Catholic religion[1]; a fact from which we may fairly infer, either that the course of his education and the incidents of his life, led him into a particular acquaintance with these, and an indignant disgust against them, or else that he, in this instance, merely echoed the voices of Pascal and Chillingworth."

I have selected the following passages from Junius, in order to contrast them with a similar selection from the writings of Lord Temple:—

" Avail yourself of all the unforgiving piety of the Court you live in, *and bless God that you are not as other men are, extortioners, unjust, adulterers, or even as this publican.*"—*Junius*, vol. i. p. 461.

" Yet he must have *bread*, my Lord, or rather he must have *wine*. If you deny him the *cup*, there will be no keeping him within the pale of the Ministry."—*Ibid.*, vol. ii. p. 249.

" If it be true that a virtuous man, *struggling with adversity*, be a scene worthy of the gods, the glorious contention between you and the best of princes, deserves a circle equally attentive and respectable: *I think I already see other gods rising from the earth to behold it.*"[2]— *Ibid.*, vol. ii. p. 243.

" Without meaning an indecent comparison, I may venture to foretel that *the Bible* and Junius will be read when the *Commentaries of the Jesuits* will be forgotten."—*Ibid.*, vol. ii. p. 316.

" The holy Author of our religion was seen in the company of sinners; but it was his gracious purpose to convert them from their sins. *Go thou and do likewise.*"—*Ibid.*, vol. ii. p. 440.

" This is the present *catholic* political faith, *which, unless a man believe*, he shall not get a place."—*Ibid.*, vol. iii. p. 43.

" I agree with your correspondent, that when a nation is governed as we are, our constant prayer should be, *Give peace* in the *time* of these Ministers, O *Lord!*"—*Ibid.*, vol. iii. p. 163.

" That we may be *quietly governed*, is a very proper petition in the service of the Church of England. If the worst men should be *put in authority* under the King, they will think it politic to counteract the

---

[1] See Lord Temple's description of some *absurdities* of this nature, *ante*, p. cxlv.

[2] " The first part of the comparison is from a well-known expression of Seneca concerning Cato. The latter part is from the mouth of Saul, when he beheld the effect of the incantations of the Witch of Endor."—*Heron*.

Junius has repeated the former part in his Letter to Lord Mansfield,—" Such a man as Mr. Eyre, *struggling with adversity*, must always be an interesting scene to Lord Mansfield."

prayers of the people, and *indifferently minister* injustice, to the punishment of virtue, and the maintenance of vice."—*Junius*, vol. iii. p. 260.

And the following are from Lord Temple—

" If you had never deviated into the higher regions of cherubim and seraphim, or the *conversion* of Wilkes, compared with that of *St. Paul.*"—*Lord Temple to Wilkes*, Oct. 12, 1754.

" What amends is it afterwards to declare him *white as the snow on Salmon?*"—*Ibid.*, Oct. 22, 1761.

" Have Beckford, Gascoigne, yourself, and many others, thundered in the Capitol? *Is the voice of your thunder gone forth into all parts?*"— *Lord Temple to Wilkes*, Nov. 25, 1762.

" By which time I hope the sick man *will take up his bed and walk.*" —*Lord Temple to Lady Chatham*, Jan. 25, 1764.

" I cannot on this occasion drive from my mind those words of the Scripture, which say, '*If a son ask bread from any of you which is a father, will he give him a stone? Or if he ask a fish, will he for a fish give him a serpent? or if he shall ask an egg, will he offer him a scorpion?*'"—*Lord Temple's Speech on the Suspending and Dispensing Prerogative.*

" —— and reduces it to the case of *Esau's necessity, who sold his birthright for a mess of pottage.*"—*Ibid.*

" *They bear witness against themselves, and their witness must be true:* out of their own mouths they are condemned."—*Lord Temple, Principles of the late Changes, &c.*

" They had approached as near the *pool* as they could, against *the angel should stir the waters* of emolument."—*Ibid.*

" It always has been, and always will be true, that *when the wicked beareth rule, the people mourn; but when the righteous are in authority, the people rejoice.*"—*Lord Temple, Letter from Albemarle Street to the Cocoa Tree.*

—— " He tells it from so many quarters, and some seemingly most authentic, that *St. Thomas himself could not doubt of it;* I, who am a sinner, know not what to say."—*Lord Temple to Mr. Grenville*, July 12, 1766.

———

One of the numerous occasions on which Lord Temple was accused of being the author or promoter of political libels, arose out of a debate in the House of Commons on the 31st of January, 1770, when Mr. Grenville having observed that—

"those who say all they like, may chance to hear what they do not like;"

Mr. Luttrell replied, and, after repeating Mr. Grenville's words, added—

"The honourable gentleman, I believe, will not much like to hear, that having been traduced by a libel, I found upon the examination of a printer, that it came from a near relation of that honourable gentleman."

Mr. Walsingham, on the part of Lord Temple, who was the person hinted at, said that he had authority to state that Lord Temple "knew nothing of the letters which he calls libels."

Horace Walpole's account of the matter is, that

"Colonel Luttrell had forced the printer to divulge the writer, one Lloyd, who had confessed on his knees with tears, that Lord Temple had forced him to practise that office. Luttrell added that he had taxed Lord Temple with it by letter, who had not deigned to make an answer. Captain Walsingham said he had gone to Lord Temple on the same errand, who had declared on his honour he was not concerned in it."—*Memoirs of George III.*, vol. iv. p. 77.

No letter from Colonel Luttrell has been preserved among Lord Temple's papers; but it appears from a letter which I have found addressed by Lloyd to some person whom he styles "My Lord" (probably Lord Camden, to whom, when Chancellor, he is supposed to have been Secretary), that the letters or libels in question had been in the possession of Lloyd, and that he had inadvertently entrusted them to a friend who desired to peruse them, and who had suffered them to pass into the hands of a printer who was determined at all hazards to print them, and they were accordingly produced immediately before the Middlesex election, in order to prejudice the interest of Luttrell, who had called upon Lloyd for the name of the person to whom he had entrusted them, as he was convinced there was some person of high rank concerned in the publication, and he mentioned the name of Lord Temple. Lloyd assured him, however, that he was not known to Lord Temple, and he did not believe that he or any other person of high rank was at all concerned in it. He absolutely refused, under any circumstances, to divulge the name of the friend to whom he has lent them, and he strenuously denies the accusation of having acted any unmanly or unbecoming part, or that he had asked Colonel Luttrell's pardon upon his knees, a proceeding which he designates as an abject and contemptible meanness of which he was incapable, and that he never did nor ever intended to ask his pardon. He concludes a very long letter by requesting that his noble correspondent will communicate the contents of it to Lord Temple, and it is signed "Thomas Lloyd, Great James Street, Bedford Row, 12th February, 1770."

The letters or libels complained of are printed in the first five numbers of a newspaper called the *Middlesex Journal*, commencing on Tuesday, April 4th, 1769. They relate to a claim of one hundred guineas made by Dr. Kelly, the Regius Professor of Physic at Oxford, for medical and surgical attendance upon a Miss Arabella Bolton, during her pregnancy, &c., and it appeared that the young woman had been seduced by Mr. Luttrell, and lived with him as his mistress.

The letters are dated in the year 1761, and were written by Mr. Luttrell, Dr. Kelly, and by Mr. Thomas Lloyd, on the refusal of Mr. Luttrell to pay the charge made by Dr. Kelly; the circumstances to which they relate took place in the years 1756 and 1757; they are extremely disgraceful to the character of Mr. Luttrell, and the publication of them at this time, for electioneering purposes, is equally disgraceful to the editor of the newspaper and the correspondent who furnished them.

In connection with the *Middlesex Journal*, I may mention that the noted Philip Thicknesse was one of the proprietors, and that Philip Lloyd, afterwards Dean of Norwich, was married to one of the daughters of Thicknesse.

It has been supposed from some of the Letters of the Author of Junius, under the signature of "Veteran," &c., that he was very conversant with the affairs of the Stock Exchange, that he knew all "*the pernicious arts practised in the Alley*," and all the mysteries of "*bulls and bears*."

On this subject, as regards Lord Temple, I have no other information but that which may be gathered from the opinions of his contemporaries.

In the year 1763 was published a pamphlet entitled *An Appeal to Facts, in a Letter to the Right Honourable* EARL TEMPLE [1]. The author begins by professing to be at a loss for a proper patron to whom he might address his discourse respecting a Loan, but he ironically adds :—

"from all this doubt and perplexity I was relieved at once by your Lordship, when I heard you make before a certain Assembly, which you never did nor ever will impose upon, the following unexpected and welcome Declaration:—That *although you had no personal business in the Alley, you had yet made Alley business as much your study, as any Jew or Christian there.* It is therefore with the utmost propriety that I address these papers to you; in which, and under your inspection, I mean to inquire into the true merits of a late bargain made for the nation. I shall likewise add a word or two on the tax that has been laid on cyder, and submit the whole to your review, which I know will be exceedingly cool, and no less candid." . . . . .

" They resolved in the second place to defer making the bargain for this Loan till after the Definitive Treaty should be signed ; 'till every event had happened that might contribute towards the rise of Stocks. How these things must operate, *every dabbler in Exchange Alley knows.* It would therefore be impertinent to detain, one moment longer, *a person of your consummate skill in the matters transacted there,* by offering at any proof of it."

I have not aspired or pretended to write an Essay upon the general question of the Authorship of Junius, but confined myself to such desultory notes upon the subject as seemed to advocate my own theory in favour of Lord Temple, and in the same unconnected manner I have continued my remarks, whenever an occasion presented itself, in the Notes to the Correspondence in the ensuing pages.

It will, I fear, be said that I have been too prone to dwell on trifles and to magnify them ; that in the many and various instances of similarity of phrases, locutions, and peculiar meanings affixed

[1] It was written by Mr. John Dalrymple, author of an Essay on Feudal Property.

to words, between Junius and Lord Temple, I may seem to have exhibited some which are not only trivial and popular, but irrelevant and inconclusive. Without however attaching undue importance to these coincidences, which were perhaps often accidental, I have nevertheless considered it my duty to produce every particle of evidence *valeat quantum;* and the more so, because other theories upon the same subject have been supported in a similar manner; and because such evidence, slight as indeed it is, and even worthless in a few cases, might from its frequency or other particularities add some little weight to the aggregate of circumstantial proof. I may also plead in excuse that all the more important topics connected with the Authorship are generally known, or have been well nigh exhausted; and besides that I am strongly impressed with the notion that if ever Junius is satisfactorily identified, it will be from the discovery of some very trifling circumstance which the Author himself, in his anxiety for concealment, had possibly overlooked.

If I have not succeeded in establishing my theory to my own satisfaction, it is chiefly from the absence of actual mathematical demonstration; for I must frankly confess that I should not be *quite* content with anything short of that decided proof; but it is my firm and deliberate conviction, that if Lord Temple were not the Author of Junius, then the Author has never yet been publicly named, and that he will then still remain that mysterious UMBRA SINE NOMINE, to exercise the ingenuity of some more successful inquirer.

I should be ungrateful indeed if I did not take this opportunity of expressing my thankful acknowledgments to the Right Honourable John Wilson Croker, for the many valuable suggestions with which he has favoured me during the progress of the Grenville Correspondence through the press.

W. J. S.

GRENVILLE PAPERS.

LORD CLIVE TO MR. GRENVILLE.

(Cape of Good Hope, January 5, 1765.)

DEAR SIR,—We have had a very pleasant and expeditious passage to this place, where we expected to have found Commodore Byron, who sailed three weeks before us from Rio Janeiro. I can now easily perceive, that if Byron be destined for the East Indies, it is South about.

The Manilla expedition has certainly proved a very unfortunate one for the East India Company, since it has given rise to a very powerful rebel, whom we have not yet been able to subdue with all our force on the Coast of Coromandel, who has not only cost us the lives of numbers of private men, but also of many gallant and brave officers, among whom may be reckoned Major Preston, than whom a better officer never served in India, as Colonel Monson will inform you.

Affairs in Bengal still remain in much confusion. The iniquity of individuals makes a thorough reformation absolutely necessary.

A French Pacquet anchored here three days ago, who left France the 22nd of October. From her we only learn that Mons. Law [1] had sailed for India with

---

[1] Baron Law, of Lauriston, Commandant General of the French Settlements in the East Indies. He was a nephew of John Law, the celebrated projector of the Mississippi scheme.

five ships full of men, military stores, masons, carpenters, &c., and that a fleet of ships were to leave France about Christmas. If there be any truth in this, they certainly mean to resettle in India; and if they do resettle, I will venture to pronounce it will not be at Pondicherry, but in the Deccan, where they are at a distance from our chief strength, where they are under no restrictions by the late Treaty, and where they may acquire what extent of territory they please by grant from Nizam Ally, the Soubah of the Deccan, for giving him that assistance which we were obliged to refuse him on account of the expedition to the Manillas.

However, I hope our enemies will be well watched, both at home and abroad, for I am persuaded they have ambitious views, by their sending out two such active men as Law and Surville to command.

I must request your acceptance of two casks of Constantia, one of red, and one of white, which the Governor assures me is genuine and good, but new [1].

Captain Collins, of His Majesty's ship *Weymouth*, has taken the charge of them, and will deliver you this letter. All that I can say of Captain Collins is, that he is a very deserving man, and hath not partaken of any of the spoils of setting up and pulling down of Nabobs. I am, &c., &c.

CLIVE.

THE BISHOP OF GLOUCESTER TO MR. GRENVILLE.

Grosvenor Square, January 12, 1765.

HONOURED SIR,—The very polite, but very general answer, which I had the honour to receive from you

---

[1] I can vouch for the excellence of this Constantia when it was at least eighty years old.

this last summer, when I took the liberty of mentioning to you my pretensions on the Bishopric of London, both encourages and necessitates me to give you this further trouble.

Sir, I presume that the marks which I have given of my duty to His Majesty, and of my zeal for his service, are not in the least equivocal; certainly not, in the opinion of the enemies of His Majesty's measures, who have insulted me with so foul a torrent of abuse and slander; indeed so infernally outrageous, that I believe no man, in my station, ever experienced the like; while that conscious innocence, which shields me from the wounds of calumny, cannot but infinitely inflame one's indignation at the villainy of the attempt.

I have, Sir, a perfect confidence in His Majesty's own gracious disposition towards me; and I would by no means doubt of yours, to promote the good effects of it, both from your love of letters, and your warmth for the public service, whose true interests you so successfully advance.

I might be thought to know little of the world,— some will be ready to say, and less of myself,—if I reckoned as anything what I have done, in my profession, for Religion in general, and for the religion of my country in particular: yet I must not conceive so very meanly of myself, as that I can be of no account, whenever the Public comes under consideration [1].

[1] Churchill dedicated his *Rosciad* to Bishop Warburton, and in allusion to his having been bred an attorney and renounced the Law for the Church, he says :—

> " But you, my Lord, renounced attorneyship
> With better purpose, and more noble aim,
> And wisely played a more substantial game.
> Nor did Law mourn : blessed in her younger son ;
> For Mansfield does what *Gloucester* would have done."

I have only, Sir, to add, that when an opportunity may offer of laying this before His Majesty, I shall esteem the favour of your doing it amongst the most agreeable of those civilities which I have had the honour to receive from you ; and which have lain the very pleasing obligation on me, to subscribe myself, Sir, &c.

W. Gloucester.

THE KING TO MR. GRENVILLE.

40 min. past 9, A.M.,
(Tuesday, January 29, 1765.)

Mr. Grenville,—When the debate [1] of this day is over, I hope to receive a line from you with the summary account of it.

MR. GRENVILLE TO THE KING.

Downing Street, Wednesday, January 30, 1765,
Six o'clock, A.M.

The House is just up, and I have the honour to enclose to your Majesty, agreeably to your orders, an account of the question first moved, and of the amendment made to it, together with the names of the several speakers in the order in which they spoke.

The amendment was opposed by all the gentlemen who were friends to the original question, and, from opposing that, they took occasion to debate the merits of the whole proposition, and to blend the original question and the amendment together, in which they were followed by those who proposed the latter.

[1] On the question of General Warrants ; renewed upon this occasion by Sir William Meredith.

Mr. C. Townshend, Mr. C. Yorke, Lord George Sackville, Lord Middlesex, Lord George Lenox, and almost all those who had voted for the question last year, voted against the amendment on the present occasion[1].

Mr. W. Pitt was not present. The debate went very much upon the same general grounds as it proceeded upon last year. There was nothing very extraordinary in the debate except an angry altercation between Mr. Yorke and Mr. Attorney-General[2] with regard to what had been the opinion and arguments of the former, concerning General Warrants, when those causes were tried. Many gentlemen spoke extremely well, and Mr. Solicitor-General[3] and Mr. Dyson seemed to be particularly approved of.

I will wait upon your Majesty at one o'clock at noon to give a more exact and accurate account, and in the meantime humbly beg your pardon for the errors con-

---

[1] The amendment was rejected by 224 against 185. A better account of this debate is given by Walpole in his *Memoirs of the Reign of George the Third*, and a summary of the arguments will be found in the *Parliamentary History*, vol. xvi. Mr. Grenville does not mention his own part in this debate, but Walpole says he " spoke his usual hour." Upon a subsequent occasion, in April, 1769, Mr. Grenville took an opportunity of declaring his opinion upon General Warrants. In a debate on Mr. Onslow's motion for declaring Colonel Luttrell member for Middlesex instead of Mr. Wilkes, Mr. Grenville remarked :— " I said originally that General Warrants were illegal. Of the then Ministry, my name and that of a noble Duke (Bedford) were the only ones not signed to those warrants. I said that the law of the land was to decide the point, not a vote of Parliament. If all those who agreed with me at that time would hold to the same opinion and agree with me now, if they who now talk of consequences would say that this question should not be carried, I venture to assert that the country would be made as happy and easy by such a determination as it was made upon the question of General Warrants."—*Cavendish Debates*, vol. i. p. 385.

[2] Sir Fletcher Norton.   [3] Mr. De Grey.

tained in this, which it is not in my power to make as perfect as it ought to be.

MR. GRENVILLE TO THE KING.

Tuesday, March 5, 1765.

I HUMBLY beg leave to express part of the joy which I feel at the happy account of your Majesty's being so much better.

I would not, however, presume at this time to trouble your Majesty with any business if the enclosed letter from the Duke and Duchess of Athol, to the Treasury, relative to the Isle of Man, did not make it necessary for me to receive your Majesty's directions to lay it before the House of Commons, in order to their proceeding upon it. By the mark of your Royal munificence referred to in the end of that letter is meant a grant of £2000 a-year to the Duke and Duchess of Athol for their respective lives, out of the Revenues of Ireland, which, from the great diminution of their income, by the particular circumstances of their case, as well as from the great benefit to be derived to the Irish Revenues from this purchase, it is hoped your Majesty will not think improper or unreasonable, any more than the other parts of this proposition, the reason of which I will beg leave to explain when your Majesty will allow me to have the honour of waiting upon you.

Lord Strange[1] has entreated me to lay the two enclosed commissions for the Judges to hold the ensuing assizes for the County of Lancaster before your Majesty for your Royal signature, as they require dispatch.

---

[1] Chancellor of the Duchy of Lancaster.

THE KING TO MR. GRENVILLE.

The Queen's House, Tuesday, March 5, 1765.

I AM obliged to Mr. Grenville for his expressions on my being so much mended; the physicians, on my naming that I feel as yet some weakness in the breast, have renewed their injunctions of not talking, and particularly on business; if there are any warrants ready for my signature, I wish Mr. Grenville would at any time send them in a box, as also a summary account of the debate of yesterday, which I am curious to hear.

The proposal of the Duke and Duchess of Athol seems modest; as to the Irish pension, if Parliament seems to beg for it, that will be a reason for my granting it to them; I return the papers signed.

MR. GRENVILLE TO THE KING.

Downing Street, March 5, 1765,
Twelve at night.

I LAID before the House of Commons the letter from the Duke and Duchess of Athol, which I had the honour of sending to your Majesty this morning for your directions, and after explaining the whole of the proposition contained in it to the House, and informing them that if your Majesty should be pleased to comply with the request at the latter end of it, it would only be in consequence of their wish and approbation of this whole measure for the public service, I had the pleasure to find the House unanimous upon this subject, and am extremely glad that this important business is in so fair a way of being settled to the general satisfaction, and to the great advantage of the revenues both of this kingdom and of Ireland.

The debate in the House of Commons yesterday was opened by Mr. Nicholson Calvert [1], who moved for a Bill for the relief of the subject on informations in the Court of King's Bench, filed by and in the name of the Attorney-General. Mr. Serjeant Hewitt [2] seconded the motion, and both of them admitted that no abuse, at least for many years past, had been made of the power vested by law in the Attorney-General for that purpose, insisting only that it might be an instrument of oppression in bad times, though not used as such at present.

The Attorney-General answered these gentlemen, and gave a very full and satisfactory account of the antiquity and legality of this power.

He urged that the Attorney-General was a sworn officer, and therefore bound to execute this part of his office to the best of his judgment, for which he was answerable both to his conscience, and to the law, like other judicial officers.

That he had the satisfaction to know that he had never filed an information upon which the party had not afterwards been convicted, and that therefore, though for his own part he could wish to be freed from the exercise of a power which brought much odium and no pleasure, yet he could not consent to strip the Crown of its just

---

[1] Member for Tewkesbury.

[2] Member for Coventry. He was afterwards Lord Lifford, and Lord Chancellor of Ireland. Lord Campbell quotes the Duke of Grafton's journal, in which Mr. Sergeant Hewitt is thus described :—" He was a true Whig, and bore a character to which all parties gave their assent of respect ; and though his speeches in Parliament were long and without eloquence, they were replete with excellent matter and knowledge of the law. His conduct in Ireland under the peerage of Lifford soon gained the esteem of the public."

prerogative in an instance in which it was not even pretended it had been abused.

In support of the motion spoke almost every gentleman who usually speaks with the opposition in Parliament, Mr. G. Onslow, Mr. T. Townshend, Mr. Rose Fuller, Sir William Meredith, Sir G. Savile, Mr. Beckford, Sir William Baker, Lord G. Cavendish, Lord John Cavendish, Mr. J. Grenville, and Lord Palmerston.

Against the question spoke almost every gentleman of the law in the House. Mr. Yorke very fully and very ably, Mr. Morton, Mr. Forrester, Mr. Wilbraham, and Mr. Wedderburn, all of whom showed the impropriety of the question in so strong a light that it was much doubted whether those who moved it would have ventured to divide the House upon it. Lord Frederick Campbell likewise spoke against the question very well, and concluded with saying that he rejoiced to find that we lived at a time when, instead of real grievances, the apprehension of grievances was all that the most disposed to find fault could complain of.

Mr. Yorke took particular notice of the many libels which had been published, and of the lenity of the Government with regard to them. He observed what strange doctrines of law had been propagated, and amongst others, that of the jury being judges of the law as well as the fact, which would deprive the subject of the benefit of moving in arrest of judgment, and of having the opinion of the Judges in point of law, as well as of the jury in matter of fact, before he could be condemned.

The other gentlemen of the law spoke very well, and Mr. Wilbraham with great weight from his character, knowledge, and long experience.

Mr. Fazakerley likewise attended to the last, and intended to have spoken on the same side, but found himself unable from his great age to go through with the fatigue.

Mr. Hussey did not speak, but voted with the majority, as did Mr. Charles Townshend (Lord Townshend's brother) and many others who have not constantly voted on that side.

Mr. Fuller having mentioned M. D'Eon's case as one of those in which an information had been filed, many gentlemen took notice of the propriety of it. Mr. Yorke represented the necessity of it in the strongest and most convincing terms, and expressed his firm belief of the injustice and outrage committed against M. de Guerchy. Upon the whole, the gentlemen of the law, who spoke against the question, treated it so very fully, and with so much approbation, that there was not any room, nor indeed the least occasion, for any one else to speak upon it.

The arguments used in support of the question turned principally upon the danger and possibility of the abuse of this power, although it had not lately been abused. It was said that there was no occasion for it, as the grand jury might be applied to in the regular course of proceedings, or the Court of King's Bench, for leave to file it, as is done in other cases.

The great increase of the power of the Crown was urged from the increase of the public debt, and with regard to libels, that there had been libels on both sides, and that they ought to be equally punished; and lastly it was insisted, that even supposing that informations of this sort ought not to be taken away, yet the Bill should be received to regulate them in whatever instances it might be proper. The House sat 'till between 7 and 8 o'clock, and the Division was 207 against the question, and 78 for it. I ought to beg pardon for this long account, if it were not given in obedience to your Majesty's command, which I obey with the utmost joy, as I flatter myself that it is a fresh proof of your Majesty's health continuing to mend, for the perfect re-establishment of which I offer my most ardent vows and prayers.

Agreeably to your Majesty's orders, I enclose with this such warrants of form as are ready for your Royal Signature.

THE KING TO MR. GRENVILLE.

30 min. past 4, P.M.,
(Saturday, March 9, 1765.)

MR. GRENVILLE,—Though I shall see you to-morrow, not to lose time I send you the letters that have passed between Lord Halifax and the Secretary at War[1], concerning the difficulties that have occurred in America with regard to the Mutiny Act; Lord Halifax appears to disregard the noise that may be made here in Parliament by extending the quartering soldiers in private houses in America[2]. As I think that at a time like this

---

[1] Mr. Welbore Ellis.

[2] The objectionable clause was subsequently withdrawn, but not until it had been the cause of considerable discussion and uneasiness. Lord Hyde sends Mr. Grenville a letter which he had received from David Barclay, who styles himself a "clamorous citizen," and adds :—" I cannot refrain availing myself of the liberty heretofore indulged me, to plead for America. The clause in the Mutiny Act, now framing for that part of the King's dominions, making it lawful to billet soldiers on a march in *private* families, is, in the opinion of every well-wisher to America, and every friend to liberty, such an innovation upon the privileges of those who justly claim the natural rights of this country, that it alarms many well-wishers to the present Administration, and is

all measures should be duly weighed before they are undertaken, I send them to you before I return them to
the office.   You will plainly perceive that the Secretary
at War, in his answer, though he feels the necessity of
some alterations to adapt the Act to the circumstances
of America, yet seems to decline approving of the mode
proposed for rectifying it.

When you have thought it over, I beg you will this
evening return me the box.

MR. GRENVILLE TO THE KING.

55 min. past 11, P.M.,
(Saturday night, March 9, 1765.)

I HAVE but just now received the honour of your Majesty's commands on my return home from my Lord
Chancellor's, where I have passed the greatest part of
the evening.   On the short examination which I
have hitherto been able to give to the letters which
have passed between Lord Halifax and the Secretary of

made use of much to their disadvantage by those who are not so; for
if any man will but for a moment place himself a resident in America,
no plausibility of argument attempting to prove the necessity, will convince him that *feels* the oppression.   At this juncture especially, it cannot fail of impressing the most disagreeable ideas upon the minds of
the Americans; and as the number professing non-resisting principles
are so inconsiderable to the whole, no man can say what may be the
consequence of a law which *avowedly* abridges them of the liberty of
English subjects, at a time when their ideas lead them to expect a
larger portion than we enjoy as a reward for the toils of their forefathers in settling those deserts.

" As this law will increase the power of the Commander-in-chief in
America, it may not be improper to remark, what every body seems to
agree in, that if America ever throws off its dependence on this country,
it will most probably be attempted by some aspiring genius amongst
the military."   This letter is dated *Hackney*, 11th *April*, 1765.

War, it seems to me that the clause which your Majesty mentions for the extending the power of quartering soldiers in the private houses in America, is that which is by far the most likely to create difficulties and uneasiness, and therefore ought certainly to be thoroughly weighed and considered before any step is taken in it, especially as the quartering of soldiers upon the people against their wills is declared by the petition of right to be contrary to law.

If I do not mistake, the same difficulty of not having either barracks or public houses sufficient for quartering the troops occurs in Scotland as well as in America, and I think there is a clause in the annual Mutiny Act to quarter the soldiers in Scotland in such houses as they might have been quartered in there at the time of the Union; perhaps some general words of the like nature referring to the former usage may be the properest precedent to follow in this instance, in case it shall be judged absolutely necessary to insert any new clause relative to it. Lord Halifax and Mr. Ellis have both mentioned to me that General Gage had been obliged to make representations concerning the defects of the present Mutiny Act with regard to America.

We have not yet had time to enter into the discussion of the particulars, but the other additions and amendments proposed do not at present appear to me to be liable to the same sort of objections with the clause for quartering soldiers in private houses.

I humbly beg your Majesty's pardon for offering these imperfect observations to your consideration, and will certainly think this matter over more thoroughly before I have the honour of waiting upon your Majesty to receive your commands to-morrow. I will direct the box with the letters to be returned early to-morrow morning, as my receiving it so late has made it impossible for me to obey your Majesty's orders of sending them back this evening.

THE KING TO MR. GRENVILLE.

(March 11, 1765.)

MR. JEFEREY's ground in the little Park at Richmond [1] was renewed August 1760. He means to sell it: asks £3,500.

Mr. Grenville to enquire into it, and see what agreement can be made.

THE KING TO MR. GRENVILLE.

30 min. past 10, (Wednesday, March 13, 1765.)

MR. GRENVILLE, I would have you come to me at one, to clear off what business my illness has kept back.

MR. GRENVILLE TO THE KING.

Friday morning, March 22, 1765.

I HUMBLY beg to receive your Majesty's directions for laying before the House of Commons the enclosed Copy of the Treaty for the payment of the money due for

---

[1] Part of the site of the old monastery at West Shene, formerly granted to Sir William Temple, and subsequently held under lease from the Crown by Mr. Jeffrey. The hamlet of West Shene stood about a quarter of a mile from the old palace; all the buildings that remained were taken down in 1769, and the site, converted into a lawn, added to the King's enclosures.—See *Manning and Bray's History of Surrey*, vol. i. p. 422.

French prisoners, and the certificate of the money paid upon that account into the Exchequer, and likewise copies of the several reports for liquidating the German demands which have been made by the Commissioners appointed for that purpose; it being necessary that these papers should be presented to the House before the general state of the supplies for the year is opened, which is proposed to be done on Monday or Wednesday next.

THE KING TO MR. GRENVILLE.

(Friday, March 22, 1765.)

MR. GRENVILLE, I should have sent for you to-day had I not been forced to fresh discipline from some little additional cough and pain in the breast : I therefore return you the papers, and perfectly approve their being laid before the House of Commons.

MINUTE OF A MEETING OF HIS MAJESTY'S SERVANTS.

Great George Street, Friday, April 5, 1765.

Present :

Lord Chancellor.   Earl of Egmont.
Duke of Bedford.   Lord Mansfield.
Earl of Halifax.   Mr. Grenville.
Earl of Sandwich.

The Lords having taken into consideration, pursuant to the King's orders, His Majesty's intention of proposing to Parliament to make a provision for the ad-

ministration of government in case of a minority
(which God prevent), are thoroughly sensible of His
Majesty's paternal care and attention to the welfare of
his people, and most humbly express their entire approbation of His Majesty's general idea, that a Regency
should be appointed ; and that it should be communicated to Parliament in a speech from the Throne ; in
which should be mentioned with precision what power
his Majesty wishes to have, and under what restrictions
and regulations, with a proper reference to the last
Regency Act.

That they understand His Majesty's idea of reserving
to himself the power of appointing a Regent is meant
to be restrained to the Queen, or any other person of
the Royal family, usually residing in Great Britain[1].

THE EARL OF HALIFAX TO MR. GRENVILLE.

Great George Street, Tuesday Evening, April 9, 1765.

DEAR SIR,—I take for granted that Lord Sandwich,
before you left town, acquainted you that His Majesty
received with seeming satisfaction the Minute of our
Friday's meeting, without either asking questions, or
expressing a doubt on any part of it[2]. Being still unable to wait on him myself, I have by letter desired my
Lord Mansfield to give the proper directions to the

---

[1] On the back of this Minute is the following note in Mr. Grenville's
hand : " *Carried to the King the same day by Lord Sandwich, and approved of entirely by His Majesty.*"

[2] The King had probably not yet been made acquainted with the
strange doctrine that his own mother was not one of his Royal Family.

Attorney-General to prepare the Bill agreeable to the
Minute, with such references to the late Regency Bill as
shall be proper. By his Lordship's answer, which I
send you, you will see he thinks nothing can be done
'till the Speech is settled, and imagines all parties will
be in town next week. I have informed him since that
I understood from you, on Friday last, that you did not
intend returning to town till the latter end of next
week.

In the meantime, if you would send me a sketch you
may have made of the Speech, it may be of use to his
Lordship for such directions as he may think necessary
to give to the Attorney-General ; and it will be essentially necessary to me, as without it (though I retain your
general idea of it) it will be difficult for me to draw the
Address, which I would willingly do as well as I am
able. I am, &c., &c. DUNK HALIFAX.

MR. GRENVILLE TO THE EARL OF HALIFAX.

Wotton, Wednesday night, April 10, 1765.

MY DEAR LORD,—The messenger brought me the
honour of your Lordship's letter this morning, together
with Lord Mansfield's to you, which I return inclosed
with this. I understand that it was settled by the
Minute taken at our meeting on Friday last, that there
is to be no variation from the former Act, except in the
power to be reserved to His Majesty, to appoint the
Queen, or any other person of the Royal family, to be the
Regent during the minority of the successor, and that
the Speech from the throne is to contain the sense of
that Minute precisely, with a proper reference only to
the last Regency Act. Lord Sandwich gave me the

pleasure of knowing before I left London that this Minute had met with His Majesty's perfect approbation. I take it for granted, therefore, that the Speech must in substance be drawn exactly conformable to it, and in that case I do not see how the draft of the Speech can be necessary to give the proper directions for preparing the Bill agreeable to the Minute. I have always felt that there would be some delicacy and difficulty in stating this matter with precision and distinctness in a Speech from the throne, and for that reason desired if possible to have had the words of the Speech settled at the same meeting, but as that was declined, I should be extremely glad to receive your Lordship's and Lord Mansfield's ideas upon this subject before I put any-thing upon paper; especially if there is the least in-tention of making any other variations from the last Act, which I was so far from thinking of doing in the draft of the Speech to be prepared here, that I have not even brought down the Act with me into the country; if therefore anything of that kind shall be found neces-sary, the Speech must be altered agreeably to such farther alterations as shall be made in the Act if they are any way material.

I explained to your Lordship my general idea upon this subject, and did not intend to reduce it into writing till my return to town about the middle of next week, when, as Lord Mansfield rightly observes, we shall be all in town, and may talk it over together.

You will see from what I have said how impossible it is for me to send you at present the sketch of the Speech as you desire, but I will endeavour to prepare it and bring it to town with me; in the meantime I hope this will be no hindrance to your Lordship, nor put you under any difficulties, the subject being confined to and explained by the Minutes of the Council, upon which alone, both the Speech and Address must be founded. I am, &c. GEORGE GRENVILLE.

I rejoice to hear of M. de Guerchy's promise to pay the money due to us from France in a few days, as it is really of consequence to shew the good faith of that country by their punctuality in making the payments according to Treaty.

THE EARL OF MANSFIELD TO MR. GRENVILLE.

(April 20, 1765.)

MY DEAR SIR,—I am most strongly of opinion against the addition [1]. It is unnecessary, because it is a condition incident by law to such an office that the person should be of age, and a Protestant, except in so far as naming the Queen personally might dispense with any objection to her. You will find that in the power given to the late King to name four, their being of age, and Protestants, is left to the general rule, and not expressed.

The description is as certain, except with regard to the Princess of Wales, as if they were all named, and they are all Protestants. It was not added in the case of the Princess of Wales in the last Act, *being a Protestant;* but if it was proper to put any new clause in the Bill, I never would mention it in the Speech; the King should take that for granted : it sounds ill to my

---

[1] The addition to the King's Speech proposed by Mr. Grenville, was to the effect that the Regent should be "a Protestant, and of the age of twenty-one years or upwards."

ears that he should add it : a person of unsound mind would be incapable of such an office, and yet it would be strange to express that restriction in the Speech.

I am clear that the Speech will be much more correct, and less liable to objection, by taking those requisites for granted, than by expressing them. I saw the Attorney-General this morning and talked the matter over with him.

The Act will be ready in time. I doubt a little whether you should say *the* Queen tout court, or whether there should not be some epithets : look into the late King's speeches, in which he acquaints the Parliament that he had left Queen Caroline guardian, &c. I believe it is *my beloved*, &c.

I am very glad we succeeded last night ; I thought the point of consequence [1].

I think the Speech now takes in everything shortly and precisely, and the idea is to re-enact the last law, only concealing the name of the Regent, but fixing the choice to a few objects. I explained it so to the Attorney this morning, who saw it in this light. Yours most affectionately, &c.   MANSFIELD.

Is not the Regent by the express provision of the Act to qualify according to law ? If there is not, he must do it. There were Acts to dispense with Queen Caroline's qualifying, which shews the thing to be necessary.

[1] This was probably upon the King waiving the point of having the power of naming four councillors besides the princes of the blood, and desiring that it might be settled for his only having five additional councillors. If the former arrangement had been adopted, the King would have had the nomination of nine out of the eighteen councillors, and thus would have annulled the power of the Officers of State.—See Mr. Grenville's Diary, *post.*

MR. GRENVILLE TO THE KING.

Downing Street, April 24, 1765,
35 min. after 5, p.m.

THE House of Commons have agreed to the Address proposed by the House of Lords to be presented to your Majesty, without any division, but not nemine contradicente.

When I moved the concurrence, I opened the general state of the proposition with the proper acknowledgments of your Majesty's goodness and concern for our welfare from which it took its rise, and I observed that the difference between this and the former Act, arose from the difference of circumstances, and from the great length of time for which the present provision was made, compared with that of the 24th of the late King.

Lord North seconded the motion very properly. Mr. Nicholson Calvert said that he did not then object to the Address, but objected to the power of appointing the Regent, and to the constitution of the Council, which he compared to that established by King Henry VIII., to which he attributed the troubles during the minority of his successor, King Edward VI.

Mr. Beckford spoke next, and carried it still further, for he declared that, with all possible duty and attachment to your Majesty, he should oppose this Act in every step of it, and must oppose the Address as implying a general approbation of it; that he thought there was no occasion for any Regency Bill whatever; that whenever that grievous calamity should befall us, the Parliament would take care of the Government, which they would do much better and more properly than by giving a power to name a Regent and a Council, which he entirely disapproved of.

Mr. Nugent then spoke for the proposition, and showed the propriety of it, and how unseemly it was that the Address should not go without a negative.

Mr. G. Onslow (the late Speaker's son) spoke next, and recommended strongly unanimity upon the Address, but laid in his claim to oppose the Bill whenever it should come before the House. He was followed by young Mr. Thos. Townshend, who went upon pretty much the same grounds with Mr. Onslow, but with more eagerness against the provisions of the Bill, which he would suppose to come, not from your Majesty, but from your Ministers. This closed the debate; the question was put, and carried without a divison, but Mr. Beckford and Mr. Calvert gave their negatives to it.

Upon the whole it appeared very plainly that the plan of the Opposition was to let the Address go, but to resist the provisions of the Bill to the utmost.

It seems to me advantageous that this plan has been thus laid open, and I am therefore glad that I moved the concurrence with the Lords in such a manner as to give occasion to it.

THE KING TO MR. GRENVILLE.

Richmond, Tuesday, 3 o'clock, (May 7, 1765.)

MR. GRENVILLE,—I am desirous to know how the Regency Bill was received yesterday, and what may pass on this day; therefore desire you will write to me when the House adjourns, and that you will acquaint one of the Secretaries of State that they should immediately transmit it to me with dispatch [1].

[1] Received in the House of Commons.—*Note by Mr. Grenville.*

MR. GRENVILLE TO THE KING.

Downing Street, Tuesday, May 7, 1765,
25 min. past 11, P.M.

I HAVE the honor to inform your Majesty that the House of Commons continued sitting 'till near ten o'clock this evening.

The Regency Bill was read the first time yesterday, and ordered to be read a second time to-day, but nothing at all was said on that occasion.

To-day, about two o'clock, Lord John Cavendish came up to me in the House, and told me that he intended to move for an Address to be presented to your Majesty, desiring that you would be pleased to name a person to be proposed to the House for Regent, and that his motion would be to the same effect, and almost in the same words, with that moved by Lord Lyttelton in the House of Peers. He made the motion for the Address accordingly just before the second reading of the Regency Bill, in a very few words, and was seconded by Mr. T. Townshend, junr.

Inclosed with this, I transmit to your Majesty an account of the several speakers in this debate, and in the subsequent one, in the order in which they spoke.

It did not seem that the proposition for the Address made great impression upon the House, especially after the answers which were given to it.

There was nothing very particular in the debate, except that several gentlemen who were for the Address, having declared against the principle of the Regency Bill, they were told that it would be highly improper to present an Address to your Majesty to name a Regent, if they intended to reject the Bill afterwards in which the Regent was to be named. This debate lasted 'till near six o'clock; the question was then put upon that motion, but was carried in the negative without a division. The Bill was then read a second time, and the question put for committing it. This was opposed upon all the general arguments against any Regency Bill whatever, and against the particular provisions and clauses in the present Bill. General Conway spoke very strongly against the latter, but declared that he would vote for committing the Bill. This debate lasted 'till past nine o'clock, and upon the question being then put, it was carried for committing the Bill without any division.

After this, Mr. G. Onslow [1], of Guilford, moved to put off the Committee to a longer day than Thursday, which was the day proposed by me to go into the Committee upon it agreeably to what had been done in the former Regency Bill, and which was agreed to accordingly, and the Committee fixed for Thursday without any division.

Mr. G. Cooke then moved to print the Bill, but this was objected to in point of time and regularity, and because there was no occasion for it, the instances in which it differs from the last Regency Bill being so very few.

After some little debate, there was a division upon this question, 18 for printing it, and 117 against it, the greater part of the House being gone away before the motion was made. In general the debate was carried on pretty regularly upon the two principal questions, and

---

[1] There were two George Onslows at this time ; one, the late Speaker's son, M.P. for Surrey, who subsequently became Earl of Onslow, and died in 1814 ; the other, a nephew of the late Speaker, and M.P. for Guilford ; he was the younger of the two cousins, and sometimes styled Colonel Onslow ; he died in 1792. One of them, probably the Speaker's son, was distinguished as *Black George*, more, it is supposed, by allusion to the character in *Tom Jones*, than from his complexion, though that no doubt gave the *colour*.

seemingly very much to the satisfaction of the House, which was the reason that they did not venture to divide upon either of them, though they declared repeatedly that they would oppose the Bill in every stage of it, and particularly in the Committee.

Upon the whole I flatter myself that every thing has gone in a manner which will be agreeable to your Majesty, though as it is now past ten o'clock, I must, in obedience to your orders for dispatching the messenger with this account as soon as I can, reserve the further particulars until I have the honour of waiting upon your Majesty to-morrow morning.

MR. GRENVILLE TO THE KING.

Downing Street, May 9, 1765, Thursday, 30 min. past 11, P.M.

I HAVE the honour most dutifully to inform your Majesty that the House of Commons continued to sit in the Committee upon the Regency Bill 'till past nine o'clock, at which time they had gone quite through the Bill, and agreed to report it with the Amendments to-morrow morning. The first debate in the Committee was upon a motion made by Mr. Rose Fuller[1] to leave

[1] The following is Mr. Grenville's Report to the King, of this debate.

HOUSE OF COMMONS, *Thursday, May 9, 1765.*

Mr. Rose Fuller.—The leaving a request to the option of His Majesty is unprecedented now, and may be made a precedent for the future. I have no objection to any one of those from whom His Majesty is to make his choice; they are all very proper and very perfectly qualified ; but there is one more peculiarly fit to be named, which is the Queen ; the nomination of any other would be inconvenient. The examples of Henry V. and of Louis XIV. shew the inconveniences of a nomination, and how uncertain it will be of its effect. I wish to work up the Regency into the Constitution. This is the only country in Europe in which it is not settled. This would

out the words *such person,* and to insert instead thereof, *Her present Majesty, our most gracious Queen Char-*

prevent such debates as that of to-day. It cannot be done just now, but it may in another sessions, and for the present I think the Queen only, ought to be named.

Mr. Onslow.—I always was of opinion that Parliament ought to know the person whom they agree to be Regent, and upon that principle second the motion. The only precedent of a like nature is that of Henry VIII., and that is disavowed. I support the motion from respect to His Majesty, who cannot but receive satisfaction from seeing his Commons make this choice.

Mr. Peter Burrell.—I should, I believe, be against this Bill, if a Regent were named. It might be the means of a faction in a Court, though not in the House of Commons. Everybody must remember the situation of this country under the very last Regency Bill, though the princess named was every way qualified for that purpose; yet there might have been circumstances which might have made it desirable that the Regency were in the hands of a man, and even of that man who was then unjustly abused, and, it is said, intended to be omitted. I can suppose circumstances which may make His Majesty to leave the Regency rather to another than to the person named, and I would leave that to the wisdom of His Majesty. The Act of Queen Anne gave a much greater power to the Electress of Hanover.

Sir William Meredith.—I hope the nomination of the mother of the minor king was not dictated in the last Regency Bill at the instigation of obloquy against the man who was just returned from saving this country. The mother is the natural guardian. To do otherwise is appointing a successor to the Crown perhaps for fourteen or sixteen years. It may be a means of disturbing His Majesty's tranquillity. The mother can have no other interest than that of her child; others may.

Lord George Sackville.—I am against this motion, because I was against the Address, which was the most respectful manner of doing the same thing. The choice is not left to His Majesty at large, but confined to persons all unexceptionable. If the Regency were for only three or four years I would say nominate the Queen, but in a long interval of sixteen years it might be improper. Will any gentleman say that at all times the Queen Consort should be Regent? The circumstances of the times must determine the choice; that is the case now. The virtues of the Queen give her now a preference, and the King will be led to a proper choice by the joint interest of his children and his people. Leave it to the King to choose a Regent of his family most like to himself.

General Conway.—To delegate the power of Parliament to the Crown

lotte, His Majesty's Royal Consort, and then to leave out all the subsequent words, by which alteration the is to me unconstitutional and unprecedented, except in the instance of Henry VIII. It is not only a new, but a dangerous power. It is not only to this King, but to the Crown irrevocably. Besides the power of substitution is a power for the King to nominate a Regent at the times of which he cannot know the circumstances. The Bill, too, does not provide for the contingency of the King not executing the power of nomination ; or he may execute it on a death, when the policy of all countries guards against the weakness of that situation in the disposition of their own property. Regencies during absence are so limited that they cannot affect this case. The only instance is the last Regency, where all the merit of the Duke of Cumberland could not get the better of the natural principle which made the mother guardian to her children.

Mr. Dempster.—I devolve with pleasure what right I may have, as far as a single vote goes, to appoint a Regent out of the Royal family, (to him?) who is so much a better judge of their virtues and qualifications.

General Conway.—To explain the situation he remained in, (in) the army, which had been mentioned by Mr. Dempster [a].

Lord North.—This can be no precedent but in the like circumstances, for His Majesty ties down his proposition to the present circumstances. He is confined in his choice to persons having all the circumstances of religion, birth, and residence, which we require in the Prince to govern us. Parliament cannot choose with judgment a Regent for a minority, which, if the King should lose many of his children successively, may not take place these thirty years, and then possibly for a long minority. Change of persons, characters, abilities, dispositions, and of a thousand other circumstances, may happen in the interval. Could there then a change be made in a nomination now fixed? The ambitious and factious would crowd round a person so named upon every prospect of a minority. It would be encouraging faction during His Majesty's life, which it is the view of this Bill to prevent during a minority. This Act will prevent all confusion ; it makes the Regent certain at the time of the event. Louis XIV.'s appointment was set aside because France has a fixed constitutional Regent. Henry VIII.'s was disputed, but the dispute was dropped as frivolous. This Bill secures a Protestant Regent of the House of Brunswick, resident in England ; and I am glad when I have secured this to the people, to restore the King to the natural right of a father to choose a guardian to his child.

Sir George Savile.—I can never comprehend that uncertainty is to be the parent of peace and quietness. I am always afraid of delegating

---

[a] Walpole says that Dempster had expressed his disapproval of the dismission of General Conway from the Army.—*Mem. Geo. III.* vol. ii. p. 140.

clause would be a complete nomination of the Queen to be Regent and Guardian. Mr. George Onslow, of Surrey, seconded this motion.

new powers to the Crown, and in considering that, I reject all consideration of his present Majesty's virtues. They ought not to be mentioned in debating a general proposition, and advantage may be taken of the last moments of the King to make the nomination, which, however improper, none can prevent, and none can be responsible for it.

Lord Frederick Campbell.—I am not afraid of leaving it to His Majesty to delegate to whom he pleases of the several persons who we all agree to be proper—a power less than he himself enjoys, the exercise of which is liable to all the checks of the constitution.

Mr. Dowdeswell.—It is difficult to argue that this Bill is unconstitutional. A minority is a blank in the constitution, and where does the constitution point out the Queen mother to be Regent? The King is the best judge who is best qualified to be Regent. We cannot debate their several qualifications. If Parliament only could nominate the Regent, it might discourage future kings from proposing any Regency Bill. I think the circumstance in which the constitution is hurt by this Bill is in the powers given to the council, whose union and whose dissensions, &c., &c.

Sir George Savile.—Mr. Dowdeswell to explain.

Lord John Cavendish.—The only sense in which this Bill can be called unconstitutional is that the power of delegating so great a power from the Crown to another person is unknown in the constitution.

Mr. Chancellor of the Exchequer.—I have already given my opinion twice upon this question, and should now leave it but for some things that have fallen from the honourable gentleman. The arguments have been urged before upon the motion for the Address; and the powers to be given by this Bill, I have the strongest authority to say, will be exercised as soon as given, and that the public will know that they are exercised.

Colonel Barré.—I should be glad to know whether it is meant that the instruments will only be sealed, or that the public will be informed of the nomination.

Mr. Chancellor of the Exchequer.—In explanation of the words he had used before [a].

Colonel Barré.—I am afraid this will be made a precedent. Queen Mary asked for the same powers as had been given to her father.

[a] According to Walpole's report of this debate, Mr. Grenville said, in reply to Colonel Barré, that " the powers would be executed, and that it would be known they were ; not the person."—(*Mem. of Geo. III.* vol. ii. p. 141.) It will be subsequently seen in Mr. Grenville's Diary, that the King's opinion was contrary to that of Mr. Grenville with respect to the question of naming the Regent.

Mr. Peter Burrell spoke against it, and then the rest of the gentlemen, who spoke for and against it in the order in which they stand in the inclosed paper.

This Bill seems to me a Bill to encourage faction. It is possible that may prevail to prevent the Queen from being Regent, and she may be deprived, at the same time, of her Royal Consort and of the guardianship of her children. She has been pointed out by the King ; can we do better than give our sanction to the intimation, and check all faction by the certainty of our supporting our own choice ? What could encourage faction more than if the King were to substitute a younger brother to the Queen, and one son only were to survive the King? The presumptive heir of the Crown could never brook the preference.

Mr. Burt.—The instance of Queen Mary proves the little danger of the precedent ; Parliament refused to do for her what they had done for her father.

Mr. Cooke.—The nomination of the Queen will please everybody. The doubt whether she or any other person, and what person, may be the Regent, will keep up continual uneasiness.

Mr. Grosvenor.—The King's knowledge of his family makes him the most proper person to choose a Regent.

                    Ayes   . . . . 258 | Noes 67

MOTION—*To insert " Her Royal Highness Augusta Princess Dowager of Wales, or."*

Mr. Morton.—Had this Bill come down from the other House agreeable to His Majesty's Speech, it would have met with an almost general concurrence ; but altered as it now is, I think it necessary to propose an amendment. His Majesty's Speech comprehended all his Royal family. One is now excluded, and if that exclusion is with her own consent it is an instance of magnanimity which makes the propriety of inserting her name the greater. Whatever may have been the reasons, they are unknown to the people ; they can never be known to foreigners or to posterity, who will not be able to account for her being the only one of the Royal family excluded. She was but lately thought the person fit to be Regent in preference even to the Duke of Cumberland.

Mr. Kynaston seconded.

Mr. Martin.—I was determined not to move this amendment. I have never expressed a wish to any gentleman of this House that it should be moved. I shall vote for it. I am not authorized to say anything from the Princess I serve, but as a private man I will declare that it is a matter of total indifference to Her Royal Highness. The

When the division was made, it was carried for the words standing in the Bill as they did without the Amendment: ayes 258, noes 67. Majority 191.

event of her son's death can suggest to her only the sentiments of maternal tenderness, not the views of ambition and power. If any gentleman or mechanic thinks otherwise, I do not pretend to convince him ; I find the Bill is different from the Speech. I do not pretend to know by whose suggestion the alteration has been made [a]. It is parliamentary to suppose that it proceeded only from the other House ; but it circumscribes the power of nomination out of the Royal family, and excludes none of that family but the Princess of Wales. Other females are admitted. Succession cannot be the rule, for the Queen is not in the line of succession, and yet she is the most proper person to be named ; and is there not a reason of equal propriety for inserting the Princess if the Queen should happen to die? I might almost call this a parliamentary brand upon her. If the other House have distinguished her unduly, I hope this House will set it right. I do not mean a panegyric upon Her Royal Highness. She has, in twenty-eight years' experience in this country, had reason enough to know how little encomiums are to be relied on. She was particularly pointed out by the late King, and all the nation approved the choice. Will not omitting her name seem to arise from some personal consideration? This personal distinction alone has induced me to second the motion.

Mr. Blackstone.—The Act of 24th George II., by which the Princess of Wales is named for Regent, is not yet expired; there is a possibility still of its taking effect, and therefore it seems to me highly improper to exclude her from this. If the Crown should devolve on a minor son of the late Prince of Wales, she would be Regent.

Colonel Onslow.—I came down determined to oppose this nomination, but I find myself under the greatest difficulties. I have been convinced by what I have here heard : if the Queen were to die, I think the Princess the most proper person to be Regent. My chief objection to the Bill is, that so many persons may be nominated; but I cannot be so invidious as to exclude the Princess on any principles of law or of honour.

Mr. Onslow.—I have always been for the absolute nomination of a Regent. Upon the same principle I think the smaller number His Majesty's choice is confined to, the nearer it approaches to an absolute nomination. It is indifferent to me which : I wish all had been left out, and disclaim all personalities. His Majesty's Speech recommended

[a] See Mr. Grenville's Diary, *post;* where the history of the alteration by which the Princess Dowager of Wales was excluded from the Regency, is fully detailed.

The arguments used by those who spoke for the Amendment were very much the same as had been used

a very different mode from what appears in that Bill His Majesty's Secretary of State moved [a].

Mr. Stanley.—(To order.) We are not to enter into the speeches made there; we may of their proceedings.

Mr. Onslow.—The Secretary of State spoke as a public man.

Mr. Dyson.—(To order.) We are not to take notice of anything that passes in the other House that does not appear in the journals.

Mr. Elliott.—(To order.) We cannot refer to what passed in a previous debate in our own House, and certainly not to a debate in the other House.

Mr. White.—It is not disorderly to refer to what appears in the journals of the other House, and the words alluded to do appear on the journals.

Mr. Elliott.—The name of the Earl of Halifax does not appear on the journals.

Mr. Burrell, Lord Barrington, Sir John Rushout.—(To order.)

Mr. Onslow.—It has been reported that a Secretary of State made this explanatory motion, and intimated that he did it by His Majesty's orders [b]. If so, that was the sense His Majesty meant to put on his words. The explanation was necessary and was made. Are we to put another construction? If it was not His Majesty's explanation, I do not know how it could be offered to that House. If the same explanation had been made here it would have prevented this motion.

Lord Catherlough.—We have no business to debate on a Bill not before us. What this was formerly is immaterial. I like it in its present state, and I wish only to alter the present Bill by enlarging the King's power so as to nominate the Princess.

Mr. Chancellor of the Exchequer. — The motion made by the learned gentleman is certainly of a most delicate nature; but as I have nothing to conceal, I am under no kind of difficulty to declare my opinion with regard to it, because that opinion is founded upon sentiments which are not peculiar to the particular situation in which I have the honour to be, but which are common to me and to every gentleman who hears me. It is of public notoriety that the alteration to which this motion refers was inserted in the Bill to obviate a doubt which had been made, by persons of the greatest authority, whether the Princess Dowager of Wales was or was not included in the words *my Royal family*, as they are used in His Majesty's Speech,

---

[a] The Earl of Halifax, as Secretary of State, was the mover of the Regency Bill in the House of Lords.

[b] See Mr. Grenville's Diary, *post.*

for the Address proposed on Tuesday last, the question
in reality being the same.

and in the Act now under your consideration. As this difficulty had
been started, and it was indispensably necessary that it should be
cleared up, and as His Majesty was desirous in every part of this Bill
that all possible satisfaction should be given to both Houses of Parliament and to all his people, these words explaining that doubt were
proposed by a great officer of state, hoping that they would be universally acceptable. I took it for granted that they were agreeable to the
wishes and inclinations of Her Royal Highness the Princess Dowager ;
I say I took it for granted, and firmly believed it, though I am not
authorized to say it was so, but I am fully persuaded that if it had been
otherwise, much more, if this had been seen in the light in which the
gentleman who spoke third (Mr. Martin, H.R.H. the Princess of
Wales' Treasurer) has represented it, of a brand and stigma upon the
Princess of Wales, no servant of the King would have been authorized
to propose them. The learned gentleman has not told us, and I do
protest I do not know, whether this motion will now be pleasing or
displeasing to Her Royal Highness, from any suggestions upon which
it may seem to be founded ; but of this, sir, I am very sure, that His
Majesty, after having manifested his gracious intentions for the public
happiness and security throughout the whole of this important business,
will see with pleasure any proper compliment which this House shall
think fit to pay to his Royal mother the Princess of Wales, which he
cannot but look upon as a mark of their duty and affection to himself.
In this situation, sir, I need not add that I shall certainly concur in
any proposition which the House shall approve, and which may be
agreeable to Her Royal Highness, in order to express the respect which
is so justly due to that great Princess, the mother of our sovereign.

Mr. Martin.—I declare again that I do not know any more than the
person most distant from her, whether this motion is agreeable or disagreeable to Her Royal Highness.

Mr. Morton.—Had the Princess wished to express her sentiments
she would have chosen a messenger of more consequence than I am.
The explanation might have been made in the other House.

Mr. Onslow.—Whoever calls this a brand, brands the House of
Lords.

Mr. Chancellor of the Exchequer.—I only rise to repeat that His
Majesty, after having provided for the safety of his people, cannot but
look upon any compliment to his Royal mother as a mark of respect
and duty to himself.

Lord Palmerston.—The King's name cannot be meant to restrain
the debate. I am a friend to this Bill, but against this motion. At

Nothing very remarkable passed in the debate, except that Mr. Peter Burrell, Mr. Dempster, and Mr. Dowdeswell, all spoke with the Majority. Mr. Beckford, Mr. James Grenville, and many of those who usually vote with the Minority, were absent, and some of them voted with the Majority.

The second question was upon a motion made by Mr. Morton, to insert the name of Her Royal Highness the Princess of Wales amongst those who are capable of being appointed Regent. This motion was seconded by Mr. Kynaston for form only, as he said nothing at all in support of it, but it was then supported very warmly by Mr. Martin, and very temperately by Mr. Blackstone. When the question was going to be put, I followed, as nearly as I could, the idea which your Majesty had pointed out to me, and had the pleasure to find that it met with general approbation, and put an end to the question in the manner which your Majesty approved without any division upon it.

After this, three more amendments were proposed. The first, a grammatical one, by omitting the word *other*, which, as it stood in the Bill, would include the Queen and the Princess of Wales as descended from the late king. The second was an alteration and explanation of the words *now and usually* residing, &c., which it was

present a great line is drawn, and it may be dangerous to set a precedent for passing it now, when even the Royal personage herself does not appear to desire it. She is not excluded from disrespect, but by that general line.

Mr. Chancellor of the Exchequer.—I do not mean by naming the King to put any restraint upon any gentleman. I spoke my own sentiments only, and without any authority.

Mr. White against the motion.

Lord George Cavendish against the motion.

The question being put, it passed in the affirmative.

thought were inaccurately expressed. The third was to make the Council removeable by the Regent upon the Address of *either House* instead of *both Houses of Parliament.* The two former can admit of no difficulty, the latter may be altered to-morrow on the Report, if not approved of.

I flatter myself that this account will not be displeasing to your Majesty, and I have ordered the Messenger, as it is now too late to be at Richmond early enough to-night, to take care to be there to-morrow morning at six o'clock. I will have the honour of waiting upon your Majesty at St. James's to-morrow, to give any further information concerning the particulars of this day's business which your Majesty may chuse to receive.

THE KING TO MR. GRENVILLE.

(Friday, May 10, 1765,) 50 min. past 2, P.M.

MR. GRENVILLE,—I have just seen Lord Sandwich, who seems of opinion that the Chancellor and others may be uneasy at the alteration proposed by the Commons of a removal in the Council of Regency being obtained by a single House of Parliament, therefore if the House can be brought to leave it as it was in the Bill, I should think it advisable.

MR. GRENVILLE TO THE KING.

Downing Street, May 11, 1765,
Saturday morning, 25 min. past 3, A.M.

I HUMBLY beg leave to acquaint your Majesty that the Regency Bill is completely passed the House of Commons, and I am ordered to carry it up to the House of Peers on Monday. We continued to sit till half an hour past eleven, in order to go through it. A great variety of alterations and debates attended almost every part of its progress. The first question was, whether the House should agree with the Committee in the amendment made for inserting the name of Her Royal Highness the Princess of Wales amongst those whom your Majesty is enabled to appoint Regent.

Mr. Rose Fuller began with opposing, though in very moderate terms; and several gentlemen, whose names are specified in the paper I have the honour to transmit to your Majesty, spoke for and against that motion, but no new arguments were urged on either side, and nothing very extraordinary happened in the course of it. Many of the opposition were absent, notwithstanding which, a division was made, and the numbers were 167 to 37. The amendment for leaving out the words " *both Houses of Parliament,*" in order to insert " *either House of Parliament,*" came next to be considered. This I desired might be kept as it was originally (agreeable to your Majesty's wishes). Mr. Nugent began by opposing it, and was followed by the other gentlemen for and against it, according to the order in which they stand in the enclosed paper : in the end it was given up without a division. The next amendment was upon the alteration and explanation of the words *now and usually.* For this purpose the Attorney-General proposed some words which were inserted, and it was agreed that a Proviso should likewise be added to the Bill, which the Attorney-General withdrew to prepare. Mr. Pryse Campbell objected, that another amendment would be necessary to disqualify all such as should marry a Papist, or intermarry with any subject without consent of Parliament. This, after much altercation, produced a motion to recommit, to which the previous question was put, those who moved the question to recommit having wished to withdraw it, the numbers upon the division for recommitting were—ayes 34, noes 156.

They then proposed to adjourn, but Mr. Blackstone offering to produce the proviso above-mentioned as settled by the Attorney-General, the House accepted that proviso, to which an amendment was proposed agreeable to the Act of Settlement, by inserting " *or in case such person so nominated or appointed Regent or Guardian shall marry a Papist :*" this, after a long debate, and a personal altercation between Mr. G. Onslow and Mr. C. Townshend, was agreed to.

Mr. Pryse Campbell then moved his Proviso, to prevent any person appointed Regent from marrying without consent of Parliament, but upon the motion to bring it up, a division ensued, in which the ayes were 37, the noes 149.

Lord John Cavendish then moved another Proviso, to declare that the Regent and Council should not grant any Peerages, pensions for lives, or reversions, without an address from both Houses of Parliament ; this was carried in the negative without any division : Mr. G. Onslow, of Surry, moved to leave out all the words relative to the Council of Regency, but that likewise passed in the negative without a division. A motion was then made to adjourn ; the question was put, and carried for going on by 150 against 24 : the Bill was then read a third time, and the question being put for its passing, another motion was made for adjournment, but no division on either of these questions.

The whole of this day's debates upon all these various propositions were so uninteresting and unimportant that it is impossible for me to think of troubling your Majesty with them, and the fatigue of the day, as well as the present late hour, renders me almost unable to do it as I ought to do, which I hope will plead my excuse for any errors or imperfections in this account.

THE KING TO MR. GRENVILLE.

(Saturday, May 11, 1765,) 55 min. past 7, A.M.

Mr. GRENVILLE,—Your account of last night's debate has given me much satisfaction, particularly the having rejected the address of either House instead of both Houses, as, by what I saw yesterday, many people would have disapproved of it in the House of Lords.

THE DUKE OF CUMBERLAND TO EARL TEMPLE.

Cumberland House, May 14, 1765.

My Lord Temple,—You will be convinced that the subject that makes me give you this trouble is of consesequence enough, when I most earnestly desire your presence in town, that you may give your sentiments on the most interesting situation of this country. Our master seals my lips 'till a personal interview.

Excuse the hurry of these few lines, and be assured I remain your very affectionate friend,   William.

EARL TEMPLE TO THE DUKE OF CUMBERLAND.

Stowe, May 15, 1765, 3 o'clock in the morning.

SIR,—I this instant receive the great honour of your Royal Highness's commands, to which I shall shew my ready obedience by the best dispatch in my power.

I will not presume to guess at the interesting situation in which my poor services can be thought of any use; but my zeal in a cause in which His Majesty and your Royal Highness are concerned can never be wanting.

I am, with the highest respect and duty, &c., &c.

TEMPLE.

THE DUKE OF CUMBERLAND TO EARL TEMPLE.

Cumberland House, past 3, (May 15, 1765.)

MY LORD TEMPLE,—If six this evening or after will be agreeable, I shall be extremely glad to lay aside discretion for openness, and to acquaint you with the reasons of my troubling you. I remain, your affectionate friend,   WILLIAM.

THE EARL OF SANDWICH TO MR. GRENVILLE.

Sunday morning, May 19, 1765.

DEAR SIR,—The Duke of Bedford, Lord Halifax, and Lord Chancellor, will be at my house this morning at 12 o'clock, to consider what language we shall hold to the King, in case His Majesty should be at St. James's this day: we shall be much obliged to you if you will be at this meeting, at the time and place above-mentioned. I am, &c., &c.   SANDWICH.

THE EARL OF ALBEMARLE TO EARL TEMPLE.

Cumberland House, Sunday, 10 o'clock,
(May 19, 1765.)

MY LORD,—His Royal Highness the Duke of Cumberland was sent for yesterday to Richmond, from whence he did not return 'till eleven at night, and where he received His Majesty's directions and commands to go to Hayes, for which place H. R. H. is just setting out, and desires to see your Lordship there about twelve o'clock [1]. I have, by express, informed Mr. Pitt of His Royal Highness's intentions. I have the honour to be, &c., &c.   ALBEMARLE.

THE HONORABLE AUGUSTUS HERVEY [2] TO MR. GRENVILLE.

May 20, 1765.

MY DEAR SIR,—'*Tis*, as the *letter* told you, that I carried you to-day, and Lord T. goes Thursday to Stowe.

I wish I could see you again by and by.

I have had such encouragement from *one* that I named to you to-day, that I wrote from his house to see Lord T. at one o'clock. I shall say nothing of you at all, but go on a subject his Lordship has often talked to me about, and feel my ground properly, and you shall

[1] Lord Temple arrived at Hayes about two hours after the Duke of Cumberland: they remained in consultation with Mr. Pitt nearly five hours.

[2] Second son of John Lord Hervey, and brother to the Earl of Bristol, whom he afterwards succeeded in that title. He was a distinguished naval officer, and some time a Lord of the Admiralty. He married the celebrated Miss Chudleigh, afterwards Duchess of Kingston. He died in 1779.

see me afterwards. Trust to a younger man than yourself for once, whose head may not be so good as his
heart, but who will never risk your name, or even a
word you have ever said to me : but I think I see a
prospect of what I wish, and every friend to you and
their country must, and wish I may soon be an instrument of bringing it about ; and you may both bid defiance then to all *dark* work [1].

You know my heart, Sir, is truly embarked in this
cause, and ever yours, &c.   A. H.

Pray do not name. I will see you again soon. Lord
T. has just sent to desire to see me.

THE KING TO MR. GRENVILLE.

(Tuesday, May 21, 1765,) 15 min. past 9, P.M.

MR. GRENVILLE,—I am surprized that you are not
yet come, when you know it was my orders to be attended this evening, I expect you therefore to come the
moment you receive this [2].

----

[1] It will be seen that Mr. Hervey refers to the hope of a reconciliation between Lord Temple and Mr. Grenville, subsequently accomplished through his exertions. For some time past, however, Lord
Temple had been drawing nearer to his brother George, as appears
from a letter to Mr. Grenville from Lord Hyde, dated *February* 12 :
" I have heard that Lord Temple should lately have said that since he
perceived the struggle was only for places, he was as well satisfied to
see his brother at the head of the Treasury as any other person."
    *   *   *   *   *   *
" It was intimated to me by great authority that Mr. Pitt would not be
well enough to attend this session."

[2] It came to Mr. Grenville while he was in council with his colleagues
at Bedford House, respecting the terms upon which they would consent
to continue in office. The King was very impatient to know the result
of their conference. See Mr. Grenville's Diary, *post*.

AT A MEETING AT MR. GRENVILLE'S IN DOWNING
STREET.

Wednesday, May 22, 1765.

Present :

Lord Chancellor.   Lord Sandwich.
Duke of Bedford.   Mr. Grenville.
Lord Halifax.

The points agreed upon by all His Majesty's servants
present at this meeting to be humbly offered to His Majesty by Mr. Grenville, in consequence of the orders
which the King gave to him last night, to know their
sentiments with regard to their continuing in his Government, were as follows, and Mr. Grenville was
desired to lay them before His Majesty as indispensably
necessary in their opinion for carrying on the public
business, viz.

1st.   That the King's Ministers should be authorized
to declare that Lord Bute is to have nothing to do in
His Majesty's Councils or Government, in any manner
or shape whatever.

2nd.   That Mr. Stewart Mackenzie be removed from
his office of Lord Privy Seal of Scotland, and from the
authority and influence which has been given to him in
that kingdom.

3rd.   That Lord Holland be removed from the office
of Paymaster General, and that office disposed of as
has been usual in the House of Commons.

4th.   That Lord Granby be appointed Commander
in Chief of the Army.

5th.   That the King would be pleased to settle the
Government of Ireland with his Ministers.

EARL TEMPLE TO MR. GRENVILLE.

Wednesday morning, (May 22, 1765.)

DEAR BROTHER,—I think of calling upon you this morning. On my part I have not the least objection to the notoriety of our reconciliation and interviews [1].

[1] *The following relates the circumstances previous to the reconciliation of Lord Temple with Mr. Grenville.*

MEMORANDUM GIVEN TO MR. GRENVILLE BY THE HONORABLE AUGUSTUS HERVEY; IN THE HAND-WRITING OF THE LATTER.

HOUSE OF LORDS, Monday, May 20, 1765, near 5, P.M.

Mr. Hervey having acquainted Mr. Grenville with his earnest wishes to be the means of a reconciliation between Lord Temple and him, and that he had been talking to Lord Temple this morning on that subject (though without Mr. G.'s knowledge), and had related to his Lordship the kind manner in which Mr. Grenville had always expressed himself towards Lord Temple, Mr. Grenville heard with the most sensible pleasure from Mr. Hervey the kind expressions which Lord T. made use of in regard to him, in the conversation which Lord T. had with Mr. Hervey, and which Mr. Grenville is very happy that Lord T. allowed Mr. H. to communicate to him.

As to the two points which Lord Temple mentioned, on which he would gladly see Mr. Grenville as a brother, the first of which was that Mr. G. should admit he was in an error to Lord Temple in preferring Lord Bute to him.

Mr. Grenville says that he should indeed have been in an error if he could have preferred Lord Bute to Lord Temple at any time before the absolute separation which was made between Lord Temple and Mr. Grenville, and Mr. Grenville does solemnly assure Lord T. that the very reverse of that was the truth.

With regard to the second point, viz., that Lord T. knew nothing of Mr. Grenville's connections, but that he himself was quite free and open (Mr. Pitt and himself being as one), if Mr. Grenville has the happiness of seeing Lord Temple, Mr. G. shall, with the utmost pleasure and freedom, explain his own situation, which he flatters himself will coincide with Lord T.'s sentiments, and he perfectly agrees with Lord T. that this critical time is the properest for their seeing each other.

MEMORANDUM IN THE HAND-WRITING OF MR. GRENVILLE.

Tuesday morning, May 21, 1765.

Mr. Grenville saw Mr. Hervey at ten o'clock this morning, and in

Who has a right to object to either ?

Let me know if you are in the same sentiments ; in which case, and if you are at leisure, I will lose no time in seeing you.   I am, your affectionate brother,

TEMPLE.

MR. GRENVILLE TO EARL TEMPLE.

Downing Street, May 22, 1765,
Wednesday morning.

DEAR BROTHER,—Nothing can make me so happy as to see you, and to express to you the sentiments which I feel towards you.   I beg you will come immediately. I have an engagement at half an hour after ten.   I wish not to conceal our interview and reconciliation, which will make so essential a part of my happiness[1].   Who indeed has a right to object to either ?   I wait for you with impatience, and am your most affectionate brother,

GEORGE GRENVILLE.

THE DUKE OF BEDFORD TO MR. GRENVILLE.

Bedford House, (May 22, 1765.)

DEAR SIR,—I waited at St. James's, expecting to be called in when the Chancellor came out, but the Duke of Cumberland, who was waiting in another room, took

consequence of an appointment which Mr. Hervey informed him of from Lord Temple, Mr. Grenville waited upon Lord T. at twelve o'clock ; but many difficulties arising in the course of the conversation upon past matters, they parted without agreeing, Mr. Grenville expressing his wishes to see Lord Temple again.

[1] The reconciliation of Lord Temple and Mr. Grenville was henceforth complete.   They ever after continued upon the most affectionate terms.

my place, and was with the King, I believe, an hour.
I was then admitted, but the King would not explain
anything to me, but will give his answer to you singly
this evening. By this I conceive, and by his manner to
me, that every thing is over [1]. I intend to be at Marl-
boro' House from 7 till 11. Ever yours, BEDFORD.

MR. GRENVILLE TO THE LORD CHANCELLOR.

Downing Street, May 23, 1765,
Thursday morning, 4 o'clock.

MY DEAR LORD,—I am just returned from the Queen's
House, the King not having sent to me to go there 'till
past eleven o'clock.

I received his orders to inform all the Lords who met
here this morning of the answers which he has given
upon the several points proposed to him [2].

The Duke of Bedford has promised me to come
hither to-morrow morning at ten o'clock, in order to
consider what we should all say upon this subject.

I therefore beg that your Lordship will, if possible,
do me the honour to call here at that time, as the King
pressed to have the answer given by us all to-morrow at
12 o'clock, at St. James's, therefore I would not lose a
moment's time to inform you of it. I am,

GEORGE GRENVILLE.

[1] The Duke of Bedford it is evident did not expect that their terms
would be acceded to.
[2] See Mr. Grenville's Diary, *post.*

THE BISHOP OF GLOUCESTER TO MR. GRENVILLE.

Prior Park, May 30, 1765.

HONOURED SIR,—You will wonder, perhaps, at the further trouble of a letter from me; but it is only to remove what perhaps you have as much wondered at before, the trouble of my former letters, which I presumed to write to you as to a patron and a friend, whom no services, and very small personal knowledge of me, entitled me to the honour of being considered by you in either of those lights.

But the truth is, I wrote to a Minister, of whom I had the highest opinion; to one, who, I was assured, had the honour of his Master and the interest of the public principally at heart; and therefore (as every man is disposed to think too favourably of himself) I concluded that my duty and devotion to His Majesty, and zeal for his service, joined to my character, not unknown in my efforts to serve the public in the way of my Profession, would make me the object of such a Minister's regard, and dispose him, in good earnest, to second our common Master's gracious dispositions towards me.

At the same time I know how reasonable, and even necessary, it is for a Minister to provide for services wanted, as well as to acknowledge services done. I know too how generous and commendable it is in such a case to promote his private friends.

All this I know, and consequently I confide in your candour to believe, that this trouble at least can be only meant to shew that that appearance of claim to your patronage and friendship was grounded solely in my high opinion of your character; for which, I beg leave to say, I have the highest esteem and reverence. I have the honour to be, &c. W. GLOUCESTER.

MR. ALMON TO EARL TEMPLE.

Piccadilly, June 15, 1765.

My Lord,—Yesterday some further business, relative to my attachment[1], came on in Westminster Hall, in a manner the most extraordinary and unexpected.

Between one and two o'clock, when the Court of Common Pleas was up, and the lawyers beginning to go away, Lord Mansfield suddenly left his Bench, and Mr. Justice Wilmot instantly called for Sergeant Glynn and Mr. Dunning. It happened the latter was in Court, but the former was gone. However, Mr. Dunning sent a message after him, who luckily found him at the Hall gate, just as he was going away. Mr. Justice Wilmot said that he had a matter to propose to them in the case of the attachment against me, to which he desired their concurrence. In the rule made out last January for me to shew cause, there was a material mistake, for the title of that rule was the King against *Wilkes*, whereas it should have been the King against *Almon*.

Your Lordship will be pleased to recollect that the offensive paragraph in the letter on Libels was that which they said alluded to the alteration of Mr. Wilkes's record; therefore this contempt of the Court was originally made a branch of that cause, and that alteration being made by Lord Mansfield at his own house, Glynn and Dunning in the shewing cause insisted that the act of a Judge at Chambers was not an act of the Court. This argument, which was pressed very strongly, it

[1] For the publication of the celebrated "*Letter on Libels and Warrants*." A letter from Almon to Lord Temple, without date, but written on the 23rd of June 1765, and upon the same subject as the above, was, by mistake, inserted in vol. ii. p. 65. It should properly have been placed in the present volume.

is thought was what divided the Judges. But although they were divided as to that single paragraph, yet they agreed that there were other paragraphs in the book, particularly those which relate to the Habeas Corpus, which amounted to a clear and undoubted contempt. Now what they wanted by this proposed alteration was, to be able to shift the ground of accusation to other parts of the book, which, while Mr. Wilkes's name stood in the title of the rule, they could not, for it confined the whole criminal matter to that paragraph.

Sergeant Glynn and Mr. Dunning complained greatly of their being entirely unprepared for this proposal, that they had no instructions from their client on this important point, and that therefore they could not consent, neither was it the practice of the Court, they said, to make such alterations. Wilmot, for near an hour, coaxed and bullied them by turns. But they remained firm. His principal point, after they had positively refused to consent, was to get them to move for a new rule to shew cause why the former rule should not be discharged. What! said Dunning, a rule upon a rule, it is contrary to all practice ; and the quarrel at length became serious, and once quite personal between Wilmot and Glynn. Aston all the while was laughing, and so were above 200 people, for the Court instantly filled after the affair began. Wilmot (who seemed quite mad) urged strongly that there was other matter in the book (meaning besides the paragraph originally excepted to) proper to be taken notice of, but of which they could not take cognizance until this rule was altered : and therefore, as a gentleman, he said, he put the question to Glynn, whether, *upon his honour*, he would not consent to the proposed alteration. This piqued Glynn ; for I, since that, find that there was always a singular friendship between them, as gentlemen, and therefore Glynn took it very ill of Wilmot to ask him in that manner. He declared *upon his honour* that, without consulting his client, he would not consent.

Yates and Aston spoke near half-an-hour each. Yates chiefly said that it was a mistake, which came to their knowledge only the night before ; (this was a lie : for on Monday last, at my own consultation with Glynn and Dunning, I told them that I had undoubted information of an intention in the Court to shift the ground of charge, to which they both said it could not be, for that they could never believe the Court would do such a thing and not allow, nor give them notice to make a defence against it :) that there was other matter of the highest consequence ; that it is true, it was not the practice of the Court to make such alterations ; but in this case he thought the proposed alteration right and necessary. Aston said, in substance, that he was not thoroughly acquainted with the alteration, yet confessed it was not altogether the practice. Glynn and Dunning still refused to consent, and the former made a motion to discharge the rule, which the Court would not do.

Norton said he would consent to the rule being discharged if Glynn would add to his motion, *in consequence of such and such a mistake.*

This Dunning opposed, as affording ground for a fresh rule, and said some very severe things of Norton. In short, the whole lasted between three and four hours, and now the whole stands in exactly the same state it was when your Lordship left London. The Court must either give judgment upon the single paragraph, or begin a new process, if they mean to punish for any other parts of the book.

Thus I am still in good fortune after all my hair-breadth escapes, but I fear I have lost my supposed favour at the Pay Office, not having heard a word more about it, and it is near a fortnight since Mr Townshend mentioned it, which makes many people think it a joke. I beg your Lordship's pardon for this long letter. I am, my Lord, &c., &c.,   J. ALMON.

MR. GRENVILLE TO THE EARL OF SANDWICH.

Stowe, June 17, 1765.

MY DEAR LORD,—I came hither from Wotton just before dinner, and was followed by the messenger with your letter an hour afterwards, the particulars of which I will answer as shortly as is possible.

I will take no further steps about what Sir Laurence Dundas and Mr. Abercrombie spoke to me upon, till they both desire it, and am extremely glad to hear that the former is in such friendly dispositions.

The vacancy of the post of Master-General of the Ordnance in Ireland, by Lord Kildare's resignation, was what I expected when Lord Weymouth was appointed Lord-Lieutenant. Mr. Rigby told me immediately that it would be so, and advised me to try if Sir Jeffry Amherst wished to succeed him, which Lord Granby and I did accordingly that day: we found him very reluctant to take that, with even the command of the troops in Ireland joined to it, but referred him to another time for a fuller answer, though I am convinced, from what passed, that he will not accept if both are offered, unless it is forced upon him by the King. I told Lord Weymouth that if this vacancy should happen, I thought his wisest way would be to propose Sir Jeffry Amherst to the King; if His Majesty should consent to it, as I am persuaded he will, there will be time for Lord Weymouth to give the answer, and to think of somebody else: if Sir Jeffry shall accept, he will really be the properest person in the public opinion, and of real use to Lord Weymouth, or to whoever shall go to Ireland, and if any less desirable subject should be proposed, there cannot be a properer person chosen to withstand it. This is my opinion, which I think Lord Weymouth already knows.

As to our political situation, and its duration, I am satisfied that it is too uncertain for any one to depend upon or to decide against, and therefore in that state I must leave it for the present, relying upon your Lordship to send me any further intelligence which you may receive, and returning you my thanks for your letter, and for that information which you have given me. I am, &c., &c., GEORGE GRENVILLE.

MR. WHATELY TO MR. GRENVILLE.

Parliament Street, June 19, 1765.

DEAR SIR,—The opportunity of a messenger has tempted me to trouble you with the occurrences which I have heard of since you left London. The most material is the determination in the Court of King's Bench of the question of General Warrants. It was argued yesterday by the Solicitor-General and Mr. Dunning, and a second argument being mentioned, the Court said it would be proper on the other parts of the case, but that with respect to the single point of a warrant to apprehend Printers and Publishers, &c., they wanted no further time to enable them to decide that it was illegal. Of that question, therefore, my Lord Mansfield said he would ease the second argument, and the other Judges agreed with him. As to the points of whether the officer had a probable cause to justify his apprehending Leach under that warrant, or whether the Secretary of State was a Justice of Peace within the Statute, they gave no opinions. The same questions were at the same time arguing in the Court of Common Pleas, who came to no decision upon any, but intimated that they thought the Secretary of State was not within the Statute, but gave no reasons, as they left it to the parties to chuse whether they would wish to have it spoken to again, if not, they said they would give Judgment in a few days.

The King's Bench have got the start of the Common Pleas with respect to the legality of General Warrants, but I suppose there is no doubt of the Common Pleas concurring in opinion, and then there will be an end of that troublesome affair.

There has been an odd confusion about the motion for an attachment against Almon. It is said that the Judges differ in opinion whether it lies for a reflection cast upon a Judge for what he did at his chambers, on which ground the present motion stands, and that therefore they wished it had been moved on the whole pamphlet as a libel in other parts also upon a Judge in his office. Whether this surmise be well grounded or not, it is certain that the Court suggested the propriety of discharging this rule, in order to make another motion, upon an exception taken up by themselves, that the affidavits bore a wrong title, being in a cause of the King and Wilkes instead of the King and Almon. The Attorney-General maintained the titles were right, that they were justified by constant practice, and that the Court was apprized of their being as they are from the beginning: they came to no decision, and thus the matter rested when it was last mentioned.

General Irwin has been offered to go to Gibraltar: he is much mortified at this turn, and greatly regrets your absence, as it is a situation very different from that he hoped for, and he fears may be given him instead of a regiment. It has, however, been put to him in a way that he finds he must accept it. I have only seen Lord George Sackville in company, but he took occasion before them to acknowledge your kindness to Irwin in strong terms.

The reports of changes continue as strong as ever; but those are not news to you.

I am very happy to address this to Stowe, as no man more sincerely shares in the domestic happiness you must there enjoy. I am, &c., &c., THOMAS WHATELY.

THE EARL OF SANDWICH TO MR. GRENVILLE.

Wednesday, half an hour past 3, (June 19, 1765.)

DEAR SIR,—I am this moment returned from Court, and by what I am going to say you will find that it is necessary I should give you a minute detail of all that I heard and saw there.

The King did not come to St. James's 'till near two o'clock; upon inquiry I found the occasion of this unusual delay was that Mr. Pitt was actually at that time at the Queen's house, where he had been for near two hours.

Lord Chancellor was at Court in consequence of a message he had received from His Majesty to attend him after the Levée; as we waited a full hour, I had much confidential conversation with him, and found him thoroughly disposed to give the King the most wholesome advice relative to the present state of men and things; when he had had his audience he took me aside and communicated to me all that passed in the closet; that the King had told him it had been suggested to him that Mr. Pitt might, if His Majesty should see him, be prevailed on to take a part in his Government; in consequence of which an intimation had been sent to Mr. Pitt that the King would see him (but by whom that intimation was conveyed I do not know; I imagine by some one from the Duke of Cumberland). Mr. Pitt went accordingly to-day to the King, and declined entering into any particular detail of the conditions on which he would serve, 'till he knew what *measures* would be pursued; that those measures must be explained and fully understood before he entered into any engagements; this he adhered to, and desired leave to return to his country retirement, without coming to any agreement whatever.

Lord Chancellor upon this narrative represented to His Majesty how unhappy these frequent events must make all those who wished well to him, that he foresaw it would end in his throwing himself upon the Duke of

Newcastle, who possibly might undertake to form an Administration, though he (Lord Chancellor) was positive he could not carry it through, and that the best advice he could give was, that His Majesty should stand by his present Ministers (who were the only people who could serve him effectually), and treat them again with good humour. This he said the King seemed to listen to attentively, and he thinks it made the proper impression, and the audience finished with the King's desiring Lord Chancellor to let him see him often, particularly to return to him again to-morrow morning; and his Lordship's conclusion upon the whole is, that Mr. Pitt has certainly done nothing, and that things are better for us than they were before.

I went into the closet after this audience, and the King went through several points of business with me, with more seeming good humour and ease than I have ever seen him since the late events, and I am inclined to think with Lord Chancellor that affairs are altered for the better.

In this critical state of affairs surely you will think your immediate presence among us absolutely necessary. I have sent a copy of the letter I am writing to the Duke of Bedford and Lord Halifax, and hope they will come up immediately to meet you. I shall press them in the strongest terms I can, as I do you, because I think the crisis is of the utmost importance, and that the fate of this nation may depend on our conduct in this delicate state of affairs. Be assured that I am, &c., &c.,

SANDWICH.

MR. GRENVILLE TO THE EARL OF SANDWICH.

Stowe, June 20, 1765, 9 o'clock, A.M.

MY DEAR LORD,—The messenger brought me your letter last night at twelve o'clock, just as I was getting into bed, which prevented my re-dispatching him 'till this morning.

I am much obliged to you for the detail you have given me of what has passed, but I hope you will excuse me if I cannot agree with you as to the propriety of my immediate return to town in consequence of it. This is the result of my opinion after having weighed the whole of the account which you have sent to me. You will consider that the King has not taken the least notice of any part of this business, even to your Lordship who are upon the spot; nor have you received through the channel of my Lord Chancellor any positive information what the King's intentions and dispositions now are, or are hereafter likely to be, with regard to his Administration, and to that influence which has suggested to him the thoughts of changing them.

In this state, whilst the favour and authority of the Crown still appear in direct opposition to each other, I own I am not eager to press my advice and services upon the King; nor do I see what benefit can be derived to His Majesty or to the public by my being in town. When I took leave of the King, I asked his permission to stay in the country 'till Tuesday next, which he granted to me. My return to town before that time, uncalled for, will have the appearance of a desire to embarrass the arrangement which he is now endeavouring to form, and which I need not tell you will come on, or go off, just the same whether I am there or not; as the

King would not in the present situation communicate it to me, and without that I certainly should not trouble him upon the subject of it.

So far therefore from thinking it necessary, I do not think it even decent for me to change the time which was fixed and settled with the King for my stay in the country, unless I receive his commands to the contrary. I imagine that these reasons will induce the Duke of Bedford and Lord Halifax (to whom I take for granted you will show this letter) to come to the same resolution, or at least that they will be of sufficient weight with your Lordship to excuse me for not complying with your wishes and opinion, which I should be extremely desirous to do wherever my own conviction will allow of it. If anything further passes, I shall be glad to hear of it; in the meantime I agree entirely with my Lord Chancellor in lamenting the difficulties which I fear the King and kingdom will fall into, and which must daily increase instead of diminishing, unless some certain plan is speedily formed and steadily pursued. I am, &c., &c.,

GEORGE GRENVILLE.

THE EARL OF SANDWICH TO MR. GRENVILLE.

Thursday, June 20, 1765.

DEAR SIR,—Lord Chancellor has had another long interview with the King, and communicated to me afterwards what had passed; he thinks the King still undetermined what to do, and he assures me he has said everything that he thought likely to induce him to determine in favour of his present servants, who he assured him were those who would serve him with most ease to himself; this he thinks made an impression, but the King, he says, considers us in a state of resignation, having understood from the Duke of Bedford that unless further terms were granted, we meant to give up our offices[1]; this his Lordship said to the King he believed was a mistake, for that he understood that our only point was, that we might have His Majesty's cordial support, and that his authority and confidence might go together. I told him that he had explained our meaning fully, and that I wished he would take an early opportunity of satisfying the King entirely upon that point, and of assuring him that we did not think of resigning, if His Majesty would enable us to serve him by really giving us his countenance, and that no further terms would be exacted, or were ever thought on, if we met with that support. He has promised to see the King again on Sunday: I would therefore wish to know whether I have said too much or too little upon that subject. I am aware that if you have acquired any additional strength it may be saying too much, and therefore if you will give me the least hint, I will stop my Lord Chancellor between this and Sunday from saying anything at all upon this subject, without letting him know my reasons; but if we stand upon our original ground, it seems extremely material that we should immediately remove the impression of our intending to re-

---

[1] Upon the authority of the MS. Diary of Sir Gilbert Elliot, one of the *King's friends*, the Duke is reported to have said to the King, that if, upon his return from the country in three weeks or a month, the Ministers were not received with greater expressions of favour and confidence, he and his colleagues were determined to resign their offices. The King replied that the confidence necessary for the dispatch of public business he had given them; that as to favour, they had not taken the way to merit it.—See *Bedford Correspondence*, vol. iii. p. 290.

sign, or of expecting that further sacrifices should be
made. No one will know how to treat this business so
well as yourself, therefore I hope this will meet you on
the road, or determine you to set out without loss of
time.

You will understand that though Lord Chancellor
thinks Mr. Pitt will not join with our adversaries, he
does not think His Majesty gives that quite over, and
he believes he means to see him again : he also understands that the Duke of Cumberland has furnished His
Majesty with a plan of Administration which he advises
him to adopt, but that the whole is still undecided, and
the conclusion extremely doubtful ; and he protests that
he will do everything in his power to make it take the
turn we wish it should. I am, &c.,   SANDWICH.

MR. GRENVILLE TO THE EARL OF SANDWICH.

Stowe, June 21, 1765.

MY DEAR LORD,—I received the honour of your
Lordship's letter by Pearson the messenger late last
night. You will have seen by mine of yesterday morning, which must have come to your hands before this
time, what my opinion is concerning my immediate return to town, and therefore to that I beg leave to refer,
adding only that it is in no degree altered, but confirmed, by the account which you have sent me of what
has since passed.

With regard to the conversation which the Duke of
Bedford had with the King, by what his Grace told us,
and by the account which he gave of it in his letter to

the Duke of Marlborough[1], I am fully persuaded that
he made no such declaration as is mentioned in your
letter, in whatever manner it may have been understood.
However, as to any representation of that matter to the
King, I can say nothing further to it, as the Duke of
Bedford himself is the only person who can authorize
any one to make it.

I come now to that part of your Lordship's letter
which relates to declarations to be made in all our names
with respect to the future.

It appears from your letter that three distinct negotiations are actually carrying on with Mr. Pitt, the Duke
of Cumberland, and Lord Chancellor, at this moment[2].

Of the two former, my Lord Chancellor seems to be
very imperfectly informed, and I know nothing of any of
the three, nor of what has passed in the course of them,
but from the very short account which you have been
able to give me of them.

In this situation, when I have not sufficient materials
to form even my own judgment, can your Lordship
think it reasonable or proper for me to empower another
to make declarations in my name? I must, therefore,

---

[1] See *Bedford Correspondence*, vol. iii. p. 286.

[2] " It was not a capricious partiality to new faces;—it was not a
natural turn for low intrigue;—nor was it the treacherous amusement
of *double and triple negotiations.*—No, sir, it arose from a continued
anxiety, in the purest of all possible hearts, for the general welfare."—
Junius, i. 390. Having quoted the ironical observations of Junius for
the purpose of showing how well he was acquainted with every occurrence at Court, it is but fair to add, that on this occasion, these *double
and triple negotiations* were rendered necessary by the difficulties with
which the King was surrounded : they had, however, but *one* object,
the introduction of Lord Temple and Mr. Pitt into administration, and
to bring that about, the King had employed the Duke of Cumberland
and the Lord Chancellor.

insist that nothing of that kind may be done as far as I am concerned, but that I may be left at full liberty to act as I shall think necessary at my return to town, which you know will be in a few days. I am, &c., &c.,

GEORGE GRENVILLE.

EARL TEMPLE TO MR. GRENVILLE.

Stowe, Friday, 9 o'clock, P.M., June 21, 1765.

MY DEAR BROTHER,—I did not see your newspapers 'till this minute. I hear the two ministers have stayed at the inn all the day for want of horses, and are gone to Buckingham. Shuvalow[1] I have kept here.

Everything remained ad referendum between the King and Mr. Pitt, who is ordered to attend His Majesty again to-morrow. It is then thought I shall be sent for. I will, if possible, call at Wotton in my way. Ever yours, &c., &c.,   T.

MR. PITT TO EARL TEMPLE.

Pall Mall, Saturday, 4 o'clock,
(June 22, 1765.)

MY DEAR LORD,—I have again this day had a long audience at the Queen's house, and am commanded by

---

[1] The favourite and supposed husband of the Czarina Elizabeth. " Absolute favourite," says Walpole, speaking of him in a letter to Montague, " for a dozen years, without making an enemy. In truth he is very amiable, humble, and modest. Had he been ambitious, he might have mounted the Throne ; as he was not, you may imagine they have plucked his plumes a good deal. There is a little air of melancholy about him, and, if I am not mistaken, some secret wishes for the fall of the present Empress, which, if it were civil to suppose, I could heartily join with him in hoping for."

the King to acquaint your Lordship that His Majesty wishes to see you at the Queen's house on Tuesday morning next at ten o'clock.

Let me now, my dear Lord, express my own most earnest desire that you will be so good to set out to-morrow morning, and if I may beg the favour, that you will come on and take a bed at Hayes the same night. I am just returning to that place, finding it quite necessary to sleep in the country. You will easily believe that a few hours will not suffice for our conversations. I write with much difficulty, having some pain in my hand; but had I the pen of a ready writer, a letter would ill convey what I have to impart. I will only say that things have advanced considerably in the audience of this day: the first audience was, as this, infinitely gracious; but not equally material. Upon the whole, I augur much good, as far as intentions go: and I am indeed touched with the manner, and *Royal frankness*, which I had the happiness to find [1].

You will say, my dear Lord, here's a man far gone : I confess I am disposed to believe that if the country were not, from past fatal errors, too far gone, that all might be well. That my wretched health will ever be so, I almost despair.

Lady Chatham desires her loves. I am ever my dear Lord Temple's most loving and devoted brother,

WILLIAM PITT.

---

[1] The tone of this letter implies that Mr. Pitt would now have been willing to accept the terms offered by the King for his resumption of office if he had found Lord Temple less impracticable. Lord Chesterfield observes, in a letter to his son, dated at this time, that "Mr. Pitt would have accepted, but not without Lord Temple's consent, and Lord Temple positively refused. There was evidently some trick in this, but what, is past my conjecturing."

THE EARL OF SANDWICH TO MR. GRENVILLE.

Belvidere, June 22, 1765.

DEAR SIR,—You may very safely assure yourself that there is no danger of my ever speaking myself, or authorizing any one to speak in your name, without your express authority.

I have had no idea of taking any step whatever in this critical situation of affairs, other than sending you and our other two friends an account of such intelligence as came to my knowledge.

As to your coming to town, as you justly say, you had given very sufficient reasons against it in your first letter; but you will observe that my second letter was dispatched before I had received your answer to the first, otherwise I should not have repeated my wish that you should think it advisable to return immediately to town.

I have not been in town to-day, and it is now 8 in the evening, and I have just received a note from Phelps[1], with no other intelligence, than that Mr. Pitt was at the Queen's house a quarter before ten this morning. The King arrived soon after, and went away from thence at half an hour past twelve directly for Richmond. Mr. Pitt went away at the same time. I am ever, &c., &c.,　　　　　SANDWICH.

[1] Richard Phelps, Lord Sandwich's private secretary. Several volumes of his papers and correspondence were in the Stowe Collection of Manuscripts, now in the possession of the Earl of Ashburnham.

MR. GEORGE ONSLOW TO EARL TEMPLE.

Tuesday morning, June 25, 1765.

MY DEAR LORD,—The confidential conversation I had the honor of having last night with you and Mr. Pitt, encourages me to trouble you with this to implore your acceptance of the Treasury, for all the reasons I mentioned; for the sake of this country; for the sake of us all; and to submit once more to your consideration and most serious reflection, what a *use will be made*, and what a language will be held, if this great Edifice falls to the ground, on your refusing to take the burthen on your shoulders, especially when Mr. Pitt has acceded to take his share of it with you. Consider only the confusion it will create, consider the great *public* points, and which are nearest to your heart, that will be gained by your acceptance, and irrecoverably lost to this country by your refusal.

Indeed, my dearest Lord, you owe yourself to the Public, and the Public will think they had a right to you. I *know* you will be supported in the House of Commons by the City of London, and the voice of the whole Kingdom; and I will venture to say, that with all the difficulties that it must be owned there are to be encountered, it will be the most *popular* administration that ever was in this country.

I know your goodness to me enough to persuade myself you will pardon this freedom, because it comes from a heart most warmly attached to you, and animated with the expectation of honour and prosperity to my country from the noble sentiments I heard avowed and adopted last night by Mr. Pitt. God grant we may soon see them put in execution.

Your Lordship's repeated favours to me, and partiality so exemplified in your thoughts of having me in public business immediately under yourself, are what I can never forget, and shall ever be proud of.

You might have many abler, but you cannot have a more faithful and devoted humble servant than myself.

GEORGE ONSLOW.

EARL TEMPLE TO MR. GRENVILLE.

(Pall Mall, June 25, 1765,) Tuesday, near 11 at night.

MY DEAR BROTHER,—A groom of the King's called here about seven with a letter from His Majesty to Mr. Pitt, with which he went on to Hayes.

Portents and Prodigies, &c. What new attempt is now to be made? Yours most affectionately,   T.

EARL TEMPLE TO MR. GRENVILLE.

Stowe, July 2, 1765.

MY DEAR BROTHER,—I should have been much mortified if you had confined yourself, on Saturday, to the heat and dust of London on my account, having nothing of material consequence to impart. The plan of the provisional administration was, I think, Butal-Ducal, and as to the propriety of forming one, equal to the times, it is no doubt indispensably necessary.

I hope our respective Post Coaches will frequently travel the road of Stowe, and Wotton; but for the great State Coach, *Tempus abire mihi est.*

Many kind compliments to Mrs. Grenville and the young and old maidens conclude the rural epistle of your most affectionate,   TEMPLE.

LORD HYDE TO MR. GRENVILLE.

The Grove, July 7, 1765.

My dear Sir,—Though most things that pass must come to your knowledge, I am so concerned for my country and you, that I can't conceal what comes to mine, or even into my imagination. Such a use is made of Mr. Pitt's answer, that was it the strongest assurance of support, it could not be repeated with more energy and persuasion. Would it be impossible to know and spread precisely the truth? Nothing stopped the report of Mr. Townshend's acceding to the new measures, but his brother and himself [1]. Before their contradiction came

[1] The following Letters from Mr. Charles Townshend to Lord Townshend, refer to the subject of the present Negotiations.

(From copies in Mr. Grenville's hand.)

Adderbury, July 3, 1765.

My dear Brother,—I had last night the favour of yours from Dereham, by which I learn how entirely our sentiments have agreed upon the subject of the late political negotiations, as far as they have come to our knowledge. My former letters were, as I told you, written upon conjecture, or, at best, loose information; but I can now speak to you with certainty. In the first place it is resolved that the present Administration shall not continue; in the next, Mr. Pitt's negotiation was on the Saturday accomplished, and broke up by Lord Temple on the Monday, against Mr. Pitt's judgment, declaration, and most earnest remonstrance; nay, more, it did not break off on Mr. Grenville's account. Mr. Pitt and Lord Temple have differed entirely; Lord Temple would assign no reasons in the Closet [a], and Mr. Pitt remains with the King, lamenting that he has not health and strength to undertake, without his family, for the relief of his Sovereign and his country. With these public declarations he set out for Somersetshire; Lord

[a] Lord Temple told Mr. Grenville that the reasons he had assigned for not accepting the offer the King made him, were two—the first was the difficulty of forming a proper plan with regard to the House of Commons; the second was of a tender and delicate nature, and which he therefore desired not to explain. If, as Mr. Townshend asserts, and as I believe with truth, the negotiation was not broken off by Lord Temple, on Mr. Grenville's account, that "*tender and delicate*" reason must still remain inexplicable.

out, the party strengthened itself by averring his union
with it. Mr. Yorke still harps on the conciliating
string.

Temple is returned to Stowe, where the Duke of Bedford is said to be
expected ; and the Ministers still attend Court only in form.

I have been assured, upon expressing my surprise at the change we
both experienced so lately in the behaviour to us at St. James's, that
my acceptance had been unpleasing to the King, from the manner in
which it had been *forced* upon him, at *such* a *time*, and with other
similar affronts to him ; upon which I have ventured to deny the fact,
and to recapitulate the circumstances of that long-depending promotion, and the explanation which accompanied the offer and appointment ;
to which I was answered, Lord Townshend and you, believe me, have
been deceived, and if ever you should return to the Closet this *very*
matter will be the *first* to be *cleared* up. I said no more, perfectly
convinced of my own fair dealing and of your affectionate part towards
me in this transaction, and of the evidences we have to produce of the
truth. I mention this for your own use, as it explains many dark
passages to us in the last mysterious month.

At present, one of three measures must take place,—either the
Ministry be received again, or a new one formed out of the minority,
or an Administration composed of the country gentlemen and the
Scotch. The former, it is avowed, the King will never permit ; the
second is under consideration, and seems very difficult ; the latter may
be the necessary final measure, but would be most offensive. In the
meantime in what distress is the King, and in what condition are these
kingdoms ? Is such a dilemma paralleled in the history of any times ?
Surely things hasten in this embarrassed country to some sudden revolution, and from this hour men of sense will review their notions of
the balance of this Government, and of the comparative strength of
the several orders of it. As to me, I am sincerely sorry to see the confusion, attended with such neglect of business, and followed by such
general discontent. I desire not to make any advantage of it to
myself, for late experience has deadened my ambition by lessening my
confidence. I only wish to have misconceptions unjustly entertained
of us, fully removed. I seek no power ; and I mean, if the tide brings
to me any communication or overture, to decline any answer until I
have seen you, that *we who* acted so honourably in the last instance
may be the *same* men in the same *union* upon every future occasion.
Conclude, therefore, that I write to you as often as I hear anything I
believe, and reject all reports of me which are not from me. The
arrangements reported had *no* authority. There would have been *no*

Lord Gower wished for a general meeting of friends to form rules of conduct.

difficulty about Mr. Grenville. I do not credit the paragraph about Ireland.

Lady Townshend writes that she means to stay later at Tunbridge; this delays our journey to Rainham; and as the assizes are in the last week of July, we propose to be with you in the first week of August.

We had fixed our time for the second week of this month, and Morton would have come with us, but his circuit will, upon this change, prevent him. However, we make no change until we hear from yourselves again.

I fear the King's health suffers from his sense of his situation, and I know the minority are divided by the division in the Grenville family. Mr. T. Townshend and his family, with many others, move with Mr. Pitt, who, it is expected, will soon give some very public testimony of his sentiments.

Thus you have a long gazette on which you may depend. Take the map, consider it well, and when we meet we shall be the better prepared to judge, agree, and act upon a plan which may be honourable and manly.

Farewell! let me hear from you. Most affectionately yours,

C. TOWNSHEND.

Adderbury, July 4, 1765.

MY DEAR BROTHER,—Since I sealed and sent my letter to you I have had a visit from Lord Rockingham, who had been desired to open the situation of public affairs, and to prepare me for the arrival of an express from St. James's. His Lordship has represented, in direct words, His Majesty's firm resolution not to continue the present Ministry, let what will be the consequence, the cause of the sudden breaking up of the last negotiation, Mr. Pitt's difference with Lord Temple, the union of Lord Temple with the Duke of Bedford, Lord Temple's refusal to assign any reason for declining employment, and His Majesty's readiness to have forgiven Mr. Grenville, his present distress, and his satisfaction in Mr. Pitt's conduct. His Lordship then proceeded to enumerate to me the parts of an arrangement under consideration, in which he was pressed to be at the Treasury with a Chancellor of the Exchequer; the Duke of Grafton to be one Secretary of State; the Boards generally changed; Mr. Conway Secretary at War; and Mr. Yorke probably Attorney-General.

He then suggested a wish to me that I would be Chancellor of the Exchequer, and upon my saying I would not be to any man living, he threw out the seals to me. As soon as he had finished this map of the

F 2

Lord Chancellor expresses objections, without reserve, to the dangerous experiment of inexperienced people.

Court, and the etching of a new Ministry, I began with lamenting the wretched state of the King and kingdom from frequent injudicious and momentary changes in administration. I then lamented the little kindness I had found at Court upon my late acceptance, which I said had made me seek the country and deadened my ambition; and I added how much I was surprised to find myself *now* so necessary, who, in the last week, was not, to my knowledge at least, in the least regarded, perhaps intended to have been forgot.

I desired leave to decline any conversation until these two extraordinary circumstances, so very expressive of indifference and of censure, were clearly explained, and repeated my resolution to enter upon no confidential conversation until I had seen you, with whom I should act entirely. I then asked his Lordship why no express had been sent to you, especially as upon former instances of distress you had both been much consulted, and acknowledged to have done essential service; and I recommended it to his Lordship to delay any express to me 'till a message had been sent to you, as I could not give any answer even to the King, separate, and without a perfect understanding.

Lord Rockingham, in his answer, confirmed the suspicion which I before had of the cause of the King's coldness to us both, and said we had been deceived; and in speaking of you, expressed some sanguine hopes that you approved *as well as Lord Granby.*

To this I said in general that the former of these points must be fully cleared up, and the latter can be known only from my brother.

It is very difficult to form any judgment in the present state of confusion; but it is necessary to form an opinion, to be prepared for the day of application to us both, and to have some consultation about the part we are to take[a].

If you will accept my first thoughts upon so cursory a view of so complex a matter, the plan opened to me has not the show of much stability nor of necessary strength in it. The Treasury where Mr. Dowdeswell would be Chancellor of the Exchequer would be unequal, at least in common estimation; the Duke of Grafton, though sensible, is very inexperienced in business; Mr. Pitt's *private* approbation would not bring weight with it, and would be for ever disputed; and most men would think the offices of trust and difficulty too generally filled with persons very respectable for their birth and characters, but not enough in the habit of business. On the other hand, it is delicate to

---

[a] " Charles Townshend, who besides not knowing either of his own minds, has his brother's minds to know too."—*Horace Walpole.*

Many monied men and merchants (among others Mr. Harley) grieve on your intended removal. I could comment on all these intelligences of yesterday, was I writing to one who wanted such assistance. I could mark out what trials might be made, if it is not too late, was I not determined to acquiesce in a better judgment. I wish the King could know through the Chancellor, or by any decent persuasive manner, how much the City, and the best part of his subjects, are alarmed at the designed dismission of his first Commissioner of the Treasury, or that Lord Bute was made sensible that his own and the public's safety has no so good chance of being secured as by the present Ministry's restoration to favour.

I a m, &c.,   HYDE.

THE DUKE OF BEDFORD TO MR. GRENVILLE.

Woburn Abbey, July 8, 1765.

DEAR SIR,—I am much obliged to you for your account of the transactions of yesterday, and do most en-

disobey the Crown in such a minute of distraction, especially after Mr. Pitt's forgetfulness of us both, in consequence of the last step which he has heard represented falsely, and as a condition imposed upon the King upon the return of the Ministry, which you know it was not, and Mr. Grenville, I dare say, will testify to others willingly.

However, let things end as they will : united, nothing can hurt us ; and all I wish is that we may meet, and, with Lord Granby, settle the part which we are to take, for the manner of it will be delicate, and must be unexceptionable.

No Captain General, nor the reported Lord-Lieutenant of Ireland.

You will write to me by the return of my servant. If I am sent for, and obliged to go to town, you know already my present answer, and if you wish to have a meeting soon, you will name some day in the next week, and I will keep it, in London.

Adieu, most affectionately yours,

C. TOWNSHEND.

tirely agree with you, that whoever has public or private feelings, must heartily wish to see an end put to these childish transactions, which must all over Europe throw disgrace on Government, and the nation in general.

I am sorry to find that Lord Granby has not had the resolution to abide by his first determination of quitting his employment. Adieu, my dear Sir; I wait for my letter of dismission with impatience, though I can hardly bring myself to believe that any people will be hardy enough to undertake an Administration, which is constructed on no better a foundation than the support of Lord Bute's favouritism. I am, &c., &c., BEDFORD.

EARL TEMPLE TO MR. GRENVILLE.

Stowe, July 9, 1765.

I AM much obliged to you, my dear brother, for the trouble you have taken, in sending me an account of the heavy loss I have sustained, in the death of the Duke of Bolton[1]; as bad news travels fast, I learnt it by express a little after six o' clock on the day it happened. I wish I could say he has left many behind him whom I have so abundant reason to love, and honour, to the

---

[1] Charles Paulet, fifth Duke of Bolton. He was succeeded in the Dukedom by his only brother, Lord Harry Paulet. Horace Walpole, writing to Sir Horace Mann at this time, says:—" The Duke of Bolton the other morning, nobody knows why or wherefore, except that there is a good deal of madness in the blood, sat himself down upon the floor in his dressing-room and shot himself through the head. What is more remarkable is, that it is the same house and same chamber in which Lord Scarborough performed the same exploit." Lord Scarborough put an end to his life in a fit of mental aberration, at his house in Grosvenor-square, in February, 1739-40.

degree my heart felt for him : but no more on this melancholy subject.

I next proceed to your own political dissolution,—

"dicique beatus
Ante obitum nemo supremaque funera debet." [1]

Whether it would have been better had you died by your own hand, than that of the executioner, I will not investigate. I only know that my political existence ended this day fortnight, that I am not in the least degree concerned in any of the subsequent transactions, that I am a stranger to every thing, but as I fear the inevitable ruin of the whole, and that I am, &c., &c.,

TEMPLE.

THE EARL OF NORTHINGTON TO MR. GRENVILLE.

Wednesday, July 10, 1765.

DEAR SIR,—I have this moment received His Majesty's commands to signify to you his pleasure, that you attend His Majesty at St. James's this day, at 12 o' clock, with the seal of your office.

I am very unhappy in conveying so unpleasing commands, as I have the honour to be, with great respect, &c., NORTHINGTON.

LORD LYTTELTON TO EARL TEMPLE.

Curzon Street, July 11, 1765.

MY DEAR LORD,—On Monday last I returned to London, after a week's excursion from thence, on a party of pleasure, which I made on purpose to be out of the way of all business. But on Tuesday morning, Mr.

[1] *Ovid, Metam.* iii. 137.

Conway came to me from the Duke of Cumberland, and pressed me to take a part in the new arrangement. My answer was, that I should have been willing and happy to do so, if Mr. Pitt and your Lordship had been at the head of it, but could not think of separating myself from you in any system of Administration.

I went to-day to Hayes, where I thought to have found Mr. Pitt, and informed him of this transaction; but, as he is with your Lordship, I must beg you to show him this letter. I am, ever, &c., &c., LYTTELTON.

EARL TEMPLE TO MR. GRENVILLE.

Stowe, July 14, 1765.

MY DEAR BROTHER,—I condole with you, as I ought, on the unfeigned mark you have received of the King's displeasure, assuring you, however, that in a private light you will not be the less welcome here, and I long to see you. The new Ministry have, I find, *at last* undertaken His Majesty's affairs, after having twice acknowledged themselves incapable of so arduous a task.

The greatest things are to be expected at their hands, and if they accomplish them who will not applaud?

Let me only add that I am sincerely your affectionate Brother, TEMPLE.

Mr. Pitt and Lady Chatham left us this morning.

MR. WHATELY TO MR. GRENVILLE.

Nonsuch Park, July 24, 1765.

DEAR SIR,—It is so short a time since you left London, that few occurrences can be news to you. You know of Jenkinson's appointment[1], and of the Attorney-General's dismission.

Mr. Yorke still hesitates, but I suppose will at last, though perhaps not immediately, accept. He has paid Sir Fletcher Norton a visit of three hours, but what he came for, or what he said, or what he intends to do, Sir Fletcher declares he does not know, so very undeterminate was the whole conversation. The Solicitor-General desired that he might go to Court with Norton on Sunday, and has behaved to him in a very becoming manner. After the drawing room, Sir Fletcher had an audience, with which he is highly satisfied : he represents His Majesty's behaviour to him as exceedingly gracious, and at the same time agitated.

Since that, the King has had a slight return of his former complaint, and was blooded yesterday, but I know for certain that his physicians are not under any apprehensions [2].

The whole Admiralty are to be removed except Lord Egmont and Lord Howe. Mr. Thomas Pitt has refused to continue. Of the Board of Trade, Soame Jenyns, Elliot and Price, will certainly remain. Dyson's situation is said to be doubtful, but I understand that his sentiments are not so, and that whatever may be their determination, he will not think himself much obliged to them : if he should stay, I shall be apt to attribute it

---

[1] Auditor of Accounts to the Princess Dowager of Wales.

[2] Mr. Jenkinson writes to Mr. Grenville on the following day :— "We have no news but that the King has been again indisposed. He was blooded on Tuesday morning; his disorder was the same as that he had in the winter. Sir William Duncan said there was very little fever, and nothing to be apprehended at present. The danger to be feared was a violent return in the winter. The King had no *levée* yesterday, but to-day he came to the drawing-room, and the Queen was there for the last time before her lying-in."

to Lord Dartmouth's wish to keep him, which he could not at first succeed in.

A warrant is made out for the Vice Treasurers of Ireland, in which Nugent's and Oswald's names are inserted, and a blank left for the third. This is filled up by the generality with Mr. Ellis, who they say is to have Mr. Finch quartered upon him. I know that he has had no offer of it; that though he expected, yet he did not know of his dismission when Lord Barrington kissed hands, but went to Court that day with papers to do business; and that he has not since, at least he had not yesterday, heard of any office intended for him.

I am much more inclined to believe that an offer is gone to Colonel Barré to be one of the Vice Treasurers. His answer cannot yet be received, and some of his friends think he will decline accepting, as Lord Shelburne is not in office. Mr. Finch is said by others to be quartered upon Mr. West, who is Treasurer of the Navy. There was a report this morning, that Lord Howe was to be Treasurer of the Navy, as it was found difficult to settle his claim of precedency, but I believe this story to be without foundation.

The new people very generally and very loudly complain of the Duke of Newcastle's engrossing all the places. Complete restitution is the rule. They have begun with the Alienation Office, where the change is almost total, and the persons removed happen to be mostly Lord Holland's friends.

Those that are reinstated are, I hear, to be paid out of the Civil List the amount of the salaries they have lost by being out of office: if this idea should be carried throughout, I fancy these Restorers will be startled at their own justice, when they come to make up the account;

the officers properly charged on the Civil List will complain of their arrears, and surely loading the Civil List with compensations to the dependants of that party cannot be an ingratiating measure.

The removal of Sir Fletcher Norton after all the circumstances you know, to which he adds an assurance given him, on his agreeing last year to continue, that nothing disagreeable to him should ever be done with respect to the office of Attorney-General, is carrying *the necessity of His Majesty's service very far*. Other instances will occur, and then perhaps a comparison will arise between the two Administrations in the article of compliance.

Wilmot has declined accepting the place of Solicitor of the Treasury, which is now to be offered to Nuthall.

Lord Stanhope I understand is not to continue, and if so, then the Secretary of State's office will be as clear as the Treasury of persons acquainted with the business. Sir Joseph Ayloffe is removed from the place you lately gave him. I have the honour to be, &c., &c.,

THOMAS WHATELY.

MR. GEORGE ONSLOW TO EARL TEMPLE.

Ember Court, July 29, 1765.

MY DEAR LORD,—Nothing would have prevented my troubling you with a letter sooner, but my almost daily intentions to do myself the honour of running down to Stowe; which I wanted much to do, not only to pay my respects to you, but also to say a thousand things to you, which it is impossible to do by letter; but the constant

attention I have been obliged to give to my friends in
Surry, have made it quite impossible.

I long to go through with you all the intricacies and
difficulties of the last three weeks, and explain to you the
extreme difficult part I had to steer through them, more
perhaps than any one man of them all, behind none of
them, I am sure, on account of affection, gratitude, and
devotion to you, which nothing in this world *can* happen
ever to lessen, and which formed the *chief* part of my
difficulty, though not the whole, knowing, as I did and do,
that your objection to accepting was founded on the most
honourable and consistent principles in the world. I
think I can convince you (which indeed I flatter myself
you do not doubt, though you *may* think me *mistaken*) that
my accepting [1] has been founded on the same, and after
having done all I did, which was all I could, I could not
take any other part than what I did.

This is all I can say by letter. I will with your kind
leave soon have the honour of coming to Stowe, if possible the time I intended, the end of August, to talk this
over more at large, to enter more fully into every circumstance of my situation, my connections, my friendships,
and my principles, which I never shall doubt till I find,
which I am sure I shall never do, that they differ from
your Lordship's. It will be the greatest misfortune I
can know, to see we differ in the smallest degree in the
application of them, as it has been the greatest honour

---

[1] He was made a Lord of the Treasury under Lord Rockingham.
George Onslow had been one of Lord Temple's most devoted followers;
therefore he probably considered that his acceptance of office needed
some apology. Junius writes to Woodfall in 1769:—"*I know George
Onslow well; he is a false silly fellow.*" So perhaps Lord Temple
thought of him upon the receipt of this letter.

of my life to have received the marks of regard and
kindness which you have shewn to one most sensible
of them all, and most sincerely and affectionately, my
dear Lord, your most attached and humble servant,

GEO. ONSLOW.

LORD CAMDEN TO EARL TEMPLE.

Camden Place, August 7, 1765.

MY DEAR LORD,—Pardon me for not writing sooner.
My reason was that I did not form any plan of rambling
'till I returned hither, and even now I am not able to
fix either the time for any expedition, or indeed the expedition itself. Yet I am so very desirous of seeing
your Lordship that I will contrive that visit if it be
possible, and therefore if your Lordship intends to be
absent from Stowe, any part of the summer, be so good
as to inform me. I am very happy in your Lordship's
good opinion of me, and am much obliged to you for
your congratulation.

The Ministry is at last upon its legs ; the Offices and
Boards are settled, so that there is the outward form
and body of an Administration, but I can't yet tell who is
that Prometheus that is to give it animation, or will undertake to steal fire from Heaven for that purpose.
Time will shew : in the mean while, let things and men
change as they please, I am, and shall always continue
with utmost respect, your Lordship's much obliged and
obedient Servant, CAMDEN.

Pray present my respects and
my wife's to Lady Temple.

MR. WHATELY TO MR. GRENVILLE.

Parliament Street, August 8, 1765.

DEAR SIR,—I enclose a copy of the Resolutions of the Assembly in Virginia [1].

They are such as in my opinion cannot escape the notice of Parliament; perhaps it may not suit the system of the present Ministers to produce them, but that may not hinder their being called for : though, indeed, if the universal opinion, both of town and country, is to be credited, the system that now is, whatever it may be, will not be the system of the winter. It cannot hold, is everybody's language. The only hopes of its continuance, Mr. Pitt's support, is at an end ; it is now so little relied on, that those who believed the assurances that were given of it, begin to charge him with inconsistency.

Mr. Yorke still hesitates : I believe that will be a paragraph in every letter I shall write this summer : the managements he wishes to keep with Norton are supposed to occasion so extraordinary a conduct, and the reason assigned for such attention there is, that *Norton has him in his power with respect to some opinions he gave on the question of General Warrants.* This is all that is said of it at present, and it is said only in a whisper : you know what the fact was, and probably it will come out now. If Mr. Yorke should decline, a reason is already prepared to account for his

---

[1] The Resolutions of the Assembly of Virginia were the first after the passing of the Stamp Act, as the Assembly happened to be in session when the intelligence arrived. One of the resolutions asserts the exclusive right of the Assembly to lay taxes and impositions on the inhabitants of that colony, and that every attempt to vest such a power elsewhere is "illegal, unconstitutional, and unjust, and has a manifest tendency to destroy British as well as American freedom."

brother's accepting : that (it is said) is only upon the principle of Restitution, but wherein the situation of the two brothers differs in that respect I do not know, for both I think resigned.

It can hardly be news to you that Mr. T. Pitt has absolutely refused to continue in the Admiralty : the question is so natural, why they did not know his sentiments before they inserted his name in the new Commission, that everybody asks it, but I do not find any reason is given [1].

It is generally understood that Colonel Barré will not accept the offer intended him : Lord Shelburne, I hear, has answered for him, and declares against the present Ministers.

Nobody, I am told, is more positive than Calcraft, that they will not last 'till Christmas. I have the honour to be, &c., THOMAS WHATELY.

SIR ARMINE WODEHOUSE[2] TO EARL TEMPLE.

Kimberly, August 26, 1765.

MY LORD,—Your Lordship has often honoured me with your sentiments upon political subjects : I am in doubt whether that entitles me to do myself the honour to write to you. However, I much mistake your cha-

---

[1] This circumstance is alluded to in Lord Temple's pamphlet, *The Principles of the late Changes Impartially Examined.* "They thought fit, also, to insert, without leave, certain names of affinity in conspicuous commissions, that the *Gazette* might circulate an appearance of connection. But this foundation failed, as false ones always will. They got an early warning of authority, which gave a check to the unwarranted use of that name of renown under which they were desirous to take shelter."

[2] M.P. for Norfolk.

racter, if you take it amiss of me to ask you one question. Does *Mr. Pitt* and your Lordship *approve of the present arrangement of Government?* I own, Mr. Grenville's not making a part of it, I look upon to be a great misfortune to the Publick. If your Lordship thinks me impertinent, I dare say it is not the only instance you have met with ; I confess your Lordship's public spirited conduct, and openness of temper, has led me to this extravagant impertinence ; I shall be mortified to find that Mr. Pitt and you have formed this Administration, which is the general opinion of this part of the Kingdom. I am, my Lord, &c.,

A. WODEHOUSE.

MR. CHARLES LLOYD TO MR. GRENVILLE.

August 29, 1765.

SIR,—I have just met Humphrey Cotes, who tells me that the paragraphs in the City Address [1], implying a disapprobation of the present Administration, were at his desire and contrivance ; that upon reading the Address over, the Secretaries of State sent to the Recorder ; that the Recorder thereupon wrote a letter to the Com-

---

[1] It had been presented the day before, to congratulate the King on the birth of another prince. The Address contained the following passage :—" Whenever a happy establishment of public measures shall present a favourable occasion, they will be ready to exert their utmost abilities in support of such wise councils as apparently tend to render His Majesty's reign happy and glorious." A well-written pamphlet was soon after published by "*An Indignant Liveryman,*" entitled *A Letter to the Common Council of London on their late very extraordinary Address to His Majesty,* in which, he says, they tell the King positively, though indirectly, that unless his affairs are in a flourishing situation he is never to expect the smallest support or assistance from the City of London.

mon Council, proposing alterations, which were unanimously rejected: the Recorder's letter I am promised a copy of.

A negative is to be put upon the Recorder's attending any more Addresses.

The Duke of Grafton is issuing some *very extraordinary* warrants : *this is a fact.*

Exeter, Bristol and Canterbury, are to echo the London Address.

(MR. MACKINTOSH TO EARL TEMPLE.)

(August 30, 1765.)

A Fragment.

* * * * *

immediately, as he did ; but he was brought back now by a special call, the purpose of which, 't is said, was to put a categorical question : the view being to know certainly the calibre of every one. For the same reason 't is handed about that Mr. Elliot and Mr. Oswald must now speak plainly out. They have not been removed because the wish is rather to have the advantage of their abilities in the penury there is of trained forces : but if they are not now explicit, they must make room for others.

By all accounts there is the greatest passiveness in the Closet, but there are no great marks of cordiality. The ——— (King) more and more hurt: obliged to absolute submission, and dare not take the least on : puts on an appearance of cheerfulness, but in his retired hours discovers the sharpest feelings, and to particulars, shews the awkwardness of his situation, and his sense of the odd appearance of things, by a visibly *out-of-countenance* look.

There was a story soon after I came to town, that L. B. (Lord Bute) had gone and taken a formal leave of the (King); but I paid no attention to it. Lately I have had information that I have reason to believe I may rely upon; and I am assured that Lord Bute did, at an interview with the (King) since the change, tell him that he saw he could not be of any use to him; that he was unhappy enough to have been the occasion of so much uneasiness to him, by the attachment; and therefore begged him to think no more of it; that he would go abroad or do anything to make matters easy, and hoped his ―― (Majesty) would give up all thoughts of any correspondence. Since that, if I can lay any stress upon my authority, which was what should be good, and I am persuaded is fair and honest, Lord Bute has not seen the (King) but in public twice, one of the times to present his son; and that there really has been no correspondence by letters. This at least has been averred, and is believed. To all this 't was to me added, from the breath of a very near quarter, that the (King) feels still the uneasiness of his present situation; that his strongest inclinations appear and are expressed for your Lordship and Mr. P. (Pitt) and an Administration on your bottom; that he wants to be at ease, and sees that only can give it him. A very strong expression was used to me " that it was believed 't would make the King a foot higher, to be able to bring that about." Some, I can say, that are personally attached to the (King), and do not chuse to take their mark from any other gnomon, avow their having no liking for, no confidence in, our present steersmen, and so much so that they have abstained going near them, though they have received broad hints, for which they give reasons that do not mark any apprehensions of pleasing the (King).

It has been expressly said to me, that this seems to be the very season for being Masters of the Closet, and with every advantage; and that if your Lordship and Mr. Pitt would come in, or there were any means to bring you, you might have the most absolute influence. I do verily believe those from whom that language comes wish sincerely 't was brought about; and I have that opinion that they think what they say, upon grounds and evidence which they are able enough to judge of, and have full access to. I only give what I have got. The difficulty, as 't was fairly suggested, is the D—e (Duke of Cumberland), who, 't is visible (I have seen * that clearly enough), is the head and soul of all. The error 't is now said is discovered, of having so totally surrendered regality into those hands, and that the fatality of the mistake is felt; which produces wishes as well as opinions of the necessity of being delivered: and 't is said that *that* was thought to have been the most probable means of satisfying your Lordship in particular, to use that mediation; because there had intervened certain marks of habitudes between your Lordship and the Duke of Cumberland or at least with P. A. (Princess Amelia?), and that the real ground was not known. Supposing things really to stand upon this foot, I 'm sure I pretend not to think what may or should be your Lordship's feelings. I am sure the true wishes of the public are as I think they ought to be; and their looks are where there is only prospect of any thing stable or salutary. But, for my own part, as these are my wishes, nevertheless I do desire full satisfaction of solid ground to stand upon before I see any risk run, by attempting to stand upon it; and nothing does or can alter my opinions upon that point, from what I have often declared 'em to be.

Mr. Y——ke (Mr. Charles Yorke), very consistently with all his conduct, went to N——n (Sir Fletcher Norton); sat four hours with him, endeavouring to persuade him that he was doing the most essential service to him, by accepting of his office. Norton said little during that long discourse, but just enough to lead the other on. At last Mr. Yorke got up to go away, and Norton said, "Good night, the next time we have occasion to talk over these matters, will probably be in the H. of C." This seemed to waken the other gentleman out of his dream; and he wanted to go back into the Chamber to resume the discussion: but Norton very coolly said, "Mr. Yorke, 't is late, so good night."

Your Lordship, I suppose, got early a copy of the City Address; as B——e (Beardmore) told me he would send one under a blank cover. He was with me before 't was adjusted, and I wished, and did try, to make it not less strong, but a little more fluent, as I thought. However, I was glad of the turn being taken, though the expressions might have been mended: and I think there never was such stupidity as in the attempt as well as proposed alteration of the R——r (Recorder). I think that body are fully at your Lordship's desires, if they only can know 'em. I was disappointed in not seeing the reception of the Address, by the late arrival of the C——Cl (Common Council), though I was at Court, but I very soon felt it had stung: and was not a little diverted to hear that the K—— (who had sent   *   *   *   *

EARL TEMPLE TO SIR ARMINE WODEHOUSE.

Stowe, September 5, 1765.

SIR,—At my return late last night from an expedition into Worcestershire, I found your letter of the 26th of August, by which you wish to know whether Mr. Pitt and I approve of the present arrangement of Government; to which I can with great truth and openness answer, first, for myself, that I do not; next for Mr. Pitt, that he neither had, nor would have, any the least share in the formation of it, as it now stands; he is retired into Somersetshire, and has not, I dare say, any the smallest communication with them.

If they pursue the measures which we stipulated for on behalf of the public, no doubt, so far, they will be entitled to our support and approbation; but, as I look upon the system to be weak and insufficient, I cannot say I entertain any hopes from it in favour of my country. I found myself under the unfortunate necessity of declining all the gracious offers of His Majesty under the circumstances which then existed, but I should be most happy, if I could see such a Government formed as could reasonably engage public confidence at home and abroad : 'till that is happily accomplished, I fear we shall continue in a weak and divided state, inviting insults, unable to repel them.

I have now fully obeyed your commands, and have at all times a pleasure in assuring you that, whether we act together politically or not, I am always much, Sir, your obedient, humble servant,   TEMPLE.

MR. EDMUND BURKE TO MR. CHARLES LLOYD.

Queen Ann Street, October 1, 1765.

DEAR SIR,—I hope you will do me the justice to believe that my long delay in answering your letter did in no respect arise from a disregard to your character, or an indifference to the success of your desires. A good deal of business, together with some returns of the same complaint I suffered under when you saw me, were the real and only causes of a delay, which I confess I cannot entirely excuse, but which you will have the goodness to forgive.

On communicating the contents of your letter to Lord Rockingham, his Lordship seemed much surprised to find that you think you have *already* received some marks of his displeasure, as you have used the expression of a fear of *further* marks of it. His Lordship thought you had been sufficiently apprised of the true cause of your removal from the office of Receiver of Gibraltar; this change having been made in consequence of a general arrangement which his Lordship and his friends apprehended to be required from them by the rules of strict justice in favour of former sufferers; and by no means from any particular dislike or resentment to you. Many persons suffered from the same disposition whose persons Lord Rockingham valued, and whose situations he sincerely pitied.

As to the expression in my letter to which you have excepted, I must beg leave to explain myself, and to assure you that it related to the substance of the question, and not at all to your motives in asking it.

It was meant to express the impropriety of giving any answer to it, from the obvious consequences which must have resulted from an answer, and not from the smallest intention of reflecting upon you, for your having desired satisfaction upon a matter concerning which you must naturally be very anxious.

I am with great esteem, and very real good wishes, &c.,   E. BURKE.

MR. AUGUSTUS HERVEY TO MR. GRENVILLE.

Park Place, October 3, 1765.

DEAR SIR,—We are here very few in number indeed, the thinnest Courts I have ever seen—only a small *family* party, and those to all appearance not the most cordial, for very few days ago it was very visible there was great confusion, and the report about was strong that Mr. Charles Townshend was to have Mr. Conway's seals, who was to be Pay-Master, en attendant quelque chose (pas de mieux) mais *plus convenable;* it is said to have gone off with a negotiation that Charles Townshend undertook with Lord Holland, who refused to take any part in the Cabinet.   Now it is said they are divided by an extraordinary step of the Duke of Newcastle, who is endeavouring to get the Duke of Cumberland to openly avow the Favourite, whose appearance for three or four times openly at Court lately, authorizes these reports : 't is certain his friends in place have been very openly censorious on the present Ministers, and appeared much dissatisfied at being made the sacrifice to their game, and 't is said they have drove their patron to come to an explanation, and to declare he would suffer no more of that game : yet in contradiction to this, I have heard for certain to-day that Lord Bute has sold his house building in Berkeley-square to Lord

Shelburne for 22,500*l.*, and is to floor, and cover it
in [1].

'T is very certain and visible their disagreement:
Conway and he [2], who first carried on the secret transactions against the Administration, had a *smart, short*
hit at each other in the Cabinet the other day, when the
Committee of the Council was called in about something
to be referred to that Board; I cannot at present *risk*
you the particulars; it is sufficient it was so, in a very
trivial affair in itself, though made a point of by one
and the other, as it broke in upon the department at
which *one* presides.

I suppose you know they have repeated the demand
for the Manilla ransom, and in strong terms; but I can
assure you they must do it with yet stronger energy
before they 'll succeed so as to be able to give the least
satisfaction on that head when called upon. I hear for
certain we shall not meet for business 'till after the
Holidays, yet I hear about for as certain that the
intimates of a young Duke [3] affirm everywhere that that
young Duke has taken no step since in power without
having the opinion of the great Commoner.

I go Sunday evening from hence, and hope Monday
to be at Stowe.

I have wrote a very long explanatory and argumental
letter to Ickworth on that which I received, and have

---

[1] Now the residence of the Marquis of Lansdowne. Lord Shelburne
gave an entertainment by way of *housewarming*, on the occasion of its
being completed, on Monday, the 1st of August, 1768.

[2] Probably Lord Egmont, who was supposed to have been secretly
in the confidence of Lord Bute. He remained First Lord of the Admiralty during the Rockingham Administration.

[3] The Duke of Grafton was at this time entirely under the guidance
of Mr. Pitt.

another in return, acknowledging the force and justness of mine, but says *he*[1] *must close his ears like the deaf adder, charm I ever so wisely :* a quoi bon d'en dire davantage sur ce sujet.

The papers go on prosperously, and you find you have many friends even there, as you have everywhere else, but none in the world who wishes you more health and happiness, or is more sincerely and warmly attached to you, than, dear Sir, &c., &c., A. Hervey.

MR. AUGUSTUS HERVEY TO MR. GRENVILLE.

London, October 12, 1765.

Dear Sir,—I was four days at Stowe, where I found Lord Shelburne, who only staid a day. I left my Lord and Lady[2] very well yesterday in their delightful and elegant Palace. What improvements! What a delightful place! How well he is served, with all the magnificence of a Palace, all the elegance of a real nobleman, and all the ease of a private gentleman! I never saw so large a house so well conducted[3], servants that have no *embarras*, no noise, but all attention and respect: 't is a miracle how they have formed them so, and rubbed off the dirt and familiarity from the Foreigners, and inattention and ill-breeding from the English ones; I wish the master of a certain very great family had the art of conducting his as well, then should we see order restored instead of confusion, respect instead of flattery, and

---

[1] His brother, the Earl of Bristol.
[2] Temple.
[3] These are compliments which Stowe continued to deserve until a much later period.

efficiency in the place of inability: if ever that happy change returns, it must be brought about by yourself, the only able upper Servant that can, in our distresses, direct the whole. In short, I mean to tell you I was delighted with my reception, and my vanity flattered by *his* obliging condescension in a full discussion of everything, and pleased to find he approved the steps you recommended, and I shall follow.

Mr. Stanley is returned from abroad, and 't is said is offered the Vice-Treasurership of Ireland, and reported that he will accept. I should much doubt.

I hear Mr. Charles Townshend declares aloud that he has now given his plan to the King, and that if Lord Bute will agree to stand out, and promise not to flinch, he will engage to carry on the Administration, himself at the Treasury, and says he will kiss the King's hand with Lord Bute if he pleases to-morrow, but Lord Holland must be a Cabinet Councillor. Lord Holland has refused, though I hear from very good authority that he is to be in town on the 20th.

They remain much divided among themselves, and this constant talk of changes raises jealousies, and alarms the individuals of them, which prevents their cementing.

The Duke of Grafton is heartily tired, and expresses it everywhere, though his people pretend to assert very confidently that Mr. Pitt approves his Grace's steps.

I hear they are in a furious dilemma at Sir George Macartney [1] having concluded the Treaty with Russia with two articles included that absolutely destroy a certain Treaty of '74, and which alarm so much, that four couriers have been dispatched thither within these

---

[1] British Ambassador at St. Petersburgh.

three weeks. He was going to be recalled on a sudden, but they now want to get the Russians to recede from these two articles. They exclaim, and say it was done purposely to destroy them, and have searched all offices to see if there were any private or public instructions that authorized it, but none appears. I assure you it is a great secret this, but a great noise among themselves and great alarm. Pour le reste, I hear nothing but common talk. I suppose you know that Keppel, the Bishop of Exeter, has the Deanery of Windsor— malgré the Duke of Newcastle's earnest solicitations for another, Lord Barrington for his brother, and the Duke of Grafton and General Conway for Lord Francis Seymour.

I think *some one* might take notice, and make the public sensible how all things are crowded into three or four people's pockets, and no other families can expect anything. I had some thoughts of making you a visit for a day or two at Bath; my sister being there gives me the opportunity of enclosing this safely to you, and if it should be opened first, it is a matter of great indifference who sees it; they will only be convinced of my sovereign contempt for them, and the great opinion, esteem and respect which, ever since I have had the honour of knowing you, has attached me most sincerely to you, and from which I shall not depart.

I forgot to tell you David Hume [1] goes from Paris to *Dublin,* to make out Speeches and answers to Addresses: that is not a bad one for Anti-Sejanus [2] *to handle.*

[1] Appointed Secretary to Lord Hertford, as Lord-Lieutenant of Ireland.

[2] A clergyman named Scott was the author of a series of letters under this title in the *Public Advertiser.* He was under the patronage of Lord Sandwich.

MR. HUMPHREY COTES[1] TO EARL TEMPLE.

Byfleet, October 13, 1765.

MY DEAR LORD,—I have been extremely impatient to transmit to your Lordship and my good Lady Temple, my poor thanks for the many and distinguishing marks of favour and civility I received when I last paid my devoirs at Stowe; the omission would have been quite unpardonable, had I not been busied in some trifling affairs, which the papers sent herewith will, *in part*, explain, if your Lordship will please to peruse them.

Upon my arrival in town, I called upon our friend Mackintosh, who told me of the conversation had with General Græme[2], Secretary to Her Majesty, and shewed

---

[1] Cotes appears to have been for some years in great intimacy with Lord Temple. The present letter shews that he had been received as a visitor at Stowe; and that Lord Temple had been Cotes's guest at Byfleet, let the parody on CHEVY CHASE be my authority:—

> " The tidings to Earl Temple came
> At *Cotes's* where he lay."

The correspondence of Wilkes and Cotes, as published by Almon, furnishes many instances of the confidential intercourse which existed between Cotes and Lord Temple. How long it continued after this time I know not; no other letters from Cotes are extant among these papers. In 1767 Cotes became a bankrupt, and it would appear from Wilkes's letters that he was a considerable loser by his failure. He died on the 1st of May, 1775.

[2] Major General David Græme, M.P. for Perth, and Private Secretary to the Queen. He was afterwards Comptroller of the Queen's Household. He had been sent to Germany, in 1761, to visit the several Protestant Courts; and it was at his recommendation that the Princess Charlotte of Mecklenburg Strelitz was selected to be the Queen of George III. Walpole says he was a notorious Jacobite, and had been engaged in the late rebellion. David Hume congratulated him on having exchanged the dangerous employment of making kings for the more lucrative province of making queens.

me the notes[1] he had taken to preserve precision. I, in turn, acquainted him with the particulars which your Lordship gave me in charge; we appointed to dine together the next day; when he assured me that your sentiments gave entire satisfaction to Mr. G.; but that he desired that the substance might be reduced into writing: this, I own, was a very delicate business, and embarrassed me not a little. We passed the whole afternoon of that day in forming this business, and inclosed you will receive a copy of what was delivered to Mr. G.: I can only assure your Lordship that the utmost caution and attention was observed in forming this paper to convey *entire* your sentiments, and it will make me extremely happy to find, that *we* have acted in this particular to your good-liking. The notes inclosed, wrote by our friend,[2] will explain the rest, and I shall only add that it gives me real satisfaction to find so much good sense and discernment in the Q. (Queen), which must in the end produce some good effect, as I hope the present business will; I think at least it will bring forth the K.'s *real* sentiments[3].

[1] These notes have, unfortunately, not been preserved.

[2] This refers to the PAPER, in the handwriting of Mackintosh, mentioned in the following letter from Lord Temple.

[3] It has not been hitherto supposed that Queen Charlotte interfered, or was ever employed by the King in any of the political intrigues at this early period of his reign. Lord Chesterfield, writing to his son about this time, thus mentions Her Majesty:—" You seem not to know the character of the Queen. Here it is—She is a good woman, a good wife, a tender mother, and an unmeddling Queen. The King loves her as a woman, but I verily believe has never yet spoken one word to her about business." The King was already tired of the Rockingham Administration, which he had accepted with reluctance, but the Ministers were entirely unconscious of the secret steps which were being taken to supplant them, chiefly perhaps in order to accomplish the King's great desire to prevent, if possible, the Repeal of the Stamp Act.

It would be doing great injustice upon this occasion not to mention the fervent zeal and indefatigable attention of our friend Mr. M. I can, with great truth, bear testimony for him in the pursuit of this great object.

Mr. G. had not an opportunity of conveying the written paper to the Q. (Queen) till last Tuesday night, when he gave it into her own hand, together with a letter he wrote himself upon the subject; copy of which I shall send to your Lordship next week, and which Mr. M. tells me was very satisfactory. He has heard nothing from G. since that time, but imagined when I left him yesterday in town, that something would come from that quarter as (ere) this. We have appointed to dine together on Tuesday next in town, when, possibly, I may have something new to convey to your Lordship, which I shall take care to do by a safe hand [1].

I have not lost sight of the two objects we talked of at Stowe : — the Fine of Wood [2] — [and the Em-

The death of the Duke of Cumberland, which happened very shortly after, probably interrupted the course of this negotiation, but we shall see that it was partially renewed a few months later, when it is mentioned in Mr. Grenville's Diary.

[1] It is, perhaps, not the least remarkable feature in this singular transaction, that the agents employed for the purpose of undermining one Administration in order to set up another, were a broken-down wine merchant, a briefless barrister (both of them subsequently bankrupts), and a Scotch adventurer, who happened to be Secretary to the Queen. I shall have another opportunity of mentioning Mackintosh, the barrister.

[2] This alludes to the verdict of 1000*l.* damages which Wilkes had obtained in an action against Wood, the Under-Secretary of State. Upon the subject of these trials, Charles Yorke writes to Lord Rockingham on the 3rd of November :—" In short, my Lord, the true complaint of all these verdicts is the *excess of damages*, which cannot be set right ; and from what has passed in both Courts, I know that it is impossible to avoid the payment of them."[a] The fine was accord-

bassy [1].] The good Lords of the Treasury have been graciously pleased to grant my request for the first, by a minute of their board, but there remain some legal impediments, such as Bills of Exceptions, and Writs of Error, to be cleared away before I can get the money. However, I doubt not success in that business [2].

ingly paid to Cotes ; and Wilkes, in a letter to him of the 1st of January following, says :—" As you have received Wood's 1000*l.*, I beg you to send me immediately some kind of remittance, &c." [a]

[1] The words within brackets have been obliterated by Lord Temple, but not effectually ; with some care they may still be perceived. I cannot conjecture why Lord Temple, in preserving this letter, has yet endeavoured to obliterate these words. The embassy to Constantinople, from which Mr. Henry Grenville had lately returned, was the object of Wilkes's ambition ; and his friends had endeavoured to induce the Ministers to confer this appointment upon him. In a letter from Wilkes to Cotes, of the same date, from Paris, he says :— " I am still in the same idea as to Constantinople ; nothing can so effectually heal all breaches of every kind. When you consider what passed as to the brother of a certain man not an Englishman [b], I believe the person you mention (the King) may be brought to yield to it. You, who are on the spot, can best judge of this. There is nothing I so much wish, on every account my busy mind can suggest to me." [c]

[2] These words end a page. If there were any other conclusion to the letter, it has not been preserved, and consequently there is no signature. The letter is, however, in the handwriting of Humphrey Cotes, and it is dated from his residence at Byfleet in Surrey.

[a] *Almon's Memoirs of Wilkes*, vol. ii. p. 222.

[b] This alludes to the dismission of Mr. Stuart Mackenzie, Lord Bute's brother, from his post of Privy Seal of Scotland in May 1765, notwithstanding the royal promise that he should hold it for life.

[c] *Almon's Memoirs of Wilkes*, vol. ii. p. 210.

EARL TEMPLE TO (MR. MACKINTOSH).

[From a draught in the hand-writing of Lord Temple.]

Stowe, Sunday night, October 13, 1765.

MY DEAR SIR,—I have perused the Minutes[1] you sent me, which carry with them every mark of being, as far as they go, strictly genuine. Nothing can be more amiable than the whole tenor of the conversation on one part, or more friendly towards me on the other, than the various explanations given both of my feelings and conduct in almost all the parts which were touched. An obligation I can never forget.

The delivery of the Paper,[2] as the result of what had passed here, is very delicate, and you know I chose to say as little as possible ; it contains, however, the result of my real feelings, and is unexceptionably drawn up ; nay, so judiciously is it worded, that I would have wished to have had an opportunity of saying myself the same things to both if called upon, with the variation only of desiring to hear the King's ideas rather than presume to think of offering any of my own.

My sense of the difficulties which late transactions have superadded to what was but too difficult before, no man who has conversed with me can be a stranger to. Mr. Pitt is in my notions indispensable, and you know I think too much regard cannot be shewn him. The determinations of his mind since he went into Somersetshire I know not, but whenever he is called upon as before, I take it for granted he will give them with the same duty and zeal. I read the latter part of your let-

---

[1] Of the conversation between General Græme and Mr. Mackintosh, mentioned in the preceding letter, but which, as I have already stated, have not been preserved.

[2] See the following page.

ter and smile,—I think we even laughed out at Stowe,—
happy here and everywhere else in assuring you that I
am sincerely, &c., &c.

Many kind compliments to Mr. —— [1] I avoid writing
more than is absolutely necessary. Infinite secresy is
indispensable.

THE FOLLOWING *is a copy of the* PAPER *above referred
to by Lord Temple ; it is in the handwriting of Mr.
Mackintosh, and Lord Temple's draught of his reply
is written upon the same paper :—*

——Have it in charge to say : That .he takes the
greatest confidence in the channel through which this
communication comes : that he has the highest opinion
of the Queen's amiable qualities and prudent conduct ;
of which he has always expressed his sense in the strongest terms, and should esteem himself very fortunate to
possess her gracious regards.

That he desires always to be stated to the King as
full of the most dutiful and affectionate attachment,
and should have the greatest pleasure in contributing to
the honor, ease, and felicity of his Government.

That he has much indulged the thoughts of retirement, but could not satisfy himself, if he did not all in

---

[1] This word is most effectually erased. I am in some doubt whether
this letter was addressed to Mackintosh or Cotes. The question is,
however, unimportant. I have been induced to ascribe its address to
Mackintosh, from the circumstance of this erasure being sufficiently
long for a word with as few letters as *Cotes*, but not for Mackintosh.
The name has evidently been erased at a subsequent time, but why
Lord Temple should have done so, I am unable to explain.

Lord Temple's letter is dated on the evening of the same day as that
written by Cotes. From the secret nature of Cotes's communication,
it was most probably sent to Stowe by a private messenger, and the reply
to Mackintosh returned by bearer.

his power, on every occasion, to promote the King's comfort and satisfaction, and to keep at a distance from him any cause of uneasiness.

That for these ends he would cheerfully sacrifice his private enjoyments, and undertake the publick service, if he can do it upon such clear ground, as may allow him to hope for success in it.

But that no consideration on earth can induce him to engage in Administration, unless he is assured he enters upon it with the King's full cordiality and confidence, because he knows these are essential to the capacity of doing His Majesty, or the country, any effectual service.

That he wishes for no negotiations, and is averse to any interposition whatever ; as nothing can be so agreeable, or so satisfactory to him, as to receive the King's pleasure from himself.

But that if ever he is called upon, by his duty, in obedience to the King's commands, he will be happy in having a fair opportunity of explaining his ideas to His Majesty, upon what he judges most conducive to his service.

MR. HANS STANLEY TO MR. GRENVILLE.

Admiralty, October 14, 1765.

DEAR SIR,—Your letter of the 18th did not reach Paris 'till I was on the point of leaving that place, and consequently in hopes of seeing you here, as soon as my answer could have found you : I am exceedingly obliged to you for your sentiments upon the inconsiderable share which I have felt of the late storm, they are proofs of your good opinion, upon which I know how to set a due value ; as the loss of place gives me no uneasiness from views of interest, so, I cannot think it a dishonour to partake in the fate of so many other good servants of the Crown.

I was not a little surprised, since my arrival here, at a note I received from Lord Rockingham, to desire an early opportunity of seeing me. I desired to have his commands in writing, and declined as long as I civilly could an interview, which I informed his Lordship could end in nothing very essential; on our meeting he was pleased to offer me restitution of office. I need not say to you how inadmissible this proposal appeared to me on all accounts; I intend when I am presented on Wednesday, if His Majesty will condescend to honour me with an audience, to give him my reasons for declining it, and to declare my resolution of supporting those measures for which I have voted during your wise and honourable administration, and which I hear are to be attacked. I shall, at the same time, submit the other place which I hold to his disposal, in case this determination should be thought a reason for my removal. In so uncertain and critical a situation of politics, I will at all events preserve the consistency and rectitude of my character.

Though this letter contains nothing of consequence, I chuse to send it by a private hand, observing that all my correspondence is opened in a very awkward and bungling manner, which I intimate in case you should chuse to write anything which you would not have publick.

You will, Sir, always be sure of the sincere esteem and respectful attachment with which I have the honour to be, &c., &c., H. STANLEY.

MR. WHATELY TO MR. GRENVILLE.

Parliament Street, October 17, 1765.

DEAR SIR,—I enclose to you a copy of a letter which I have received from Boston, and which relates the behaviour of the populace with respect to the Stamp officer there: I am told that after that, they proceeded against Mr. Hutchinson, the Lieutenant-Governor, who, though a very popular man, yet having issued warrants for apprehending some of the Rioters, was become the object of their resentment: in Rhode Island the Collector of the Customs and the Distributors of the Stamps have been obliged to take refuge on board a ship.

There are some disturbances also in Virginia: and the Assembly of Deputies from the several provinces, in order to apply jointly for a Repeal of the Act, is soon to be held at New York. The instructions given by one of the Colonies to their Deputies on this occasion are come over, and, as I hear from one who has seen them, are directly treasonable. I suppose no representation from such a Convention of States will be received by Parliament, at least it is worth considering whether it should or not. The rage of the people seems not to be confined to the Stamp Act; the Officers of the Customs are also the object of it, and if that should be avowed, then the clear point is, whether the Parliament has a right to impose any taxes at all there.

The language of the Ministry is I am told resolute, and they have certainly written to Governor Bernard, directing him to enforce the execution of the law vigorously, but I believe they are undetermined about the measures to be taken, and the mode of proceeding if the tumult continues.

The rescue of the murderers of the Cherokees in

Virginia is another very serious affair; these people seem to profess that killing an Indian is not a civil offence, and will, I doubt, bring on an Indian War. The report you have heard of the dissolution of the Parliament is not prevalent here. The opinion is very current that the meeting will not be before Christmas, but I cannot still believe that business will be postponed 'till the beginning of February, which must be the case if that report should be true. Some change before the meeting is universally expected. The Lie of yesterday was, that Lord Bute, Lord Holland, and Charles Townshend were to form an Administration. Another story was, that there was a violent competition between the Duke of Grafton and Lord Albemarle for the vacant Garter; but I believe that both reports are equally without foundation.

I hear again that the design is to pay off all the unfunded debt, in preference to the Navy Annuities, and I believe you will find that to be the plan of operations. The fall you may observe of the Stocks is owing only to the Bulls and Bears taking perhaps some little advantage of the disturbances in America. I have the honour to be, &c., &c., THOMAS WHATELY.

The Duchess of Argyll is probably dead by this time, and Charles Townshend has been sent for on that account, and I believe is now in town [1].

MR. PITT TO EARL TEMPLE.

Burton Pynsent, October 29, 1765.

MY DEAR LORD,—This brings the best wishes of Burton Pynsent, that sickness may long since have bid

[1] Lady Dalkeith, the wife of Charles Townshend, was one of the daughters of the Duchess of Argyll.

adieu to Stowe, and that your Lordship may be, at this present writing, immersed in the amusing cares of building and gardening, with the whole train of the Arts.

As for your Somersetshire friends, our bill of health is somewhat fairer than it has been : Lady Chatham, thank God! is quite recovered, and the small flock tolerably well.

I propose carrying my legs, since they will not carry me, to Bath, towards the middle of November, if I hold out so long, and try once again to prop up a little a shattered tenement with the help of steel waters.

Besides expressing the joint wishes of this place for the health and happiness of Stowe, I have a business to trouble your Lordship with as a Trustee : it is this ; Lady Chatham and I being quite agreed also in another wish, which is to part with our dear Hayes, we desire the favour of your Lordship and the other Trustees to concur therein, and should an Act of Parliament be necessary for this purpose, that you will be so good to promote it.   I have not the Marriage Settlement here, and am doubtful as to the powers of the Trustees, but if Mr. Nuthall's memory be right, he thinks that the Trustees have power to consent to the sale of Hayes, the lands whereof were bought with a part of the £5000.

My intention is that the whole sum produced by the sale of house and lands should be disposable in the purchase of other lands, and follow the terms of the Settlement upon our children, &c.

Mr. Thomas Walpole [1] is ready to treat with me upon the purchase.   Thus you see, my dear Lord, how the passion of dirty acres grows upon a West Saxon of yes-

---

[1] At this time M.P. for Ashburton.   He was a younger son of Horatio Lord Walpole, and in business as a merchant in the city of London.

terday, and that I meditate laying rapacious hands on a considerable part of the County of Somerset; but this under Peter Taylor's good pleasure.

I advance apace in brick and mortar; but the monumental Column[1] must wait the return of Spring to lift its head upon a weather-beaten Promontory, where I trust fortunate chance may one day lead your Lordship's peregrinating steps.

Jemmy is gone to Bath, not without sensations of Gout, which I hope, however, may pass away.

Lady Chatham joins in affectionate compliments. I am ever dear Lord Temple's truly affectionate Brother,

WILLIAM PITT.

MR. AUGUSTUS HERVEY TO MR. GRENVILLE.

Sunning Hill, October 29, 1765.

DEAR SIR,—I should have acknowledged the receipt of your kind letter sooner, had I not intended going down to make you a visit as this day at Bath, but hope my sister will soon let me hear of Mrs. Grenville's recovery. As to news, I live out of the way of it, and only have it at second hand. Lord Sandwich staid with me four days with a friend of his from Cambridge.

Rigby dined with me Friday in his way to town, and was in great spirits; I see no reason to be otherwise. The Parliament you find is to meet the 17th, but I find it will be but for a few days, and the report of its dissolution is not credited. You see that has been touched upon in the Papers, from some very good hint.

I find *A. E.* is a *true friend* to the Cause, whoever he

---

[1] Which he was erecting to the memory of Sir William Pynsent.

is : there are many ; but I agree fully with you in thinking *another place* the properest place to answer any
attack made on Principals : but I am not sorry to find
your friends will not tamely bear your being so unjustly
attacked, and though I detest personal abuse, yet one must
not let it pass without expressing that contempt for, and
dislike of it, which it deserves. I make no doubt but
you have seen the *Political Apology*[1]; 't is to the purpose.
Lord Sandwich believes it to be wrote by one, that I
assured him it was not, though I think I guess at the
author ; but I was pleased to find that even Lord S.
was not always sure of styles, which he has often told
me he was ; in this he was mistaken.

I suppose you know how Lord Rockingham submitted
to send over and over again for Mr. Stanley, and at last
only to say, that he really knew nothing of his being out
of the Admiralty, that it was a mistake absolutely, and
such nonsense, and begging of him to come in again,
which I heard afterwards even another *personage* offered,
and when Stanley would have resigned the Government
of the Wight, he was desired to remain, in the same
language that Lord Granby and others were.

I have a letter last night tells me that most assuredly
there will be a change of *hands* not *measures*, before
the House meets, but that if 't is so, that the Duke of
Grafton and Conway come out : the last to be Secretary
of War, and Barrington Vice Treasurer of Ireland;
at the same time, you may assure yourself, that the *Conference* on the *Sea Coast* has brought up that *Lord*[2] to

---

[1] " *The Political Apology, or candid reasons for not taking part with
the present system, in a letter from a man who never had a place, to a
Right Honourable Gentleman who has lately accepted of an high
office.*"

[2] Probably Lord Holland.

assist in private, though he will not appear in publick; and the same correspondent assures me, the *Great Man* is returned short from the North, where he -was absolutely gone : a few, very few, weeks will unveil much. I hear the Tamworth affair is over, which I am glad of. Adieu, my dear, dear Sir. I hope you are convinced of the warmth of my attachment, and the *sincerity of my determination.*

MR. AUGUSTUS HERVEY TO MR. GRENVILLE.

London, Saturday afternoon, (November 2, 1765.)

DEAR SIR,—Though I wrote to you yesterday, yet as I have heard all the particulars of the event from the *first hand*, I will not omit letting you know them.

I saw Lord Albemarle at the Duke of York's this morning; he told me that the (Duke of Cumberland) was to have had a Council that evening about American Affairs ; that he himself had been with His Royal Highness 'till near four,—that the Duke dined well ; one of his servants after dinner went into the room where the Duke was, and the Duke bid him put the window up. Immediately His Royal Highness said he felt an odd catching in his hand ; the man perceiving the Duke changed colour, took hold of his hand, and as the Duke drew towards a settee, he asked him if he should send for Sir Cliff: Withrington : the Duke said, not yet, and expired immediately. He was bled, and bled freely, but was cold before Lord Albemarle could get to him, though he was only at his own house in Arlington Street when sent for.

He has been opened, and it seems died of an excrescence on the head that grew downwards like a tooth, and which pressed on the blood-vessels when they filled, and they being then particularly full, one burst, which was like a ball to him.

The King sent to Lord Albemarle by Lord Rockingham to-day, that he knew the Duke wished him to have the Garter, and that though His Majesty had not intended to give any away yet, he would give this mark of his regard for the Duke's memory, and give it to Lord Albemarle immediately.

Lord Albemarle says the Duke's debts he will engage to pay before Christmas, if the King pleases ; they will not exceed £24,000. There is no Will found, which makes strange confusion, and there are several papers, I mean various letters of correspondences of particular people, that will all fall into the King's hands I hear.

This stroke causes great uneasiness to these people, as I told you yesterday. The talk to-day is that Mr. Pitt is to be immediately negotiated with, and that the Duke of Grafton is to endeavour to put this on foot, and if he will only accept of a Councillor's place that Charles Townshend will undertake all, and how they boast that Lord Temple's great objection is removed.

Others say that Lord Albemarle is to try the Duke of Bedford again ; but I hear the great *Northern* Earl [1] (related to the *very Great one* [2]) says that the Grenville faction (as he calls them) must not at any rate come in.

'T is currently reported that ―― has been paid £500 within these three days for having brought home the news of landing the troops at Martinico : I think that is the highest piece of profligacy yet done : this is

---

[1] Northumberland.   [2] Lord Bute.

all I can hear to-day ; to-morrow I go out of town, as mourning will not be put on till Sunday next.

I forget to tell you the poor young Prince Frederick is at the very last stage, and can't live but very few days. Some said he was gone to-day, but I heard at York House to-day, that he was to be tapped as to-night.

MR. WHATELY TO MR. GRENVILLE.

Nonsuch Park, November 8, 1765.

DEAR SIR,—I was in London on Wednesday, but did not hear of any measures to be taken in consequence of the Duke's death ; indeed I believe that none are resolved on, and in the meanwhile the adherents to the Ministry treat it as an event of no consequence, for that he took no part in the conduct of affairs. I have, however, heard some of the Duke of Newcastle's friends express their opinion, and it seemed to be also their wish, that it might throw everything into Mr. Pitt's hands ; and others go no further than to surmise that it will make the opening more easy for Charles Townshend.

Lord Bute's particular friends are in the highest state of disgust. The advances supposed to be making towards them have ended in some unmeaning civilities to a few individuals which have given more offence than satisfaction ; and the indisposition from that quarter against the present set, is certainly very great ; but the reports of intended Motions against him keeps them in suspense.

The Tories, it is said, are endeavouring to form themselves into one body, to act together ; I doubt they will not completely accomplish that, but the majority of them is greater than was at first imagined.

I have now got all the particulars of the riot at Boston from the persons I have seen, and the letters I have received.

The first mob was certainly countenanced by the better sort of people, who most severely repented of the part they had taken, when they saw the outrages of the second, and were so sensible of the danger, that in a few minutes after the Council had ordered the Alarm drum to be beaten, five hundred of them appeared in arms. Fifty of these who formed a corps of Cadets meeting the mob, and preparing to fire, dispersed them instantly. No precautions were taken after the first riot to prevent another, and in the meanwhile, Dr. Mayhew, one of their pastors, preached on a text out of the Galatians, *I would they were cut off which trouble you : for, Brethren, ye are called unto Liberty,* and in his sermon inveighed with the utmost vehemence of expression and gesture against the Stamp Act, which, however ridiculous it may seem to us, so irritated his heated audience, that it was with difficulty they were restrained by the observance of the Sabbath, and the next day burst forth into all the violence you have heard of.

The principal mischief was done to Mr. Hollowell and Mr. Hutchinson, whose furniture and wainscot they cut into shivers with hatchets, and carried off £600 in cash from the one, and £200 in cash, with a £1000 Province Bill, from the other.

Since that time a guard has been kept in the Town, and at the Custom House : some of the rioters are taken, but, as I hear, they wish to proceed against some one, if they can find any such, of no consequence, instead of chusing the most considerable as the most guilty. I have some reason to believe, what you will hardly expect, that you will be told that the appointment of natives to be Distributors was improper, and the smuggling Cutters especially in America are to be decried. The fire which happened yesterday was in a very alarming place, just in the centre between the Bank, thè South Sea House, and the India House. The wind, however, soon blew it from the Bank, but it reached the Church which is parted from the South Sea House by a very narrow street, and burned it. The India House was not safe for three hours that they were without water, but then the progress that way was soon stopped [1]. I have the honour to be, &c., &c.,

THOMAS WHATELY.

MR. KNOX[2] TO MR GRENVILLE.

Great Marlborough Street, November 28, 1765.

SIR,—I was yesterday prevented mentioning to you, in the conversation you did me the honour of, a little Pamphlet which I writ last year immediately after the Stamp Act passed the House of Commons, in order to

[1] The fire began at a barber's house in Bishopsgate Street. It burnt the church of St. Martin Outwich, at the corner of Threadneedle Street, five houses in Cornhill, and twenty in Leadenhall Street. In the *Gentleman's Magazine* for November 1765 there is a plan of the site of this fire, shewing the houses which were injured or burnt.

[2] Mr. Knox was a zealous supporter of British authority against America, and the author of several pamphlets on that subject. His principal performance was a tract entitled *The Present State of the Nation*, which was replied to by Edmund Burke, in a pamphlet entitled *Observations*, &c., upon the supposition that the former was written by Mr. Grenville. Mr. Knox was afterwards Under Secretary of State to Lord Hillsborough. The pamphlet alluded to in this letter was probably entitled *A Letter to a Member of Parliament, wherein the power of the British Legislature and the case of the Colonists are briefly and impartially considered.*

transmit to America with the account of the passing of that Bill. I did not think it necessary at that time to disperse them here, and very few of them were seen in England, as I sent almost the whole edition to such of the Colonies as I had any correspondents in, and as those Colonies have not been intemperate since they had them, I have some reason to hope they were of use. I did not send you any of them, nor acknowledge myself to be the Author whilst you were Minister, lest what was thoroughly my opinion, should seem to you as a tribute to your power.

I have now confidence to acknowledge my attachment to you, and therefore request to know if a second edition of this Pamphlet would not be disagreeable to you.

I think I could also say something in another way, which might tend to recall to the minds of the dispassionate people here, the essential services this nation had done it, during your Administration, but I am apprehensive of saying what you would chuse to reserve for Parliament, and will not therefore adventure without your permission.

In whatever manner you shall please to direct me, I will endeavour to render you all the little service I am capable of, nor shall I fear to hazard the loss of what you give me by so doing, as I have the honour to be, &c., &c., WILL. KNOX.

MR. JENKINSON TO MR. GRENVILLE.

Sunday night, 10 o'clock, December 15, 1765.

I HAVE just heard in confidence what has passed at the meeting in my neighbourhood: it was very numerous, but many were at it who had no right to be there, and never used to be at such meetings before.

Among others there was Beckford, Sir William Baker, Black George Onslow, and Dempster : Ellis was also there.

I hear that the Speech as it stands at present was not finished till to day at two o'clock : it begins with saying that in the present tranquillity of Europe, His Majesty would not have assembled the Parliament 'till the usual time after the holidays, if certain occurrences in America, of which His Majesty expects further accounts, and which he then intends to lay before them, had not made it necessary : that he calls them therefore together that they may take the proper methods for filling up the vacancies in the House of Commons : this, with a short conclusion, recommending I suppose unanimity, &c., is the whole of the Speech : it takes no notice of the Duke of Cumberland's death, nor of the birth of the Prince.

The Address [1] says that they will apply themselves with the utmost dispatch to take into consideration the important occurrences in America, as soon as the accounts are laid before them, and that they will exert their utmost endeavours to support the honour of His Majesty, and the true interests of his people, through his wide extended dominions. I think I am pretty accurate in these words : there then follow congratulations on the birth of the Prince, and other paragraphs with compliments of condolence, and a most luxurious panegyric on the Duke of Cumberland. I am still so much out of order that I cannot write. You will know from whom this comes without my signing my name to it.

P.S. Lord George Sackville was also there, and so was the Speaker.

---

[1] To be moved in reply to the King's Speech.

MR. GRENVILLE'S DIARY

OF

MEMORABLE TRANSACTIONS.

(Continued from Vol. ii. page 535.)

1765. *Tuesday, January 1st.*—The King told Mr. Grenville that the Duke of Cumberland is ill, and that the Princess Amelia had sent to let the King know that he was coming to the Drawing-room, and that she begged His Majesty would send to prevent him, which the King accordingly did, but before his message could reach the Duke, H. R. H. had sent to desire His Majesty would excuse his not coming to Court, as he found himself unable to do it.

Mr. Grenville spoke upon business of various sorts to the King, but still found him cold and unwilling to give decisive answers upon anything.

Mr. Grenville had at different times mentioned Lord Granby's earnest recommendation of Dr. Ewer, for being Primate[1], to His Majesty, but he always found him averse to him from ill impressions that had been given of him; Lord Northumberland pushed eagerly for Dr. Robinson, Bishop of Kildare, to whom the Duke of Bedford was much disinclined, as were all the rest of the King's servants, namely, Lord Halifax, Lord Sandwich, Lord Chancellor, &c. Mr. Grenville wished to have gratified Lord Granby's recommendation, but Lord

[1] Of Ireland.

Northumberland was so earnest for Dr. Robinson that he carried his point.

Thursday, January 3rd.—Mr. Grenville, after speaking upon other business to the King, told His Majesty that he was extremely concerned to acquaint him how greatly Lord Granby was dissatisfied with the appointing Dr. Robinson to the Primacy; that Lord Granby's services and attachment to His Majesty were very eminent, and that he (Mr. Grenville) could see nothing with greater uneasiness than anything that could alienate a person of so much consequence from His Majesty's service. The King said Lord Granby was a good man, that he esteemed him much, and hoped a little time would calm his mind upon this. The King seemed uneasy at this conversation.

Friday, January 4th.—Mr. Grenville received a message from the Duke of York to appoint him to come to him the next morning.

Saturday, January 5th.—When Mr. Grenville went to the Duke of York, His Royal Highness told him he desired to know if the fifteen thousand per annum was the utmost allowance the King meant to make to him. Mr. Grenville said he understood it was. He then said, if that was the case he must lessen his expense by retrenching the unnecessary part of his family, viz., the grooms and equerries, whom he must recommend to His Majesty's goodness; but that he would do nothing in it without first speaking to the King.

He seemed much dissatisfied, and upon Mr. Grenville's stating how little the King was able to spare at this time, considering the great and necessary expenses at his accession, and His Majesty's unwillingness to burthen his people still more than they are already, the

Duke of York said Lord Bute ought to have taken care to have provided for the necessary expenses of the King's accession. H. R. H. desired Mr. Grenville to acquaint the King with the reason of his sending for him, which Mr. G. promised to do.

Sunday, January 6th.—Mr. Grenville stated the Duke of York's business to the King, who seemed displeased with his brother, said he could not increase his allowance, and in regard to his family he might do as he pleased, but that the Duke of Gloucester had told him that with 15,000*l.* per annum, he should find no difficulty, and why could not the Duke of York do the same?

Monday, January 7th.—Mr. Grenville went in the evening to the Duke of Bedford, who talked with great friendship and cordiality to him, and told him he knew Lord Bute was doing him (Mr. Grenville) ill offices, but that if he did, he (the Duke of Bedford) would pull the House about his ears, for that there was nothing in the world he would not consent to sooner than to see that man minister.

Wednesday, January 9th.—The King seemed cold and distant, but very civil. The Meeting at the Cockpit was large, but none of the Yorke family there.

Lord Litchfield and Lord Pomfret proposed amendments to the Address when it was read at Lord Halifax's.

Lord Litchfield was a good deal in liquor, and made Lord Halifax an excuse before he left the room, but nevertheless this step appeared singular from two immediate friends of Lord Bute's, and the more so because Lord Denbigh and Lord Le Despencer did not come to the meeting, though they appeared the next day at the House of Lords.

Thursday, January 10*th.* — The Address passed unanimous in both Houses.

Mr. Conway made a hot, angry attack upon Mr. Grenville, which he answered with spirit and with the approbation of all his friends.

Friday 11*th.*—Mr. Grenville went to the King, found him embarrassed and distant; His Majesty asked him what had passed in the House of Commons ; Mr. Grenville related everything ; the King heard him with coldness.

Lord Bute saw Lord Botetourt in the House of Lords, said he was sorry for what Lord Litchfield had done. Lord Botetourt told him he thought it was the effect of wine.

Saturday, January 12*th.*—Mr. Grenville saw the King, and found him rather less cold but still much embarrassed.

Lord Halifax told Mr. Grenville that Mr. Yorke's chariot had been seen two or three nights ago, at seven o'clock at night, waiting at the Queen's house.

It was, however, Mr. Hawkins's chariot which was mistaken for Mr. Yorke's.

Mr. Thomas Pitt told Mrs. Grenville that he knew from undoubted authority, that when Mr. Yorke had his audience of the King, he made a long deduction and explanation of his sentiments to His Majesty, and at the close the King had said to him, " I understand, Mr. Yorke, that you accede to me, and not to my ministers."

Sunday, January 13*th.*—Sir William Duncan came to let Mr. Grenville know that he had been with the King, who had a violent cold, had passed a restless night, and complained of stitches in his breast. His Majesty was blooded 14 ounces ; he told Sir William

I 2

he felt the cold seize him as he came out of the House of Lords.

Monday 14*th.*—The King is better, but saw none of his ministers.

Tuesday 15*th.*—Mr. Grenville went to the King, he found him perfectly cheerful and good-humoured, and full of conversation.

Friday, January 25*th.*—Mr. Grenville went to the King, who began to talk to him upon the debate [1] of the Thursday before, but with not the least word in commendation or approbation to Mr. Grenville.

Mr. Grenville made a pretty strong remonstrance to His Majesty upon the general state of things, and the independency avowed by the Gentlemen of the Army, and that of those lukewarm friends to Government who professed attachment to His Majesty, but at the same time thought themselves at liberty to oppose his measures and ministers. The King heard him patiently, though with a good deal of confusion and embarrassment.

Sunday, January 27*th.*—Mr. Grenville again renewed his remonstrance to the King, who received it in the same manner as the preceding day, assenting to the evil, but neither pointing out the remedy, nor enquiring into the cause of Mr. Grenville's alarm, nor saying any word of approbation of his services or past conduct. Upon other subjects he was easy and civil.

Before Mr. Grenville went into the Closet, he had a long conversation with Lord Mansfield, to whom he imparted his fear of the confusion into which the Government was likely to be thrown, while men's minds were kept at a gaze for want of a thorough support and countenance from the King to his principal servants,

---

[1] On the dismission of officers.

and whilst that sort of distinction was suffered to be made between His Majesty and his ministers.

Lord Mansfield seemed much struck with the deduction Mr. Grenville entered into, and a good deal alarmed at the disgust Mr. Grenville expressed; said he was sorry to find so much reason for it, and was surprised the King could forget how much he owed to Mr. Grenville. He went in to the King after Mr. Grenville came out, and staid with him till half-past five.

Tuesday, January 29th.—The House of Commons sat upon the question upon the legality of General Warrants till five o'clock the next morning.

Mr. Grenville received a note from the King, desiring him to write him a summary account of the debate; said it had been a very good day, that many people had done well, but Mr. Grenville best of all; that he had already heard so from several people.

Tuesday, February 12th.—Mr. Grenville received a letter from Mr. Henry Grenville from Constantinople, dated January 3rd, stating to him the uneasiness of his situation there, and his earnest wish to be recalled. Mrs. Grenville went to Lady Temple on Wednesday the 13th, to communicate this to her, and to acquaint her with the proposition Mr. Grenville intended to make to Mr. Henry of the office of one of the Commissioners of Customs then vacant, which, as it would oblige him to vacate his seat in Parliament, would exempt him from involving himself in the unhappy differences in his own family.

Lady Temple seemed pleased with the kindness of this scheme towards Mr. Henry, and said she would take an occasion to apprize Lord Temple of it. Mrs. Grenville told her she was at liberty to do it if she pleased, but that she brought no message from Mr. Grenville to Lord Temple.

Monday, February 18th.—Mr. Grenville opened to His Majesty his wishes in regard to Mr. Henry Grenville's return, and his appointment to the Customs, to which His Majesty graciously consented, enquired the reasons which had induced him to go to Turkey, and what part he had taken in the family differences.

Saturday, Feb. 23rd.—Mr. Grenville dined with Lord Townshend, who took him aside to tell him that his brother, Mr. Charles Townshend, had made a very explicit declaration to him of his firm resolution to take a firm and cordial part with Mr. Grenville; that he had dined with the Duke of Newcastle and many others of the Opposition, from whom he had withdrawn himself, and endeavoured to dissuade them from bringing on the question upon General Conway's dismission, telling them nothing could give it weight or popularity, but the getting Mr. Pitt to come down that day, and that even then they would probably make but a poor figure; saying to his brother in the relating it, " that the wings of their popularity rested upon Mr. Pitt's shoulders." Lord Townshend further said that his brother wished to have a conversation with Mr. Grenville, in which he would explain himself in the fullest manner. Lord Townshend told Mr. Grenville he thought it would be right to have two people present at this meeting; that he himself might be one and Lord Hyde the other.

Mr. Grenville said he thought so too; that he should be glad to see Mr. Charles Townshend taking a part that became him in support of Government, but that he must again repeat what he had so often said, viz., that if he wished to attain any situation in the King's service through any channel but Mr. Grenville's, whilst he held the high rank he does in the King's service, Mr. Grenville would quit that moment.

Sunday, February 24th.—Mr. Grenville went to the King and made a strong remonstrance to His Majesty upon his having yielded to the solicitations of Lord Halifax and Lord Sandwich to permit Lord Rochford's chaplain to be appointed Secretary to the Embassy in Spain, which office, since Colonel Ligonier's return, Mr. Grenville wished to have suppressed, apprehending that Lord Hertford might require the same appointments for Mr. Hume at Paris.

The King looked confounded, and tried to excuse himself upon the pressing instances of his two Secretaries, who, he said, did not do fairly in urging these expenses without Mr. Grenville's participation.

Monday, Feb. 25th.—The King was blooded, and kept his bed with a feverish cold; Mr. Grenville was confined at the same time.

Tuesday 26th.—Mr. Grenville was able to go to the House of Commons upon the business concerning the purchase of the Isle of Man, in which he met with universal approbation.

Lord Granby earnestly pressed him to the interview with Mr. Charles Townshend, telling him that Lord Townshend and himself would answer for the sincerity of Mr. Charles Townshend's professions, and that he (Lord Granby) desired to be present. The meeting was agreed to be at Lord Townshend's on the Sunday following. The King all this time continues ill, and sees none of his ministers.

Sunday, March 3rd.—The King had a good night,

but waked in the morning with a return of fever and pain upon his breast; he was blooded in the foot.

Mr. Grenville went according to his appointment to Lord Townshend's, where he met Mr. Charles Townshend. Lord Granby did not come.

Mr. Charles Townshend made the fullest declaration imaginable of his intentions to unite cordially with Mr. Grenville, assuring him that he was under no engagements whatsoever with the Opposition, and that he had told them that he was tired of that plan, that he meant to act with the Government, and would on no other footing continue in Parliament. He gave the most cordial assurances to Mr. Grenville of his firmness, and readiness to assist him in everything in his power; that he desired no situation of any kind, and did not wish to have any arrangement made for him, but that in regard to the question relating to General Conway he must reserve to himself the choice of acting as he should think best; that he hoped and believed the Opposition would not bring on the question, but that if they did, he reserved to himself the entire liberty of doing as he pleased. He assured Mr. Grenville he was in no communication with Lord Bute, whom he had not seen these four months. Mr. Grenville asked him whether or no this interview was to be talked of, but he said he thought it was better not, to which Mr. Grenville agreed.

Tuesday, March 5th.—Mr. Grenville went to the Queen's house to inquire after the King, and sent up a letter to His Majesty relating to the Duke and Duchess of Athol's pretensions, to which the King returned an answer in his own hand, desiring Mr. Grenville to transmit to him by letter any necessary business, and to send any warrants which required his signature.

The King sees nobody whatever, not even his brothers. Lord Bute saw him on Monday for a quarter of an hour, for the first time, though he (Lord Bute) had desired and pressed to see him before.

Wednesday, March 6th.—The King was not so well as he had been; his pulse rose in the morning, but sunk again at night, and he was much better and quite cheerful in the evening.

Saturday, March 9th.—Mr. Grenville went to the Queen's house to inquire after the King; His Majesty sent him out word, that he would see him if he wished it. Mr. Grenville sent in an answer, that he had nothing to trouble him with which required immediate haste. The King then ordered him to come the next day at two o'clock.

Sunday, March 10th.—Mr. Grenville went to the King according to his orders; he found him very cheerful, and his complexion clear, but a good deal thinner than before his illness. His Majesty talked very easily with him, told him he had seen nobody, and should still keep quiet for some time, and that he would send to him again soon. Mr. Grenville asked him for the vacant Prebendary of (Canterbury) for Dr. Dampier, which His Majesty granted.

Saturday, March 16th.—Mr. Charles Townshend came by appointment to Mr. Grenville: nothing remarkable passed.

Sunday, March 17th.—The King sent a note [1] to Mr. Grenville (differently worded from what they usually

[1] Of which the following is a copy:—

"Sunday, 10 P.M.

"Mr. Grenville,—I would have you attend me to-morrow at two."

were) to appoint him at two o'clock the next day. Mr. Grenville went to the Drawing Room, where the Queen told him she was afraid he would not agree with her in wishing that the King would not see his servants so often, nor talk so much upon business[1].

Mr. Grenville told Her Majesty, that for his part he never wished to break in upon His Majesty : she again repeated that she thought he had better not speak much upon business. Mr. Grenville said again, that he had never pressed upon His Majesty, but had waited his commands.

Monday, March 18th. — Mr. Grenville found the King's countenance and manner a good deal estranged, but he was civil, and talked upon several different subjects, and upon Mr. Grenville's proposing the Government of Cork for Sir George Pigott's brother, which Lord Northumberland wanted for Colonel Cooke at the desire of Mr. Ponsonby, but Mr. Grenville had spoken the first in favour of Mr. Pigott, His Majesty was averse, and said he had been much pressed upon that subject by Lord Northumberland for another person. Mr. Grenville made answer that it was too hard to prefer Lord Northumberland's request, who was upon the point of leaving Ireland, and added that His Majesty would lose his English Parliament to please the Parliament of Ireland ; upon which His Majesty answered, he would think upon it.

The Queen asked Lady Egremont if Mr. Grenville was not angry with her for what she had said to him in the Drawing Room the day before. Lady Egremont told her she knew nothing of it, but supposed Mr.

---

[1] It is probable that the Queen had accurately observed the state of the King's mind during his illness.

Grenville could not be angry with Her Majesty. Upon which she said, Yes he is, and repeated the conversation, adding, that she still wished the King would follow her advice.

Friday, March 22nd.—Mr. Grenville went to the Queen's house to carry a written note for His Majesty, in case he did not see him. The page told him the King was not so well as he had been, and that the physicians had seen him in the morning, and desired him to keep quiet. Mr. Grenville sent up the note, and received the answer in writing.

The King was cupped the night before. The Duke of Bedford was with him the Thursday morning by appointment for a considerable time, and found him well and cheerful. The Duke of Bedford told Mr. Grenville that the King had mentioned him to him with great approbation.

Monday, March 25th.—The King sent Mr. Grenville a note [1] to appoint him at two o'clock : he found His Majesty well to all appearance—he had been out to take the air ; he kept Mr. Grenville a long time, talked a great deal with good humour, and coughed but once during the whole conversation.

Mr. Grenville renewed his application for the Government of Cork for Mr. Pigott: the King said he would, if Mr. Grenville wished it, give Mr. Pigott one of the English Governments then vacant, but that Lord Northumberland expressed so much uneasiness about Cork, that he did not care to disappoint him.

Mr. Grenville opened to His Majesty the idea of ap-

---

[1] Of which the following is a copy :—

"10 min. past 10 A.M.

"Mr. Grenville,—I shall be ready to see you a little before two this day."

pointing Lord Weymouth to succeed Lord Northumberland in Ireland. The King paused and made some objections, though in the main he commended Lord Weymouth.

Mr. Grenville told His Majesty he would find himself much confined in his choice, especially upon the present idea of the constant residence of the Lord Lieutenant.

The King's confinement makes a great deal of talk, as few people believe him to be as ill as is given out by Lord Bute's friends.

Mr. Grenville recommended Mr. Duff, Lord Fife's brother, to Mr. Mackenzie, to hold the office of Registrar to the Order of the Thistle. Mr. Mackenzie told him he had many applications for that office, but that he would lay Mr. Duff's pretensions before the King. Mr. Grenville answered, that he, Mr. Grenville, could do that; but what he desired of him (Mr. Mackenzie) was, to back those pretensions, and really to prefer Mr. Duff at Mr. Grenville's desire, saying, at the same time, that Mr. Mackenzie had made several applications to him for offices in the Revenue for his friends, with which he had complied; and if Mr. Mackenzie meant to co-operate with him, he must have regard to those he wished well to.

Friday, March 29th.—The King sent a page to order Mr. Grenville to come to him : he asked him how business went on in the House of Commons. Mr. Grenville said, very well. The King asked few questions upon that subject, nor made no particular complaint to Mr. Grenville. His Majesty gave him leave to go out of town for the holidays, but took no notice that he himself intended to go to Richmond.

Saturday, March 30th.—Lord Sandwich saw the

King, and in relating what had passed in the House of Lords upon the Poor's Bill, showed a list of those who were against the Bill, among which was Lord Bute's name. The King asked why he put Lord Bute's name, for he believed he did not attend it. Lord Sandwich said it was true, but that he heard he was in inclination against it, and that Lord Denbigh had told him so.

Monday, April 1st.—The King went to Richmond.

Wednesday, 3rd.—Mr. Grenville received notice from Lord Sandwich that the King was to have a Levée. Mr. Grenville went to it : the King spoke civilly to him at the Levée, took notice of his having a very bad cold, and said he had told Dr. Duncan that Mr. Grenville would be ill, if he did not take more care of himself.

Mr. Grenville went afterwards to the King in his Closet ; His Majesty told him that, before he spoke upon any other subject, he desired to apprize him of one of a very serious nature—namely, a Bill of Regency, which he had thought upon during his illness, but would not enter upon 'till he was quite well, and able to appear. He said he wished his servants to have a meeting upon it, such of them as by their offices would be of the Council of the Regency, and had therefore settled a meeting for the next day, with the Chancellor and the Duke of Bedford, to whom His Majesty said he had that day named it, and that he, the King, had appointed it for the next day at the Chancellor's, that it might not keep Mr. Grenville in town.

(N.B. The King wrote to Lord Chancellor with his own hand, to order him to come to him, and sent to the Duke of Bedford, but Mr. Grenville and Lord Halifax received no notice of His Majesty's being in town but from Lord Sandwich.)

The King talked a good deal upon the subject; said that he approved of the plan of the Bill made in the late King's time, except that he wished to have the power of naming the Regent left to himself, by instruments in writing, without specifying the particular person in the Act of Parliament, which he thought would be a means to prevent any faction or uneasiness in his family upon this subject. Mr. Grenville expressed his general approbation of the King's goodness in thinking of a Regency, but avoided saying anything with regard to the change by the proposal of reserving the nomination to the King, which then appeared to him liable to great objections, some of which he mentioned to the Duke of Bedford and Lord Sandwich as soon as he left the Closet. The King was averse to having the Princes of the blood in the Council of Regency, and said he thought it would create jealousy and uneasiness.

Mr. Grenville, after this conversation was ended, among other things named Mr. Duff to the King for the Secretary to the Order of the Thistle. His Majesty made no other answer than desiring to see the names of all the persons soliciting that office, which in all probability is to take Mr. Mackenzie's recommendation, and seemingly to make it his own choice.

Thursday, April 4th.—The King came to the Drawing Room, and looked very well. Mr. Grenville saw him afterwards in his Closet. His Majesty told him he had sent Sir William Duncan to him, and had told Sir William that if Mr. Grenville did not take care of himself he would be ill, and have as long a confinement as his own had been.

When Mr. Grenville renewed his application in favour of Mr. Duff, the King told him he had determined to give that office to Sir Henry Erskine, who he understood had applied for it, and to whom he long had promised a Government. Mr. Grenville argued and pressed strongly for Mr. Duff, but in vain.

The House of Commons sat till eleven o'clock at night, for which reason the meeting at Lord Chancellor's was put off till next morning between nine and ten, at Lord Halifax's.

Friday, April 5th.—Lord Sandwich reported the deliberations of the Council to the King, and came to acquaint Mr. Grenville that His Majesty was perfectly pleased with what had passed there, and entirely approved the Minute [1].

Saturday, April 6th.—Mr. Grenville went to Wotton.

Wednesday, 17th.—Mr. Grenville came to town.

Thursday, April 18th.—Mr. Grenville saw the King; his behaviour to him was nothing remarkable.

Mr. Grenville told His Majesty that he had been thinking of the important business of the Regency Bill, and showed His Majesty the Speech, which he entirely approved. The King had now altered his opinion with regard to the Princes of the blood, and said he would have them all of the Council, reserving still to himself the power of naming four more according to the former Act.

Mr. Grenville threw out at a distance his apprehensions that the reserving the power of naming the person of the Regent might be attended with difficulty; the King said nothing to that, but told him that he had seen the Duke of Cumberland, and had named his design of having such a Bill brought in, but without opening his particular idea to him, and that the Duke had said it

---

[1] See *ante*, page 15.

would be best, if possible, to form a general Bill to establish a Regency for all future times, which opinion the King did not adopt. His Majesty told Mr. Grenville that he thought the Duke was then very ill, and that he heard he was worse since.

Friday, April 19*th.*—The King was very temperate about the Regency Bill, and not desirous of having the power of naming four Councillors besides the Princes of the blood. Lord Chancellor had objected to it; His Majesty, therefore, desired it might be settled for his only having five additional Councillors.

Mr. Grenville again threw in his doubts upon the security of the whole, by not immediately naming the Regent, and said it would be better and safer to follow the former plan, and recommend the person in the Speech from the Throne, but His Majesty did not alter his opinion in that particular.

Sunday, April 21*st.*—The King seemed more easy in his behaviour than he had been of late.

Monday, April 22*nd.*—A Council was appointed at St. James's, at which the King was to propose the Regency Bill.

Mr. Grenville went into the Closet before the Council, and upon His Majesty asking who was already come, Mr. Grenville named the Archbishop, with whom he said he had been talking about the Bill. His Majesty asked what the Archbishop said to it. Mr. Grenville told him that he had been asking what answer was to be given to such people as might ask why this Bill was altered from the former, in the Article of not immediately appointing the Regent, to which Mr. Grenville said he had told the Archbishop that it was with a view to prevent faction, considering the youth of all the branches of the Royal family, and then asked His Majesty if that was not the answer to be given.

The King, in some agitation, said, " Mr. Grenville, you have more‘ than once thrown out an idea of this being attended with some difficulty, particularly you did so on Friday last : is that your opinion, and from whence does it arise ?"

Mr. Grenville told His Majesty that he thought it his duty to acquaint him that he believed it would be much more secure to name the Regent, as men's minds would by degrees accustom themselves to what they were hereafter to expect, and be more ready to confirm it, from the habit of seeing it, and consequently the fear of faction would be less ; but at the same time it was a subject of a very delicate nature, in which so much of His Majesty's own particular feelings and domestic happiness was concerned, that he did not mean to press his own opinion upon him, nor to make an act of goodness from His Majesty to his people (for which he and all his subjects must be filled with gratitude) grievous to him in the execution.

The King paused, seemed agitated and embarrassed, asked if it would meet with difficulty in the House of Commons; to which Mr. Grenville answered him that he believed it would be opposed, but that was not the difficulty which operated upon his mind—it was from a cause much more remote. The King said, "What shall I do ? shall I propose the doubt to the Council ?" Mr. Grenville said, that must be as His Majesty pleased, that he could not say that the objections he himself had made, were those of any of the King's other servants. The King asked him if he thought the Council would give their opinion if he asked it ; Mr. Grenville said he could not tell ; that possibly such of them as had known of this measure for some time past might ; that he for his part was ready to do it in publick, in private, or in any place where it should be required, but that in a matter of such magnitude, those to whom it was entirely new might not care, on such short notice, to give a decisive answer.

His Majesty then said he would open the affair in general terms, without proposing the doubt.

When the two Secretaries of State went in, His Majesty mentioned to them the objection Mr. Grenville had made ; he did the same to the Chancellor, and to the Duke of Bedford, but with great temper, as they afterwards told Mr. Grenville.

Wednesday, April 24th.—Mr. Grenville saw the King before he went to the House of Lords, and found him easy and good-humoured. His Majesty asked Mr. Grenville if the Archbishop had said any thing more upon the Regency Bill ; Mr. Grenville said he had not seen him since.

His Majesty ordered him to send him an account of what should pass in the House of Commons.

Thursday, April 25th.—While Mr. Grenville was waiting to go into the Closet, the Dukes of York and Gloucester came to him in the King's outward room, and told him that now this great business of the Regency Bill was set on foot, the Duke of York (who spoke for both) said they thought that, as a proper corollary to it, some provision should be made for them, that they might not be left at the mercy of they did not know who, and in a situation which no one was ever in before.

Mr. Grenville told the Duke of York that His Royal

Highness must be sensible that in this business he could only receive the King's commands, and that he supposed His Royal Highness meant that he should lay this before the King. He said, " We mean to speak to the King about it."

(N.B. The two Princes had been in the Closet just before this conversation passed.)

When Mr. Grenville went into the Closet, he told His Majesty what had passed. The King said the end of the Sessions seemed not a proper time for it.

Friday, April 26th, 1765.—Lord Halifax, before the Levée this morning, was told by the King that he heard there would be a great deal of opposition to the Regency Bill, and that it would be very disagreeable if they should move to name the Princes, his brothers, and the Duke of Cumberland, to be of the Council, and for his Ministers to put a negative to them : that he thought it might therefore be better to name them. He said the same thing afterwards to Lord Sandwich, and still more strongly after that, to the Duke of Bedford, to whom he added that this thought came into his mind yesterday upon the conference which he had with his two brothers, the Dukes of York and Gloucester, and which was before he saw Mr. Grenville, who informed the King yesterday that both their Royal Highnesses had come up to him that day in the Anti-chamber, and that the Duke of York had said to him in both their names, that which has been already stated, and which Mr. Grenville understood to refer to a Parliamentary Settlement of the provision made for them.

The King took no notice to Mr. Grenville that he had seen both his brothers about two hours before, nor of what had passed, though that was the conversation which

His Majesty referred to when he spoke to the Duke of Bedford to-day, on the subject of adding the names of his brothers and of the Duke of Cumberland in the Regency Bill.

After speaking to the Duke of Bedford, the King sent in again for Lord Halifax, and ordered him to summon a meeting of those Lords who had been at the former meeting, for to-night, in order to consider of this subject, and of the means to carry it into execution.

Mr. Grenville being at the Treasury, did not go to St. James's till after two o'clock, when the King was set out from thence upon his return to Richmond, and therefore did not see him to-day.

Lord Halifax went to the House of Lords to speak to the Lord Chancellor upon this business, to whom the King bid him say that His Majesty would have writ to him to have seen him upon it, but that the thought came so suddenly into his head that he had not time to do it.

When Lord Halifax informed Lord Chancellor of this, he found him much dissatisfied with it, and His Lordship refused upon any account to attend at any meeting upon it, saying that he had already given his opinion upon it, but that he should not oppose what the King should think fit to do with respect to his Royal family.

Lord Halifax afterwards spoke to Lord Mansfield, who said that this question about the King's appointing his brothers and his uncle to be of the Council of Regency, could not be proper for a Cabinet meeting, which he therefore advised against, but consented to meet with Lord Halifax, Lord Sandwich, the Duke of Bedford, and Mr. Grenville, this evening.

From him, Lord Halifax and Lord Sandwich went to the House of Commons, and sent to Mr. Grenville, to whom they told what had passed, to his great surprise.

He told them that he agreed in thinking that this was no business for a meeting, nor could any opinion about it be given at one.

Lord Halifax then wrote to the King, and informed him that Lord Chancellor had declined coming to any meeting about it, but would not oppose what the King should think fit to do with respect to his Royal family; that he (Lord Halifax) would try to see such of His Majesty's principal servants as he should be able, and consult with them what would be proper to be done.

At eight o'clock in the evening, Mr. Grenville went to Lord Halifax's, where he found his Lordship and the Duke of Bedford, and immediately after came in Lord Sandwich and Lord Mansfield, but just before the two last came in, the messenger, whom Lord Halifax had sent to the King at Richmond, returned with an answer from the King to Lord Halifax's note, which answer was in the following words :

"Lord Halifax, I approve of your attention in transmitting to me the Chancellor's declining attending the meeting to-night, though not disinclined to a provision being made for my Royal family, if I think that the circumstances of the times makes (make) it expedient. I desire Lord Halifax will send me to-morrow a copy of the Minute, that I intend to keep, and that he will accompany (it) with a line, if anything particular has been said *by any Person.*"   " 20 min. after 6."

This letter of the King's was shewn to the four who were present, and they all agreed that no opinion could be given at any meeting concerning the fitness of appointing the Princes of the Royal family to be of the Council, but seemed to think that the properest manner of doing it, if it was to be done, would be by message from the King, specifying it, as was done in the former instance in the late King's reign.

It was insisted upon, that Lord Halifax should not shew any Minute in writing of this meeting, and that what was said was only for his information with respect to the language which he should hold when he should see the King, which he proposed to do to-morrow by going to Richmond, and it seemed resolved between them that Lord Sandwich would go thither with him.

Lord Mansfield, after the meeting, set Mr. Grenville at home, and observed to him how very unfortunate this air of fluctuation and of difference in Councils would be; to which Mr. Grenville agreed, and represented the particular difficulties it would lay him under in the House of Commons.   Friday, April 26, past 12 at night.

In consequence of what passed this day (*Friday, 26th*) Lord Halifax and Lord Sandwich wrote a note to the King, desiring leave to wait upon His Majesty at Richmond at three o'clock, after his return from riding on Saturday, or any other hour His Majesty would please to appoint, to give him an account of the result of what had passed that night. This was sent early on Saturday, the 27th. The messenger got to Richmond by seven o'clock: when he came, he found that Lord Bute was already with the King. They received an answer from the King to this effect:

"Lord Halifax, I chuse to have my time when I am at Richmond to myself, and not to have it broke in upon, and as it will make no difference in the going on with the Regency Bill, I will not fail being in town to-morrow at ten o'clock to receive Lord Sandwich and you. I am a little surprised that Lord Halifax did not send me a line with a sketch of what had passed, though it might want more explanation, and I do insist on the doing it to satisfy my curiosity before I hear the rest to-morrow." (Dated 8 o'clock, A.M.)

To which Lord Halifax and Lord Sandwich returned an answer to the following effect, that Lord Mansfield and some other of the Lords had been of opinion that this was no subject for a meeting, but that Lord Halifax had prevailed with Lord Mansfield, the Duke of Bedford, and Mr. Grenville, to meet Lord Sandwich and himself at his house, where they were still of opinion that the determination of this matter must be left entirely to His Majesty, and that the best means of carrying his orders into execution would be by a message to the House, after the reading of the Bill on Monday. That Lord Halifax and Lord Sandwich imagined a verbal account of this would have been more satisfactory to His Majesty, which was the reason of their asking leave to wait upon him at Richmond, and that they would punctually obey his commands in attending him the next day (Sunday) at St. James's at ten o'clock. Lord Halifax and Lord Sandwich came early in the morning (Saturday) to relate all this to Mr. Grenville, and to settle with him what they should say to the King the next day, which they all agreed should be the same as before, viz., that it was no subject for Council, and must be left to His Majesty.

Mr. Grenville soon after saw Lord Granby, to whom

he told the whole affair, in which Lord Granby said Mr. Grenville had acted wisely and honestly, and that it was a snare laid for them.

In the evening (Saturday) Mr. Grenville went to Lord Chancellor ; he found him very warm and eager against this strange transaction, but cordial and friendly to Mr. Grenville, to whom he shewed a letter he had received the Thursday before from the King, in which His Majesty said, that as he had not seen him at St. James's that day, he wrote to acquaint him that upon mature deliberation he thought it expedient to name the Dukes of York, Gloucester, and Cumberland, of the Council of the Regency, and his two other brothers when they came of age, and that he desired His Lordship would appoint a meeting of those of his servants who had already met upon this subject, to consult together upon it ; to which the Chancellor returned in writing, that it was his opinion that this could be no matter of Council ; that what regarded so nearly the Princes of His Majesty's Royal blood, must be decided by himself ; that as to his own part, having already given his opinion in Council, he must desire to be excused giving any other upon that subject ; that he did not mean to oppose what His Majesty had suggested with regard to the Princes, but that he thought it his duty to lay before His Majesty, that if besides the Princes of the blood His Majesty meant to name five Councillors to the Regency, it would be nine out of eighteen, which would entirely alter the whole idea upon which it was formed, and totally disannul the power meant to be lodged in the great Officers of State [1]. The King in his letter ordered

---

[1] The *ex officio* Members of the Council of Regency were as follows, namely :—The Archbishop of Canterbury, the Lord Chancellor,

the Chancellor to come to him on Sunday. The Chancellor told Mr. Grenville he had shewn this letter to nobody but himself: he was highly discontented, and said he looked upon this affair as the overthrow of the present Ministry.

Sunday April 28th.—Lord Halifax and Lord Sandwich came between ten and eleven o'clock to Mr. Grenville, to let him know they had seen the King, who received them with good humour, and said he found that they were all of opinion that the manner of proposing the alteration he had made was by a message. They said that in talking it over it had appeared so to his servants with whom they had prevailed to talk upon it, that they heard the Bill would meet with great opposition.

The King never departed from his purpose, repeated often that he would have it laid before his Parliament, said he had had a very civil letter upon it from the Chancellor, and then dismissed them.

The King agreed with them that it was no subject to be discussed at a meeting, seemed impatient to dismiss them, and kept them a less time than they ever staid upon any business before.

The Duke of York had an interview, either Saturday or Sunday, with the Duke of Cumberland, and came to the King on Sunday immediately after the Drawing Room ; but Mr. Grenville does not know that the King told anybody what passed between them.

After the Drawing Room the Chancellor went into

the Lord President, the Lord Privy Seal, the First Lord of the Treasury, the two Secretaries of State, the First Lord of the Admiralty, and the Lord Chief Justice of the King's Bench. In case of an equality of voices in the Council, the Regent would be entitled to decide.

the Closet according to the King's order, and in the conversation settled with His Majesty that he should content himself with naming the five Princes of his blood, as Councillors to the Regent, giving up the nomination of the four others by instruments under his hand, and only filling up the places of any of the five upon the death of any of them.

The King then sent for Lord Halifax to communicate this to him, and when he came out Mr. Grenville went into the Closet. The King began by telling him the alteration he had made in concert with the Chancellor, and asking Mr. Grenville if he did not think that this would be agreeable to everybody ; to which Mr. Grenville answered with a firm and steady countenance, that he really had been honoured with so little of His Majesty's confidence and communication in this important business, that he was at a loss to form any opinion upon it, or to know what it was that had drawn upon him this degree of His Majesty's displeasure.

The King started, seemed surprised, and asked Mr. Grenville what was the matter, and said that he had ordered Lord Halifax to tell him of the alteration, as he himself had not seen him on Friday. Mr. Grenville told him it was true, that he did not come that day to Court till after His Majesty was gone, having been kept at the Treasury till half an hour after two o'clock ; that Lord Halifax had sent for him out of the House of Commons, to tell him that the King had ordered him to call a Council upon the change he proposed relating to the Princes of the blood; that His Majesty must remember that when he first opened this matter to him it was on a Wednesday (Lord Sandwich having sent him word that His Majesty was that day to have a Levée) that he received his orders, sat all that day and the next 'till eleven at night, in the House of Commons ; met the Council upon it on Good Friday (April 5), at Lord Halifax's; went the next day into the country, where, whatever might be his own opinion upon it, in duty to His Majesty, he immediately set about drawing the Speech, which at his return to town he shewed to His Majesty, who approved it ; that he thought it his duty to offer his objections against it to His Majesty's consideration, which he had done; that on Thursday the 25th he had the honour to see His Majesty after the Dukes of York and Gloucester had been with him, but that he was not pleased at that time to mention any alteration to him; that His Majesty was certainly at liberty to name his business first to such of his servants as he thought proper, but that he must observe to His Majesty, that whatever difficulty there was in this affair, it would fall heavier upon him who was to carry it through the House of Commons, than upon any one of his other servants whatever, and that if it should be represented to him, that Mr. Grenville had done it coldly or with slackness, he must take the liberty to observe how much injustice would be done to him, since, notwithstanding his own opinion, he had forwarded it in the best manner he could, not only in the opening of it in the House of Commons, but likewise in the earnest manner in which he had pressed it upon his own friends, many of whom had great difficulties about it, and if His Majesty doubted of this, he referred him for the truth of it to the Duke of Bedford, who by various accidents had come to the knowledge of some of the particular instances; though he thought himself bound in honour as a gentleman not to name or particularize the individuals ; that he had in the most dutiful, and, as far as he was able, in the most effectual manner, endeavoured to serve His Majesty, and that if he had had the misfortune to displease him, he begged to know in what it was; that he felt the marks of it sensibly and grievously, both as it disabled and discouraged him in the execution of His Majesty's commands; that he entreated His Majesty for his own welfare to suffer nobody to persuade him to weaken those to whom he had entrusted his Government, since the ill effects of it must inevitably fall upon His Majesty; that as to his Ministers, it was of little consequence whether this or that person filled the station, but His Majesty must still be King, and he hoped a glorious and happy King; that as long as he (Mr. Grenville) had the honour to continue in his service, it should be with duty, zeal, and affection; but he could not wish the continuance of it from the moment he withdrew his confidence and approbation from him. He then said it was late, he would not detain His Majesty any longer, and presented a paper to him which was a matter of form only. The King, during this conversation, seemed exceedingly agitated and disturbed, he changed countenance, and flushed so much that the water stood in his eyes from the excessive heat of his face; he two or three times interrupted Mr. Grenville, to say that he had bid Lord Halifax tell him of the alteration in the Regency Bill; that he agreed in opinion with his servants that what regarded the putting in the Princes of the blood was not a proper subject to be discussed by a Council, that he did not think of it 'till some time after he had seen the Duke of York, and therefore had not named it to Mr. Grenville; besides that, he thought he would not like to interfere in a matter between him and his family.

The King endeavoured to seem to understand Mr. Grenville's complaint, as regarding the present instance alone : Mr. Grenville extended it to the general withdrawing of his confidence.

The King neither denied nor admitted the charge, said no words of anger, nor none of excuse or softening, but seemed surprised, and rather put on a smile of good humour when Mr. Grenville made his bow [1].

Tuesday April 30th.—Mr. Cadogan came to acquaint Mr. Grenville that the Duke of York desired to see him at any time that was convenient to him, to talk over the making a settlement upon him and the Duke of Gloucester, agreeable to what had passed between His Majesty (who had received H. R. H. very graciously) and H. R. H. upon that subject.

Mr. Grenville named the next day between eleven and twelve o' clock.

Wednesday May 1st.—Mr. Grenville went to York House, where he found the Dukes of York and Gloucester, who made three propositions to him, desiring in the first place that their separate revenues might be augmented from £15,000 to £20,000 per annum ;

---

[1] It may be readily imagined, after the scene which has just been described, that the King's *smile of good humour*, when the happy moment arrived for Mr. Grenville's *making his bow*, was extremely natural and unaffected. The grievous *charge* made against the King on this occasion amounted only to this,—that on Friday the 26th inst., when Mr. Grenville had delayed his attendance upon the King until His Majesty had left St. James's for Richmond, Lord Halifax had been commissioned by the King to convey a message of formal information with respect to the Regency Bill, which would otherwise have been communicated by the King himself ; and for this offence, it appears that the King had given an explanation almost amounting to an apology. It is probable that His Majesty had not made up his mind upon the matter in question until the evening of the previous day, when he had committed an additional offence by writing to the Lord Chancellor on the same subject.

secondly, that it should be perpetual, instead of during pleasure ; and, thirdly, that it should be laid before Parliament, where it should be proposed to be taken off the Civil List, and put upon the Revenue ; that is to say, £5000 per annum to each, upon Ireland, and £15,000 upon Great Britain.

The Duke of York said he had talked upon this with many people, who told him it might easily be done. Mr. Grenville said it was easy for those who had nothing to do with raising the money, to be generous for others, but that His Royal Highness must know that the distress of the publick was very great ; that all he could say to it was that he would lay it before the King, and give every facility in his power to whatever His Majesty thought expedient. They approved of his speaking to the King about it, but desired it might not be to-day. The conversation was very long. The two Royal Dukes desired Mr. Grenville to apprize all the King's principal servants of it, which he immediately did to the Duke of Bedford, Lord Sandwich, and Lord Halifax, who were all of opinion that this was not the proper time for such a measure, the Sessions of Parliament being so near an end. It was, therefore, better to wait at least 'till another session, when, if in the meantime any accident happened to the Duke of Cumberland, it might meet with less difficulty. From York House Mr. Grenville went to the King, who received him with a countenance of good humour, began to talk of indifferent things, and from thence to the business of the preceding day in the House of Lords. When His Majesty had done, Mr. Grenville told His Majesty that he hoped he had given some consideration to what he had had the honour to say to him on Sunday, which arose from the concern and uneasiness he felt at the apprehension of having displeased him; that if that was the case, he only desired to know in what it had been. The King said, "Why do you think so, Mr. Grenville? you know I told you for what reasons you did not hear of this business sooner." Mr. Grenville said the moment His Majesty told him he meant no slight to him in it, it was enough for him to believe he did not, but that he must repeat to him that His Majesty's general conduct to him of late had been such as not only induced him to believe that he had withdrawn his confidence, his countenance, nay even his approbation from him, but that it was likewise visible to all the world. The King said he wondered he should listen to such idle tales and reports, asked if he ever had complained of him, and said if he had had any reason he would have told him so. Mr. Grenville said he was far from listening to idle tales and reports, but to prove to His Majesty that he had not lightly taken this idea, he desired His Majesty would be pleased to ask any one of his servants of the truth of this opinion; that when His Majesty ordered him to undertake his affairs, he had been pleased to promise him his utmost support and protection; that without it, he had told His Majesty he could not engage in the scene; that even with it, he scarce could answer for the success, but on that, and that only, he would risk it, which he had accordingly done, forming no party to himself nor endeavouring at any; that the success of His Majesty's affairs had exceeded his (Mr. Grenville's) most sanguine wishes, that he was therefore much at a loss to know in what he could have displeased him; that he had neither pressed him for grants, honours, nor pensions, that the secret service money was by a great deal less than under any other minister[1]; that hitherto no untoward accident had happened which had risqued his safety; but should such a misfortune befall him, what had he to rely upon if His Majesty's favour and protection was withdrawn?

[1] On the subject of *Secret Service money*, I found among Mr. Grenville's papers the following curious statement. It is in the handwriting of Whately, Secretary to the Treasury, and is endorsed by Mr. Astle, of the State Paper Office, and Keeper of the Records, "SECRET and SPECIAL SERVICE from 1760 to 1769":—

"*Monies paid out of the late King's Civil List Revenues.*"
In 1761, £30,000; in 1762, £116,702 12s. 5½d.; in 1763, £22,477 0s. 11d.; and in 1765, £3,425 12s. 0d.; amounting in the whole to £172,605 5s. 4½d[a].

Pensions, &c., payable at the Exchequer from 1752 to 1760	£192,312
Pensions, &c., payable by Paymaster from 1752 to 1760 .	339,610
Secret Service from 1752 to 1760	323,000
	£854,922

Pensions, &c., payable at Exchequer from 1761 to 1769 .	£224,400
Pensions, &c., payable by Paymaster from 1761 to 1769 .	373,745
Secret Service from 1761 to 1769	156,000
	£754,145

"SECRET and SPECIAL SERVICE from other Accounts."

Ending 25th Oct., 1761.

J. West	£47,735	
N. Magens	10,507	
		£58,242

Ending 25th Oct., 1762.

J. West	£30,000	
J. Richardson	1,046	
S. Martin	10,000	
J. Nichol	26,289	
G. Amyand	14,853	
		£82,168

Ending 25th Oct., 1763.

S. Martin	£41,000	
G. & R. Udny	10,000	
C. Jenkinson	5,000	
J. Nichols	5,000	
		£61,000

Ending 25th Oct., 1764.

J. Richardson	£1,840	
J. Nicholl	22,915	
G. & R. Udny	10,805	
W. Young	1,277	
		£36,837

[a] This sum was probably part of the late King's large accumulation of money, found by George the Third upon his accession to the throne.

The conversation on Mr. Grenville's part was much to this effect, and never produced any thing stronger from the King, than the general words of asking him, why he believed this and that, (and that) if he had reason to complain he would tell him so.

Ending 25th Oct., 1765.		
J. Nichols	£12,631	
Sir G. Amyand	8,318	
W. Mellish	8,425	
		£29,374

Ending 25th Oct., 1766.		
Sir G. Amyand	£12,128	
L. Dutens	533	
A. Cleveland	323	
C. Lowndes	29,216	
C. O'Hara	700	
C. S. Cadogan	293	
Walter Cope and Bignell	205	
Rogers, Sibell and Co.	2,386	
		£45,784

Ending 25th Oct., 1767.		
C. Lowndes	£14,000	
Rogers, Sibell and Co.	326	

Ending 25th Oct., 1767.—cont^d.		
Colonel Tunykins	£533	
C. S. Cadogan	293	
Executors of Sir G. Amyand	1,030	
A. Drummond and Co.	323	
Grey Cooper	8,213	
		£24,718

Ending 25th Oct., 1768.		
Grey Cooper	£28,000	
Drummond and Co.	2,255	
Amyand and Co.	5,022	
Earl of Morton	4,207	
Captain Cosby	500	
M. Morgan, Esq.	400	
		£40,384

Ending 25th Oct., 1769.		
Grey Cooper	£16,000	

This account of 1769 is only from 25th of October, 1768, to 25th of February, 1769.

The following characteristic letter may serve as an interesting illustration of the mode in which some part at least of the Secret Service Money was disposed of:—

"LORD SAY AND SELE TO MR. GRENVILLE.

"London, November 26, 1763.

"HONOURED SIR,—I am very much obliged to you for that freedom of converse you this morning indulged me in, which I prize more than the lucrative advantage I then received. To shew the sincerity of my words (pardon, sir, the perhaps over-niceness of my disposition), I re-

Mr. Grenville then passed on to his common business, and then withdrew.

He told much of what had passed to the Duke of Bedford, Lord Halifax, Lord Sandwich, and Lord Granby, who all approved, and said he had acted like a man of honour and spirit, and the three former assured him they would bear testimony to the appeal he had made to them, if ever the King put the question to them.

When Mr. Grenville reported this conversation to the Chancellor, that day, at the House of Lords, he seemed colder upon it than any of the other Lords.

Thursday, May 2nd.—Mr. Grenville went to the King, who received him with ease and good humour, and talked to him of what had passed the day before in the House of Lords, saying that he thought every point relating to it ought to be made as clear as possible.

turn enclosed the bill for 300*l.* you favoured me with, as good manners would not permit my refusal of it, when tendered by you.

" Your much obliged and most obedient servant,

" SAY AND SELE."[a]

" P. As a free horse wants no spur, so I stand in need of no inducement or douceur to lend my small assistance to the King or his friends in the present Administration."

The above letter, it may be presumed, explains the style of conversation implied in the phrase of " being authorised *to talk to the members of the House of Commons* upon their several claims and pretensions."—See *ante*, vol. i. p. 483.

[a] Richard Fiennes, sixth and last Viscount Say and Sele. He married the daughter of Sir John Tyrell, a Buckinghamshire Baronet. This lady had been previously twice married, first to John Knapp, and secondly to John Pigott of Doddershall, both of them Buckinghamshire 'Squires.

Lord Say and Sele died at Doddershall, an ancient residence of the Pigott family, in Bucks, and the Viscountcy became extinct, but the Barony was subsequently revived in the Twisleton family.

Mr. Grenville then acquainted His Majesty with the business upon which the Duke of York had talked to him, according to His Royal Highness's desire.

The King seemed very much surprised, and said he wondered the Duke should press for a permanent settlement at this moment; that he must have misunderstood him very much if he thought that he approved of his applying to Parliament at this time; that he should have expected that the Duke should have spoken to him himself upon it first, rather than to have communicated it to him through his servants; that he wondered he had done it, especially as the Duke had been with him not above ten minutes before Mr. Grenville came in, and that when he asked the Duke of York why he had not spoken to him himself, the Duke of York said he did not then think of it, though, the King added, Mr. Grenville knew that the Duke had mentioned it to him, and through him to the King, in the beginning of the winter, but that having done so, the Duke had given him an opportunity of taking his servants' opinion upon it, who all universally were against the making any such proposition at this time; the King seemed also much averse to augmenting the revenue of the Princes, and said he hoped the Duke of Gloucester had not desired it, for that he had repeatedly told him (the King) that his income was sufficient for his expenses.

Mr. Grenville said the Duke of Gloucester had been present all the time, but had said but little. The King ordered Mr. Grenville to tell the Duke of York that he was very much surprised that he had directed Mr. Grenville to take *his* (the King's) orders in relation to a proposition to be laid before Parliament for a permanent settlement upon him and the Duke of Gloucester, when he so well knew by what had passed between them that it was contrary to his opinion.

Lord Halifax, Lord Sandwich, and Mr. Grenville dined at the Duke of Bedford's after the House of Lords was up. The Duke of Richmond had put several questions to the House relative to the ascertaining the extent of the words Royal Family—whether or no a person born out of the kingdom could come within that description, &c., &c.

Lord Halifax and his Grace had been very warm, and the Judges were ordered to deliver their opinion the next day upon the questions relative to the Queen being enabled to hold the office of Regent. The Chancellor declared that the Queen's marriage constituted her naturalization, and gave her all the privileges of a natural-born Englishwoman.

The Duke of Bedford differed from the Chancellor, who said he thought, and was of opinion, that the words Royal Family included the Princess of Wales; whereas the Duke of Bedford said that it was his opinion that the words Royal Family extended only to those who were in the line of succession to the Crown.

Lord Halifax told Mr. Grenville that in talking upon the Bill in the morning with the King, His Majesty had empowered him to confine it to the words "born in England," if he saw the least occasion for it. This surprised Mr. Grenville extremely.

The Duke of Bedford behaved with great friendship and cordiality to Mr. Grenville, but seemed greatly heated and incensed against the Chancellor for his whole conduct in regard to the Regency Bill.

The words of the question settled at the Duke of Bedford's, to be proposed to the Judges for their opinion, and which Lord Halifax was to lay before the King for his approbation, in order to ascertain whether or no the Princess of Wales was, or was not, included in the words Royal Family, were as follows :—

"What is the interpretation of the words Royal Family according to the legal sense thereof in any Act or Acts of Parliament, where these words have been used?" And in case His Majesty was of himself disposed and inclined, as Lord Halifax imagined from what the King had said the day before, to put an end to this doubt, by inserting other words which would not include Her Royal Highness, that then the description might be by inserting the following words : "or any person of the Royal Family descended from the late King, His Majesty's Royal Grandfather."

The Ministers who dined together agreed that it was indispensably necessary to ascertain the doubt which had been raised in the House of Peers, what persons could be appointed Regents under the words "Royal Family," and that if the Opposition in the House of Commons should insist upon an explanation of it, it would be impossible to refuse it.

Lord Halifax and Lord Sandwich went to Court on Friday the 3rd of May, and on mentioning this difficulty to the King, His Majesty proposed to them to explain it by words which would exclude the Princess Dowager; in consequence of which the words above-mentioned were immediately agreed to and settled by the King, of which Lord Halifax informed Mr. Grenville by a word as he passed by his Lordship to go into the Closet : and when Mr. Grenville waited upon the King, His Majesty told him he hoped he had settled it with Lord Halifax in such a manner as would obviate all difficulties, and repeated to him the words above-mentioned, and informed him at the same time that he had authorized Lord Halifax the day before to put an end to this doubt; that Lord Halifax had told him it would make the whole easier, and particularly in the House of Commons, where some gentlemen might otherwise have difficulties about the meaning of the general words.

When Lord Halifax went to the House of Lords, Lord Bute came up to him as if by chance, and said some indifferent thing to him (which he had not done before of a long time), and said to him, My Lord, what have you to move? to which Lord Halifax said, "the words *now* and *usually* residing in Great Britain." Lord Bute said, "Why do you not put an end to the doubt at once by adding the words 'born in England,' which would explain the whole, and exclude the Princess." This Lord Halifax said he was authorized to do, if it should be found expedient. "Why then do you not do it at once? I think it would be the better way, but you know your own business best." This conversation passed on Thursday the 2nd of May.

The King had himself suggested the words to Lord Halifax. This conversation Lord Halifax repeated again to Mr. Grenville on the 8th of May, which is the reason why it is twice in these papers.

Lord Bute asked Lord Halifax what he had to move. Lord Halifax told him it was to use the words, "now and usually, &c." Lord Bute said to him, "Why do you not put an end to the doubt at once by adding the words 'born in England,' which would explain the whole and exclude the Princess, which he (Lord Bute) thought would be better, and he was sure Her Royal Highness would think so too." This the King had empowered him that day to do, if it should be thought expedient.

The King told Mr. Grenville that he had seen the Duke of Gloucester, who did by no means ask for an augmentation, and was very well satisfied, and had told the King that he had been led further into this affair than he had at first intended.

The King told Mr. Grenville that he had informed the Duke of Gloucester that Mr. Grenville had done justice to H.R.H. in saying that he had not been forward in the proposal, though he was present all the time.

Mr. Grenville told the King he had delivered his message to the Duke of York, and showed it His Majesty in writing.

The Duke of York received the King's message very properly, said His Majesty was the best judge, and best knew the time at which this ought to be proposed. Mr. Grenville asked H.R.H. if he should wait upon the Duke of Gloucester to apprize him of His Majesty's message, or whether His Royal Highness chose himself to tell it to him. The Duke of York said he would undertake it, and before he had done speaking the Duke of Gloucester came in, and both readily acquiesced to the King's commands.

Saturday, May 4th.—Mr. Grenville met the Chancellor and several other Lords at the meeting of the Governors of the Charter House in the Prince's Chamber, and stayed a considerable time with him alone when they were gone. He found him very much out of humour, and dissatisfied with the last alteration, throwing out many alarms of questions from the Opposition concerning the omission of the Princess Dowager of Wales. Mr. Grenville said that he should do his duty, and was very indifferent concerning the event as far as it regarded himself or his political situation, and they parted with some degree of dryness.

Sunday, May 5th.—The Chancellor was the first of the Ministers who went into the King's Closet ; he stayed a great while, and came up to Mr. Grenville when he came out, and spoke to him of his own health, but took no notice of what had passed between the King and him.

The Duke of Bedford went in next, stayed but a very little while, but said nothing to Mr. Grenville as he went by, but waited 'till Mr. Grenville, who went in next, came out.

As soon as Mr. Grenville came in, the King coloured, and, with great emotion, said that he had something to speak to him upon, which gave him the greatest uneasiness, which was the mark of disregard shown to the Princess of Wales, his mother, by the words which excluded her alone from the Regency ; that he had talked upon that subject to the Chancellor, who agreed with him in the impropriety of it, and had told him that many people were much offended at it, and that a Motion against it would be made by the Opposition. The King added that Mr. Grenville must see how strange a thing it would be to have this proposal come from the Opposition, and to be opposed by his servants ; that besides, the offence it marked to his mother was what he could not bear, and therefore was desirous to have some means of altering it found out ; that the Chancellor had said it could not now be done in the House of Lords, but that it might be by a message to the House of Commons.

Mr. Grenville told His Majesty that he could not be surprised at any of the feelings of regard from His Majesty to Her Royal Highness, which could make him see with concern anything that could look like a slight to her ; but that Lord Halifax having been authorized by His Majesty to propose them, the King seemed to throw it upon Lord Halifax, and to make a distinction upon the words " born in England, and descended from the late King," which singly excluded his mother, but that his uneasiness was very great, and asked Mr. Grenville if it could not be done in the House of Commons by adding the words " Princess Dowager of Wales, and the descendants of the late King."

Mr. Grenville then endeavoured to show His Majesty how impossible it was for him to propose the alteration ; that His Majesty's Secretary of State having, with his authority, proposed those words, which excluded Her Royal Highness, how could his Chancellor of the Exchequer by the same authority propose the adding her name ? that people must and would suppose that either the one or the other had mistaken His Majesty.

The King then asked him if it could still be done in the House of Lords. Mr. Grenville said he imagined in point of form it might be done ; but if there was any difference between their proceedings and those of the Commons, Lord Mansfield was without, from whom His Majesty could be informed.

He appealed to the King if he (Mr. Grenville) had ever mentioned the exclusion of Her Royal Highness ; that he had been from the beginning for naming the Regent, and had afterwards agreed with the King upon the necessity of ascertaining who was capable of being named under the words of the Act of Parliament [1].

---

[1] I have endeavoured, but in vain, to reconcile to my own satisfaction, the conflicting evidence which is to be collected from these various

The King seemed much agitated, and felt the force of what Mr. Grenville said in regard to the different direc-

conversations between the King and his Ministers on the subject of this remarkable alteration in the Regency Bill.

On Thursday, May 2nd, Lord Halifax declares that the King had empowered him to use the words, "*born in England,* if he saw the least occasion for it." This would clearly have excluded the Princess Dowager of Wales from the Regency, and no wonder therefore that when Lord Halifax communicated it to Mr. Grenville, he was *extremely surprised.*

On the evening of the same day there arose a debate in the House of Lords upon the exact meaning of the words "Royal Family:" the Duke of Bedford, in opposition to the Chancellor, contending that they comprised only those who were in the line of succession to the Crown. After this discussion in the House of Lords, the Ministers dined together at Bedford House, and it was proposed to submit this question to the Judges for their opinion. But Lord Halifax seems to have imagined, or wished it to be believed, that the King was willing to exclude the Princess, and therefore it was arranged at this Cabinet dinner that the following words should be inserted :—" or any person of the Royal Family, descended from the late King, His Majesty's Royal Grandfather."

It is then stated that Lord Halifax and Lord Sandwich in their joint audience of the King on the following morning (Friday) submitted this alteration to His Majesty, that it was immediately agreed to and settled by the King, and that when Mr. Grenville subsequently saw the King on the same day, His Majesty said he hoped he had settled it with Lord Halifax in such a manner as would obviate all difficulties : repeating the words above-mentioned, and informing Mr. Grenville that he had authorized Lord Halifax the day before to put an end to this doubt.

Mr. Grenville may here be considered perhaps as in some measure writing a defence of his own conduct in these transactions ; but if any surprise or deception were practised upon the King, it must have been by the contrivance of Lords Halifax and Sandwich, with the Duke of Bedford. Lord Halifax seems to have been particularly desirous of deluding the King into a belief that the Bill would encounter great difficulties in the House of Commons, if the Princess Dowager were within the possibility of being Regent.

It cannot be supposed that the King would have permitted himself to be made the spontaneous agent of so marked an insult on his mother, and therefore either Lord Halifax must have greatly misunderstood, or treacherously misrepresented the King's meaning, or that the full effect of the words which had been submitted to him did not strike His

tions given to his servants in the two Houses, but still enforced the argument of this being moved by the gentlemen of the Opposition. Mr. Grenville said, that even without any directions from His Majesty, he should never have opposed any mark of respect offered to Her Royal Highness ; that on the contrary he meant to have said, that he could not but suppose that every degree of duty and regard from that House to any part of His Majesty's Royal Family could not be displeasing to His Majesty, and that this might be done in case the question was proposed.

Lord Mansfield went in after Mr. Grenville, and the Duke of Bedford and Mr. Grenville waited for his coming out. Lord Mansfield stayed with the King a very considerable time, urged very strongly to His Majesty the unhappy appearance of wavering and fluctuation which this affair must inevitably give to his councils, and declared it as his opinion that the Bill was now gone too far in the House of Lords to admit of any alteration taking its rise there, and used the same language with regard to the different language to be holden in the two Houses, by His Majesty's two principal servants, as Mr. Grenville had done.

The King was in the utmost degree of agitation and emotion, even to tears.

Mr. Grenville saw Lord Mansfield again in the evening, who then told him more fully what had passed

Majesty's mind so forcibly, until they were more fully and more candidly explained to him by the Lord Chancellor on the Sunday following, immediately before the King saw Mr. Grenville, and when he appeared to be so painfully affected at the slight and disregard which had been evinced upon this occasion towards the Princess of Wales. A few days afterwards the King assured Mr. Grenville that he had never had any talk upon this affair with his mother since it happened.

in the Closet, where his Lordship had shewn the King how wisely and ably Mr. Grenville had conducted himself through all the difficulties he had had to struggle with; told His Majesty that Mr. Grenville was the great stay upon which his Government rested, advised His Majesty for the future to consult with fewer people upon his business, merely two or three at most, and to take his decisions firmly to destroy the idea of instability and wavering, so destructive to his business, and with which men's minds were so strongly possessed, and would still be more so from this last affair; shewed him the uneasiness it must give his servants, to have his approbation and authority for a measure on the Friday, which was to be changed again, without any of them having had access to him, on the Sunday.

Lord Mansfield told Mr. Grenville in the course of this conversation that Lord Bute, talking with him upon the subject of the Bill, had asked him why they did not at once put an end to all doubt upon the Princess of Wales, by moving for the words "born in England," that he was sure the Princess would be much obliged to anybody who would do it; and Lord Denbigh told Lady Blandford that Lord Bute had said much the same to him.

Lord Mansfield assured Mr. Grenville that he spoke to the King with great freedom upon the whole, and not restraining himself from naming any person whatever, which Mr. Grenville understood to refer to the Princess of Wales and Lord Bute. The King spoke very civilly of Mr. Grenville, and with asking Lord Mansfield if his Lordship and Mr. Grenville were in confidence together. The King in the course of the conversation seemed to excuse himself upon not having mentioned the first change in the Bill to Mr. Grenville, whom he did not see that day, and said Mr. Grenville had thought there was some mystery in the plan proposed by His Majesty for the Bill, which the King assured Lord Mansfield was not the case, and that he had avoided naming the Regent merely to avoid faction.

Mr. Grenville told Lord Mansfield that what he intended to do in the House of Commons in regard to the Princess of Wales was, in case any opening was given which brought her name in question, to take for granted that whatever had been done relative to Her Royal Highness, must certainly have proceeded from her own wishes, but that he was persuaded that any mark of respect to her, could not but be pleasing to His Majesty, and most certainly so to all who had the honour to serve him ; and so in that manner to give in to the proposition which the Opposition would probably make for inserting her name. Lord Mansfield entirely approved of this plan.

Monday, May 6th.—As soon as Lord Halifax came to town, he came to Mr. Grenville, who apprized him of what had passed the preceding day.

Lord Halifax repeatedly assured Mr. Grenville that the words " born in England " had been first proposed by the King to him and Lord Sandwich, and that he (Lord Halifax) had rather held back in it, telling His Majesty that it might possibly not be necessary.

The King though in his talk to Lord Mansfield seemed angry with Lord Halifax, and said he had surprised him into the message, yet when he met his Lordship on Monday morning in Richmond Park in his chaise, His Majesty rode up to it, and spoke to him upon his health in the most gracious manner.

Tuesday, May 7th.—The King writ to Mr. Grenville

to order him to send him an account of the proceedings of the House of Commons, on that and the preceding day.

Wednesday, May 8th.—Lord Mansfield went into the Closet before Mr. Grenville, and when he came out Mr. Grenville just asked him as he went by, how things went ; he said to him, You have reason to be contented. Mr. Grenville found the King in the most perfect good humour, and speaking to him with great ease and civility. His Majesty said to him that he had all the reason imaginable to believe that he served him well, and desired that he would freely give him his opinion in regard to the question upon the Princess. Mr. Grenville said it was his duty to do so, and told the King he heard that the question declaring her to be capable of being Regent, was not to be moved by the Opposition, who meant to resist it, but by people well affected to Government, and who formerly had been attached to the late Prince of Wales ; that Mr. Morton had told him that he should move it ; that Mr. Grenville had told Mr. Morton that he could not but suppose that the steps already taken had been agreeable to what Her Royal Highness wished, and asked him if he had now her authority for the question he meant to propose, to which Mr. Morton said he had not.

Mr. Grenville told the King that in his opinion the most advisable step for Her Royal Highness would be, to authorize somebody to say that she was perfectly well satisfied with what had already passed, and to decline this motion. The King said he saw it was so, but that he could do nothing in the affair.

Mr. Grenville said that undoubtedly all His Majesty's servants would give in to the proposition.

The King, in this conversation, never denied Lord Halifax having his authority for the last amendment in the House of Lords; though Lord Bute's friends give out everywhere that Lord Halifax had misunderstood His Majesty. The King mentioned in the course of the conversation that he never had had any talk with his mother upon the affair since it had happened.

Thursday, May 9th.—The King was in very good humour, and seemed desirous to be particularly civil to Mr. Grenville, and to express more approbation of his conduct than he had done of a long time. He desired Mr. Grenville to write him an account of the debate, which Mr. Grenville accordingly did.

The House of Commons sat 'till nine o'clock. Mr. Morton made a motion for inserting the name of the Princess Dowager of Wales in the Regency Bill. Mr. Martin seconded this motion, but both declaring that they had no authority from Her Royal Highness to make this proposition. Mr. Grenville got up when the question was called for, and spoke. Lord Halifax and Lord Sandwich came home to dinner with Mr. Grenville; they had been all the time present at the debate, and Lord Halifax was most perfectly satisfied with all that Mr. Grenville had said upon his subject, concerning the amendment proposed by his Lordship in the House of Lords.

Lord Sandwich told Mr. Grenville that the Duke of Bedford had been in with the King, and had spoken very strongly to His Majesty upon the reports which were got about of an intended change, which he told His Majesty it was in vain to conceal from him, as they did at this time prevail very much; that for his own part, he had entered His Majesty's service merely to support his Government, and add what little strength he could to it; that as long as he remained in it he should always endeavour to do so, but that he should never wish to continue in it a moment longer than his service was agreeable to His Majesty; but he must at the same time observe how destructive to his affairs this belief of uncertainty and wavering must be. He likewise pressed the King upon Ireland, but could never get anything beyond general civility upon either subject[1].

Friday, May 10*th.*—Mr. Grenville went to the King, who was very civil, and as Mr. Grenville was giving an account of what he had said in the House of Commons, he said at the different periods, that he had done perfectly right; but, upon the whole, his manner was colder than it had been the two former days.

His Majesty told him that, the day before, Lord Denbigh had asked him what His Majesty wished the country gentlemen to do in this affair; that he was sure their inclination was, to do what was agreeable to His Majesty, and therefore begged he would tell him, that he might know what answer to give them; to which His Majesty answered him that the House would probably sit very late, and then added to Mr. Gren-

---

[1] The Duke of Bedford's version of this interview with the King is contained in a letter to the Duke of Marlborough dated May 19th, in which his Grace says:—" We have long been apprehensive (I mean the King's Ministers) that Lord Bute had for some time past been operating mischief with the King, and Mr. Grenville and I, so long ago as the beginning of last week, took the liberty to mention to the King our suspicions, to which we could obtain no more satisfactory answer but that he would explain himself more fully hereafter." And again:—" I took the liberty to remind the King upon what conditions, proposed by himself, namely, the excluding Lord Bute from his presence, and any participation in public affairs, I was called by him into his service, and how very unfaithfully these conditions had been kept with me."—*Bedford Correspondence,* vol. iii. p. 279.

ville, Does he think I am such a fool as to be catched so [1] ?

The King sent Mr. Grenville a note to the House of Commons relative to the propriety of informing the Lords of the alteration of the Bill.

Mr. Grenville wrote His Majesty an account of the debate, which lasted 'till past eleven at night.

Saturday, May 11*th.*—Lord Mansfield came to see Mr. Grenville in the evening, talked to him in a very friendly and kind manner, and repeated to him a great deal of the conversation he had had upon his subject with the King.

His Majesty said he believed Mr. Grenville was a very honest man, and well intentioned to him and his Government; that he had very good judgment and abilities when he acted from his own opinion : His Majesty asked Lord Mansfield if he did not think this was true. His Lordship parried the question, but the King still pressed it, and said, I am sure, my Lord, you agree with me. Lord Mansfield said Mr. Grenville had certainly great abilities, and that he was not in general thought to be too easy in giving up his opinion.

Mr. Grenville understood this conversation to be aimed at the Duke of Bedford, and that Lord Mansfield sounded to try to detach him from him, especially as his Lordship dropped that, in the course of the conversation, he had said to the King that he should some day or other tell Mr. Grenville part of this discourse, at which the King smiled.

Mr. Grenville commended the temper and moderation

[1] Meaning, perhaps, that after what had passed in the House of Lords, His Majesty would not be induced to express any opinion upon the subject.

of the Duke of Bedford's conduct through the course of the last twelvemonth, but made his Lordship observe that in the Regency Bill his Grace and Mr. Grenville had totally differed in opinion upon several points, particularly the appointing the Regent, which Mr. Grenville thought better to have been done directly; the Duke thought otherwise; and likewise in naming the Princes of the blood of the Council, which the Duke of Bedford had thought expedient, and Mr. Grenville not.

Mr. Grenville added, that when he himself had taken the management of His Majesty's business, the Government would have been in confusion in a very short time, had he not endeavoured to reconcile men's minds by yielding where he could, and managing their different tempers and passions : to which Lord Mansfield replied, " Yes ; and I told the King it was necessary for you to do so."

Sunday, May 12*th.*—Mr. Grenville met Mr. Elliot at dinner at Lady Blandford's; he had dined the day before at Lord Bute's ; and he told Mr. Grenville that Lord Bute in his discourse did not seem pleased with what Mr. Morton and Mr. Martin had done in the House of Commons with regard to the Princess Dowager ; but never pretended to say that Lord Halifax had not authority for what he did. Mr. Elliot said to Mr. Grenville that things were in a sad situation ; he was sorry to see it, but whilst the King distinguished between his favourite and his ministers, they must be so.

Mr. Grenville saw the King after the Drawing-room : nothing remarkable passed, he was rather cold, and expressed discontent at Lord Halifax, who, he said, had wrote to him to ask what His Majesty would have him

do when the Regency Bill was to come up the next day
to the House of Lords; to which the King said he had
writ him word he had no directions to give him, but
that he thought it should be left as it came from the
Commons.

The Duke of Bedford had some discourse with Mr.
Grenville about Ireland. Mr. Grenville endeavoured
a little to turn his thoughts from Lord Weymouth, who,
he said, they could not force upon the King, if he objected to him, particularly upon the distress of his
fortune. The Duke of Bedford agreed with Mr. Grenville; was extremely reasonable upon the subject, and
said he would employ the Duke of Bridgewater to
induce Lord Weymouth to settle his affairs by selling
part of his estate, to prevent any public éclat of seizures,
&c., which Mr. Grenville had said he heard was much
talked of; and Lord Weymouth's friends all agree that
he is very averse to the selling his estate.

Monday, May 13*th.*—Mr. Jenkinson told Mr. Grenville he knew for certain that Lord Bute disapproved of
Mr. Morton and Mr. Martin, for what they had done
in the Regency Bill, and that he was very sure of it.

Mr. Rigby told Mr. Grenville that he heard from
authority he could not doubt, and from a well-wisher to
Mr. Grenville, that Lord Mansfield had been seen to go
in this morning to Lord Bute's house, where he had
stayed for two hours.

Lord Halifax grows uneasy, and thinks he shall be the
victim.

Wednesday, May 15*th.*—Mr. Grenville saw the King,
and found him uneasy, and very much disturbed upon
account of the weavers, who had been the day before in
a large body at Richmond, to petition for redress, upon

the House of Peers having rejected the Silk Bill. His Majesty pressed Mr. Grenville very earnestly to see what could be done, and to see two or three of the principal amongst them. Mr. Grenville told His Majesty that nothing could be done now, the sessions of Parliament being in a manner closed; but that in obedience to His Majesty's commands, he would see some of them. The King seemed much displeased with the proceedings of the House of Peers. The body of weavers followed the King to the House, where he went to pass the Regency Bill: a party of them insulted the Duke of Bedford in his chariot, and threw stones at him. Mr. Grenville went to see the Duke of Bedford in the evening, who shewed him a stone of five or six pounds' weight, which had been thrown into his chariot: he parried the blow with his hand, which was wounded by it, notwithstanding which it had struck his temple. He said the mob had followed him home; that when he got out of his chariot he spoke to them, asked what they had to say to him, and that he would hear any two of them that would come in, which accordingly two of them did; he shewed them the outrage he had received, complained of it, and asked them if he was to be insulted for giving his opinion in Parliament.

Those he spoke to disclaimed the insult, and said they should be very sorry that any harm should happen to him; that they had no thoughts of assembling, but had been summoned by beat of drum; that they were starving and wanted redress.

The Duke of Bedford talked a great deal with Mr. Grenville, with respect and temper, of the King, although thoroughly persuaded that some machination is in hand against the present Ministry, and very angry at Lord

Mansfield, who, he said, he heard from the same quarter as before, had been a second time with Lord Bute, and had stayed a considerable time.

Thursday, 16th May.—Mr. Grenville went to the King; he talked to him for some time upon common business, and then Mr. Grenville took the Speech out of his pocket, for the close of the Parliament, and offered to shew it to the King ; His Majesty said he would see it some other time, that it was time enough to think of that, and that he would have the Parliament adjourned.

Mr. Grenville asked him with some surprise, for what reason, for that all the business was done ; the King said because there was so much confusion. Mr. Grenville said he knew of none, and asked in what respect; the King said, the rising of the weavers : Mr. Grenville said that was over, and besides, what could the Parliament do to that ; it was the law that must operate there, and not the Parliament.

Using the words "confusion" and "weavers," Mr. Grenville asked what reason he must assign for the adjournment ; that the world would suppose His Majesty meant to change his Government ; to which he said, "Mr. Grenville, I will speak to you another time about that [1]: I promise you I will speak to you ; you may depend upon it I will speak to you ;" and in this kind of emotion and disorder parted with him.

Mr. Grenville came back to remind His Majesty that the House of Commons was now adjourned 'till Tuesday : the King said he should speak further to him between this and then, and that it could be afterwards adjourned for a little time.

---

[1] The Duke of Cumberland had written to Lord Temple two days before, by the King's orders, to come to London for the purpose of negotiating a change of Ministry.

The Chancellor and the Duke of Bedford both went in, and the King held much the same discourse to them : His Majesty had said nothing of it to the Secretaries of State.

The Duke of Bedford, Lord Halifax, and Mr. Grenville, dined at Lord Sandwich's, who pressed strongly for their all agreeing to hold one uniform language—to which Mr. Grenville consented ; whereupon Lord Halifax said that he must speak out, and confess that he had for a good while past felt great uneasiness at Mr. Grenville's conduct towards him, which he thought had been unkind : to which Mr. Grenville replied, he must speak out too, and say that if Lord Halifax had thought this of him, he had at least felt it as strongly from his Lordship, but that he now declared, nay more, insisted, that upon this occasion he would never be made the obstacle to anybody's situation, and that he entreated them all three, that if the King meant to make his Government without him, no one of them should make the least difficulty about it : the Duke of Bedford declared he would not stay a moment in the King's service without him.

From Lord Sandwich's, Mr. Grenville went to Lord Granby, at Knightsbridge, and told him the whole affair. Lord Granby expressed himself in the kindest manner imaginable to him, was extremely uneasy at the news, and said the King was infatuated, and was running on to his ruin : that as for himself he could not be transferred from one administration to another ; that he had told the King he had no personal acquaintance with any of his ministers but Mr. Grenville ; that the more he had known him, the more he had found reason to respect him, which he did from the bottom of his heart, and had no other political attachment ; that he had long seen that they were playing foul with him, and had prepared his father (who thought upon Mr. Grenville's subject as he did) for it.

The Chancellor told Lord Halifax what the King had said to him, and that he had told the King he was tired of the seals, and that his health made him unfit for them; but said, however, to Lord Halifax, that he desired to be at liberty to take what part he pleased. Lord Halifax said to be sure he was so, but that they would certainly take the seals from him to give them to Lord Chief Justice Pratt.

Friday, May 17th.—Lord Sandwich and Lord Halifax came early in the morning to Mr. Grenville, who insisted with them, that when they saw the King they should in no shape interfere for him; that they were most perfectly at liberty to do or say whatever they thought became their own situations, but as for him, as on the one hand he was determined never to hold a publick situation by the interposition of any person whatsoever, so on the other, he was too indifferent about it to be anxious for the continuation of that he now held, and earnestly pressed them never to mention him at all, as he would never be an obstacle to whatever they should think right for themselves, nor call on anybody to take part with him. They said this declaration was very handsome, and seemed very well satisfied.

Mr. Grenville went afterwards to St. James's, expecting to see the King, but was told by the Page that he was not to come to town. Lord March, the Lord in waiting, had a message to say the King had got a cold, and would have no Levée, but that he should come on Sunday as usual.

The two Secretaries of State and Mr. Grenville dined

at Bedford House: the Duke of Bedford had been prevailed upon not to go out of his house, upon the intelligence he received of the outrage with which he was threatened by the mob: they began to gather round Bedford House from five o'clock, and between six and seven the numbers were so great, and they grew so outrageously bent upon forcing open the gate, that they would unavoidably have prevailed, had not a reinforcement of troops been sent with all possible expedition to surround the house, which was now beset and attacked both before and behind.

The Proclamation was read, but totally disregarded, upon which, finding that the civil magistracy could not prevail, the cavalry was ordered to endeavour to disperse them by riding in amongst them. This had the effect. They all run into the neighbouring streets, the horse scampered after them, and they got away as they could; but great numbers went together and forced open two armourers' shops, and took away what arms they could find; they then went to Carr's shop[1], and broke all his windows. Six or seven people were taken up by the Justices who were at Bedford House, and examined, not one of which were weavers, but said they were ordered by their masters to come there, and were paid their day's wages for so doing; and many others of them said the same to different people who questioned them. The body of troops remained all night at Bedford House, and all the avenues to Bloomsbury Square were guarded. This body of people had assembled in the morning in Palace Yard, to wait the rising of the House of Lords. The Guards were ordered down to prevent disturbance. The mob standard was placed by the door of the House

---

[1] A fashionable mercer and dealer in French silks.

of Lords, next to the Royal Standard. They were very importunate in asking the Lords as they came out, what they had done; and when the House was up, they marched away directly to Bedford House.

Sir John Fielding was examined before the House of Lords. The House came to the same resolutions as had been made in the Excise year, when Sir Robert Walpole was insulted in the Court of Requests.

Lord Mansfield came in the evening, after the mob was dispersed, to Bedford House, expressed great concern and indignation at the disturbance, and great surprise and disapprobation at the idea of the King's changing his Government, of which he solemnly vowed he knew nothing; said it was madness and infatuation to attempt it, and utter ruin to the King's authority for ever. It was yielding to the mob, to do it at this instant, even if he had otherwise intended it; but he looked upon it as impossible, and as an idea crude and undigested, which could not take effect, assuring them he knew nothing of it, and appealing to Mr. Grenville if he could doubt the truth of this, considering what had lately passed between them.

Saturday, May 18th.—The troops continued all day at Bedford House : there was a mob continually about the door, but seemingly more from curiosity than anything else. The body of people carrying the standards, &c., did not appear, but it is said their language still continues the same, vowing revenge against the Duke of Bedford. The Duchess of Bedford was ill, and forced to be blooded, in consequence of the hurry and agitation of the preceding day.

Lord Mansfield saw Mr. Grenville in the morning; still held the language of disapprobation of the change, but said he would not go to Court the next day; he would have nothing to do with it; the King, he said, would not listen to his advice, and therefore he would not go.

Lord Temple went to Stowe on Tuesday or Wednesday; was sent for by the Duke of Cumberland to come back with all possible speed the next day, which he accordingly did; went to Mr. Pitt at Hayes on Thursday, and it is said saw Lord Bute the same night. Lord Albemarle was at Hayes on Friday, and so was Lord Shelburne, who went from thence to Mr. Calcraft's[1].

Lord George Cavendish told Mr. Lyttelton, whom he met in the Park on Saturday, that the administration was changed; the Duke of Bedford and his friends were all to be out, and he believed Mr. Grenville, but of that he was not sure; and upon Mr. Lyttelton's expressing surprise, he said his father could have told it to him, for that he had known it for some days.

Sunday, May 19*th.*—Mr. Grenville went to the King, who talked to him a great deal about the riot at Bedford House, and asked him a great many questions about it: Mr. Grenville observed to His Majesty that it seemed a well-disciplined mob, that those who were examined said they were paid their day's work. The King talked in a higher tone about it than he had done before, and said all possible means ought to be taken to quell it.

He then signed the papers Mr. Grenville brought to him, and was going to have bowed him out of the room, when Mr. Grenville told His Majesty that he believed he had forgot to give him his orders relating to the change of his Government. The King said he wished

---

[1] At Ingress, in Kent.

to speak to him about it, and should soon do so. The King told him he would have him adjourn the Parliament till Monday fortnight. Mr. Grenville said he could not do it; that he trusted His Majesty would put nothing upon him that was disgraceful and dishonourable to him, and that it was unfit for him to be the person to adjourn the Parliament for a change in the Government made without his advice, and which he could not approve. The King several times repeated, " I will speak to you upon it. I wish to speak to you upon it." The King said he should not do that by any man (referring to the words disgraceful and dishonourable), and least of all to Mr. Grenville, and asked him who then ought to adjourn it according to rank. Mr. Grenville said there was no rank, that it must be whoever His Majesty pleased; and upon the King pressing him again to say who, Mr. Grenville answered, " The man whom your Majesty destines to be my successor;" and then added, " But, Sir, let me entreat your Majesty to consider well what you are about to do, and how far this change will affect your future happiness or reputation. I do not say this in respect to my own situation, for I would not, Sir, for any consideration under heaven, continue in your service after I had lost your confidence."

The Duke of Bedford went in next; the King had been very civil to him in the drawing-room. When he came into the Closet, he told the King that Lord Bute was the exciter of this mob, that he was at the bottom of it. The King told him he was mistaken, that it could not be; but the Duke of Bedford persisted in his opinion, and with terms of reproach to Lord Bute for his perfidy. The King told him of the adjournment of the Parliament, and with regard to the intended change, said he should speak to him soon upon it. Much the same was said to the two Secretaries of State.

The Chancellor said he had spoken warmly and strongly to the King against the change.

The Duke of Cumberland was with the King for three hours on Saturday night, and went the next morning (Sunday, 19th) to Hayes.

Monday, May 20th.—Lord Halifax came early in the morning to Mr. Grenville, to shew him a letter from the Duke of Bedford, giving an account of the mob having gathered again before Bedford House the night before, where they had been very outrageous, and the Guards were again obliged to disperse them. Lord Halifax sent an account of this to the King at Richmond, at one o'clock in the morning[1]. The King returned an answer wrote in great alarm, desiring that all possible means might be taken to quell the tumult, and ordering Lord Halifax to go to the Chancellor to ask his opinion whether at this time it would be expedient to adjourn the Parliament.

Lord Mansfield soon after this came to Mr. Grenville, expressing his fullest disapprobation and detestation of

---

[1] Lord Halifax, in his letter to the King, suggested the immediate appointment of Lord Granby to the chief command of the troops, to be assisted by Lord Waldegrave and the Duke of Richmond; and believing that the King might wish to nominate the Duke of Cumberland, he adds: "Lord Granby is a very popular man, and might save the lives of these deluded wretches, which may be exposed and sacrificed by another commander, equally well intentioned, but less a favourite with the people." The King upon this immediately wrote to the Duke of Cumberland, desiring him to take the command as Captain General. The riots were, however, fortunately suppressed by the ordinary measures adopted, and this nomination therefore did not take effect, but it displays a firm determination on the part of the King to have acted in a very decided manner upon this occasion.—See the correspondence in *Memoirs of Lord Rockingham*, vol. i. p. 208.

the intended change of the Ministry, arraigning Lord
Bute in the strongest terms, and saying, upon his
honour, that though he had seen Lord Bute the Saturday
and Sunday se'ennight, he had not said the least word
to him that tended to a change ; and he protested to Mr.
Grenville that he knew nothing of it.

Mr. Augustus Hervey came in much about the same
time, and told Mr. Grenville that Lord Sandwich had
just shewed him a letter, which said that after the Duke
of Cumberland had stayed five hours at Hayes, he had
not been able to prevail on Mr. Pitt to have anything to
do with the change of Government; that Mr. Pitt had
made the banishment of Lord Bute a preliminary article,
without which he would consent to no terms whatsoever [1].
The Duke of Cumberland was not empowered to grant
this, and came away with an absolute refusal from Lord
Temple and Mr. Pitt; the former goes directly to
Stowe, where Mr. Pitt and a party of ladies are to go
on Thursday ; and Lord Bristol shewed a letter to Mr.
Hervey which he had just received from Lord Temple,
saying, "Come to me, my dear Lord, and share my
satisfaction."

[1] In the Duke of Cumberland's account of his interview with Pitt
and Lord Temple at Hayes, it does not appear that any such *stipulation* was made with regard to Lord Bute. It is true that Lord Frederick Cavendish subsequently mentioned, partly on the Duke's authority,
that Mr. Pitt had said, " he did not see a possibility of his being of
any service, for as yet he had heard nothing that gave him room to
hope the Closet would be *propitious* to him. On the contrary, my
Lord Bute, whose influence was as strong as ever, and whose notions of
government were widely different from his, would disincline the King
to his system. * * * He drew a conclusion from the situation of
the present Ministers, that if they were turned out for no other reason
than supporting the measures they advised, it *augured* ill for him, and
therefore he must know why they were turned out."—*Albemarle's Memoirs of Rockingham*, vol. i. pp. 202—211.

The Duke of Bedford, the two Secretaries of State, &c., are determined to oppose the adjournment of the Parliament. Mr. Hervey pressed strongly to Mr. Grenville to unite and reconcile himself to Lord Temple. Mr. Grenville expressed himself with great decency and temper upon Lord Temple's subject, and Mr. Hervey asked if he might tell Lord Temple what had passed. Mr. Grenville said he had no objection to it, provided he carried no message from him to Lord Temple, and assured his Lordship that Mr. Grenville had charged him with none. Mr. Hervey met Mr. Grenville again in the House of Lords, reported to him what had passed between him and Lord Temple, who said he thought Mr. Grenville and he could meet upon this subject, having both equal reason to complain of Lord —— (Bute). He empowered Mr. Hervey to tell him so, and Mr. Grenville agreed to see Lord Temple [1].

Mr. Grenville had been pressed to this union by Lord Halifax, Lord Sandwich, and many other people, even before Mr. Hervey had made any overture.

Mr. Grenville told it the same night to the Duke of Bedford, who entirely approved of and rejoiced at it.

The Guard was doubled at Bedford House upon many advices received of intended disturbances from the watermen, shoemakers, and many other trades, but no riot happened in the course of that day.

Lord Mansfield met Mr. Grenville at Bedford House, and talked the same strong language which he had held on the Saturday.

The King had several messages sent to him to Richmond from Lord Halifax and Lord Sandwich, to apprize him of the situation of things here. He ordered them

---

[1] See letters on this subject, *ante*, page 42.

to take all possible care to prevent disturbances, and sent word that he would come to town the next day.

The Committee of the House of Lords sat 'till very late, so that the House of Lords was not up till past six o'clock.

They came to a resolution to address the King to issue his proclamation for every means possible to be used to put an end to the riots.

The Dukes of York and Gloucester came up separately to Mr. Grenville in the House of Lords, lamenting the horrid situation of the kingdom, and saying they hoped Government would exert their utmost powers to prevent the bad consequences which might attend it.

Mr. Grenville agreed with them in the fact, and deplored the misfortune of such a calamity befalling us, when with a mob at our doors there is no Government within to repress it.

Lord Bute was at the House of Lords and at the Committee, with an affectation of ease and serenity; Lord Egmont sat by him; Lord Talbot, Lord Le Despencer, and others of his friends, were absent.

Lord Northumberland is known to have been on Saturday night at Richmond with the King, who waited for him in the garden, and let him in himself. He stayed but a very short time, returned to London, and soon after the Duke of Cumberland came to Richmond. There have been several meetings at Northumberland House[1].

[1] Lord Northumberland, under private instructions from the King, had been for some weeks past in secret communication with the Duke of Cumberland, both at Newmarket and in London. An interesting account of the negotiations conducted by the Duke of Cumberland with the leaders of Opposition at this crisis, is contained in a statement drawn up by His Royal Highness, and for the first time printed in Lord Albemarle's *Memoirs of Lord Rockingham*. There is, however, such a strange confusion of dates throughout this document,

Lord and Lady Northumberland made a visit at Bedford House while Mr. Grenville was there. Lord Northumberland had a very cold reception, and the language which passed before him could not be very pleasing[1].

The Duchess of Bedford said that the only persons who on this occasion had neither sent nor come to her were Lady Bute and Mrs. Anne Pitt, and that she was very glad of it, as it put an end to all difficulties of situation between her and Lady Bute.

Tuesday, May 21st.—Mr. Augustus Hervey came early in the morning to Mr. Grenville, to let him know that Lord Temple would see him at half an hour past ten. The Duke of Cumberland was to go to him at ten. Mr. Grenville went at the time appointed, but the interview did not prove satisfactory. They came to an agreement not to relate any part of what passed between them. Lord Temple was going directly to Hayes.

The Council was appointed at St. James's at twelve o'clock. The King came to town soon after ten, and drove directly to St. James's, without stopping at the Queen's house. Her Majesty was with him. The Duke

---

that very careful attention is necessary to understand it correctly. The dates of several of the transactions appear to have been retarded one week. It is much to be regretted that Mr. Bancroft, in his very valuable "History of the American Revolution,"[a] in which he is usually so accurate, has been led into error by too great a reliance on the *correctness* of the Duke of Cumberland's narrative.

[1] "Words cannot describe," says Walpole, "the disdainful manner in which they were received. The Duke of Bedford left the room; the Earl was not asked to sit, nor spoken to; but was treated with visible marks of neglect and aversion." It should be remembered that the Earl's son, Lord Warkworth, was married to a daughter of Lord Bute, and against the latter it appears, at this time, the Duke and Duchess of Bedford had conceived a most inveterate hatred.

[a] Vol. ii. p. 293.

of Cumberland went to the King, and stayed with him a considerable time. His Majesty then sent for the Chancellor, who saw the King first alone, and afterwards was a great while with him and the Duke of Cumberland. The purport of this interview was to desire the Chancellor to continue in the King's service.

Mr. Grenville went in next. The King spoke to him first upon the state of the rioters. He seemed in great disorder and agitation. Hurt with people thinking he had kept out of the way from fear, said he would put himself at the head of his army, or do anything to save his country. His Majesty then told Mr. Grenville that he had had a design to change his Government, but not the part which was under his care ; that as to him, he never had had any complaint against him, that he knew he had served him faithfully, ably, and with attachment, but that he (Mr. Grenville) must know that in other parts of his Government there had been slackness, inability, precipitation, and neglect[1]; that this had induced him to think of the change ; but it was now over, and he

---

[1] This is partly corroborated by the Duke of Cumberland's statement to Lord Temple, that the King was " displeased with his present Ministers, both for their behaviour in the Closet, and that he found them extremely dilatory in public affairs." But it is not easy to understand in what manner the King proposed to include Mr. Grenville in any new combination, or how that part of the Government which was under Mr. Grenville's care was to remain unchanged, when, as the Duke of Cumberland also said to Lord Temple, " His Majesty had chalked out,·for the beginning of an arrangement, Mr. Pitt and Mr. Charles Townshend Secretaries of State, the Earl of Northumberland First Lord of the Treasury, the Duke of Newcastle and Lord Temple —one President, the other Privy Seal, and Lord Egremont (Egmont) First Lord of the Admiralty, and had been pleased to order me to treat with him and Mr. Pitt, as well as with those Lords that formed the head of the Whig party, whom the King looked upon as his best friends, and who had always supported his Royal family."—Lord Albemarle's *Memoirs of Lord Rockingham*, vol. i. p. 195.

earnestly desired to know if Mr. Grenville was willing to serve him.

To which Mr. Grenville answered, that to his willingness and desire to serve him he had hitherto sacrificed every consideration of interest, pleasure, leisure, and happiness, nay, of health too, which was scarce able to resist the load of business he had laboured under ; but as to the power of serving him, he knew not how far his Majesty, by this unhappy step, might have disabled him. The King pressed for a categorical answer. Mr. Grenville said it was impossible for him to give it without consulting those with whom he was engaged in His Majesty's service. The King then threw in some expressions tending to show that there had been uneasiness amongst his servants. Mr. Grenville owned it, and acknowledged the dissatisfaction he himself had sometimes expressed to His Majesty on that head; but added, that though he strictly relied on His Majesty's secrecy as to whatever passed in the sacred recess of his Closet, yet he did assure him he never had said more in that place than he had to Lord Halifax himself; and that it had ever been his care, since he had the honour to come into his service, to conciliate men's minds to the utmost of his power ; that in the forming the Government he had showed that to be his inclination, for the Duke of Bedford had been the person who had advised the King, in August, 1763, to remove Mr. Grenville [1], notwith-

[1] "You will be surprised to hear in France that I advised the King to send for Mr. Pitt, but it is true, hoping and having some reason to believe that he would have been moderate, as well with regard to the Peace as to the persons he would have expected to have brought in with him. It was far otherwise ; but I do not repent of the counsel I gave, as I am convinced by showing themselves the party will be weakened, and the King's hands strengthened."—*The Duke of Bedford to Mr. Neville, Sept.* 5, 1763.—*Bedford Correspondence*, iii. 242.

standing which he had united himself with his Grace
for His Majesty's service; that Lord Halifax, indeed,
had been in it before, and " as to Lord Sandwich," said
the King, " neither you nor I placed him." Mr. Grenville said it had been his endeavour to manage the
Chancellor's mind, so as to unite him firmly with His
Majesty's other servants ; that upon this plan of general
conciliation he had proceeded ; that the publick business
had gone on with a degree of success surpassing his
most sanguine wishes ; and that after all this it was
mortifying and cruel to him to find himself no further
advanced, nay, rather less acceptable to His Majesty
than he had been, even at the period of August was
two years. The King used many gracious expressions
to assure him that he never had displeased him, that he
did not mean to have removed him; nor he did not
know that anything could induce him to do it ; but he
desired him to give him a positive answer whether he
would now serve him or no.

Mr. Grenville urged the necessity of consulting with
the other Ministers before he could give His Majesty an
answer ; showed the King the fatal consequences of the
step he had taken; said it was in vain for him to conceal
from His Majesty that all the world knew that the
Duke of Cumberland had been empowered by His Majesty to make offers to everybody from right hand to
left, which offers had been rejected [1] ; that there was but

[1] During their short interview in the morning, Mr. Grenville had
probably received from Lord Temple some secret particulars of the
negotiations which had been carried on for a change in the Government, and perhaps at the same time Lord Temple had encouraged him
to make a firm stand against the influence of Lord Bute, as he himself
had done in refusing to accept office under " Lord Bute's Lieutenant,"
as he termed the Earl of Northumberland, who was proposed for First
Lord of the Treasury in the new arrangement.

one voice upon this subject, that all the world saw it to be Lord Bute's doing, and contrary to the express declarations made to his present Administration when they undertook the Government, contrary, I will not say to stipulation, sir, for I made none; I pressed no demands upon you; your Majesty regulated yourself Lord Bute's situation, told it me, and authorised me to make it known. Your Majesty cannot but recollect that you did so. The King said, I do not deny it; but it is not Lord Bute that has done this. Mr. Grenville said the world would have difficulty to be persuaded of that, and that it was now, more than ever, essentially necessary that Lord Bute should have nothing to do in His Majesty's councils. The King said he had not; he ordered Mr. Grenville to go and consult with these gentlemen with all haste, and to bring him the answer immediately. The King then went at three o'clock to the Council (with the Duke of Cumberland with him) which had been summoned about issuing the Proclamation, and eight o'clock was appointed for the Chancellor, the two Secretaries of State, and Mr. Grenville, to meet at Bedford House.

At nine o'clock, or a little after, the King sent a letter [1] to Mr. Grenville, pressing him to come to him that minute. He was forced to break off the conference and go.

The King showed great impatience, and pressed for the answer. Mr. Grenville stated to him how short a time had been allowed them for a deliberation of so much moment, and which, by His Majesty's command, had been obliged to break off so abruptly. The King asked what conditions they meant to ask. Mr. Gren-

---

[1] See *ante*, page 40.

ville said that previous to everything else they must
have the strongest assurances of Lord Bute never having
anything to do, in any shape whatever, in His Majesty's
councils or business. The King asked what else. Mr.
Grenville added that they could not longer consent that
Mr. Mackenzie should hold up the standard of ministry
for Lord Bute in Scotland. The King asked what else.
Mr. Grenville said they had got no further then, and
were to meet again the next morning at half an hour
after ten. The King seemed impatient to know the
demands that would be made upon him. Mr. Grenville
told him not such as Mr. Pitt had twice made to His
Majesty, but that they must be satisfied whether or no
the Duke of Cumberland was to have the forming of
the Ministry. The King said no. Mr. Grenville said
it was necessary for him to ask all these questions, because he could not serve two masters. The King told
him and assured him he meant to give him his fullest
countenance and support. Mr. Grenville took notice
to him how much he had been mortified to find both
withdrawn from him; that he had taken an opportunity
of telling His Majesty so not long before. The King
said he remembered it. Mr. Grenville then conjured
him, in the most earnest and solemn manner, if ever he
had served him faithfully, or in a manner acceptable to
him, that he would grant him the request he was then
going to make to him. The King asked him what it
was. Mr. Grenville said that what he entreated of him
was, that if the continuing him in his service was in any
degree a force upon his inclination, or done with any reluctance, he did conjure him not to do it on any consideration whatever; that he always had endeavoured to
serve him with the fidelity, duty, and attachment, which

had been the rule of his conduct towards him; and that he hoped that during the whole course of this conversation no word had dropped from him in which he had been wanting in respect and duty to His Majesty. The King said he always did behave to him in the most respectful and becoming manner[1].

Mr. Grenville added that no consideration under heaven could make him go through the task, or sacrifice every enjoyment of his life, as he now did, if he had not His Majesty's approbation while he did it. The King said : " Mr. Grenville, the affecting manner in which you speak to me touches me; I feel the kindness of your behaviour to me, and you shall find that I mean to give you my confidence and my countenance in the fullest manner." Mr. Grenville told him that if he had wished to change his servants, and had been pleased to have

---

[1] And yet in the modern style of writing history, or rather the romance of history, Mr. Grenville has been accused of "holding language to which, since the days of Cornet Joyce and President Bradshaw, no English King had been compelled to listen."[a]   It has been the fashion, too, to say that George the Third " hated Mr. Grenville beyond all living men;" and that he would " sooner see the devil come into his Closet than Grenville;" and other similar phrases which chiefly rest upon the authority of Horace Walpole, who personally disliked him, and who never lost an opportunity of sneering at him, not improbably because Mr. Grenville had refused to perpetrate some *job* in which Walpole was interested.   It may be that Mr. Grenville was tedious and verbose in the Closet, and that in his official communications with the King, his austerity of manner, and his scrupulously attentive habits of business, may have frequently rendered him an unwelcome visitor; but no man knew better than the King how to appreciate the sterling good in Mr. Grenville's character, and it has been said, upon authority quite as trustworthy as that of Horace Walpole, that upon the death of Mr. Grenville the King expressed to Lord Suffolk his great regard for his memory, and that he lamented the loss of his friend, " that great and good man Mr. Grenville, who was an honour to human nature."

had so much reliance on him as to have consulted him in it, he would, though it had regarded his own situation, have given him every facility to it in his power, but the doing it without him had mortified him in the most sensible manner ; that he had seen it coming ever since that *unhappy* Regency Bill had been on foot.

The King enquired whether they meant to restrain him from civility to the Duke of Cumberland, who had acted well on this occasion : had offered to head the troops in case of any insurrection, and to do everything in his power for the safety of the King and kingdom. Mr. Grenville said that nobody could be so unreasonable as to wish to restrain any civil intercourse between His Majesty and his Royal family, but that His Royal Highness must have nothing to do with the Government.

The King in the course of the conversation repeated several times that he was an honest man, and he hoped Mr. Grenville thought that he was so : he seemed very impatient for a decided answer, and desired to have it as soon as possible.

Wednesday, May 22nd.—Mr. Grenville received a letter from Lord Temple at eight o'clock in the morning, saying he would come to him, &c., which he accordingly did by a little past nine o'clock ; their meeting was of the most friendly kind, and upon the foot of the most perfect reconciliation. Mr. Grenville told the King of the reconciliation as soon as he went to him. Lord Temple afterwards came up stairs to see Mrs. Grenville and the children.

The Ministers met in Downing Street between ten and eleven, and came to five resolutions which they were to lay before the King, viz. :

Lord Bute to have no share whatever in any shape in the King's councils.

Mr. Stuart Mackenzie to be removed from his office of Privy Seal of Scotland, and no business whatever to be transacted through him.

Lord Granby to be made Commander-in-Chief. Lord Holland to be removed from the office of Paymaster.

Ireland to be settled by the full approbation and recommendation of the Ministers.

Mr. Grenville went at twelve to communicate this to the King, who asked him if they all concurred in these resolutions: Mr. Grenville said yes. He asked if it was his own opinion: he said he would not have been the hand to have brought them if that had been otherwise. He then asked if they were absolutely sine quâ non: Mr. Grenville said they would not have troubled His Majesty with them if they had not thought them all indispensably necessary.

The King said he would consider of them, and give Mr. Grenville his answer in the evening.

The Chancellor went in next, and the Duke of Bedford meant to go in after the Chancellor came out, but the Duke of Cumberland took his place, stayed above an hour with the King, and when the Duke of Bedford went in, the King would not explain himself to him, but said he would give his answer singly to Mr. Grenville.

In the afternoon His Majesty sent for Lord Granby, who was above an hour with him, in which time His Majesty explained to him a promise he had made to the Duke of Cumberland, that His Royal Highness should command in case of an insurrection, and endeavoured to dissuade Lord Granby from the proposition of his being declared Commander-in-Chief; to which Lord Granby replied that he never had solicited that honour, and even had some points in his own mind upon it different, perhaps, from what any minister, even Mr. Grenville who was so much his friend, might perhaps think right, but that he begged His Majesty to be assured that, though Mr. Grenville had asked it, he had not done it in consequence of any solicitation of his, but as a mark of regard for which he must feel himself greatly indebted to him, and that his attachment to M r. Grenville was greater than to any man breathing, but that he desired that no pretension of his might stand as an obstacle to any arrangement which might be for the advantage of the King's service.

The Duke of Cumberland was again with the King in the afternoon, and so was Lord Chancellor.

At eleven o'clock at night the King sent for Mr. Grenville, and told him he had considered upon the proposals made to him : he did promise and declare to them that Lord Bute should never directly nor indirectly, publicly nor privately, have anything to do with his business, nor give advice upon anything whatever : that as to what related to Lord Granby, he found by the conversation he had had with his Lordship that he was willing for the present to decline the proposition made for him, and particularly as His Majesty had explained to him the situation of the Duke of Cumberland : that as to what respected Mr. Stuart Mackenzie, he would consent that the business in Scotland should go through other hands, but he strongly deprecated the depriving him of his office, saying that at the time he gave it him, he might have had a place for life, and that His Majesty had promised him that he should not be removed from this: that His Majesty did consent to remove Lord Holland, and likewise to take the recommendation of his servants for Ireland, either in favour of Lord Weymouth or any other person they should agree upon.

Mr. Grenville strongly pressed Mr. Mackenzie's removal, urging how strongly the refusal would stand as a continuation of Lord's Bute's influence, but he made little impression, and the King desired to have the final answer whether his servants would or would not serve him. Mr. Grenville refused to give any answer 'till he had consulted with the other Ministers. Twelve o'clock the next day was named by the King for the final decision, and Mr. Grenville wrote to the Chancellor, and the two Secretaries of State, to appoint them to meet in Downing Street the next day at ten ; he had seen the Duke of Bedford, who had named that hour.

The Chancellor in his interview with the King had yielded to his idea of Mr. Mackenzie's retaining the office deprived of the power, but Mr. Grenville stood firm to the point.

Thursday, May 23rd.—The Ministers met at the hour appointed, were unanimous in their resolution not to depart from the propositions laid down by them, except the Chancellor, who held the same language which he had done the night before to the King, and accordingly it was agreed that Mr. Grenville should report it to the King.

Lord Granby came to Downing Street by a little after nine o'clock: he explained his ideas fully to Mr. Grenville, and told him what had passed ·between His Majesty and him the night before, and desired to be no obstacle to any good arrangement. . Mr. Grenville told him that they proposed to waive his appointment at present, but to ask for the promise of it in case of the Duke of Cumberland's death.

When Mr. Grenville reported the ultimate resolution of the Ministers to the King, he fell into great agitation upon the article relating to Mr. Mackenzie, and strove in every manner possible to have saved him, going so far as to say, "he should disgrace himself if he did it."[1] Mr. Grenville begged His Majesty would consider how hard it was to use such an expression to a servant for an opinion which His Majesty ordered him to give, and begged he would rather dismiss him (Mr. Grenville) from his service than to put him under the cruel dilemma of thinking that he was forcing his inclination. The King said, "Mr. Grenville, I have desired you to stay in my service. I see I must yield. I do it for the good of my people."

Lord Sandwich was ordered to write a letter of dismission to Mr. Mackenzie, and Lord Halifax the same to Lord Holland.

The office of Privy Seal of Scotland was destined to Lord Lorne : he was set out upon his journey to Scotland the day before, and was fetched back express for Mr. Grenville to propose this to him ; he returned directly, but declined the office in favour of Lord Frederick Campbell, his brother, but with all possible expressions of gratitude and attachment to Mr. Grenville.

The Duchess of Hamilton was told at the last place

---

[1] The King's reluctance about Mackenzie's dismissal arose from the same delicacy of *personal honour* towards a faithful servant, that he showed on another occasion for "*poor George Grenville*"[a] himself.

[a] See Memoirs of Lord Hardwicke, iii. 379.

where she changed horses, that she could not drive into the yard, because Lord Bute's family filled it up, but it proved to be only Lord Bute and his sons from Winchester school.

Friday, May 24th.—Lord Frederick Campbell kissed hands for the Privy Seal of Scotland, and Mr. Charles Townshend for the office of Paymaster [1].

When Mr. Grenville went into the King's Closet, he found him very gloomy, and with an air of great dissatisfaction.

---

[1] Some months before this time, Mr. Charles Townshend had made professions of political attachment to Mr. Grenville, and said that he was tired of the plan of opposition, and that he meant to act with the Government. Immediately after the failure of the negotiation with Mr. Pitt and Lord Temple in 1763, Mr. Townshend had declared his firm resolution never to be withdrawn from them and the principles which they maintained. The following letter, written at that time, though without date, was omitted in the place where it should have been inserted :—

MR. CHARLES TOWNSHEND TO EARL TEMPLE.

Adderbury, Saturday, (September 11, 1763.)

MY DEAR LORD,—I cannot express the satisfaction your very friendly and affectionate letter has given me.

I heard of your sudden journey to town only by report. I had received no authentic account of the result or passages of Mr. Pitt's audience, and I confess I grew impatient to learn something from authority. At first sight, and judging from this distance, it seems to have been a measure conceived in a short interval of temper and reason, submitted to in despair, repented of as soon as resolved, and disgraceful in the highest degree to those, who having had the courage to advise the measure, had not constancy enough to persevere in the steps necessary to the complete execution of it.

This is the manner in which this singular transaction now strikes me, but I shall be able to determine, where I can now only conjecture, after I have had the benefit of your information.

Shall I come to you early to-morrow ? I would have dined with you this very day, if I had not company with me I cannot leave ; in the meantime, give me leave to assure you that if I have been named, in the course of this negotiation, as one whom Mr. Pitt thinks of any

Mr. Grenville laid before His Majesty the duty and respect which Lord Lorne had expressed to His Majesty for his intended goodness to him ; to which the King replied, " It 's your goodness, Mr. Grenville, not mine ;" and he expressed the same to Lord Sandwich, saying to him, " When Mr. Grenville made the vacancy, I let him fill it up as he pleased."

The physicians were ordered to attend the King. They waited a considerable time while the Dukes of York and Gloucester were with the King ; at last the King opened the door himself and called them in. He gave Sir William Duncan his hand to feel his pulse, which was quick, but bid him not mind it, because he had been hurried for some days past, but that he had eaten very little and had no fever. He inquired earnestly of Sir Clifton Wintringham how the Duke of Cumberland did after all his fatigue, and if he stood it well, and that, for his part, he never had slept above two hours for several days past. The physicians were appointed to see His Majesty again on Sunday.

importance to an Administration formed upon his idea, sufficient to me is the honor of being thus described and remembered by him, and, if my own conduct of late has manifested my firm though quiet resolution never to be withdrawn from men whose names, whose characters, whose principles I love, revere, and hold by any emoluments or honors, I have obtained my point, and am the very man, and in the very situation I wish to be.

I cannot conclude, without particularly acknowledging the kindness of several expressions in your Lordship's letter, nor without repeating to you how sensible I am of your candour, generosity, and friendship to me   Believe me, you waste not such qualities in exercising them upon me, who am, and ever shall be, with the warmest regard, my dear Lord,
&c., &c.,   C. TOWNSHEND.

Lady Dalkeith desires her best compliments to your Lordship and Lady Temple, to whom I beg to be remembered with every expression of respect and real regard.

During all these days the King saw the Duke of Cumberland constantly, and many other people, and offers were made to people of all sorts and all parties, but the general tone was to refuse.

The King complained bitterly of the hardship put upon him in making him dismiss Mr. Mackenzie. His Majesty asked Mr. Grenville if he might not go that night into the country, for he felt that he wanted the air. Mr. Grenville said by all means, and he was glad to hear that His Majesty intended it, as he thought it would do him good.

The Duke of Cumberland went to Windsor. Lord Bute came back to London.

Saturday, May 25th.—The King came to town at eleven, went to the House of Peers to prorogue the Parliament at twelve, and returned at one to Richmond, and saw none of his Ministers.

Sunday, May 26th.—The King and Queen did not come to chapel, and there was no drawing-room upon account of its being Whit Sunday. The physicians had notice that the King was not very well, and would not come to town, but ordered them to attend him on Wednesday morning at the Queen's house.

Tuesday, May 28th.—General Græme came to Mr. Grenville's Levée and made professions of wishing well to him, and desired to speak to him the first day that was convenient.

Wednesday, May 29th.—The King had his Levée as usual. Mr. Grenville saw him in the Closet before the Council ; his behaviour was not remarkable, but when Mr. Grenville asked his leave to recommend to the vacancy made in the Queen's family by Lord Weymouth, who had kissed the King's hand on being appointed

Lord Lieutenant of Ireland[1], the King said, that was no office of State, that the Queen had thought of a proper person for it, and had even named it that morning for the Duke of Ancaster, and it was reasonable for her to please herself. Mr. Grenville bowed and said no more. The Duke of Ancaster went to Windsor Lodge to consult the Duke of Cumberland before he kissed hands.

Thursday, May 30th.—Mr. and Mrs. Grenville went with Lord Temple and Mr. James Grenville to dine at Hayes. Mr. Pitt expressed pleasure at the reconciliation of the family, and early in the course of conversation took occasion to say to Mr. Grenville, that in politics each had taken their separate walks and opinions, and therefore wished that their intercourse might be of a friendly domestic nature, without entering upon political topics. Mr. Grenville gave readily and cheerfully in to this idea, said he sincerely thought it best, and each kept strictly to it.

Friday, May 31st.—Mr. Grenville saw the King, who appeared more easy and less reserved than he had been the former days, and talked easily upon business. Mr. Grenville told him he had received a letter from Mr. Henry Grenville on Wednesday full of thankfulness for His Majesty's condescension and goodness in allowing him (Mr. George Grenville) to propose the office of Commissioner of the Customs to him, which he most readily accepted. Mr. Grenville asked leave to make

[1] Lord Weymouth was nominated to the appointment, but he never went to Ireland as Lord Lieutenant. Junius accuses him of plundering the Treasury of the first fruits of an employment which it was well known he was never to execute, and states that he received three thousand pounds for plate and equipage money. Lord Weymouth had been Master of the Horse to the Queen.

out the warrant, which was accordingly agreed to by His Majesty, and Mr. Grenville told him that in consequence of a former agreement made with Mr. Frederick Frankland, the vacancy in Parliament was to be filled up during this Parliament by some of Lord Temple's family, which would be Mr. James Grenville's eldest son.

The King asked if Mr. James Grenville had more than one son. Mr. Grenville said yes, one of them was in the Army, a very pretty man, and much commended in his profession. He then asked if the eldest was of age, and which of them had an office in the Privy Seal.

Lord Halifax went in afterwards, and when he had done speaking upon business, the King asked him if he knew who was to come into Parliament in Mr. Henry Grenville's room. Lord Halifax said no; to which the King said with a kind of sneer, " Mr. James Grenville's eldest son." [1] Lord Halifax told it to Mr. Grenville as soon as he saw him.

Mr. Grenville received a letter from General Græme excusing himself for not waiting upon him next morning according to appointment.

Sunday, June 2nd.—Mr. Grenville found the King more easy and cheerful than before ; he talked with great civility to Mr. Grenville upon the necessary business of the day. Lord Gower told Mr. Grenville he had found the same towards him.

Tuesday, June 4th.—The King appeared much the same in his behaviour to Mr. Grenville as he had done on Sunday, but never begins the conversation as he used to do, but waits 'till Mr. Grenville speaks. The Duke

---

[1] Afterwards Lord Glastonbury. He was to come into Parliament for the Borough of Thirsk.

of Bedford told Mr. Grenville that it was now known from Lord Albemarle that the King had told the Duke of Cumberland, that the reason why he wished to change his Ministry was the disunion which reigned amongst them; that Sandwich and Halifax were pretty easy to be dealt with, because they were afraid to lose their places, but that they did no business; that the Duke of Bedford and Mr. Grenville were inflexible, not loving each other, and only agreeing to give him the law.

Wednesday, June 5th.—Mr. Grenville recommended General Mostyn to the King to succeed Sir R. Rich as Governor of Chelsea Hospital, to which he had been earnestly pressed by Lord Granby. The King heard him civilly, and by his manner of speaking of General Mostyn, seemed not averse to do it.

Friday, June 7th.—The King spoke to Mr. Grenville without waiting for him to begin : he appeared civil and easy. Mr. Grenville recommended Lord R. Manners for Sir R. Rich's Dragoons in case they became vacant. This he did at Lord Granby's request, and the King did not object, and answered civilly upon some other military promotions, but sent afterwards to Lord Granby to speak to him himself, in order that he might feel that he owed the grace singly to him; and he had done the same to General Mostyn, but there is no vacancy at present, as Sir R. Rich is not dead. The King's countenance is certainly calmer, and his manner civiller than it was, but Mr. Grenville has no reason to think that it proceeds from anything but disguise.

Saturday, June 8th.—Mr. Grenville went to Short-grove, where he stayed 'till Monday night.

Tuesday, June 11*th.*—Mr. Grenville went to the Princess Dowager's Drawing-room. She received him very coldly, talked very long to Mr. Mackenzie and to Lord Egmont, and a great deal to Lady Bute, &c.

Wednesday, June 12*th.*—The Duke of Bedford went into the Closet to ask leave to go out of town, and took that opportunity to remonstrate to the King upon the little countenance he showed to his Ministry, and how difficult it was for them to go on under such difficulties; that for his own part he knew that His Majesty was surrounded by his (the Duke of Bedford's) enemies, amongst whom he chiefly named Lord Bute, and said he feared that the pernicious advice given to His Majesty would soon or late throw the kingdom into great disorder; that those who gave it ought to consider that, as well as the consequences it might produce. The King heard him civilly and temperately, and said nothing towards disculpating himself from the want of confidence in and countenance to his Ministry, but absolutely denied Lord Bute's having ever made any representation to him against the Duke of Bedford, but on the contrary, that he had always spoken of him with great regard [1].

[1] This interview with the King has been described by the Duke of Bedford himself in a letter to the Duke of Marlborough, printed in the *Bedford Correspondence,* vol. iii. p. 286. " I took the liberty," says the Duke, " to desire leave to recapitulate to him what had passed between him and his Ministers, from the time he avowed the design of changing his Administration to their being called back again by him to resume their functions. Whether his countenance and support had not been promised them? Whether this promise had been kept? but on the contrary, whether all those who are our most bitter enemies had not been countenanced by him in public? And whether we and our friends had not met with a treatment directly opposite to this?" Lord Albemarle, in his "*Memoirs of Lord Rockingham,*" has adopted a ridiculous invention of Horace Walpole's brain, to the effect that upon

When Mr. Grenville went in, the King's behaviour was the same as it had been for some time past.

There was a Council at night, at which Lord Egmont, who used always to be silent, was very free in giving his opinion. Lord Halifax and Lord Egmont differed, and were pretty warm. The Duke of Bedford declared he had no opinion to give, except in support of that which Mr. Grenville had delivered.

Thursday, June 13th.—The Duke of Bedford, Lord Halifax, and Lord Sandwich, dined with Mr. Grenville, and after dinner the Duke of Bedford told Mr. Grenville that as he was going into Buckinghamshire, where he would see Lord Temple, he did desire that whatever arrangement he could make with him for strengthening the general system, might be done ; that he confided in Mr. Grenville as a man of honour, that nothing would be expected from him that could condemn his conduct in the Peace, which he should ever support, and could not tread back upon his own steps, but that if the resig-

this occasion " the Duke of Bedford, accompanied by Grenville, Sandwich and Halifax, waited on His Majesty with a remonstrance, which the Duke had drawn up, which took an hour in reading, and which the King had the greatest difficulty to command himself enough to hear it read to the end. The King made no answer ; but when they were gone he said that if he had not broken out into the most profuse sweat, he should have been suffocated with indignation." [a] The story told by Junius is equally remote from the truth : that " the Duke of Bedford demanded an audience of the King, reproached him in plain terms with his duplicity, baseness, falsehood, treachery, and hypocrisy —repeatedly gave him the lie, and left him in convulsions." It may be admitted that the Duke's language to the King, however supposed to be "justified by the occasion," was somewhat unbecoming in a subject towards his Sovereign personally, and his " behaviour," as it is described by a more moderate contemporary writer, " such as no private man could have suffered in any one of his inferiors."

[a] *Memoirs of Geo. III.* vol. ii. p. 182.

nation of his office could facilitate measures, or make an agreeable arrangement for Lord Temple, he was ready to do it at a moment's warning. All this was heightened by the warmest and most cordial expressions to Mr. Grenville.

Lord Halifax and Lord Sandwich made the same professions to Mr. Grenville, and expressly told him that he might dispose of them and of their offices, and repeated it several times. Very many people have said the same to Mr. Grenville upon this occasion.

Mr. Elliot came to Mr. Grenville in the morning; his language was deploring the state of the kingdom, complaining of Lord Bute for the state to which he had brought the King's affairs, exclaiming against the Duke of Cumberland, and lamenting Lord Bute's conduct in transferring his friends backwards and forwards from one man to another. He said he had seen Lord Bute but twice of a long time, and had talked no politics. Lord Bute affects to say to everybody that he knows nothing of all the present transaction, and that he meddles with nothing.

Friday, June 14*th.*—Mr. Grenville saw the King; his behaviour was in nothing different from the former days. He did not speak 'till Mr. Grenville began, nor ever has done, except the time before mentioned. Mr. Grenville renewed his desire to go into the country, to which the King said yes, and inquired how long he proposed to stay.

Sunday, June 16*th.*—Lord and Lady Temple came to dine at Wotton, and brought Mr. and Mrs. Onslow, Lady Pembroke and Mr. Barnard, and Lord Harry Paulet with them.

Monday June 17*th.*—Mr. and Mrs. Grenville went

to Stowe, where they were received with the most cordial affection.

In the evening Mr. Grenville had a letter by express from Lord Sandwich, in which, after writing upon other business, he tells him the report in town is very strong, that the duration of their political life is not to exceed many days, and that he knows that Mr. Phelps [1] has been consulted by a friend of his attached to Lord Northumberland, to know the value of Private Secretary-ship to a Secretary of State, or Lord Lieutenant of Ireland; and this report seems confirmed by Mr. Onslow, who went this day to dine at Wakefield Lodge, but did not find the Duke of Grafton at home. A person who was there told him that the Duke of Grafton had been sent for to London; had since been one day at Wakefield, and said everything seemed to go on as well as possible, and that he was to go to Hayes on Tuesday the 18th, to talk with Mr. Pitt, and that he was determined to agree to nothing but in concurrence with Lord Temple and Mr. Pitt.

Lord Lyttelton went this day to Wotton, but not finding Mr. Grenville there, followed him to Stowe. He told Lord Temple that Mr. Pitt seemed to doubt whether or no the present Ministry had done wisely in removing Mr. Mackenzie, but that he (Lord Lyttelton) approved it.

Wednesday, June 19th.—Lord Thomond came to Stowe, and at the same moment arrived a messenger from Mr. James Grenville, apprising Lord Temple that Lord Villiers had been sent by the Duke of Cumberland to Mr. Pitt to desire him to attend the King the next morning at ten o'clock. Mr. James Grenville desired Lord Temple to hold himself ready to set out for London

[1] Lord Sandwich's Private Secretary.

immediately if he heard further. Lord Temple determined not to go upon this notice. At twelve o'clock at night Mr. Grenville received an express from Lord Sandwich, telling him that Mr. Pitt had been that day three hours with the King; that His Majesty had afterwards sent for the Chancellor, to whom he had said that he had been advised to see Mr. Pitt himself, it having been intimated to him that he might by that be induced to take some share in the Government. His Majesty related what he thought proper of the conversation, the result of which was, that they had not come to any agreement, nor yet were totally and finally separated.

The Chancellor's advice to the King was to adhere to his present Administration, giving them his cordial support and countenance. The King heard it attentively and civilly, and afterwards, when Lord Sandwich went in to talk upon the common business, His Majesty seemed in good humour.

Thursday, June 20th.—Mr. Grenville had a letter from Lord Sandwich, with the contents of which he was much displeased. It contained an account of a conversation which had passed between the Chancellor and him, in which the Chancellor had told Lord Sandwich that the King, since the last conversation with the Duke of Bedford, looked upon his present Ministers as in a state amounting to their having resigned; that his Majesty was as yet come to no resolution, but understood that if he continued to employ them they had further demands to make upon him. This Lord Sandwich positively denied, and told the Chancellor that all the present Ministers had to ask was His Majesty's full support and countenance. Lord Sandwich refers to Mr. Grenville whether he had on this subject said too much or too little, saying that the Chancellor was to see the King again on the Sunday following, when, under Mr. Grenville's directions to him (Lord Sandwich), he would set the Chancellor right in what he was to report, unless Mr. Grenville would come to town himself, which he earnestly pressed him to do.

Mr. Grenville was highly displeased at the declaration Lord Sandwich had made, which Mr. Grenville totally disavows as his sentiments in his answer to Lord Sandwich, and insists that no person whatever shall give any opinion for him, though at the same time he will not hasten his journey one moment without the King's express command. Lord Sandwich adds in his letter, that he understood the King was to see Mr. Pitt again, and that the Duke of Cumberland had an Administration ready to propose.

The Duke of Grafton dined this day at Stowe, and had a great deal of talk with Lord Temple, but had left London before the King had seen Mr. Pitt.

Friday, June 21st.—Mr. Grenville, &c., went to Wotton; he met Mr. James Grenville in his chaise coming to Stowe, but nothing but common civility passed between them. A servant came to Wotton late at night from Lord Temple, bringing some packets which had been directed to Mr. Grenville at Stowe, and with them a letter from Lord Temple, saying that Mr. James Grenville brought word that all that Mr. Pitt had said to the King was taken *ad referendum*, and that he was to see His Majesty again on Saturday.

Sunday, June 23rd.—Lady Temple, Lord Bristol, and Mr. James Grenville's two sons came to Wotton. Lady Temple brought Mr. Grenville a letter from Lord Temple, in which he told him that he had received an express from Mr. Pitt the night before, telling him that His Majesty desired that Lord Temple would attend him at the Queen's house on Tuesday morning at ten o'clock.

Other letters to Mr. Grenville mentioned the Duke of Cumberland having seen Mr. Pitt previous to Mr. Pitt's first audience of the King, and having stayed with him 'till four o'clock in the morning. Lord Temple was to set out from Stowe immediately, to lie at Hayes on Monday night, and earnestly pressed Mr. Grenville to let him see him on Tuesday morning before the appointed hour.

Monday, June 24th. — Mr. Grenville and Lord Thomond went early in the morning to Woburn, and were to be in town late at night. Mr. Grenville found the Duke of Bedford in the most friendly dispositions imaginable towards him, approving entirely of all he had done, and giving him full powers to dispose of him entirely as he should think fit, telling him that he wished much not to stir from Woburn; but that if Mr. Grenville saw the least use in his coming to town, he would be ready to do it at a minute's warning.

Tuesday, June 25th. — Lord Temple came to town from Hayes early in the morning. Mr. Grenville went to him in Pall Mall before breakfast. His conversation was of the most cordial and affectionate kind to Mr. Grenville, but he appeared under great agitation. He went at ten to the King, with whom he stayed about an hour. He absolutely declined coming into the King's service, and wrote Mr. Grenville a note at twelve to tell him so. He came afterwards to dine with Mr. Grenville, and then related more at large what had passed, and tol him the reasons he had assigned for not accepting the offer the King made him were two, the first of which was the difficulty of forming a proper plan with regard to the House of Commons; the second was of a tender and delicate nature, and which he therefore desired not to explain. The King pressed him to come into his service, and wished him to consider upon it.

Mr. Pitt saw the King after Lord Temple, and went out of town before dinner. Lord Temple told Mr. Grenville he intended to go to Stowe on Thursday or Friday. It was generally understood that Mr. Pitt had agreed to form the Administration. Measures had been settled with the King in the conference with Mr. Pitt on the Wednesday, and Men on the Saturday. The first were principally a treaty with Prussia, the repeal of the Cyder Tax, and the question upon General Warrants, &c. The latter was pretty near as follows:—Lord Temple, First Lord of the Treasury; the Duke of Newcastle, President of the Council; the Duke of Grafton and Mr. Pitt, Secretaries of State; Lord Northumberland, Chamberlain; Lord Lyttelton, Privy Seal; Lord Shelburne, First Lord of Trade; Lord Bristol, Lord-Lieutenant of Ireland; Sir George Savile, Secretary at War; and Mr. Mackenzie some office equivalent in value to that he had quitted, but without the power, in Scotland; and all Lord Bute's friends to keep their offices. Lord Chief Justice Pratt to be made a Peer.

The King went out of town before dinner.

Late at night Mr. Grenville received a note from Lord Temple, telling him that one of the King's grooms had just called at his house with a letter from the King to Mr. Pitt, and was gone with it to Hayes. Nothing can be more truly affectionate than Lord Temple's conduct towards Mr. Grenville in all this transaction.

Wednesday, June 26th.—Mr. Pitt was about an hour with the King, who again pressed him to come into his service, but he declined. The King came very late to the Levée: he spoke civilly to Mr. Grenville; but his particular mark of grace seemed to be to Lord Granby. The Chancellor went into the Closet before the Levée, and when he came out told everybody that the negotiation with Mr. Pitt was broke off. The Chancellor had a great deal of discourse with Mr. Grenville, told him how much he had pressed the King to continue his old Ministry, and said the King had told him that the Duke of Cumberland had answered for Mr. Pitt's taking the Administration, which had induced His Majesty to take this step, and that it was singly by H. R. H.'s advice that he had done it. The Chancellor seemed to understand that Mr. Pitt was a good deal displeased at the Duke's having answered for him, and the Duke as much so at his not having answered his expectations [1]. The

---

[1] On this day the Duke of Cumberland wrote to Lord Albemarle:—
"I fear by what I understood last night from His Majesty, that we are all afloat again, Lord Temple having most peremptorily and determinately refused bearing a part in any shape, great or small, in the Administration to be formed. This declaration of Lord Temple's prevents Pitt from taking a share, which indeed most thoroughly and most heartily he had done. * * * * These circumstances, so different from what I hoped, and really thought were in a manner settled, must, I suppose, bring me to town again. * * * * By what I can pick up, Pitt is completely mortified, and I am heartily sorry for it, as he had entered more sincerely and cordially into the King's service, nay, and went further almost than the King's views." [a] That Pitt was really disappointed there can be little doubt. The often-quoted, but

[a] *Lord Albemarle's Memoirs of Lord Rockingham*, i. 214.

King seemed to have told the Chancellor all the political points which Mr. Pitt had insisted upon, such as the Prussian Treaty, General Warrants to be explained and settled, and Cyder Tax repealed. He likewise blamed the taxation of the Colonies, the unfunded debt, and the measures taken against smuggling in America, and disapproved the turning out Mr. Mackenzie. Some of these opinions Mr. Grenville heard from the Chancellor, others from Lord Lyttelton, as being fundamentals laid down by Mr. Pitt.

When the Levée was over, Mr. Grenville went into the Closet. The King spoke first, and began with ease and seeming good humour to talk to him about his journey into the country. Mr. Grenville then gave him the papers necessary to be signed, and spoke about the common business, and nothing else passed between them. The two Secretaries of State said the King's behaviour to them was exactly the same. The King went soon after three o'clock to Richmond.

Lord Temple dined with Mr. Grenville, and said he should go out of town the next day, after having been at the Drawing-room. Lord Temple went at nine o'clock to the Duke of Bolton's. The Duke of Cumberland is said to have been on Tuesday night with the King at Richmond.

Thursday, June 27th.—Lord Temple went to Hayes in the morning, and returned to go to the Drawing-room, but came too late: he went to Hayes that night, and

---

very apt and pathetic quotation from Virgil, which he is said to have pronounced to Lord Temple upon this occasion, fully proves it—

" Extinxti me teque, soror, populumque, patresque
Sidonios, urbemque tuam."—*Æn.* iv. 682.

said if he came back time enough, he would dine with
Mr. Grenville.

Friday, June 28th.—Mr. Grenville saw the King,
who received him civilly, began to speak first, but only
upon the common business.

Mr. Grenville received an intimation from Mr. Augustus Hervey that Lord Egmont had dropped that he
was surprised Mr. Grenville did not upon this occasion,
now that all negotiation was at an end, endeavour to
gain the King; that His Majesty must have a shyness
upon him, after what had passed, and an unwillingness
to speak first upon it, and that a gentle behaviour to
him, from his Ministers, might have an effect upon him.
Lord Temple did not come from Hayes 'till late at
night; he stayed about an hour with Mr. Grenville, took
his leave of him, and said he should set out the next
day after dinner for Stowe. Mr. Grenville receives fresh
assurances every day from a great variety of people of
their indignation at the ill-treatment he has received,
and of their determination to follow him through all
situations. Mr. Grenville went to dine at Shene: at
his return late at night, he found a letter from Lord
Temple, desiring to see him for a moment before he
went, but upon inquiry, he went out of town at three
o'clock.

Sunday, June 30th.—Mr. and Mrs. Grenville went
to the Drawing-room, and were very coldly received.
Mr. Grenville did not go into the Closet.

Monday, July 1st.—Mrs. Grenville met Lord Bateman
in Hyde Park, who told her that the Duke of Newcastle and General Conway were at Windsor Lodge on
Saturday with the Duke of Cumberland, and that nego-

tiations seemed to be carrying on there, though at the
same time Lord Albemarle's language was the blaming
the timidity of people who were afraid to undertake to
serve the King, and wondering at the situation.

Lord Thomond was told to-day that the Duke of
Cumberland is come to town.

Tuesday, July 2nd.—The report of this day is that
the Ministry is forming under the Duke of Cumberland
and the Duke of Newcastle, with Lord Rockingham at
the head of the Treasury.

Wednesday, July 3rd.—Mr. Grenville went into the
Closet; the King was civil; did his business, but said
nothing relative to the change of his Ministry. Mr.
Grenville asked His Majesty if he would give him
leave to recommend a person to him for the vacancy
in the Board of Excise, in Mr. Vernon's room. The
King said he would think of it. Mr. Grenville
knows very authentically that the management of the
King's business in the House of Commons has been
offered to Sir Wm. Baker, who declined it.

Thursday, July 4th.—Mr. Grenville did not go to
Court. The report prevailed of the new Administration being settled, and it was said that Lord Rockingham went to Adderbury to endeavour to persuade Mr.
Charles Townshend to take on with it. Mr. Grenville
saw the Chancellor in the evening, who slighted and
contemned the idea of the new arrangement, and said
the kingdom was lost if Mr. Grenville retired, and that
everybody universally agreed in the same language.

Friday, July 5th.—Lord Granby came to Mr. Grenville in the morning with the warmest assurances of his
attachment to him, and him alone; he told him that
he was determined to speak to the King; that he did

not think himself at liberty, after the many graces and
honours the King had conferred upon him, to throw
up his office, but that he meant to tell his Majesty that
he must remember that he came unwillingly into his
service upon the Duke of Newcastle's retiring, to whom
he had been attached : that when he was pleased to give
him the office of the Ordnance, he had signified to him
that he wished him to support his Government under
Mr. Grenville's administration, which he had done to
the utmost of his power in obedience to His Majesty's
commands ; that he had known Mr. Grenville 'till then
but as a common acquaintance, but that he thought
himself bound in honour to bear testimony to the fair-
ness and openness of his conduct to him, both as a friend
and a relation ; that he had examined his public conduct as far as he was able, and never had seen a circumstance in it, in which his own conviction had not concurred ; that he sincerely lamented the unhappy step
His Majesty meant to take in the parting with him, but
that if that was his determination, he did most humbly
entreat His Majesty to resume the office he now held,
as it was impossible for him to hold it in support of a
new Ministry, of which he must say he disapproved ;
that he did not mean to resign or to distress His Majesty's affairs, but most humbly to entreat him to resume
the office, and thereby to spare him the cruel alternative
of holding it under the imputation of doing it from
lucrative views, or of resigning it, which he should most
unwillingly do.

Lord Granby told Mr. Grenville that Lord Rockingham had sent to desire to speak to him, and that
he would come the next day and tell him what had
passed.

Mr. Grenville went to the King after the Levée, and took occasion to say to him that there were several things relating to his Revenue with which, from respect to His Majesty, he forbore to trouble him in the present situation of things, but that it was from respect alone that he did not do it: to which the King answered, " It is very true, Mr. Grenville, there are a good many things ;" and immediately turned the discourse. Mr. Grenville again named the vacancy in the Board of Excise, but the King said he would think of it.

The Chancellor told Mr. Grenville that he understood from the King, that nothing was as yet settled.

Mr. Charles Townshend came to town in the evening.

Saturday, July 6th.—Lord Townshend came to town : he had been sent to by Lord Egmont : he came to Mr. Grenville and made very strong professions to him, but did not mean to resign his office, though he would not engage to support the new Administration, nor to deviate from any of his former opinions : he told Mr. Grenville that his brother Charles had refused the offer Lord Rockingham had made him, of Chancellor of the Exchequer, and in his talk wanted to put it as a sacrifice to Mr. Grenville, who would never admit of it in that light ; said he called upon no man to resign, and that if Mr. Charles Townshend thought that situation under the new Ministry consistent with his honour, or desirable for his advantage, he was at liberty to take it.

Mr. Pitt was in town Friday morning to go to the Levée, but came too late.

Saturday, July 7th.—Mr. Grenville went to the Drawing-room, but not into the Closet : the King asked him two short questions.   Lord Mansfield was at the Drawing-room, and spoken to as usual, but the King did not wish to see him in the Close t: he had a great deal of conversation with Mr. Grenville, lamenting the deplorable state into which the King was bringing his affairs; that it was madness and desperation ; that in the new Ministry, he neither saw the man capable of directing the foreign business, nor of managing the revenue, nor what relates to the interior of the kingdom ; that he had a great personal regard for Lord Rockingham, who he thought was a man of sense, but unequal to the task he had undertaken from want of ability, experience, and health : that this system might be appointed, but so far from continuing could not even set out; and upon Mr. Grenville's saying that for his part he was weary of the scene, and glad to retire, Lord Mansfield entreated him to keep himself in such a situation as to return to it to save the kingdom from utter ruin, and to which without his assistance it would inevitably go.

Lord Granby went into the Closet, and when he came out reported to Mr. Grenville what had passed, and which had been conformable to what he said before to Mr. Grenville. The King seemed much agitated, pressed him earnestly to continue in his service, and upon Lord Granby pressing him to resume the office, which he did not see how he could hold without imputations dishonourable to him, as it was impossible for him to support a Ministry he disapproved, the King begged him not to leave his service and thereby add to the distress of his affairs ; that he left him entirely at liberty to act as he thought fit, which he did not doubt would be like an honest man, and a man of honour.

Lord Granby made a very strong encomium on Mr.

Grenville, and declared his attachment to him in the strongest terms, and with declarations that he hoped it would continue as long as they lived. The King heard him patiently; and upon Lord Granby telling him that Lord Rockingham had pressed him to take part in the Government, which Lord Granby had absolutely refused, and that Lord Rockingham had then desired him to give his support to the new Ministry, Lord Granby had said it was impossible for him to support an Administration which he disapproved,—the King said Lord Rockingham had done unwisely in asking that.

The King spoke to Lord Townshend in the Drawing-room to come to him into his Closet. He there pressed him very earnestly to persuade Mr. Charles Townshend to take the office of Chancellor of the Exchequer, which Lord Townshend continued to refuse both on his brother's account and his own, declaring strongly his disapprobation of the new Ministry, and his firm adherence to his former opinions, and telling His Majesty that he could never act in contradiction to them, nor persuade his brother to what he could not do himself: that he had been called upon by His Majesty to oppose the very men His Majesty was now taking into his service, and that he should disgrace himself by supporting them.

The Chancellor went into the Closet, and spoke to Mr. Grenville when he came out, but did not care to narrate exactly what had passed, though he told Mr. Grenville that he had still blamed the change of the Ministry in strong terms, and had exposed to the King the danger of the measure. The King heard him patiently, but seemed determined, and showed him a long list of names and offices, but not finally settled. He told him that it had been proposed to him to make Lord Chief

Justice Pratt a Peer, with the reversion of a Teller's place for his son, but he had given no answer upon it.

The King spoke to the Lord Chancellor about calling the Parliament in September, to which the Chancellor objected, and said he must certainly do so if his opinion was asked in Council. He told Mr. Grenville that he meant to give no facility whatever to the new Administration, and that if ever he did come to Council, it would be to oppose everything that was proposed.

Mr. Grenville received a letter from Lord Sandwich inclosing a note he had just received from the Duke of Bedford, in which he told him that on Thursday the Duke of Marlborough had received a proposition of making him Master of the Horse, and giving any place he should wish to his brother Lord Charles, if he would take on with the new Administration, but that the Duke of Marlborough had in the handsomest manner declined. The King, notwithstanding this transaction on the Thursday, said to Lord Granby at the Review, at eight o'clock on Friday morning, that he hoped his Lordship knew that he had no thoughts of removing the Duke of Rutland from his office, whatever reports he might hear.

Monday, July 8*th.*—Things continued much in the same situation.

Tuesday, July 9*th.*—The King came very early to the Queen's house, where he saw Lord Townshend, and again endeavoured to prevail with him to persuade his brother Charles to take the office of Secretary of State, which they now offered him; but Lord Townshend still persisted in his refusal, alleging for reason that it would be inconsistent with his former conduct to support a Government formed of the very people he had been called in to oppose, and measures directly contrary to his former opinions : he likewise alleged the injury he felt as having been done to him in attempts having been made to seduce his brother from him, by negotiating with him at least ten days before he himself had received any message. The King afterwards saw Mr. Charles Townshend, who, in conformity to his brother, still refused to accept the Seals.

The King went out of town about eleven o'clock.

Wednesday, July 10th.—Mr. Grenville received a letter from my Lord Chancellor at half-past ten, signifying to him the King's commands to attend him at twelve o' clock at St. James's with the Seal of his Office.

When Mr. Grenville came into the Closet, the King told him that from what the Duke of Bedford had said to him the last time he saw him, he understood that the Duke had resigned himself, and in the name of the rest of the Ministers, and that he had therefore found himself at liberty to form another Ministry, which he had accordingly done. Mr. Grenville said he was apprized that His Majesty had understood it so ; that the Duke of Bedford had shown to Mr. Grenville the substance of what he had said to His Majesty, viz., "that he hoped His Majesty would be pleased to give his countenance to his Ministers, and for the future let his support and his authority go together, or else that he would give his authority where he was pleased to give his favour :" that for his (Mr. Grenville's) own part, he had not resigned, nor even if he had intended it, should have employed another person to do it for him, having the honour of such constant access to His Majesty, and having seen him both the day before and after the Duke of Bedford had been with him, but that he certainly concurred in opinion that it was absolutely necessary that His Majesty's favour and authority should go together; that he must remind His Majesty that he had told him about two months ago, when he saw that he had withdrawn his confidence from him, that he did not wish to continue in his service after he had lost his favour, that the situation was every way too responsible and too irksome. The King said he remembered he had said so. Mr. Grenville said he had repeated this to His Majesty when, after having intended to dismiss him from his service very lately, he had again recalled him to it, and had besought His Majesty not to suffer him to serve him, if it was with any force upon his mind : that he was utterly ignorant for what cause he had forfeited his favour and good opinion, and the more, as he did not recollect, in more than two years that he had been in the office of First Lord of the Treasury, that he had ever proposed any measure to His Majesty which had not met with his approbation, or that His Majesty had ever expressed a dislike to, 'till after His Majesty had thought fit to desire him to continue in his service, after having dismissed him.

He had mentioned Mr. Mackenzie's removal, which was the opinion of His Majesty's other servants as well as his own ; that upon that occasion indeed His Majesty had marked much uneasiness and reluctance, but that, as he must observe, could not be the cause of His Majesty's displeasure against him, since his own former dismission had been previous to it. He therefore most earnestly entreated His Majesty to apprize him by what means, either omission or commission, he had drawn down his displeasure upon him, since that circumstance alone gave him any uneasiness.

The King said in general that he had found himself too much constrained, and that when he had anything proposed to him, it was no longer as counsel, but what he was to *obey*.

Mr. Grenville started at that word, said he did not know how to repeat it, that surely His Majesty could not mean that word to him, who knew that there was not that power on earth in whom His Majesty ought to acknowledge superiority, but that it was the duty of his servants, sworn to that purpose, to deliver their opinions to him upon such things as were expedient for his Government; but that as he could not recollect any instance bordering upon anything that could have given His Majesty such an impression, he begged he would mark it to him. The King named the proposing Lord Weymouth for Lord Lieutenant of Ireland; that he himself had thought well of Lord Weymouth, and had a good opinion of him, but thought there were objections to him for that situation. Mr. Grenville desired His Majesty to remember that Lord Weymouth was no nomination of his. The King said he knew that; but that he had espoused him because the Duke of Bedford did. Mr. Grenville begged His Majesty would recollect that he had at the same time asked him if he had any person for whom he wished it, and had shown His Majesty how little choice he had of proper subjects from various circumstances; the King said it was true.

Mr. Grenville then entreated His Majesty, from his known justice and honour, to clear him from the malice of his enemies, who he found had ventured to spread about that he had been wanting in respect to His Majesty, so far as to threaten to quit his service, and to leave the Seals at the Closet door. The King with some emotion said, "Never, Mr. Grenville, never: it is a falsehood," and repeated it once or twice.

He then said he must trespass still further on His Majesty's goodness, and desire him to say whether he had engaged with Lord Bute to share the power with him, and had since betrayed him, which was another report propagated by his enemies, and he appealed to His Majesty's honour whether he had not the most express declaration both from His Majesty and Lord Bute, that Lord Bute should never publicly or privately intermeddle in any business whatever, and whether in consequence of this declaration, Lord Bute did not, at the time of Mr. Grenville's leaving the Admiralty to take the office of First Lord of the Treasury, go to Harrogate, in confirmation of it, to Lord Halifax, Lord Egremont, and Mr. Grenville. That at the time when Mr. Grenville had the Seals given him as Secretary of State, he came in to act with Lord Bute, who was then at the head of the Treasury; that His Majesty had been pleased by Lord Bute's advice to take the Seals from him, and to appoint him to the Admiralty; that however hard this usage had appeared to him, his respect and attachment to the King, which was unbounded, and which had been the means of his making such sacrifices to his service as no other servant had it in their power to make, made him obey without repining. That in August, 1763, when His Majesty had been pleased to send to Mr. Pitt, upon that treaty not taking effect, His Majesty had called him back again to his service, and again upon the strongest assurances and declarations that Lord Bute was absolutely to retire, and not to intermeddle in any shape with the Government, and

that he had His Majesty's authority to make these
assurances to all his friends. The King assented to all
this, and Mr. Grenville went on to remind His Majesty
of the success with which his service had been attended,
—success far beyond Mr. Grenville's most sanguine
hopes, notwithstanding which he had the mortification
to see his service unacceptable, and himself lost in His
Majesty's confidence by the malice of his enemies. The
King took occasion to assure Mr. Grenville in some part
of this conversation that Lord Bute had no hand in
advising the present change. Mr. Grenville answered,
that he was glad that a person whom His Majesty
honoured with his favour and confidence had not
advised a measure which he feared would be productive
of so much weakness and disorder to his Government.

The King's whole conduct was civil, imputing no
blame, but giving no word of approbation throughout
the whole conversation. Mr. Grenville told him he
understood that the plan of his new Administration was
a total subversion of every act of the former; that nothing
having been undertaken as a measure without His
Majesty's approbation, he knew not how he would let
himself be persuaded to see it in so different a light,
and most particularly on the regulations concerning the
Colonies ; that he besought His Majesty, as he valued
his own safety, not to suffer any one to advise him to
separate or draw the line between his British and
American dominions ; that his Colonies was the richest
jewel of his Crown ; that for his own part he must
uniformly maintain his former opinions both in Parliament and out of it ; that whatever was proposed in
Parliament must abide the sentence passed upon it there,
but that if any man ventured to defeat the regulations
laid down for the Colonies, by a slackness in the exe-

cution, he should look upon him as a criminal and the betrayer of his country.

Mr. Grenville thanked the King for the justice he had done him in his appeal against the aspersions of his enemies, gave him his papers to sign, went through an account with him, which the King gave him his word should never go out of his own hands, for which he likewise thanked him, saying there were those now in his service to whose honour he should be sorry to trust, and withdrew.

Lord Thomond went to the King after the Levée, and told His Majesty that his personal attachment to Mr. Grenville, which proceeded not only from his love for him as a friend and brother, but likewise from his great abilities and integrity as a public Minister, joined to the strictest friendship, had united him to him in such a manner, that neither his honour nor his opinion could justify him in continuing in His Majesty's service after his dismission : he therefore most humbly begged leave to resign his office[1]; that wherever his new Administration proceeded upon the views and principles Mr. Grenville had pursued, he should with the same cheerfulness support his Government out of office as he had done while he was in it, but that he much apprehended that would not be the case. The King answered, " My Lord, I always took you for a very honest man, and your behaviour now confirms it." The King then took up his words about opposition, and said he thought he understood by what he had said, that in such points as were not contrary to his former opinions, he would support his measures.

Lord Thomond explained that still further by saying

---

[1] Lord Thomond was Cofferer of the Household ; he was succeeded in that office by Lord Scarborough.

that having entirely approved of Mr. Grenville's plan of government, his support must go in proportion as these gentlemen did or did not deviate from that system.

The King looked struck and uneasy while he was talking. Mr. Grenville went to the Levée, where the King asked him one cold question.

Lord Rockingham was declared First Lord of the Treasury; Mr. Dowdeswell, Chancellor of the Exchequer; Duke of Grafton, Secretary for the Northern department; Mr. Conway for the Southern.

The Duke of Newcastle was above an hour in the King's Closet. Mr. Charles Townshend went in for a minute. The Duke of Newcastle was more caressed than anybody at the Levée.

Thursday, July 11th.—Mr. Grenville let in everybody that visited him : a great variety of people came, among others the Duke of Richmond, who spoke rather not warmly of the new Administration, and commended Mr. Grenville extremely.

Lady Egremont said the Drawing-room was thin : the King did not speak to her.

Friday, July 12th.—Lord Winchilsea was declared President ; Lord Ashburnham kissed hands for the great Wardrobe. Lords Besborough and Grantham for the Post Office ; Lord Scarborough for the Cofferer ; and Lord Villiers for Vice-Chamberlain.

Monday, July 15th.—The King came to town early in the morning. Lord Winchilsea was named President, and Lord Chief Justice Pratt made a Peer by the name of Baron Camden, and the Duke of Newcastle Privy Seal, which the Duke of Marlborough had resigned : the King pressed him to keep it, and to consider of it again.

Mr. Pitt and Lady Chatham came to Downing Street in the evening, stayed about an hour, and then went on to Hayes.

Tuesday, 16th July.—The Board of Treasury consists of Lord Rockingham, Lord John Cavendish, Mr. Dowdeswell, Mr. Onslow, and Mr. T. Townshend.

Wednesday, July 17th.—The Duke of Bedford came to town to dine with Mr. Grenville, was extremely warm and cordial in his expressions to him. Lord Powis (who resigned on Sunday) was of the dinner; so were Lord Halifax, Lord Sandwich, Lord Weymouth, Lord Farnham, Sir L. Dundas, Mr. Rigby, Lord Thomond, &c. Lord Granby sent his excuse. Lord Mansfield came to Mr. Grenville in the morning, deploring the situation of the kingdom, and the disorder into which the King had plunged his affairs : he said he did not see any prospect of amendment, for that things were now in that situation, that if the offer was to come to Mr. Grenville to-morrow, he scarce knew what it would be possible for him to do with it. Mr. Grenville agreed with him, and lamented the general state of things.

Mr. Thomas Pelham kissed hands for Treasurer of the Household, and Lord Edgecumbe for the office of Comptroller.

Thursday, July 18th.—Lord Granby came to Mr. Grenville in the morning, and after a long conversation upon his future ideas, and the state of affairs in general, the sum of his declaration amounted to his supporting Mr. Grenville in Parliament, in everything that had been a measure of his, and in particular the question of General Warrants, or any personal attack upon Mr. Grenville; but that whatever could carry with it the air of a peevish or factious opposition was contrary to his ideas, and what he never would give in to, though at the same time he never would be sent down to attend by the present Administration. He concluded with great personal attachment to Mr. Grenville, and said he would come to see him at Wotton.

Mr. Yorke came to Mr. Grenville to notify to him that he should take the office of Attorney-General, assigning for his reasons that he could not see another Attorney-General put over his head, who should have precedence, and priority of audience; that he had received the King's commands to take the office, with which he could now the more willingly comply, as many of the old Whigs and those with whom he had formerly acted composed the Administration; that he had endeavoured and wished to have something done in this instance that might be agreeable to the present Attorney-General. Mr. Grenville said he must know that could not be the case, since they meant to turn him out, but that he could say nothing as to all this, but that every man was the best judge of his own situation. The conversation was long, and ended with great personal civility from Mr. Yorke to Mr. Grenville.

The Duke of Bedford came in the evening, renewed his professions to Mr. Grenville, spoke with a good deal of uneasiness of his own particular situation, and said he had had a stone thrown at him twice that day; he said he was going to France immediately to stay a month; (this Mr. Grenville highly disapproved, but having often shown his Grace his dislike to it, he said nothing to it then;) that as soon as he returned, the Duchess and he would come to Wotton in their way to Blenheim, and that he should afterwards fix at Woburn, except when his health required the Bath waters, for that in his particular circumstances he did not see how he could attend Parliament.

Friday, July 19*th.*—The Governors of the Bank came to Mr. Grenville, said they did it as a mark of respect, that they sincerely lamented his dismission, and could never do business with any man with the same ease they had done it with him ; that they understood Lord Rockingham gave it out that he did not mean to continue in the situation, and only held it for a time ; that they most heartily wished to meet Mr. Grenville in the same public station he had held, at the next meeting of Parliament, and seemed sanguine in their hopes of its being so. Mr. Grenville discouraged those hopes, thanked them for their particular civility to him, and begged them to give every facility they could to Lord Rockingham to prevent any national distress.

Lord Dartmouth kissed hands for the Board of Trade, and Lord Barrington for Secretary at War.

Mr. Jenkinson came to Bath in *November,* 1765, where he had several conversations with Mr. Grenville, all tending to the justification of Lord Bute's conduct, and particularly upon the late change of Ministry, which he endeavoured to persuade Mr. Grenville had not been brought about by Lord Bute's influence, saying that he never had seen the King but twice during his illness in the spring, which fact Mr. Grenville could not be brought to believe. He owned, however, to Mr. Grenville that the intercourse in writing between His Majesty and Lord Bute always continued, telling him that he knew that the King wrote him a journal every day of what passed, and as minute a one as if, said he, " your boy at school was directed by you to write his journal to you."

Mr. Grenville came to London from Bath on November 14th, and on Friday the 15th he went with Lord Thomond to the Levée. The King received them both very coldly, asking them each two questions; and was still colder at the Drawing-room on Sunday, the 17th; but the Queen was extremely gracious to Mr. Grenville, particularly in her inquiries after Mrs. Grenville's health, and continues to ask very particularly after her of Lady Egremont.

December 9th, 1765.—Lord Halifax came to Mr. Grenville, and told him he had just had overtures made to him from a Peer who was in the present Administration, whose name he was not at liberty to mention, but who told him he came to him by authority to tell him how reluctantly the King had parted with him, and how much he wished to have him in his service again; that he would do well to turn his thoughts that way, and see whether a proposition of this kind ought to be disregarded by him, and the more so as some of those who Lord Halifax thought his friends were now making up for themselves and their family without any regard to him; nay, that even whilst they were acting with him in Government they had wanted to have disposed of the Seals if the King would have consented to it.

Lord Halifax's answer was, that as to the first part he had little reason to think that the King had parted with him reluctantly, since he had dismissed him from his service at half an hour's warning; that as to the joining the present Administration, he so thoroughly disapproved of them that he could never think of it, but should continue to act with those friends with whom he had been in Government, and of whom he had not the least reason to complain, neither then nor now; nor could he add any credit to the suggestions made against them.

Mr. Grenville told Lord Halifax he had acted very honourably; that he found from all hands the Ministers were everywhere trying to detach individuals, and were looked upon by most people to be in a falling state; that as to the suggestions thrown out to his Lordship against those who had been with him upon the scene, he must know that union was their crime and not division, for that he (Mr. Grenville) might have remained First Commissioner of the Treasury if he would have consented to a change of the Secretaries of State, and that, on the other hand, the Secretaries might have remained, giving up the First Commissioner of the Treasury and the President; that the Chancellor, who had given them all up, proved the truth of this by having been continued.

DETACHED FRAGMENTS IN THE HANDWRITING OF MRS. GRENVILLE, FORMING A SEQUEL TO MR. GRENVILLE'S DIARY.

1765. *Tuesday, March 5th.*—I was told that Mr. Beckford went down the Saturday before to Mr. Dickenson's, near Dunstable, and from thence sent over to Lord Bute at Luton, to desire leave to wait upon him, but Lord Bute declined the visit.

Tuesday, March 19th.—Lord Fife made me a visit, and told me he had lately seen the Duke of York, who had expressed himself with great civility towards, and approbation of, Mr. Grenville, commending particularly his conduct in the proposing the American Tax, and the purchase of the Isle of Man. His Royal Highness had some time before insinuated as if he thought Mr. Grenville had been backward in the transactions between the King and His Royal Highness, but seemed now to think that he acted properly in an affair of so delicate a nature; he said Mr. Grenville had much to struggle with, and that during the King's late illness he had been sorry to see Mr. Grenville come twice to the Queen's house, without being admitted to see the King, though Lord Bute's chair was both times waiting in the court, and that once His Royal Highness told the King that Mr. Grenville was there, but he believed he did not see him that day, having (as His Royal Highness said) been perhaps fatigued with too long a conversation with Lord Bute.

1765. *Tuesday, April 30th.* — The Regency Bill was read for the second time in the House of Lords. Lord Lyttelton made a motion to address the King to name the Regent, but the Lords having another question before them, would not then go upon a new one. Lord Wycombe (Shelburne) spoke against any Regency Bill whatever. Lord Temple spoke warmly but with guard against this particular Bill, so did the Duke of Newcastle. The Duke of Grafton very short. Lord Halifax, Lord Sandwich, the Duke of Bedford, the Chancellor, and Lord Mansfield spoke in favour of the Bill; when the question was put upon the commitment, the numbers were—Contents 124, Not Contents 9. After the Question, Lord Lyttelton renewed his Motion, the consideration of which was postponed till the next day.

1765. *Friday, May 3rd.*—Lord Hillsborough told me that he knew, from the best authority, that the Princess of Wales was extremely offended at the Amendment proposed that day in the House of Lords to the Regency Bill, declaring the Royal family to be such only as were lineally descended from King George II., which was a direct affront to her. Lord Hillsborough said he understood that Amendment to come from the King, to which Lady Bute said she knew nothing of that, but if it did it must have been much misrepresented to him [1].

Lord Botetourt told me that Lord Despencer had mentioned that very Amendment to him at the first reading of the Bill as they sat together in the House of Lords.

Monday, May 13th.—The Silk Bill was thrown out by the House of Lords. The same night Lord Northumberland went to the Duke of Cumberland and began a discourse upon general topics of hounds and horses, &c., and then insensibly led it to politics, and opened the idea of the intended change of the Ministry [2].

On *Tuesday, the 14th of May*, the weavers marched in a large body to the King at Richmond, and sent in

---

[1] See *ante*, page 150.

[2] See Lord Albemarle's *Memoirs of Lord Rockingham*, vol. i. p. 191, where this transaction is, in error, referred to *Monday, 6th of May.* The Duke of Cumberland states that Lord Northumberland came to him by the King's orders, and with a desire that he " should endeavour to see whether Mr. Pitt and Lord Temple, with the other great Whig families, could not be brought to form him a strong and a lasting Administration, which might empower him to form systems at home and abroad, such as the dangers of the times might require : desiring withal that this negotiation might be carried on with the utmost secrecy and celerity, as its magnitude would allow of."

a message demanding redress, and saying they were starving. The King sent them a message telling them to go home, and that he would do all he could for them.

Lord Temple went to Stowe the day before, and on Wednesday morning at two o'clock he received a letter sent to him by express from the Duke of Cumberland, desiring him to come to town with all speed.

Wednesday, May 15*th.*—Lord Temple came to London, sent to the Duke of Cumberland to acquaint him with his arrival, and received a message from His Royal Highness desiring him to be at Beaufort House that evening. Lord Temple went there, and His Royal Highness opened to him the plan of the change of the Ministry, proposing Lord Northumberland to be at the head of the Treasury : Mr. Pitt and Mr. Charles Townshend Secretaries of State, and Lord Temple President, or Privy Seal. Lord Temple made his objections to this plan, saying particularly that he would not make himself a party to the propping up Lord Bute's power, nor would he act under Lord Northumberland, who he looked upon as Lord Bute's lieutenant. Lord Temple was desired by His Royal Highness to go to Hayes, which he accordingly did, but brought back the same unfavourable answer on Thursday the 16th.

Friday, May 17*th.*—The Duke of Cumberland sent Lord Albemarle to Hayes to treat with Mr. Pitt, but he had no better success than the former messages had produced.

Saturday, May 18*th.*—The Duke of Cumberland went to the King at Richmond in the evening, and stayed extremely late.

Sunday, May 19*th.*—The Duke of Cumberland sent early in the morning to Lord Temple to let him know that H.R.H. had the King's commands to go down to Hayes, and desired Lord Temple would meet him there. Lord Temple set out as soon as he could, but His Royal Highness had been there two hours before he came there. His Royal Highness told both Lord Temple and Mr. Pitt that he came with *carte blanche* from the King. Lord Temple and Mr. Pitt were determined not to take the Administration whilst Lord Bute's power existed. The Duke always evaded any explicit declaration on that head, which determined them to throw all possible difficulties in the way. They therefore made five propositions : the first was a new system of foreign politics ; the second, that provision should be made for the unfunded debt ; the third was the making Lord Chief Justice Pratt a Peer, and bringing him on to the head of the law ; the fourth was the settling the question of General Warrants by a Bill or Declaration ; the fifth was restoring the officers who had been dismissed.

The Duke took all these proposals *ad referendum,* which still made them more determinate in their resolution to break off the negotiation, and have nothing to do with it [1]. The Duke stayed five hours at Hayes, and then went to report the result of this conference to the King.

---

[1] It would appear from this statement that Mr. Pitt and Lord Temple agreed in their *mutual determination* not to accept the King's offers, and that it was not from any difficulties created by Lord Temple *alone,* as has been generally supposed, that the formation of a Government was prevented at this crisis ; nevertheless, it is most probable that Mr. Pitt had a real inclination to have attempted it, if Lord Temple would have concurred.

Monday, May 20th.—Proposals were made to Lord Lyttelton to make him First Lord of the Treasury, in order to form an Administration without Lord Temple or Mr. Pitt.

EARL TEMPLE TO MR. GRENVILLE.

Wednesday morning, January 15, 1766.

MY DEAR BROTHER,—I heard you last night [1], so much to your honour, give the lie direct to the vile misrepresentations which had been so industriously propagated against you, and I feel so much pleasure in it that I must beg you will accept of the small pittance of a thousand pounds transferred this day to your account at Mr. Coutts's in testimony of my joy and conviction. I am, &c.   TEMPLE.

MR. GRENVILLE TO EARL TEMPLE.

January 15, 1766.

MY DEAR BROTHER,—Your approbation I shall always think my greatest honour, and feel your friendship and kindness as my greatest comfort. Judge, then, how sensibly I must be affected by the assurances and proofs

---

[1] In a debate on the Address at the meeting of Parliament, when the subject of the Stamp Act was introduced. Mr. Grenville's policy was attacked by Pitt on this occasion in one of his celebrated speeches. Wilkes has alluded to this speech in a letter to Cotes, dated Feb. 15, 1766. " I hear from every quarter that Lord Temple and Mr. Pitt are entirely separated; and that when Mr. Pitt made the American speech, Lord Temple was in the House under the gallery, and made use of the same expressions against his brother-in-law, which he used against his brother George in the same place three years ago. I hear that Bedford, Sandwich, Halifax, &c., are united with Lord Temple and George Grenville."—*Almon's Memoirs of Wilkes*, vol. ii. p. 226.

which you have given me both of the one and of the other. The honourable testimony which your affection has prompted you to give me upon this occasion, I accept with the sincerest thanks and gratitude. It makes me proud and happy that you should think I deserve it. May I ever continue to do so, and to show you by every means in my power how cordially and truly I am your most affectionate Brother,

GEORGE GRENVILLE.

LADY CHATHAM TO EARL TEMPLE.

Hayes, Monday morning, January 20, 1766.

DEAR BROTHER,—You being in town and I here, which prevents my having the pleasure of seeing you, I desire to take this way of expressing the real satisfaction I have in hearing so good an account of your health. I am besides truly anxious to express to you my unalterable affection under all circumstances, and my constant wishes that no misapprehensions may ever suggest to your mind that I am or ever can be changed in my sentiments towards you, being ever, your loving Sister,

CHATHAM [1].

I desire my compliments to Lady Temple.

EARL TEMPLE TO LADY CHATHAM.

Pall Mall, January 20, 1766.

MY DEAR LADY CHATHAM,—I am much obliged to you for the kind inquiries contained in your letter, and I shall certainly call upon you as soon as I know you

[1] Lady Chatham signs thus, as a Baroness in her own right.

are in town. I did wish to be sure to hear an account both of your own health and Mr. Pitt's from the Bath, but you deprived me of that pleasure[1].

Many unfortunate events have fallen out both for the public, and affecting the comfort of my private life. Misapprehensions I believe are, oftener than realities, the cause of much unhappiness, and I refer myself only to your recollection of what has passed betwixt you and me in many unreserved conversations, manifesting towards you such real esteem and affection in one who is above dissimulation, and very much your affectionate Brother, TEMPLE.

LADY CHATHAM TO EARL TEMPLE.

Hayes, Thursday, January 23, 1766.

MY DEAR BROTHER,—Was it not for a violent cold which I have, as well as four of the children, I would have had the pleasure of coming to you myself instead

---

[1] There had been a cessation of correspondence, and much coolness between Mr. Pitt and Lord Temple for some months past. The "*misapprehensions*" to which Lady Chatham refers, probably took their rise from the failure of the negotiation in the July preceding, when it was supposed that Mr. Pitt was compelled to decline the King's offers in consequence of difficulties on the part of Lord Temple. Wilkes, writing to Humphrey Cotes on the 4th of December, 1765, after mentioning Pitt as "the best orator, and the worst letter-writer of the age," adds, "I grieve at the coldness between Lord Temple and Pitt. I wish that, like most bosom friendships, it does not end in an inveterate hatred. George Grenville had better have continued as he was * * * * * * * * * * * I foresee all the consequences of a disunion, and there is nothing I desire so earnestly to hear of as their reconciliation. United, they were too weak against the favourite. Separated, I fear both will be undone. Nothing can so effectually do the business of the favourite, as the quarrel between the two brothers."[a]

[a] *Almon's Memoirs of Wilkes*, ii. 217. I regret that I am unable to explain the passage which relates to George Grenville : the suppression indicates something important.

of this letter; and will call upon you as soon as ever I am able to go to London. In the meantime I desire to assure you my not writing to you from Bath did not proceed from any resolution to the contrary, but from many uncertainties about my own motions, and from various occurrences. I am deeply grieved for whatever affects your private comfort, and feel too sensibly for my health, how much my own has been wounded from the day of your unfortunate dissent from Mr. Pitt.

One of the dearest pleasures to my mind, and which gave me the most heartfelt joy, was the persuasion, that I was possessed of your real esteem and sincere love. I acknowledge to the full, the instances of your confidence in me, and all your goodness to me in the different marks of your friendship towards me.

For misapprehensions, I can only say, that there may be such, though I do not know any, and that misapprehensions will arise where false appearances (if they are such) are so sustained, as to have in general the same effects as if they were realities. However things are, this I am sure of, that I have invariably wished your happiness, and never have ceased to be at any time, your most loving Sister,   CHATHAM.

EARL TEMPLE TO LADY CHATHAM.

Pall Mall, January 24, 1766.

MY DEAR LADY CHATHAM,—It is no small satisfaction to me to find by your letter of yesterday that the long discontinuance of our correspondence, on your part, did not proceed from any resolution of putting an end to it, but from various occurrences which prevented me from hearing from you at all during a very considerable and interesting period.

I do not mean to enter into observations upon all or any part of what has passed since the day of my dissent from Mr. Pitt. I have my recollections, and events have verified my opinions. I can appeal to my own heart, and I know the purity of my own intentions sufficient to vindicate me to myself, and to enable me in some degree to bear up against new scenes of family disunion. I share in every grief you feel, and I am sure happiness of every sort was at hand.

Whenever your cold permits you to visit this devoted city, I shall be very happy in your affording me the melancholy satisfaction of assuring you that I am inviolably, my dear Lady Chatham, your most affectionate Brother, TEMPLE.

I am sorry the amiable little family are indisposed.

MR. PITT TO MR. GRENVILLE.

Bond Street, Saturday morning, (February 8, 1766).

MR. PITT presents his compliments to Mr. Grenville, and understanding that his retiring from the Committee last night, when Mr. Grenville was beginning to speak, gave him displeasure, he desires to assure him that nothing could be further from his thoughts than to mark the least want of personal regard to Mr. Grenville, being, in truth, not in a condition to remain in the Committee, and having requested their leave to retire[1].

---

[1] Mr. Grenville had moved an Address to the King to give orders for enforcing the laws in America, and carrying all Acts of the English

Mr. Pitt begs to inquire after Mrs. Grenville's health, which he sincerely hopes is much better, and to present his compliments to her.

MR. GRENVILLE TO MR. PITT.

Bolton Street, Saturday morning, February 8, 1766.

MR. GRENVILLE presents his compliments to Mr. Pitt, and is sorry that he was not in a condition to remain in the Committee last night after he had spoken, as Mr. Grenville found himself under the necessity of giving an answer to many passages contained in Mr. Pitt's speech, in which he apprehended himself to be personally called upon, and to which he earnestly wished Mr. Pitt could have heard his answer.

Mr. Grenville is obliged to Mr. Pitt for his assurances that nothing was further from his thoughts than to mark the least want of personal regard towards him; and Mr. and Mrs. Grenville join in returning their thanks for his inquiry after Mrs. Grenville's health, which they hope is better than it has been, and shall be glad to receive the like favourable account of Mr. Pitt and Lady Chatham.

MR. WILKES TO EARL TEMPLE.

Holles Street, May 15, 1766.

MY LORD,—If I could have seen Mr. Cotes the hour of my return, I should then have desired him to assure your Lordship that I am come to my native country with

Parliament into execution. Pitt retired from the House after making a speech in opposition to Mr. Grenville's motion, which was negatived by a majority of 274 to 134.

a heart not in the least changed, but always full of the infinite personal obligations I have to Lord Temple, and of gratitude to him as an Englishman.

I am returned without the knowledge of any one person in or out of the Administration. I declared to all my friends at Paris, three days before I set out, that I was coming on a tour to England, and I sent for an order for post-horses in my own name.

I believe that I shall soon have my pardon to plead the first day of next term. I find universal good humour with respect to myself. I have entered into no political engagements, but I have declared very explicitly to the friends of the present Ministers that no consideration whatever shall induce me, in any moment of my life, to do anything offensive, or in the least disobliging, with respect to Lord Temple[1].

I beg to assure Lady Temple of my sincere regard and esteem.

[1] Wilkes had no personal communication with Lord Temple upon the occasion of this hurried visit to London. His arrival, it appears, was unexpected even by his friend Humphrey Cotes, who afterwards furnished Almon with an account of Wilkes's negotiations with the Ministers at this time. (See *Anecdotes of Lord Chatham*, vol. ii. p. 154, ed. 1792.) In this narrative he says that Wilkes desired him " to assure Lord Temple of his best respects ; and that he would have paid his respects in person, but as he was in an interesting negotiation with the present Ministers, he hoped his Lordship would excuse him. I went immediately to Lord Temple's bedside, and related the above to him. He seemed extremely well satisfied with Mr. Wilkes's conduct, and wished most heartily that the Ministers might be as good as their promises. He desired me to convey his kind compliments to Mr. Wilkes, and to assure him of his friendship and approbation of his conduct upon the present occasion ; at the same time he told me that he was very certain that Lord Rockingham had not the least intention of serving Mr. Wilkes, and feared they would deceive him." Lord Temple was right. Wilkes was disappointed both of a pardon or a pension, and he made a precipitate retreat from London, and returned to Paris.

I am ever, my Lord, your Lordship's most obedient
and devoted humble servant,   JOHN WILKES.

MR. WHATELY TO MR. GRENVILLE.

May 23, 1766.

DEAR SIR,—Inclosed I send you the Bill for opening
the Free Ports in Dominica and Jamaica, as I imagined
you might wish to look it over. I am not master of the
subject, and therefore cannot point out the imperfections
of the scheme, but at first view I think every one must
be disappointed to see so great a liberty guarded by
so few restrictions, and no additional provisions made
against the new dangers to which this licence will expose the commerce of the Colonies. I suppose the Bill
will be proceeded on next Monday, but there is other
business to be brought on before the rising of Parliament.

A provision for the Dukes of York and Gloucester is
to be made out of that fallen in by the death of the
Duke of Cumberland, and though very proper to be
done, seems to be introduced very improperly so late in
the year; though I see the precedent of the 15,000*l.* to
the Duke of Cumberland may be quoted, which was
brought into the House on 3rd May, 1739, and carried
through in five days. That was by message; this, it is
said by some, is to be moved in the revived Committee
of Supply; and by others, it is to be only an Address to
His Majesty to desire him to pay it out of the Civil
List, and to promise to replace it out of the next Aids.
This, I believe, will be the proceeding, and against this
I have heard a very strong language held, that it is the
most ungracious way of doing an agreeable thing; that

it is loading the Civil List, already oppressed; that if it should be necessary to apply to Parliament for a Civil List debt, why add this sum to it? that it is unfair to bring this in at a time when many will by their absence be deprived of an opportunity of expressing their zeal for the Royal family; why throw a slur upon such a transaction by bringing it in at the end of a Sessions, as if a full House would not have approved of it; that the greatness of the boon from His Majesty to the people in altering the Civil List revenues, is not sufficiently known, and ought to be stated, &c., &c. [1]

You know best whether you would choose to be present when the Address is moved for, or how far you wish to say anything, which at least you had not written before.

There will at the same time, I hear, be a motion for the Queen of Denmark's portion, which must be made in a Committee of Supply.

The Duke of Richmond is to be Secretary of State for the Southern department [2], General Conway for the Northern, and the Colonies (at least those of the Continent) to be restored to the Board of Trade, with more active powers than were ever vested in Lord Halifax; even so far (it is said) as to make the first Lord of Trade Secretary of State for the Plantations.

Charles Townshend's account of his transaction about the Seals is, that when he was first offered them, he refused them because the system would never do, with all the abilities of the House of Commons against Administration, and no power trusted in anybody there; that he was next offered them with a Peerage, which he said was worse and worse, as his family were not in circum-

---

[1] See *Walpole's Memoirs of George III.*, vol. ii. p. 328.
[2] On the resignation of the Duke of Grafton.

stances to make that situation desirable, and he himself too young to retire into an Hospital [1] ; that he was then offered to be Secretary of State for the Plantations, and on declining that also, he was told that it was very extraordinary such offices should go a-begging ; that if the present system broke up, it must be laid at his door ; that the Ministers had too much spirit to be Ministers only for a summer ; and the conversation growing warm, he was desired to explain himself, to which he answered that he meant to keep his place, and that they durst not take it from him if they could, and could not if they durst, which he hoped was sufficiently explicit.

It has been proposed to Lord Townshend, and he has refused to go either to France or Spain ; upon which Lord Rochford is to be removed from Madrid to Paris, which just at this moment seems to be the worst choice that could be made, as he, by knowing exactly the present state of the Court there, and by being an object of the attention of the people, may be of more service where he now is than any other man can be.

The reason assigned for Lord Egmont's refusing the Seals is, that he did not choose to make a part of the present Ministry, upon which it is said that Lord Rockingham has made some representations, which have been very ill taken.

A rumour universally prevails of some very bad news from America, but I cannot hear anything of it authentically. The story is, that they are in arms. This I do not find any foundation to believe. I have been told that private letters say they will not be content with the Repeal, which they say is of as little consequence as the

---

[1] It was, I believe, Lord Chesterfield who first called the House of Lords *the Hospital for Incurables.*

Stamp Act, both being nullities, but I have not met with anybody who has received letters[1]. I have the honour to be, &c., &c.   THOMAS WHATELY.

[1] I found the following letter among Mr. Grenville's papers. The writer, Dr. Thomas Moffatt, was a Physician at Newport, in Rhode Island, and Dr. Styles an Independent Minister residing in the same town. Dr. Moffatt's house having been pulled down by the populace, he was obliged to retire to London. He was examined by the House of Commons about the tumults in America on account of the Stamp Act, and after its repeal he was asked by the Marquess of Rockingham to write this letter to Dr. Styles, who was a leading man in New England. I am not aware that it has been printed.
A note in the handwriting of Mr. George Chalmers certifies that it was copied from Dr. Moffatt's original draft, which was *corrected by the Marquess of Rockingham and Sir George Savile* [a]. Another note in the handwriting of Mr. Thomas Astle, afterwards Keeper of the Records, is to the same effect, and he adds, " that this letter is important, because it shows the arts used by the noble Marquess and his friends to quiet the Americans after the repeal of the Stamp Act. The Rockingham Administration did not seem to know at this time that the leaders of the factions in America despised them. Knaves generally despise those whom they have duped."

DR. THOMAS MOFFATT TO DR. STYLES.

London, March 18, 1766.

SIR,—I persuade myself that you are under no expectation of receiving a letter from me, but as I am under an influence neither necessary nor very proper for me to explain to you, I cannot very easily refrain from acquainting you that the Stamp Act of America is now repealed by Parliament, nor from endeavouring to communicate to you an idea of the great difficulties that have attended this work from the first moment it was known to be adopted by the King's servants, who with their combined influence and interest in both Houses of Parliament, have happily effected it against a sea of hindrance and opposition from many quarters felt, known and unseen. The difficulty of repealing this Act was also greatly increased by the conduct of the Colonies, who continued to assist and co-operate in embarrassing an administration that was warmly inclined to relieve America from every *bondage*, and who had undertaken it against opposers that were very considerable and powerful in respect of their quality, capacity, connexions, and influence, and of whom I shall say no more than that they lost not the

[a] See *Bancroft's History of the American Revolution*, vol. ii. p. 521.

MR. WHATELY TO MR. GRENVILLE.

Parliament Street, Saturday, May 24, 1766.

DEAR SIR,—It is hard upon you to be pestered every post in a holiday week with politics and news, but the shadow of any opportunity either to prevent or retard the passing of the Bill for repealing the Stamp Act.

But the present Ministers of State, full of the tenderest and most benevolent sentiments towards America, set out in this undertaking upon a principle of reclaiming the British Colonies by marks of their moderation and grace rather than by instances of their power and resentment, which last was much and eagerly insisted on by many, but prudently averted by those at the helm of Government, who never have been, nor are yet insensible how much they have hazarded on this occasion for the sake of North America, and how much they have now depending upon the instant and future behaviour of the British American Colonies.

If, therefore, the repeal of the Stamp Act is received in North America with the expected and becoming spirit of gratitude and obedience really manifested by the restoration of public and private tranquillity, order and safety, then may the King's Ministers and all the true stedfast friends of America have abundant cause to rejoice, and be well satisfied with what they have now accomplished.

But if, on the contrary, the repealing of the Stamp Act should be received and considered by the colonists as a condescension or submission extorted from Sovereign and Supreme Authority, or if the occasion shall be celebrated with extravagancy and triumph indicatory of such sentiments or opinion, then may the Americans be said to have conspired in betraying their redeemers, and even of bringing them to open shame, *and what the ensuing consequences would be to America* and them is but too plain to require any explanation from me to you.

Your function, station, and regard to your country, with many other motives, will naturally point out to you how necessary and incumbent it is to impress the minds of all people with a dutiful sense and spirit of gratitude, submission, peace, and good order, on an event so very favourable and gracious to North America.   I am, &c.

THOMAS MOFFATT.

The word *bondage* in the first paragraph was objected to by the Marquess of Rockingham, and the following words, "*from every degree of hardship, or degree of oppression,*" were substituted in the room thereof.

The words, *and what the ensuing consequences would be, &c.*, in the fourth paragraph were objected to by Sir George Savile as not suf-

present Administration are so active that not a day can escape without an occurrence; and it would not be doing them justice to omit any of their transactions. That no time, for instance, might be lost, they chose this for passing the Bill of Indemnification to those who have not used stamps in America, which, though formed upon your motion, is now amended to the very reverse of your idea. To conform to the resolution which provides for *certain restrictions* to accompany the Indulgence, the Bill was brought in with a clause to require the previous payment of the duties; but that has been struck out in the Committee, and the Bill now gives an absolute indemnification without any restriction. By great accident Mr. Thurlow[1] was yesterday in the House, when it was proposed to have it read a third time, and on his representation of the impropriety of pressing it, Mr. Fuller agreed to postpone it to Wednesday.

The Vice-Treasurership of Ireland has been again offered to Lord North, who has behaved with great propriety on the occasion, and sent yesterday a peremptory refusal to accept it[2].

It is said that in Ireland the Castle has lost another question by a majority of nine, but not having yet heard what the question was, I do not give entire credit to the report.

ficiently explicit, and the following words were substituted in room thereof, "*and will be even instrumental in overturning the present Administration, and of introducing into North America a different police founded in, and supported by, force and rigour.*"

[1] Afterwards Lord Thurlow, and Lord Chancellor.

[2] "It cost him bitter pangs," says Walpole, "not to preserve his virtue, but his vicious connections. He goggled his eyes, and groped in his money-pocket; more than half consented; nay, so much more, that when he got home, he wrote an excuse to Lord Rockingham, which made it plain that he thought he had accepted."

The provision now said to be intended for the princes is to divide the whole 25,000*l.* among the three. I think this probable; and that some provision will be made this Session is, I apprehend, certain.

The more I consider the Free Port Bill, the more it alarms me. There is no provision to prevent the importation of French manufactures, provided they be the produce of the West Indies; on the contrary, it is presumed that such produce will be brought in manufactured to a certain degree, and if to the greatest degree it is nowhere prohibited. I do not see why the French may not set up two or three looms for cotton stuffs, and in like manner establish other fictitious manufactures in their Islands, and under that colour supply our colonies with whatever they please, which can by possibility be made of the produce of the West Indies, especially as no proof is required of its being actually produced there; and they are allowed to import all goods and commodities, the growth or produce of any colony or plantation, without specifying the particulars, which would not have been difficult. I have the honour to be, &c.

THOMAS WHATELY.

THE BISHOP OF CARLISLE TO MR. GRENVILLE.

London, May 27, 1766.

MY DEAR SIR,—The motion for a provision to be made by Parliament for the two Dukes and Prince Henry, is dropped for this Session, as I am well assured. Lord Hardwicke has accepted the Cabinet, though he refused the Secretary of State's seals. Lord Rochford is certainly to go Ambassador to Paris, and the Ministry are at the greatest loss to find a proper person to succeed him at the Court of Spain.

I don't find any one has heard a word of a revolution in New Spain, so conclude your friend's intelligence was ill-founded.

There is a whisper about commotions in our North American colonies; and some people go so far as to say that the *Declaratory Act* has been publicly burnt by the Sons of Liberty; but whether this be so or not, the profound silence of the Ministers about the contents of the last letters received from thence, gives great room to apprehend things are not in a very agreeable situation.

The Ministers are embarrassed to the last degree how to act with regard to Wilkes. It seems they are afraid to press the King for his pardon, as that is a subject His Majesty will not easily hear the least mention of; and they are apprehensive, if he has it not, that the mob of London will rise in his favour, which God forbid.

Tom Pitt[1] arrived at Paris about ten days ago from Flanders; as he has a good deal to do, and many places to see there and in the environs, I suppose he will not be able to obey Mrs. Grenville's summons of meeting you all at Shortgrove on the 4th of June. His friend, the Duke of Roxburgh[2], has let his house in Windsor Forest to Prince Henry for seven years, at 900*l.* per annum rent.   I remain, most cordially yours.

---

[1] Thomas Pitt, afterwards Lord Camelford.

[2] John, third duke of Roxburgh in the peerage of Scotland, and second Earl Ker in that of Great Britain. He died in 1804, when the British honours became extinct. The Duke will be long remembered as a book-collector at a period when the Bibliomania was raging with its greatest virulence. The dispersion of his very curious library, which was sold by auction in 1812, gave rise to the celebrated Roxburgh Club.

THE BISHOP OF CARLISLE TO MR. GRENVILLE.

London, May 29, 1766.

My dear Sir,—The House of Lords did not rise 'till seven yesterday evening, having for about four hours debated the Window-Tax Bill. We divided on the Question for Commitment, and the Contents were 57 and Non-contents 16. Proxies were not called for. The Bishops of Bangor and Carlisle were alone in the minority, Lord Abercorn voted with the majority. Before the Order of the Day was called for, Lord Temple moved for the reading the Bill touching the *Seizure of Papers*, and Friday was appointed for taking it into consideration, when all the Judges are ordered to attend, but as that is the first day of the term, if the Judges cannot conveniently attend, then Monday next is fixed for this business. Lord Chancellor took occasion to tell the House that he should oppose this Bill.

Lord Weymouth began the debate on the Window Bill by calling on the Administration in a very proper and brief manner, to explain the general purport of the Bill, the sum that was proposed to be raised by the tax, and the necessity there was for laying a new tax on the people in time of peace. To this, not a single word was answered, and the Chancellor having waited some time, and seeing no one rise, put the question for commitment; on this the Duke of Bedford rose, and in some heat, cried out shame on the Administration for endeavouring to cram down a tax of this kind merely by force of numbers, and without vouchsafing to say a word in justification of it. This brought up the Duke of Richmond, and afterwards Lord Rockingham, from both of whom the House received very little edification, as you will easily believe. I shall not trouble you with more particulars relating to this debate, except that the Duke of Bedford in the course of it made very honourable mention of the late Minister, Mr. Grenville; and Lord Temple, as usual, spoke very ably, and proved the immense loss this country sustains by the repeal of the Stamp and Cider Acts.

I must not indeed omit telling you that the Duke of Grafton spoke very plausibly in support of the Bill, and concluded with informing the House that he had not gone out of office from a love of ease, and indulgence to his private amusements, as had been falsely reported, but from finding that the man who had raised the reputation of this country higher than ever it was before, while he had the principal direction of public affairs (or words to that effect), was not again employed, which he thought would alone give that dignity and weight to Government which it seemed to have wanted for some time past; that for himself, though he had carried a *general's staff*, he was ready to take up a *mattock or spade* under that able and great Minister, whenever he shall be called upon, so far was he from consulting his own private ease.

Lord Howe's resignation surprises everybody; the sole reason he assigns is, Mr. Pitt's not being in office. His Lordship would have done himself more honour had he resigned his seat at the Admiralty last July, and not accepted the Treasurership of the Navy.

I am assured from very good hands, notwithstanding what we heard last week, that no offers were made to Mr. Mackenzie; but if they had been, he would certainly have rejected them.   Adieu, &c., &c.

MR. FRASER[1] TO MR. GRENVILLE.

Suffolk Street, June 10, 1766.

DEAR SIR,—You have been so very good to me that I am not afraid of your thinking me impertinent, of however little consequence you may think the matter that occasions you the trouble of reading these lines.

You must have heard of, and have probably seen, a political piece which has appeared within these few days, called a History of the late Minority[2]; it is now published, and advertised in the daily papers; I met to-day, at Leicester House, two or three of Lord Bute's friends, who seemed nettled at it, and I could gather that he was himself hurt and surprised that such a publication should be made at this time: they talked as if Lord Temple was the hero, and Lord Bute the butt, and from thence concluded it wrote by a friend, and with the approbation of Lord Temple; and a friend of Lord Bute's, who is at the same time very much your's, said to me since, that praise of Lord Temple and abuse of Lord Bute was an unlucky association of ideas at this juncture; upon the whole, would it not be a pity that a thing of this sort, which, so far as I hear of it, tends to nothing less than that union of ability and integrity so much wished,—would it not be a pity that it should have a

[1] Eldest son of Simon Lord Lovat, who was executed in 1747 for his share in the rebellion. He was at this time M.P. for Inverness, and as a colonel in the Army he had distinguished himself at Louisburgh and Quebec. He died in 1782.

[2] This tract was published and partly compiled by Almon, and notwithstanding the denials that were circulated for Lord Temple, it appears most probable that the materials were principally furnished, if not directly from himself, in some indirect manner, by his authority. Humphrey Cotes was a likely man to have had a principal share in the compilation.

chance of creating a suspicion any way adverse to the amicable (I hope I may call it so) train, in which matters are at present ? If so, I humbly submit how far it would be proper that some person should be authorized to say that it had not Lord Temple's sanction : if this would not be improper, I am certain it would have a good and most conciliating effect : at any rate, pray, dear Sir, pardon my zeal ; if it is blind it is become so from being over keen ; for to the respect I bore the Minister, believe me upon the word of a gentleman and a soldier, you have added such an affection for the man, as can never be eradicated. I have the honour to be, &c., &c.

S. FRASER.

MR. GRENVILLE TO SIMON FRASER, ESQ.

Petworth, June 11, 1766.

DEAR SIR,—With regard to the subject of your letter, I informed my brother, Lord Temple, who is now here, of the publication of the pamphlet which you mention, and can very truly assure you that he has neither advised nor encouraged the writing or publishing of any political paper whatever, and more particularly not this pamphlet, which, he says, contains many mistaken facts, and is contrary to his opinions and plan, as this History of the late Minority attacks both friends and foes, and amongst others your humble servant. I have not read this performance, but from its general tenor and the account I have heard of it, I could have been very sure that this was the case even if I were not authorized to say so. I am, &c., &c.   GEORGE GRENVILLE.

MR. WHATELY TO MR. GRENVILLE.

June 13, 1766.

DEAR SIR,—I take the opportunity of Mr. Lloyd's meeting you at Salt Hill to write to you on a subject which I am desired to mention to you: it is in relation to a pamphlet or rather book just published, entitled, I think, a Defence of the Minority[1] during the former Administrations, and containing a narrative of all the proceedings of party since the present King's accession.

It abuses Lord Bute very liberally, and as it appears to have been written by some person attached to Lord Temple, occasion has from thence been taken to surmise that his Lordship might be privy to the publication. You know the sensibility of the person abused in this work to such abuse: Wedderburn has been more than once with me, greatly vexed at the affair, and very anxious to have it in his power to say that Lord Temple knows nothing of the matter. Perhaps you may be able to assert it, if that pamphlet has been accidentally mentioned amongst you at Petworth; if not, you best know whether, and in what manner, you could mention it to Lord Temple, without his being offended either at the suspicion, or at the question. If you can furnish a satisfactory answer to the surmise, Wedderburn thinks it of consequence to have one, and if you will favour me with a line upon it, couched in such terms that it may appear only an answer to my having told you that the publication was ascribed to a friend of Lord Temple, and supposed to be countenanced by him, without mentioning Wedderburn's name, I will read the paragraph

---

[1] He means a "*History of the late Minority.*" The "*Defence*" was written by Charles Townshend, and published subsequently.

to him, and he will know how to make the best use of the information.

I have had some conversation with Dr. Lloyd on the subject he is engaged in [1]. His idea seems to be to publish extracts from the papers, which, after the care taken to conceal them from the public eye, will certainly be obnoxious to enquiry, and perhaps raise a general resentment. The substance might be given at large without copying words or affixing names, and would be as effectual. I mean this with respect to the advices from America, the writers of which would be exposed by a publication : as to Conway's letter that has been already published in the newspapers, and may appear to be taken from thence ; as to the facts, they are of general notoriety, and it is easy to express the sentiments of persons there, as advices received from thence without taking the very terms they use : you are best judge of the weight of these considerations, but I know that if I had been of opinion against printing them by authority of the House, I should be offended at their being published by any other.

There is but little political news stirring : the same set of new peers are talked of, though not with great certainty : and the report of a negotiation for Lord Tyrawley's regiment is stronger than ever. The terms mentioned are a pension to him of 2000*l*. for fourteen

---

[1] About this time was published a pamphlet, entitled " *A Collection of all the remarkable and personal Passages in the Briton, North Briton, and Auditor. London,* 1766, 8*vo.*" But the description of Dr. Lloyd's work would rather imply that it was a collection of extracts from the correspondence from America relating to the Stamp Act, and the proceedings consequent thereupon. It does not appear whether the Dr. Lloyd here mentioned was Dr. Philip Lloyd, Dean of Norwich, or Dr. Pierson Lloyd, one of the Masters of Westminster School.

years, and a provision by places for two natural children, which terms are so high, as I suppose the regiment worth little more than 2000*l.* per annum, that I can hardly believe them.

I have delivered your message to Lord North, who would have waited upon you, if he had known you were in town, and will pay his respects to you at Wotton during the summer.

MR. NUGENT[1] TO MR. GRENVILLE.

Great George Street, June 17, 1766.

My DEAR SIR,—I received by yesterday's post a letter from Reeve, the Quaker, dated from Bristol, June 14th, informing me that by letters from America received the day before, he is informed that the repeal of the Stamp Act, and the Declaratory Act, were known there, and produced universal joy. He does not name the ports from whence his intelligence came. I do not hear a word of news that can be depended upon, except that after having undone everything within the reach of power, which you did for Old England, in Parliament; the arrangements made in Scotland, during Lord Bute's and his brother's administration there, are treated with the same unsparing and subversive hand by the Administration; what the particulars are I do not know.

A pamphlet has made its appearance under the title of a History of the late Minority, stuffed with the most virulent abuse upon Lord Bute, and full with the praises of your brother and Mr. Pitt. This last circumstance, added to its publication by Almon, renders it an object

---

[1] Afterwards Viscount Clare and Earl Nugent.

of much speculation, from which many are willing to infer, what they wish should be believed by others, that Lord Temple's enmity continues unabated[1].

The Chancellor, I am told, talks as freely of his adjuncts as he was wont to do, and I suppose acts with them, although, it is said, there is great variance in the councils held at his house.

As I cannot bear the jolting of a horse, I pass my mornings in reading; and the new Act for repealing the late American Duties and substituting others has been this day the subject of my contemplation, in which I find by the last clause but one, that Ireland can be supplied with no one article from America after the 1st of January next. There are other curious particulars, too many for a letter, which will occur to you upon reading the Act. N.B. I had no share in the consultations upon this Act. It is the genuine production of the maiden and spotless Treasury. But I must not laugh : it hurts my bowels. When I can trust them in a journey, I will visit Stowe and Wotton. All I know for certain is, that my physician gives me no hopes of being free under a fortnight or three weeks, and that I am tired to death of him and his cooling, purifying draughts : less purification and more warmth have ever suited my constitution best. Our friend of Bucks has set out this morning for Devonshire. We drank your health at parting last night : he in pure wine, and I in wine and water, but with the same unmixed affection and regard with which I shall ever be, &c., &c. R. NUGENT.

---

[1] The same report coming from three several correspondents proves how general was the belief that Lord Temple was concerned in the publication of this pamphlet.

MR. GRENVILLE TO MR. NUGENT.

Wotton, June 21, 1766.

My dear Sir,—I have not the least doubt that our brethren in America will express great joy at the repeal of the Stamp Act, especially if they understand by it, as they justly may, notwithstanding the Declaratory Bill passed at the same time, that they are thereby exempted for ever from being taxed by Great Britain for the public support even of themselves, which this kingdom is to pay for them. I think they will be very ungrateful to our American patriots and our American merchants if they do otherwise; and if your correspondent, Mr. Reeve, and the rest of those gentlemen, will do the same by Buckinghamshire, and double tax themselves to take off our taxes, I will engage for my countrymen here that they shall express as universal joy and more gratitude for the future than we shall meet with from Mr. Reeve's correspondents in America. The event, however, will show the merit which those who have contributed to this measure are entitled to from this kingdom for the plan which they have followed in Great Britain, Ireland, and the colonies; and I do assure you that I do not envy them all the praise which they will reap from it. I know not the particular measures which you refer to concerning Scotland; but I suppose it is a relaxation of the laws of revenue there, which they are certainly as well entitled to, and will receive as gladly, as if they lived in America. I have the strongest reason to be satisfied that my brother, Lord Temple, has neither advised nor encouraged the publication of the History of the late Minority which you mention, and consequently all reasonings derived from a contrary supposition fall to the ground. I am, &c.   George Grenville.

MR. WHATELY TO MR. GRENVILLE.

June 25, 1766.

DEAR SIR,—I am afraid you will think I give the business upon which I now trouble you too much importance, by sending a messenger on purpose about it; but I could not write upon the subject by the post, and have therefore sent my servant with this letter. The occasion of it is, Mr. Lloyd's having informed me by a line this morning, that you had desired him to avoid being concerned in any publications, and he takes your injunction so strictly *au pied de la lettre,* as to decline proceeding in that which he had begun for me, the consequence of which is, that it is absolutely stopped; for as it is already in the press, there is no possibility of altering the course in which it has been put[1]. I cannot go to the printer myself, or have any direct intercourse with him, as I would not on any account appear: if Mr. Lloyd attempts to withdraw the papers, he might probably meet with a refusal, and certainly would exasperate the printer to tell all he knows, and to trace the pamphlet when he sees it published by another; whereas if permitted to proceed, it will be his interest to keep the secret, and I see no danger of a discovery; I am sure there is greater danger of his naming Mr. Lloyd, should

---

[1] The pamphlet in question was probably that of which Mr. Whately was the author, entitled " *Considerations on the Trade and Finances of this Kingdom, and on the Measures of Administration with respect to those great National Objects, since the Conclusion of the Peace.*" A cotemporary critic says that it contains a clear and concise account of the various branches of the public revenue, and the application of them. Mr. Whately was also the author of a tract called " *Remarks on the Budget,*" in answer to one written by Hartley, called " The Budget," and he wrote besides an Essay on Landscape Gardening.

the work be taken out of his hands. For these reasons I should be very glad that you would give me leave to tell Mr. Lloyd that you do not mean to prevent his finishing what he has begun, and which, unless he continues it, will never be finished; I will then let him know your intention, and you may depend upon both our discretions.

Mr. Wedderburn has had a long conversation this morning with Lord Bute, which his Lordship began by asking him what had passed between him and you; Wedderburn related it not as propositions, but merely as discourse, and Lord Bute expressed himself highly pleased with your sentiments, and agreed in all. He is entirely satisfied with respect to the late publication [1], and thinks as you do of Mr. Pitt, particularly he said that he was told Mr. Pitt was eager to come into office; by which he says I understand very well that he is ready to receive a message from the King, which is not a measure I should ever have a hand in, unexplained as his sentiments are.

The Lord Chancellor had an audience of considerable length a few days ago, in which it is said that he told the King that affairs could not go on as they were, and advised the sending for Mr. Pitt [2]; to which the answer was, I do not mean to be a slave; and the reply to that was, that slavery would be better than the present situa-

---

[1] "*The History of the late Minority.*" I suppose Mr. Whately means that Lord Bute is satisfied with Mr. Grenville's assurance that Lord Temple was not concerned in that publication, and it was no doubt strictly true, as far as Mr. Grenville had any knowledge of the matter.

[2] In a fortnight after this date the Lord Chancellor wrote to Mr. Pitt inclosing a letter from the King (see *Chatham Correspondence,* vol. ii. p. 434), desiring his presence in town, and "having his thoughts how an able and dignified Ministry may be formed."

tion ; I do not give entire credit to this account, though I have heard the Chancellor himself quoted for it ; but it is certain that he is very declared against the present people ; and it is added that in the Closet he said, he must resign if they continued.

Accounts are come from America since they received the news of the repeal ; I think the date of the letters is about the 12th of May. I do not find that the Ministry give out any particulars, from whence I conclude that they have received none they like. I hear from New York that since the rejoicings for the repeal, the Sons of Liberty assembled in a body of above 500, to rescue a person committed for a trespass, and did rescue him : this is true. I hear too, but I doubt whether it is true, that the Assembly of South Carolina have, since the rejoicing, voted themselves independent of Great Britain.

I fancy there is some mistake in this, as it comes only from one quarter, and through three or four hands.

I must trouble you for an answer by the bearer, and I hope that it will be such as will in this one instance permit Mr. Lloyd to proceed just so far as may be necessary for finishing what is begun, as the completing it will be less hazardous than the breaking it off abruptly.

MR. WHATELY TO MR. GRENVILLE.

June 29, 1766.

DEAR SIR,—I am favoured with yours by my servant, and entirely agree with you on the propriety of that caution you recommend to ——¹, but in this instance I

---

¹ Charles Lloyd. Mr. Grenville had replied that he was only desirous that Lloyd should not subject himself to a charge of breach of trust and its consequences, with regard to the offices he held under the Treasury, and recommended the utmost caution.

verily believe it would have been more dangerous to retract than to proceed; and it is settled in a method
which will be perfectly secure, and in which he will not
personally interfere.

As soon as my business is completed, I shall pay my
respects to you. I have seen to-day the person [1] you
wish me to come with; he has had more conversation
on the same subject, and in the same strain; but for my
own part, I question whether anything will be done immediately; my conjecture is, that the wish will be to
wait for an event; but if none happens soon, I believe
it may not be waited for, and some sudden step may be
taken. I am pestered every day with the reports of
changes; my answer is that I know of none, but that
I conclude from the general expectation, that it is the
general opinion there ought to be one; and indeed the
expectation is universal. I believe I told you in my last
that the Ministers had failed in their attempt to remove
Lord Eglintoun and Mr. Dyson [2]: they have this week
failed again in their creation of peers, which affair is
now entirely at an end. I hear no more particulars from
America. Some of their Assemblies must, however, have
sat before another mail can arrive, and we shall then see
what reception they give to the requisition.

The news from the East Indies, which you see in the
papers, sunk that stock about one per cent., and yet I
think it cannot be true : the French letters which mention it are of the 27th of August, from Chandanagore,
and the Company's letters of the 1st of October from
Calcutta, which is but four hundred miles from Chanda-

[1] Mr. Wedderburn.
[2] Lord Eglintoun was a Lord of the Bedchamber, and Jeremiah
Dyson was a Commissioner of the Board of Trade; both of them were
in the intimate confidence of Lord Bute.

nagore, and that down the river Hoogly, take no notice
of it. I forgot to tell you in my last the general idea
which your visitor [1] last week gave of the discourse he
had with you ; he said when he was asked what had
passed, that your sentiments were invariably the same as
those you had expressed at the interview in the winter,
and that your conversation with him was a comment on
that text. I think the reference was good, and should
not be lost sight of.

Sir J. Lowther has had a disagreeable squabble with
one Gale, of Whitehaven, whom he met, and who insulted him at Carlisle races, but Sir James acquitted
himself with credit ; behaved with temper at the time ;
endeavoured to prevent any interposition, but by the information of his adversary, was put under arrest.

MR. WILLIAM GERARD HAMILTON [2] TO EARL TEMPLE.

Hampton Court, July 1, 1766.

My dear Lord,—I have declined making use of the
liberty you are so obliging as to allow me, and have
denied myself, for some days past, the pleasure of writing
to you, because I could not satisfy myself that any of the
reports which prevail at present were authentic enough
to justify my troubling your Lordship with a communication of them. As I have been entirely in the country,
I had not 'till this morning an opportunity of an inter-

---

[1] Mr. Wedderburn.

[2] M.P. for Pontefract, well known by the *sobriquet* of *Single Speech.*
The celebrated speech which gained him the name was made in the
House of Commons in November, 1755. His subsequent career dis-
appointed the expectations which had been raised by his first exhibition
of parliamentary eloquence. He was for some time Chancellor of the
Exchequer in Ireland, and died in 1796.

view with my friend[1], or of inquiring into the manner in which your Lordship's answer was received by those to whom he promised to report it immediately, and whether anything, and what, was likely to be the consequence of it. He assures me, in the most positive manner imaginable, that the dispositions of the Court are as favourable to your Lordship as they possibly can be; and even as they who have the honour of being acquainted with you as well as I am, know they ought to be; and that everything must end, at no very great distance of time, in the manner which the friends of the public and your Lordship would wish.

The Chancellor has been into the Closet to execute what he has so long threatened, and to inform His Majesty that he should prefer resigning his office, to holding it with an Administration so unqualified for the service of the Crown or the public. This is his own report of his conduct, and it is credited by those who would have the means of contradicting it if it were untrue.

The friends of Lord Bute assert that Lord Hertford has made an offer, and a very submissive one, of his own services and of his relations' at Court, but that they were absolutely rejected; and my friend bears positive testimony to the truth of this fact.

I think your Lordship may rely upon these two particulars, that Lord Holland left London much dissatisfied with the Court, and the Court with him; and that Lord Egmont is the most desponding part of a very desponding Administration. He certainly has lost the ground which he once had, and will fall a sacrifice upon any

---

[1] The friend alluded to was probably Sir Fletcher Norton, and Mr. Hamilton seems to imply that there had been some communication between Lord Bute and Lord Temple at this time.

change of system. Lord Holland made some request, but what I can't learn, the success of which he had much at heart[1]. It was countenanced by the Administration, and discouraged by the Closet.

You may possibly be entertained, but I think you will not be surprised, when I tell you that the Duke of Newcastle has been of late imploring the protection of the Princess of Wales, for himself and his friends. He has laboured this point by every method in his power, but I have not as yet heard that he has succeeded in it. The plan of the Court is evidently and avowedly, not to remove these Ministers from their employments, if it can be avoided; but to reduce them to the necessity of relinquishing them.

The Duke of Richmond, Lord Hertford, and General Conway regularly oppose, upon occasions serious and trifling, Lord Rockingham, the Duke of Newcastle, and Winchilsea; and Mr. Conway is particularly free in declaring his utter ignorance of every thing except the mere business of his office.

Nothing seems to have declined more rapidly than Lord Albemarle's influence. The refusal of some military requests, and the appointment of the three Princes as joint Rangers of the Park at Windsor, which it is said is now to take place, and which was known to be a very favourite object with his Lordship, has diminished exceedingly the reputation of the weight which he affected.

I understand from my friend that Mr. Wedderburn has lately paid a visit to Mr. Grenville, and is soon to be with your Lordship at Stowe. I flatter myself that

---

[1] Perhaps an Earldom, which it is well known was the object of Lord Holland's ambition.

he will confirm everything which I had the honour of communicating to you, and that I shall be found to have executed both your commands, and those with which my friend entrusted me, with tolerable exactness, and with an attention which I must ever show, where your Lordship's interests are so nearly concerned.

A mixture of friendship and of business may possibly bring me within a few miles of Stowe towards the 20th of this month, and rather I think before it.

If that time should not interfere with Princess Amelia's visit, and you will permit me, I am not without thoughts of troubling you for a single day, provided your Lordship grants me another favour, and will suffer me not to consider this visit as an exclusion of the pleasure I propose to myself from being at Stowe in autumn.

Believe me, my dear Lord, most faithfully and affectionately yours, &c., &c.   — — —[1]

Lord Rockingham's part of the Administration are (by what means I can't learn) exasperated beyond measure with Mr. Townshend, and have informed him that nothing but their removal shall prevent his being either absolutely dismissed, or obliged to take an office, where he shall be active and support them, instead of being indolent and ridiculing them.

MR. JENKINSON[2] TO MR. GRENVILLE.

Paris, July 6, 1766.

MY DEAR SIR,—I take the liberty to send you some account of myself, though I have little to say that can

----

[1] All Mr. Hamilton's letters to Lord Temple are signed with three dashes instead of his name.

[2] Afterwards Viscount Hawkesbury, and Earl of Liverpool.

be in the least interesting to you. I have now been five
weeks in this country, which I have spent either in the
great towns of Normandy, or at the house of Duc
d'Harcourt.

The recommendation of Mons. de Guerchy has procured me everywhere the politest reception, so that I
have hitherto every reason in the world to be satisfied
with my journey.

The Duc d'Harcourt is a fine old man of about seventy,
and is as fond of farming as his namesake in England.
He is Governor of Normandy, the richest province in
France, and as in that quality he keeps constantly an
open house, the noblesse of the Province flock in to him.
I have seen frequently between twenty and thirty persons
who lay in the house, and I am told that towards the
autumn, when they have Comedies there, the number is
much greater, and there is in their manner of living a
degree of magnificence and splendour which I have
never seen in England.

I left Harcourt on Wednesday last, and came here
on Friday evening. I saw in my way two remarkable
places—Navarre, the house of the Duke of Bouillon,
which Henry IV. gave that family in lieu of Sedan ; and
Rhosny, the birth-place and residence of the great
Duke of Sully. The first of these is a very fine thing ;
it is surrounded by the noblest woods I ever saw, and
though the gardens are laid out in the taste of this
country, yet they are good in their kind. The last is a
good old house in the midst of a great estate, and carries with it many marks of ancient splendour. But alas !
the present inhabitants of these houses are strangely
different from those who were the ancient possessors of
them. The house of Navarre still belongs to the family

s 2

of Bouillon; but that family depends on two young men, the eldest of which is a decrepit idiot, and the second a lame dwarf. The eldest is just going to be married to a Princess of Hesse, in hopes that by this junction the family may not only be perpetuated, but a little of their ancient vigour restored to it. But Rhosny no longer belongs to the House of Sully: it is in the possession of one who has gained a great fortune in the finances, by those means which it was Sully's merit to oppose, and thereby saved his country. I was so struck with the place, the different characters of the two possessors, and the several circumstances of their history, that I returned to my inn full of meditation, and if I had been in England, and the Parliament sitting, I should certainly the next day have spoke a philippic against the present Administration.

I have not seen much of this place yet; Mons. de Guerchy is returned to France, but he is at present at Versailles. I have heard no politics since I left England, except what a few letters from thence have brought me, and if I knew any, it would not be proper to trust them to this conveyance. I am, &c., &c.

C. JENKINSON.

MR. WEDDERBURN TO MR. GRENVILLE.

Lincoln's Inn, July 9, 1766.

DEAR SIR,—I have been flattering myself from day to day with the hopes of waiting upon you this week, and have been constantly disappointed. As often as I have thought I saw the period of my business in town approaching, new matters coming in upon me have obliged me to go on reluctantly, and I now find myself under

the disagreeable necessity of leaving several things un-
finished that all the industry I could employ has not
been able to accomplish. Whately will testify for me
that I have laboured very hard to get out of town two
or three days before the circuit; and as I never had so
strong a motive, I can with great truth assure you I
never took half the pains to get business, that I have
now done ineffectually to get rid of it. As soon as the
circuit is finished I propose returning to this part of the
world, and hope you will give me leave to take the
earliest opportunity of making myself amends for a disappointment I feel very much.

Lord Temple was so good as to mention me to a
friend of mine, who had the honour of seeing him at
Stowe the day before yesterday, and told him he expected me there. It is a very sensible addition to my
disappointment in not waiting upon you, that I am likewise deprived of this opportunity of paying my respects
to Lord Temple; and as you was so good as to propose
carrying me there, I have the pleasure to think you will
do me the justice to assure Lord Temple of the regret
I have in not being able to profit of it at present.

The approach of a circuit used generally to be very
pleasant to me. It happens now to be quite the reverse;
I have many reasons for wishing to remain in this neighbourhood; and though some of them are very interesting to a man's own heart, I cannot impute my reluctance
to them alone, for I am sensible my journey would be
much less unpleasant if it did not remove from me an
opportunity of assuring you of the very sincere regard
with which I have the honour to be, &c., &c.

AL. WEDDERBURN.

MR. WHATELY TO MR. GRENVILLE.

Friday, July 11, 1766.

DEAR SIR,—I have very little to inform you of, not knowing what has passed at St. James's; but Mr. Pitt arrived this morning, and has been there. The message was sent for him on Monday last; the Chancellor wrote the letter [1], and is the only acting person in the transaction. The world, you may be sure, suppose another [2] to be privy to it, upon which a friend [3] of yours, who was to have been with you this week, and to have gone over with you to Stowe, desires me to tell you that the appearances are, that no other person took any part in it, and that he is persuaded there has been no previous communication. He bids me add, that his own sentiments are what they always were, and I understand that those of another person [4] with whom he is much connected are the same. I stay in town to be in the way to communicate to you any intelligence which may concern you; and I wish you would let Lord Temple know (as he is expected here to-morrow) that if he has occasion for any particular communication to you, and wants a person to convey it, I am ready to set out for Wotton at a moment's warning. If I did not fear he might think it presumption in me, I should myself offer my services [5].

The speculations of the day are, that Lord Temple

---

[1] See *Chatham Correspondence*, vol. ii. p. 434.

[2] Lord Bute.   [3] Mr. Wedderburn.   [4] Sir Fletcher Norton.

[5] " This poor man (Whately) with the talents of an attorney, sets up for an Ambassador, and with the agility of Colonel Bodens, *undertakes to be a courier.*"—*Junius*, iii. 310.

will be at the head of the Treasury; and that General Conway is not to be dismissed; the Duke of Grafton a Secretary of State: but all this is mere speculation.

Lord Rockingham's friends express great resentment. Lord Hertford appears not displeased, and the Chancellor is very happy. I shall hardly miss writing to you every post.

THE LORD CHANCELLOR TO EARL TEMPLE.

London, July 13, 1766, 4 p.m.

My Lord,—I have just now received His Majesty's commands to let your Lordship know that the King desires to see you in London, as soon as you can with convenience to yourself. Mr. Pitt is in London, and I believe His Majesty wishes to have a conversation with your Lordship on the subject of giving force and effect to his Government. This charge from His Majesty was, your Lordship must think, a very agreeable one to me, who have always had so just a regard for your Lordship and your family. I have the honour to be, with the greatest respect, my dear Lord, your Lordship's most obedient and most humble Servant, NORTHINGTON.

EARL TEMPLE TO THE LORD CHANCELLOR.

Stowe, July 14, 1766, 7 a.m.

My Lord,—My zeal to obey His Majesty's commands signified to me by your Lordship, will carry me to town with all the dispatch in my power at so short a warning.

No man in the kingdom can wish more ardently than

I do to see force and effect given to the King's Government, having long lamented for my country, as your Lordship knows, the want of it.

Permit me to assure your Lordship that I cannot receive the honour of the King's orders through any channel more agreeable to me than that of your Lordship, for I have always been with the greatest truth and respect, my dear Lord, your Lordship's most obedient and most humble Servant,   TEMPLE.

THE LORD CHANCELLOR TO EARL TEMPLE.

July 15, 1766.

MY LORD,—Though I dispatched my messenger as soon as I rose, yet the King being out, and not returning 'till 12, I have but now, 5 min. past 2, received His Majesty's answer, which is that he desires to see your Lordship between 5 and 6 this evening at Richmond[1]. I have the honour to be, with great respect, my dear Lord, &c., &c.   NORTHINGTON.

THE DUKE OF BEDFORD TO MR. GRENVILLE.

Woburn Abbey, July 16, 1766, half past 3, P.M.

DEAR SIR,—The account you give me of some late

---

[1] Lord Temple had notified his arrival in London on the previous evening, and had received the following from the Chancellor:—" My dear Lord, I am just awake, and can only say to your Lordship that as I transmitted the King's commands to your Lordship, who is now at Richmond, I will notify to him as soon as I rise, your Lordship's arrival, and communicate to you his further commands on the intended interview. I am, &c.   NORTHINGTON.
14th, half-past 11, in bed.

transactions[1], though you call it an imperfect one, is much more perfect than any that I have hitherto received.

The first notice I had of Mr. Pitt's being sent for to town by His Majesty's command, was by a gentleman who came hither from London on Thursday evening, on which day Lord Gower arrived here from Trentham, in order to be of the Stowe party, to which Lord Temple had invited him : he left this place on Sunday, in order to go to London, but as I have heard nothing from him since that time, I suppose nothing yet transpires of what has passed in the Cabinet. I had fixed likewise to have gone for London for two days on Sunday last, in order to have seen my son and Lady Tavistock, but this report of the great transactions carrying on in London induced me to postpone that journey, as I was sensible many idle reports would probably be propagated on Lord Gower's and my coming up to town together at this critical time. I expect to see Lord and Lady Walde-grave here this evening, who will at least bring me the common talk of the town, but I believe no intelligence worth detaining your servant for.

Mr. Rigby left me to be at the Chelmsford Assizes to-morrow. If he hears anything material this evening in London, I have desired him to send me word of it. I wish a solid and permanent Administration may now be fixed on. I shall rejoice (though a private man) to be able to act in Parliament in support of it.

It has been told me from pretty good authority that the King expressed himself to General Conway in the presence of the Duke of Richmond, as wishing to be able to continue the former in his service : this was a severe stroke on the Duke. I can't help mentioning a

[1] See Mr. Grenville's letter in *Bedford Correspondence*, iii. 340.

very improbable report Lord Essex brought us, after we were set down to dinner, from the Assizes at Hertford, where Lord Mansfield was not present, and the reason assigned for it was, that Mr. Pitt was to dine with him that day at Kenwood. I am, &c., &c.   BEDFORD.

THE LORD CHANCELLOR TO EARL TEMPLE.

12 o'clock, July 17, 1766.

MY LORD,—I have just received His Majesty's commands to signify to your Lordship that the King will be glad to see your Lordship at the Queen's house at 3 this day, after the Drawing-room [1]. I have the honour to be, with great respect, &c., &c.   NORTHINGTON.

---

[1] This was Lord Temple's last audience ; he had previously seen the King on the 15th, and in the interim had long consultations with Mr. Pitt. The King's letter to Mr. Pitt, (*Chatham Correspondence*, vol. ii. p. 443,) describing his interview with Lord Temple, and his inclinations " to quarters very heterogeneous to my and your ideas," did not afford much expectation of a favourable result, and Mr. Calcraft, who had formed his judgment from Lord Temple's own report, writes to Mr. Pitt on the same day, that he has " some reason to fear Lord Temple's reception at Richmond was not the most flattering." At the second audience, however, Lord Temple mentions that the King was " very gracious," but he adds, " and I believe not a little delighted at my declining." It is most probable that Lord Temple upon this, as upon other similar occasions, had much over-rated his own importance ; and the King's having made the first application to Mr. Pitt, besides having distinguished him by letters written with his own hand, were circumstances which did not tend to conciliate the natural haughtiness, or to soften the usual impracticability, of Lord Temple's political character.

EARL TEMPLE TO MR. GRENVILLE.

Stowe, Friday, 6 o'clock, A.M., July 18, 1766.

My DEAR BROTHER,—I am this instant returned from London, which I left last night a little after nine. You will easily foresee that I have declined. The intended basis of the new, virtuous, and patriotic Administration is to be the Rump of the last, strengthened by the particular friends of Mr. Pitt, the whole consisting of all the most choice spirits who did in the last Session most eminently distinguish themselves in the sacrifice of the rights and honour of the whole Legislature and Kingdom of Great Britain. At the head of this I might have stood a capital cypher, surrounded with cyphers of quite a different complexion, the whole under the guidance of that great Luminary, the great Commoner, with the Privy Seal in his hand.

It was thought extraordinary that I should dream of a Cabinet place for Lord Lyttelton, but as an act of special grace to me, he might have been indulged with a place, and called to the Cabinet, as I suppose of the hanging Committee.

Lord Gower, Secretary of State, could not be thought of.

I had my last audience of the King yesterday at three o'clock. I stayed with him an hour: very gracious, and I believe not a little delighted with my declining.

Illuminations, City Address, &c., all preparing: whether any damp will be cast upon them, I know not.

I have not stated you as a Candidate for anything, but most expressly declined it, as a thing of more dignity for you, and a proof of my infinite moderation compared with all the insolence in return.

I suppose I shall be much abused, as the public is much disappointed, but I am more sinned against than sinning. Thus ends this political farce of my journey to town, as it was always intended, and I am now going to bed to get a little sleep, and to rise very happy.

Nugent will not be Vice-Treasurer. I just learn, my cook, drunk from the Assizes, has tumbled off his horse[1]. I have one coming from London, but if he does not recover, I believe I must send a file of musqueteers for yours.

MR. WHATELY TO MR. GRENVILLE.

Saturday, July 19, 1766.

DEAR SIR,—The impossibility of writing all my sentiments by the post, occasions my sending a servant with this letter, by which conveyance you may return me an answer as freely, as there really is occasion for some communication, for the reasons of Lord Temple's departure not being known has given rise to a variety of reports, and authority is wanting to contradict them. The first cause assigned was, that it was proposed to restore Mr. Mackenzie; the next, that there was too much consideration of Lord Bute in the intended arrangement. While these were current, I went to Sir Fletcher Norton, whom I found in the best disposition that could be, but totally uninformed.

---

[1] A serious inconvenience on the eve of a Royal visit. The Princess Amelia and a large party, including the Duke and Duchess of Bedford, the Duke and Duchess of Marlborough, Lord Gower, Lord Waldegrave, &c., were expected at Stowe in the following week.

The account which took place of these were, that Mr.
Pitt refused to admit Lord Lyttelton to the Cabinet,
and another is now told of his objecting to Lord Gower
as Secretary of State. I have again seen Sir Fletcher
this morning, and met Lord Darlington with him:
there are no others of Lord Bute's friends in town, and
Lord Bute himself stays pertinaciously in the country,
postponing his return from day to day. Both these
gentlemen took a side against Mr. Pitt, and talked of
opposition. No notice has been taken of Lord Bute;
they do not like Mr. Pitt, and they expressed themselves
in the strongest terms with respect to you. After Lord
Darlington was gone, Sir Fletcher wished me to set out
for Wotton, only to ask of you the real reasons, and the
circumstances of this transaction, both to have a story
for the world, and to furnish him with facts on which
he might know what to do. I told him I would set out
this afternoon if *he* had anything he wished to say to
you; upon which he recollected himself, and said, that
things were not quite ripe yet; in a day or two he should
know more, and desired me to see him on Tuesday next.

Against that time I wish to be furnished with such
facts as may be material, and with your sentiments upon
the present situation: I do not mean a letter to be
shown, but to be apprised myself of whatever you may
think proper in confidence to me, either to be used or
not as you may direct, or occasions may offer. Sir
Fletcher's declared opinion is to prefer you to all others,
and that no settlement is good which has not that object
at least *ultimately* in view; to establish an union between
Lord Bute, Lord Temple, and yourself; and in short,
to pursue the plan which he has laboured all the winter.
He says that he has prevailed on Lord Bute, as he

thinks, to give up the idea of restoring Mr. Mackenzie
to the *same* office, and is persuaded that neither Lord
Temple nor you mean to insist that he shall never be in
any office; he wishes even for an English one. He
doubts whether Mr. Pitt will venture to go on: if he
does, he supposes that an Administration formed on the
narrow bottom which he is now confined to will not last,
and has every prejudice against his conduct. I find
that he has a constant correspondence with Lord Bute,
and he told me that if anything particular occurred he
would send for me from Nonsuch, where I am going for
a little fresh air, to stay 'till Tuesday.

From all these symptoms I thought he had a mind to
write to Lord Bute, before he saw me again, and at the
same time to give me an opportunity of knowing your
sentiments; and if in giving them to me, you would take
an opportunity which the subject naturally leads to, of
saying something favourable of Lord Bute, of his friends,
and of Sir Fletcher particularly, either from yourself
alone, or from both Lord Temple and you, I might
perhaps use it to advantage.

The point I drive at is, to have it said where it will
have weight, that an Administration formed on a narrow
bottom will not remedy the present disorder. I hinted
that the King might without impropriety wish to extend
it. He let the insinuation pass without reply, but it is
evident as Lord Bute disavows the present transaction,
and seems to be neglected, that this is an opportunity,
if you choose it, to strengthen a connexion with that
quarter, without the appearance of soliciting to court
favour. You know Sir Fletcher always desired it. Lord
Darlington took occasion to show that he wished it, and
said you were the first man in this kingdom for abilities.

I saw yesterday a letter from Lord George Sackville, in which he observed that if the new arrangement included Mr. Grenville it would have stability; if not, it would be an Administration of *Parade*, not of business, and I am happy to hear from all sides the wishes of all men enter into the same sort of idea: but still that popularity of Mr. Pitt will, in my opinion, bear him up against many difficulties, though it is not so great as it was, yet for some time men will not see that it is declining. The general supposition is, that he will go on to form an Administration, which now cannot be very different from the last, or the present, for I do not know which to call them. He has sent Nuthall round to Lord Chancellor, the Duke of Grafton, Lord Shelburne, and General Conway. He is better in his health, but I do not find he has seen the King. The present people are in spirits since Lord Temple's departure, for they feared him more than they do Mr. Pitt; but still it is supposed that the Duke of Newcastle and Lord Rockingham will have no pretensions with him. It is given out that Lord Rockingham says he wishes Mr. Pitt may be able to form an Administration which he can support, and the saying ascribed to the Chancellor is, that he must make it out somehow or other; else these fools will turn him out, if they are not greater fools than he takes them to be.

It is rumoured that Lord Shelburne has agreed to accept of the Admiralty, but this and every other report is so very vague, that I give no credit to any of them.

I have heard that you are to be at Stowe this week, and should be obliged to you if you will let me know your motions, as it is not impossible I may suddenly set out

for Buckinghamshire, and shall be glad to know where
to find you if I do.

EARL TEMPLE TO EARL GOWER.

(From a draft in Lady Temple's hand.)

Stowe, July 19, 1766.

My Lord,—At my return from the Queen's house
on Thursday I did myself the honour of calling upon
your Lordship to ask your pardon for the liberty I had
taken, without your knowledge or approbation, to state
your Lordship as a person who I wished to see one of
His Majesty's Principal Secretaries of State. The service which I was sure your Lordship would do to your
King and country, led me to that nomination, and the
conviction of it was so strong upon my mind that I hope
I shall be forgiven by your Lordship.

This idea did not meet with Mr. Pitt's approbation.
Other circumstances concurred to make it impossible for
me to engage in the King's service in the high station
to which His Majesty has been graciously pleased again
to call me. The plan of an administration, formed
entirely of those who had in the course of the last sessions so disgracefully sacrificed the honour and interests
of the King and kingdom, could not meet with my approbation; and if a lead of *superiority* was claimed, it
was rejected, on my part, with an assertion of my pretensions to an *equality*.

I will apprize your Lordship, and my other friends, of
more particulars when I have the honour of seeing you
and them. In the meantime, be so good to communicate
this letter to the Duke of Bedford.

Lady Temple and I join in begging the favour of your Lordship to assure the whole House of Woburn of our best respects; and I have only to add for myself, that if you forgive me you will make happy, my Lord, your Lordship's, &c., &c.   TEMPLE.

I returned to this place in the night of Thursday, as I was resolved no family considerations should prevent the formation of a Ministry upon a plan of general union. I entirely waived any pretensions for my brother, and in so doing I thought I gave a high proof of my moderation and real desire to facilitate the success of this new negotiation. My brother, who called here with Nugent last night, and left us this morning, did not intend to write to the Duke of Bedford, as he knew I was so soon to have the honour of seeing his Grace.

MR. GRENVILLE TO MR. WHATELY.

Wotton, July 20, 1766.

DEAR WHATELY,—However desirous I am to enable you to contradict the various falsehoods which have been, and I know will be, industriously spread concerning the late transaction, yet I am sure you will see the utter impossibility of entering into a full detail of all that has passed, within the bounds of a letter, or of doing more than to give you some general outline of it and reserve the rest 'till I see you here, which for many reasons I wish may be as soon as is convenient to you. Lord Temple's sudden return to Stowe on Thursday night sufficiently shows that he had determined not to give his concurrence, and engage in the new, or rather old, system of men and measures. He saw Mr. Pitt but once, which was at Hampstead, on Wednesday. The proposition made to him was, to stand as a capital cypher in the most responsible situation in the kingdom, surrounded with other cyphers of a different complexion, the whole under the absolute guidance and nomination of Mr. Pitt, who was to hold the office of Lord Privy Seal, and consequently to run no risk or have any trouble but as far as he chose it. Every dependant of Mr. Pitt's was to be brought into office, and no other changes to be made but what were necessary for that purpose. It was not pretended that there was any change of *measures*, and the change of men consisted in giving three or four of the first offices of the kingdom to some of the immediate friends of Mr. Pitt, who, joined with General Conway, and the Rump of the last Administration, were to compose the present Ministry. This was the modest proposition to which Lord Temple was invited to accede, and which Mr. Pitt well knew that he would not consent to, before the King, in consequence of Mr. Pitt's advice, sent for him to come to town. His wish was union, but not obedience, which neither his rank, fortune, nor inclination will allow him to admit of in contradiction to the public opinion which he had declared last Sessions, and in support of some new measures which he foresees that he may probably not approve. He immediately rejected it as highly unfit to be made to him by one who knew that he would not accept it, and to whom in the like case he would not have offered it.

He expressed his desire of union to strengthen the King's Government, and to give it both credit and stability, for which purpose he had endeavoured to divest himself of private affections and prejudices, and, as far as was possible, to bring into His Majesty's service as much weight and ability as could be got together at this critical conjuncture; that he was sorry to find that Mr. Pitt's plan was so very different from it, and that ideas of so little moderation and temper had taken possession of his mind; that as this was the case, it was needless to talk further upon principles so totally inadmissible. Here he wished to close it, and I rejoice extremely to be able to tell you that he expressly declined making any mention of me upon this occasion, which I think is much more for my dignity and honour, and for his own, as his refusal cannot now be attributed to personal views for his own family.

The causes assigned for his refusal, that it was because it was proposed to restore Mr. Mackenzie, and that too much consideration was had of Lord Bute in the intended arrangement, are, I am confident, without the least foundation, and I am still persuaded that neither Mr. Mackenzie's nor Lord Bute's name were ever mentioned in the whole conversation; but the account of Mr. Pitt's having refused a Cabinet Council office to Lord Lyttelton, and of his having objected to Lord Gower as Secretary of State, is I believe very true. I understand that his intention was to take the Privy Seal himself, to give the office of President of the Council to the Duke of Grafton, and those of the two Secretaries of State to Lord Shelburne and Mr. Conway. This is the great comprehensive plan as far as I have heard of it for giving that vigour, experience and ability to the public offices, and for restoring that union of all parties, that temper and harmony, that confidence and permanency in Government, which have been said to be so much wanted, and for the attainment of which the

King has been prevailed upon to take the extraordinary step of sending for Mr. Pitt out of Somersetshire in contradiction to the opinion which His Majesty was said to have adopted last Sessions, of not seeing him except upon a plan and principles which had been previously explained to him. I do not hear how it was determined to fill up the vacancy made by Lord Temple's refusal, which must have been foreseen, and was certainly expected, and whether any alterations may now be made in this system, formed upon such disinterested, temperate, conciliating, and extended views. I take it for granted that they will all serve the King and the public *without salaries,* as we have been solemnly assured by the newspapers that they would, or at least that they would let them lie *in the Treasury,* where we have been repeatedly told with equal modesty and veracity, and half England really believes, that the three thousand pounds a-year which was payable to Mr. Pitt as Secretary of State now lie unapplied. To speak seriously, I am glad to hear from several hands that Lord Bute disclaims the present transaction, which is certainly founded upon principles widely different from those which I am told he laid down with such general approbation in the House of Lords last Sessions, and which I hear from many of his friends he is determined to abide by. As to my sentiments on this subject, I may be too much prejudiced to form them impartially, but at least you can bear me witness, as well as Sir Fletcher Norton, in the conversations I have had with him, that the language I have holden has been that of temper and moderation with respect to my own feelings, and a desire to promote it in every other man. I am very much obliged to Sir F. Norton for his good opinion of me, and

for the manner in which you tell me he has expressed
it, and still more so for the justice he does me. I at
no time contended that Mr. Mackenzie should *never*
hold *any* office, not even at the time when, for variety of
reasons which you know, I carried to the King the proposition for removing him from the office of Lord Privy
Seal of Scotland. Sir F. Norton, therefore, very justly
thinks that it would be a strange thing if after what has
passed, when he believes that Lord Bute has given up
the idea of restoring him to the *same* office, and wishes
even for an *English* one, that in return for it I should
now take up and insist upon the contrary opinion. As
to Lord Temple, I have not talked to him upon this
subject. I cannot take upon me to give any answer, but
Sir F. Norton must have heard his general sentiments
from a friend of his, who has often talked to Lord
Temple about Lord Bute and his friends. I am, &c.,
&c. GEORGE GRENVILLE.

I trust this letter to your discretion, as the subject is
of a delicate nature, to contradict any falsehoods which
have been raised, or any wrong impressions which have
been given.

EARL TEMPLE TO ——————[1]

Stowe, July 20, 1766.

MY DEAR LORD,—I received the honour of your Lordship's most obliging letter last night.

I left London on Thursday night after two conferences
with His Majesty, and one with Mr. Pitt; I could not

----

[1] This letter is from a rough draft without any address.

lend myself to the ideas of the latter, whose plan of the future *Ministry* consisted entirely of those who, in my opinion, sacrificed in the last Sessions most ignominiously the honour and interests of the King and kingdom, the consequence of which would have been the making me a cypher, at the head of the first department in administration. For the sake of public and general union I was willing to accommodate myself to Mr. Pitt's negative to my brother Grenville being a part of the intended Ministry, and I never proposed it. I felt it was impossible to give a higher mark of my desire of universal conciliation; after which I claimed an equality, and have no idea of yielding to him in a bystanding situation, or indeed in any other, a superiority which I think it would be unbecoming in me to give. Thus am I deprived of the means of accomplishing what it is pretended I was called to, having only to add that both in and out of government, I am, my dear Lord, much your obedient humble servant, TEMPLE.

I stated Lord Lyttelton for a Cabinet Council office, which was not agreed to, nor was my idea of making Lord Gower a Secretary of State consented to, Mr. Pitt having objections to both. The nomination of Chancellor of the Exchequer, and of my whole Board, was left to me.

MR. NUGENT TO MR. GRENVILLE.

London, July 22, 1766.

MY DEAR SIR,—I saw Lord Shelburne yesterday in the evening, who expressed himself sorry and hurt at the late event. He spoke of Lord Temple and you in the same terms which he has always used with me, and seemed convinced that Mr. Pitt's idea of an union with your brother was founded on a perfect equality. No plan has yet transpired, and if none has yet been formed for a new treasury, as is generally believed, the inference seems pretty clear that Mr. Pitt depended upon Lord Temple's acceptance.

The Rockinghamites are, I am told, extremely elated on your brother's departure, and now say they always wished for Mr. Pitt, and only feared him. I am, &c., &c.   R. NUGENT.

LADY CHATHAM TO EARL TEMPLE.

North End, July 22, 1766.

YOU will not wonder, my dear Brother, that my answer to your last kind letter is dated from hence. Mr. Pitt's fever returning again, he very well knowing what I should feel in continuing at so great a distance from him, in so painful a circumstance, kindly left to me to decide upon my own motions, when he writ to give me an account of his health. Our dear children being, thank God, happily all well, I was under no suspense about my determination, but set out immediately, and went Friday evening part of my way in company with the little ones, who are gone to Weymouth, much I hope both for their health and pleasure. I arrived here yesterday morning, and had the comfort to find Mr. Pitt considerably mended, but with not half so good looks as when we parted. I cannot express to my dear Brother the sensible joy it is to me to understand from Mr. Pitt, that, though you upon the whole did not agree in sentiments upon things in question, yet your differing was with the greatest kindness and friendship imaginable towards him, and which I assure you is felt by no less pleasing satisfaction by him than by me. I indulge a hope that now some way or other it may be possible for a visit to be made to Stowe by no less rapturous admirers than the Prince de Cruy himself. I am extremely glad that your own passion for it is revived again, though it seems as if it were a little indebted for it to foreign praises, which by confirming its merits, reproves your inconstancy. I desire to put you in mind in return for your twigs, that your over-grown timber is not upon the scale of a garden, and that the competition is not between parks. In short, I will not give Stowe up to any place. As your own, *in civility*, you may if you please. I long to show you Burton Pynsent, because it belongs to us, and because there is something not quite common about it. You know I have your promise. Adieu, my dear Brother, I don't know but you are still amidst your grandeurs, and therefore I will break in no longer upon you than to assure you of the constant affection of your friends here. Your most loving Sister,   CHATHAM [1].

MR. WHATELY TO MR. GRENVILLE.

July 29, 1766.

DEAR SIR,—I have been detained a day longer in town than I proposed to stay, and have thereby an op-

---

[1] See Lord Temple's reply to this letter in *Chatham Correspondence*, ii. 467.

portunity of sending you the latest reports, though I will not always answer for their being the most authentic; though the general arrangement is certain, and will take place to-morrow: the Duke of Richmond and Mr. Dowdeswell having resigned their Seals this morning. I believe it to be true that the Duke of Grafton and Mr. Townshend both declined their respective offices; the latter assigned for the reason of his reluctance, that he was already in an office of more honour, more profit, and more ease, which he did not choose to quit unless by His Majesty's command: he has nominated Mr. D'Oyley to be Secretary to the Chancellor of the Exchequer: I heard this first from D'Oyley, whom I had called upon to mention the business you desired me, but this circumstance silenced me, and I conclude now there is an end of it, at least for the present. Lord John Cavendish will not stay at the Treasury; but in hopes that he may alter his mind, I am told that the Commission is to be made out for only four Lords; if he persists, either Lord Villiers or Pryse Campbell will succeed him, but I believe the latter. Both the Secretaries continue: Mr. Dowdeswell is to be provided for.

The story of the day is, that Sir John Cust is to be a Peer, and Mr. Dowdeswell, Speaker; but I am told from better authority that he will be Treasurer of the Navy, and Lord Howe one of the Joint Treasurers of Ireland. Both Lord Barrington and Mr. Stanley are talked of for the other, and both also for Secretary at War, but I suppose nothing is settled about either of them. It is said Lord Townshend is to be an Earl, which I do not believe, and that Lady Dalkeith is to be a Peeress, which is not improbable. I can learn no certainty concerning Lord Northumberland either way, but I rather incline to think he is not to be Chamberlain, and this afternoon it is said that the Duke of Portland has been told he may continue.

Lord Northington is President of the Council, and Lord Camden, Chancellor. The offer has been made to Hussey of being either Attorney - General or Chief Justice. The opinion is that he will accept the former, and then the Solicitor resign. I fancy he will prefer the easier situation. Mr. Yorke will, it is said, take nothing if anything should be offered to him. Mr. Pitt's patent is making out for Earl of Chatham, &c. He has been to pay a visit to Lord Rockingham, and was let into the hall, but his Lordship sent out word that he was busy.

It is reported that Lord Hertford is to continue Lord Lieutenant of Ireland, but the Duke of Richmond to go there to the next Sessions.

The violent fluctuation of the India Stock to-day is mere Stock-jobbing.

At New York a Bill has been brought into the Assembly for compensation to the sufferers. The Representatives for the upland Counties opposed it, saying that the Yorkers did the damage, and ought to bear the expense; on the first division, 11 for the Bill, against 10. On the second division, 13 to 10.

If Hussey is Attorney-General, Judge Wilmot is to be Chief Justice.

MR. CHARLES LLOYD TO MR. GRENVILLE.

Salt Office [1], Tuesday, July 29, 1766.

DEAR SIR,—The new arrangements are to take place

---

[1] The Salt Office was in Buckingham Street. Charles Lloyd held no appointment there; but he seems to have resided with his mother,

to-morrow. The Duke of Grafton, first Lord of the Treasury; Charles Townshend, Chancellor of the Exchequer. Lord John Cavendish is to go out, and Lord Villiers to replace him. Lord Shelburne and Mr. Conway, Secretaries of State. Lord Egmont continues. Mr. Pitt to be Privy Seal, and immediately created Earl of Chatham, Viscount Pynsent, of Burton Pynsent, in the County of Somerset. This last is an *assured* fact, officially coming to my knowledge. Mr. J. Grenville is said to have Mr. Dowdeswell for his adjunct in the office of Paymaster. Mr. Yorke gone out of town, and out of humour. Lord Bute is said to take no part in all this. Lord Townshend is to be an Earl, and Lady Dalkeith a Baroness: this seems apocryphal. Lowndes and Cooper both continue Secretaries. D'Oyley is to be made Secretary to Charles Townshend as Chancellor. Wilmot to be Chief Justice of the Common Pleas.

Lord Rockingham has bearded Mr. Pitt in letting him come in as far as his hall last Sunday, and then sending word by a footman that he could not see him. The explanation he gave of this at the Board to-day, is, that as a private man he would on every occasion that he could, resent Mr. Pitt's contemptuous usage of him; as a public one, he should neither oppose nor support his measures. Pitt says, I hear, that he is resolved never to be angry again, but that if this had happened twenty years ago, Lord Rockingham should have heard of it, for he would have taken no such usage from the first Duke in the land. I expect, dear Sir, that you

Mrs. Catherine Lloyd, who probably had apartments as House or Office keeper.

will believe this and the Peerage story; the rest, comme
il vous plaira. At all events, pray believe me, &c., &c.

C. LLOYD.

MR. HANS STANLEY TO MR. GRENVILLE.

Admiralty, July 29, 1766.

DEAR SIR,—After returning you a great many thanks
for the favour of your last letter, the immediate purpose
of my writing to you at present is, that you should know,
not by reports, or by newspapers, but from myself directly, what relates to me. I left London a few days
after Lord Temple, when my hopes were disappointed
of seeing your family united, and placed where I have
always humbly wished them in the State. I was scarce
arrived at Paultons, when I received the King's commands to return here, which were followed with an
offer of my choice between the two vacant Embassies of
Madrid and Petersburg. I need not say that nothing
can be further from the plan of life I had proposed to
myself, or from my wishes, than either of them; I can
with great truth add, that I neither sought nor thought
of any employment, but tired and disgusted with all the
late scenes of domestic politics, and anxious about the
future, I have accepted the Embassy to Petersburg [1], as
a temporary retreat from the present confusion; if any
circumstance can render it acceptable to me, it is the
reflection that I shall stand as free as a military officer

---

[1] Mr. Stanley's appointment did not take effect. See many letters on
the subject in the *Chatham Correspondence*, vol. iii. Sir George
Macartney was soon after made Ambassador Extraordinary and Pleni
potentiary to the Court of Russia.

in his command, and be merely a servant of the publick in the most extensive sense of the word : I hope I shall have the pleasure of seeing you again before I set out, and of receiving any commands you may have for me. I suppose you have heard from persons much better informed than myself, the various changes which are to take place, and I write this merely to assure you that my absence will never diminish the inviolable esteem and high respect with which I shall ever be, &c., &c.

H. STANLEY.

COUNTESS TEMPLE TO MR. GLOVER.

Stowe, July 29, 1766.

I BEG the favour to know, my good Mr. Glover, whether you are in the land of the living or the dead, that I may guess what you are about; if you are alive, I know your mind is wholly occupied with your French Mademoiselle, but yet I presume you might turn one thought towards a true English dame, who has a real friendship for you. If you are in the shades below, I know you are trotting after Leonidas like St. Anthony's pig, 'till your poor feet are worn to skin and bone (if one may make use of that expression to a shade), for you are resolved never to lose sight of him. Good Lord! how I should laugh to see Melissa puffing and blowing to keep pace with you ; for since you have been favourite and first Minister to Apollo, she licks the dust under your feet, as Conway did to the great Commoner. I think you might write me a letter, for letters from the Dead are allowed, and you may be sure I have correspondence from Elysium, or I could not so exactly know how you spend your time. You departed loaded with various Politicks. I hope you threw them all into the river Styx, for they must be useless in a place of bliss, or sent them to Pluto by the hands of Mercury : they may be of use to the Judges in the trial of some people. My Lord insists upon it you are dead, or else you would never have been so long without seeing us, and desires you may know he loved and respected you to your last moment. If you should take a trip to this world, pray don't come and open my bed-curtains in a winding sheet, with a pale visage, and a taper in your hand, but come in the evening in your brown cloaths, with a healthy complexion, and a smile, reading Leonidas : be sure not to speak in a hollow voice. These prelimi-naries being settled, I shall not be afraid of seeing you ; nay, I can even say I shall be glad to see you, and my Lord promises not to make use of the broomstick and David's Psalms, as he once did against the Devil : greatest and best of Manes, the rough Spartan himself not excepted, farewell.   A. T.

MR. WILLIAM GERARD HAMILTON TO EARL TEMPLE.

Hampton Court, July 30, 1766.

MY DEAR LORD,—Though the *Royal Party* should leave you both in town and country [1], my satisfaction in coming to Stowe, and my affection for the owner of it, will never I think be diminished by such sort of calami-ties ; and I am full as anxious to be of your party in your present choice of quiet and retirement, as I ever

---

[1] The Princess Amelia had been Lord Temple's guest at Stowe about this time.

can be in any change that may possibly happen to you, of sentiment, or of situation.

I have, I believe, already mentioned to your Lordship, that my friend Mr. Hutchinson, whose arrival from Ireland I expect every hour, was to pass a few days with me at Hampton Court. As soon as I am released from that engagement, I shall certainly have the honour of waiting upon you, of which I will take the liberty to give your Lordship notice; lest you should be absent from home, or so circumstanced as may possibly make my coming to you inconvenient.

Lord Rockingham, who acquired so little reputation during his continuance in office, has, and I think deservedly, gained some approbation by his conduct in one instance since he left it. Mr. Pitt went to wait upon him to apologize for his Lordship's being removed from the Treasury, and, it is said, to offer him the Lord Lieutenantcy of Ireland. Lord Rockingham came home while Mr. Pitt's chair was at the door, upon which it was carried into the hall, but his Lordship went up stairs and sent word by his servant to Mr. Pitt, that he was extremely busy, and could not possibly see him.

Mr. Yorke will certainly throw up his office upon Lord Camden's having the Seals. De Grey, and not Norton, is to be Attorney-General. Who is to be Solicitor I can't learn, but I am told it is to be neither Wedderburn nor Dunning. The prevailing opinion is that Wilmot will have the Common Pleas. Lord Bute declares as usual that he knows nothing of all these changes; and is at a loss to conjecture how they were brought about. His ignorance of all these matters is not more affected than Norton's and Wedderburn's was real.

After your Lordship's party at Stowe, and at Blenheim, it may appear idle to relate to you the language of the Duke of Bedford's friends in London ; but they declare one and all, loudly and universally, that though your Lordship may possibly have behaved generously to them, it is a generosity which has undone them. That they are thrown into the most hopeless situation imaginable by your refusal : and that rather than you should have declined, they would, had they been consulted, have pressed your Lordship to accept without one of them. And they take care to hint in guarded, but at the same time in very intelligible, terms, that if Mr. Pitt would have consented to Mr. Grenville's being of the Cabinet, it is probable they might have been totally overlooked. This is the language which is circulated. What attention ought to be paid to it, your Lordship is a much better judge than I am ; I thought it right to communicate it, and the more so as it comes from quarters which I have always considered as the best informed in regard to the real sentiments of that connection. I must add that nothing can be more observable, nor is more observed, than the attention paid by the Duke of Grafton to the Duke of Bedford's friends who happen to be in town, and Fitz Roy, I know, said that his brother would be empowered to offer them such terms as he hoped they would accept.

Inclosed I send your Lordship an account I have this moment received of what was done to-day at Court. I can't help observing that Charles Townshend has *not* kissed hands. Your's, my dear Lord, most faithfully and affectionately,   — — —

THE COUNTESS OF CHATHAM TO EARL TEMPLE.

North End, Saturday, August 2, 1766.

DEAR BROTHER,—I have to say in return to your last letter, that it was extremely unexpected, and that the mistake (since it is one,) which I proceeded upon was very natural both for my Lord and me to have made, for certainly our past conversations encouraged me to an easy belief, that private friendship and affection would remain, though disagreement upon public situations should unfortunately happen between Mr. Pitt and you.

You know my faith, and I hold it fast, that the blessing of Heaven will still be given to upright and virtuous intentions.

There remains for me only to desire you to receive my most sincere wishes for your health, honour, and happiness, remaining, under all circumstances, your most affectionate Sister, HESTER CHATHAM.

MR. WILLIAM GERARD HAMILTON TO EARL TEMPLE.

Hampton Court, August 3, 1766.

MY DEAR LORD,—I have passed these last two days in town with Mr. Hutchinson, whom I have made exceedingly happy by informing him of the permission you gave me to bring him with me to Stowe, and, unless you forbid us, we shall probably have the honour of waiting upon you in less than a fortnight.

Having no opportunities of receiving any information which is authentic, I can only relate to your Lordship what is reported, and what, extraordinary as it may seem, is universally believed.

Lord Camden is said to have complained loudly of Mr. Pitt's having accepted a peerage ; and of his having adjusted everything without the least communication to any one friend. The bargains which his Lordship and Lord Northington are reported to have made with the Court are scarcely to be credited. Lord Camden, according to the notion which prevails, is immediately to have the reversion of a Tellership for his son, and a pension of 5000*l.* per annum, if he should at any time be removed from the Great Seal. Lord Northington, in addition to his present employment, is to have a pension of 3000*l.* for life, and, in case of his being displaced, a further addition of 1500*l.* per annum.

Dowdeswell is so much offended at his being removed for Mr. Townshend, that he has refused to accept of being Speaker, of being at the head of the Board of Trade, or of being Joint Paymaster, the last of which has been given to Lord North, but who is to have the remaining half I understand continues as yet unsettled.

Mr. Yorke has changed his resolution of quitting his profession with the resignation of his office, and it is thought that Lord Rockingham and his friends, from the language which they hold, will connect themselves with the present Administration, though there has been a sequel to the history which I wrote to your Lordship of what had passed between him and Mr. Pitt. Lord Rockingham went up to him at Court, and said that though it was possible his refusing to see him might upon the first view of it appear to be improper, yet he was persuaded that if Mr. Pitt would be at the trouble of recollecting the many marks, not only of inattention, but of actual disregard, which had been shown to him during the course of the late transactions, his behaviour could not but appear, even to Mr. Pitt himself, extremely justifiable.

The Duke of Newcastle has refused a pension of 4000*l.* per annum, and Hussey declines being a Judge in the King's Bench. There are those who still think that Norton, and not Wilmot, will be Chief Justice of the Common Pleas.

In the letter I had last the honour of writing to your Lordship, I mentioned the ideas which prevailed here in regard to what were the real wishes, and to what would be the probable conduct, of the Duke of Bedford's friends, under their present circumstances. I think I can now speak with authority better than what I then had, though I thought that extremely good : you may rely upon it as certain that the Duchess of Bedford does not scruple to declare her very sanguine wishes for a junction with Mr. Pitt; that her language is, that the present system must be a permanent one; that it ought to be so; and that Mr. Pitt, by his talents and address in the Closet, will establish his power by ingratiating himself with the King. Knowing the Duke of Bedford's dislike to Lord Bute, her Grace adopts the opinion, which is very industriously circulated, that these last changes were brought about without the knowledge, and contrary to the wishes, of Lord Bute.

If the Duke of Bedford was left entirely to himself, I should think it probable his good wishes for Mr. Grenville would prevail. His Grace had thoughts of making a visit to Wotton, but, if I am not mistaken, great pains are taking to prevent it.

It is asserted by very high authority that your Lordship had peremptorily refused making a part of the new system upon your very first interview at Richmond [1]. The use made of this declaration is to show that your declining could not have been occasioned by any disagreement with Mr. Pitt, your resolution having been not only formed, but declared, before you ever saw him. Another particular is mentioned, upon which much stress is laid; that in a letter to Lord Gower your Lordship, after having informed him of the reasons why you did not accept, mentioned that the new system was to be formed entirely by Mr. Pitt; and added these words, "*that you hoped it would be permanent.*" [2]

This is construed as meant to imply, if not an actual disclaimer, at least a great indifference.

(*Imperfect.*)

MR. CHARLES LLOYD TO MR. GRENVILLE.

Tuesday, August 5, 1766.

DEAR SIR,—You may perhaps have seen a Pamphlet advertised, entitled "An Enquiry into the Conduct of a Great Commoner," [3] together with an account of a late

---

[1] The King's letter to Mr. Pitt, written immediately after the interview, certainly conveys an impression that Lord Temple was by no means satisfied with the proposed arrangements, and the King probably anticipated the difficulties which subsequently occurred between Lord Temple and Mr. Pitt. Lord Temple is said to have told Lord Northington that "his Lordship need not have sent for him from the country, for there was no real wish or intention to have him in the Administration."

[2] This passage does not occur in the letter written by Lord Temple to Lord Gower when he desired to be excused for having named him to Mr. Pitt, for Secretary of State. See *ante*, page 272.

[3] This "scurrilous and scandalous pamphlet," as Lord Chesterfield calls it, was compiled by Humphrey Cotes and Almon, but the prin-

Conference. Mr. Roberts told me yesterday that Almon, the publisher (who says that he had authority for the particulars of what he intended to publish), had received orders not to publish it. I hear to-day that notwithstanding this he resolved to publish to-morrow. I will send it to you when published.

Your paper of to-day will contain, copied from yesterday's Gazetteer, a letter supposed to be written by Sir Robert Walpole to the late King. *It is commended*[1].

Lord Northington is to have 5000*l.* per annum as President of the Council, and whenever he quits it, 4000*l.* per annum pension during his life, and a reversion of Clerk of the Hanaper for two lives.

cipal materials, particularly the private conversations which it describes, were unquestionably derived from Lord Temple, and that was the general opinion at the time of publication. Walpole, alluding to Lord Chatham's unpopularity, says, " The great engine of this dissatisfaction was Lord Temple, who was so shameless as to publish the history of their breach, in which he betrayed every private passage that Mr. Pitt had dropped in their negotiation and quarrel, which could tend to inflame the public or private persons against him. This malignant man worked in the mines of successive factions for near thirty years together. To relate them is writing his life." A refutation of this pamphlet, written as Lord Chesterfield adds, " by some friend of Mr. Pitt, gives an account of his whole political life, and at the latter end there is an article that expresses such supreme contempt of Lord Temple, and in so pretty a manner, that I suspect it to be Mr. Pitt's own. I here transcribe the article : ' But this I will be bold to say, that had he (Lord Temple) not fastened himself into Mr. Pitt's train, and acquired thereby such an interest in that great man, he might have crept out of life with as little notice as he crept in ; and gone off with no other degree of credit, than that of adding a single unit to the bills of mortality.'" I cannot, however, agree with Lord Chesterfield in ascribing this passage to Mr. Pitt; it is very inconsistent with his character that he should condescend to write in this manner of himself, and it is as little likely that he should so express himself of Lord Temple, the loss of whose affection and friendship he constantly and bitterly deplored.

[1] Sir Robert Walpole's advice to George II. to make Pulteney a Peer, is applied by the writer to the case of George III. and Pitt.

Lord Camden has got a reversion of a Tellership for his son, and a grant of 1500*l.* per annum on the Irish Establishment, if he quits the Seals before the Teller's office is vacant. The new Treasury Board sat for the first time yesterday. There is but one opinion about Mr. Pitt's Peerage.

I am just going to Chiswick to dine with Lord Townshend, who I hear is sorry for the acceptance of his brother [1]. Mr. Dowdeswell has refused the Joint Paymastership, and the First Commissionership of Trade, chiefly owing, I understand, to his great uncertainty as to his re-election.   I am, &c., &c.

CHARLES LLOYD.

THE EARL OF HILLSBOROUGH TO MR. GRENVILLE.

Hanover Square, August 6, 1766.

DEAR SIR,—When I had the pleasure of writing to you on Monday night, I had not the most distant idea of what has since happened. It was very well known that had I not been dismissed, I could not have continued at the Board of Trade upon the footing I held it. I must have resigned unless some alteration was made, and I knew none was intended, and therefore I gave it up in my mind, even if I could have reconciled it with my going abroad. Many other circumstances conspired to prevent my regretting the loss of my employment, which I need not trouble you with.

On Tuesday last I received a very gracious message, accompanied by a wish that I would return to the Board,

---

[1] Charles Townshend was now Chancellor of the Exchequer in place of Mr. Dowdeswell.

and ordering me to return my answer the next day in
the Closet. This message was delivered to me in the
most obliging manner by the present Minister. I
turned it in my mind; not whether I should come to
the Board as it was constituted while you was Minister,
for I knew I could not carry on the business in that
manner; nor whether I should propose, what is certainly most desirable for the public, that it should be
made an independent department upon an extensive
plan, for I know the disposition of some too well, to
suppose that would be complied with, by parting with
any powers or patronage; but whether I could not contract the plan so as that I might do the business in an
easy manner to myself, and free from that very unpleasant, and in some measure unbecoming, attendance upon
others, which is the consequence of unexplained connections of departments in business, and always very
disagreeable to that which is considered as in the inferior situation.

I wished at the same time to accept, because I do,
and shall always, wish to show a disposition to support
Government, being resolved, as you say, to judge by
actions, and not by words; and whatever my wishes
may be with regard to particular persons whom I love,
not to support or oppose men, but measures. After
therefore considering the office in this light, I resolved
to accept, provided the Board should be altered from a
Board of Representation to a Board of Report upon
Reference only; that the order to the Governors in
America to correspond with the Board of Trade *only*,
should be rescinded; and that every executive business
that has by degrees crept into the Board should revert
to the proper offices, particularly all Treasury business;

and that I should not be of the Cabinet (which was also offered to me). In this manner, which has been agreed to, I have accepted the office ; my own business will go on with ease and satisfaction to myself; the load of business that this will throw elsewhere, will, I hope, meet with strength of abilities to support it, and application to dispatch it. I give no opinion about it ; it is not my affair.

I thought it right to give you an account of this transaction, as you are so kind to me as to interest yourself in what regards me in the most friendly and obliging manner. I beg your pardon for writing so long a letter about myself; I think you will discern through it, that I have wishes, which possibly time and mutual calm reflection may bring to pass ; it would make me very happy to be instrumental. I am, with sincere and affectionate attachment, &c., &c.   HILLSBOROUGH.

MR. GRENVILLE TO SIR JOHN GLYNNE[1].

Wotton, August 7, 1766.

DEAR SIR,—There is no occasion for you to make the least apology for your letter which I received last night ; on the contrary, if upon this or any other subject I can give you any information or do anything which may be of use to you it will give me a very sincere pleasure. As to the question which you ask of me whether Dr. Blackstone is right in his "Stemmata Chicheleana,"

---

[1] Of Hawarden Castle, County Flint. He was the sixth Baronet. He married Honora, daughter of Henry Conway, and grand-daughter of Sir John Conway, of Bodryddan, who was a grandson of Sir Kenelm Digby and Venetia Stanley, and through them descended in direct line from the Stanleys and the Percys. Sir John Glynne died in 1777.

No. 135, when he makes Sir Peter Temple marry Eleanor Tyrrel, as this does not agree with Willis's account of Buckinghamshire, and therefore whether Peter Temple, the father of John, might not be a knight and married to Eleanor Tyrrel, I apprehend that it is very easy to give you a satisfactory answer, though I have only one of the books which you mention, viz. "Willis's Account of Buckinghamshire." In page 276 of this book you will see that the eldest son of *Sir Thomas Temple of Stowe* was *Sir Peter Temple of Stowe*, who was grandfather to Lord Cobham, and to my mother; you will likewise see in the same page of the same book that the second son of Sir Thomas Temple of Stowe was Sir Thomas Temple of Stanton Barry. This Sir Peter Temple of Stanton Barry married Eleanor Tyrrel, and by her was father to Eleanor Temple, who intermarried with my grandfather Richard Grenville of Wotton, and was mother to my father and to Lady Conway, and another daughter who died young. By this account it appears there were two Sir Peter Temples, the one of Stowe, who was my mother's grandfather, the other of Stanton Barry, who intermarried with Eleanor Tyrrel, and was my grandmother's father. This is a full answer to the question which you ask. I have not the "Stemmata Chicheleana," but I suppose that book states it truly. If you have any further doubt, you may consult the new edition of the " Peerage of Great Britain," by Mr. Edmonstone, in which you will find the pedigree, I believe, very exactly stated under the article of Earl Temple, but I have not the book here, having left it in town. This I hope will be sufficient to clear up any difficulty on this head, and that your son will succeed in his application for a Fellowship of All Souls.

I do not write anything to you about the late extra-ordinary political transactions, the particulars of which you must have seen and read long ago: I will only say that I have had nothing to do with them in any shape, having expressly declined to have my name mentioned, and I rejoice extremely that Lord Temple has refused to engage upon a plan which was neither consistent with his honour nor safety, and of which there is no example; the express claim being to *guide everything* in a sine-cure office and to be *responsible for nothing*. I cannot think that such a proposition can be attended with that good-will, credit, and permanency which the state of the kingdom so much requires, as private intrigue and the public distress and indignation will in all likelihood join to overturn it. I am very sorry to hear so bad an ac-count of Mrs. Conway's health, which I fear is in a very dangerous situation. I shall at all times be glad of any opportunity to express the esteem and regard with which I am, &c., &c.   GEORGE GRENVILLE.

MR. GRENVILLE TO MR. CHARLES LLOYD.

Wotton, August 8, 1766.

DEAR LLOYD,—The several packets containing the pamphlet published by Mr. Almon[1], together with your letter, came safe last night. There are certainly some mistakes in it, but I shall make no comments upon the general purpose of it, nor take any notice of the mis-takes in it, except of one pretty essential one which re-lates personally to myself.

[1] " An Enquiry into the Conduct of a late Right Honourable Commoner."

It is said, page 41st, that notwithstanding my being entirely " out of place, and excluded from all connection with the intended system, I would nevertheless support *the Measures of their Administration.*" I desired Lord Temple not to clog or embarrass this transaction in any shape by mentioning me, but that if he could find it consistent with his honour and safety to engage in it, I would nevertheless give him all the assistance and support in my power, as far as I could consistently with my friends, and former opinions, and as far as *he* was concerned in it, but desired it might not be understood to *go any further.* I never engaged myself in any shape, either in or out of office, to support *Mr. Pitt's Measures or Administration.* This I desire you will tell everybody whom you see, and take some means to let Mr. Almon know it, and of having it contradicted as fully and effectually as you can. I would have assisted and supported *my brother, Lord Temple,* if *he* had taken the Treasury[1], as cordially and affectionately as I could, but I have so long and so highly disapproved Mr. Pitt's public conduct, his principles and his measures, that I never could make any such general declaration of support to *him*, though at the same time if *he* should change his sentiments, as *he* has so frequently done, and make any proposal which was really for the public service, I would not do as *he* has done by me, and oppose it from personal rancour and jealousy.

I am sorry to see Lord North in half an office, joined with that able statesman, Mr. George Cooke.

I desire you will return my sincerest thanks to Lord Townshend for the cordial manner in which you tell me

---

[1] Mr. Grenville's " support " is only mentioned upon that supposition.

he has expressed his good will, and his good opinion of me   I have writ to nobody about the late transaction, who had not writ first to me, and have therefore omitted many of my most intimate friends, as you know ; but if I had known in any way that Lord Townshend would have liked it, I certainly should have writ to him upon this occasion, which you may tell him from me, with my best compliments, whenever you see him.   I am, &c., &c.   GEORGE GRENVILLE.

THE EARL OF SUFFOLK TO MR. GRENVILLE.

August 8, 1766.

DEAR SIR,—Your account of the late extraordinary transactions squared much with what I had heard from others : indeed with respect to yourself, it has been ingeniously reported that Lord Temple's conferences with Mr. Pitt broke off upon your account ; that such stipulations were made in your favour as the latter could by no means acquiesce in.   Conjecture has variously explained what they were, and too absurdly for me to say how ; but this has been represented to me with an air of truth and importance, and by people who ought to know better.   Upon the whole it appears to me that Lord Temple has been most contemptuously treated, that the propositions made to him were disgraceful, such as his situation in every respect could only reject and disdain, and that they were made to him only with a view to obtain his refusal.

I am sorry to draw so hostile a conclusion to my favourite ideas of *union, comprehension,* and *moderation.*

I earnestly wished it.   I expected to have seen it ; but without it I do not expect to see that stability in Government which never people stood more in need of than we do.   I am, &c.   SUFFOLK.

MR. JENKINSON TO MR. GRENVILLE.

Paris, August 10, 1766.

MY DEAR SIR,—I am obliged to you for the account you have sent me of your conduct in the late transactions. I entirely approve of it. I think it honourable, disinterested, and public spirited, and what must do you good with all men whose opinions are worth regarding. As to myself, I first delayed my journey into the south, that I might have the earlier intelligence of what was transacting at London. This delay, and the friendship of Lord Holdernesse, has procured me the acquaintance of the people of the first fashion here, and I have found this acquaintance so agreeable, that I shall continue here or at Compiègne, where the Court is at present, some time longer. I have been presented at Court and to the Prime Minister of this country, Monsieur de Choiseul. From the conversation I had with him, which was very short, I can form no judgment of his talents ; his aspect is very much against him.

I have presented your compliments to all the Maison d'Harcourt. They all desire me to return their compliments to you, and particularly Monsieur and Madame de Guerchy. They often inquire after you and Mrs. Grenville, and the last desired me to inform Mrs. Grenville that she has sent the needles for working of tapestry, which Lady Egremont had desired her to buy.

As I have found much amusement in this place, I think I have drawn, also, some information from it. I see more reasons every day to apprehend that France will extricate herself sooner from the difficulties which the war has brought upon her than we shall. I am sorry that this question, which goes so far to decide the whole of modern politics, should be so much against us. As to Monsieur de Nivernois, though we have frequently interchanged visits, yet I am not likely to see him except by chance. His establishment is so small that he lives in the summer with his wife's mother, where he can invite very few people. You would be surprised to see the number of English that come to this town. From what the people of this country see and know of their expenses, they must be sensible that they are at least their rivals. I am afraid, as Englishmen, we ought to lament we give this proof of it. I am, &c., &c.

C. JENKINSON.

MR. GRENVILLE TO EARL TEMPLE.

Wotton, August 20, 1766.

THE intelligence which you sent me, my dear brother, by my nephew, Jemmy, was well founded, as you will see by the account I am going to give you.

I went to Woburn on Saturday last, the day that Lady Egremont left us, and found the Duke of Bedford, who received me with great friendship and openness, and said that if he had not seen me, he proposed to come to Wotton in the course of this week. He told me that he had heard nothing since he saw you, except that Lord Hertford, whom he had met in town, had assured him of his own wishes, and of the wishes of those with whom he was connected, to see the Duke of Bedford and his friends in Government; but this was in general only, and went no further.

On Saturday evening Lord Tavistock, who brought Lady Tavistock into the country that day, after her lying-in, informed the Duke of Bedford that the Duke of Grafton had sent to him on the Thursday preceding, desiring to see him the next day; that when they met, the Duke of Grafton began by making excuses for troubling him on a subject which possibly he might not like to intermeddle in, but that having something to say to the Duke of Bedford, he rather chose to do it by Lord Tavistock than to employ any underlings.

He then expressed himself in very high terms concerning the Duke of Bedford, and dwelt upon it a great while, adding that though they had differed in Parliament, yet he hoped he had never been wanting in personal regard to him. That the Administration wished to see the Duke of Bedford and his friends in Government, and that, therefore, he desired to know how the Duke of Bedford stood affected towards the present Administration. That by Lord Egmont's resignation [1] there was a vacancy in a great office, which they should be glad to see supplied by Lord Gower, through the Duke of Bedford's mediation and approbation, but that it must be understood that this proposal came only from them, and that if it was accepted, they would propose it to the King. On Lord Tavistock wishing to know whether anything further was intended besides this offer to Lord Gower, the Duke of Grafton said that no further offer

---

[1] He had recently been First Lord of the Admiralty.

was meant at present; that he knew Lord Chatham's idea was *a great comprehensive and conciliating plan*, but that he did not mean at present to turn out any of those who would act with the Administration. That he, the Duke of Grafton, was so desirous to see an union established which might bring together as much strength and ability as might be; that notwithstanding his attachment to Lord Chatham, he would not have come in if he had thought that Lord Chatham did not intend it.

In answer to this, the Duke of Bedford wrote to the Duke of Grafton and to Lord Gower on Sunday, and showed me the letters to both of them [1]. He told the Duke of Grafton that his son had informed him what passed; that he was extremely sensible to the many obliging expressions which the Duke of Grafton had used concerning him; that he had wished to see the Duke of Grafton in office, because he thought him a friend to his country; that he had a great regard for him, and some others in the Administration, but that as to the question which was asked of him, he must freely declare that he and his friends having opposed the totality of the measures proposed by the last and supported by the present Administration, he must entirely decline taking any part by his mediation in this business, but left it to Lord Gower, upon any application made to him, to do as he should think best.

The Duke of Bedford's letter to Lord Gower contained an exact narrative of what I have writ to you, and a copy of his letter to the Duke of Grafton, telling him that by this means he had *quite washed his hands of it,* and that having done so, Lord Gower would act

---

[1] See *Bedford Correspondence*, vol. iii. pp. 342-3.

in it, if he heard anything more, as his own judgment should direct him.

The Duke of Bedford enjoined me secrecy, as Lord Tavistock was very unwilling that what passed in private conversation with him should be publicly discussed, but upon my desiring to communicate this to you, the Duke of Bedford very readily agreed to it, but under the seal of secrecy, which, as this is a matter of a delicate nature, is indispensably necessary to be observed.

The evident purpose of all this is, to break and divide us if possible, for which end your own words are now to be adopted, and a proposition made through another channel to those whom, when proposed by you, it was thought necessary absolutely to reject[1].

If I can trust my accounts from London, the indisposition even amongst those in office *augments*, as well as the public clamour both there and in the country. Adieu, my dear Brother, &c., &c.

GEORGE GRENVILLE.

EARL TEMPLE TO MR. GRENVILLE.

August 21, 1766, Thursday morning.

MY DEAR BROTHER,—I learn that things go very lamely on at St. James's, that the great and little Earl[2] are already upon ill terms, the great Earl demanding from the little one the immediate execution of certain

---

[1] Lord Temple, in his last interview with Mr. Pitt, on Wednesday the 16th of July, had proposed Lord Gower for Secretary of State, as a means of conciliating the Bedford connection, and restoring unanimity by a combination of parties. Mr. Pitt, however, at that time objected to the appointment of Lord Gower to any office.

[2] The Earls of Bute and Chatham.

stipulations, which diminutive wishes to postpone. He affects to be very indifferent upon the subject of the city of London, says he has held the cap to them long enough, that for the future he shall devote himself to the King's service *entirely*, and execute that so long as His Majesty shall approve of his counsels and measures; if not, he shall withdraw from all, and retire to Burton Pynsent.

Q. How Lord Gower's judgment will direct him[1]; the Duke of Bedford once refused to come into office himself, put Lord G. in, and in a little time accepted likewise himself.

I know authentically that my conduct in refusing is not applauded by that quarter, and that the offer has been invited, as far as certain expressions of longings for office do invite, and I believe much further too; however, we shall now see, and the event is very indifferent to me[2]. The testimony of adopting my plan, after refusing to me the execution of it, is, I think, advantageous to me; and as to the rest, I see nothing within the possibility of things which can give me real satisfaction on behalf of the public. Yours affectionately,

TEMPLE.

EARL TEMPLE TO MR. HUMPHREY COTES.

Stowe, August 24, 1766.

I AM very miserable, my dear Cotes, at what I this moment read in the papers with your name affixed to it.

[1] Lord Gower declined the offer of the Admiralty, according to Horace Walpole, because "he could not stand *alone*, in so responsible a place, and was connected with none of the present Ministry."

[2] Lord Temple never seems to have had entire confidence in the good faith of the Bedford party.

I am sensible that you have been hurried into this step by an honest indignation and warm zeal for my honour, but were I to see you, I am sure I could convince you of the numberless mischiefs attending it. The Enquiry itself which you allude to contains *many* mistakes, and particularly on the subject of pensions; it was a lucrative office and not a pension that was proposed for Lord Lyttelton, with the Cabinet Council annexed: and as to the assertion which angers you, forgive me if I hold it not worthy of notice; I scorn to think it possible, any man who knows me can be misled by such an invention, which I am certain Lord Chatham would not countenance a moment[1]. There now remains only for me to beg of you, on every account, not to proceed further in anything of this sort; all your friends and mine will join, I dare say, in the same request. Let me also add, that I am with much concern, though very sincerely, your faithful and obedient   TEMPLE.

MR. WILLIAM GERARD HAMILTON TO EARL TEMPLE.

London, Monday, (August 25, 1766.)

MY DEAR LORD,—The intelligence which I sent you of Lord Gower's having refused to accept of the Admiralty, is undoubtedly true: and it is as true that some

---

[1] The author of a pamphlet entitled *Seasonable Reflections*, &c., commenting upon the *Enquiry into the Conduct of a late Right Honourable Commoner*, and in allusion to Lord Temple, has the following passage:—" But in all this wonderful Enquiry we meet not with one word of his Lordship's (Lord Temple) afterwards offering to accept a place in the new Ministry, and of his being told he was then too late in his application." Humphrey Cotes, in a letter to the printer of the *Public Advertiser*, on the 23rd of August, designates the above as " a wicked, infamous, and wilful lie."

negotiation is still going on between Lord Chatham and the Duke of Bedford's friends.

The persons employed are the Duke of Grafton and Lord Camden, who declare everywhere their wish that Lord Gower may be placed in any situation which may be most agreeable to him.

I have reason to think that Lord Chatham has proposed to make Lord Tavistock Master of the Horse, which it is, however, reported the Duke of Rutland is very much disinclined to resign. An express was sent late last night to overtake Lord Granby upon his road to Scarborough, for which place he set out only a few days since. This message is a subject of much speculation.

The Duke of Grafton has declared that he is ready to resign his pretensions to the next vacant Garter to the Duke of Marlborough, and I know that Colonel Fitz-Roy was authorized to say, that if other arrangements could by any means be adjusted, Lord Weymouth might again be made Lord Lieutenant of Ireland. The offer of the Admiralty for Lord Gower, with a liberty of nominating to the two vacant seats at that Board, was made by the Duke of Grafton to Lord Tavistock, and was reported by him to the Duke of Bedford, who refused giving any opinion upon the proposal, but desired that the whole of it might be submitted to Lord Gower.

I am persuaded that the Duke of Bedford's friends will not accept without at least a communication of their design to Mr. Grenville. I think I can discover distinctly that they have strong apprehensions lest your Lordship should use your influence with Mr. Grenville to oppose their taking any employments under Lord

Chatham : but it is the universal opinion that their present difficulty is not occasioned by the nature of their engagements, but by some dispute about the advantageousness of the terms.

Lord Ligonier has got the pension for his nephew increased from 1000*l.* to 1500*l.* per annum, and a promise of the second regiment that becomes vacant ; the first being engaged to Colonel Clinton.

Lord Bute, who affects at least to be much dissatisfied with everything which is going forward, had a meeting with Lord Ligonier at Lord Townshend's, where he declared that he had not been in the least instrumental in the *disgrace* which his Lordship had suffered by the promotion of Lord Granby, and added that upon his honour, he had not seen the King, even once, during the last twelvemonth.

Shelley is to have Lord Edgecumbe's white staff, and Admiral Keppel declares he has not so much as a thought of resigning.

I am persuaded there must have been some mistake in your accounts relative to Sir Richard Lyttelton.

Shelburne tried all his tricks to prevail on Lord Lyttelton to pay a visit to Lord Chatham, and would, I am disposed to believe, have succeeded, had it not been for the interposition of Sir Richard. I was charged with a commission from him which I forgot to execute when I was at Stowe. It was to beg that you would give directions for the sending a buck to him at Chelsea. I shall probably have the happiness of drinking your Lordship's health with him, over a part of it.

There is one piece of intelligence more, to which, much as I wish it, I can give but little credit : it came, I believe, from Lord Hertford : "that some arrangement was under consideration which might be agreeable to Mr. Grenville."

Mr. Conway is much hurt at Lord Granby's promotion, and particularly as everything relative to it was settled without his knowledge. Yours, my dear Lord, &c., &c.   — — —

P. S. Your Lordship may now depend upon it that Sir Charles Saunders is to be First Lord of the Admiralty.

Lord Chatham was seized last night with a fit of the gout, and is confined to his bed.

MR. CHARLES LLOYD TO MR. GRENVILLE.

York Buildings, Friday, August 29, 1766.

DEAR SIR,—I delivered to Mr. Morin this morning your letter to General Conway, and the books having been previously packed up and sealed with your seal, were fetched away to the office [1].

Lord Palmerston and Sir George Younge are named Puisne Lords of the Admiralty. Mr. Pitt so ill at Hampstead that he will not see anybody.

Many people insist upon it that Lord Gower has declared his willingness to accept. They go further, and assert that his Lordship would upon no account have joined in Lord Temple's plan, but that he has a high respect and veneration for Lord Chatham. This may

---

[1] Mr. Grenville returned to the Secretary of State's Office some books of Prussian Correspondence, and in a letter to General Conway on the subject, he says:—" I have always been desirous that the correspondence with the Ministers at the different Courts should be preserved entire, and therefore when I quitted the office I left in it every public paper which had passed during the time that I held the seals, though I knew it had been the practice and had even been insisted on as a right by some of my predecessors to do otherwise."

be a story worthy of the populace, but I assure you it is vouched by people in high office, and repeated by men of distinction.

I am told there is a great fracas at the Post Office about a letter from the Duke of Bedford to the Duke of Grafton having been opened. Mr. Saxby is named as the person doing it, and is under strict examination, I hear, to name who set him on to do it[1].

[1] On the following Tuesday Charles Lloyd writes to Mr. Grenville, " Saxby is turned out of an office of 1200*l.* a year for opening the Duke of Bedford's letter, it is said, to the Duke of Grafton."—And again, " The Duke of Grafton has declared that if ever Saxby is put into any office, he will move the House of Lords to address the King to remove him."

The system of opening letters at the Post Office was the subject of very frequent remark in the correspondence of this period ; indeed it was so universally known or suspected, that few persons were so indiscreet as to send anything by that medium which they would object to have read in the " *Secret Office.*"

Mr. Anthony Todd, the Secretary to the General Post Office, in a " *Private Memorial,*" to Mr. Grenville, dated August, 1763, communicates the following statement of the Secret Service Money applied to the payment of the several allowances on the " Secret List," for one year to the 5th of April, 1763 :—

The Bishop of Bath and Wells	£500	Brought forward £3375	
Thomas Ramsden . .	500	Peter Hemet . . .	300
Edward Willes . .	500	Stephen Dupuy . .	300
Thomas Willes . .	300	John French . . .	300
James Wallace . .	400	John Ernest Bode, jun. .	300
James Rivers . .	200	William Augustus Bode .	200
Peter Morin . . .	250	John Ulrick Selshop .	100
Cuchet Juvencel . .	150	John Calcott . . .	60
John Ernest Bode, jun., £400 ; extra allowance, £100	500	James Holcome . .	40
		James Sanders . .	60
		Anthony Todd . .	750
The same person for Seals, &c.	75	The same person for distributing these allowances	25
			£5810
Carried forward £3375			

Peter Hemet, whose name stands for £300, and who had been super-

The great Earl says this Administration, though not what he wishes it, is still better than the last, and that he shall support the King's measures.

You may depend upon it, the present idea is that the Parliament should meet in November.

Saturday, August 30.

The East India Directors, it is said, have been twice this week before the Privy Council, where notice was given them that a Parliamentary inquiry would be made next session into their management. This has been so well understood that the stock of that Company has fallen from 230 to 210.

Mr. Pitt (Lord Chatham), I hear, complains that Lord Temple is the encourager of all the abuse against him. I am, &c., &c. C. Lloyd.

MR. WHATELY TO MR. GRENVILLE.

September 5, 1766.

Dear Sir,—I fear I shall have raised your expectations of the contents of this letter by the conveyance I have chosen for it; but though my intelligence is not very decisive, yet as I could not write upon it freely in any other way, and I can give you, I believe, the real situation of a party, with some particulars which you did not know, I imagined you would think it worth while to send a servant to Aylesbury for it.

annuated for above twenty years, being dead, Mr. Todd requests permission to increase the salary of his nephew, John Madison, who had been sent to St. Petersburgh to learn the Russian language in order to copy and translate, as well as to attempt that cypher. He also desires to increase the allowance of Mr. Bode, "*for engraving the many seals we are obliged to make use of.*"

The manner of Mr. Mackenzie's appointment clears, in a great measure, the speculations it has given rise to. He received in Scotland a letter, merely official, from General Conway, acquainting him that His Majesty had appointed him to the office of Privy Seal. When he waited on the King, His Majesty spoke of it as his own act, in which the Ministers had concurred. He met Lord Chatham at Court, who talked to him of the roads and the weather, without mentioning the subject. He has not seen any of the Ministers, but has heard that the Duke of Grafton is inclined to see him. The office is not given him for life, nor has there been any intimation of annexing any power to it. Hitherto, therefore, the Ministers seem to decline the reputation of having any share in the nomination. He himself expresses a satisfaction in being possessed of the office, and defends his accepting it as not being a means of incumbering his friends, nor tending to connect them with the Ministers; but I do not find any confirmation of his using so strong an expression as the calling Lord Chatham the Dictator. Lord Bute faintly defends Mr. Mackenzie's acceptance, on the ground of its being impossible for him to refuse it from the King, but is highly irritated at the manner in which the Ministers conduct themselves with respect to it. As to Lord Bute's general language, I hear that he said to Lord Townshend that he wished to have seen a more comprehensive plan; but that, however, this Administration is better than the last, and that he shall support the King's measures. But I hear from another quarter, which I take to be more accurate, that the language is, "Mr. Pitt had it in his power to have formed a more comprehensive plan. I am sorry he has missed it, and I wish that his measures may be such as I can support, because I think this Administration better than perpetual changes." Upon stating to him that though such reasons might satisfy his friends in office, yet those out of office and neglected would think it unbecoming them to support an Administration that defied them; he acknowledged that they could not; and upon his whole conversation, as I have heard it, he seems to me to have taken no resolution; that he means to hold a general language, and to be equally far from being pleased with the present arrangement, or inclined to be active in opposing it. Some of his friends will, however, I am persuaded, be in opposition, and try to prevail on him to follow them. He is hurt, again, at a pamphlet, *The Enquiry*, which is, you know, ascribed to Lord Temple, and contains the same sentiments with respect to him as *The Narrative*. I said as to that, that I had heard Lord Temple speak of that pamphlet as containing many mistakes; that his Lordship disavowed all connection with any author of any pamphlet on the present occasion; but that he professed to make no secret of the late transactions, told it to right and left, and supposed that some zealous person [1] had picked up facts, and published them without his knowledge.

You will receive a visit from Mr. Wedderburn in a few days, and you will find his sentiments and his conduct exactly the same as they have been. You may be as open to him as to anybody, and he loves openness.

Lord Rockingham holds a language almost of opposition, and complains much of the usage he has received;

[1] This " zealous person " was no doubt Humphrey Cotes, who was thus enabled to glean all the information necessary for the compilation of the pamphlet. It is signed N. C. M. S. C., a combination of letters of which I have never heard any explanation.

but still I imagine he will in general support, unless a fair opportunity offered to oppose particular measures.

The negotiation with some of the Duke of Bedford's party is said to be still going on; but I hear no particulars, and doubt whether they are of consequence. There is some bustle among the Ministers, expresses having been sent yesterday to bring the President of the Council and the Chancellor of the Exchequer to town; but I have seen nobody to-day to tell me more.

The abuse of Lord Chatham is to the full as virulent as ever. Lord Northington comes in for a share. Lord Shelburne, it is said, is disgusted.

It is now generally known that Lord North repents of accepting. The *Considerations*, &c.[1], are not yet published, owing to an absurdity of the printer, but I suppose that will soon be over.

MR. WHATELY TO MR. GRENVILLE.

September 5, 1766.

DEAR SIR,—I have enclosed in two covers which accompany this, some newspapers which you do not take in, and in which Mrs. Grenville may find two or three pieces not unworthy of places in her collection[2].

I have endeavoured in vain to get the *Ledger* of yesterday, which contains a very saucy paper from America with respect to the letter from the Committee of Merchants. There is another still stronger in the *Virginia*

---

[1] Mr. Whately's pamphlet before-mentioned.

[2] Mrs. Grenville had a small book in which she kept a collection of cuttings from the newspapers, chiefly on political subjects, and among them are some of the early letters of the author of *Junius*, before he adopted that more celebrated signature.

Courant just come over, but not yet published here; well written as I am informed, and supposed to be the work of Delany, telling the Americans that they have more reason to grieve than to rejoice at the repeal of the Stamp Act, as the British Parliament came into the measure on commercial considerations only, and still refuse to acknowledge the rights of the Colonies.

New York has granted the compensation in the shape of a grant of, I think, 5000*l.* to the Crown for *charitable purposes*.

The Assembly at Boston have broke up without coming to any resolution relating to it, except appointing a committee to inquire for the authors of the last disturbances. The Secretary of State's letter was read to the Assembly at Rhode Island, but nothing done upon it.

The affairs of the East India Company are now very much the subject of conversation, and the designs of Government with respect to them the subject of many speculations; for my own part, I do not see that much at this juncture can be, and I doubt whether anything will be, done concerning them. The ideas of private property and public faith will prevent any material alterations in the situation of the Company.

I have endeavoured to trace the author of that paper which you thought so well done, but can only find that it is not any of the persons we guessed.

It is said that Lord Bristol's brother [1], who goes with him as chaplain, is to have an English bishopric: Lord Bristol is to hold the Lieutenantcy for five years, and to reside constantly.

---

[1] Frederick, third son of John Lord Hervey; he was Bishop of Derry when he succeeded his brother Augustus as fourth Earl of Bristol. He died in 1808.

LORD CLIVE TO MR. GRENVILLE.

Calcutta, September 8, 1766.

DEAR SIR,—I have impatiently waited to receive a few lines from you, and to hear from your mouth that you are well; at last I have attained that satisfaction by the hands of Mr. Crotty.

You could not do me a greater pleasure than putting my gratitude to the test by recommending to me this young gentleman. I gave him a commission instantly in preference to every gentleman that came out this year; he is gone up the country to join the army, and carries with him a letter to Colonel Sir Robert Barker, who I am persuaded will let slip no opportunity of serving him, and you may be assured my attention shall be constantly fixed upon his welfare, whether I am in India or in England. I have heard with some surprise that this young man might have come out in the civil, but that he preferred a military station; although the military service in India is certainly the best in the world, it is not to be compared to the civil service. Before my departure, I will sound his inclinations on that subject, and on my arrival in England, it will be no difficult task to get him appointed to a civil station.

The Revolution which has happened was to me unexpected, unaccountable, and surprising. I cannot conceive how any one man can dare, through the influence he has with his Prince, thus to endanger, if not to sacrifice, the interests of so great a nation.

As an individual not slightly concerned, I can't help feeling for the deplorable situation of my country: may the Almighty Disposer of kings and kingdoms save this from impending ruin, and inspire our great men with sentiments of moderation and zeal for the public good, in preference to private pique and resentment; and may I, Sir, be so happy as to hear that you are restored to that share of power and confidence with your Prince, which you was so universally allowed to deserve, at the time I left England.

Last year I troubled you with a long detail of India affairs: the Company's prospects are great, and their condition permanent and stable, but such a work could not be brought about without violent convulsions. A general mutiny among the officers, attended with circumstances shocking and dishonourable to our nation, had nearly deprived us of all our possessions; however this great evil has been productive of good; subordination and discipline are restored; moderation and frugality have taken place of insolence and extravagance [1].

A general Court-Martial of Field Officers is now sitting for the trial of the principal offenders, and you will be much surprised that Lieutenant-Colonel Sir Robert Fletcher is accused of being the author and principal promoter of the late mutiny, in which no less than 173 officers resigned their commissions.

The general Court-Martial has already sat six weeks, and will probably sit six weeks longer before the whole be concluded. The only officer as yet on whom sentence has been pronounced is Lieutenant Virtue, who was tried for desertion and disobedience of orders, but for want of sufficient proof that he received his pay, although it was drawn for in the usual manner, he has

---

[1] Some account of this mutiny of officers will be found in Malcolm's Life of Lord Clive, the details of which are derived from a narrative written by the late Sir Henry Strachey who was Lord Clive's private secretary, and inserted in the Report of a Committee of the House of Commons on the subject.

only been sentenced to be broke with infamy, by having his sword and spontoon broke over his head, and his sash cut in pieces in presence of the whole army.

Captain Stainforth, who has had the honour to bear His Majesty's Commission, is under an arrest for making a proposal to cast dice who should assassinate the Commander-in-Chief, and afterwards proposing that the officers should all have fusees at the next review, that he might have an opportunity of shooting me.

It gives me pain to relate any of these circumstances, but they must be soon made public, and will bring with them great disgrace upon the Company's service. Indeed I do not think such a horrid combination can be paralleled in any age or country. Solemn oaths taken, penalty bonds executed, subscriptions put on foot, and every other method devised to ensure success. To enter more minutely into this disagreeable affair would take up volumes; give me leave therefore to refer you to Mr. Walsh or some of our Directors for further particulars.

It will give you pleasure to hear of Mr. Strachey's prosperity; the principles upon which I have proceeded, of adding more to my own fortune, would not admit of my doing great things; however I have the satisfaction to assure you, he will return a richer man than he came out, without having greatly impaired his constitution.

Without something very extraordinary happens I propose leaving India next January, 1767, and hope to have the pleasure of kissing your hands some time next July. Wishing you health and prosperity, I am, with the greatest sincerity, &c., &c. CLIVE.

MR. WEDDERBURN TO MR. GRENVILLE.

London, September 9, 1766.

DEAR SIR,—I was in hopes upon my return from the North to have had the pleasure of paying my respects to you at Wotton.

Though I have been forced to stay in London for these ten days past, I have lived so little in it that I have hardly seen anybody but paviors and bricklayers. The only other profession which is carried on here at present is politics ; but as I know none of the workmen employed in it, I am not able to give you the least account what they are about. The master politician keeps himself invisible upon the pinnacle of Hampstead Hill, from whence he surveys all the kingdoms upon earth ; but how he intends to dispose of them nobody presumes to guess. Fame says, indeed, that he has began at one extremity of the world, and that

" Hydaspes, Indus, and the Ganges,
Dread from his arm impending changes." [1]

Something, too, is said of the great northern constellation of alliances, which is to be the polar star of the European hemisphere, and it is supposed that this new discovery in astronomy is to be the object of Mr. Stanley's mission [2] ; but except a few such sounding meta-

[1] Lord Chatham had projected a Parliamentary inquiry into the affairs of the East India Company.

[2] Mr. Stanley had been appointed Ambassador to the Court of Russia, and it would have been part of his duty to negotiate a triple defensive alliance between the Courts of Great Britain, Russia, and Prussia, with a provision for adding thereto any other powers which were not engaged in the Family Compact of the House of Bourbon. For various reasons, however, this project failed, and Mr. Stanley's appointment did not take effect.

phors, that I am very unable to express to you in plain prose, there has as yet, I believe, been no talk of any of the intended measures of the new Administration. A few weeks it is to be hoped will enable us to form a better idea of their schemes; for all accounts agree in this, that Parliament will meet early in November. I have the honour to be, &c., &c. AL. WEDDERBURN.

EARL TEMPLE TO MR. GRENVILLE.

September 20, 1766, Saturday morning.

MY DEAR BROTHER,—I have little more to say than that we returned from Woburn on Wednesday, and that we are both in high health and feeding.

You have seen the great Rigby, so you best know what judgment to form. He and the Duke were lavish in your praise; *the Duchess*[1], entirely silent as to politics. The Duke says his day was fixed for town before the Parliament was summoned; he shall, therefore, be there for the first day, and then to Woburn. Nothing to do but lie by and wait events. Lord Gower refused the Admiralty, offered in a letter, not very wise, by the Duke of Grafton. From this you will judge of the state of things. Extremely civil in all respects, which satisfies me perfectly, who only want barely to acquit myself, and to have done.

I suppose you learnt by last post that Mrs. Conway[2] is dead. Yours most affectionately, TEMPLE.

[1] Gertrude, the sister of Lord Gower, of whose influence Walpole tells so much.

[2] Aunt to Lord Temple and Mr. Grenville: see *ante*, vol. i. p. 135, *note*.

MR. GRENVILLE TO EARL TEMPLE.

Wotton, September 21, 1766.

MY DEAR BROTHER,—Mr. Rigby gave me exactly the same account of the Duke of Bedford's dispositions with that contained in your letter; but I found his own wishes and opinion was to take an active part at the meeting of the Parliament, instead of laying by and waiting for events, as you tell me the Duke of Bedford proposes. I told him that must very much depend upon the part which our friends in general would take. That the consideration of the King's Speech was a kind of state of the nation, in which we were in some degree called upon to declare our sentiments, and that I should be under no difficulty to deliver mine, and should then see how far others were disposed to adopt them.

The account which the present Ministry have industriously given of the great civility and willingness of Lord Gower's letter, is, I find, one lie more added to the daily heap, as, by what I hear, that letter was, on the contrary, an answer of slight and even ridicule to the proposal, which was as weak in its manner as in the matter of it.

You will hear from Mr. Wedderburn, who told me that he should go to Stowe to-day or to-morrow, what he thinks of Lord Bute's situation; notwithstanding which I think it very possible that the Chamberlain's staff may be given to Lord Northumberland, who, it is generally thought, would not be unwilling to receive it.

The East India business, I am told, engrosses all conversation in town, and grows very serious. The people can hardly believe, notwithstanding the threats thrown out to the Directors, and the language holden by Alderman Beckford, &c., that after what passed last year with regard to North America and the West Indies, they will this year break through the charter of the East Indies which was purchased by the Company, and which has been repeatedly confirmed by many solemn Acts of Parliament.

This would be a stroke indeed worthy of their wisdom and consistency, and which will be a proper crown to the whole. There is to be a general Court of the Proprietors, I am told, next Wednesday, and we may then probably hear more of what is intended.

Lord Trevor has this moment left us; but the message which Mr. Rigby brought me from the Duke of Bedford, that he would come hither if a visit from the Duke of Marlborough did not stop him, keeps me at home for some days. I am, my dear Brother, &c., &c.

GEORGE GRENVILLE.

MR. WEDDERBURN TO MR. GRENVILLE.

Lincoln's Inn, September 25, 1766.

DEAR SIR,—Instead of paying my compliments to Lord Temple from Mr. Morton's, as I intended, I found myself obliged to set out for London, by a mistake of my correspondent here, who had neglected to send me down a letter of attorney for transferring some stock which stood in my name as a trustee.

The India Court yesterday was very fully attended, and the measure of raising the dividend to ten per cent. seemed to meet with the general approbation.

The Directors opposed it, and were supported by Mr.

Walpole, Salvador, and one or two more of the monied people. The reasons given by the Directors were very unsatisfactory, for they admitted the value of their late acquisitions; the very rich returns now made, and annually to be expected from the trade; they allowed that in June next the dividend must be increased, and perhaps beyond ten per cent.; and only insisted that it should be postponed 'till that time, because they said the money coming in would not greatly exceed the debts to be discharged in that period. The foundation of their whole argument was to consider the effects in their hands as of no value 'till they were actually sold; and they carried this so far as to consider their stock of tea as a distressing circumstance, because it could not all be brought to market in one year.

Their arguments had not much weight in general; those who supported them relied chiefly upon the credit that ought to be given to the Directors, and both they and the Directors threw out a great many terrors of the interposition of Parliament.

The Chairman read an account of the message sent to the Directors, which, I think, was to this effect: Mr. Dudley and Mr. Rous received a message from the Duke of Grafton, desiring them to attend upon His Majesty's Ministers, at his house, on the 28th of August. When they came, the Ministers told them that the East Indian affairs would probably come under the consideration of Parliament, and that the Parliament would be called before Christmas, and it was thought a mark of regard to the India Company to give them that notice.

This account was received with profound silence, and the mention of a Parliamentary interposition in the course of the debate seemed to give great alarm, and was by no means well received. Some people suppose the Directors, in opposing an increase of dividend, were a little under the influence of Administration, who wished to delay it 'till it might be of use to sweeten some potion they have been brewing for the Company, and I think there were many appearances to support that supposition.

Lord Clive's despatches will come under consideration on Thursday. I find he has not omitted writing to every quarter from whence he could expect assistance; but the popular opinion is not at present in his favour.

I have troubled you with a very tedious account of these matters, and shall take the liberty of troubling you again, because they begin to be very interesting.

I have heard no other news except that Lord Beauchamp[1] has got the place of Constable of Dublin Castle, with an additional salary of 1000l. to the old 500l., and for life: this with Orford, and the Mastership of the Horse[2], is a very reasonable compensation, methinks, for a troublesome office. I am ever, &c., &c.

AL. WEDDERBURN.

MR. WHATELY TO MR. GRENVILLE.

September 26, 1766.

DEAR SIR,—I have received your favour of the 21st instant, and am glad to have it in my power authentically to contradict the accounts which have been so confidently given of Lord Gower's answer.

---

[1] Eldest son of the Earl of Hertford.

[2] The members for the borough of Orford were returned to Parliament by the influence of Lord Hertford, and he was at this time Master of the Horse.

I should not, however, be surprised to see that negotiation revived, or some new one opened before the
meeting of Parliament, as the Ministry are provided
with a tolerable broad basis to begin with; for I look
upon it as certain that the Duke of Portland[1] will
continue only 'till a successor can be found for him, and
so long, I understand, he will continue, being determined not to resign. Lord Huntingdon[2], too, it is said,
is removable whenever there shall be occasion for it; and
with two such places to dispose of, they may treat with
any party who is inclined to listen to them. I suppose
the early meeting of Parliament is occasioned by the
dearness of corn, and that the first business will be the
prohibition to export it, as a popular measure, though the
rise upon it now, which with us is up to fifteen guineas
per load, is owing to the expectation of such a measure.

The East Indian business, though it will be brought
on immediately, would hardly have been a reason for
calling them so soon together; that subject does, as you
are informed, engross all conversation. What the parliamentary motion is to be does not yet appear; the
most probable conjecture is, that it is intended to deny
the right of the Company to possess themselves of
territory, and that consequently that which they have
lately acquired is taken by them for the benefit of the
Crown: out of this may arise a proposition that they
shall advance a gross sum, or be charged with an annual
rent to the Crown, or else that the Crown will take
possession. This is however but conjecture, nor did
anything appear at the general Court on Wednesday to
give a further light into the design. The Directors communicated the message, which occasioned no debate.

[1] Lord Chamberlain.   [2] Groom of the Stole.

The claim of the Navy to a donation from the late Nabob, assigned by him for payment on the revenues of the country now in possession of the Company, was also brought before them. This being considered a debt charged on those revenues, was voted to be paid, whenever it shall suit the Company's affairs, to the amount of 150,000*l.* But the principal business was a motion founded on the late dispatches from Bengal, for an addition of four per cent. per annum to the present dividend. I do not know what arguments were used on either side, but only hear that the Directors declared that they had made the most accurate computation they could of what might be expected to be the state of the Company's treasury in June next, when the increased dividend is proposed to take place, and that they did not think there would be assets in hand to pay it; notwithstanding which it is supposed the question, which is to be decided by ballot to-day, will be carried by a great majority.

On Thursday next is to be another Court, when an attempt will be made to re-instate Mr. Johnstone and others in the Company's service. This, I think, must necessarily bring on all Lord Clive's proceedings in India: the party against him here is strong, and if they carry any question I shall look upon it as decisive for Mr. Sullivan against the present Directors.

THE EARL OF BUCKINGHAMSHIRE TO MR. GRENVILLE.

London, October 9, 1766.

DEAR SIR,—One of His Majesty's messengers arrived at Blickling on Sunday last with a letter from Lord

Shelburne, desiring to see me in town. Accordingly I arrived here on Tuesday, and in the evening waited upon his Lordship.

After the first compliments, he entered into a dissertation upon the critical state of affairs in Spain, which I interrupted before he had well concluded his first period, by telling him it would not be candid in me to hear his Lordship enlarge upon the subject, as I had no thoughts of accepting the mission. But not unnecessarily to trouble you with the detail of a conversation of near two hours, it will be sufficient to inform you that the proposition was flatteringly stated, strongly pressed, and decently declined.

The world in general guess the occasion for which I was summoned, but I would avoid, as it appears to me illiberal, parading a refusal, and therefore let these particulars sleep with you.

I went yesterday to the Levée to present an Address from Norwich, and afterwards had an audience of His Majesty to acquaint him with my having received a letter from the Vice-Chancellor of Russia, informing me that the Czarina had sent me her picture for their Majesties, and a compliment to them upon the occasion.

Nothing passed upon the subject of Spain.

It concerns me to hear that Mrs. Grenville's indisposition continues. I return to Blickling to-morrow, where a line from you, informing me of her better health, would give particular satisfaction to your faithful and affectionate BUCKINGHAM.

MR. WHATELY TO MR. GRENVILLE.

October 10, 1766.

DEAR SIR,—I have been accidentally in town this week for a day or two, and I find the reflections on the creation of a Duke of Northumberland such as the occasion must naturally suggest.

The first thought is, that it must disgust all the nobility, and that it proves an understanding between Lord Bute and Lord Chatham. On the other hand, I can tell you for certain, that Lord Bute says he thinks the Ministry mad, for they draw upon themselves all the odium which a supposed connection with him can raise, without obliging him; by doing what he does not desire, and neglecting those whom he wishes to see advanced. I am assured from more quarters than one, that this has no relation to any correspondence between them, nor gives any satisfaction to Lord Bute, and indeed the manner of its being done confirms the supposition; for Lord Northumberland was it seems always of that party among Lord Bute's friends who were inclined to Mr. Pitt, and thought himself therefore very ill-used in the preference of Lord Hertford to be Master of the Horse. He went to Lord Chatham upon it, who endeavoured to soothe him with the prospect of other arrangements in which he might come into office, but Lord Northumberland told him flatly, that if Lord Hertford kissed hands, there was no office that he would accept of: upon which Lord Chatham held out title, &c.; first tried a marquisate, but as that did not do, the Dukedom was proposed and taken [1]: so that Lord

---

[1] Lord Northumberland was created a Duke on the 18th instant. He had been Sir Hugh Smithson, but having married the Lady Eliza-

Bute really was not privy to the transaction. My idea of this conduct of Lord Chatham is, that he means to gain the King and Lord Bute by distinctions shown to Lord Bute's friends, and to keep in reserve, ground to say to the people that he never brought them into power. If he should propose Sir Fletcher Norton to be Chief Justice without a Peerage, I shall consider it as part of this plan, for it will be removing him out of the way by means of rank and pension, without any political nfluence; but I have heard a more refined idea suggested, and it comes from one of Lord Shelburne's party, which is, that by such proceedings he will enable himself to say even in the Closet, that he has shown the greatest attention to Lord Bute's friends, and all will not satisfy him; and this suggestion is so far supported, that it accounts, whereas nothing else will account, for his doing these things without communication with Lord Bute. But however, be his plan this, or any other, I apprehend that party is dissatisfied, and I guess their conduct will be much the same as it was last year, supporting Ministers at the beginning of the Session, and flying off upon some measure before the end of it.

The necessary consequences of the hauteur with which Lord Chatham treats all mankind, will be to disgust many persons during the course of the winter, and therefore it will be worth while to endeavour to form as respectable a party as we can for malcontents to resort to. It will not be so bad as is imagined:

beth, daughter and heir of Algernon, Duke of Somerset, he succeeded, according to a limitation in the Patent, to the Earldom of Northumberland upon the death of his father-in-law, in 1750. The Duke of Northumberland died in 1786. See *Chatham Correspondence*, vol. iii. p. 74.

though some are lost, there will be some accessions; Lord George Sackville and Mr. Dowdeswell must be in opposition directly, and others will insensibly drop in, if we do not discourage them by seeming to despair of a party. I think that pains should be taken to get people to attend before Christmas; that the Duke of Bedford should be desired to get his friends together; that some of the country gentlemen should be informed that business of consequence will probably come on, and they should be pressed to attend; and that the Duke of Bedford, Lord Temple, yourself, and some others should be in town at least a week before the meeting, see one another, see your friends, and hold out the appearance of a steady opposition. This is my little plan of politics for the present occasion, not formed upon a supposed possibility of carrying any question against any ministry, but merely upon the necessity of showing a strength to which individuals, or the people, or even the Court, may resort, when disgusted with the proceedings of the Administration.

MR. WHATELY TO MR. GRENVILLE.

October 20, 1766.

DEAR SIR,—Since I sent away my last letter I have had a confirmation of all I wrote to you by that conveyance with respect to Lord Bute's situation. I hear from the Northumberland quarter that the connection between his Grace and his Lordship is not so strong as it was. It was weakened (as I understand) before the ducal creation, and I do not believe that will tend to reunite them. I hear from another quarter that Lord Bute appears more and more dissatisfied with the pre-

sent Ministers every day; but the disgust is not confined
to him, it extends very wide among the principal families of the kingdom. Lord Mansfield's observation upon
it is, that though it is impossible to say when it will
show itself, yet that it certainly must break out. He,
himself, speaks with the utmost contempt of the late
proceedings. He has been lately much with the Duke
of Newcastle and the Marquis of Rockingham, and says
that though they hold a moderate language, yet they are
exasperated to the highest degree. They will, however,
and so will Lord Bute's friends, as parties, at first give a
faint support, though individuals belonging to each will
take the line of opposition perhaps from the beginning;
but angry men cannot be long lukewarm; parties cannot
subsist in a state of indifference; and the Session will
probably furnish fair occasions enough for them to show
their resentment. I hear nothing precise of Mr. Yorke,
but that he does not leave the bar; I think it however
impossible that he should support this Administration.
I believe too that we shall see Burke in opposition, but
I have a particular reason for desiring this may not be
mentioned: when I know more with certainty I will
inform you. Dr. Hay and Mr. Ellis I take for granted.
Wedderburn's sentiments, and Sir Fletcher Norton's,
you know. I find opinions divided on the part Sir
Gilbert Elliot will take, but I think he will avoid
playing a deep game after the disappointment he has
met with in the estate he inherits from his father, which
does not turn out half so much as he expected. I have
a long letter from Lord North, strongly marked with
the uneasiness of his situation. Charles Townshend's
language is very discontented. He disclaims all share
in administration, abuses their inactivity, and says that

he shall confine himself to his department. By his account (which he gave yesterday) the Duke of Grafton is totally Lord Chatham's; that General Conway is ill with his Lordship, hardly ever sees him, and seems to think that he is not much concerned in the parliamentary proceedings, though to be sure he must conduct them; and that nothing is done; that the Manilla ransom, the East India prisoners, and the American affairs, are just where they were, but that he (Mr. Townshend) has nothing to do with them, they are ministerial objects; that in his own department he finds the finances in a very flourishing condition, but the immensity of the debt weighs them down; and speaks with moderation of his own operations. He says Lord Townshend is to be a Marquess; but when he tells the state of the application he makes it appear improbable that he should be; for his account of it is, that Lord Townshend wrote to the Duke of Grafton desiring that when Marquesses were appointed he might be one; but the answer he has received is, that the King has it in his intention, but has not formed a resolution to do it. The singularity of which is, he says, its being done without any communication with Lord Chatham, whom Lord Townshend hates mortally. Charles Townshend has also desired the Duke of Grafton to apply for a peerage for Lady Dalkeith; the Duke declined it, and told him he had better mention it himself, to which Townshend answered that he was sure the King would give him no answer, and Lord Chatham, when consulted, would put a negative upon it. This conversation arose on Lord Maynard's new patent[1], and there it

---

[1] Charles, sixth Baron Maynard. He was advanced to the title of Viscount, and died in 1775 at the age of eighty-five.

rests : but both instances prove the truth of your observation on the other claims which the new creations will
raise. Townshend's language yesterday with respect to
the India Company was, that nothing could be more
absurd than to think of taking away any of their
acquisitions, or sharing the power in India between
them and the Crown ; that some regulations might be
made at home with respect to the management of the
General Courts, and also to bring their affairs in some
measure before Parliament every year ; that the best
thing which could be done would be to make a bargain
now for the renewal of their charter, but that he did not
know whether the Ministry had any such thoughts ; he
rather believed not, and it was not his affair. As to his
own schemes in the finances, he is reserved ; but the
truth is, that nothing is determined in that, any more
than in any other department ; I have, however, heard
from a variety of hands, some of the projects which are
in agitation, most of which will, and perhaps all of them
may, come to nothing, but they are the present ideas.
To increase the consumption of tea is one object, with
which view the duty retained on the exportation to
America and to Ireland is to be given up, and some
some say sixpence to be taken off from the home consumption. Some scheme is in contemplation with respect
to tobacco ; I do not know what, but the end of it is
purely commercial. A wild project is talked of for
paying off the Civil List debt, and providing an American revenue, both together. It is only supposing that
the quit-rents in the Colonies, if properly collected, will
be sufficient to support the military establishment there,
and then the Crown may sell them to the public for four
or five hundred thousand pounds. As extravagant as

this may seem to you, the Auditor of the Plantations is directed to make out accounts and calculations which lead to such a proposition. The produce of the sinking fund is certainly prodigious ; I shall be able in a few days to make a tolerable guess, and will send you the accounts I get ; but from what I have heard already, I imagine it will be at the least 2,500,000*l.* surplus. I have not heard the selling of the Crown Lands mentioned lately, but I do not know that it is dropped. Jersey and Guernsey I informed you of before. Lord Mansfield observed with pleasure that the *Considerations,* &c., had precluded the Administration from any merit on that and on other accounts. He has read that pamphlet, I hear, and says it is very satisfactory ; I believe it is a good deal read and approved of [1].

It is thrown out that the Parliament will probably enter upon no business except the corn before Christmas ; it is also said that the Opposition mean to arraign the illegality of the embargo. I own I shall be sorry if it be much insisted on ; the measure is certainly popular, and few will choose to appear against it ; but there is a way of attack which to me seems practicable. The dearness of provisions, as of everything else, is in a great measure owing to the multiplicity of taxes, and to the increase of fictitious wealth by the increase of the stocks. Half the taxes and half the debt were for the German war, and the author of that measure is responsible for this consequence of it : it is to him, and not to the shortness of the crop, that the present distress is owing ; for a light crop of wheat would not make meat, butter, and cheese dear. He has reduced the poor to

[1] It has been already stated that Mr. Whately was the author of this pamphlet.

such necessitous circumstances as tempts Ministers to illegal measures for their relief, and occasions the dangerous precedent of such exertions of Prerogative. This relief, too, is but a temporary expedient. The only effectual remedy is the diminution of that debt and those taxes ; for which service he is the least qualified of any man, and which he particularly has rendered more difficult by cutting off the resources which the equality of taxation intended by the Cyder Act, and by the American Stamp Act, had opened. I the more earnestly wish that whatever is said on this or any other occasion be put upon popular ground, because the people now want an object to look up to, and I hear again since I wrote to you, that you are rising very fast in the public opinion. I should be glad if any popular topic could be thought of, to make a stand upon it. A reduction of the Land-tax to one shilling in the pound, is to a degree, though not entirely, of that nature, and with such a sinking fund would not be improper; but perhaps better subjects will occur to you, and I am sure they deserve your attention.

I do not understand this Dukedom of Montague. Lord Cardigan[1], who claimed an old promise, was yet so offended at a letter from the Duke of Grafton, as to refuse the offer, and now he accepts it. Sir Fletcher Norton is to be in town this week, and I hope will call upon you in his way to his place in Surrey. Wedderburn has been with me some days[2], which, with some other company, has prevented my writing to you sooner.

---

[1] George Brudenell, fourth Earl of Cardigan. The Dukedom now created became extinct upon his death in 1790.

[2] Probably at Nonsuch, Whately's residence in Surrey.

MR. GRENVILLE TO EARL TEMPLE.

Bolton Street, November 10, 1766.

MY DEAR BROTHER,—The conversation which I had last night with the Duke of Bedford was as civil and obliging, personally to me, as was possible, but his sentiments with regard to the public business in many respects extremely different from mine.

He seemed fully convinced that the Minister was highly blameable in not calling the Parliament, instead of proroguing it to the 11th November, notwithstanding which he was uncertain what part he and *his friends* could take even upon that question, doubting whether it would not be very improper *to give any disturbance whatever*, though he should always avow and adhere to the principles and opinions which he declared last year. This is sufficient to give you an idea of the whole.

I send you the paper you desired, though I fear it is scarcely exact enough to be absolutely depended upon, but you will send it me back when you have done with it. If you will call upon me when you come from the city I will show you the motions which we propose to make in the Hou of Commons, which may save you some trouble in forming yours for the Lords. I am ever, my dear Brother, &c., &c.

GEORGE GRENVILLE.

THE EARL OF MANSFIELD TO MR. GRENVILLE.

Bloomsbury, November 10, 1766.

DEAR SIR,—I think it due to friendship to tell you that yesterday morning I turned a little in my thoughts the matter you talked of, and cast my eye over the Corn Acts.

An embargo is a term well known, and the power exercised in all maritime countries. It differs from a prohibition to export or import merchandize, though it has that effect when laid on ships going out or coming in. Our constitution trusted the executive power with this. It could not be exercised by Parliament. The nature of it is adapted to sudden emergencies of short duration. I incline strongly to think that no authority can be found which confines an embargo to time of war, though the occasions happen most frequently then. The reason may hold equally in time of peace, as in case of famine, or upon apprehension, or preparation. I have a notion that some of the late embargoes as to provision ships from Ireland were before an actual war. The Address from the House of Commons in 1756 is immensely strong. The power is admitted; the only doubt was whether the occasion justified the exercise of it merely as a prohibition to export.

In all or most of the Corn Acts before the Restoration there is a power to the King by proclamation to suspend the permission to export.

In the Acts after the Restoration that power is omitted; but these permitting Acts all have in view the general prohibition to export, perhaps by that law without licence, by the Statute of Edward III. and Philip and Mary, and certainly have not in contemplation the cases of an embargo; and I am very clear that whatever power the Crown had before, as to embargoes, remains notwithstanding these permitting Acts. That may bring the question to this, whether this embargo is not a colour to prohibit contrary to the permission given by the Acts, and therefore an abuse of a power vested in the Crown for one purpose, by applying it to another; but popular opinion and the sense of mankind is in favour of the exertion of the power if the Crown had it.

It is clear that when the Parliament gives leave to export from general policy, the King ought not, upon general policy, to prohibit under the colour of an embargo; but an immediate danger of famine resembles the danger of a sudden hostile attack.

I send you these confused hints or sudden thoughts, for I am far from being master of the subjects; I have not the materials, and have had no opportunity of searching for them; but this uncertainty may be of use to you as to your measure or manner. A wrong attack positively made upon a popular step would turn into occasion of triumph.

The proclamation itself betrays a doubt, and warrants the asking how it is founded in law, with a view to an indemnity.

Tell Lord Lyttelton this, because when I saw him I had not thought of it, though in part it struck me in the same light, especially as to the late Acts.

MR. GRENVILLE TO THE EARL OF MANSFIELD.

November 10, 1766.

MY DEAR LORD,—I have endeavoured to consider the hints contained in your letter with that attention which every thought of yours so well deserves, but I own I cannot see how it is possible to consider the Proclamation in any other light than as a *Prohibition* to export corn. It is meant as *such* and as *such* only, and if it is a *Pro-*

hibition, it is not only within the meaning, but within the very *letter*, of the 22 C. II. That Act does not extend to other *Provision Ships*, nor to Ireland, and therefore no argument can be drawn from thence ; and yet with respect to corn, even to be exported from Ireland, an Irish Act of Parliament was passed last year to enable the King to prohibit the exportation from thence by the advice of the Privy Council of Great Britain or Ireland; and this was done, as I have been told by those concerned, after great consideration had here, and it was certainly founded upon an opinion, after a good deal of enquiry, that the King had not that power, even in Ireland, without it.

However pleasing it may have been to the people to stop the exportation by any means, yet the contending for such a prerogative, against the positive words and plain intention of an Act of Parliament, will, I believe, be too odious even for those concerned to insist upon, and this I am persuaded will be the case in the House of Commons, where, by what I have heard, there will not be one gentleman of the Law who will maintain it.

This is my present opinion, not lightly taken up, for I have given all the attention to this question which I am able, and shall continue to do so, from the weight which the least doubt of yours must have with me.

I am much obliged to you for having communicated your thoughts to me upon this subject, and am with the most affectionate regard, my dear Lord, &c., &c.

                    GEORGE GRENVILLE.

P.S. I do not know whether I shall have an opportunity of communicating your letter to Lord Lyttelton before this business comes on, but if I have, I will certainly do it.

MR. GRENVILLE TO EARL TEMPLE.

Bolton Street, November 18, 1766.

MY DEAR BROTHER,—An event has happened to-day, which fully shows in how different a light the House of Commons considers the doctrines of a dispensing power in the King superior to the Laws, from that in which it was represented in the House of Peers by those great State luminaries the Earls of Northington and Chatham and the Lord Chancellor.

Mr. Conway proposed a Bill of Indemnity for all those who acted *under* the Proclamation and Order of Council for prohibiting the exportation of wheat. I thought this ground too narrow, and proposed that those *who advised* it might be included in the Bill, but said that if the proposition was not consented to, I would not make the debate in a thin house, though I assured them that after the desperate doctrines which had lately been holden, of a power in the Crown superior to the Laws, this question should not be evaded, but be agitated to the bottom, when I saw how this Bill was framed.

Mr. Conway, in answer, did not insist upon the legality, though he refused the words extending it to advisers, &c. Many others spoke in doubtful terms, others were clear for the words of extension, amongst whom Mr. Pitt[1] did very well. Alderman Beckford then spoke, and after many flourishes, said these words: " If the public was in danger, the King has a dispensing power." I immediately called him to order, and made the Clerk of the House take down the words, to censure them in the strongest terms. Many got up to excuse him from

[1] Thomas Pitt, afterwards Lord Camelford.

weakness, inadvertence, ignorance, &c., but not one to support the doctrine. Alderman Beckford, after some debate of this kind, said I had stopped him too soon, for that he meant to have added, "with the consent of the Council, whenever the Salus Populi requires it." These words I again excepted to, and said that the explanation was at least as criminal as the first words, and directed those words to be taken down by the Clerk likewise, and endeavoured to show them as totally subversive of our Constitution, protesting that if the dispensing power were to be thus established, I thought every man dishonoured who would set his foot in the House afterwards. After this, many tried to palliate, but none to justify, and upon my insisting that the words should be *retracted*, or I would immediately move a censure, and that the House must either approve or censure, for the words must now stand upon the Journals; after an hour or two more, and an universal *disapprobation* of the doctrines contained in those words, Alderman Beckford thought fit to consult Mr. Hussey, and by his advice drew up the following explanation in these words, or to this effect: "That he meant to say, that in the most urgent necessity, it might be *excusable* to act contrary to law, which was only to be justified by Act of Parliament." As these words contained exactly my sense in almost my own words, I immediately consented to them, provided they were entered upon the Journals as the proof of our sense of the Law and Constitution. This was done, and thus this day's debate ended.

I know not what preamble they will have to their Bill, but if there is not a full declaration of the *Illegality*, I shall certainly treat the question fully.

What will the three great Ministers say? What a

triumph to Lord Mansfield, and to you and your friends! It seems to me that this will produce curious scenes in the House of Peers, if made the most of, as it is most probable that the Bill will come up in a shape very different at least from the opinions laid down there, which however will, I believe, be softened, if not retracted. I would not delay to inform you of this for your curiosity and judgment. The Bill will not be brought into our House for some days. Adieu my dear Brother. I am, &c.   GEORGE GRENVILLE.

EARL TEMPLE TO MR. GRENVILLE.

Stowe, November 20, 1766.

I CONGRATULATE you most warmly, my dear brother, on your glorious triumph, not only over the wild alderman, but in him over the whole crew of new converts to tyranny and despotism.

Your victory is so complete, that I think it impossible the enemy can rally; their own proposition of indemnity to those who have acted under the *Royal Authority* admits the illegality, and requires that the indemnity should be extended as you propose. I am impatient to hear the further progress of so wonderful an outset as we were all witnesses to at the first meeting, distinguished for ever by neglect, ignorance, and high prerogative doctrines.

But of this, no more at present; if there is likely to be any debate in your House on the second reading, that is, should the Ministry persist in refusing to be indemnified, I will fly up time enough to be present, and in all events will not be absent when it is *brought*

up to us, for I shall delight to be present at least at the
quibbling retractation of principles odious and diabolical, which these ears have already heard, with an indignation equal to the prostitution[1]. You know if you
send any answer to this to my house on Friday night, it
may be with me on Saturday night.

Judge how impatient I must be. Sure Lord Suffolk
and Lord Buckingham should be apprized in time.

I have had another wonderful epistle from George.
As you say nothing of Mrs. G., we take no news to be
good. Adieu! I am, &c., &c.   TEMPLE.

MR. GRENVILLE TO EARL TEMPLE.

Bolton Street, November 21, 1766.

MY DEAR BROTHER,—As I thought that in the present critical situation you would be impatient to hear
from time to time how things go on, I desired Mrs.
Grenville to write last night to Lady Temple, both
because I came home so late that I could not have done
it so fully myself, and because in all likelihood a letter
from her would go safer, and have a better chance to be
unopened, than one from me by the post. I shall send
this to your house to-night, from thence to be conveyed
by the stage coach to you to-morrow.

Our Bill of Indemnity is to be brought in on Mon-

---

[1] Junius mentions the subsequent debate in the House of Lords upon
this subject, which he says " *I myself heard;* " and, perhaps in allusion
to " *the prostitution,*" and the "*principles odious and diabolical,*" he
says also:—" There is no act of *arbitrary power* which the King might
not attribute to *necessity,* and for which he would not be secure of
obtaining the approbation of his *prostituted* Lords and Commons."—
Junius, ii. 362–364.

day, and we then propose to move for the printing it, and fixing a day for reading it a second time, which probably will be on Wednesday, or, at latest, Thursday. I am assured, that with regard to the preamble the Court will give way, and that they intend in it to assert the illegality of the measure in point of law; but the advisers are not to be included, and if so, we shall be able to enter into the whole debate, upon an instruction to the Committee to insert them, to be moved at the second reading. At all events, I think we shall certainly find some ground on which we shall differ, and be able to gall them with the repetition of this odious subject.

As to the state of parties, there are many marks which show them to be in a great ferment. Lord Edgecumbe's[1] dismission for Mr. John Shelley has exasperated the friends of Lord Rockingham, who had a meeting the night before last to consider what to do, and the news of this day is, that they are determined to resign, particularly Mr. Conway, who, it is asserted, has had a very angry interview with Lord Chatham, and says publicly that he knew nothing of Lord Edgecumbe's dismission. The Duke of Grafton says, as we are told, that he would have stopped it if he could, and Lord Shelburne likewise disclaims it, so that the whole of it is laid at Lord Chatham's door. I have no great faith myself in these general resignations, notwithstanding they are so positively asserted, but the air of

---

[1] George, third Lord Edgecumbe; a naval officer, and at this time Rear Admiral of the Blue. Being the patron of four boroughs, he was possessed of considerable parliamentary influence. He was dismissed from his office as Treasurer of the Household, because he declined exchanging it to be a Lord of the Bedchamber, which Lord Chatham considered an affront to the King.

discontent does certainly appear very strongly among them. Lord Bute's friends still manifest the same, or rather greater, dissatisfaction than when you went out of town.

Sir Gilbert Elliot and Mr. Dyson spoke very fully against the legality, on Tuesday; and Sir Fletcher Norton, Mr. Wedderburn, Mr Thurlow, and almost every lawyer, with all the judges, as 't is said, but one or two, hold the same language. The lawyers, and almost all our friends, were gone out of the House on Tuesday, when Mr. Alderman Beckford thought proper to adopt the doctrines of his friends and patrons in the House of Peers, so that we beat them with their own troops.

Lord Northington, I hear, swears like a trooper, that we " know nothing of the constitution in the House of Commons, but that this is Bute's villainy; and that he will go to the King and tell him so." The other sage of the law, the Lord Chancellor, says " that men are mad, and that they may force him to submit, but that his doctrines are good law, and that he will maintain them."

Lord Chatham is said to complain of Lord Bute, and to declare that either he or Lord Bute's friends must go out.

The Duke of Bedford is gone out of town, as you know, but Mr. Rigby came to me the night before last, and assured me in the strongest terms, that they had not had the least intercourse either *directly* or *indirectly* with Lord Chatham, *since he left Bath.* He said, that he and all the Duke of Bedford's friends would support me to the utmost upon this occasion; that he was going into the country for two days, but would stay if I chose it, and promised to return to town on Sunday. He said he was confident that the Duke of Bedford would come up on purpose from Woburn, if I wished it. His language in general and in particular was as open and explicit as possible. Suspend, therefore, your belief of the reports about them 'till you see further[1]. I have writ to Lord Suffolk[2], to apprize him of this state, and will write to the Earl of Bucks. Adieu, my dear Brother, ever yours, &c., &c. GEORGE GRENVILLE.

Mr. Burke, Lord Rockingham's Secretary, spoke for the Bill of Indemnity, to vindicate and avenge, as he said, the Constitution.

I send you enclosed the memorable words, as they stand on our Journals:—

"Whenever the Public is in danger, the King has a dispensing power."

"With the advice of Council, whenever the Salus Populi requires it."

"That on great and urgent occasions, where the safety of the people called for the exertion of a power contrary to the written law of these kingdoms, such exertion of power is excusable only by necessity, and justifiable by Act of Parliament."

THE EARL OF SUFFOLK TO MR. GRENVILLE.

Charleton, November 24, 1766.

DEAR SIR,—I feel infinitely obliged to you for your circumstantial account of a very interesting event which

---

[1] Lord Temple again suspects the Bedfords.

[2] Mr. Grenville's letter to Lord Suffolk contains, in other words, precisely the same information, and therefore I have not inserted it.

must have its consequences in both Houses of Parliament. I honour your firmness, and rejoice in its success.

As to my thoughts and intentions, which you are pleased to inquire after upon it, I shall very explicitly and confidentially declare them, subject, nevertheless, to revision, when we meet, upon further information from lights which it is impossible to be benefited by at this distance from the scene of action.

You say many are disposed to take the matter up in the House of Lords. If by that is meant an early reconsideration of the former debate, an inquiry into the legality of the prohibition, without its coming, of course, before us in the Bill of Indemnity, I am clearly of opinion (supposing everything as I left it ten days ago), that Lord Temple, Lord Lyttelton, and your humble servant, without (I suspect it very much) having half a dozen adherents in the House, can effect little by this kind of attack upon Ministry. In such a situation, the contenting ourselves with speaking our sentiments like men above being biassed or intimidated, seems to me to be, for the present, our only rule of conduct.

But you express a confidence that the Duke of Bedford's connection decline taking part with the present Ministers; and add, that the two other great parties begin very publicly to show their dislike.

If this be so, the case is much altered, and that becomes very eligible in the one which would not be at all so in the other.

If people will speak out; if there are doctrines broached which from public or private considerations they scorn or do not dare to adopt; if they will stand by those who, from principle, are ready to put themselves in the front, I should then advise the immediate reconsideration of this state-necessity law as you term it, in any manner that is parliamentary, without waiting for its being brought again upon the *tapis* by the intended Bill of Indemnity, or any other Ministerial mode whatever. The decision of the House of Commons will afford abundant reason and argument for such reconsideration. But if we are still to blunder on in the dark, to be played fast and loose with, and have no certain support to depend upon, I should then, in such a case, think it improper and absurd to make ineffectual efforts, or attempt anything further than what becomes our own honour and character as individuals. In this consideration, nothing under heaven shall ever induce me to acquiesce in, or sit silent when I hear it advanced —a doctrine of so dangerous a tendency as the justification of the legality of any power superior to law. * * *

(*Imperfect.*)

MR. NUGENT TO MR. GRENVILLE.

Great George Street, December 4, 1766.

MY DEAR SIR,—I have this day accepted His Majesty's gracious offer of being made First Lord of Trade, and have communicated my acceptance only to two persons, with whom I am obliged to take some necessary arrangements. It is of some importance to me that it may not be authentically known to many for some days. I flatter myself with hopes that a change of situation will produce no abatement of that friendship with which you have honoured me, and which I shall ever endeavour to deserve by every testimony of affection and respect, with which I ever shall remain, dear sir, your most faithful and obedient servant,   R. NUGENT.

THE EARL OF HARCOURT TO MR. GRENVILLE.

Cavendish Square, December 7, 1766.

DEAR SIR,—I had the misfortune to call at your door this morning about five minutes after you went out, which was the more unlucky, as I wished much to have some talk with you about Jenkinson, who is very much concerned to hear that you are displeased with him on account of a late transaction, of which, if you was apprized of the circumstances, I am inclined to believe that you would not think unfavourably of him [1].

Lord Chatham wrote to him last Sunday to desire him to call upon him : he waited upon him, and stayed with him an hour. His Lordship pressed him very much to go to the Admiralty, which Jenkinson declined, not only from a dislike to an office which by no means suited him, but on account of some other difficulties which he thought insurmountable. He was told that his refusal would displease the King, more especially considering Mr. Jenkinson's particular situation. He, however, persevered in his refusal, thinking that the difficulties he had mentioned were sufficient to justify the resolution he had taken. Before they parted a second interview was desired, and declined by Jenkinson as not likely to answer any purpose.

He heard no more of Lord Chatham 'till Tuesday, when he was pressed to attend him a second time, when he was told the obstacles were removed and the difficulties surmounted, which left him no room any longer to decline the office, unless he had urged the imprudence of accepting a place which no man can insure him the

---

[1] See Mr. Grenville's Diary, *post*.

possession of three months hence. He actually refused the employment on the Sunday, when there was, according to appearances, a probability of the Duke of Bedford's acceding, and accepted the office on the Tuesday, when the Administration was in a far more critical, dangerous, and uncertain state.

I own I think he has not consulted his interest upon this occasion, but the untoward situation he was in, left him no possibility of taking a different part. I was unwilling that you should be unacquainted with that part of the late transaction that came to my knowledge, and which I believe is precisely true. I ever wish, dear Sir, to see my friends deserve your good opinion, because I have the greatest respect and value for it, and am, dear Sir, your most faithful and obliged humble servant,

HARCOURT.

Mr. Jenkinson communicated the above transaction to me in confidence, therefore would beg it might not be mentioned.

MR. WILLIAM HAMILTON [1] TO MR. GRENVILLE.

Naples, December 30, 1766.

SIR,—I have now the satisfaction of assuring you that this charming climate has entirely restored Mrs. Hamilton's health, and I am convinced that she owes her life to your goodness in having sent us hither. We shall never be able to express sufficiently how much we think ourselves indebted to you; but to a heart like

---

[1] Afterwards Sir William Hamilton, K.B., and for so many years Ambassador at the Court of Naples. He was a son of Lord Archibald Hamilton, by a daughter of James, sixth earl of Abercorn. He died in 1803.

yours, the reflection of having done good is its own reward.

My situation is comfortable now that I am settled; at first I experienced Monsr. de Guerchy's having been in the right, et que la première mise est furieusement à craindre, especially for a married man in such a country as this, where the whole is expended in exterior parade, the nobility living upon macaroni and greens in order to support a greater number of servants, and to have finer equipages and liveries than their neighbours.

The numberless changes and extraordinary events that have happened since I left England, have often brought to my mind the character the Duc de Sully gave of us when he was Ambassador at our Court: "Environnés de la mer," says he, "on croiroit qu'ils en ont contracté l'instabilité;" however, I am convinced that though you have met in these bustles with some disagreeable circumstances, yet it is not in the power of man to make you unhappy, as you can sit by your own fireside with the comfortable reflection of having ever acted the part of an honest man, which, begging their pardons, few Ministers can boast of after having been so long employed.

Excuse my having taken up so much of your time, but I could no longer resist the pleasure of assuring you that I am, and ever shall be, with the utmost respect and gratitude, Sir, your most obedient and most obliged humble servant,   WM. HAMILTON.

MR. GRENVILLE'S DIARY

OF

MEMORABLE TRANSACTIONS.

(Continued from page 227.)

1766. *Friday, January 31st.*—Lord Hyde came to Mr. Grenville, and told him that Lord Harcourt had been in with the King on Thursday 30th, to make a representation to His Majesty of the present state of things, and to show His Majesty with how little weight and ability his present Administration went on. The King heard him patiently, and when he mentioned the Stamp Act, the King said he was strenuously for supporting and asserting the right of Great Britain to impose the tax, was against the repeal of the Bill, but thought it could perhaps be modified. (Mr. Grenville observed to Lord Hyde that these were the very words Lord Bute had used two nights before in a conversation with Lord Lyttelton.) Lord Harcourt suggested at a distance that His Majesty might make these his sentiments known, which might prevent the repeal of the Act, if his Ministers should push that measure. The King seemed averse to that, said he would never influence people in their parliamentary opinions, and that he had promised to support his Ministers. Lord Harcourt threw in doubts of their being able to support themselves, and then endeavoured to look round and name such people of ability as could form an Administration, named Mr. Grenville as the only man in the House of Commons capable of carrying on the business there, and commended his conduct during the time of his Administration. The King heard him patiently, but as Lord Harcourt reported no precise answer to Lord Hyde, Mr. Grenville imagines nothing gracious was said, because not repeated, and knows that if His Majesty expressed himself angrily Lord Harcourt would conceal it. The King spoke graciously of Lord Hyde, both as to his conduct abroad and at home ; said that a few days would show more of the state of things ; spoke civilly of the Opposition, and said he was glad to hear they were inclined to come into his service, if called to it. These words Mr. Grenville took up, and told Lord Hyde he hoped these words did not regard any declaration made by anybody for him, for that he never yet had said whether he would or would not go back to the King's service, and that he did desire his Lordship would understand that he was no party to all this transaction, and that he knew nothing of it, took it as no message, nor would he be understood to know that Lord Harcourt had had such a conversation. Lord Hyde assured him that Lord Harcourt should not know that he had told him of it. The conversation with the King passed at two different times, for the Queen came in with the young Princes in the morning, and interrupted it, and the King bid Lord Harcourt come again at night, which he did. Lord Harcourt, when he left Lord Hyde, went directly to Lord Bute, probably to report what had passed between the King and him, by all which Mr. Grenville sees this is a manœuvre of Lord

Bute's to change the present Ministry, and not to appear in it himself, saving himself under the subterfuge of Lord Harcourt going to the King, and he himself not seeing him. The King expressed himself angrily against Mr. Pitt, and said he was glad he had not committed his dignity by seeing him.

Lord Suffolk came to me at three o'clock this afternoon in the House of Commons, and told me that he was desired by a person of consequence to let him know whether, if a message were brought from the King to the Duke of Bedford or me, through Lord Bute, it would be received and attended to. I said it was a matter of great delicacy to give any answer, especially as I did not know the party who proposed it, and therefore could only say for myself that I was not disposed to negotiate but with principals; that therefore I thought Lord Suffolk's best way would be to ask the person who had spoken to him whether he would allow his name to be disclosed, and whether it was meant as a commission to one of us only, or to the Duke of Bedford and me together, in order that he might deliver it accordingly.

To this Lord Suffolk agreed, and at eleven o'clock that night, on my return home from the House of Commons, which sat till then on the American papers, I found the Duke of Bedford and Lord Suffolk at my house, the latter of whom had writ to me desiring me to take no notice of what had passed between him and me.

He opened to the Duke of Bedford and me the proposition, and informed us that it came to him from Lord Marchmont; that he had explained to him that he believed we would not be willing to negotiate but with principals, to which Lord Marchmont replied, that it was only to found an advice from a *person of the greatest consequence* (whom I guessed to be my Lord Chancellor) and to open the door, that the Duke of Bedford and I might negotiate an Administration with the King himself immediately; that he did not trifle with us, and wished that Lord Suffolk would tell this to the Duke of Bedford and me together. They both agreed with me in my guess that the person giving the advice was the Lord Chancellor, and after some talk together, it was determined to give the following respectful and formal answer, in both our names: "That any message which the King should send to us by any person whatever, would certainly be received with all respect and duty, and with that attention which His Majesty's commands would always require." [1]

We all agreed that this was the only proper answer, as it left us entirely at liberty not to negotiate with Lord Bute, even if he should come in consequence of this message, which we did not think likely; and on the other hand, a more negative answer might be called indecency to the King, and throw Lord Bute, with all the weight he can carry, into the scale of the Administration upon the present important question of exerting the sovereignty of Great Britain over America, which once gone is irretrievable, and which in the present situation, by Lord Bute's defection from the Ministry, there is a very fair prospect of preventing.

Saturday, February 1st.—Lord Suffolk reported this answer to Lord Marchmont, who said it was a very wise and guarded answer, and such a one as he should have expected from those who made it, and that he would report it to his friend, but said it would now soon be in

---

[1] See *Bedford Correspondence*, vol. iii. p. 326.

other hands, that indeed the cat was already out of the bag, for Mr. Elliot, Mr. Oswald, &c., had voted with Mr. Grenville the night before.

The King sent for his physicians, having a little cold; he was blooded, looked flushed and heated, but had not much fever.

Sunday, February 2nd.—The King did not go to the Drawing-room, he had still some feverishness,[1] but not much, and seemed in a good deal of agitation, and burst out into an expression before the physicians, saying he was willing to do anything for the good of his people, if they would but agree among themselves.

Monday, February 3rd.—The King's cold was better, but there was no Levée.

Lord Chancellor and Lord Rockingham were with him separately for near five hours the day before.

The House of Lords and Commons sat upon the American business, the Lords 'till ten at night, the Commons 'till three in the morning. The Duke of Grafton proposed a resolution to the House for establishing the right of Great Britain over her colonies: many Lords spoke, Lord Camden against the right, Lord Mansfield for it: the resolution was carried in the affirmative by 125 against 5; viz. Lord Shelburne, Lord Poulet, Lord Camden, Lord Cornwallis, and Lord Torrington. The Commons debated on the same resolution proposed by Mr. Conway, who at the same time declared he should be for the repeal of the Stamp Act. They had no division in that House: Mr. Pitt was there, and spoke with much more moderation than usual.

Tuesday, February 4th.—The House of Lords met

---

[1] The reader will not fail to remark how often these feverish attacks follow the King's political perplexities.

again upon the same business. The Duke of Grafton proposed a resolution to the House to *recommend* to the Governors of the American provinces to *give* compensation to those who had suffered by the late riots. Lord Suffolk proposed an amendment, by putting the word *require* instead of recommend. Lord Dartmouth and the Duke of Grafton consented to the amendment, but in the course of the debate retracted it again; had a division upon it, which was carried for the amendment by 63 against 60.

The King was better, and seemed in great spirits in the morning when his physicians saw him.

Wednesday, February 5th.—The House of Commons met again upon the American business, and continued sitting until two in the morning. The House agreed to the Resolutions proposed by Mr. Grenville: he moved two or three, but when he came to the last, Mr. Elliot and Lord Bute's party (who had conceived some jealousy upon observing that Mr. Pitt and Mr. Grenville had spoken with more civility to each other than on the former days) dissented. Mr. Grenville's friends would have had him divide the House upon it, but he thought it more prudent to give up the words objected to than to furnish them perhaps with a pretence for leaving him in the main question of the repeal whenever it should come on.

Thursday, February 6th.—The House of Commons adjourned 'till the next day, but the Lords met again upon the same business. It was proposed that thanks should be returned to such governors and officers in America as should have obeyed the English Acts of Parliament.

Lord Temple proposed the specifically naming the

Stamp Act, and his amendment was carried by five. Lord Bute spoke in support of the Act, and all his friends voted with Lord Temple, so did the Duke of York.

The Chancellor still holds the language of a change of Ministry, and says it must be Mr. Grenville and his friends : he desired the Duke of Bedford would adjourn the House, hoping something might be settled.

Sir Fletcher Norton talks in the same style to Mr. Grenville, but the Ministry seem determined not to resign, which indeed Mr. Grenville does not seem to think they could do with safety, leaving such a charge against them as their neglect in the accounts of the disorders in America in their enemies' hands ; and it does not look at present as if the King would dismiss them.

Friday, February 7th.—The House of Commons sat 'till eleven o'clock. Mr. Grenville proposed the address of thanks similar to that of the Lords, with the *Stamp Act* specified : there was a debate upon it. Mr. Pitt came down at four o'clock, made a very insolent overbearing speech, with great personal animosity to Mr. Grenville, and when he had done walked out of the House. Mr. Grenville got up after him, called to him to stay, but upon his going out, said he found himself under the necessity of answering that gentleman, as if he was present, and did it in very strong terms and with great applause. The House divided upon the words *Stamp Act*, which was carried in the negative by a majority of 140, and the Court party seemed much elated.

Saturday, February 8th.—Mr. Grenville received a letter from Mr. Pitt to excuse his having withdrawn the night before, to which he returned a cold answer[1].

[1] See *ante*, page 231.

Sunday, February 9th.—Mr. Grenville received advice from a fresh quarter[1], that Lord Bute wished to have a personal interview with Mr. Grenville, to which Mr. Grenville made answer that he concluded the Duke of Bedford was included in any proposition to be made to him, and that with him he was ready to hear any proposition Lord Bute should be authorized to make. The Duke of Bedford came in the evening, and Mr. Grenville and he talked the matter over together.

In the meantime, Lord Temple had intelligence from other hands of the Queen's favourable dispositions towards him, and of the King's dislike to his present Ministry. Lord Temple made professions of his zeal for the King's service at this dangerous crisis, saying he was willing to shew that all heat was subsided in his mind, and that he should esteem himself happy to be the instrument to rescue the King out of the hands of those who wanted and meant to take him prisoner ; that

---

[1] The following memorandum is thus endorsed in the handwriting of Mr. Grenville :—

"Paper delivered to me by Mr. Cadogan, writ in his own hand, containing an account of what he had said in consequence of the proposition which he brought to me on Sunday the 9th of February, 1766, to see Lord Bute, and which he said he had authority to make to me. This paper was given to me by Mr. Cadogan on Thursday, February 13th, 1766, the day after I had seen Lord Bute, to satisfy me that no part of the mistake attending that transaction had been owing to Mr. Cadogan, who was the only person whom I saw concerning it."

"That Mr. Grenville is ready to receive any proposition Lord Bute thinks proper to make. Then in conversation that it is wished that the proposition should come jointly to the Duke of Bedford and Mr. Grenville, whether it comes by interview or otherwise ; if by interview, there is no disposition in either of the above parties to look back to what is past, or consider anything but what is *now* best for the King's service. If pressed on the subject of the Duke of Bedford, to hint that as something of this kind has been lately made to them jointly, the leaving him out now would have an odd appearance ; but all this must be distinguished from any idea of a proposition on their parts, it being only to clear the ground for anything Lord Bute has to say."

even if the King had delicacies about sending to him after what had passed in May last, he would save His Majesty the blush by asking an audience. These thoughts he set down on paper, and the person took away the paper with them[1].

Lord Bute was known to have been four hours on Saturday with the King, but the Ministry give out that his favour is declined. They likewise plead the King's name for the repeal of the Stamp Act.

Monday, February 10th.—Lord Bute had it conveyed to Mr. Grenville that he wished to meet him at two o'clock at Lord Eglintoun's, to which Mr. Grenville agreed, but said he must send to the Duke of Bedford to be present: there was some mistake in the delivering the messages, and nine o'clock at night was named by Mr. Grenville, and agreed to by Lord Bute, who not only desired to have the Duke of Bedford

---

[1] This was probably a recommencement of the advances which had been made towards Lord Temple through the medium of the Queen, in October, 1765. It corroborates in some degree the circumstances related by Almon (*Political Anecdotes*, vol. ii. p. 58), with the exception that the agency is by him referred to the Princess Dowager of Wales and Lord Bute. He says:—" By the assistance of a great Lady at Carlton House, he (Lord Bute) contrived to amuse Lord Temple during the months of March and April, 1766, with the daily expectation of a *carte blanche*. Lord Temple was for several weeks the dupe of this device ; and notwithstanding Lord Bute's visits at Carlton House were notorious, yet this matter was so unreservedly declared to be totally independent of him, that had not, by accident, the *cloven foot*, as Lord Temple called it, appeared unexpectedly, the deception might have been continued some time longer; until perhaps some measure or arrangement might have been produced by it."   *   *   *   *
" But while he (Lord Bute) remained obstinately attached to the continuation of his secret influence, Lord Temple, who was always furnished with correct information of certain secret visits and meetings, received with submission and examined with jealousy every proposition that came from the Court. To this sedulous attention he owed the peculiar honour of being the only English nobleman who had not been deceived and subdued by the intrigues of Lord Bute."

present, but Lord Temple too, if he chose it. Lord Temple declined it; but Mr. Grenville did not receive the answer, so Lord Bute went and waited at Lord Eglintoun's, but neither the Duke of Bedford nor Mr. Grenville came. Lord Temple came to Mr. Grenville in the evening, and told him that by the channel from which he himself (Lord Temple) drew his intelligence, he had information of all that had passed between him and Lord Bute by message.

Lord Strange[1] went into the King's Closet, where, whilst he was speaking to him upon business, His Majesty interrupted him, and said he heard his name had been unjustly made use of, as if he wished the repeal of the Stamp Act; that he was so far from doing it, that he wished the Act to stand, but with such modifications as Parliament should judge necessary.

Many of His Majesty's Ministers went in to endeavour to get leave to dismiss some of those of his servants who had voted with the Opposition, but could not prevail; and Lord Strange told everybody he met of the discourse His Majesty had held to him, which was in direct contradiction to what had been propagated for the last two days by the Ministers.

Tuesday, February 11*th.*—The Duke of Bedford and Mr. Grenville thought they were to meet Lord Bute at Lord Eglintoun's at half-past nine at night, and went there accordingly; but, when they came, Lord Eglintoun told them Lord Bute was not to be found,

---

[1] Chancellor of the Duchy of Lancaster. The eldest son of the Earl of Derby had assumed the title of Lord Strange, although it had really passed as a Barony in fee, by females, to the Duke of Athol. In the next generation the Derby family took Stanley as their *courtesy* title, but it was not until 1832 that a Barony of Stanley was really created in that House, into which the present Earl of Derby was called up in *vitâ patris*, in 1844.

and gave them to understand that he was with the King.

Wednesday, February 12*th.*—Lord Eglintoun came to Mr. Grenville to acquaint him that Lord Bute would be at his (Lord Eglintoun's) house, at one o'clock, to meet the Duke of Bedford and him.

They went to the time appointed, and Lord Bute came soon after, but denied, and made it clear to a demonstration, that he had never sent any message, but on the contrary, he thought, from what was told him, that the Duke of Bedford and Mr. Grenville had wished to see him; but he was very civil, and said, if Lord Eglintoun had done it, either ignorantly, or wishing to bring them together, he was obliged to him for it; that he desired not to look back, but to look forward, and was glad to find himself upon the same ground as them, in the great measure now before Parliament, and which had called him out as a public man; that he never looked but to a private line, and meant never to deviate from it. All this was answered with great civility, both by the Duke of Bedford and Mr. Grenville. Lord Bute told them he lamented the unhappy state of the King, but knew none of his opinions, as he never saw him [1]. The Duke of Bedford declared he would never come into Government again, and Mr. Grenville said, that if this Act was repealed, nothing should ever make him come into the King's service to carry it into execution [2].

---

[1] This is inconsistent with Mr. Grenville's information that on the Saturday previous Lord Bute had been *four hours with the King*, and only the day before, when the Duke of Bedford and Mr. Grenville were waiting at Lord Eglintoun's to have an interview with Lord Bute, they were informed by Lord Eglintoun that he was not to be found, and gave them to understand *that he was with the King.*

[2] There are several conflicting accounts of this negotiation and of the interview which took place between Lord Bute, the Duke of Bedford,

Lord Rockingham sent to desire Lord Strange would come to the Levée, which he did. They had some angry words about the declaration made by Lord Strange and Mr. Grenville, at the house of Lord Eglintoun. Mr. Grenville's narrative is now before the reader: the Duke of Bedford's statement is in the third volume of the *Bedford Correspondence ;* and Almon's account is contained in the second volume of his *Political Anecdotes,* and it is said to be derived from the information and even from the language of Lord Temple. Horace Walpole, too, has given, with an air of probability, the opinions of the Duke of Bedford upon what had passed between Lord Bute and himself. Walpole asserts that Lord Temple had intended to be present, but that at the hour of meeting he excused himself from attending it. He adds, " The Favourite, however, had the triumph of beholding the Duke of Bedford and George Grenville prostrate before him, suing for pardon, reconciliation, and support. After enjoying the spectacle of their humiliation for some minutes, the lofty Earl, scarce deigning to bestow upon them above half a score monosyllables, stiffly refused to enter into connection with them; on which the Duke of Bedford said hastily, ' He hoped, however, that what had passed would remain a profound secret.' ' A secret !' replied the Favourite, ' I have done nothing I am ashamed of,—has your Grace?' and quitted the room. As if Lord Bute's refusal of secrecy made it prudent to expose even more than Lord Bute could tell, the Duke went home, and at dinner with sixteen persons, and before all the servants, he related what had passed ; and then said to the Duchess and his Court, ' I was against taking this step, but you would make me.'" [a]

Although Lord Eglintoun afterwards professed to be in great distress at having so much mistaken the business or misrepresented it, there can be no doubt but that the meeting was the result of a preconcerted arrangement between himself and Lord Bute, and it seems equally certain that the latter was disappointed at the absence of Lord Temple, who was by far the most important person to be gained ; he knew that George Grenville would be sure to follow his brother, and the Duke of Bedford was also at this time in close alliance with Mr. Grenville, besides that in conciliating Lord Temple, there was also a remote chance of, at least, moderating the opposition of Mr. Pitt, in his views with regard to the repeal of the Stamp Act. That Lord Bute was disappointed in not seeing Lord Temple is in some measure corroborated by his having taken no further notice of this meeting of the 12th of February. The Duke of Bedford observes in his " Minutes " of the affair : " Hearing nothing of any sort from Lord Bute, on Monday the 17th, I took the liberty to speak to the Duke of York upon the circumstances of the

[a] *Memoirs of George III.,* vol. ii. p. 295.

of the King's opinion, upon which Lord Strange went into the King's Closet, to ask if he had mistaken the sense of what he had been pleased to say to him ; the King confirmed it, and said he had not.

Lord Rockingham declared the King had told him he was for the repeal of the Act, set it down upon paper, and went into the Closet to ask if that was not what His Majesty had said to him. The King wrote under it in pencil that he had said so, but it singly was in answer to the *two* propositions *only*, of enforcing or repealing, and that of those two he thought the last the best [1].

present times." [a] Last of all comes the commentary of Junius upon these transactions, who a few years later accuses the Duke of Bedford of descending to " the humility of soliciting an interview with the Favourite, and of offering to recover, at any price, the honour of his friendship." Junius subsequently added in a note, "Lord Bute told the Duke that he was determined never to have any connection with a man who had so basely betrayed him."

[1] The insinuation of double-dealing here implied against the King, has been very satisfactorily refuted in the *Quarterly Review*, vol. lxxvii. pp. 285-6. "The King avowed what he had said to Lord Strange—he rebuked Lord Rockingham for telling but *half the story*, and boldly, we dare say somewhat indignantly, *wrote*—so as to admit of no misrepresentation, on Lord Rockingham's paper, the important qualification of his opinion, which Lord Rockingham had suppressed."

The following passage is from Lord Temple's Pamphlet, entitled *The Conduct of the late Administration examined, &c.*, 1767. " But this was not the only instance in which they represented the sentiments of their Sovereign : when they were to influence by authority those whom popular tumult could not terrify to consent to the repeal of the Stamp Act, they had recourse to the name of the King; assuring those who would hear them, that the King wished it might be repealed [b]. The part of honest and affectionate servants was the very reverse of this; supposing the measure itself to have been just, all mention of that name should have been suppressed, till the success of the repeal being ascertained, the wishes which he expressed for the relief might be held out as the object of the gratitude of his people;

[a] *Bedford Correspondence*, vol. iii. p. 329.

[b] "The reputation of public measures depends upon the Minister, who is responsible, not upon the King, whose private opinions are not supposed to have any weight against the advice of his counsel, whose personal authority should therefore never be interposed in public affairs. This I believe is true constitutional doctrine."—*Junius*, ii. 126.

This Lord Strange told to Mr. Grenville on Thursday the 13th, and said, the King had said that the Duke of Grafton and Lord Rockingham had often endeavoured to persuade him of the expediency of repealing the Bill, but without effect.

Lord Temple came to Mr. Grenville in the evening, and told him he knew, by the same private channel as before [1], all that had passed in relation to their interview

but to quote this authority, and to risque thereby this reputation for the promotion of their own party purposes, was a conduct neither suggested by their duty to their Sovereign, nor by regard for the constitution : this reserve would have been necessary had the opinion of the King been that which they attributed to him ; but it is certain that they falsified as well as *prostituted*[a] the sentiments of the King : it is certain, although when contradicted on this subject by those who could do it with authority, they endeavoured to avoid the disgrace of this contradiction by an expedient borrowed from their only school of business, those clubs of gaming in which gentlemen do not trust the unwritten words of gentlemen, and demanded in writing the words of their Sovereign. His words were the genuine dictates of his wisdom and love for his people ; careful of the safety of all his subjects, he wished to unite them all by the bands of mutual support, and by a community of duties as well as of rights. They can claim no merit towards the Crown, who by their artifices prevented the execution of that royal wish ; but must with terror look forward to that hour, for it will come, when Augustus, grieved with the remembrance of the only loss which can obscure the glories of his successful reign, shall demand from them a restitution, not of a province, but of an empire more extensive than that of Rome ; not of three legions, but of whole nations of subjects."

[1] This is the second occasion on which Lord Temple has lately professed to have a " private channel " of information relative to the doings of Lord Bute. (See *ante*, 362.) The same system of secret *espionage* is described by Almon (" *Lord Temple's man* ") to have occurred in the following June and July, when for eighteen successive days, the movements of Lord Bute, and his evening visits to the Princess Dowager of Wales at Carlton House, were most vigilantly recorded by some unknown chronicler ; not improbably the same person from whom Lord Temple now " drew his intelligence." This "*faithful journal,*" as it is called, will be found in Almon's *Anecdotes of Lord Chatham,* vol. ii. p. 168, edit. 1792. It should be remembered that in the presentation copy of this work, which Almon sent to Lady Chatham, he wrote,—

[a] A very favourite word with *Junius,* and often used by him in this sense.

with Lord Bute, and said that Lord Eglintoun had been in great distress at having so much mistaken the business, or misrepresented it.

Saturday, February 15th.—Lord Harcourt came to Mr. Grenville at ten in the morning, had a long discourse with him, lamenting the general state of things, the situation of the King, and particularly with respect to the present business of the Stamp Act; giving Mr. Grenville to understand that he and Lord Temple were the people on whom everybody's eyes were turned, and wishing the King would come to the resolution to make the change. Mr. Grenville said in general, that neither Lord Temple nor he were desirous to come into Government, considering the desperate situation of affairs, and more especially if the Stamp Act was to be repealed ; that he, for his own part, would never come in to be the instrument to carry that repeal into execution, nor did he wish to force himself into the King's service at any rate; that the task of a Minister was always difficult enough, but in times like these, much too hazardous without the full countenance and favour of the King; that, on the other hand, he was not desirous to disturb the King's Government; that if His Majesty thought proper to form such a Government as could carry on his affairs, though he himself was not part of it, he should be glad to support it, and give every facility to it in his power.

Lord Harcourt commended his moderation and the good sense of what he said, and told him he would take care the King should know it, and asked if he should

" From your Ladyship's noble brother, the late Lord Temple, I received the most interesting part of these anecdotes : his Lordship honoured me with his friendship and esteem many years."

find him at home in the evening in case he could call upon him again : Mr. Grenville said yes, but he did not return.   Lord Temple called upon Mr. Grenville in the evening, and told him he had met Lord Denbigh at dinner at Lady Blandford's, with whom he had had a great deal of discourse ; that Lord Denbigh had said how necessary Lord Bute thought it that some great Lord should go to the King to represent to him the distressed situation of affairs.   Lord Temple told him what he had already done upon that head, and repeated the same to Lord Denbigh, who said he would go the next morning to the Queen's house to report it to the King.   They agreed that Lord Denbigh should write a letter to Lord Temple recommending this, to which he should send an ostensible answer.   Lord Denbigh saw Lord Bute that night, and at twelve o'clock sent to Lord Temple for his letter.   The next morning Lord Denbigh came to Lord Temple, said he had considered the matter fully, that the King did not like to be spoken to on these subjects, that he (Lord Denbigh) should be the victim of it, and that he desired to have his own letter back, and would restore Lord Temple's, which accordingly was done, and the two letters burnt, which Lord Temple suspects was by Lord Bute's suggestion.

Monday, February 17th.—Lord Temple wrote a note to Mr. Grenville, telling him hearts had failed [1], and nothing had been done, and soon after came and told him that Lord Denbigh went to Lord Bute, talked the matter over with him, and they both thought it best to say nothing of it.   Lord Gower came to Mr. Grenville

---

[1] In allusion, I presume, to the timidity of Lord Bute.   The words of Lord Temple's note are :—" Their heart has again failed.   I will tell you particulars when I see you.   This only inter nos."

to acquaint him that the Duke of York had desired him
to use the same language from his Highness to the Duke
of Bedford, namely, the necessity of some person of
consequence desiring to see the King to represent the
present dangerous crisis to him. The Duke of Bedford
said he was ready to do it provided it would not be disagreeable to His Majesty; that he would ask an audience, and deliver his own sentiments to His Majesty,
saying at the same time that Mr. Grenville concurred
in them : this was writ down on paper, but Mr. Grenville desired his name might not be mentioned, repre-
senting to Lord Gower the impropriety of it, from the
difference of situation, viz., the Duke of Bedford going
to the King as a great Peer, determined to take no office ;
whereas it would seem as if Mr. Grenville came to solicit the office from which he had been dismissed.

This was in consequence of the Duke of Bedford
having reported to the Duke of York what had passed
between Lord Bute, his Grace, and Mr. Grenville, when
Lord Bute had assured them both, that having no intercourse with His Majesty, nor never seeing him, he could
not make any representation to him, upon which the
Duke of York desired to have a memorandum from the
Duke of Bedford, the copy of which Lord Gower
shewed to Mr. Grenville[1]. His Grace therein refers
to the conversation he had had with Lord Bute, and
the declaration Lord Bute had made of his not being
able to make known his Grace's sentiments to the King.
He therefore desires his Royal Highness will be pleased
to acquaint His Majesty that if he thinks to stop the
further progress of the measure now before Parliament,
and to change his Ministry, his Grace was ready to re-

---

[1] See *Bedford Correspondence*, vol. iii. p. 326.

ceive his commands to come and lay open his sentiments
to him, and he believed Mr. Grenville was in the same
disposition.   Mr. Grenville objected to the words relating to him for the reasons already mentioned.

The motion for the repeal of the Stamp Act in the
House of Commons is fixed for Friday.

Tuesday, February 18*th.*—Mr. Rigby came to Mr.
Grenville in the House of Commons, told him that he
had seen Lord Gower, who reported from the Duke of
York that His Majesty had given a favourable hearing to
the suggestions His Royal Highness had made to him,
and was very well pleased with what the Duke had said
to him from the Duke of Bedford, namely, that if His
Majesty still continued in sentiment against the repeal
of the Stamp Act, and for the modification of it, he (the
Duke of Bedford) was ready to receive his commands
whenever he should please to allow him to lay his sentiments before him, and would give every assistance in his
power to the modification of the Bill.

The King told the Duke of York that he was firm in
his opinion for the modification, and against the repeal
of the Bill; that he had told his Ministers so very often,
who had always endeavoured to persuade him to give
in to the repeal, and to avail himself of the popularity
of the measure, but that he had told them he never
would, and that they would ruin him, themselves, and
the nation, by trying for popularity; that as to what the
Duke of Bedford had conveyed to him, he must take
some little time to think of it, and seemed afraid, lest
the seeing the Duke of Bedford might be deemed treating with him.

The Duke of York intended to go in the evening to
shew the paper to the Princess of Wales.

Wednesday, February 19*th.*—Mr. Cadogan came to Mr. Grenville and acquainted him with all that had passed between the King and the Duke of York on the preceding day, saying that the Duke of York was extremely satisfied with the manner in which the King had received what he had said to him, and that his behaviour had been full of affection to the Duke of York. Mr. Cadogan repeated all that Mr. Grenville had already heard from Mr. Rigby, particularly the King having strongly disclaimed to his Ministers the availing himself of a vain popularity, which he said would undo his people, in giving up the rights of his crown; that to this he would never consent; that they gave him bad advice in it, and would ruin him and the nation by affecting popularity. In regard to the Duke of Bedford's proposition, His Majesty said he had made it a rule never to refuse an audience to any nobleman whatever, but seemed apprehensive that in the present conjuncture it might be deemed *treating.*

The Duke of York said that must be as His Majesty pleased. The King said he heard that the Duke of Bedford, Lord Bute, and Mr. Grenville, had acted very much like men when they met, in laying aside all private prejudice, and resolving to act for, and to consider the good of, the public alone. The Duke of York always deplored the sad state of the kingdom, and the danger of the repeal of the Act.

The King by a letter he wrote to his brother the same evening thanked him for having spoken to him upon the subject, but said when a measure was once before Parliament, it must abide the decision of Parliament, deeming it unconstitutional and improper in any way to interfere, but that his sentiments were as strong as ever against the repeal[1].

The Duke of York saw the Princess of Wales on Tuesday evening, and told her what had passed ; she seemed under very great anxiety, lest it might prejudice the Duke in the King's opinion, and seemed very apprehensive of the consequence for him, though pleased with what she heard of the King's manner of taking it.

The Duke rode with the King in the morning, and they talked a great deal upon the same subject, and bid the Duke of York come to him again the next morning.

Mr. Grenville told all this to Lord Temple, who did not expect that anything would happen in consequence of it, and was full of approbation of Mr. Grenville having desired to have his name omitted in the paper, and the

---

[1] These sentiments appear strangely inconsistent with some letters not dated, but supposed to have been written about this time, by the King, to Lord Rockingham and General Conway, and printed in Lord Albemarle's *Memoirs of Lord Rockingham.*

"Talbot," says the King, "is as right as I can desire, in the Stamp Act—strong for our declaring our right, but willing to repeal ; and has handsomely offered to attend the House daily, and answer the very indecent conduct of those who oppose with so little manners or candour." When leave was given to bring in the Bill for the Repeal of the Stamp Act, by a large majority, the King thanks Lord Rockingham for the particulars of the debate in the House of Commons, "which, by the great majority, must be reckoned a very favourable appearance for the Repeal of the Stamp Act in that House." To General Conway the King writes:—"Nothing can in my eyes be more advantageous than the debate in the House of Commons this day." Again, on the following day, to Lord Rockingham:—"I am much pleased that the appearance was so good yesterday."

Nevertheless, it is tolerably certain that George III. was at this time very desirous of getting rid of the Rockingham Administration, and he would have been equally willing, if possible, to have prevented the Repeal of the Stamp Act.

Duke of Bedford was likewise very well satisfied that it should be omitted.

The Duke of York in the House of Lords came to Lord Aylesford, spoke long to him upon the Stamp Act, declared his sentiments against the repeal, and said he was happy in knowing the King to be in the same opinions, notwithstanding his name had been so improperly dealt out to the contrary, but that he was very sure of what he advanced, having seen the King that morning.

Thursday, February 20th.—Mr. Grenville went to the Queen's Drawing-room (her birth-day being kept that day), and was very civilly received both by King and Queen.

Friday, February 21st.—The repeal of the Stamp Act was moved by Mr. Conway, and seconded by Mr. Grey Cooper. The House sat 'till four in the morning. The question for the repeal was carried by a majority of 108 voices.

Thursday, April 10th.—Mr. Grenville went to see Lord Mansfield, who told him that he had seen the King the day before; that he had asked an audience to acquaint the King with Lady Stormont's death, and, in consequence of it, to obtain a discretionary leave for Lord Stormont to come for some time to England, when his private affairs should require it[1]. His Majesty received him with the utmost graciousness, expressed his concern for whatever affected Lord Mansfield, saying he should be ungrateful if he did otherwise, being more

---

[1] David, seventh Viscount Stormont, probably held some diplomatic appointment at this time. He was afterwards Ambassador at Paris in 1772, and subsequently Secretary of State and President of the Council. He succeeded to the Earldom of Mansfield on the death of his uncle in 1793, and died in 1796. He married a daughter of Count Bunau, a Privy Councillor to the Elector of Saxony, and his Minister to the Court of London.

obliged to his Lordship than to any man in the kingdom; inquired much after his health, and upon Lord Mansfield's asking His Majesty how he did, said he had got his pain again in his breast, which he feared he never should get rid of, saying it was the same complaint as the Duke of Leeds has, but that he was otherwise well.

His Majesty naturally enough led the conversation to business, by inquiring how Lord Mansfield had borne the fatigue of the House of Lords, where there had been a great deal of business, particularly in relation to the repeal of the Stamp Act.

Lord Mansfield lamented that unhappy step, which he said he feared had given a mortal blow to Great Britain, of which God grant that His Majesty might not feel the fatal effects in the extent in which he (Lord Mansfield) apprehended.

He took notice of the King's name having been bandied about in a very improper manner, to which the King assented, saying he had been much displeased at it, as thinking it unconstitutional to have his name mentioned as a means to sway any man's opinion in any business which was before Parliament; that all those who approached him knew that to be his sentiment. Lord Mansfield said he differed from His Majesty in that opinion, for that though it would be unconstitutional to endeavour by His Majesty's name to carry questions in Parliament, yet where the lawful rights of the King and Parliament were to be asserted and maintained, he thought the making His Majesty's opinion in support of those rights to be known was very fit and becoming.

Lord Mansfield told the King that he knew not in what light his own conduct through that whole affair might have been stated to His Majesty, but that he could assure him he had entered into no set plan of opposition ; that he was no party man, but a hearty and sincere well-wisher to his King and country, and both as such, and from his thorough approbation of the propriety and wisdom of the measure of laying the Stamp Duty, he had endeavoured to support it to the utmost of his power, and to show his full disapprobation of the repeal, but that what he had done had been from opinion only, in no concert with any man whatever, for he could safely say no man knew his opinion upon it 'till he delivered it in the House; and, as a proof of it, told the King of his having refused to take Lord Bathurst's proxy, because he would charge himself with no man's conscience but his own.

The King said he had had justice done him by those who had reported the debates to him, saying that Lord Mansfield had some friends among the Ministers, but that the reports were made with certain colourings conformable to the sentiments of those who reported, as for example, that he had been told that Lord Mansfield had spoken much better upon the *right*, than upon the *repeal*, at which they both laughed. The King heard all he said with ease and seeming assent, and in the course of the conversation Lord Mansfield mentioned Mr. Grenville, saying he was the man in all England of whom he thought the best; that he had lived long with him in great intimacy, but had concerted no measure of opposition with him, nor did he understand that the part Mr. Grenville had taken, or meant to take, was that of saying anything whatever in opposition which he should be obliged to unsay in any other situation; that as to the resisting the repeal of the Stamp Act, or any other thing done by him whilst in the Administration, it was what, as a man of honour, he was obliged to do, in support of those opinions which had led him to those measures.

Wotton, July 11th, 1766.—Mr. Grenville received a letter from Lord Thomond, acquainting him that the day before (the 10th of July, the same day on which Mr. Grenville had the preceding year delivered up the Seal) the King had declared to his Ministers that he had sent to Mr. Pitt to come and form an Administration, assigning for his reason their having taken no steps to strengthen his Government. Several other letters confirmed the same, and all agreed that the measure was totally unexpected by them. Lord Chancellor wrote the letter by the King's order to Mr. Pitt [1].

Sunday, July 13th.—Mr. Grenville had a letter from Lord Temple, repeating much the same intelligence, but saying he had it from no head-quarters. In the evening letters came in, saying that Mr. Pitt arrived on Friday, and saw the King on Saturday. Lord Bute's friends say he knew nothing of the measure, that it was not his doing, and that his language seems to disapprove it.

Monday, July 14th.—Mr. Grenville went to dine at Sir William Lee's [2], where, soon after he arrived, they brought him word that Lord Temple was there, and desired to speak with him. His Lordship told him that he had received a letter [3] that morning from the Chancellor, signifying the King's pleasure to him, that he should come to town to consider upon settling a Govern-

---

[1] Enclosing one from the King himself, for which see *Chatham Correspondence*, vol. ii. p. 436. The King wrote several letters to Lord Chatham upon this occasion.

[2] At Hartwell.   [3] See *ante*, p. 263.

ment to carry on the King's business with ease. He set out immediately, and hearing that Mr. Grenville was at Hartwell, called there to apprize him of it. Lord Temple and Mr. Grenville conversed together for near an hour, and then Lord Temple went on.

Thursday, July 17*th*.—Lord Temple returned to Stowe, and sent an account to Mr. Grenville, in a letter, of what had passed between Mr. Pitt and him [1].

Mr. Grenville immediately set out with Mr. Nugent for Stowe, where Lord Temple related all particulars to him at large.

Mr. Grenville went to Woburn, on *Saturday, the* 16*th of August.* The Duke of Bedford received him with great marks of friendship and kindness, and said he meant to have come over to Wotton, if he had not seen him there. He declared very strongly to Mr. Grenville that he continued firm in his former opinions, made many declarations of the strongest and most friendly dispositions towards him, and that he would nor could have nothing to do with Lord Chatham, the *totality* of whose measures he disapproved.

The Duchess expressed great jealousy and apprehension of a reconciliation between Lord Temple and Lord Chatham, which Mr. Grenville endeavoured to destroy.

Sunday, August 17*th*.—Lord Tavistock came to Woburn to acquaint his father with the offer made to Lord Gower, the particulars of which are in the copy of a letter from Mr. Grenville to Lord Temple [2].

Mr. Rigby came to Wotton on [. . .] of [. . . .], saying the Duke of Bedford would, if possible, come to Wotton before he went to Bath, expressing in the same

[1] See *ante*, p. 267.   [2] See *ante*, p. 302.

strong manner as before his preference to Mr. Grenville. Mr. Rigby was as warm in his declarations, and eagerly pressed Mr. Grenville to enter, upon the very first opening of Parliament, into a warm opposition. Mr. Grenville said he should be ready to take his part, as he ever had done; but after having done that, if he found himself deserted as he was last year, and left to speak to empty walls, he should withdraw, and follow his ease and pleasure as others did theirs. Mr. Grenville received many letters during the course of the summer, and saw a great many people; the letters will best explain what they meant to convey, and the conversations were agreeable to the different sentiments of the people, but there always appeared a great deal of manoeuvre in Lord Bute, through such of his friends as were not in office, to keep a degree of communication with Mr. Grenville, though in a manner not clearly avowed.

1766. *Monday, November 3rd.*—Mr. Grenville came to town.

Wednesday 5th.—Mr. Grenville, Lord Temple, and Lord Lyttelton went to the King's Levée; he received them civilly and with an open countenance.

In the evening Mr. Grenville saw Mr. Wedderburn, who held a very hostile language to the present Administration, continued to confirm all he had said and wrote during the summer, concerning Lord Bute's dissatisfaction; said he had great reason to believe the Duke of Northumberland was not pleased, and that he believed Earl Percy would oppose the measures of the Ministers.

Reports still prevail of the Duke of Bedford and his friends having resolved to act with Lord Chatham;

these are strengthened by the Duke and Lord Chatham having frequently met at Bath[1], and great civility having been shown by the Duchess of Bedford to Lady Chatham.

Thursday, November 6th.—Mr. Rigby came in the morning to Mr. Grenville, and had a long conversation with him, in which he declared firmly and roundly that he would support and maintain all his former opinions; that the thing in the world which he wished the most was to see Mr. Grenville again at the head of affairs; that the Duke of Bedford was disgusted at all public situations, and saw nothing but ruin; but that so far from having made any arrangement for his friends with Lord Chatham, he was ready to oppose if he saw any ground held out to him to act upon; that he preferred Mr. Grenville to any man in England; that he meant to see him as soon as he came to town, which would be on Sunday; and that he wished to hear what he had to say before he saw anybody else whatever. He told him, that Lord Tavistock declared a detestation of all public business, and most particularly of the House of Commons; that this dislike led him to wish to be called up to the House of Peers; not that anything was then in agitation about it, on the contrary, that he spoke slightingly of Lord Chatham, but that he was persuaded that Lord Tavistock meant, if possible, to decline standing again for Bedfordshire.

Mr. Grenville received a letter since he came to town

---

[1] "Gilly" Williams, in a letter to Selwyn, dated from Bath, at this time says,—"Lord Chatham is here with more equipage, household, and retinue, than most of the old patriarchs used to travel with in ancient days. He comes nowhere but to the Pump-room; there he makes a short essay and retires."—*George Selwyn and his Contemporaries,* vol. ii. p. 60.

from Mr. Fraser, which had been round by Wotton, pressing him earnestly to come to town, and with words as if some immediate change was on the carpet. He came this evening to Mr. Grenville. The business referred to was the desire Sir Fletcher Norton and others of Lord Bute's friends had to act with Mr. Grenville, but more particularly Sir Fletcher Norton. Mr. Fraser at the same time said he had dined with Lord Bute, who had inquired what passed at Wotton and Stowe, knowing he had been at both; spoke with great regard of Mr. Grenville, but expressed surprise that Lord Temple should have allowed of the Pamphlet published immediately after his interview with Mr. Pitt. Mr. Fraser assured him, that he knew from Lord Temple himself that he was a stranger to that publication, and thought it an absurd pamphlet, with many false facts[1] though some true ones, particularly with regard to what passed between him and Mr. Pitt; that those might easily be known, and to many people, because he had told them to right hand and left, thinking it right for his own justification so to do.

Lord Bute was inquisitive what sort of plan Mr. Grenville meant to proceed upon in case he should be sent for, and his whole language was to disapprove of the Administration as it now stands.

Friday, November 7th.—Lord Gower came to Mr. Grenville, talked with great personal regard of and to Mr. Grenville, but for the rest held the same language as Mr. Rigby had done, but rather with stronger symptoms of the Duke of Bedford and his party taking no

---

[1] If this solecism were the expression of Lord Temple, it was also used by Junius in a letter to Draper:—" I am sorry to tell you, Sir William, that in this article, your first *fact* is *false.*"—*Junius,* i. 415.

active part, and saying that he could not separate himself from the Duke of Bedford.

Mr. Jenkinson came likewise, saying the same in regard to Sir James Lowther, from whom he could not divide himself, being brought into Parliament by him, and knowing no other person who would give him a seat there.

Sir Fletcher Norton's language was great anger and disgust at the ill-treatment he had met with, but yet did not seem inclined to take any active part.

Sunday, November 9th.—Mr. Grenville went to Bedford House: the Duke received him with great cordiality, with many expressions of his personal approbation of him, and his earnest wish to see him again at the head of Government, but as that could not be at present, he thought the melancholy and disordered state of the kingdom such as required all the assistance it could receive; that therefore he doubted whether he and his friends should disturb the Government; that he knew Lord Chatham disapproved of him, but that some of his errors he might possibly correct, and time at least should be given for the trial; that he himself should always adhere to and continue in the principles and opinions he had professed last year, but that as to the rest, the disturbing Government might in the present exigence be a remedy worse than the disease.

Mr. Grenville differed from his Grace in this opinion, staggered him by his reasoning, but did not bring him off this ground; on the contrary, when Mr. Grenville said that the Court laboured industriously to divide his Grace and his friends from him (Mr. Grenville), the Duke said how could it be otherwise, where their opinions differed.

Mr. Grenville went from thence to Lord Mansfield, who talked with the highest blame of the Ministry.

Monday, November 10*th.*—Lord Thomond dined with Mr. Grenville, and told him that he heard from the Duke of Bedford's friends, that his Grace declared himself to be extremely satisfied with the language Mr. Grenville had held to him. There was a meeting at Bedford House, in the morning, of the Duke's family and friends.

At the Cockpit meeting[1] Lord Lisburne[2] was called upon, having promised to move the Address, but he excused himself, saying he was ill, and found himself utterly unable : this a little disconcerted Mr. Conway, but he immediately meant to have recourse to Mr. Augustus Hervey, who had been induced by Lord Bristol's earnest and peremptory solicitation (though very much against his will) to second the Address, and accordingly his name was echoed round the room, but in vain, for he was playing at Quadrille with Mrs. Grenville instead of attending the meeting.

Tuesday, November 11*th.*—Mr. Nugent came to Mr. Grenville in the morning, holding a language so different, and seeming in opinions so contrary to Mr. Grenville's, that he did not communicate to him the motions that were intended to be made relating to the Address in the House of Commons that day. He was just returned from Bath, where it was said he had been the Pacificator between the Duke of Bedford and Lord Chatham.

Mr. Augustus Hervey moved the Address in the

---

[1] To hear the King's speech read.

[2] Wilmot, fourth Viscount, and afterwards Earl of Lisburne. He died in 1800.

House of Commons, accompanied with a direct *opposition* speech. Sir Alexander Gilmour[1] seconded the Address.

Mr. Grenville spoke to arraign the illegality of the laying the embargo upon the exportation of corn, instead of calling together the Parliament for their sanction for so doing in case it was necessary. Mr. Conway answered him in a very unsatisfactory manner.

Mr. Grenville afterwards made a motion for the giving a sum of money towards the relief of the poor, but it was rejected without a division.

The speakers on the side of the Court were Mr. Conway, Mr. Onslow, Mr. T. Townshend, Mr. Beckford, &c. ; on the contrary party, Mr. Grenville, Mr. Harris, Mr. Whately, Mr. Pitt, Mr. Luttrell, Mr. Wedderburn, not to the question and motion proposed by Mr. Grenville, but in answer to something thrown out upon general warrants.

In the House of Lords the Address was moved by Lord Spencer, and seconded by Lord Hillsborough. The speakers on the side of the Court were Lord Chatham, Lord Botetourt, Duke of Grafton, the Chancellor, Lord Northington, Duke of Richmond. Against the Court were Lord Temple, Lord Suffolk, Lord Lyttelton, Lord Buckinghamshire.

The Duke of Bedford spoke strongly to the illegality of laying on the embargo without the advice of Parliament, but was against the amendment of the Address proposed by Lord Temple[2].

[1] M.P. for Edinburgh.

[2] The Amendment proposed by Lord Temple was to express their intention of bringing in a Bill to indemnify those who had advised the embargo, in order that the Ministers might be included in the operation of the Bill. The Amendment was rejected.

Mr. Rigby being near Mr. Grenville in the House of Commons, Mr. Grenville asked him what they were to do. He answered, " We are to do nothing ; but so help me G—, as I am a man of honour, it is not by my advice."

Wednesday, November 12*th.*—Mr. Grenville was told that Sir Fletcher Norton, who had all the day before intended to speak, had a whisper given him in the House, which advised him to sit still. Mr. Grenville met Sir Gilbert Elliot at Mr. Jenkinson's, who spoke with great eagerness upon the illegality of the laying the embargo without the sanction of Parliament, and said these were the tyrannical principles of Lord Chatham and Lord Camden ; that Mr. Dyson was of his (Sir Gilbert Elliot's) opinion, and that they had both declared to Mr. Conway that they should both be against him if he meant to maintain the legality of that measure.

Thursday, November 13*th.*—Mr. Pitt told Mr. Grenville that Lord Percy did not go to the meeting at the Cockpit, that he held the language of opposition, and told Mr. Pitt that the manner in which his father had obtained the Dukedom was as follows :—Lord Northumberland went to Lord Chatham, and asked him whether he was to be Master of the Horse, or Lord Hertford, that if it was the latter, he should look upon himself as excessively ill-used, and should be mortally offended, thinking that his own services in Ireland deserved at least as well to be rewarded as Lord Hertford's. At this Lord Chatham seemed startled, said the arrangements were taken, and the offices disposed of. Lord Northumberland said that did not signify, for unless he could get a mark of the King's favour before

Lord Hertford kissed hands, he should look upon it as the greatest affront to him and his friends, and should act accordingly. Lord Chatham said the time did not allow of it, for Lord Hertford was to kiss hands the next morning. Lord Northumberland still continued to urge his pretensions, and Lord Chatham then proffered honours to him. Lord Northumberland asked of what sort. Lord Chatham said the highest, a dukedom, if he wished it; to which Lord Northumberland said the King would not do it. Lord Chatham said he would, told him he could not then see the King himself, nor write, having the gout, but desired Lord Northumberland to go to the King from him to ask it, and to use his name, saying he came from him. This was in the evening, and Lord Northumberland objected to the lateness of the hour, and likewise to His Majesty's being at Richmond, where he was to stay till eleven at night. Lord Chatham set all these objections aside, and Lord Northumberland went to the Queen's house, sent in to the King to acquaint His Majesty that he was come to speak to him upon earnest business. The King came out to him, and Lord Northumberland laid his suit before him, saying he was come from Lord Chatham, and by his direction. The King coloured and looked embarrassed, said he must take some little time to consider what engagements he was under, and named Lord Cardigan. He then went into his Closet, from which he returned in a short space, and told Lord Northumberland he would create him a Duke.

The report is in everybody's mouth, that the Duke of Bedford's party have made their bargain, which it is said Lord Chatham confirms, and their conduct on Tuesday seems conformable to this report, though Lord

Temple thinks the Duke of Bedford's speech was directly upon the ground of opposition.

Tuesday, November 18*th.*—Mr. Conway moved for the bringing a Bill into the House of Commons, to indemnify all those who shall have acted under the Order of Council to prohibit the exportation of wheat, &c.

Mr. Grenville declared his satisfaction upon hearing such a Bill was intended, but said he thought the ground on which it was proposed too narrow, and wished to have it extended to the advisers of that measure. Mr. Conway did not seem inclined to adopt the extension, and many people spoke their different opinions upon it, Alderman Beckford among others, and said that the King had a dispensing power in times of necessity. Mr. Grenville took down those words, and moved to have them taken down by the Clerk, in order to take the sense of the House upon this dangerous doctrine, which he said had already prevailed too strongly in another place.

Mr. Beckford, very angry, desired he might explain himself, and said he had been interrupted too soon, that what he meant to say was, that in cases of necessity, for *salus populi,* and with the advice of Council, the King had a dispensing power.

Mr. Grenville ordered these words likewise to be taken down, saying they were more exceptionable and unconstitutional than the former, and that he insisted upon having the sense of the House upon them, unless the gentleman would retract them. Mr. Conway, the two Onslows, and others, got up to deprecate and to explain away what had been said, begging Mr. Grenville to suffer the words to be withdrawn; but he continued firm, saying he meant not to be hard upon the gentle-

man from personality, but to censure such unconstitutional doctrine; and that if the House meant to avow
it, and support it, it must remain on the books as an
eternal blot upon that House of Commons which had
let it pass without censure.

Mr. Beckford was then advised by his friends to
recant, which he did, and Mr. Grenville suffered the
motion to be withdrawn.

This was a severe censure on the Lords Northington,
Chatham, and Camden, who had all holden the same
language with Mr. Beckford in the House of Lords.

The House of Commons did not venture to assert the
legality of the act, though the Lords did.

Mr. Grenville was greatly applauded and approved
for this affair; none of the Duke of Bedford's people
were down, nor any of Lord Bute's, but the House was
clearly with him, from the force of his arguments, and
the temper with which they were delivered.

In the evening Mr. Grenville went to Lord Mansfield,
who was in the highest joy imaginable upon the slur
thrown upon the opinions of the three Lords.

Wednesday, November 19*th.*—Many people came up
to Mr. Grenville in the House of Commons to express
their satisfaction of the preceding day, particularly Mr.
Rigby, who complimented him very highly, and desired
to come to him in the evening, which he accordingly
did, resumed all the cordiality and warmth of his former
conversation with him, assuring him of the strongest
attachment from himself and all the Duke of Bedford's
party, blaming the resolution the Duke had taken at
first coming to town, of lying by, and not acting, dis-
claiming the having been a party to it, and throwing it
all upon Lord Tavistock, swearing that as he was a man

of honour, there had been no negotiation, nor even intercourse, between them and Lord Chatham since they
came from Bath.   Lord Gower, Lord Weymouth, and
himself, had had the strongest offers made to them, that
he himself might have been restored to his office, but
that neither then nor now could he bear the thoughts
of being separated from Mr. Grenville[1]: then said all
that was possible to be said in approbation and commendation of Mr. Grenville, both as a man and a Minister;
said Lord Gower was in the same ideas, that the Duke
of Bedford thought more highly of Mr. Grenville than
of any man breathing, was perfectly satisfied of the
honour of his conduct towards him, and of the language
he had holden to him, and that the Duke had directed
him to assure Mr. Grenville, that though he was now
gone into the country, if Mr. Grenville had the slightest
wish or desire to have him return, he would do it upon
the first notice.   Mr. Rigby said further, that he knew
how temperately Mr. Grenville had spoken concerning
all the reports of their union with Lord Chatham, that
he wished Lord Temple had been as temperate, but
that he knew his Lordship had said "*that the Bedfords
were hungry,*" but that if they had been so their hunger
might have been satisfied if they had chosen it.

[1] See the Duke of Bedford's Diary in the *Bedford Correspondence,*
vol. iii. p. 352; where it appears that it was from no particular
delicacy with regard to a separation from Mr. Grenville, that they were
prevented from accepting the offers of Lord Chatham, but that the
terms were not considered sufficiently advantageous.   The Duke of
Bedford says, " They agreed unanimously that they ought not at present
to accept these terms, especially as there was no immediate room for
any but Lord Weymouth, and feared that many might be disgusted at
no further earnest being given immediately, but wished me to explain
it in such a way to Lord Chatham, as not to show their dislike of
entering into the King's service, but that they must wait till the bottom
should be enlarged."

Mr. Grenville desired him to believe no reports. Mr. Rigby said it did not much signify, for they all, as a party, desired to have it understood that their wishes went to Mr. Grenville, and not to Lord Temple. There was a meeting the night before at Lord Rockingham's, supposed to have been upon account of the removal of Lord Edgecumbe, whose white staff was given to Mr. Shelley, which greatly angered all the Rockingham party.

The Bedchamber was offered to Lord Edgecumbe, but he refused it, and wanted to have the Post Office; to this Lord Chatham would not consent, and said the King's honour had been already too much compromised.

The resolution was then taken by the Rockingham party to resign.

Tuesday, November 25th.—Mr. Beckford moved in the House of Commons for the House to enter into the Committee to consider of the state and wealth and conquests of the East India Company: this occasioned great debate, in which Mr. Grenville bore a very principal share with an universal applause. Lord Rockingham's friends were all in the minority. Lord John Cavendish made a farewell speech to the Administration; Mr. Charles Townshend inclined much to the same side; Mr. Rigby and some others of the Duke of Bedford's party voted with Mr. Grenville; Mr. Wedderburn supported him ably and roundly, but Sir Fletcher Norton and all the young people of Lord Bute's party went away; but Sir Fletcher Norton excused himself for it the next day, saying he thought the business would not come on that day, and Lord Percy, Sir James Lowther, &c., went away upon seeing him go.

Wednesday, November 26th.—Lord Lichfield's chariot was seen for two hours at Lord Chatham's door, and it is said the office of Master of the Horse was offered to him, and that he refused it.

Reports of negotiation with the Duke of Bedford's party again prevail, and it comes authentically from that quarter that Lord Gower and the Duchess are strongly for engaging with Lord Chatham, and Mr. Rigby as strongly against it.

Mr. Grenville went to see Lord Mansfield last night; his opinion is that the Ministry cannot stand; he thinks (as many others do) that the King is tired of Lord Chatham, and that the Queen is particularly averse to him.

He quoted some conversation he had had in the Drawing-room with Her Majesty, in which she reproached him with being a great stranger at Court, and her discourse (at a distance) expressed discontent.

Other intelligence confirms the same.

Thursday, November 27th.—The Duke of Portland, Lord Scarborough, Lord Besborough, and Lord Monson resigned their offices.

The Chamberlain's staff was immediately given to Lord Hertford.

Lord Gower was two hours in the evening with Lord Chatham.

Lord George Sackville sent to Mr. Grenville to devote himself to him, and came to him that evening.

Friday, November 28th.—Sir Charles Saunders went to Court, meaning to resign, and with him Sir William Meredith and Admiral Keppel, but had a long conference with Lord Chatham in the outward room, and at his desire deferred it 'till Monday. Lord Chatham told him the other resignations were indifferent to him, but that his and Admiral Keppel's went to his heart.

Lord Gower went this morning to Woburn, where Mr. Rigby went the day before, each to endeavour to persuade the Duke of Bedford to act according to their different opinions. In the meantime Lord Bute's party seem to talk and to act with hostility to Lord Chatham.

Saturday, November 29th.—Lord Gower returned from Woburn, and was at the Opera. When people asked him for news he said he knew none, but seemed to have an air of satisfaction.

Sunday, November 30th.—It has transpired from some of those who returned from Woburn that the Duke of Bedford is to come to town to-morrow, and to see Lord Chatham at seven o'clock, from which everybody concludes the treaty is very near completed, and that nothing now remains but to settle the final terms. The Duke of Marlborough is likewise to be in town.

Monday, December 1st.—Mr. Grenville went to see Mr. Rigby, who told him it was true that the resolution was taken to accept, and that the Duke of Bedford was coming to town to settle the terms; that for his own part he had not altered his opinion upon it; that he thought they ought never to have separated themselves from Mr. Grenville; that it disgraced and dishonoured them for ever; that he had made every representation of this kind that was possible to the Duke of Bedford, even so far as to entreat that he (Mr. Rigby) might accept of no employment 'till the end of the Session (if it lasted so long, which he did not believe it would), but the Duke of Bedford said he must not hear of that, it would be so public a mark of his disapprobation; that in this situation, Mr. Grenville must see how impossible it was for him to separate himself from the Duke and Lord Gower, but that he saw both ruin and disgrace in the measure. Many more of the Duke's party are as averse as he, and none for the measure except the Duchess and Lord Gower.

At twelve o'clock at night, Mr. Grenville received a note from Mr. Rigby, giving him to understand that he had reason to believe the consultation had failed.

Tuesday, December 2nd.—Mr. Rigby came to tell Mr. Grenville that the Duke of Bedford and Lord Chatham had disagreed, that both grew warm: Lord Chatham offered nothing more than the office of Master of the Horse for Lord Gower, Postmaster for Lord Weymouth, and Cofferer for Mr. Rigby. He spoke in a very high tone, and told the Duke more than once that the Cabinet was not afraid. The Duke took up these words after they had been twice repeated, and said he did not know what his Lordship meant by him; that the King best knew whether he wished to have his friends in employment, and for what reason he had sent to him; that for his part he neither wished nor meant to force open the door of the Cabinet. They parted, having concluded upon nothing. Lord Chatham desired to see him again, which he is to do accordingly to-morrow. The Duke of Bedford asked Mr. Rigby what language Mr. Grenville held; he told him, that of a man of honour and a gentleman, and with great temper and civility to his Grace.

Sir Edward Hawke is appointed First Lord of the Admiralty, and Sir Percy Brett and Lord Lisburne the two minor Lords. (Mr. Jenkinson came into the Admiralty in the room of Lord Lisburne, because the latter could not be chosen again for Berwick, where Lord Percy refused to give him his interest.)

Colonel Harcourt to be Groom of the Bedchamber in the room of Mr. Keppel. Lord Chatham came to Bedford House as soon as he had been with the King, and told the Duke of Bedford that His Majesty had taken his resolution to dispose of all the vacant offices, which put an end to all further negotiation. He brought words of civility to the Duke of Bedford, saying that His Majesty thought very kindly of Lord Tavistock, and would very willingly make him a Peer; this the Duke refused, and Lord Chatham, with many professions to the Duke, withdrew.

The Princess of Brunswick was to go the next day to Woburn, but sent word she was ill, and could not go: she is supposed to have been the person employed by the King to move Lord Gower to bring about all this absurd negotiation, in which the poor Duke of Bedford is so much disgraced.

His Grace brought a long list of friends to Lord Chatham, for whom he required offices. Lord Chatham offered Master of the Horse, Postmaster, and Cofferer; said his Grace might take them or leave them, and would never advance a step further [1].

Wednesday, December 3rd.—Mr. Grenville received a letter from Mr. Jenkinson, acquainting him that he was going to kiss hands for one of the Lords of the Admiralty, to which Mr. Grenville returned no answer, and forbid his porter ever to let him into his house again [2]. He was part of Saturday night with Mr. Gren-

---

[1] See *Bedford Correspondence*, vol. iii. page 358, and *Chatham Correspondence*, vol. iii. pp. 134–8.

[2] Wraxall, in his *Historical Memoirs*, thus describes the appearance

ville at a meeting with Sir Fletcher Norton, Mr. Wedderburn, and others.

The Duke of Ancaster kissed hands for Master of the Horse: all this looks so like Lord Bute and Lord Chatham having an understanding together, that it can no longer be doubted.

Sir Fletcher Norton and Mr. Wedderburn as yet remain firm to Mr. Grenville, and are very angry with Lord Bute. They both supported Mr. Grenville in the House of Commons upon the second reading of the Indemnity Bill to-day.

Lord Mountstuart moved for Mr. Jenkinson's writ.

Thursday, December 4th.—Mr. Grenville received a letter from Mr. Nugent, acquainting him that he had accepted the office of First Commissioner of the Board of Trade. Mr. Stanley is appointed Cofferer, and the Duke of Bolton Governor of the Isle of Wight.

Friday, December 5th.—Lord Harcourt called upon

and character of Mr. Charles Jenkinson, afterwards Baron Hawkesbury and Earl of Liverpool :—" In his person he rose above the common height, but his lank limbs and figure were destitute of elegance or of grace. The expression of his countenance I find difficult to describe, as, without having in his face any lines strongly marked, it was not destitute of deep intelligence. Reflection and caution seemed to be stamped on every feature, while his eyes were usually, even in conversation, directed downwards towards the earth. Something impervious and inscrutable seemed to accompany and to characterize his demeanour. His manners were polite, calm, and unassuming; grave, if not cold; but not distant, without any mixture of pride or affectation. In society, though reserved, he was not silent, and though guarded on certain topics, communicative on ordinary subjects. No man in official situation was supposed to understand better the principles of trade, navigation, manufactures, and revenue. As a speaker in the House of Commons he rose seldom, nor did he ever weary the patience of his auditors. No ray of wit, humour, or levity pervaded his speeches. All was fact and business. Such qualifications, even independent of the supposed favour of the Sovereign, necessarily rendered him an object of respect and attention to every party."—Vol. ii. p. 209.

Mr. Grenville, but not finding him, writ him a letter to say how sorry he was to have missed him; he then endeavours to palliate Mr. Jenkinson's conduct.

The Indemnity Bill was reported this day. Mr. Charles Townshend spoke warmly on the side of Administration, and attacked Mr. Grenville and Lord Temple: the former repulsed the attack, and was much applauded.

Mr. Conway said little. There was a division: the numbers were 48 to 166. All the Rockingham party, and most of the Bute party, voted with the majority. Sir Fletcher Norton and Mr. Wedderburn supported Mr. Grenville.

Saturday, December 6th.—Mr. Grenville sent to desire Lord Harcourt would appoint a time to see him. He came to him in the evening, endeavoured to say what he could in favour of Mr. Jenkinson, but was forced to own that he had behaved unhandsomely to Mr. Grenville. He said Lord Chatham had sent to him on the Sunday to make the offer, which he then declined, that he was pressed again upon it on the Tuesday, when he accepted, after having seen Lord Bute, and received the Princess of Wales's commands, &c. He never seems to have remembered his connection with Mr. Grenville, which Lord Harcourt could not nor did not attempt to justify. Lord Harcourt had a long conversation with Mr. Grenville, in the course of which he told him that he had no intercourse with Lord Chatham, that he disliked him; that he saw and lamented the sad state of the kingdom, but did not think this Ministry could last three months, and that he believed there was great interior discontent among them; that, as a proof of it, the Duke of Grafton asked in the House of Lords whether Mr. Keppel had been dismissed from the Bed-chamber, or had resigned, for that, for his part, he knew nothing of it.   Lord Harcourt told Mr. Grenville that the appointment of Colonel Harcourt came from the King to him, and not from Lord Chatham, whom he did not even visit, and had been much surprised at his Lordship's having left his name at his door the day before, though he had not the smallest acquaintance with him.

Monday, December 8th.—The Indemnity Bill came for the last time into the House of Commons, Mr. Conway agreeing to some words of alteration proposed by Mr. Grenville, which prevented any debate.

Tuesday, December 9th.—The East India business came before the House.   Mr. Beckford made a motion for some papers to be laid before the House.   Mr. Grenville opposed it, and proposed to have the business put off for three months ; there was a division upon this, of 54 to 164.   Many people spoke on that day, parti-cularly all the new converts, such as Lord North, Mr. Nugent, Mr. Stanley, &c.

The most memorable event of the day was Mr. Con-way's speech, who spoke doubtfully upon the perma-nency of the Administration, and twice affectedly called himself a passenger.   The House sat till past eleven o'clock.

Wednesday, December 10th.—The Indemnity Bill was read the second time in the House of Lords.   The debate was opened by the Duke of Richmond with great warmth and inveteracy against Lord Chatham, whose insolent behaviour to the first nobility in the kingdom he described in high colouring.   Lord Chatham answered with great heat and anger ; the House interposed upon Lord Chatham defying the Duke of Richmond to produce the instances of such a behaviour, and the latter saying *that* was perhaps not a proper place, but that if he would come to him in private he would satisfy him upon that subject. They were called to order, and their words given that it should go no further. The Duke excused himself to the House, and said he was sorry if he had given any offence *to the House*, but that he knew *truth* was not to be spoken at all times, nor in all places. The Chancellor and Lord Northington stuck to their dispensing doctrine, and maintained it to be law. Lord Chatham shuffled between necessity and law. Lord Shelburne attacked Lord Mansfield, who made the most eloquent speech, with the most spirited attack upon Lord Chatham and the two lawyers, that ever was heard. Lord Temple, Lord Suffolk, Lord Lyttelton, and others spoke on the side of opposition, but Lord Mansfield far the best of any[1].

Mr. Grenville went into the country for the Christmas holidays. The House met again on the 15th of January.

Lord Chatham had the gout at Bath, came as far as Marlborough in his way to London, but saying he was worse, turned back again and went to Bath.

[1] The debate upon this occasion was published by Almon in the form of a pamphlet, written by Lord Temple, assisted, as was supposed, by Lord Lyttelton and Mr. Mackintosh. It was entitled *A Speech against the Suspending and Dispensing Prerogative*. Although it ran through several editions, it is now of uncommon occurrence, but it will be found reprinted in vol. xvi. of the *Parliamentary History*.

END OF VOL. III.